REALIZATION OF FRENCH HOPES. *General Henri Giraud watches as the first convoy bearing war matériel for his forces approaches North Africa.*

UNITED STATES ARMY IN WORLD WAR II

Special Studies

REARMING THE FRENCH

by

Marcel Vigneras

MILITARY INSTRVCTION

OFFICE OF THE CHIEF OF MILITARY HISTORY

DEPARTMENT OF THE ARMY

WASHINGTON, D. C., 1957

Library of Congress Catalog Card Number: 57–60000

Reprinted 1969

For sale by the Superintendent of Documents, U.S. Government Printing Office
Washington, D.C. 20402

UNITED STATES ARMY IN WORLD WAR II
Kent Roberts Greenfield, General Editor

Advisory Committee
(As of 30 June 1956)

Office of the Chief of Military History
Maj. Gen. John H. Stokes, Jr., Chief

. . . to Those Who Served

Foreword

Every thoughtful American interested in the history of our present mutual assistance program should find this a profitable and illuminating book. In rearming the French the War Department and the U.S. Army became agents of an Allied policy which not only enabled this country to further a friendship for France that dated from the Revolution, but in addition served the military interests of both nations. It equipped Frenchmen with the means to fight and by so doing increased at minimum cost the forces available to the United Nations. The Army can take pride in the success with which it administered a policy involving both political and military matters. The policy of mutual aid has since been extended throughout the world with the Army again designated as the agency principally responsible for its administration. The present thorough and objective study of an early large-scale American experiment with mutual aid should therefore be highly instructive to all concerned.

JOHN H. STOKES
Maj. Gen., U.S.A.
Chief of Military History

Washington, D.C.
30 August 1956

Introductory Note

The original intent of the European Theater of Operations series was to portray the history of ground combat as carried on by U.S. forces in western and central Europe during World War II. Very early in the planning devoted to this series it became apparent that two subjects were of such grand import and interest as to require separate treatment. For this reason volumes were prepared and published on the history of the supreme command and the logistical support of the U.S. armies that fought in the European Theater of Operations. Research for these two volumes unraveled one continuing but tangled thread which did not quite fit into the fabric of the series as a whole. This was the problem posed by the French national forces serving under U.S. command and by the rearmament of these forces to permit their effective employment in the fight for the liberation of their homeland. The problems of command and decision involved in French rearmament and in the logistic support furnished to the French forces reached outside of the European Theater of Operations. It was decided, therefore, to devote a special study to the history of French rearmament. This decision was supported by the fact that the United States had once again embarked on the business of supplying weapons and other material assistance to potential Allies, and that such military assistance appeared to have become a continuing feature of U.S. policy.

An author was available who had exceptional qualifications for a task recognized from the first as complex and delicate. A scholar who had studied history at the Lycée of Limoges, France, and received his Ph.D. at Western Reserve University, Marcel Vigneras had served in the French Army in both World Wars, although in World War II seconded to duty as an American citizen with the Office of Strategic Services in 1943. He was a member of the faculty at Smith College before World War II. At the close of the war he joined the Historical Division, European Theater of Operations, then in France. At present Dr. Vigneras is continuing research on military problems as a member of the Operations Research Office, from which he was granted leave to complete the present volume.

HUGH M. COLE
Chief, European Section, 1947–1952

Preface

This volume tells how the French forces were rearmed from the time they re-entered World War II after their temporary eclipse from the battlefields of Europe. The text inescapably focuses attention on the part played by America in the undertaking if for no other reason than that the undertaking itself, while shared between the United States and the United Kingdom, was largely American.

The purpose of this volume is twofold. It is a historical account of a sizable and laborious enterprise that enabled a friendly military establishment in dire need of assistance to take its place among the forces aligned against the Axis. It is intended also to serve as a guide for the solution of problems likely to arise out of similar future enterprises. While this volume is not primarily concerned with operational matters, it contains sufficient operational material to establish the extent of the contribution made by the rearmed French forces toward the final victory of the United Nations. The reader is warned that only such French political developments that had a definite influence on the course of rearmament are discussed, and the discussion is limited to that sufficient to place the evolution of French rearmament in its proper perspective.

Rearming the French is the product of co-operative effort and it is a pleasure to acknowledge indebtedness to the many individuals, too numerous to be listed here, who offered advice and help. While I express my deep appreciation to them, I wish to emphasize that they are in no way responsible for the handling of the material used, or for errors of fact or presentation.

I am especially grateful to those French and U.S. officers who granted me interviews which enabled me to clarify a number of points. Some provided me with information from their private files. Others were kind enough to read part or all of the manuscript. Their names have been listed in the Bibliographical Note.

Several members of the Office of the Chief of Military History were particularly helpful in suggesting improvements. I should like to thank Dr. Gordon A. Harrison for generous and skillful assistance in achieving better organization and clarity of text; Col. Leo J. Meyer for valuable comments on the substance of the preliminary draft; Dr. George F. Howe for guidance in interpreting controversial points; finally Dr. Kent Roberts Greenfield for his critical review of the revised draft.

For assistance in exploring the tons of files held by the War Department, I am indebted to Mr. Royce Thompson, of the European Section, OCMH,

Mrs. Blanche Moore and Mr. Albert Whitt, of the Departmental Records Branch, AGO, Mrs. Mary Greathouse, of the Historical Section, G–3, Mr. Israel Wice and members of his Reference Branch staff in OCMH.

The task of extracting pertinent data was greatly facilitated by the diligent help of Miss Katharine C. Jenkins. I am indebted to her for assembling and analyzing the material now appearing in the section on French assistance to the American Expeditionary Forces in World War I, and in the chapter on the Joint Rearmament Committee.

Miss Ruth Stout edited the entire manuscript and her suggestions greatly contributed to improving the narrative. The excellent map is the work of Mr. Wsevolod Aglaimoff, Deputy Chief Historian for Cartography. Miss Margaret E. Tackley selected and prepared the illustrative material. The copy editors were Mrs. Marion P. Grimes and Mr. Arthur C. Henne.

Rearming the French was prepared at the suggestion and under the general direction of Dr. Hugh M. Cole, Chief of the European Theater Section. It was my good fortune to have his wise and learned counsel throughout the period of research and writing.

30 August 1956   MARCEL VIGNERAS
Washington, D. C.

Contents

PART ONE

The North African Forces

PART TWO

The Metropolitan Forces

Tables

Charts

Map

Illustrations

    The illustrations are from the files of the Department of Defense except for those from the following sources:

        Service Cinématographique des Armées, *Frontispiece*.
        National Archives, page 7.
        Acme Photograph, page 216.

Prologue

In October 1942 Maj. Gen. Mark W. Clark, representing the U.S. Army, and Brig. Gen. Charles Mast, spokesman for General Henri Giraud, met secretly in Cherchel, seventy-five miles west of Algiers. The subject of their conversations was a momentous one—the imminent re-entry of French North Africa into the war. General Clark, acting on instructions from President Roosevelt, gave positive assurances to General Mast that the United States would furnish the equipment necessary to outfit the North African forces.[1]

Clark's commitment was timely, for Anglo-American forces were about to land in northwest Africa. More important, it heralded an event of great significance: the forthcoming assumption, by the United States, of direct responsibility for re-equipping the French armed forces. The British had been discharging this responsibility by maintaining the small band of Frenchmen stubbornly fighting on their side and under their control since mid-1940.

Before World War II had ended, the Americans had fully equipped and trained eight French divisions in North Africa, partially outfitted and trained three more in France, furnished equipment for nineteen air squadrons, and carried out an extensive rehabilitation program for the French Navy. They had supplied some 1,400 aircraft, 160,000 rifles and carbines, 30,000 machine guns, 3,000 artillery guns, 5,000 tanks and

self-propelled weapons, and 51,000,000 rounds of ammunition.

An occurrence of historic import was thus re-enacted in reverse. Twice France had similarly undertaken to assist an unprepared America at war. In 1781, in addition to sending an expeditionary corps to help the young colonies in their fight for independence, France supplied weapons and matériel to the infant Continental Army. Much later, in World War I, France, herself at war with Germany, again provided matériel to the American Expeditionary Forces (A.E.F.) sent to the European continent. In that second episode, the nature and extent of the help rendered were vastly different from what they were to be in World War II. Yet the parallel is striking enough to warrant, for the sake of historical comparison, a brief account of the aid extended by the French to the American forces in 1917–18.

French Assistance to the A.E.F. in World War I

The entrance of the United States into World War I, on 6 April 1917, found the American forces totally unprepared for the arduous tasks which they were later to carry out on the battlefields of western Europe. Initially, these forces, transported to the Continent as fast as they were raised and as shipping facilities would allow, lacked the most essential weapons of the armies then at war, namely, artillery, tanks, and aircraft. Their plight was made worse by the fact that, at home, most ordnance and munitions plants were not prepared to go

---

[1] These instructions were relayed in Msg R–2080, Gen George C. Marshall to Lt Gen Dwight D. Eisenhower, 17 Oct 42, CM–OUT 5682. (See Bibliographical Note.) "Clark . . . should state . . . the U.S. will furnish equipment for French Forces which will operate against the Axis."

into large-scale production for months to come. In the case of airplanes, it was reported that American manufacturers could not begin to furnish them before the summer of 1918.[2]

On reaching the Continent, in early June 1917, Maj. Gen. John J. Pershing, Commander-in-Chief, American Expeditionary Forces, at once investigated the possibility of obtaining from Allied sources the implements of war so urgently needed for his forces. The depredations of enemy submarines on Atlantic shipping made such a procedure even more advisable, and General Pershing began urging the War Department to make use to the fullest extent possible of French and British factories, already geared to wartime production, for the manufacture of war matériel for the A.E.F.

To the A.E.F. Commander-in-Chief, speed was the essential consideration, for his objective was to forge, as rapidly as possible, a well-organized and adequately equipped striking force to be employed as a separate and autonomous component of the combined Allied armies. Without such a force, he would have no other alternative than to submit to the already strong pressure exerted by top Allied authorities for the use of his troops as replacements for their own armies.[3]

While Allied recognition of the principle of a separate American task force was delayed for some months, the need of getting equipment into the hands of U.S. troops for training and combat purposes was at once recognized. To this end, all available resources, it was agreed by everyone concerned, must be tapped immediately. General Pershing himself strongly supported this view. "It matters little whether we have a particular kind of artillery; if we cannot get the French, we should get the British. The same can be said of small arms and personal equipment. If our ordnance cannot furnish them, the French and British have them. So in equipment and armament there should be no delay." [4]

Investigation convinced General Pershing that French industry was in a far better position than its British counterpart to supply a large part of the needed war matériel. Although not fully supplied themselves, the French were said to be industrially so situated as to be capable of increasing their production rapidly and substantially. With this realization and the assumption that American troops would operate in proximity to the French armies, A.E.F. officials decided to adopt the French types of artillery for the usual calibers and to seek French assistance in obtaining the guns needed at least for the first two years. "We secured an agreement that our troops, as they came along, would be provided with French guns and ammunition, including not only the 75's and 155's, but 37-mm. guns and 58-mm. trench mortars as well." [5]

Although "France was responding generously," her resources were not inexhaustible.[6] Unless energetic measures were taken to provide French factories with the necessary raw materials, their output could not be expected to reach the required levels. With this in view, War Department officials enlisted the help of American industry and business in establishing a vast supply program. Figures on the tonnage of raw ma-

[2] John J. Pershing, *My Experiences in the World War* (New York: Frederick A. Stokes Co., 1931), I, 161.

[3] *Ibid.,* I, 159.

[4] *Ibid.,* II, 112.

[5] *Ibid.,* I, 107.

[6] *Ibid.,* I, 258.

terials supplied to the French up to the Armistice for the production of munitions of war are illuminating. For the artillery pieces and ammunition of French manufacture fired by the A.E.F., the United States supplied, in metals alone, over 700,000 tons of steel, 30,000 tons of pig iron, 5,000 tons of brass and zinc, 50,000 tons of copper, as well as all the principal materials used in loading the entire supply of shells. For the finished airplanes used by the Air Service, 34,500,000 feet of spruce, fir, and cedar, 7,000,000 feet of mahogany and walnut, 4,000 tons of aluminum, and miscellaneous aircraft materials and supplies were furnished by the United States. All together, the French received from America, up to November 1918, over 800,000 tons of raw materials and semifinished products.[7]

On the other side of the ledger, available figures on the weapons of war manufactured by the French for use by the A.E.F. are no less impressive. The forty-two divisions, representing a total of 1,390,000 combatant troops, which at the time of the Armistice made up the A.E.F. in France, were equipped almost exclusively with French artillery, artillery ammunition, tanks, and planes. It has even been said that, if given the necessary raw materials, France could have supplied all the artillery, ammunition, tanks, and aircraft for an American army of any size that could have been sent to Europe.[8]

The French produced 3,532 of the 4,194 pieces of artillery used in combat by the A.E.F. up to 11 November 1918, 227 of the 289 tanks, and all of the 240-mm. and 58-mm. trench mortars. As General Pershing

observed: "It was most fortunate that we were able to get these guns from the French, as up to the end of the war no guns manufactured at home for our army, of the types used, except twenty-four 8-inch mortars and six 14-inch naval guns, were fired in battle.[9] Almost all of the railroad artillery used by the U.S. forces consisted of equipment loaned by the French. The entire supply of ammunition fired by American artillery up until the last days of the war was of French origin because practically none of U.S. manufacture (other than shrapnel) had reached the front. As for automatic weapons, reports show that the first twelve U.S. divisions were completely equipped with Hotchkiss heavy machine guns and Chauchat rifles purchased from the French Government.

Another striking figure is the number of aircraft. By the time of the Armistice, equipment in the hands of the Air Service consisted of 3,210 combat and 3,154 training airplanes, or a total of 6,364, of which 4,874 had been supplied by French industry. Of the forty-three American squadrons engaged in operations on 31 October 1918, only ten were equipped with aircraft manufactured in the United States and three with planes of British manufacture, as compared with thirty equipped with French-made planes.

Besides manufacturing and supplying munitions of war, the French also provided t r o o p s and facilities. The practice, adopted by agreement between General Pershing and the War Department, of giving priority of shipment to infantry and machine gun units left the A.E.F. woefully short in supporting arms and services. This condition never was corrected and General Pershing was compelled to obtain from the

[7] Benedict Crowell, *America's Munitions: 1917–1918* (Washington, 1919), pp. 590–92.

[8] Grosvenor B. Clarkson, *Industrial America in the World War* (Boston and New York: Houghton Mifflin Co., 1923), pp. 236–38.

[9] Pershing, *op. cit.,* I, 107. See Table 1, below.

TABLE 1—EQUIPMENT FURNISHED AMERICAN EXPEDITIONARY FORCES IN WORLD WAR I, BY TYPE AND SUPPLYING COUNTRY: 6 APRIL 1917–11 NOVEMBER 1918

Type	Total	From France	From Great Britain	From United States
Artillery [a]	4, 194	3, 532	160	502
Howitzer, 9.2-inch	40	0	40	0
Howitzer, 8-inch	208	0	120	88
Howitzer, 155-mm.	798	796	0	2
Gun, 10-inch, Sea Coast	15	0	0	15
Gun, 8-inch, Sea Coast	6	0	0	6
Gun, 6-inch, Sea Coast	74	0	0	74
Gun, 155-mm., (GPF)	233	233	0	0
Gun, 5-inch, Sea Coast	26	0	0	26
Gun, 4.7-inch	71	0	0	71
Gun, 75-mm.	2, 022	1, 862	0	160
Gun, 37-mm.	701	641	0	60
Railroad Artillery [a]	158	[b] 140	0	18
Howitzer, 400-mm.	4	4	0	0
Gun, 14-inch	84	66	0	18
Gun, 340-mm.	2	2	0	0
Gun, 32-cm.	12	12	0	0
Gun, 24-cm.	24	24	0	0
Gun, 19-cm.	32	32	0	0
Caissons	9, 023	2, 658	0	6, 365
Howitzer, 155-mm.	1, 994	796	0	1, 198
Gun, 4.7-inch	219	0	0	219
Gun, 75-mm.	6, 810	1, 862	0	4, 948
Trench Mortars	2, 555	237	1, 427	891
Mortar, 240-mm.	101	101	0	0
Mortar, 8-inch, Stokes	1, 757	0	914	843
Mortar, 6-inch, Newton	561	0	513	48
Mortar, 58-mm.	136	136	0	0
Automatic Weapons	124, 352	40, 484	0	83, 868
Browning Machine Gun	30, 089	0	0	30, 089
Vickers Machine Gun	10, 411	0	0	10, 411
Hotchkiss Machine Gun	5, 255	5, 255	0	0
Browning Rifle	43, 368	0	0	43, 368
Chauchat Machine Rifle				
8-mm.	15, 988	15, 988	0	0
.30-caliber	19, 241	19, 241	0	0
Tanks	289	227	26	36
Renault	237	227	0	10
Mark IV	24	0	12	12
Mark V and Mark VI	28	0	14	14
Airplanes	[c] 6, 345	4, 874	258	1, 213
Balloons	295	20	0	275
Horses	225, 598	136, 114	21, 759	67, 725

[a] Nearly all artillery ammunition used up to 11 November 1918, approximately 10,000,000 rounds, was of French manufacture.
[b] Loaned by France.
[c] Excludes 19 airplanes furnished by Italy.

Source: Artillery, caissons, mortars, automatic weapons, and tank data: Historical Branch, War Plans Division, General Staff, *Organization of the Services of Supply, American Expeditionary Forces*, Monograph 7, WD Doc. 1009 (Washington, 1921), p. 75. Data on airplanes, balloons, and horses: Col. Jacques de Chambrun and Capt. Charles de Marenches, *The American Army in the European Conflict* (New York: The Macmillan Company, 1919), pp. 205, 213, 231. Ammunition information: Benedict Crowell, *America's Munitions: 1917–1918* (Washington, 1919), p. 590. Railroad artillery data: Historical Division, Department of the Army, UNITED STATES ARMY IN THE WORLD WAR: 1917–1919, XIV, *Reports of Commander-in-Chief, A.E.F., Staff Sections and Services* (Washington, 1948), 81.

French a great part of the corps and army artillery, aviation, and other services necessary to support his armies. For the movement of his supplies, the A.E.F. Commander-in-Chief likewise obtained from the French the use of their facilities such as harbors, railways, depots, warehouses, and supply dumps. At the time of the Armistice, American cargo was utilizing 98 berths in French ports of which 86 were French-constructed and 12 American-built. During the three-month period from September to November 1918, an average of 300 trains per day, representing a daily haul of 22,000 miles, were operating at the disposal of the American General Headquarters.[10]

When plans were first discussed for setting up a supply system for the A.E.F., the French strongly urged General Pershing to adopt their own for the sake of simplification. The proposal was turned down for a variety of reasons, not the least of which was the firm American intent to preserve the integrity of the U.S. forces as a separate military establishment. Yet, in superimposing the American supply system on the existing French organization, efforts were made, whenever possible, to harmonize with the latter so as to prevent needless complications.[11] As a concession to the French plea for unification, U.S. administrative sections generally were made to conform to the boundaries of French military regions. This resulted in simplification and greater Franco-American co-operation. One important feature was borrowed from the French supply system—regulating stations. Located near advance depots, these stations controlled the flow of supplies from the zone of interior to the units at the front. At the time of the Armistice, the A.E.F. had constructed one such station, was in process of organizing another, and was making use of French stations whenever necessary.[12]

Another major contribution to molding the A.E.F. was the valuable assistance the French rendered in the field of training. The critical shortage of Allied manpower had made it necessary to send untrained troops to France immediately after the entrance of the United States into the war.[13] Although General Pershing, President Woodrow Wilson, Secretary of War Newton D. Baker, and the American public were insistent on the creation of a unified American Army, trained and commanded according to U.S. methods, the urgency of the operational situation during the first year of American participation in the war required that every expedient be used to get U.S. troops in battle as speedily as possible.[14] For lack of time and better practices, Allied training methods were adopted, with the result that no completely American training organization was set up before hostilities came to an end.

---

[10] Col. Jacques de Chambrun and Capt. Charles de Marenches, *The American Army in the European Conflict* (New York: The Macmillan Company, 1919), p. 205; Lt. Col. Edouard Jean Réquin, *America's Race to Victory,* with Introduction by General Peyton C. March, Chief of Staff, U.S. Army (New York: Frederick A. Stokes Co., 1919), p. 185.

[11] Historical Branch, War Plans Division, General Staff, *Organization of the Services of Supply, American Expeditionary Forces,* Monograph 7, WD Doc 1009, (Washington, 1921), p. 14.

[12] *Report of the Military Board of Allied Supply* (Washington: Government Printing Office, 1924), pp. 344–46.

[13] As an illustration, over 50 percent of the component elements of the first U.S. division to reach the Continent were completely untrained. Historical Division, Department of the Army, UNITED STATES ARMY IN THE WORLD WAR: 1917–1919, III, *Training and Use of American Units With British and French* (Washington, 1948), 426.

[14] *Ibid.,* p. 2.

Except for two divisions,[15] U.S. units abroad were trained by the French since they were to fight alongside the latter at least initially. This procedure was strongly recommended by the chief of Liaison Group, General Headquarters, who declared on 28 May 1917: "If the French Army is to be our model and if the American is to fight beside the Frenchman according to the latter's methods, then the training of the American troops should be done in as close contact as possible with the French troops, not only from the technical point of view but from that of mutual acquaintance, mutual understanding, mutual respect."[16] After the proposed procedure was approved, an effective method was adopted by which officers and enlisted men of both armies were exchanged. American troops were detailed to French training camps as students, and the French came to U.S. stations as instructors. Also, the practice was established of billeting a French division in proximity to a corresponding American organization for the purpose of giving them both thorough instruction. The French division would stay about a month, lending its officer and technician personnel to the American unit, and would arrange for the parallel instruction of the two divisions. After this initial training period, American cadres would spend tours of duty with the French in

quiet sectors of the front for additional experience in trench warfare.[17]

For the training of pilots, arrangements were made for U.S. troops to enter flying schools in France and in other Allied countries until such a time as American training centers could be established.

From this brief summary, it can safely be assumed that the services rendered by the French, and to a lesser degree by the British, both in supplying munitions of war and in providing training and other facilities shortened by many months the time it took the American Expeditionary Forces to become a well-equipped and well-trained striking force ready to take a decisive part in operations. Even so, a year elapsed before the A.E.F. was in a position to undertake offensive action, and then with the strength of but a single infantry regiment. It is probable that without the generous assistance they received from the French, American troops, except for a few individual units, might well not have engaged in combat in 1917–18. It is equally probable that the record of this assistance influenced the U.S. decision in World War II to extend similar help to the nation that had proved itself a loyal provider in the earlier conflict.[18]

The American Decision To Rearm the French in World War II

The American assurances given the French at Cherchel in October 1942 auto-

---

[15] Which were among the American units to be trained by the British for participation in combat alongside British troops, in accordance with the Six Division Plan agreed to by the United States and the United Kingdom in January 1918 (and revised later in June to include ten divisions). Eight of the ten divisions were withdrawn before the training program was completed, leaving only two entirely British-trained. *Ibid.,* pp. 2–3.

[16] *Ibid.,* p. 238.

[17] Serious consideration was given to the possibility of sending French and British officers to the United States to give advanced courses in tactics. General Pershing opposed this procedure which, he felt, would tend to reduce the sense of responsibility and initiative of American officers. Furthermore, he was not entirely in agreement with the military tactics taught by the French. Pershing, *op. cit.,* II, 237.

[18] See Bibliographical Note for list of World War I source material used in this section.

VICTORY PARADE, PARIS, 1918. *Leading Army troops is General John J. Pershing.*

matically became a firm commitment the moment the North African forces threw their weight on the side of the Anglo-American allies barely a month later. The re-entry of these forces into the war climaxed a long period of painful uncertainty for the Allies themselves, as well as for the French. This period, which began at the close of the ill-fated Campaign in the West of May–June 1940, probably constitutes the most crucial page of France's recent history.

French Political and Military Situation June 1940–November 1942

By the time of the Franco-German armistice of 22 June 1940, the German forces had penetrated deep into French territory. They proceeded at once to establish themselves in a zone of occupation comprising northern and western France, or approximately one half of the country, and, by a demarcation line, virtually severed it from contact with the other half. A French government headed by Marshal Henri Pétain organized in the "free zone" and from the small city of Vichy undertook to repair the physical and moral havoc caused by the blitzkrieg just ended. Fearful of further German encroachments on what was left of French sovereignty, Marshal Pétain and his associates resolved to abide strictly by the stiff armistice terms imposed by the Germans. Under these terms the French Army was being reduced to a skeleton police force, or "Armistice Army," of some 100,-

000 men for Metropolitan France and a like number for the overseas territories in Northwest Africa. The fleet, still intact, was to remain in French harbors on sufferance so long as the French respected the armistice.

It has now been established that, during the ensuing years, a number of officials in the government and on the General Staff in Vichy secretly endeavored to strengthen the Army, at home as well as overseas, beyond the limitations imposed by the armistice clauses. These patriotic individuals, undaunted by a defeat which they regarded as only a temporary setback, were preparing for the day when the Army would take up arms once more against the Germans. Their main effort was directed at building up a cadre force and a reserve of weapons and maintaining organizations and services then unauthorized in anticipation of the eventual mobilization of former combatants.[19]

At the end of June 1940, General Maxime Weygand, Minister of National Defense, issued a secret directive on the hiding of weapons and requested military region commanders in the free zone to conceal all antitank and antiaircraft guns in their respective areas. These instructions appear to have had the full support of both the high military command and the heads of services. The SR (Service de Renseignements, or Intelligence Service), ordered to disband, managed to retain the framework of its organization and continued to function

underground at the cost of many lives. New civilian organizations sprang up which absorbed part of the General Staff and a number of Medical, Engineer, Ordnance, and Quartermaster officers. Military transport units reappeared under the guise of civilian transport agencies. Even civilian organizations created by the Vichy regime for national rehabilitation purposes underwent some unauthorized military instruction. Students attending a training center for the Chantiers de Jeunesse in 1941–42 were taught guerrilla warfare, a subject for obvious reasons taboo in the regular schools of the Armistice Army. On the basis of the experience gained at that center, the commanding officer later prepared and distributed *sub rosa* a 200-page manual on the organization and operational employment of guerrillas.[20]

In addition to, and often at odds with, these efforts on the part of regularly constituted authorities, other insurgent movements without official connection or backing developed after June 1940. Unwilling

---

[19] Général Revers, "L'O.R.A.," *La France et son Empire dans la Guerre,* ed. Louis Mouilleseaux (Paris: Editions Littéraires de France, 1947), II, 119–22; Maxime Weygand, *Mémoires: Rappelé au Service* (Paris: Flammarion, 1950), pp. 303–21; Intervs with Lt Gen Augustin Guillaume, Dec 48, and with Brig Gen Marcel Pénette, Jul 50. (See Bibliographical Note.)

[20] After the Franco-German armistice of June 1940, the Vichy Government created the Chantiers de Jeunesse (youth work camps somewhat similar to the CCC camps established in the United States in the thirties) for the purpose of putting to work, both in France and in North Africa, young men who had not yet reached the age of military conscription. Dressed in a green uniform of semi-civilian type, these men were primarily employed in tasks of public utility. The training center referred to above was the Ecole des Cadres located at Collonges, near Lyon, barely eighty-five miles from Vichy. For the role played by Chantiers de Jeunesse in North Africa, see p. 68, 68n, below.

The manual was *Instruction Provisoire sur l'Emploi des Corps Francs,* prepared by Maj. Charles de Virieu in 1943, clandestinely printed and distributed under German occupation in early 1944. Copy found in file "Material zur Freischzerlerfrage" (Material on Partisan Problem), Military Commander France, Oct 43 to Jul 44, GMDS No. 75486, located in German Military Documents Section, AGO.

to bow to the enemy, many citizens, especially in the German-occupied zone, began to organize into Resistance movements. These were generally sponsored and controlled by political parties. Their aim was to resist by force the occupying power as well as the Vichy Government, which they regarded as a defeatist, or even a pro-German, regime. The dubious behavior of some high officials, plus the increasingly harsh measures—such as the conscription of young men for forced labor in Germany and the deportation of political enemies of the "New Order"—taken by both the occupant and the more collaborationist element of the Vichy Government, forced many of the "resisters" to take refuge in remote areas. There they organized themselves into Maquis or guerrilla groups.

Eager to strengthen the spirit of resistance of the French in view of its potential military value, the British undertook as early as November 1940 to assist the underground forces morally and materially. Later, in 1943, the Americans joined in the task of supplying ammunition, equipment, and even personnel such as leaders, radio operators, and instructors in sabotage and guerrilla warfare.[21]

On 18 June 1940, four days before the signing of the Franco-German armistice, Brig. Gen. Charles de Gaulle, who had just made his way to London in a British plane, issued his now historic appeal over the BBC to the people of France urging them to continue the battle. Although on 23 June he was stripped of his military rank by the Vichy Government, the general rallied around him all Frenchmen willing to re-

main in the fight on the side of the British Commonwealth. In a letter dated 7 August, the British Prime Minister, Winston Churchill, recognized him as "head of all free Frenchmen, wherever located, who rally around you to the support of the Allied cause." [22] This recognition was followed, on the same day, by a formal agreement between the British Government and General de Gaulle which constituted the Charter of Free France.

A year later, on 24 September 1941, the Free France organization established in London a French National Committee under the presidency of General de Gaulle. To the world at large and more especially to an increasing number of the French people then under German occupation, General de Gaulle was fast becoming the symbol of the ultimate resurrection of France.

Meanwhile, a number of French overseas possessions had broken with the Vichy Government and announced their shift of allegiance to General de Gaulle. By the end of 1942 de Gaulle had control over French Equatorial Africa, the Cameroons, Syria, Madagascar, Djibouti, and Réunion. Military manpower available in these areas, added to Frenchmen who had escaped to the United Kingdom, produced a potential army of about 100,000 men. In late 1940 General de Gaulle had begun converting it to reality by creating staffs as well as ground, naval, and air units. These organized groups, known as Forces Françaises Libres or Free French Forces, grew to some 35,000 men by October 1942.[23]

---

[21] A brief evaluation of this Anglo-American undertaking and of the American share in providing material assistance to the Resistance forces is given in Chapter XVIII, below.

[22] Ltr, Churchill to de Gaulle, 7 Aug 40, quoted in Philippe Barrès, *Charles de Gaulle* (New York: Doubleday, Doran and Co., 1941), p. 147.

[23] Theoretically, they were renamed Forces Françaises Combattantes (Fighting French Forces) when, on 19 July 1942, the Free France organization changed its name to Fighting France in order

From the start, the Free French Forces operated under the control of the British who assumed the responsibility for feeding and equipping them. In mid-November 1941 President Franklin D. Roosevelt declared them eligible to receive American lend-lease equipment, not directly, but through the British.[24] Soon after the entry of the United States in the war, their status was re-examined as British and Americans studied the division of responsibility for equipping members of the United Nations. On 24 March 1942 the topmost Anglo-American military body, the Combined Chiefs of Staff, agreed on what amounted to a system of adoption by which the members of the United Nations would look for all their military supplies either to the United Kingdom or the United States. By this arrangement, the Free French Forces remained under the tutelage of the British, who would provide for the rearmament as well as the training of these forces except for the few stationed in the Pacific.[25] Thus, from the time they were organized in the fall of 1940 to the end of the Tunisian campaign in May 1943, the Free French were

almost entirely British-equipped and British-trained. During those two and a half years, they took an active part in military operations.

Their ground forces consisted of two main units. The first was the L Force, also known as the Leclerc Column, from the name of its commanding officer, Col. Jacques Leclerc. After making a spectacular dash from Lake Chad across northeastern Africa, the column reached Tripolitania where it fought gallantly under the operational control of the British Eighth Army. It was subsequently engaged in southern Tunisia. Later it was raised to the strength of a division, operating as the 2d Free French Division (2d DFL) under the command of Brig. Gen. Jacques Leclerc. The second unit was initially composed of the 1st and 2d Free French Brigades, of which the 1st, under the command of Brig. Gen. Pierre Koenig, distinguished itself, also under the British Eighth Army, at the battles of Bir Hacheim in Libya and El 'Alamein in Egypt. The two brigades having been reorganized, in February 1943, as the 1st Free French Division (1st DFL), the unit

---

to include the members of the Resistance forces. In practice, however, they generally retained their former appellation throughout the war. They will be referred to as Free French Forces or the Free French throughout this volume. Most important of the staffs created was the BCRA (Bureau Central de Renseignements et d'Action), whose function was to carry out clandestine operations in France. See p. 299–300, below.

[24] Ltr, Roosevelt to Edward R. Stettinius, Jr., 11 Nov 41, DAD Authority File of President's Ltrs.

[25] Min, CCS 13th Mtg, 24 Mar 42. (See Bibliographical Note.)

The Combined Chiefs of Staff, organized in January 1942 with headquarters in Washington, consisted of the British Chiefs of Staff or their designated representatives in the United States (British Joint Staff Mission) and the U.S. Joint Chiefs of Staff. Their task was to formulate and execute, under the direction of the heads of the countries involved, policies and plans relating to

the strategic conduct of the war, broad war requirements, allocation of munitions, and transportation requirements.

The British Chiefs of Staff were Field Marshal Sir Alan F. Brooke, Chief of the Imperial General Staff, Admiral of the Fleet Sir Dudley Pound (later replaced by Admiral of the Fleet Sir Andrew B. Cunningham), First Sea Lord, and Air Chief Marshal Sir Charles Portal, Chief of the Air Staff.

The U.S. Joint Chiefs of Staff were Admiral William D. Leahy, Chief of Staff to the Commander in Chief (President Roosevelt, later President Harry S. Truman), General George C. Marshall, Chief of Staff of the Army, Admiral Ernest J. King, Commander in Chief, U.S. Fleet, and Chief of Naval Operations, and General Henry H. Arnold, Commanding General, Army Air Forces.

See Gordon A. Harrison, *Cross-Channel Attack*, UNITED STATES ARMY IN WORLD WAR II (Washington, 1951), Ch. I.

was subsequently engaged, under the command of Maj. Gen. Pierre Koenig, in southern Tunisia along with the Leclerc Column. From their earliest commitment to combat up to the end of operations in that area the Free French Ground Forces had suffered nearly 3,700 casualties, including 1,160 killed in action. Likewise participating in Allied operations were the Free French Naval Forces and the Free French Air Forces. By October 1942 the Air Forces had grown to five squadrons. Two were operating from the United Kingdom, one in the Middle East, and one in Libya in conjunction with the Free French Ground Forces. Shortly afterward, the remaining squadron departed for the USSR, there to participate in operations on the Russian front under Russian control.[26]

Not all of the overseas possessions had rallied to General de Gaulle. In French North Africa (Tunisia, Algeria, and French Morocco) and West Africa, military authorities had chosen the policy of "unity of the French Union behind the Marshal." The African Army had been greatly reduced in numbers and efficiency as a result of its participation in the campaign in France of May–June 1940 and subsequent demobilization. Its chiefs—Generals Maxime Weygand, Alphonse Juin, Auguste Noguès, and others—first undertook the task of reorganizing, re-equipping, and training such forces as were authorized under the terms of the Franco-German armistice.[27]

The strength of these forces was set successively, with German agreement, at 100,000, 120,000, and finally 137,000 in 1942. By waging an active recruiting campaign especially among the native population, and by obtaining from the General Staff in Vichy additional French cadres, the North African military authorities gradually built the army to its authorized strength. Simultaneously they took steps to reorganize the necessary services, find equipment, and rekindle the morale of the troops.

As in the case of the Metropolitan Armistice Army, it appears that individual staff officers or groups of officers exerted considerable effort to increase the African Army over and above the authorized level.[28] They put into effect a bold, secret program which had a twofold objective: immediate concealment of extra troops and equipment, and mobilization of additional men in the event of hostilities. The program, unlike that undertaken in continental France, proceeded with relatively little interference from Axis armistice commissions. It was particularly successful in mountainous French Morocco; the geographical situation at the westernmost end of North Africa encouraged and facilitated clandes-

---

[26] Figures on losses are taken from Lt. Col. P. Santini, "Etude statistique sur les pertes au cours de la guerre 1939–1945," *Revue du Corps de Santé Militaire*, X, No. 1 (March, 1954).

Les Forces Aériennes Françaises de 1939 à 1945, ed. Pierre Paquier (Paris: Berger-Levrault, 1949), pp. 53–65, a semiofficial publication prepared by a group of French Air Force officers. See also pp. 195, 376, below.

[27] Although the avowed purpose of the rehabili-

tation of the North African Army was to provide for the defense of that area against *any* invader, recent written and oral statements from various Army officials then in control leave little doubt that their secret hope was that their forces would take up arms once more against the Axis in conjunction with an eventual Allied intervention on French territory. Evidence in this connection: Weygand, *op. cit.;* Gen Noguès, Corres with OCMH; Intervs with Gen Guillaume, Nov 48, with Gen Juin, Dec 48, with Gen Pénette, Jul 50.

[28] Adm. Pierre Barjot, *Le débarquement du 8 Novembre 1942 en Afrique du Nord* (Paris: J. de Gigord, 1948); René Richard and Alain de Sérigny, *L'Enigme d'Alger* (Paris: Librairie Arthème Fayard, 1947), pp. 203–14; Weygand, *op. cit.,* pp. 395–405; info provided by Gen Pénette, Jul 50.

tine activities. The results were impressive: some 60,000 men, including short-term volunteers, civilian workers, laborers, auxiliary police, and goumiers (or Moroccan riflemen), were secretly maintained in various mountain areas. A secret plan was worked out to mobilize 109,000 men and requisition transport vehicles, animals, and supplies in the event of hostilities.[29]

As for equipment, 59,000 weapons and 22,000,000 rounds of ammunition above the levels authorized under the armistice were hidden away. Most of this matériel had been concealed immediately after the armistice on orders from local commanders. Some weapons in time were manufactured locally from odds and ends.

Finally steps were taken to increase the capabilities and efficiency of important services such as the radio communication system and the medical corps, and to replenish quartermaster stocks. Additional roads, trails, and rail lines were constructed to improve the transportation network.[30]

In French West Africa armistice commissions had not determined the number of men or the amount of equipment to be authorized in that area. French military authorities as a result had the opportunity to play up their defenseless position in the face of Allied threats to Dakar, and to convince the Germans of the need for strengthening West African garrisons. A force of some 50,000 men was eventually raised. But it received little equipment, no tanks, and no antitank guns.[31]

Pre-TORCH Negotiations on Supplying the French

By the spring of 1942, General de Gaulle was confident that in the event of an Allied landing in France, large numbers of Frenchmen would rally to the common cause and assume under his leadership a substantial share of the fighting. To implement the ambitious rearmament program which he had just completed, he decided to tap the real source of equipment, the United States. In May and again in June, he and members of his National Committee asked American officials in London whether or not the United States would agree to allocate and deliver equipment, under the Lend-Lease Act, directly to the Free French Forces instead of through the British as was the practice.[32] Before American authorities could take action on the matter, Free French headquarters submitted in July and again in August and September of the same year a series of concrete proposals. These called for re-equipping with U.S. matériel not only the existing Free French units but the much larger forces expected to be raised once an Allied assault on continental France had been launched.[33]

---

[29] Info furnished by Gen Pénette, Jul 50. General Pénette, a captain assigned to General Weygand's staff in North Africa in early 1941, is credited with having initiated the program. See also Weygand, *op. cit.*, pp. 395–405.

Col. Augustin Guillaume, then on General Noguès' staff, was in charge of recruiting, equipping, and training the goumiers. With the connivance of officials in the Vichy Government, he obtained substantial appropriations with which to carry his work on and secured additional cadres from France. In this manner, he was able to conceal several thousand goumiers. Interv with Gen Guillaume, Nov 48.

[30] Info supplied by Gen Pénette, 1952.

[31] Maj Gen Emile Béthouart's statement at 6th MRP Meeting, 7 Jan 43, CCS 334, Military Representatives of the Associated Pacific Powers (5–26–42); see also Interv with Gen Pénette, Jul 50.

[32] Memo, Adm Harold Stark, 2 Jun 42, in Comdr U.S. Naval Forces in Europe, US-French Relations, App. B, Pt. I, copy in OCMH.

[33] Notes 2 and 3, Gen de Gaulle's Special Staff, 21 Jul and 4 Aug 42, OPD 336 France, Sec 1;

The proposals were turned down for a number of reasons. First, there were at the time more pressing needs for armament and matériel elsewhere. In the opinion of General George C. Marshall, Chief of Staff of the U.S. Army, the limited striking power of the Free French Forces did not warrant such increased allocations of matériel as those requested by General de Gaulle. In addition, there was considerable reluctance on the part of American authorities to have dealings with the Free French military headquarters. Not that the integrity of General de Gaulle himself was in the least questioned, but experience had convinced Anglo-American planners that his organization was "extremely leaky" from the standpoint of security.[34] More important still was the fact that at the very moment when the Free French armament request was being submitted, U.S. military authorities in London and Washington were putting the final touches to plans for an assault not on France but on northwest Africa (Operation TORCH). In line with the policy of avoiding all official exchange of information with the Gaullists, the latter were being excluded from planning for, and participation in, the contemplated operation. At the same time, however, American planners were negotiating with other French authorities for active French support.[35]

General Giraud, who had been in southern France since late April 1942 after his daring and spectacular escape from intern-

ment in Germany, was regarded by American officials as the available military figure most likely to be successful in leading French North and West Africa back into the war on the side of the Allies. A soldier first and foremost, General Giraud cut a legendary figure in the eyes of most Frenchmen. His recent escape was the second such exploit in his life, the first having taken place in World War I. At the outbreak of hostilities in September 1939, he was leading the French Seventh Army. In mid-May 1940, soon after the German break-through at Sedan, he took command of a group of armies and desperately attempted to stem the German advance only to be taken prisoner. In early 1942, after his return to France, American representatives approached him secretly and obtained his promise of support. General Giraud felt that the Allies should consider a landing on the Mediterranean coast of France simultaneous with the invasion of North Africa. For the forces that he expected to assemble in the bridgehead from available French manpower, he urged the Allies on 27 October to include in their logistical planning the provision of some 150,000 tons of war matériel to be brought from Gibraltar to a port in southern France.[36] Such a proposal was out of the question for, unknown to General Giraud, TORCH had long passed the planning stage. In fact, the assault troops were already at sea. Finally persuaded that he must accept Allied plans and expecting that they would go into effect in an operation beginning several months later, General Giraud signified his readiness to be brought to North Africa at the opportune moment.

In North Africa, meanwhile, the heads of a small band of determined French offi-

---

Memo, Col Emmanuel Lombard for Adm Stark, 26 Aug 42, OCS A–45–523 (France).

[34] Memo, Gen Marshall for Secy State, 20 Nov 42, OPD 336 France, Sec 1.

[35] Memo, Marshall for Adm Ernest J. King, 1 Oct 42, OCS A–45–523 (France) ; Memo, Brig Gen Albert C. Wedemeyer for Maj Gen George V. Strong, 29 Oct 42, OPD 336 France, Sec 1 ; Memo, Marshall for President, 3 Sep 42, WDCSA 381 TORCH (9–3–42).

[36] Général [Henri] Giraud, *Un seul but, la Victoire* (Paris: R. Julliard, 1949), pp. 336–38.

cers and civilians who had long pledged
themselves to the Allied cause and had welcomed General Giraud's promise of leadership were preparing for the role they
expected to play at the time of the Allied
landings. In the course of the secret meeting held at Cherchel on 23 October, at
which General Clark relayed President
Roosevelt's pledge of assistance to the African forces in the event of their re-entry in
the war, he and General Mast, military
leader of the French "dissidents" and
spokesman for General Giraud, discussed
the nature and amount of armament that
would be required. A week later, in two
letters addressed to General Giraud, Robert
D. Murphy, the U.S. political representative in North Africa, confirmed the President's intent as disclosed at Cherchel:
"During [the period following the land-
ings] the Government of the United States
will bend its efforts to furnish the French
forces with arms and modern equipment. . . . The United States Government will extend the benefits of the
Lend-Lease Act to the requisitions for matériel from the United States intended to
give the French Army the means to participate in the common struggle. The United
States Government will facilitate the negotiation and implementation of these
requisitions." [37]

On the strength of the assurances he had
been given, General Mast submitted at
once and in great secrecy an extensive
and detailed rearmament program, known
thereafter as the Mast Plan. The program
was based on the assumption that French
North Africa would be able to raise, by the
end of the first month after the landings,
eight infantry and two armored divisions,

together with a number of tank, artillery,
air, and service units. Actually the Mast
Plan was the third rearmament scheme to
be submitted before TORCH to American
representatives in North Africa. It was
drawn up by Lt. Col. Louis Jousse, a Resistance member on the staff of General
Mast, who had already proposed (in December 1941 and June 1942) the equipping of two armored and six infantry divisions. Neither the first Jousse program nor
the still earlier rearmament study submitted
in March 1941 by Capt. André Beaufre,
another Resistance member on the staff of
the Governor General of Algeria, was officially acted upon. [38] In point of fact the
possibility that the United States would
some day undertake a French armament
program had not yet been seriously considered by the War Department, and for
a number of reasons.

First, it was not until July 1942 that
British and American planners decided on
an invasion of northwest Africa as part of
the Anglo-American "Grand Strategy," a
strategy which involved operations on many
fronts. For some time before, they had
tossed back and forth a plan to land in
France itself, but had abandoned the
project in favor of the North African venture, thus removing for the time any consideration of an armament program for
Metropolitan France. [39]

Even after plans for TORCH began to
take shape, there could be no question of
an armament program for the North African forces. Allied planners were being
faced with crucial issues, in particular a

---

[37] Text of both letters, dated 2 November, in
French Records, File 221, OCMH.

[38] Intervs with Col. André Beaufre, 7 and 9 Sep
50; Barjot, op. cit., pp. 34–36, 54–55.
[39] See Maurice Matloff and Edwin M. Snell,
Strategic Planning for Coalition Warfare: 1941–
1942, UNITED STATES ARMY IN WORLD
WAR II (Washington, 1953), Chs. XII and XIII.

shipping and equipment situation rendered critical by the heavy demands from China and the USSR for matériel. An ambitious American armament program known as the Victory Program had been initiated in late 1941; it visualized a maximum U.S. ground force of over 200 divisions as necessary to accomplish the defeat of America's potential enemies.[40] The program still was in its early phase of implementation. Even to equip the American divisions earmarked for TORCH required that other divisions in training in the United States be "scalped" of their matériel.[41] To provide arms for forces such as the North African Army would necessitate stripping more U.S. units. At any rate the question was premature in view of the uncertainty regarding North Africa's eventual reaction to TORCH itself.

By September the encouraging results of the secret negotiations carried out with the dissidents gave hope that the North African forces would join the Allies. The problem of providing them with arms was now in the foreground. In October the assurances given at Cherchel forced the issue: the Mast Plan would have to be taken into serious consideration in Washington.

In transmitting to the War Department a partial list of the Mast requirements, Lt. Gen. Dwight D. Eisenhower, commanding general of the TORCH forces, urged that he be informed as to the ability of the United States to furnish the necessary items of equipment and the rates at which they could be made available. His intention was to include the matériel in later shipments "in

accordance with the situation as it develops." [42]

After rapid examination of the Mast Plan, War Department officials concluded that, in general, the items on the partial list of requirements could be made available for shipment by 20 December 1942. To carry out the entire plan, they warned, would require stripping twelve American divisions. They urged therefore that only such matériel be provided as was necessary to supplement existing French equipment.[43] Their recommendation was submitted to General Marshall, who approved furnishing supplementary equipment when it could be determined that the French would take an active part in operations.[44] Commenting on the French request for aircraft, Lt. Gen. Henry H. Arnold, Commanding General, Army Air Forces, urged that caution be exercised in the employment of French pilots. He recommended that as soon as practicable after the initial phases qualified French pilots, once their loyalty had been determined, be incorporated in American combat and service units. When their ability had been ascertained and as their numbers increased, flights within American squadrons might be formed, progressing gradually to all-French combat and service units using U.S. equipment. In his opinion, the factors of importance to be considered included determination of loyalty, need for security, language differences, ability to absorb training, and familarization with American equipment.[45]

The invasion of northwest Africa thus

---

[40] See Richard M. Leighton and Robert W. Coakley, *Global Logistics and Strategy: 1940–1943*, UNITED STATES ARMY IN WORLD WAR II (Washington, 1955).

[41] Matloff and Snell, *op. cit.*, p. 318.

[42] Msg 4259, Eisenhower to AGWAR, 30 Oct 42, ABC 400 (11–11–42), Sec 1.

[43] Memo, Chief, Logistics Gp OPD, for Lt Gen John E. Hull, 31 Oct 42, OPD 400 France, Sec 1.

[44] Planning Div Diary, ASF File, 1 Nov 42.

[45] Msg R–2728, Arnold to Maj Gen Carl Spaatz, 3 Nov 42, ABC 400 (11–11–42), Sec 1.

brought suddenly to a head the question of American large-scale and rapid rearmament of the French. By November a plan was in being and it had been tentatively approved. Yet all the thorny problems of rearmament still lay ahead as the Allied armada steamed toward the coast of Africa to deliver the first Anglo-American blow for the liberation of Western Europe.

The French North and West African Forces Throw Their Weight on the Side of the Allies

Operation TORCH, directed by General Eisenhower, was launched on the night of 7–8 November 1942.[46] The assault troops numbered some 83,000 Americans and 26,000 British, or a total of 109,000 men, the British in addition furnishing almost all the shipping and carrier air support. As they landed, the invaders eagerly hoped that the French would welcome them or offer no more than token resistance. In the Algiers area, the timely and effective intervention of the French dissidents circumscribed hostilities and rapidly brought them to an end. At Oran and more particularly in and around Casablanca, the Allies met with strong, even bitter, resistance.[47]

When, on 9 November, General Giraud reached North Africa after much unexpected delay, another French official, Admiral François Darlan, commander in chief of all the armed forces of the Vichy Government, was already in control and had assumed the role of leader of the forces opposing the Allies. He had agreed on the previous day to a local cease fire at Algiers and was negotiating with the Allied authorities there for a broader understanding while in communication with Marshal Pétain. Not until 10 November did Darlan order all resistance in French North Africa to cease, and not until 13 November did he succeed in arranging with other French officials for a provisional French government in Algiers under his leadership which would renew hostilities against the Axis Powers. On 14 November he appointed General Giraud commander in chief of all French ground and air forces in the territory. An agreement signed by Admiral Darlan and General Clark on 22 November set forth the terms under which French North Africa was joining the Allied camp. The North African Army was back in the war.[48]

The Germans, meanwhile, alarmed at the turn of events across the Mediterranean, had made two quick moves. On 9

---

[46] For a detailed account of TORCH, see George F. Howe, *Northwest Africa: Seizing the Initiative in the West,* UNITED STATES ARMY IN WORLD WAR II (Washington, 1957).

[47] French authorities in control at the time have, since then, ascribed this resistance to a lack of understanding, before the operation, between the Allied command and themselves. They were caught off guard, they claim, and had no opportunity of releasing officers under their respective command from the loyalty pledge which the latter had been required to give to their commander in chief, Marshal Pétain. The dissident leaders, on the contrary, have blamed it on faulty or insufficient co-ordination between their own forces and the Allies, and on the fact that General Giraud had not reached Africa by D Day. Whatever the reasons,

a brief but bloody encounter ensued accompanied by considerable political and military confusion on the side of the French.

[48] For detailed information regarding the relations of Darlan with the Allied authorities, see William L. Langer, *Our Vichy Gamble* (New York: Alfred A. Knopf, 1947), and Howe, *Northwest Africa.* The English text of the Clark-Darlan Agreement may be found in Arthur Layton Funk, "A Document Relating to the Second World War: The Clark-Darlan Agreement, November 22, 1942," *The Journal of Modern History,* XXV No. 1 (March, 1953), 61–65; a French translation, in René Richard and Alain de Sérigny, *L'Enigme d'Alger* (Paris: Librairie Arthème Fayard, 1947), pp. 270–76.

November, taking advantage of the confusion prevailing among the French North African authorities, they had gained a foothold on the eastern coast of Tunisia and were hastily building up strength in that area. On 11 November their occupation forces in France had crossed the demarcation line, overrun the free zone, and ordered the Armistice Army disarmed. Not only would this German action cause the large French fleet harbored in Toulon to scuttle itself,[49] on 27 November, rather than to fall in enemy hands, but it would wipe out many of the valuable gains laboriously achieved in great secrecy by the French General Staff. Resigning themselves to the fact that the Allies had chosen not to land in France proper at this time, a small number of officers and personnel of the Armistice Army prepared to escape from France in order to join French forces overseas. A larger number formed a secret organization known as Organisation de Résistance de l'Armée for the purpose of continuing underground the activities they had c o n d u c t e d in semiclandestinity. Working now in conjunction with other existing underground forces, they resolved to prepare for the day when they could again fight in the open alongside the Allies for the liberation of their country.

With French North Africa, except for the eastern coast of Tunisia, securely on the side of the Allies, the active participation of France in the common struggle suddenly assumed considerably larger proportions. Until then it had been limited to the relatively small force of General de Gaulle. Now another much larger French force was swelling the ranks of Allied military manpower by some 197,000

men, including the North African Armistice Army and the 60,000 troops heretofore maintained in mountain hide-outs. By the end of November, when the effects of the secretly prepared mobilization had been felt, another 68,000 men had answered the call to the colors, bringing the total number of effectives under arms in North Africa to 265,000 men, or nearly twice the size of the Armistice Army. Meanwhile the rallying of French West Africa, on 22 November, had provided a further increase of 50,000 men, thus raising the effectives available to General Giraud in both North and West Africa to over 300,000 men.[50]

Initially these effectives were distributed as follows: one infantry division in Tunisia; three infantry divisions and one light mechanized brigade in Algeria; two infantry divisions, one light mechanized brigade, and 5,000 goumiers in French Morocco. In addition, scattered throughout the three areas were several regiments of general reserve troops, service units, Territorial and Sovereignty troops and installations, some naval and merchant ships for the most part in need of much repair, and a few air squadrons.

Figures on equipment and war matériel in the hands of these forces as they were re-entering the war cannot be accurately

---

[49] This fleet represented approximately one half of the French Navy.

[50] Although the secret mobilization program contemplated the recall of 109,000 reservists, only 68,000, of whom half were natives, answered the call to the colors. The partial response has been attributed to three main factors:

1. inaccuracies in the mobilization program itself caused by the conditions of secrecy existing at the time the program was drafted;

2. last-minute decision not to call up reservists engaged in or needed for defense work;

3. near paralysis of the mobilization operations because of the Allied requisition of most available transportation and housing facilities.

Interv with Gen Pénette, Jul 50; notes and statistics from Gen Pénette, Jul 50, Aug 52.

given. The only available statistics, as shown in Table 2, are dated 1 October 1942 and therefore apply to the pre-TORCH period. Of the equipment listed, an indeterminate percentage was used up or destroyed in the course of the brief period of resistance, 8–11 November. Losses were light in infantry weapons but particularly heavy in tanks, light armored cars, and airplanes. Over 50 percent of the latter are said to have been destroyed.[51]

As it passed under General Giraud's command, the African Army, half-organized and ill-equipped, could be regarded only as a "transition" force. Yet General Eisenhower, now Commander in Chief,

Allied Forces in North Africa (hereafter referred to as Allied Commander in Chief), was already depending on it to cover the continuous flow of incoming Allied units, to maintain internal security in North Africa, and to reinforce his own Anglo-American troops then rushing to meet the mounting threat in the east. By his first directive of 15 November, General Giraud committed this transition force to the pursuit of the German units established in Tunisia.[52] Four days later, French elements, now part of the combined Allied armies, were firing their first shots at their former enemy in the hills west of Tunis, a prelude to a bitter campaign to come.

[52] Dir 1, in Fr Rcds File 220, Vol. I, Reorgn of Fr Army, OCMH.

[51] *Ibid.*

TABLE 2—EQUIPMENT, BY TYPE, AVAILABLE TO THE NORTH AFRICAN FORCES:

1 OCTOBER 1942

Type	Total	In Hands of Troops and in Stock	Concealed
Weapons (Except Combat Vehicles)			
Flame Thrower	72	0	72
Gun, Artillery	515	358	157
Gun, Machine	4,525	3,014	1,511
Mortar, 81-mm.	550	340	210
Rifle (Including Automatic Rifle)	310,700	253,200	57,500
Ammunition (Rounds)			
81-mm. Mortar Shell	420,000	376,000	44,000
20-mm. Machine Gun, AA	88,000	38,000	50,000
8- and 7.5-mm. Rifle	178,000,000	152,000,000	26,000,000
Artillery, All Calibers	1,494,380	1,199,000	295,380
Light Tanks and Armored Cars	388	335	53
Airplanes	700	(a)	(a)
Food and Clothing	(b)	(b)	(b)

a Distribution not available.
b Stocks exceeded the needs of the Armistice Army.

Source: From information furnished by General Pénette, July 1950.

PART ONE

THE NORTH AFRICAN FORCES

CHAPTER I

Early Attempts To Formulate a Rearmament Program

The alignment of French North and West Africa on the side of the Allies posed a multitude of problems, political as well as military. On the political scene, Admiral Darlan's assumption of power, which the Allies had accepted as a temporary expedient at a time when resistance to the landings was going on, had produced a situation fraught with danger. The admiral's ties with Marshal Pétain's government at Vichy made impossible the merging of his following with General de Gaulle's and created instead a condition highly conducive to French factionalism rather than national unity in prosecuting the war. The problem was suddenly removed, on 24 December, when Darlan was struck down by an assassin's bullet. On orders from the Imperial Council which Darlan himself had created, General Giraud replaced him as High Commissioner for North and West Africa while remaining Commander in Chief of all armed forces including naval units. The political calm was to be short-lived. For the ensuing sixteen months one crisis after another would erupt on the French political scene and create for General Giraud increasingly difficult problems. The evolution of French internal politics during that period will not be treated in detail. However, inasmuch as the situation did at times affect, to the point of endangering them, the good relations established at an early

date between the Anglo-American authorities and the French High Command, notice will be taken of at least those political events that had a decisive influence on the course of French rearmament.[1]

Procedures

On 13 November President Roosevelt hailed North Africa's shift to the Allied camp by extending to its forces the benefits of the Lend-Lease Act, benefits heretofore enjoyed by General de Gaulle's Free French. The North African forces now were eligible to receive munitions from the Anglo-American pool of equipment. Because of the promises made at Cherchel, which placed them squarely within the American sphere of influence, equipping them would be a responsibility to be assumed by the U.S. Government and the matériel involved would be provided from American production. The Free French, on the other hand, would continue to receive armament through the British, who still held operational control of their larger units.

The procedure expected to be followed for the assignment and delivery of matériel to French North Africa would be that nor-

---

[1] For additional information on the French political situation from November 1942 to July 1943, see Howe, *Northwest Africa.*

mally applicable in the case of the United Nations whose re-equipment was similarly charged against U.S. production. Each requirement submitted by any one of these nations was transmitted to Operations Division (OPD) of the War Department. If approved by OPD, it was forwarded to the International Division of the Army Service Forces (ASF).[2] The various branches and sections of the International Division then screened the requirement, broke it down according to technical service, determined production possibilities in the light of other requirements, charged it against U.S. production, and included it in the over-all Army Supply Program. From then on, ASF was responsible for the production and distribution of the items involved. In the case of airplanes and air force items, the same procedure was followed except that the Army Air Forces instead of the International Division was responsible for processing the requirement and for including it in the Air Forces section of the Army Supply Program. In both instances, however, the decision to accept the requirement was one to be made by the War Department alone.[3]

The decision to assign the equipment involved bilateral action since it could be effected only through the combined Anglo-American Munitions Assignments Boards established, one in Washington (MAB), and one in London (LMAB), as part of the Combined Chiefs of Staff machinery. The United States having assumed the burden of furnishing matériel to the French, assignments to them became the responsibility of the MAB, the board charged with

allocating American munitions production.

The MAB operated through three subcommittees: the Munitions Assignments Committee (Ground), MAC (G); the Munitions Assignments Committee (Air), MAC (A); and the Munitions Assignments Committee (Navy), MAC (N). The Air and Navy committees assigned items peculiar to the Air Forces and Navy respectively. The Ground committee was responsible for the assignment of all other items. Since the membership of these committees was a combined one, unanimous agreement was required before action could be implemented.

The MAB and its subcommittees considered U.S. production of military items as a pool production without regard to the particular requirement for which production had been initiated. Assignments of current production were made at weekly meetings of the board and its subcommittees in the light of existing shipping and matériel availability and of the over-all strategic and operational requirements of the United Nations including the United States. Assignments normally followed accepted requirements. There were instances, however, where production of a given item was initiated as a result of a requirement stated on behalf of one member of the United Nations, while delivery of the item so produced was made to another member nation because of changes in circumstances and operational requirements between the time when production was initiated and the time when the item became available. Whether or not such delivery would be authorized and when it would be effected was left to the decision of the MAB.

Since the MAB received its policy from the CCS, it follows, therefore, that the

---

[2] Known as Services of Supply (SOS) before March 1943.

[3] Tab D to Memo, Maj Gen Wilhelm D. Styer for Eisenhower, 10 Feb 43, JRC Misc Doc, Item 5–a.

latter held the final authority in the matter of the granting or rejecting of munitions requests from individual members of the United Nations. In practice this CCS authority limited itself to laying down the general policy to be followed with respect to the member nation concerned. To arrive at their decision, the U.S. Joint Chiefs of Staff (JCS) sought advice from the various sections of their respective General Staff agencies. Of these, Operations Division was largely responsible for influencing or determining rearmament policies on the basis of recommendations from theater commanders and in the light of global U.S. commitments.[4]

Initial Groping Toward a Policy

Armament negotiations, suspended at the close of the Cherchel meeting pending the outcome of TORCH, could now be resumed. As they got under way, it soon became clear that the main protagonists, General Giraud, General Eisenhower, the War Department, and the Combined Chiefs of Staff, were approaching the rearmament problem from different points of view. The problem itself, moreover, was complicated by the fact that it involved two distinct yet closely related issues. One was the emergency provision of minimum matériel, chiefly arms, to the French units being sent to the Tunisian front in increasing numbers; the other was the large-scale rehabilitation of all African forces, such as the Mast Plan advocated, for participation in subsequent operations. From mid-November to late January 1943, divergence of opinion regarding the immediate as well

---

[4] For detailed information on acceptance of requirements and assignments of matériel, see Leighton and Coakley, *Global Logistics and Strategy: 1940–1943.*

as future employment of the North African forces, anxiety over operational developments in Tunisia, and the still critical shipping and equipment situation facing the Anglo-American allies all combined to impede attempts to formulate an armament program.

In the judgment of the French Commander in Chief, emergency equipment of the forces in action was urgent, of course, but the main issue was the conversion of his large yet poorly equipped transition army into a striking force capable of intervening in Tunisia as well as on future battlefields. Only a reconstituted French Army could restore French prestige. It was essential, then, that a large-scale rearmament program be instituted at once.

General Giraud's estimate of French capabilities was highly optimistic. From the outset he took the position that he would have no difficulty in putting into the field an effective fighting force of 250,000, even 300,000 men. These figures included the troops already available, several classes of natives and Frenchmen, soon to be mobilized, Frenchmen who were expected to escape from France in increasing numbers, as well as French nationals residing in foreign countries who were likely to enlist.

If the question had been mere numbers, General Giraud's planning would not have been unduly optimistic. But a modern army needs a high percentage of technicians. General Giraud had very few Europeans, and it soon became apparent that Moroccan, Algerian, and Tunisian natives either could not be used at all in specialized combat and service units or needed a very long period of training. The lack of white manpower was to be the source of increasing difficulties for General Giraud. In the beginning, however, the French commander, confident of his ability to raise a sizable fighting force, directed his headquarters to draft a large-scale rearmament program along the lines of the Mast Plan.

The CCS were still studying the Mast Plan. On 13 November they directed the MAB to review assignments for November and December in order to determine what matériel (except aircraft) could be made available to the French before the end of the year.[5] Simultaneously they requested the Allied Commander in Chief to submit his views and recommendations on the plan, warning him to keep in mind that shipments of matériel for the French would necessarily be at the expense of the build-up of his own forces.[6] General Eisenhower replied that the extent to which the African forces should be re-equipped by the United States depended on how they would be employed ultimately—a matter still to be determined—and on the number of first-line troops the French High Command would produce. He felt that if General Giraud could activate the number of units he claimed he could raise, "which was doubtful," it would be possible to eliminate some of the last U.S. divisions planned for shipment to the theater. He pointed out that a detailed study of the matter would soon be prepared by his headquarters and the results forwarded to the CCS.[7]

General Eisenhower was not at first convinced of the value of arming the French in view of the uncertainty regarding their combat effectiveness against the Axis. Reports reaching him during the first week of Franco-Allied collaboration seriously questioned the offensive spirit of the North Afri-

can forces. He felt, then, he could expect little of them for the present at least. He would use them initially as garrison forces in the theater. Later he might employ certain selected units in combat operations. In the belief that an early token shipment of equipment "as a political gesture" would produce beneficial effects "in every way," he recommended to the CCS, on 18 November, that small arms, antitank, and antiaircraft armament, with spare parts and ammunition, be sent forthwith to the French. As an initial shipment, he suggested 8,000 rifles, 36 37-mm. antitank guns, and 32 antiaircraft automatic guns of any type available.[8] The next day, French and German forces already were coming to blows.

Before long, reports from Tunisia indicated a marked stiffening of the French fighting spirit. This in turn suggested that the French had succeeded in solving the complex morale problem which had faced them in the second and third weeks of November. They seemed to have recovered from the successive psychological shocks of that early period: the "token" resistance directed against the Allies, the conflicting orders to which they had been subjected, the sudden breaking off with the mother country, their shift of allegiance, finally their being thrown into battle almost without equipment. Now they were reported to be doing well in combat. Gradually General Eisenhower was acquiring the conviction that he could count on them.

For the Allied commander, then, the immediate question was how to keep French units in the line in Tunisia. In his opinion the emergency issue of minimum equipment to enable them to fight must be the primary concern of any rearmament program. The

---

[5] Min, CCS 48th Mtg, 13 Nov 42.
[6] Msg, CCS to Eisenhower, 13 Nov 42, FAN 18.
[7] Msg 866, Eisenhower to CCS, 18 Nov 42, AFHQ 0100/12C G–3 Div Ops Fr Equip.

[8] Ibid.

wholesale rehabilitation of the entire North African Army, a long-range issue related to future, unpredictable campaigns in the Mediterranean or in Europe, must be given second priority.

Setting Up the Joint Rearmament Committee

Providing equipment to the French already was posing serious problems for General Eisenhower and his headquarters, Allied Force Headquarters (AFHQ), established in Algiers shortly after the Allied landings. As problems kept multiplying the Allied Commander in Chief ordered, on 16 December, the organization at AFHQ of a special agency to act both as a clearinghouse and as the authority responsible for developing an armament program. He then placed the agency, known as the Joint Rearmament Committee (JRC), directly under the authority of his chief of staff.[9] The creation of the JRC had been urged by the Chief, Liaison Section, AFHQ, whom the French had for some time queried with mounting insistence regarding a variety of matters, such as the procurement of token issues of British and American equipment, probable dates of delivery, specifications of American matériel, establishment of schools of instruction, translation of technical manuals, and other problems.[10]

The responsibilities and functions of the JRC were as follows:

a. To centralize all equipment requests from the French.

b. To develop a program for the rehabilitation of the French armed forces.

c. To ensure that the executive action necessary to implement the approved program was placed with the responsible section of AFHQ.

d. To undertake all matters of co-ordination with the French authorities, the Lend-Lease Administration, and others concerned with the rearmament of the French.

The committee, composed initially of nine members—four American, four French, and one British—met for the first time on 23 December under the chairmanship of the senior U.S. member, Col. William Tudor Gardiner.[11] It operated for approximately twenty-two months, its functions, responsibilities, membership, and place in the staff structure varying from time to time. Throughout the entire period the committee played a major role in the rehabilitation of the French African forces.[12]

While the JRC and its parent organization, AFHQ, were charged with the overall problem of equipping the French from Allied sources, the responsibility for handing over American matériel assigned in Washington rested solely with the commander of the U.S. forces in the theater. The responsibility was that of General Eisenhower, who commanded not only AFHQ but also Headquarters, European Theater of Operations, U.S. Army (ETOUSA), operating in London. The responsibility continued to be his after 3 February 1943, when he took command of the newly created Headquarters, North African Theater of Operations, U.S. Army (NATOUSA), established in Algiers as a headquarters separate from ETOUSA.

---

[9] AFHQ Staff Memo 52, 16 Dec 42, AFHQ 0100/12C G–3 Div Ops Fr Equip.

[10] Memo, Col Julius C. Holmes for CofS AFHQ, 5 Dec 42, JRC 320/001 Orgn of JRC.

[11] Min, JRC Mtg, 23 Dec 42, JRC 320/001 Orgn of JRC.

[12] For information on organization, membership, and activities of the JRC, see Ch. XVII, below.

LT. GEN. DWIGHT D. EISEN-
HOWER, *commanding general of the
TORCH forces.*

General Giraud Sends a Military Mission to Washington

Eager to obtain from the United States an early decision on the provision of war matériel, General Giraud, in the first week of December, announced his intention of sending to Washington a military mission empowered to discuss with the War Department all questions of supply. General Eisenhower greeted the proposal with some skepticism. In a message to General Marshall, he pointed out that missions of this kind were "usually only a source of annoyance to the CCS" and could accomplish "little or nothing" in their dealings with the MAB, and that recommendations from his headquarters would be required in any case. He suggested, however, that the mission be allowed to proceed as

"it might be a good thing for these people to realize at first hand the complications involved in supplying a world conflict." [13] The JCS having approved the proposal, the mission, headed by Maj. Gen. Emile Béthouart, departed from Algiers on 20 December. Its function, as defined by the French Commander in Chief, was to negotiate and expedite the delivery of matériel on the basis of the requirements set up by the French High Command and within the framework of agreements to be concluded with the U.S. Government.[14] Temporarily assigned to the mission was Jacques Lemaigre-Dubreuil, then chief of the Research Section of General Giraud's headquarters, whose duty was to obtain the production and shipping priorities necessary for the speedy delivery of matériel to the French forces and, incidentally, to act as the French commander's civilian representative in the United States. Both General Béthouart and Mr. Lemaigre-Dubreuil were stanch friends of the United States. Members of the North African "dissidence" of long standing, they had, a month earlier, distinguished themselves in their valiant attempt to prevent opposition to the American landings.

The mission arrived in Washington on 24 December.[15] Throughout the war, it formed the principal link between the French High Command and the War Department. Liaison, however, remained almost its sole function as General Eisenhower had foreseen. The entire responsibility for initiating and implementing the rearmament programs subsequently estab-

[13] Msg 1812, Eisenhower to Marshall, 12 Dec 42, ABC 334.8 (12–4–42).
[14] Memo, Giraud for Béthouart, 10 Dec 42, in same file.
[15] AFHQ 0100/4 SACS Rcd Sec, Béthouart, Nov 42–Jan 43.

lished by decision of the CCS rested with the Allied Commander in Chief in the theater of operations.[16]

Emergency Provision of Equipment

On 20 November the CCS approved the recommendation submitted two days before by General Eisenhower, and directed the MAB to assign the equipment. They stipulated that the United Kingdom would furnish the 8,000 rifles (from the stock of Enfields sold to the British by the United States after Dunkerque), in spite of some objection on the part of the British Chiefs of Staff since the transfer of these weapons to the French was to be effected at the expense of the Home Guard. In the eyes of the CCS, approval of this first request from the Allied Commander in Chief for the re-equipping of the French was given as an emergency measure. At the suggestion of the British members of the committee, they agreed that all further similar requests from him would be referred to the MAB for action.[17] On 22 November the MAB assigned the equipment. In a sense this action marked the real start of the International Division's responsibility for French rearmament, a responsibility which it was to carry through to the end of the war.

Some equipment had been assigned, but no date was yet set for its shipment. On 12 December General Eisenhower, in a

GENERAL GEORGE C. MARSHALL, *Chief of Staff, U.S. Army.*

personal message to General Marshall, stressed the urgency of sending this equipment. He pointed out that the French had no antitank weapons at all, and that he could do little to help them because of his own pressing needs. "If we had available at once antitank and light antiaircraft weapons for just one French regiment, it would have a tremendous moral and material advantage. It would even help if I could inform Giraud that the equipment for several AT and AA battalions, with some motor transport, was being shipped immediately." [18]

By then General Giraud had already placed at the disposal of the Allied Commander in Chief for the battle of Tunisia a

---

[16] In September 1943, General Giraud's mission and General de Gaulle's Free French Military Mission (established in Washington in 1941), until then two separate agencies, merged into one single organization under the name of French Military Mission in the United States. OPD 336 France, Sec III.

[17] Min, CCS 49th Mtg, 20 Nov 42; Msg R–3415, AGWAR to USFOR, 21 Nov 42, JRC Cable Log.

[18] Msg 1825, Eisenhower to Marshall, 12 Dec 42, JRC Cable Log.

substantial task force commanded by General Juin. This force, then numbering approximately 7,000 men, would increase to 40,000 combat troops within the coming months. For the moment, the units were unable, because of their still meager and for the most part obsolete matériel, to take offensive action against an enemy equipped with tanks and all the modern weapons of war. It was clear that they could be used only as a holding force until either adequate equipment or Allied reinforcements arrived.[19] Even if they were to hold their present positions, it was urgent that they be issued weapons without delay. Pending the arrival of the equipment ordered from the United States, Eisenhower turned to the theater for help.

On 13 December he authorized the Commanding General, Eastern Task Force, to provide French units engaged in combat under his command with such equipment, supplies, and matériel as they needed to conduct operations current or imminent. The supply of this equipment was to be on temporary loan without prejudice to any arrangements likely to be concluded with French authorities for the permanent re-equipment of their forces. A few days later the Allied Commander in Chief also appealed to the Commanding General, Western Task Force, with a request to send any surplus equipment such as automatic rifles, rifles, submachine guns, and light machine guns for loan to French units in Tunisia.[20]

Cognizant of the fact that technical instruction on the proper use of matériel was as important as the issue of the equipment itself, Eisenhower took a number of measures in this connection. He requested U.S. Fifth Army then stationed in French Morocco to assist in organizing, equipping, and training French forces located within its zone. Simultaneously, he directed AFHQ to ensure that "all possible assistance" be given by American troops to the French African forces in their training with American arms and equipment. Pursuant to these instructions, the various responsible commands and agencies in the theater proceeded to establish technical training programs and arranged to get them under way without delay.[21]

Finally, pending definite arrangements on the provision of lend-lease supplies and equipment to the French, the Allied Commander in Chief prescribed the manner in which items currently being issued to them on an emergency basis were to be transferred and accounted for.[22]

By the third week of December, no word had yet been received from Washington regarding the equipment requested on 18 November. As the situation in Tunisia was growing critical, Eisenhower appealed directly to the CCS for a decision that would enable him to tell General Giraud precisely how much equipment was being sent and when it would arrive. The CCS promptly replied, on 24 December, that the promised rifles would be shipped from the United Kingdom within forty-eight hours, and the antitank and antiaircraft guns as well as 2,000 grenade launchers from the United States on 6 January. Only a shortage of

---

[19] For detailed information on the part played by the French in Tunisia, see Howe, *Northwest Africa.*

[20] Dir, Eisenhower to CG Eastern Task Force, 13 Dec 42, AFHQ AG 400/042–C; Msg 2481, CinC to CG Western Task Force, 19 Dec 42, AFHQ 0100/12C G–3 Div Ops Fr Rearmt.

[21] Ltr, CinC to CG Fifth Army, 30 Dec 42, quoted in Fifth Army History, I, 2, DRB AGO; Ltr AG 353/082 C–M, AFHQ, 31 Dec 42, AFHQ 0100/12C G–3 Div Ops Fr Rearmt, Vol. II (3); see pp. 230 ff., below.

[22] AFHQ Cir 5, 10 Jan 43, JRC 400.2/001 Admin of Sup—Gen.

shipping, they pointed out, prevented the inclusion of more matériel for the French in the 6 January convoy. Some 3,400 additional weapons including machine guns, mortars, and howitzers were available from the United Kingdom and the United States if required. They warned, however, that these weapons, if shipped, would take the cargo space allotted to organizational equipment for Anglo-American forces in North Africa. They asked the Allied Commander in Chief to make specific recommendations as to the amounts and types of armament required for the French.[23]

Reviewing the French operational situation as it stood at the close of the year 1942, Eisenhower urged the U.S. Joint Chiefs of Staff to give constant consideration to the question of equipping and maintaining the French forces engaged in Tunisia as it had "a strong influence on morale." Their most immediate need, he explained, was for light antiaircraft and antitank equipment. Since these items were not bulky, he recommended that they be shipped to the full extent of space available. A few days later, General Eisenhower appealed once again directly to the CCS. "If we can provide General Giraud with only a few tanks and some additional AA and AT equipment, he may be able to help us when the more critical phase of the battle arrives. It must be clear to all that the enthusiastic and effective co-operation of the French forces is a vital factor in all our calculations." Having cabled anew for emergency deliveries of clothing, tentage, and other matériel, he felt he had done everything in his power to assist the French. In his judgment, the

problem of their re-equipping was definitely one for the governments of the United States and the United Kingdom to solve.[24]

So far, only a small amount of matériel, largely from U.S. sources in the theater, had been or was in process of being transferred to the French, It consisted of equipment for approximately one light tank company, two tank destroyer companies, and three to four antiaircraft batteries.[25] A number of miscellaneous weapons also had been turned over directly by U.S. commanders in Tunisia to their French neighbors in the field.

General Giraud Eyes the Larger Program

While pleading for more weapons for his hard-pressed troops in Tunisia, General Giraud was giving increased attention to the larger armament objective, the rehabilitation of all his forces. By mid-December members of his staff had prepared a revised and more detailed version of the Mast Plan, based on their latest estimates of French capabilities. They submitted it first to AFHQ where it was subjected to the scrutiny of the Joint Rearmament Committee. Later, General Béthouart handed another copy of it to War Department officials.[26] The new program was slightly larger than the Mast Plan, the proposed number of divisions being raised from ten to eleven. Briefly it called for the delivery, in order of priority, of:

---

[23] Msg 2392, Eisenhower to CCS, 18 Dec 42, ABC (11–11–42), Sec 1; Msg, CCS to Eisenhower, 24 Dec 42, FAN 47; Memo, Maj Gen Thomas T. Handy for Marshall, 26 Dec 42, OPD 400 France, Sec I.

[24] Msg 3664, Eisenhower to Marshall, 31 Dec 42, AFHQ 0100/12C G–3 Div Ops Fr Equip; Msg 4141, Eisenhower to CCS, 4 Jan 43, NAF 84; AFHQ Commander-in-Chief's Dispatch, The North African Campaign: 1942–1943, pp. 29–30, copy in OCMH.

[25] Memo, ACofS G–3 for Gen Clark, 21 Dec 42, AFHQ 0100/12C G–3 Div Ops.

[26] Ltr, Brig Gen Roger Leyer to AFHQ, 30 EMG/IM/S, 14 Dec 42, and Memo, Béthouart for WD, 26 Dec 42, JRC Misc Doc, Item 5–a, Tab P.

a. The matériel necessary to maintain the normal life of the North African forces, such as medical supplies, railway equipment, coal, gasoline, motor transport, and the like.

b. The entire equipment for one army headquarters, two infantry corps headquarters, one armored corps headquarters, eight infantry divisions, three armored divisions, and miscellaneous tank destroyer, antiaircraft, and air units.

c. The matériel for the service units and depots required for the support of the above forces.

As the Mast Plan still had not been acted upon by the CCS, General Marshall transmitted the new French proposal to ASF for examination and again asked General Eisenhower for comment. The Allied Commander in Chief replied that the composition of the forces as indicated in the revised program was agreeable to him. However, since activation, equipping, and training had to be governed by a long-term policy and be influenced by United Nations strategy, he felt that the last word was not with him but with the CCS. As for the suggested sequence of shipments, he pointed out that the phasing of any approved program would be affected by changes likely to occur in the military situation in North Africa. With regard to the rehabilitation of the North African Air Forces as proposed by the French, Eisenhower, after summing up the action already taken in the theater, offered the following comment: The French, he explained, were reported to have sufficient personnel for eight hundred aircraft of various types; it was important for him to know if and when he could expect this number of aircraft; in the meantime he was considering sending selected French student pilots,

bombardiers, gunners, and radio operators to training schools in the United States.[27]

The Deadlock Over a Firm Plan

The six-week debate on French rearmament at the end of 1942 had produced no decisions, but it had served to define the points of view of the various parties concerned. The French, now definitely in the fight, were impatient to receive modern weapons of war. To them speed was the essential factor. As General Béthouart pointed out on 7 January, in the course of a meeting of Allied military representatives in Washington, equipment must be furnished to French troops rapidly so as to avoid their "complete paralysis" and to prevent a "serious blow to morale."[28] The Allied Commander in Chief, while fully convinced of the French desire to fight and ready to provide all possible material assistance, considered French rearmament in relation to his over-all requirements. These, in turn, were conditioned by the amount of shipping allocated to his theater and more particularly by the current and probable operational developments. For the moment, the failure of the Allied drive on Tunis and the rapid westward movement of the German forces had created an urgent need for the earliest possible presence in southern Tunisia of a strong Allied force. In General Eisen-

[27] Msg 3664, Eisenhower to Marshall, 31 Dec 42, AFHQ 0100/12C G–3 Div Ops Fr Equip; Msg 3503, Eisenhower to Arnold, 29 Dec 42, JRC Cable Log. The North African Air Forces is discussed in Ch. XII, below.
[28] Min, MRP 6th Mtg, 7 Jan 43, CCS 334, Military Representatives of Associated Pacific Powers (5–26–42). This was the first meeting to which France was invited to send representatives. (The name of the committee was subsequently changed to Military Representatives of Associated Powers.) The last meeting of the committee was held on 18 June 1943.

hower's judgment, therefore, the initiation, at this juncture, of a full-scale, long-range rearmament program was untimely. This point was made clear in a message addressed to General Marshall on 31 December. Excluding the needs of French troops engaged in combat which "must receive constant consideration," he set forth the shipping priorities for his requirements as follows: (1) the logistical build-up, still incomplete, of the Anglo-American forces under his command; (2) the rehabilitation of the North African civil economy so as to prevent unfavorable repercussions on the political and military situation.[29]

War Department officials, on the other hand, were weighing French rearmament in relation to world-wide logistical commitments and in the light of its probable impact on the U.S. war effort. Yet their conclusions regarding the practicability of a large-scale French rearmament program were almost identical, for reasons quite apart, with those of the Allied Commander in Chief. The report which the Logistics Division of Army Service Forces issued on 9 January on the implications of Béthouart's proposal pointed out that American production would probably make it possible to equip the 272,000 troops required under the French program, and to equip and maintain the U.S. troops already overseas or planned for shipment abroad in 1943. However, equipping the French would interfere seriously with equipping units in the United States. Furthermore, the shipping necessary to float equipment for the French had to be provided principally by the United States. This would defer the shipment of approximately 250,000 to 270,000 American troops to the Mediterranean theater in

1943 and interfere considerably with the equipping and maintaining of U.S. troops already in the theater, unless convoy restrictions were relaxed and port capacities augmented. In the light of these considerations, the report recommended, in part, that the equipping of American troops in North Africa take priority over that of the French; that only those French troops be activated and equipped which could be utilized in Allied operations; and that their initial equipping be restricted to the minimum required for their maintenance and training.[30]

To the CCS, finally, French rearmament was a matter to be viewed in relation to its likely effect on global strategy. A program of the size proposed by General Béthouart was bound to cut across the lines of Anglo-American logistical plans. The question, to the CCS, boiled down to this: would the commitment, if accepted, be feasible in view of the world-wide shipping situation? If so, what would its strategic advantage be?

Shipping, then, and not production—except in the case of some critical items of equipment—would be the main factor to be considered in drawing up any large-scale French rearmament program. This was made unmistakably clear to General Béthouart and Mr. Lemaigre-Dubreuil when, on 10 January, they called on Assistant Secretary of War John J. McCloy, himself a stanch proponent of French rearmament. "Every American," Mr. McCloy declared, was "anxious that there should be a strong French Army in North Africa." But it was well not to lose sight of the enormous difficulties involved. As an illustration he pointed out that to float the equipment necessary for eleven divisions, exclusive of all other matériel listed in the

---

[29] Msg 3664, Eisenhower to Marshall, 31 Dec 42, AFHQ 0100/12C G–3 Div Ops Fr Equip.

[30] Rpt, Logistics Div SOS, 9 Jan 43, ASF Planning Div A–47–147.

Béthouart program, would require 325 cargo vessels. These, quite simply, were not available.[31]

Increasingly alarmed over the severe losses incurred by his ill-equipped forces in Tunisia, General Giraud was prone to brush aside the unfavorable logistics of the situation facing the Allied Commander in Chief. In an effort to dispel his apparent misconception of the facts, Maj. Gen. Walter Bedell Smith, Chief of Staff, AFHQ, accompanied by the British and American political representatives in the theater, called on him on 12 January. General Smith described the "extraordinary efforts" made by the Allies to overcome the many obstacles hampering the delivery of armament. He referred to the inadequacy of port and railroad facilities, the limitations of shipping and other obstacles. General Giraud then countered that all available French merchant shipping was being turned over to the Allied shipping pool. Some of it, he insisted, ought to be used to transport equipment for his forces.[32]

The next day, 13 January, Mr. Lemaigre-Dubreuil was leaving Washington for Algiers, his mission completed. In the course of his talks with State Department officials, he had stressed the political aspect of French rearmament. General Giraud, he had pointed out, was primarily concerned with bringing Frenchmen back into active participation in the war. To succeed, he was dependent on the fulfillment of a number of conditions, moral as well as material. Among the latter was the speedy issue of U.S. equipment to his troops. At a time when General Giraud and General de Gaulle were discussing the unification of their forces, it was imperative that Giraud's hand be strengthened by all possible means. In Mr. Lemaigre-Dubreuil's opinion, only then could the French Commander in Chief pursue the war with maximum efficiency, dispel French anxiety, and establish himself as the leader of French military resistance.[33]

That General Giraud was fully confident of the intent and ability of the United States to re-equip his forces cannot be doubted. Answering a New Year's message from President Roosevelt, he declared:

The responsibility which I assume is made much lighter by the military support brought by the United States and the Allied Nations and by the promise of help which you were kind enough to send me. Thanks to American matériel, the restored French Army will be able to resume at the side of the United Nations a strong and effective action for the liberation of France and of Europe, and for the achievement of a just peace.[34]

Still, by mid-January, approximately ten weeks after the Allied landings, no decision was yet in sight on "the subject closest to Giraud's heart.[35]

[31] Min, Conf McCloy with Béthouart and Lemaigre-Dubreuil, 10 Jan 43, JRC Misc Doc, Item 5–a.

[32] Msg 3585, Eisenhower (from Murphy) to CCS, 13 Jan 43, NAF 100.

[33] Msg 1049, Marshall to Eisenhower (State Dept for Murphy), 13 Jan 43, JRC Cable Log.

[34] Msg 3731, AFHQ to AGWAR (Giraud for President), 1 Jan 43, AFHQ AG Sec 336.91.

[35] Msg 3585 cited n. 32.

CHAPTER II

The ANFA Agreement

Franco-Anglo-American Conversations

The question of French rearmament, both immediate and long range, drew considerable attention from the Combined Chiefs of Staff when, having shifted the scene of their next deliberations from Washington to French Morocco, they assembled for the sessions of the Casablanca Conference. Presiding over the conference held at Anfa, a suburb of Casablanca, from 14 to 26 January 1943, were President Roosevelt and Prime Minister Churchill. Both Generals Giraud and de Gaulle were expected to attend. In inviting them, the President and the Prime Minister had intended to bring them together in the hope that they would conclude an agreement on the unification of their forces. General Giraud reached Anfa on 17 January and immediately began a series of consultations with the President, the Prime Minister, General Marshall, Lt. Gen. Brehon B. Somervell, Commanding General, Army Service Forces, and others. The head of the Free French at first declined to come to the meeting. This rebuff angered Churchill, who had given strong backing to the Gaullist group, and prompted both him and the President to question "whether or not de Gaulle was a leader who merited their support."[1] The general finally relented and, on 22 January, toward the end of the

conference, left London for Anfa where he met briefly with Allied officials and with General Giraud.

At their first meeting, held on 15 January, the CCS heard General Eisenhower himself stress the urgency of providing immediate assistance to the North African units engaged in Tunisia. Called upon to report on the latest developments in the campaign there, the Allied Commander in Chief emphasized that a serious situation would develop if the French were unable, for lack of equipment, to stand firmly on the line they now held between the British in the north and the Americans in the south.[2]

To the CCS the two issues of immediate and long-range assistance to the French could not be separated. In their judgment, the question was simply this: how much rearmament and how soon? To answer, they had first to determine what use they intended to make of the North African forces, and this, in turn, depended on how much they were prepared to trust these forces. British and Americans were in sharp disagreement over this particular point. The British seemed hesitant to rely on an army which until recent weeks had remained obstinately loyal to Marshal Pétain's government, in their eyes a defeatist, even pro-German, regime. The Americans, although they had cause to be resentful after the costly resistance put up by

---

[1] Min, ANFA 2d Mtg, 18 Jan 43, Casablanca Conf. (See Bibliographical Note.)

[2] Min, CCS 57th Mtg, 15 Jan 43, Casablanca Conf.

that same army in November 1942, never-theless were willing to forget the distasteful episode and accept the pledges of the new ally at their face value. The U.S. Joint Chiefs of Staff had discussed this matter of trust in the North African forces. Admiral Ernest J. King had urged his colleagues to "insist" on making the "maximum use" of these forces by giving them appropriate tasks and relying on them to carry through their assignments. He realized that there would be "some British opposition," and he considered it essential to convince the British Chiefs of Staff of the "necessity of trusting the French fully." [3]

Two subsequent CCS meetings under-lined the reluctance of the British to place full confidence in the North African forces and as a result their disinclination to con-sider more than a limited rearmament. On 16 January, General Marshall, speaking for the JCS, voiced the belief that the French could be used effectively and economically. He proposed therefore that selected divi-sions be re-equipped as soon as practicable. Field Marshal Sir Alan F. Brooke, Chief of the Imperial General Staff, agreed on maxi-mum employment of the North African forces, but regarded their usefulness as con-fined largely to "garrison work." The pos-sibility of wider employment, he thought, would depend greatly on whether a satis-factory government could be established in North Africa, for good leadership was re-quired to "rekindle in the French the desire to fight." [4]

At the next CCS meeting, held two days later and attended by the President and the Prime Minister, Roosevelt urged that every

effort be made to provide equipment for the army of 250,000 men which General Giraud expected to raise. Field Marshal Brooke then observed that the British forces in North Africa had offered to transfer to the French some used tanks once they them-selves had received their new American ve-hicles. The proposal elicited from General Marshall the remark that the North African units must be given "the best equipment obtainable." This, he continued, he pro-posed to provide out of U.S. resources sub-ject to shipping limitations. If the Allies intended to equip the French, he pointed out, they must make "good units" of them. [5]

Apparently concerned over the diver-gence between the British and American attitudes toward General Giraud's forces, Admiral King brought up the subject at a meeting of the JCS on 19 January. He again urged his colleagues to place full confidence in these forces and to equip them as rapidly as possible. General Marshall agreed, saying that he thought it "imprac-ticable to go halfway with the French." They must be trusted "either completely or not at all." Personally, he had "every reason" to believe that certain divisions, when equipped, would be excellent. He felt that the objections to placing full confi-dence in the North African forces were based on technical matters rather than on anything else. True, he foresaw difficulties as to control or command, but he was cer-tain that such difficulties could be overcome as they arose. [6]

Later that same morning, the CCS heard General Marshall declare that he was in favor of proceeding with a definite rearma-

---

[3] Min, JCS 50th Mtg, 13 Jan 43, Casablanca Conf. For a list of the British and U.S. Chiefs of Staff, see page 10, above.
[4] Min, CCS 58th Mtg, 16 Jan 43, Casablanca Conf.

[5] Min, Anfa 2d Mtg, 18 Jan 43, Casablanca Conf.
[6] Min, JCS 55th Mtg, 19 Jan 43, Casablanca Conf.

ment program for the North African forces. Such an undertaking would of course imply acceptance by the French of Allied organization and training methods and would inevitably delay the progress of equipping U.S. forces. He considered, however, that the undertaking should be carried out "wholeheartedly." He was prepared, subject to General Eisenhower's views, to modify the American logistical program in order to equip French forces up to a strength of 250,000 men. The necessary matériel would be provided at the expense of U.S. units forming in America. He proposed to ship it to North Africa in French bottoms. General Somervell disclosed that General Giraud had agreed to turn over to the Allied shipping pool 160,000 tons of shipping of which he expected about 75,000 tons to be earmarked for transportation of equipment to his forces. Somervell estimated that this would make it possible to equip approximately one division per month.[7]

The most important debate on French rearmament took place on the afternoon of the same day. Appearing before the CCS at their invitation, General Giraud outlined his plans for the rehabilitation of his forces. He explained that with the cadres then at his disposal he could form an army of thirteen divisions, including three armored and ten motorized infantry divisions. In addition, he wished to raise as "an indispensable accompaniment to a modern army," an air force consisting of 50 fighter squadrons, 30 light bomber squadrons, and a number of transport squadrons—with a total of 1,000 airplanes. He was fully aware, he admitted, of the

serious difficulties that his program would involve, considering the shortage of shipping and the needs of other United Nations forces. He felt confident, however, that the French Army, if properly equipped, could make a great contribution to the European campaign.

Speaking for the U.S. Army, General Marshall asserted that he had undertaken to determine how quickly modern equipment could be provided for the North African forces. He then proceeded to outline the steps already taken in this connection by various American authorities. Admiral King had begun discussions with French naval officers on the shipping question. General Arnold had conferred with French aviation personnel on the provision of air force equipment. General Somervell had examined with General Giraud the problem of delivery of matériel. Two points still remained to be taken up with the French Commander in Chief, namely, the desired priority of items and the procedure for equipping his units. General Marshall then emphasized that it was to the interest of the United States to bring the North African forces to a high state of efficiency. It was "not a question of whether to equip the French Army, but rather of how to do it." Transport, he pointed out in conclusion, and not availability of equipment was the limiting factor.

Whether they were impressed by the determination evident in General Giraud's statements or reluctant to appear unfriendly to the French in his presence, the British members of the CCS expressed great sympathy for his aims. While they made no specific commitments, at least they raised no objection to the principle of rearmament. Speaking for the British Chiefs of Staff,

---

[7] Min, CCS 61st Mtg, 19 Jan 43, Casablanca Conf.

Field Marshal Brooke assured the conferees that he fully realized the important part which General Giraud's forces would play in bringing the war to a successful end. The British, he asserted, would do what they could within the more limited resources at their disposal to provide modern equipment. Admiral Sir Dudley Pound then declared that, in view of the growing U-boat menace, the help of the French naval forces would be most welcome. As for the French air forces, Air Chief Marshal Sir Charles Portal expressed the hope that they would be equipped as soon as possible to fight once more alongside the Allies. He too felt sure that, within the limits of British resources already considerably strained, the United Kingdom would do everything possible to hasten the day of this collaboration. Field Marshal Sir John Dill closed the discussion by declaring that it was "a matter of great pleasure" to have General Giraud back to lead France to victory.[8]

By this time, the Americans had made unmistakably clear their stand on the rearmament issue. Confident of the ability of the North African forces to put up a good fight, they were determined to see these forces used to the maximum and, to this end, rearmed fully and speedily. Eager to translate this determination into action, General Marshall, on 23 January, proposed that the JCS set forth a policy with respect to the contemplated employment of the North African forces, and the scale of equipment to be provided.[9]

---

[8] Min, CCS 62d Mtg, 19 Jan 43, Casablanca Conf. Field Marshal Dill was head of the British Joint Staff Mission and senior British member of the CCS organization. He took part in the CCS meetings as a representative of the Minister of Defence (Mr. Churchill).

[9] Memo, CofS for JCS, 23 Jan 43, JCS 206.

President Roosevelt and General Giraud Negotiate an Agreement

The issue was settled on 24 January when the President, having taken the matter in his own hands, reached an agreement with General Giraud which, in principle at least, committed the United States to a program of rearmament. This unexpected action on his part was the culmination of exchanges of views between himself and the French Commander in Chief regarding the French situation in general and the rearmament question in particular.[10] These informal meetings had proceeded in an atmosphere of mutual confidence. Apparently disregarding the adverse criticism of General Giraud's ability as an administrator which had just reached him,[11] the President had shown keen understanding of the many difficult problems then facing the French Commander in Chief and expressed great interest in his plans for the reorganization and rearmament of the African forces. On the basis of these and other discussions, and in line with his statements before the CCS, General Giraud had prepared a mem-

---

[10] President Roosevelt and General Giraud appear to have met three times during the Casablanca Conference. The first meeting was on 17 January, 1630–1730 hours, and was attended by Captain Beaufre, then Giraud's military aide. After this meeting, General Giraud had a short interview with the British Prime Minister. The second meeting, on 19 January, about 1200 hours, was attended by Harry L. Hopkins, Mr. Murphy, Lt. Col. Elliott Roosevelt, Capt. John L. McCrea (USN), and Captain Beaufre. The third, on 24 January, appears to have been a brief one with no other participants present, before the meeting at which Churchill and de Gaulle were also present. It is to be noted that the Prime Minister did not take part in these Giraud-Roosevelt meetings. Interv with Col Beaufre, Sep 50; Robert E. Sherwood, *Roosevelt and Hopkins: An Intimate History* (New York: Harper & Brothers, 1948), Ch. XXVII.

[11] Sherwood, *Roosevelt and Hopkins*, Ch. XXVII.

MEETING AT CASABLANCA, 24 JANUARY 1943. *From left: General Henri Giraud, President Franklin D. Roosevelt, General Charles de Gaulle, and Prime Minister Winston Churchill.*

orandum embodying the substance of his several conversations and submitted it for the President's concurrence.[12]   The Presi-

dent, on 24 January, recorded his approval on the margin of the memorandum.

The part of the memorandum pertaining to rearmament, together with the Presi-

---

[12] Title of the memorandum: Résumé of the Agreements in Principle Resulting From the Conversations at Anfa.   Complete text in English and in French in OPD Exec 1, Item 13.

The exact time at which General Giraud submitted this memorandum has yet to be determined. At any rate, this was one of two memorandums submitted by the general to the President and approved by the latter in the course of their meeting of 24 January.   Both later became known as the ANFA Agreements.   The second memorandum, the text of which had been prepared by Mr. Lemaigre-Dubreuil, was a résumé and a synthesis of

the conversations just ended in Washington between the French representative and the Department of State regarding the political relationship between General Giraud and the Anglo-American authorities subsequent to the Allied intervention in North Africa.   In effect it officially sanctioned the Murphy-Giraud agreements of 2 November and officially recognized General Giraud as the sole military "trustee" of French interests.

Copies in English of both memorandums were sent to General Giraud on 24 January and to General Eisenhower on 28 January.

dent's marginal comments, was known thereafter as the ANFA Plan.[13]   It read as follows:

It has been agreed between the President of the United States and General Giraud that the French forces will receive, by priority, the equipment which is indispensable to them and that this shall be made up of the most modern matériel.

In subsequent talks with General Marshall and General Somervell, it was agreed that the delivery would amount to matériel for three armored divisions and eight motorized divisions as well as for a first-line air force consisting of five hundred fighters, three hundred bombers and two hundred transport planes, and that of this equipment, there would be delivered in the weeks to come four hundred trucks and the equipment for two armored regiments, three reconnaissance battalions, three battalions of tank destroyers and three motorized divisions, and such of the aviation equipment as can come by air.

In regard to transport, it has been agreed with General Somervell that the resupplying of French Africa would be assured by the monthly allocation of 65,000 tons (50,000 tons of wheat, 12,000 tons of sugar, and 3,000 tons of fabrics) and that the shipment of the matériel would be effected before next summer.   France would furnish to the interallied pool 165,000 tons of shipping and the allies would furnish the remainder necessary for the delivery to be completed within the agreed time.   The aviation matériel [coal and fuel excepted] would be sent, as far as possible, by air.[14]

---

[13] The rest of the memorandum dealt with minor financial and political problems.

[14] The phrase "coal and fuel excepted" was omitted in the official English translation.   Incidentally, this version (as distinguished from the one, correct in all respects, prepared by General Béthouart's staff) contained at least two errors in translation: "étoffes" (fabrics) was incorrectly rendered as "matériel," and the words "le transport du matériel" (the shipment of *the* matériel) was improperly translated as "the shipment of *this* material," thereby giving the erroneous impression that only the shipment of civilian supplies (wheat, sugar and the like) would be effected before the summer.

Basically the ANFA Plan did not differ greatly from the pre-TORCH Mast Plan which called for ten divisions.   It was somewhat less ambitious than the thirteen-division program outlined by General Giraud himself in the course of his appearance before the CCS.[15]   In practice, it was a restatement of the eleven-division program submitted by General Béthouart to the War Department on 26 December, except that the air portion of the new plan was substantially larger.

Well might General Giraud rejoice. After weeks of anxious waiting, he had at last a definite promise of American assistance.   The Chief Executive of the United States Government himself had sanctioned the principle of French rearmament and had agreed to a target of eleven divisions plus a substantial air force.   Greatly encouraged by the turn of events, the French Commander in Chief returned to Algiers eager to expedite the reorganization of his forces in anticipation of the delivery of the much-needed matériel.

Clarification of the Agreement

The ink was hardly dry on the ANFA Plan when its far-reaching implications became the subject of considerable speculation. Some commitment had clearly been made by the President, but precisely what? Moreover, how would the British, who had so conspicuously not been consulted, react? There was no evidence that the Prime Minister, who had not been invited to attend the Roosevelt-Giraud conversations, had even discussed the rearmament problem with the President.   When on 5 Feb-

---

[15] It is most likely that, during his various consultations at Anfa, the general was made aware of the impracticability of a thirteen-division program.

ruary, two weeks after the close of the Casablanca Conference, Mr. Churchill chanced to be in Algiers, he did not fail to point out to Mr. Murphy this and other political and military implications of the ANFA Agreements. He emphasized in particular that General de Gaulle, the then protégé of the British Government, had been practically left out of the new Franco-Anglo-American relationship. In an attempt to meet the Prime Minister's objections, Mr. Murphy revised the text of the agreements and submitted a single memorandum to General Giraud. The French Commander in Chief endorsed the new document, a copy of which was cabled to the Foreign Office, and to Washington where the President approved it on 22 April. The text of the ANFA Plan reappeared as Part II of the new memorandum and was worded as follows:

1. On the military plane it has been agreed between the President of the United States and the British Prime Minister on the one hand and General Giraud on the other that the French forces will receive equipment which is indispensable and with that priority which their military situation demands and as may be determined by the Combined Chiefs of Staff, and this shall be made of the most modern matériel.

2. [Same as in original agreement.] [16]

Although a belated party to the rearma-

---

[16] Title of the new memo: Memo of the Points Agreed Upon at the Casablanca Conference Between the President of the U.S. and the British Prime Minister on the One Hand, and General Giraud on the Other. Text in Crusoë, *Vicissitudes d'une Victoire* (Paris: Les Editions de l'Ame Française [1946]), p. 147. The copy approved by the President: Memo, Brig Gen John R. Deane for JCS, 22 Apr 43, OPD 400 France, Sec 1.

The main difference between the original and the new document was that the latter limited the trusteeship of General Giraud to the territories of North and West Africa, thus leaving General de Gaulle in control of other areas, pending an ultimate fusion of the two administrations.

ment agreement, the British at any rate were now fully informed as to the scope of the commitment.

Another serious question arose as soon as American officials responsible for implementing armament programs began examining the ANFA Plan in relation to worldwide strategy, other armament commitments, production, and shipping. How binding was the agreement just concluded? Was it really an agreement "in principle" only? If so, emphasis could reasonably be placed on the spirit rather than the letter of the text, and a rearmament program established in the light of, and in proper relation with, the many aspects involved. Or was it, as the French were already insisting, a firm commitment to a specific program? There was of course the possibility that the President, although quite conversant with the French language, had not realized that the words "Oui en principe" as written by him in the margin of the original document had a much stronger meaning than the less binding translation "yes in principle" subsequently used in the official English text.

Ten days after the conclusion of the agreement, General Béthouart, at the request of the French Commander in Chief, called on General Marshall to discuss the implementation of the ANFA Plan. The conversation, from the outset, elicited considerable surprise on both sides. General Marshall first informed his caller that he had not yet been advised by the President of any specific agreements with General Giraud other than the confirmation of what he himself had already assured the French Commander in Chief during their conversations at Anfa, namely, that the United States would proceed with the greatest speed to equip his troops and that the matter of cargo space, character of equipment as to priorities of shipment, and the like would be determined later.[17]   General Marshall then assured General Béthouart that he did not contest the principle of French rearmament. Generals Eisenhower and Clark and Maj. Gen. George S. Patton, Jr., whom he had consulted, all agreed that North African units could be made effective for battle provided they received modern equipment. It was a foregone conclusion, he continued, that the Americans would feel justified in delaying the organization of U.S. divisions now on the War Department program in favor of equipping French divisions overseas. However, he pointed out, there were practical and technical aspects of the problem to be taken into consideration. The rearmament of the French would have to be undertaken in the light of other similar commitments, as the war was being fought on many fronts throughout the world. In addition, it was agreed that the requirements of matériel for the North African Army should be met, both in quality and quantity, under the same conditions as those of the U.S. Army. Hence it was obvious that the provision of such matériel must be made according to an order of priority to be determined for the whole of the United Nations forces. Finally, there was shipping to be reckoned with. At the present time, he explained, it was not possible to determine delivery dates with any exactness. But, since it was considered important that at least a part of the French forces be re-equipped at once,

War Department officials were taking steps to have matériel ready to fill available cargo space.[18]

On 5 February, the Combined Chiefs of Staff, meeting in Washington, examined the status of the negotiations on French rearmament. Lt. Gen. George N. Macready inquired, on behalf of the British Chiefs of Staff, whether any agreement on the matter had been reached at the Casablanca Conference. General Marshall explained that "a favorable view" had been taken by Generals Eisenhower, Patton, and Clark regarding the "potentialities" of the North African forces but that no decision had been reached with regard to what equipment should be sent.[19] Shipping, he pointed out, would be the limiting factor. One of the effects of providing equipment to the French, concluded General Marshall, would be to delay equipping U.S. units. The CCS then agreed that they should, as soon as possible, give guidance to the Munitions Assignments Board with respect to French rearmament.[20]

In the theater, officials of Allied Force Headquarters also were discussing the implications of the ANFA Plan. On 6 February, pending further instructions from Washington, the chief of staff, General Smith, issued the following statement: "The President's promises to General Giraud deal with matters which are beyond General Eisenhower's scope because they

---

[17] General Marshall was absent from Casablanca during the last days of the conference and had not seen the President since his return to Washington. The first knowledge he had of any agreement was when General Béthouart handed him, in the course of the above interview, a memo on the subject as well as a copy of the ANFA Agreements.

[18] Min, Marshall-Béthouart Mtg, 3 Feb 43, JRC 902/II Rearmt Plan; Memo, Marshall for McCloy, 4 Feb 43, OCS A–45–523 (France).

[19] It is most likely that General Marshall, who had been apprised only two days before by General Béthouart of the Giraud-Roosevelt agreement in principle, had not yet talked to the President to ascertain the facts regarding that commitment. General Macready was a member of the British Joint Staff Mission in Washington.

[20] Min, CCS 70th Mtg, 5 Feb 43.

involve additional tonnage which has not yet been allocated to him. General Giraud must deal with these matters with Washington through the Béthouart Mission." [21] In the opinion of the Allied Commander in Chief, therefore, it was clearly up to the CCS and the War Department to carry out the ANFA Plan, and to arrange for the necessary additional tonnage.

General Giraud, meanwhile, on his return from Casablanca had publicly proclaimed that he had been promised "substantial equipment to arrive by the summer." Subsequently his staff submitted a request for the immediate shipment of the matériel constituting the first part of the ANFA Plan. The Joint Rearmament Committee was then working on a schedule of shipments based on the allocation of 25,000 tons per convoy which General Eisenhower had approved on 26 January as being "the maximum tonnage which could be spared for French military equipment." The figure, incidentally, represented about one sixteenth of the total maximum tonnage per convoy (approximately 400,000 tons). It was somewhat lower than the figure of 30,000–35,000 tons allocated for civilian consumer goods as a result of Eisenhower's decision to place the requirements of the North African economy above those of the French military. Considering that convoys were contemplated at the rate of about one per month, the 25,000 tons thus allocated monthly to French military requirements would permit no more than a start on the rearmament program before the summer.[22] On 10 February General Béthouart informed General Giraud that, as now envisaged by the War Department, the composition of the next shipments under the 25,000-ton allocation was to be limited to 400 vehicles and the medical and training equipment requested on 26 December. He added, however, that War Department officials had undertaken a study of the "possibility" of equipping a first increment consisting of three divisions, a few tank battalions, and corresponding antitank and antiaircraft units. Delivery dates had yet to be determined, as shipments were dependent on production and shipping.[23]

These and other disclosures brought General Giraud's rejoicing to a sudden end. Greatly disturbed because the re-equipping of his troops was not being pushed with more vigor, the French Commander in Chief called on General Eisenhower on 16 February and made "strong representations." Believing the ANFA Agreements to be a firm commitment, Giraud expected at least the first part of the plan to be accomplished without delay. Under the allocation of 25,000 tons per convoy, the eleven-division target set at Anfa would never be reached. The negligible material assistance now offered by the Americans was inconsistent with his recent understanding with the President and General Marshall. Moreover, it gave credence to a

[21] Memo, DCofS AFHQ for Liaison Sec, 6 Feb 43, JRC 902/II Rearmt Plan.
[22] As an illustration, 25,000 tons (or less than three cargo ships) represent no more than the vehicles of the three infantry regiments and divisional artillery of a division. FM–101–10, Staff Officers' Field Manual: Organization, Technical, and Logistical Data, 1941.
Msgs 1453, Eisenhower to OPD and Marshall, 17 Feb 43, 7433, Eisenhower to Marshall, 26 Jan 43, and 1768, Marshall to Eisenhower, 3 Feb 43, JRC Cable Log; Msg 3664, Eisenhower to Marshall, 31 Dec 42, AFHQ 0100/12C G–3 Div Ops Fr Equip; Memo, International Div ASF for OCT, 26 Apr 43. ASF ID 400.318 France, Free Fr, Vol. 1.
[23] Ltr, Béthouart to Giraud, 10 Feb 43, and Memo, Styer for Eisenhower, 10 Feb 43, JRC 902/II Rearmt Plan.

rumor that had lately reached him, to the effect that it was the policy of the American government not to equip his forces in such a manner as to permit them to take part in overseas operations, but to furnish them only matériel sufficient to defend North Africa. If that was the American intent, he would withdraw from his position as French Commander in Chief.[24]

General Eisenhower, reporting Giraud's stand, urged the War Department to set forth a definite policy which would enable him to deal with the French Commander in Chief. He needed to know in particular in how many monthly increments the commitment made at Anfa could be met. His staff could then determine shipping priorities and proceed intelligently with the rearmament of forces available for immediate combat as well as those later to be employed. In the meantime, he was reassuring General Giraud, on his own authority, that the Allied governments had "no disposition other than to carry through their original promises" and that it was "their intent and desire" that the North African forces participate in the liberation of France. Stressing the urgent need for immediate action, General Eisenhower added this grave warning: "I have here to face the insinuation that we are not straight-forward, that we are long on promises and short on performances. . . . This impression must be dispelled before the situation deteriorates."[25]

To make his position unmistakably clear, General Eisenhower, on the same day, sent a personal message to General Marshall. He stressed his own and General Giraud's concern over the serious results likely to follow from American failure to deliver equipment. He feared a further lowering of morale among French units and a corresponding weakening of General Giraud's hold on his army. Discontent was already rampant among the troops fighting in Tunisia. They contended that, just as in 1940, they had been sent to battle without proper equipment with the result that they were suffering heavy losses. It was difficult for them to reconcile this situation with General Giraud's repeated optimistic statements following his return from Casablanca. Prompt action, asserted General Eisenhower, was imperative to fulfill in part the "obligation implied at Anfa." The "immediate situation" could be met, he suggested, if about 100,000 tons of military supplies and equipment were earmarked for delivery from the United States during the following two or three months. If this action was supplemented by a definite schedule for future deliveries, "the matter would be settled." The necessary tonnage, he explained, would have to be provided by General Somervell from shipping at his disposal including French tonnage. With a probable reference to those officials who might be objecting to French rearmament on the ground that it was politically inopportune, Eisenhower concluded with this pointed observation: "The plan for equipping eleven divisions has no relationship to the great question of whether France shall be rearmed after the war. The latter would be a gigantic undertaking covering many years."[26]

---

[24] Msg 1453 cited n. 22. The rumor, allegedly of American origin, had been picked up in Algiers by French officers. Approached on the matter, Mr. McCloy hastened to furnish formal assurance to the French that the rumor was without foundation. Memo, Jacques Tarbé de Saint-Hardouin for Béthouart, 26 Feb 43, OCS A-45-523 (France).

[25] Msg 1453 cited n. 22.

[26] *Ibid.;* Msg 1620, OPD Algiers to AGWAR,

In a subsequent message addressed to the Secretary of State for transmittal to President Roosevelt, Mr. Murphy corroborated General Eisenhower's disclosure of the critical situation arising from the rearmament issue. The French, asserted Mr. Murphy, were manifesting a growing feeling that they were being "hoodwinked." They had listened with "respectful credence" to repeated announcements of U.S. armament production. On the other hand they realized fully the seriousness of the shipping problem. But what they could not understand was that three months after the landings in North Africa, during which time the Allies had of necessity depended on them for many things, no evidence of a substantial armament program was yet in sight. Mr. Murphy then reviewed the military and political implications of the current fumbling on French rearmament. The security of the North African base required that the fighting spirit of the French be stimulated. Instead there was a growing fear among them that France would be "excluded from real participation in the peace settlement." In addition, General Giraud's forces, aware that the Gaullist troops had received modern equipment from the British, were now looking more and more toward the United Kingdom for practical encouragement. Finally the French Commander in Chief felt that "somewhere along the line" there was "opposition if not deception." The American political adviser then urged that "we lay at least some cards on the table and enter into franker discussions as to the future of French participation if this is at all practicable. Our prestige and policy are being challenged." If possible, he finally recommended, General Eisenhower should have more support. Additional tonnage with necessary escort vessels should be allocated to him for the purpose of rearming the French.[27]

Impressed by the gravity of the situation as described by General Eisenhower and Mr. Murphy, General Marshall referred the entire matter to President Roosevelt.[28] The President's reaction was immediate. Within a few hours after Murphy's message had been communicated to him, Roosevelt requested the American political representative in Algiers to tell the French that "at no time did [he] or General Marshall promise equipment for the French divisions on any given date." What had been agreed to, he asserted, was "the principle of rearming them." The rearmament itself was to be carried out "as soon as practicable from the shipping point of view." His agreement in principle, therefore, did not involve detailed commitments. The President then added this somewhat caustic advice: "Tell your good friends in North Africa that they ought not to act like children. They must take prompt steps to deny the silly rumors that they have been let down in equipping an expeditionary force to go into France or that slowness in supplying armament is delaying political progress. . . . They must remain calm and sensible." [29]

In a message of the same date addressed to Eisenhower, Marshall first restated the President's own interpretation of the ANFA Agreement, then disclosed some rather startling facts concerning the conversations held immediately before the President's

---

Eisenhower to Marshall, 18 Feb 43, OPD Exec 1, Item 13; Msg 1628, Eisenhower to OPD, 18 Feb 43, JRC Cable Log.

[27] Msg 252, Murphy to Secy State for President, 20 Feb 43, OPD Exec 1, Item 13.
[28] Memo, Marshall for President, 20 Feb 43, OCS A–45–523 (France).
[29] Msg, President to Murphy, 20 Feb 43, OPD Exec 1, Item 13.

approval of the Giraud memorandum. Specifically, the Chief of Staff referred to paragraph 2 of the document. As worded, it implied that, after Giraud and the President had reached an understanding on the general principle of French rearmament, Generals Giraud, Marshall, and Somervell had subsequently agreed on the details of the program. The U.S. Chief of Staff now wanted to have clearly understood that neither he nor General Somervell had made any detailed commitments such as were specified in the paper submitted to the President for his signature. In their conversation with General Giraud, they had dealt "only in general terms," and agreed solely to a rearmament program "as speedy as could be managed." They had informed the French Commander in Chief that, because of shipping limitations, his program would be impossible of immediate attainment in view especially of American commitments with the USSR and China, and requirements in the southwest Pacific. General Marshall further disclosed that the President had had no opportunity to see him or General Somervell after his receipt of General Giraud's memorandum. The President's agreement in principle, therefore, was "based on General Giraud's statement of a detailed arrangement with Generals Somervell and Marshall which had *not* been reached." [30]

Both American and French observers were later to express the opinion that General Marshall's implication that Giraud had knowingly misrepresented the facts and had secured the President's approval on false pretenses did not square with Giraud's character. It seemed to them far more likely that the French Commander in Chief, carried away by his eagerness to see his forces rearmed, was misled by the encouragement he received and that he readily translated preliminary agreements into firm commitments because he wanted so badly to have such commitments. [31] As for the President, the haste with which he had approved the document suggests the possibility that he had not examined its terms and implications with sufficient care. His endorsement was ambiguous to say the least. Under the circumstances, it was bound to lead to misunderstandings.

In an effort to dissipate General Giraud's misgivings, the MAB dispatched to Algiers, at the request of the French Commander in Chief and with the approval of the President and of the British Government, Mr. Jean Monnet, the French financial expert then in Washington. The purpose of his mission was to acquaint Giraud with the situation as seen from Washington, to review with him and with General Eisenhower the entire matter of French rearmament in relation to over-all Allied requirements, and generally to "give through appropriate channels every assistance to the solution of questions arising in connection with the rearmament of the French forces." [32] The details of the rearmament program still had to be established.

---

[30] Msg 2641, Marshall to Eisenhower, 20 Feb 43, JRC 902/II Rearmt Plan.

[31] Intervs with Col George L. Artamonoff, Dec 49, with Brig Gen Jean Regnault, Sep 50, and with Lt Gen Paul Devinck, Jun 50.

[32] Ltr, Hopkins to Monnet, 22 Feb 43, JRC 902/II Rearmt Plan.

CHAPTER III

Phase I of the Program
(January–July 1943)

Phase I Is Launched

General Giraud had been correct in
assuming, as he had in the course of his
conversation with General Dwight D.
Eisenhower on 16 February, that no definite
schedule had yet been established for giving
full effect to the ANFA Plan. Still it did
not follow that War Department officials
had detached themselves altogether from
the question of furnishing large-scale material assistance to his forces. On the contrary, they had already begun to make
available some of the matériel required
under the plan. In their opinion, such
provision represented the first increment in
a program still to be elaborated by the
Combined Chiefs in the light of the ANFA
Agreements.

At the request of the War Department,
the Munitions Assignments Committee
(Ground) had acted favorably on one
armament requisition for the French and
was about to act on a second, such action
being taken subject to the ultimate approval
of the CCS and pending final decision by
the latter regarding the over-all program.
On 1 February, the MAC (G) had recommended, and the MAB had subsequently
approved, the assignment of the matériel—
vehicles and medical and training equipment—requested for the North African

forces by the theater on 26 January.[1] This
matériel, incidentally, was much the same
as that listed under Priority I of the Béthouart program. Two weeks later, on 16
February, the MAC (G) also approved
the immediate transfer to the French of
some 400 machine guns, 24 medium tanks
for training purposes, as well as the matériel
requested earlier by General Eisenhower for
re-equipping one infantry division, two
truck companies, one service company, and
one ordnance battalion.[2] Army Service
Forces then made arrangements for the
shipment of the equipment as filler cargo
on the next convoys to North Africa.

These measures clearly indicated that
War Department officials were no less determined than General Eisenhower to begin

[1] Min, MAC (G) 74th Mtg, 1 Feb 43. (See
Bibliographical Note.)
[2] Msg 8496, Eisenhower to AGWAR, 2 Feb 43,
JRC Cable Log; Min, MAC (G) 78th Mtg, 16
Feb 43. MAC (G) withheld the 17,500 rifles
requested by General Eisenhower because there
existed at the time a shortage of 1,300,000 in the
United States. As rifles were available from British
sources, the London Munitions Assignments Board
was requested to release them to the French complete with bayonets and scabbards, accessories, and
maintenance spare parts. These rifles, all .30-
caliber, were from the old U.S. stock turned over
to the British after the battle of Dunkerque. Msg
5826, AFHQ to USFOR, 21 Apr 43, JRC Cable
Log. On the question of rifles and other infantry
weapons issued to the French during the war, see
pp. 246–53, below.

U.S. VEHICLES FOR NORTH AFRICAN FORCES, *Casablanca, 22 February 1943.*

rearming the French while awaiting a decision of the CCS on the extent of the program. They intended to proceed generally within the framework of the Béthouart proposal of 26 December, and on the basis of recommendations of the Allied Commander in Chief as to armament and shipping priorities. They concurred fully in General Eisenhower's position that matériel and shipping priorities must be decided by him, except when the CCS might have to intervene.[3] To avoid dual shipping procedures, they recommended, and the theater agreed, that shipments for the French, distinctively marked, should continue as U.S. Army shipments consigned to Commanding General, NATOUSA, and handled like any other U.S. military shipments.[4]

On 16 February Marshall referred to Eisenhower a request he had just received from General Béthouart for the equipment to complete the initial phase of the ANFA Plan. Béthouart was asking for an allocation of 100,000 tons monthly, for the next two months, over and above the 25,000-ton allotment authorized by the theater. War Department officials, explained General Marshall, considered that the decision in the matter was up to the theater, not them.[5]

The Allied Commander in Chief, on 18 February, confirmed General Giraud's eagerness to complete the initial phase of the ANFA Plan as speedily as possible. He

---

[3] In the course of a conference held at AFHQ, it had been agreed that Eisenhower would be the final authority on the matter of French requisitions. Min, CofS Conf, 29 Jan 43, AFHQ AG Sec 337.2.

[4] Memo, Styer for Eisenhower, 10 Feb 43, JRC 902/II Rearmt Plan. In accordance with an earlier request from the theater, the following distinctive markings were subsequently adopted:

all packages containing equipment for the French bore the code symbol NAFUS (for North African French-U.S.) and were stenciled with vertical red, white, and blue stripes. Msg 8496 cited n. 2.

[5] Ltr, Béthouart to Marshall, 15 Feb 43, OCS A–45–523; Msg 2399, Marshall to Eisenhower, 16 Feb 43, JRC Cable Log. The submission of Béthouart's request to the War Department was entirely consonant with General Smith's statement of 6 February (see p. 41, above) that the French must take up shipping problems directly with the War Department.

then submitted a detailed request for the necessary equipment. On the question of shipping, he pointed out in a subsequent message that for him to allocate more tonnage for the French forces from his present shipping allotment would be to compete directly with his other military requirements. He fully realized that the "apparent commitment of Anfa as understood by the French" might require an immediate increase in rearmament tonnage. Existing demands, however, were "quite beyond" his capacity to meet if future plans were to be executed, as he hoped, within the period of time currently contemplated.[6]

Without waiting for Eisenhower's reply, Marshall had instructed ASF to explore at once the possibility of allocating more tonnage for the shipment of military equipment to the French. On 19 February General Somervell had announced that a special convoy of approximately 125,000 tons could be arranged for this purpose.

The request submitted by the theater on 18 February called for the shipment of matériel to equip two infantry divisions, two armored regiments with Sherman tanks, three tank destroyer battalions, three reconnaissance battalions of the type contained in armored divisions, and twelve antiaircraft battalions. Operations Division gave the request a very high priority, so high in fact that American ground units in the United States were to be stripped of equipment, if necessary, to meet the French requirements.[7]

So far, the organization of the special convoy was an American project. The precipitate American action prompted the British to point out with perfect accuracy that to date the Combined Chiefs had made no basic policy decisions on French rearmament. To assign equipment without benefit of direction from the CCS was, in their judgment, "putting the cart before the ox." Despite the British demurral and pending final action by the MAB, arrangements for the convoy proceeded. Arms and equipment, on order of ASF, were moved into ports and the convoy was assembled. The Combined Chiefs meanwhile continued the debate on long-range policy.[8]

The convoy, known as UGS 6½[9] and consisting of fifteen cargo ships, was to leave about 19 March and arrive in North Africa around 11 April. It had been arranged with great difficulty for it represented a "terrifically stiff demand on a very, very tight shipping situation." Not all the equipment assigned on 20 February, amounting to some 150,000 tons, could be lifted in the fifteen ships. It was agreed that items left behind would be shipped as soon as practicable. Also to go later was a substantial amount of the air equipment requested by the theater on 14 February.[10]

All together, the matériel to be shipped on UGS 6½ and on convoys immediately following, for which assignment either had been obtained or was then pending, ex-

---

[6] Msgs 1628, Eisenhower to OPD, 18 Feb 43, and 1930, Eisenhower to Marshall, 20 Feb 43, JRC Cable Log.

[7] Memo, Secy for Chairman MAC (G), 18 Feb 43, attached to Min, MAC (G) 80th Mtg, 20 Feb 43.

[8] Min, MAC (G) 80th Mtg, 20 Feb 43. It was not until 24 March 1943 that the MAB, acting in accordance with a decision taken by the CCS twelve days earlier, approved the assignment recommended by the U.S. members of the MAC (G) on 20 February.

[9] The conventional symbol UG was used to identify a cargo convoy originating in U.S. ports (whereas KM signified a convoy from the United Kingdom). The added symbols "S" and "F" meant "slow" and "fast" respectively.

[10] Quotation from Memo, Lewis Douglas for Somervell, 19 Feb 43, Somervell File, Shipping; Msg 2833, Somervell to Eisenhower, 25 Feb 43, JRC Cable Log.

ceeded substantially the equipment listed by
General Béthouart on 15 February. With
it, General Giraud would be able to equip
3 infantry divisions, 2 armored regiments,
4 tank destroyer battalions, 5 reconnaissance battalions, 14 40-mm. antiaircraft
battalions, 12 truck companies, and air
units representing more than 200 airplanes.[11] In actuality, these shipments
would complete the first phase of the ANFA
Plan.

General Béthouart could well be pleased
with the arrangements just concluded.
Aware of the important part which General
Marshall had played in shaping them, the
French representative expressed to him his
personal appreciation in a letter of thanks.[12]

The announcement regarding the special
convoy could not have reached General
Eisenhower at a more appropriate time, for
he was about to convey to General Giraud
the President's interpretation of the ANFA
Agreement. In his letter General Eisenhower first stressed the United States Government's desire and policy to equip the
French forces properly as fast as shipping
could be allocated for that purpose. He
then broke the news about the special convoy. The decision of the War Department
to set it up, he pointed out in conclusion,
was "a further evidence of our desire to
share with you to the fullest extent possible
consistent with the means at our disposal." [13]

At the close of the six-week period just
ended, extending from the opening session
of the Casablanca Conference to 23 Febru-

ary, when Eisenhower wrote to Giraud, the
Americans as well as the French could point
with satisfaction to the great strides being
made toward the rehabilitation of the North
African forces. The principle of a rearmament had been recognized by the American government and made the subject of an
agreement. The implications of the agreement had been analyzed and subsequently
clarified. Finally, a substantial amount of
equipment was about to leave the United
States for North African ports, a tangible
proof of the American intent to carry
through the promises made at Anfa and
earlier at Cherchel.

The question now uppermost in the
minds of all was this: How soon and how
often could shipments be made? The divergence of views demonstrated by the British
and American members of the MAB on
20 February was clear proof that the board
was not in a position to make further assignments unless it received the necessary
guidance from the CCS. Obviously no
policy would be forthcoming until such time
as the CCS had considered the French rearmament problem in its entirety and agreed
to the establishment of a firm over-all program.

The CCS Agree on a Rearmament Formula

Eager to obtain the formalization of the
action taken by ASF as well as a definite
policy with regard to equipping the French,
the U.S. Chiefs of Staff brought the entire
rearmament question before the CCS. The
memorandum which they submitted on 23
February first pointed out that as a result
of discussions held at Anfa between President Roosevelt and Generals Marshall,
Somervell, Giraud, and Eisenhower, it had
been agreed that equipment would be

---

[11] Memo, Marshall for Béthouart, 24 Feb 43,
OSC A–45–523 (France).

[12] Ltr, Béthouart to Marshall, 25 Feb 43, OCS
A–45–523 (France).

[13] Msg 2641, Marshall to Eisenhower, 20 Feb 43,
JRC 902/II Rearmt Plan; Ltr, Eisenhower to
Giraud, 23 Feb 43, AFHQ 0100/4 SACS Fr Mat-
ters.

furnished "as expeditiously as practicable in accordance with requests submitted from time to time through and coordinated with the CinC [Allied Forces in North Africa]." The CCS, asserted the JCS, had been informed of this "policy," [14] and had further been advised that the U.S. Chiefs of Staff intended to "delay the organization of combat units in the U.S. in approximate proportion to French units to be rearmed." The U.S. Chiefs of Staff now proposed that the CCS approve the following directive to the MAB for guidance in allocating equipment to General Giraud: "Munitions of war will be assigned to French land and air forces in North Africa from the common pool to the extent that these forces can be organized as units around a nucleus of trained officers and NCO's in accordance with priorities to be established by the CinC, Allied Forces in North Africa, and to the extent that shipping can be made available for the transport of these munitions." Naval forces were specifically excluded as they were to be the object of a separate paper. [15]

The memorandum, it must be noted, was strangely silent regarding the scope of the proposed rearmament. It made no mention of the eleven-division target as agreed

to by President Roosevelt, an omission possibly due to the fact that the revised version of the ANFA Agreements had yet to be approved by the President.

The reaction of the British Chiefs of Staff was prompt and vigorous. On 25 February, they expressed their views on the proposal just offered by their American colleagues. The rearmament of the French in the immediate future and on a large scale would, they asserted, cut across the agreements reached at Casablanca regarding future strategy. They pointed out that the North African forces could not be reequipped in time to take part in current operations in Tunisia and were "unlikely to be required" for any of the subsequent operations decided upon at the conference. [16]

The British Chiefs considered further that any shipping allocated to French rearmament above that actually required for operations then contemplated would be at the direct expense of these operations, thereby seriously prejudicing them. The directive proposed by the U.S. Chiefs of Staff, they pointed out, made no mention of the fact that the commitment to rearm the French was to be carried out at the expense of the activation of U.S. units. They now understood this was "the policy agreed on at Anfa." Since French rearmament involved a problem of assignment which differed in no way from similar problems in other theaters, they considered that it should be dealt with by the MAB in the light of other global commitments and be accorded such assignments as its strategic priority merited. In conclusion, the British Chiefs of Staff

---

[14] Obviously a reference to the disclosures made in this connection by General Marshall at the 61st and 62d CCS Meetings on 19 January.

[15] Memo, JCS for CCS, 23 Feb 43, CCS 181. The memorandum was approved by the JCS at their 63d Meeting, 23 February 1943. It is interesting to note that before submitting the draft of this paper to the JCS for their approval, Brig. Gen. John R. Deane, secretary of the committee, made this rather startling statement in a memorandum for General Marshall: "The President agreed in principle with General Giraud that French Forces would be re-equipped but did not specify any particular number even though General Giraud believes that he did." Memo, Deane for Marshall, 22 Feb 43, OPD 400 France, Sec 1.

[16] The contemplated operations were: ANAKIM, consisting of a large land operation for the reopening of the Burma Road and an amphibious operation for the recapture of Rangoon; and BOLERO, a preliminary build-up of the forces required for an operation across the English Channel.

urged that the proposed directive to the MAB be revised to indicate the priority to be given to French rearmament "in its proper relation to the requirements of other military operations already agreed upon." They recommended further that the MAB be informed of the ultimate scale of rearmament and the speed at which it should be accomplished.[17]

On 26 February, the CCS engaged in a lively debate centering on the American proposal and the British answer. Admiral William D. Leahy prefaced the discussion by emphasizing that a commitment had been made "on a higher level than the CCS" and that the question now confronting the committee was "the manner" in which the commitment should be implemented. In his opinion the agreement reached at Anfa could not be voided. General Marshall then called attention to the "inconsistency" of some statements in the British memorandum. If equipment was to be furnished the North African forces at the expense of U.S. units, "it was hardly a question about a common pool." Speed of deliveries and amount of equipment involved, he pointed out, were matters still to be determined. He felt, however, that it was important, both politically and strategically, that "some measure of the agreement be carried out in the near future" so as to bolster Eisenhower's position, especially in French Morocco where his strength had been depleted by preparations for future operations. Asked whether the dispatch of equipment to the French would prejudice other planned operations, General Somervell expressed the belief that it would not. The present major shortage, he explained, was in troopships, not in cargo carriers. Gen-

eral Somervell then voiced his "great surprise" at learning that there was any question regarding the rearming of the French, as it was his understanding that the matter had been agreed on at Anfa. He urged that the MAB be authorized to assign the equipment then being loaded on the special convoy.

Speaking for the British Chiefs of Staff, General Macready first questioned the wisdom of leaving the decision as to the extent of French rearmament to the theater commander, who, he felt, was not in a position to judge all the rival claims of other planned operations. While fully recognizing the "political necessity" for delivery of a minimum amount of equipment, he feared that the contemplated shipments to North Africa would conflict with commitments in the Indian Ocean where General Sir Archibald P. Wavell was asking for an additional 126,000 tons monthly. However, added General Macready, the British Chiefs of Staff were prepared to authorize the MAB to go ahead with the present proposed assignments, "provided any delay which might thus be caused to British assignments would be made good later in the year." In an effort to reconcile the American and British stands on the matter, General Marshall proposed that the directive to the MAB be amended to read "without jeopardizing other commitments." [18]

The directive, thus amended, was referred to the British Chiefs of Staff in London. On 2 March they signified their willingness to accept it provided it was amended further as follows: "Munitions of war will be assigned to the French Forces up to the limits and at a speed to be decided by the CCS . . . without prejudicing other commitments." Their own proposed amendment, they de-

---

[17] Memo, Representatives of COS for CCS, 25 Feb 43, CCS 181/1.

[18] Min, CCS 73d Mtg, 26 Feb 43.

clared, was prompted by their feeling that assignments of vital items in short supply should not be made to the French for operational use at the expense of assignments to U.S. or British troops. Since, in addition, existing shipping was insufficient to meet all present combined commitments, they considered it essential to leave it to the CCS to decide, "on purely military grounds and after due consideration of the situation in all theaters," what was to be assigned.[19] It was now clear that one of the fears experienced by the British regarding French rearmament as proposed by the U.S. Chiefs of Staff was that the commitment would jeopardize the delivery of American equipment to their own forces.

At their next meeting, the JCS took up the controversial directive to the MAB. Admiral Leahy first informed his colleagues that the President had directed that the loading of the special convoy be continued. He then called attention to the statement contained in the British memorandum of 2 March that the Prime Minister had confirmed that he had not discussed the question of French rearmament with the President while at Anfa. The President, declared Admiral Leahy, had just informed him to the contrary. Admiral King then pointed out that, since there was no agreement such as that reached with the USSR, and since the JCS had not clearly defined the extent of the proposed rearmament, the British obviously were concerned lest the matter be carried too far. He felt that some definite statement should be made to the British indicating that for the moment not more than three divisions or their equivalent were to be re-equipped.

In a less conciliatory mood, Admiral

Leahy urged that a definite program be "made, held to, and the British so informed." This was important, he pointed out, in view of a possible United Nations manpower shortage. General Somervell, chief of ASF, then explained that there existed no shortage of equipment, not even of tank destroyers for which the British had also made a request. Shipping, he asserted, was the only question that mattered. And he believed that when French ships, once repaired, had been added to the Allied pool, it would be possible to increase the current 25,000-ton allocation for French military supplies by some 40,000 additional tons per convoy. There was no intention, he added, to continue shipments at a heavy rate, but only at the rate provided by French shipping plus the tonnage allocated by General Eisenhower. In the case of the special convoy, he explained, ships had been taken out of the U.S. shipping allocation and had been made available by the War Shipping Administration. Admiral Leahy then offered this advice: "The best attitude to adopt is to inform the British that the US JCS intend to ship the equipment." Asked by Admiral King what stand the British Chiefs of Staff had taken at the Casablanca Conference, Brig. Gen. John R. Deane, secretary of the committee, replied that at no time had they acquiesced to the American plans to rearm the French; they had listened without comment and had never agreed or disagreed.[20]

In the opinion of General Somervell, British objections to sanctioning the measures already taken by the War Department to arm the French appeared groundless. Only the matériel for three divisions had been assigned to date, a commitment "apparently concurred in by the British Chiefs

---

[19] Memo, Representatives of COS for CCS, 2 Mar 43, CCS 181/3.

[20] Min, JCS 64th Mtg, 2 Mar 43.

of Staff." In addition, very few of the items involved could be considered in short supply and even in their case the amounts assigned represented but a small proportion of the monthly production rate. Finally, in allocating the necessary tonnage, the War Shipping Administration had advised that the allocation had been made "without prejudice to the fulfillment of other operational shipping needs considered as urgent." [21]

Operations Division officials had come to the conclusion that the amendment to the MAB directive as proposed by the British would make action by the CCS mandatory on every armament request for the French. The CCS, they feared, would then be assuming the role of a munitions assignments board. Brig. Gen. John E. Hull, Chief, Theater Group, OPD, declared flatly that, as written, the British proposal was not acceptable. He offered as a possible compromise the following counterproposal:

Munitions of war will be assigned to the French forces . . . from the common pool to the extent that these forces can be organized as units . . . in accordance with priorities to be established by the Allied CinC in North Africa and to the extent that shipping and equipment can be made available without jeopardizing other commitments. Equipment allotted by the MAB will not, without prior reference to the CCS, exceed that necessary to equip eleven divisions, an air force of 450 planes, and appropriate supporting and auxiliary troops.

General Hull considered that his proposal, if adopted, would fulfill the President's "agreement in principle" and would not commit the British Chiefs of Staff to the granting of blanket authority to the MAB.[22]

On 5 March, the CCS resumed their discussion of the terms of the draft directive. First, Admiral Leahy restated the American position and reminded his British colleagues that at Casablanca they had raised no objection to the U.S. proposal to arm the French. It would now be "as impossible as it would be inadvisable" to withdraw from the commitment given General Giraud by President Roosevelt. Speaking for the British Chiefs of Staff, General Macready stated that the point of disagreement concerned the details of the commitment. What the MAB required were instructions as to the amount of equipment to be furnished and the approximate speed of delivery. Without such instructions, he explained, the MAB would not be in a position to fit the assignments to the French into the over-all claims upon available munitions. The fact was, he concluded, that "no document existed" which indicated what was to be supplied to the French.

Admiral King agreed with General Macready. Referring to the minutes of the Casablanca Conference, he asserted that, to his knowledge, no definite decision had anywhere been recorded regarding equipment for the North African forces.[23] He felt that some sort of protocol similar to that for the USSR should be agreed on for the French. It was quite right, he added, that a "brake" be put on the French project so as "to insure that other existing commitments would not be prejudiced." Admiral Leahy, on the other hand, considered that the U.S. Chiefs of Staff could not subscribe to the amendment proposed by the British as it ran counter to their own commitment. For the benefit of the British representatives, General

[21] Memo, Somervell for Deane, 3 Mar 43, OPD 400 France, Sec I.

[22] Memo, Hull for CofS, 4 Mar 43, OPD Exec 1, Item 13.

[23] The minutes of the Casablanca Conference did not record the conversations between the President and General Giraud.

Somervell, Lt. Gen. Joseph T. McNarney, then Deputy Chief of Staff, and Admiral Leahy in turn outlined briefly the ANFA Plan and explained how they proposed to meet it. Field Marshal Dill observed that the British Chiefs of Staff might take the view that eleven French divisions were more than could ever be made use of in Tunisia, particularly as a large part of this force would not become available until long after the fighting in that area was expected to cease. However, in the light of the commitment which had been made, he recognized that equipment would have to be delivered. He proposed to refer the matter to the British Chiefs of Staff and inform them of the suggested ceiling of 11 divisions and 450 aircraft. He would explain to them that "it was the impression of the U.S. Chiefs of Staff that the matter had been fully discussed at Casablanca and approved in principle." [24]

In the belief that a clearer statement of their aims might dispel British objections, the U.S. Chiefs of Staff, on 6 March, offered a revised version of their draft directive to the MAB which read as follows: "Equipment allotted to the French by MAB will not, without prior reference to the CCS, exceed that necessary to equip 11 divisions, 450 planes, and appropriate supporting and auxiliary troops." [25]

The proposed amendment failed to win over the British Chiefs of Staff. On 11 March, they flatly declared that a diversion of shipping at the present critical stage, for the rearmament of forces not required to implement agreed strategy, "could not be justified militarily." It was now clear, they continued, that the CCS could carry the matter no further in view of the commit-

ment which the President was "understood to have given" to General Giraud. The President, they pointed out, had probably not been aware of the gravity of the shipping situation or of the certainty that operations agreed to at Casablanca could not be carried out if even a fraction of the United Nations shipping resources was diverted to other purposes. As they understood that the Prime Minister would be taking the whole matter up with Mr. Roosevelt, they suggested that, in the meantime, the U.S. Chiefs of Staff consider steps to obtain French shipping then lying idle in Martinique and other French West Indies ports. This shipping comprised several small vessels whose commander, Rear Adm. Georges Robert, had refused to rally to the Allies. [26]

In the opinion of the U.S. Chiefs of Staff, there was no question of diverting shipping for the rearmament of forces not required to implement agreed strategy. Their proposed directive in fact placed the responsibility for the allocation of shipping squarely on the Allied Commander in Chief in North Africa, and specifically stated that the allocation of munitions to the French was contingent on the shipping that could be made available without jeopardizing other commitments. They considered further that the British argument over the shipping question was inconsistent. In papers submitted by them concerning projects of their own in which shipping was involved, the British had made no mention of the critical shipping situation. [27] As for their proposal regarding French shipping then lying idle in Martinique, the U.S. Chiefs of Staff

---

[24] Min, CCS 74th Mtg, 5 Mar 43.
[25] CCS 181/4, 6 Mar 43.

[26] Memo, Representatives of COS for CCS, 11 Mar 43, CCS 181/5.
[27] The projects were: AFLOC, a trans-Africa supply route for the supply of vehicles and equipment to the Middle East and east Africa; and FREETOWN, the development of the port of Freetown.

discussed it in curious language as "a good but worthless suggestion." The use of such shipping, they added, would not affect materially the issuance of a directive to the MAB.[28]

At the next meeting of the CCS, held on 12 March, negotiations came to a complete deadlock. The committee first discussed a report (CCS 142/1) from the Combined Staff Planners (CPS) concerning the allocation of aircraft to the French under the ANFA Plan. The report showed that the Staff Planners had been unable to agree on the matter. The American members had recommended an initial allocation of aircraft for one light bomber group and one fighter group, and of fifty light transports. While agreeing to the principle of an initial allocation, the British members were unwilling to have specific numbers set at this time. Commenting on the U.S. proposal, Air Vice Marshal W. F. MacNeece Foster asserted that the British Chiefs of Staff were gravely concerned at the prospect that French rearmament might prejudice the requirements for future operations. He urged the CCS to ascertain, before reaching any decision on the matter, whether or not General Eisenhower and his Air deputy in the theater, Air Chief Marshal Sir Arthur Tedder, considered that any particular allocation of aircraft to the North African Air Forces was "in the best interests of operations in Tunisia." The CCS then took up the question of equipment for the North African Ground Forces. The British Chiefs of Staff, asserted General Macready, did not object in principle to a rearmament spread over a period when it could be achieved without prejudicing other operations. Their feeling was that, with the very serious shipping situation then existing,

operations such as HUSKY and ANAKIM would suffer if equipment was shipped to the French in large quantities at this time.[29] In view of the imminence of these operations, "it might be right," he added, "to go so far as to stop the ships now earmarked for French equipment and to divert them to other uses." General Macready reiterated that the theater commander was not in a position to weigh shipping priorities as between his own and other theaters. He pointed out that General Eisenhower himself might hesitate to recommend the shipment of matériel to the French if he thought that it might result in prejudicing Operation HUSKY. Thereupon General Somervell emphasized that there was no question of HUSKY being prejudiced. Admiral Leahy then flatly declared that there could be no stoppage of the presently planned shipments. Realizing that they were not likely to get out of the impasse, the CCS finally agreed to suspend further action pending the result of the exchange of views then taking place between the Prime Minister and the President. They "took note," however, that the initial ground and air equipment set up with General Eisenhower's concurrence would be sent to North Africa.[30]

From available evidence, it appears that the high-level exchange of views referred to by the CCS was not concerned with the issue at stake and as a result was not likely to produce the expected clarification. In a message to the President, Churchill had broached not the question of French rearmament, which he regarded as merely one of the conflicting demands on shipping, but the broader problem of global shipping

---

[28] CCS 75th Mtg, Notes for the Mtg, 12 Mar 43.

[29] Operation HUSKY: an assault on Sicily; Operation ANAKIM: see note 16, above.
[30] Min and Suppl Min, CCS 75th Mtg, 12 Mar 43. Rpt, CPS to CCS, 142/1, 10 Mar 43.

requirements. That was the problem which Foreign Secretary Anthony Eden discussed with American officials in the course of his subsequent visit to Washington, 13–19 March.[31]

It will be recalled that, on 23 January, General Marshall had urged the JCS to set forth a policy with respect to the contemplated employment of the North African forces and the scale of equipment to be provided. At the request of the JCS, the U.S. Joint Staff Planners (JPS) had undertaken a study of the problem. Their recommendations, submitted on 20 March and subsequently endorsed by the Joint Chiefs, constituted in effect the basic declaration of U.S. policy on French rearmament.

In full recognition of the important part that French air and ground forces will play not only in the forthcoming operations in the Mediterranean region but also shoulder to shoulder with American and British troops in the ultimate liberation of continental France, the CCS accept herewith the obligation to equip with modern equipment and to maintain a French Army of approximately 250,000 officers and men, in accordance with the following which will be considered an integral part of the agreement:

a) Munitions of war will be assigned for French land and air forces from the common pool to the extent that these forces can be organized as units around a nucleus of trained officers and noncommissioned officers in accordance with priorities to be established by the CinC, Allied Forces in North Africa, and to the extent that shipping and equipment can be made available without jeopardizing other commitments.

b) Equipment allotted to the French by the MAB will not, without prior reference to the CCS, exceed that necessary to equip the units listed below:

11 divisions
air force of 450 planes
appropriate supporting and auxiliary troops

c) Equipment for French Forces, either already sent to North Africa or now on the way, shall be considered part of, and not in addition to, the equipment referred to in paragraphs (a) and (b) above.

d) The US and UK shall share equitably in equipping the French African Air Force, the ultimate strength of which shall be regarded as approximately 450 aircraft.

e) French forces will be employed to the maximum practicable extent (1) in the forthcoming battle in Tunisia, (2) for garrison duty in North Africa after the Axis is ejected therefrom, and (3) in such other operations as the Theater Commander may desire.

f) This agreement applies only to French forces in North Africa, and nothing herein shall be construed as binding the US and the UK to equip the French continental Army, either upon the liberation of France or after total victory over the Axis is won.

g) Although the need therefor cannot now be foreseen, in view of the speed with which the strategic situation in a global war can change, the US and the UK must reluctantly, but necessarily, reserve the right to modify the specific provisions of this agreement, should future circumstances so demand.[32]

This declaration, laid before the CCS, reflected the official American view that the United States and the United Kingdom were fully committed to a program specifically established as to scope if not as to time schedule. In line with this view, Maj. Gen. Thomas T. Handy, chief of OPD, on 15 March informed Army Service Forces that "it [had] been decided" to furnish sufficient matériel from the common pool of

---

[31] Memo, E. I. C. Jacob (LMAB) for Brig Gen William F. Tompkins (MAB), 10 Apr 43, CCS 400.17 (7–6–42), Sec 4.

[32] Rpt, JPS to JCS, sub: Equip for Fr Forces in North Africa, 20 Mar 43, JCS 206/1. A first draft of the report, completed 8 March, was examined at the 64th Meeting of the JPS on 10 March, and a revised version subsequently sent to JCS on 15 March.

munitions manufactured in the United States to equip eleven French divisions. He then requested ASF to study the impact which the provision of such matériel was likely to have on the equipping of American forces, and to examine in particular to what extent it would be necessary to defer the activation of U.S. units during 1943. ASF replied that there was no serious conflict and that the activation of U.S. units could proceed as scheduled. The 1943 Army Supply Program as then established was adequate to take care of existing units and those presently planned for activation. With a contemplated cushion of matériel for some sixteen divisions, French rearmament could easily be carried out without dislocating the 100-division program scheduled for the U.S. Army in 1943. At General Somervell's direction, ASF promptly incorporated the French requirements in Section V–A and V–B of the Army Supply Program.[33]

The inability of the CCS to arrive at a decision could not but produce a climate of uncertainty, even apprehension, in the theater. As pointed out by Colonel Gardiner, chairman of the Joint Rearmament Committee, the absence of a directive setting forth the aims of French rearmament "left room for discussion of the merits of the question and opened the way to the expression of diverse views on the subject." The French, he insisted, needed encouragement as well as "an example of decisive action" and should be given an objective as soon as possible.[34]

Still the Combined Chiefs seemed in no hurry. They did not even discuss the matter from mid-March until the middle of May when they convened for the Trident Conference in Washington. Then the situation had changed. The ending of the Tunisian campaign had placed the French armament issue in an entirely new light.[35] In addition, President Roosevelt, earlier in April, had authorized the redrafting of the Anfa Agreement leaving out the controversial paragraph which set forth the extent of the program at eleven divisions.[36] As they met, on 18 May, the CCS were now free to discuss the matter without having to feel any longer that they were committed to a specific program.

Even so, the argument at first picked up about where it had left off in March. To the Americans, it still seemed wise to speed up the arming and training of the North African forces in view of their potential value for operations in France. Admiral Leahy pointed out that, while somewhat more than three divisions had been reequipped, eight others already activated were almost without modern equipment. The French had been promised the equipment at Anfa, recalled General Marshall. Lt. Gen. Walter Bedell Smith then explained that AFHQ had been guided by the Anfa decisions. Since French units had "in general fought excellently" in Tunisia, he declared, General Eisenhower now wanted to use them not only to defend French Morocco, guard lines of communications, and man antiaircraft defenses in North Africa, but possibly to assault Corsica and Sardinia. General Giraud, he added, was especially

---

[33] Memo, Handy for CG SOS, 15 Mar 43, Memo, Maj Gen Lucius Du B. Clay for ACofS, 27 Mar 43, and Memo, Hull for CofS, 10 Apr 43, OPD 400 France, Sec 1; Control Div ASF, The Determination of Army Supply Requirements, Hist MS File, OCMH.

[34] Memos, Gardiner for Brig J. F. M. Whiteley, 12 and 30 Apr 43, copies in Col Gardiner's Private File.

[35] Hostilities ended on 13 May with the capture of the remaining Axis forces in Tunisia.

[36] Memo, Deane for JCS, 22 Apr 43, OPD 400 France, Sec 1.

anxious to equip his forces "on an expeditionary basis." Unless the Combined Shipping and Adjustment Board arranged to provide additional tonnage, General Giraud's requirements of 100,000 tons monthly would not be met.

The British reiterated their earlier cautions. While agreeing to the importance of rearming the French, Field Marshal Sir Alan Brooke voiced once again the British belief that it was a matter of timing and availability of shipping. Shipping, he asserted, should not be diverted to re-equip the North African units at the expense of a build-up of Allied forces for important operations. He agreed that, in general, the "correct policy" was initially to equip the French for the static role of relieving Allied forces for offensive operations. At a later stage the French then could be equipped as an expeditionary force.

Both sides having thus again affirmed their separate points of view substantially unchanged from the earlier debates, the CCS settled suddenly on a compromise formula: "The rearming and re-equipping of the French Forces in North Africa should be proceeded with as rapidly as the availability of shipping and equipping will allow, but as a secondary commitment to the requirements of British and U.S. Forces in the various Theaters." They agreed further that the possibility of using captured German matériel to re-equip the French should be explored.[37]

The wording represented a considerable if not total surrender to the view of the British Chiefs in providing the double safety valve for which they had consistently argued: that the commitment be not firm as to the amount of equipment to be delivered and that it be made contingent on the prior claims of British and American forces. It seems likely that the Americans conceded the point for two main reasons—a sense first that it had become critical to have some kind of decision, and second that agreement in principle would permit, even if it did not require, the carrying out of the original ANFA commitment. The Americans were convinced that neither shortage of equipment nor shortage of shipping would interfere with the arming of the eleven divisions as agreed. They were equally convinced that the North African troops had proved their usefulness and that therefore it would be militarily justifiable, if necessary, to arm them at the expense of American units.

In effect the TRIDENT decision simply reaffirmed the primary responsibility of the United States for rearming the French in North Africa and gave the U.S. Joint Chiefs of Staff a comparatively free hand in carrying out that responsibility. That point was underlined in a meeting with the President and the Prime Minister when Air Chief Marshal Portal, after pointing out that the British were supplying the North African Air Forces with aircraft for patrol duties off the West African coast, emphasized that except for this contribution "the entire project was in the hands of the United States." [38]

While the TRIDENT decision for the time being settled the rearmament policy to the satisfaction of the British and Americans, it left something to be desired from the French point of view. The urgency of rearmament had been forcibly brought to the French by their recent experience in

[37] Min, CCS 87th Mtg, 18 May 43, TRIDENT Conf.

[38] Min, 4th Mtg with President and Prime Minister, 21 May 43, TRIDENT Conf.

GENERAL EISENHOWER DELIVERING AN ADDRESS *at the ceremony, 8 May 1943, in Algiers in celebration of the fall of Tunisia and the arrival of U.S. matériel for the French. General Giraud is at the right.*

Tunisia. The 40,000 North African troops thrown into the battle had suffered some 9,600 casualties (including 2,300 killed in action) or 24 percent of the forces engaged.[39] For these heavy losses, the inadequacy of equipment had been in large measure responsible. To General Giraud, facing the prospect of perhaps again committing troops to such an ordeal, the compromise formula of TRIDENT, with its indefinite program of rearmament to be carried out only as it could be fitted into more pressing obligations, offered little comfort. "The French," one American observer had warned, "are deadly serious about the matter."[40] For the moment, however, they had no choice but to go along with the *ad hoc* solutions permitted by the CCS decision.

---

[39] Figures on losses are taken from Lt. Col. P. Santini, "Etude statistique sur les pertes au cours de la guerre 1939–1945," *Revue du Corps de Santé Militaire,* X, No. 1 (March, 1954).

[40] Memo, Gen Tompkins for Maj Gen J. H. Burns, 29 Mar 43, CCS 400 France (11–3–42), Sec 2.

LT. GEN. MARK W. CLARK PRESENTING NEWLY ARRIVED U.S.
EQUIPMENT *to the French Ground Forces in a ceremony held at Casablanca, 9 May 1943.
General Auguste Noguès is at the left.*

Implementing Phase I

Ten days before the formula on French
rearmament was finally agreed to in Washington, a significant event had taken place
in North Africa. On that day, 8 May, an
imposing ceremony was held in Algiers in
the dual celebration of the fall of Tunisia,
just wrested from Axis control, and of the
formal handing over to General Giraud of
U.S. matériel recently unloaded in North
African ports. The speech that General Eisenhower made on this occasion included a special message from President
Roosevelt to the French. "American workers," said the message in part, "are proud
to deliver the goods and weapons to be used
by French soldiers." [41] In accepting the
armament in the name of the French Army,
General Giraud echoed the feelings of pride
and gratitude of his countrymen when he
declared:

Today the pledge that was made at Anfa
by the President of the U.S. and the British

---

[41] Memo for Rcd, SGS, 9 May 43, AFHQ 0100/4
SACS Politics.

Government has been fulfilled. The convoys are arriving. The news is spreading through the country and among the troops and brings them comfort and hope. Today's ceremony, simple and great, allows us to express our gratitude to the workmen of America who have wrought that precious matériel and brought such a contribution to the restoration of Liberty in the world.[42]

Later in the day several North African contingents, formerly horse cavalry and now re-equipped as armored units, paraded through the flag-decked streets of the city and exhibited their newly acquired tanks, tractor-drawn artillery, jeeps, and combat cars to the enthusiastic populace. In the eyes of the French, the occasion symbolized the rebirth of their armed forces. The new French Army, proud of its modern weapons, was "taking its first steps." [43]

This and other similar demonstrations were vivid proof of the American determination to proceed with the re-equipping of the French.[44] In fact, even before the campaign in Tunisia had come to a close, the

first phase of rearmament was well on its way to completion. No development could have been more welcome at this time. For, if a few units were proudly displaying their newly acquired U.S. matériel, the remaining combat forces were still woefully lacking in equipment. Early in the Tunisian campaign, the French High Command had rushed to the units engaged there nearly all the matériel of French origin painstakingly accumulated before Operation TORCH. This matériel was now considerably reduced through damage, wear, and capture. What was left of it might possibly serve to equip part of the forces assigned to guard the lines of communications. Even for this purpose it would be necessary to obtain from other sources a substantial number of additional small arms. As for the British and American matériel loaned in the heat of battle, which consisted of miscellaneous quantities of Sten guns, British 2-pounder guns, 75-mm. guns, Valentine tanks, and approximately 500 assorted vehicles, it was understood that the items still serviceable at the end of the campaign were to be returned when the troops left the forward area. Considering in addition that only a small quantity of captured enemy matériel was likely to become available for use by the French, it was clear therefore that the only equipment on which the North African forces could rely for participation in further operations would be that received from U.S. sources.[45]

Of the 256,000 tons of equipment assigned by the MAB in February and March for the French Ground and Air Forces, approximately 193,000 tons (including the 126,151-ton special convoy) had reached North African ports by the end

---

[42] Rpt, C. Phillips, Import Div North African Economic Board, to L. L. Short, 14 May 43, AFHQ 0100/26 Liaison Sec, Rpts.

[43] Georges Marey, "Le Réarmement français en Afrique du Nord (1942–1944)," Revue Politique et Parlementaire (October and November, 1947).

[44] A ceremony of similar character was held on 9 May at Casablanca, at which General Clark, on behalf of the Allied Commander in Chief, presented some newly arrived U.S. equipment to the commanding general of the French Ground Forces in Morocco. There followed a parade of motorized equipment before a large crowd which could not fail to be impressed by this "tangible demonstration of the determination of the United Nations to put the French Army in the field as an effective, modern fighting organization." Rpt, Liaison Sec Fifth Army to Liaison Sec AFHQ, 15 May 43, AFHQ Liaison Sec 0100/12C Fr Rpts From Fifth Army. Likewise, in the course of a ceremony held in liberated Tunis on 10 May, a Spahis regiment, hurriedly re-equipped with U.S. matériel for the occasion, paraded through the city, a third tangible demonstration of the rehabilitation now going on in the North African Army.

[45] Memo, Artamonoff for Col Clément Blanc, 10 Jul 43, JRC 902/II Rearmt Plan.

of April. The backlog, amounting to about 63,000 tons, had been inventoried and was to be shipped on the next available convoys and at the 25,000-ton monthly rate authorized by the theater. Some 8,000 tons of supplies, including 200 airplanes, ground equipment, vehicles, and matériel for one parachute regiment, were intended for the air units. The remainder, or 248,000 tons, would serve to equip the ground troops provided for in the initial phase of the ANFA Plan. These, it will be recalled, included 3 infantry divisions, 2 armored regiments, 4 tank destroyer battalions, 5 reconnaissance battalions, 14 antiaircraft battalions, 12 truck companies, and 3 ordnance battalions. The distribution of equipment to individual units had already started and in some cases was completed, as the enthusiastic witnesses to the parade held on 8 May could testify.[46]

---

[46] Msg 4688, Marshall to Eisenhower, 26 Mar 43, JRC Cable Log; Memo, Artamonoff for Gardiner, 1 May 43, JRC 902/II Rearmt Plan. The 256,000 tons included the training equipment requested by the theater on 26 January (Msg 7433), special items and organizational equipment requested on 2 February (Msg 8496), equipment for the balance of the first phase requested on 18 February (Msg 1628), and air equipment requested on 14 and 27 February (Msgs 776 and 3271). (All msgs in JRC Cable Log.)

CHAPTER IV

Early Organizational Problems

The process by which American matériel was being channeled into the hands of French units, from the time it was requisitioned by the Joint Rearmament Committee to the time of its actual distribution, was a complicated one. It involved a number of important problems the solution of which required much patient labor and close teamwork on the part of the staffs and services concerned.

AFHQ Spells Out Rearmament Policies

The mission of the JRC consisted chiefly of determining, in collaboration with the French High Command, what units could be activated from available manpower, when they could be activated, what equipment they would need first, and how they best could be trained. In carrying out this mission, the JRC was guided by directives issued from time to time by the Allied Commander in Chief. General Eisenhower, on 31 January, had set forth the policy to govern the first phase of rearmament:

a. The French authorities will submit their requisitions periodically to this headquarters. However, the Allied CinC remains the approving authority and may modify the requisitions to conform to the availability of equipment and shipping, and to the terms of the general policy.

b. The JRC will maintain an up-to-date schedule showing:

1) How equipment issued by this Headquarters has been assigned by the French authorities.

2) How the French authorities intend to assign future issues of equipment.

He also stated that the initial rearmament phase was designed to provide forces for the defense of North and West Africa, as well as a picked force to form part of an Allied overseas expedition. Generally, the objective to be reached was "quality, not quantity." Finally, he defined the policy with regard to the rehabilitation of the naval and air forces in the light of their probable employment.[1]

It will be recalled that General Eisenhower, on 30 December 1942, had instructed the U.S. Fifth Army to assist the French in equipping and training their units. It was imperative therefore that the Fifth Army should familiarize itself with the rearmament problem. On 26 March, the deputy theater commander recommended that a procedure be arranged with the JRC whereby Fifth Army would "definitely enter the rearmament picture," and "act as a balance-wheel" to ensure that equipment was turned over to the French at a rate commensurate with proper care and maintenance.[2]

Later, on 30 March, the Allied Commander in Chief restated Fifth Army's obligation to assist the French military authorities with organizing and training the

---

[1] Dir AG 400/322–A–M, AFHQ, 31 Jan 43, AFHQ 0100/12C G–3 Div Ops Fr Rearmt, Vol. II (3).

[2] Memo, Maj Gen Everett S. Hughes for Gen Clark, 26 Mar 43, AFHQ 0100/12C G–3 Div Ops Fr Rearmt, Vol. II (Pt. I).

forces stationed in French Morocco.[3] The next day General Clark and his chief of staff, Maj. Gen. Alfred M. Gruenther, discussed ways and means to effect proper coordination between Fifth Army and AFHQ on the rearmament question.[4] Five days later, representatives from various AFHQ staff sections, including the JRC, met to determine the respective responsibilities of AFHQ, Fifth Army, and other interested headquarters. The basis for their discussion was a study prepared by G–3 Section, AFHQ, in which, curiously enough, it was stated that the rearmament policy "had already been fixed by the CCS." Nothing could have been further from the truth, for in that first week of April the CCS debate on French armament was in a state of complete deadlock. Except for this erroneous assertion, the memorandum furnished valuable data on the status of rearmament operations and made several important recommendations. It proposed in particular that AFHQ alone be made responsible for contact with the French High Command, the drafting of a rearmament program, and the control of requests for shipping, and that Fifth Army be given the responsibility for the "mechanical and tactical training" of the French.[5] On the basis of the decisions reached at the meeting, the Allied Commander in Chief, on 13 April, set forth in detail the policy to govern the entire rearmament process. His directive first described how the rate of provision of equipment was to be regulated; the role of U.S.

base sections in assisting the French with the immediate reception, storage, assembly, and issue of equipment; the assistance which the U.S. land forces in North Africa were to give in familiarizing French personnel with the technical details of storing, assembly, care, and maintenance of U.S. equipment. He then defined the respective responsibilities of AFHQ, the Commanding General, NATOUSA, and the Commanding General, Fifth Army, in the matter of French rearmament. AFHQ was charged with initiating programs and obtaining the necessary equipment from the United States. The Commanding General, NATOUSA, was responsible for handling equipment from the moment it reached North African ports to the time of its transfer to the French. The Commanding General, Fifth Army, was charged with assisting in the re-equipment and technical training of French Army units stationed throughout the U.S. Communications Zone.[6]

Eisenhower issued other directives at various intervals which set forth the manner in which French requisitions were to be processed and transfers of matériel accounted for so that proper charges could be made to the French lend-lease account in the United States. A separate directive was issued which governed the accounting procedure for transfers of matériel from British sources. Subsequent administrative memorandums established on the basis of directives from the War Department regulated the procedure to be followed by the bases at Casablanca, Oran, and Algiers for turning U.S. equipment over to the French.[7]

---

[3] Dir, CinC AFHQ to CG Fifth Army, 30 Mar 43, JRC Misc Doc, Item 5–a, Tab K.

[4] Note, Conf between Clark and Gruenther, 1 Apr 43, JRC Misc Doc, Item 5–a, Tab K.

[5] Note for Mtg, G–3 Sec AFHQ, 4 Apr 43, AFHQ 0100/12C G–3 Div Ops Fr Rearmt, Vol. II (Pt. I) ; Min, Mtg, 5 Apr 43, JRC 902/II Rearmt Plan.

[6] Ltr, CinC to CG Fifth Army and Deputy Theater Comdr NATOUSA, 13 Apr 43, JRC 902/II Rearmt Plan.

[7] See pp. 266–70, below.

INSPECTING U.S. EQUIPMENT *to be used by the French Army. From left: Col. Clément Blanc, General Henri Giraud, and Brig. Gen. Roger Leyer.*

Allied Assistance in Handling Matériel

The arrival in North Africa of matériel for the French posed physical and technical problems of considerable importance. From the outset AFHQ officials feared that the French military authorities might not be able, by themselves, to handle, assemble, sort out, distribute, and maintain the vast quantities of highly specialized equipment, much of which was entirely new to them. If units were to be equipped within the briefest possible time and with the least possible confusion, if, in other words, the optimum use was to be made of American matériel, it was indispensable that responsible Allied agencies come to the assistance of the French High Command by providing the skill and means to handle it.

In this initial phase of the rearmament operations, the French were particularly lacking in qualified administrative and technical personnel. The roster of the French General Staff and services included many very able officers, the foremost in the field of rearmament being Brig. Gen. Roger Leyer and Col. Clément Blanc, whose superior qualifications as organizers and technicians made of them then and thereafter the artisans of the rehabilitation of the French Army.[8] But in the services espe-

---

[8] From December 1942 to May 1943, General Leyer served under General René Prioux, then chief of Administrative Services, as first assistant for organization. In May, he became chief of staff of the General Staff War, a post which he occupied until November 1944, first as a major general, later as a lieutenant general. Colonel Blanc served under

cially, many of the officers, including some of the chiefs themselves, were unqualified and inefficient by American standards. Officials of the JRC were distressed over the slowness of action displayed by various headquarters. They quoted an instance when equipment delivered to French authorities in Algiers did not reach the front line in Tunisia until one month later. Even urgent inquiries, they complained, were "delayed for days notwithstanding repeated followups." The situation had led General Eisenhower, earlier in the year, to suspect that General Giraud had "no idea of Administration." [9] It was clear that little improvement could be expected until the French Commander in Chief had corrected the defects of his organization. Changes in administrative personnel and in methods of work were urgently required. It should be pointed out, however, that the difficult task of setting up almost from scratch and on short notice an entire command and service organization, with limited and often untrained help, made some fumbling almost inevitable. "Il fallait faire vite et avec presque rien." [10]

The shortage of material means was an even greater obstacle to establishing an effective organization. Office equipment was worn out or nonexistent. As late as June 1943 few typewriters were available and the JRC was urging the War Depart-

ment to send adequate supplies of them to the French. [11] Most of the indispensable facilities, such as covered space and depots, transportation, communications, and the like, had been requisitioned by the Anglo-American forces for their own use.

As General Giraud undertook to set his house in order, a task in which he gradually achieved a substantial measure of success, he found himself in need of friendly advice, "encouragement as well as tactful help and guidance." [12] The American and British members of the JRC did not fail to respond generously and loyally. He needed also considerable material assistance. Again the JRC spared no effort to have the necessary means placed at his disposal. No better illustration could be given of this determination on the part of the Allies to facilitate his task than a brief account of the manner in which the large shipment that reached North Africa in April was handled.

The magnitude of the organizational problem facing the French High Command upon the arrival of UGS 6½ with its 126,151 tons of matériel can easily be appreciated. For some days before, American, British, and French staff officers sought ways and means to supplement the limited reception and sorting facilities available to the French. At a G–3 meeting held at AFHQ on 5 April, a detailed program was laid out for the reception of the matériel. It was decided that at Casablanca, where four of the fifteen ships were to dock, the U.S. base section in charge of the port would unload, assemble, and deliver the equipment "complete and in running order." At Algiers, the British who ran the port and the base were to unload the eleven ships due

---

General Leyer first as assistant chief of staff, G–1 and G–4, later as deputy chief of staff, a post which he occupied until September 1944. He was promoted to brigadier general in April 1944. For the role played by Blanc in the rearmament operations, see pp. 280, 285, below.

[9] Statement by Eisenhower at CCS 57th Mtg, 15 Jan 43, Casablanca Conf; JRC quotation from Memo, Artamonoff for Delaney, 3 Mar 43, JRC Misc Doc, Item 5–a, Tab I.

[10] "We had to work fast and with practically nothing." Statement by General Giraud in the course of an interview, December 1948.

[11] Msg W–2573, AFHQ to AGWAR, 12 Jun 43, JRC Cable Log.

[12] Memo, Gardiner for Whiteley, 12 Apr 43, copy in Gardiner's Private File. See Chart 1.

CHART 1—ORGANIZATION OF THE FRENCH HIGH COMMAND IN NORTH AFRICA: 1 APRIL 1943

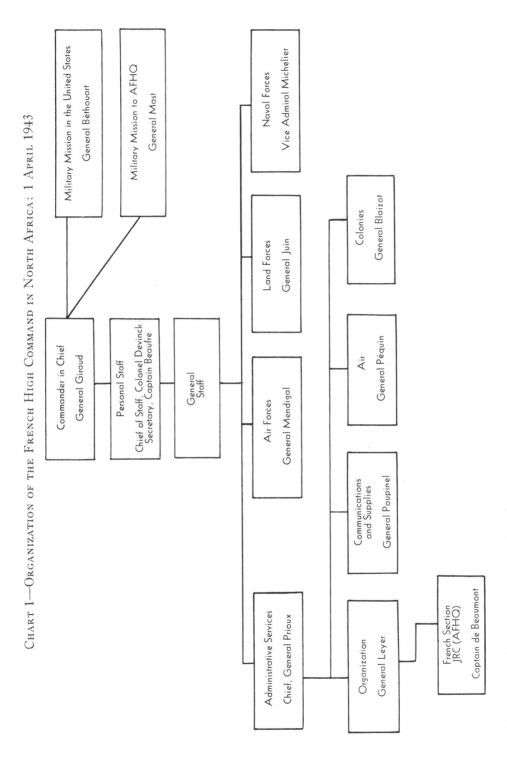

Source: Chart in JRC 320/001 Organization of French Army.

VEHICLE ASSEMBLY LINE, *Algiers, April 1943.*

to dock there and transport the matériel to eight local French depots.[13] At one of these, the French were to have the use of a vehicle assembly line operating under U.S. management. Once they had assembled the equipment, they would then distribute it.

Setting up and operating the assembly line at Algiers constituted one of the most remarkable instances of efficient planning and teamwork. First, AFHQ requested the

War Department to ship if possible on convoy UGS 6½ the necessary tools and gear to assemble about 200 vehicles daily.[14] Later, at a meeting between French and American staff officers, an understanding was reached regarding the extent and nature of the assistance to be furnished by SOS, NATOU-SA, in setting up the assembly line. It was agreed that the Mediterranean Base Section (MBS) at Oran would be responsible for organizing and operating the assembly facilities until such a time as the

[13] French headquarters had strongly urged that five vessels only be unloaded at Algiers and the other six at Oran. However, anticipated port conditions necessitated the unloading of all eleven at Algiers. Msg 7575, AFHQ to AGWAR, 19 Mar 43, JRC Cable Log.

[14] Msg 6400, AFHQ to AGWAR, 13 Mar 43, JRC Cable Log.

REVIEWING AMERICAN TROOPS
*who placed the French vehicle assembly line
in operation. General Eisenhower and General
Giraud are riding in the back of the
vehicle.*

French were qualified to take over.[15]   On
10 April, barely four days before the arrival
of the first ship, the MBS supply officer, Col.
Ernest A. Suttles, together with some forty
U.S. officers and men, arrived in Algiers
and began organizing the line.[16]   They had
brought with them crane equipment, black-
smith, welding, machine, and carpenter
tools, and related items essential for the
operation of assembly plants.   Within five
days, Colonel Suttles and his team had im-
provised five such plants: one twin-line

General Motors plant capable of assembling
one $2\frac{1}{2}$-ton truck every three minutes, one
Dodge-Chevrolet plant with a capacity of 70
vehicles a day, one jeep plant with a capacity
of over 200 $\frac{1}{4}$-ton vehicles daily, one
trailer plant with a capacity of over 150
vehicles per day, and one tank and armored-
vehicle servicing and testing plant.

The ships arrived on 14 April.   Unloading began immediately and was completed
by 21 April.[17]   The matériel was unpacked
and assembled as fast as boxes could be
brought to shore.   A French team of some
75 officers and 2,300 men, mostly from the
Chantiers de Jeunesse, assisted by Colonel
Suttles' team, accomplished the work in record time.[18]   In spite of language difficulties
and the fact that lack of proper tools and
equipment often necessitated improvisation,
1,900 vehicles were assembled in the first
week of operations, and 5,100 more during
the following two weeks, making a total of
7,000 in less than one month.[19]   French

---

[15] Memo, Artamonoff for CG SOS NATOUSA,
1 Apr 43, JRC Misc Doc, Item 5–a, Tab J.

[16] Notes extracted from *A Photographic Story
of the Assembly of T. U. P. Motor Vehicles by the
New French Army in the North African Theater
of Operations.*   Text by Col. E. A. Suttles, Maintenance Div, MBS, Ord. Copy in OCMH.

[17] Unloading proceeded with such efficiency and
speed that the British port commander thanked all
personnel concerned, American, British, and French,
for what had been "a record for the port."   JRC
Weekly Rpt 5, 24 Apr 43, JRC Rearmt Rpts.

[18] From the time of their creation in French North
Africa in 1941, the Chantiers de Jeunesse (see
above, pp. 8, 8n) quickly developed into a well-
disciplined body of approximately 3,000 men.
Although they were officially organized for peace-
time purposes, their leader, Lt. Col. Jean Van
Hecke, himself a member of the North African
Resistance, had prepared them secretly for the role
which they were to play in conjunction with an
eventual Allied operation in that area.   They de-
serve an honorable mention not only for the valuable assistance they rendered the Allies at the time
of the landings in November 1942, but for the
work which they subsequently performed on important military and public projects.   In late 1943 they
were incorporated in the North African Army as the
7th Chasseurs d'Afrique Regiment (a tank destroyer unit) under the command of Colonel Van
Hecke.

[19] The highest production rate reached 776 vehicles in a single day.

officials watched this mammoth operation with keen interest. On one occasion General Giraud accompanied by General Eisenhower visited the assembly line and expressed to the American personnel his deep appreciation of their valuable assistance.

Not all the equipment brought over by UGS 6½ could be assembled at the time. For a number of vehicles, tanks, and antiaircraft guns, necessary parts were not due to arrive until later with the shipment of the backlog of equipment.[20]

On 5 May, with the work nearly completed, the U.S. officers and men officially turned the whole assembly line over to their French associates who continued to operate it by themselves.

The French Organize an Expeditionary Corps

Unless modifications had been ordered and arranged beforehand, the equipment shipped to French units was identical with that authorized for corresponding U.S. units under War Department tables of organization and equipment current at the time. It included everything from uniforms and medical supplies to rifles, machine guns, and tanks. It included in addition two units of fire, a thirty-day replacement allowance of major items and major assemblies, and a six-month supply of spare parts. Once unloaded, the equipment was turned over to the French military authorities for assembly, warehousing, if necessary, and distribution through the French Supply Services according to priorities fixed by the French General Staff. AFHQ had agreed, on 7 April, that the French themselves would be responsible for designating which units were to receive American equipment. This, it was recognized, was an organizational matter for the French High Command alone to settle.[21]

As they prepared their distribution plan, the French military authorities were urged

COL. ERNEST A. SUTTLES, *MBS Supply Officer, relinquishes control of the assembly plant to Col. Jacques Simon, French Army, at a ceremony in Algiers.*

---

[20] JRC Rpt 4, 17 Apr 43, and JRC Progress Rpt 1, 4 May 43, JRC Rearmt Rpts.

[21] Memo for Rcd, JRC, sub: Responsibility for Fr Rearmt, 5 Apr 43, AFHQ 0100/12C G-3 Div Ops Fr Rearmt; Ltr, Loomis to Brig Gen Willis McD. Chapin, 12 Jul 44, JRC 400.2/002 Stock Control System; Min, CofS Conf, 7 Apr 43, AFHQ AG Sec 337.2. A unit of fire is a specified number of rounds of ammunition for each weapon, varying with each type and caliber of weapon. A major assembly is a combination of several major items. The 155-mm. howitzer is an example of a major assembly as it includes three major items: the howitzer, the recoil mechanism, and the carriage.

by AFHQ not to mix new and old equipment within units. This was to prevent, in particular, an undesirable demand for spare parts and service in efforts to make unserviceable matériel serviceable. They were also reminded that thereafter their headquarters must cease submitting requests for equipment to Allied depots. All their requirements, they were told, must be met from their own sources. This was essential if U.S. reserves in the theater were to be maintained at their normal level. As the French kept on submitting direct requests to British Ordnance for items of equipment, AFHQ on 15 May reminded all concerned of the established policy and pointed out in addition that the British had no rearmament commitments to the French.[22]

The matériel issued on loan to units engaged in Tunisia was now to be returned to Allied depots since the French were receiving new equipment from the United States. The policy was confirmed on 14 May in the course of a conference between representatives of various AFHQ sections. It was agreed that the equipment in question would be regained as a result of showdown inspections upon departure of the units from Tunisian area.[23]

The French had decided that the troops engaged in Tunisia should be the first to be rearmed. Accordingly, they had, early in April, pulled out of the Tunisian front for immediate re-equipping the equivalent of one infantry division. By the beginning of May they had rearmed one infantry division, the 2d Moroccan Infantry (2d DIM), and were in process of equipping two more, the 3d Algerian Infantry (3d DIA) and a division later to be known as the 4th Moroccan Mountain (4th DMM). It was the French Commander in Chief's belief that in general his units would reach an efficiency of 100 percent in eight to ten weeks from the time they had received their matériel. At least six weeks, he thought, would be required for technical training. This estimate appeared reasonable to AFHQ officials although they considered that an additional period of one month would be needed to bring armored units to a satisfactory state of readiness.[24]

In this initial rearmament phase, the French military authorities organized units according to tables of organization and equipment substantially similar to those currently in use in corresponding U.S. units. In the case of infantry divisions, however, they requested, for tactical reasons of their own, that the U.S. table of organization and equipment be modified to provide one reconnaissance battalion instead of troop, four Quartermaster truck companies instead of one, and one 40-mm. antiaircraft battalion.[25] The modifications, which the War Department approved at the urging of the JRC, were designed to provide stronger initial cover for deployment, facilitate the quick locating of hostile positions and flanks, and hasten the deployment of

[22] Memo, Brig Gen Lowell W. Rooks for G–4, 15 Apr 43, AFHQ 0100/12C G–3 Div Ops Fr Rearmt, Vol. II (2); Memo, Gardiner for Fr Sec JRC, 14 Mar 43, JRC 908 Policy and Plan—Misc; Memo, DCofS AFHQ, 15 Apr 43, AFHQ 0100/4 SACS Rcd Sec, Fr Matters; Memo, AFHQ To All Concerned, 15 May 43, JRC 908 Policy and Plan—Misc.
[23] Memo, Rooks for Fr Liaison Sec AFHQ, 22 Apr 43, AFHQ 0100/12C G–3 Div Ops Fr Rearmt, Vol. II (2); Diary of a Certain Plan, 14 May 43, ASF File Planning Div, 433–a–5.

[24] JRC Progress Rpt 1, 4 May 43, JRC Misc Rpts; Ltr, Giraud to Eisenhower, 28 Apr 43, and Memo, Rooks for CofS AFHQ, 4 May 43, JRC 902/II Rearmt Plan.
[25] Memo, Handy for CG SOS, 15 Mar 43, OPD 400 France, Sec 1.

infantry elements. The same modified table was adopted for all infantry divisions subsequently reequipped.

The intentions of the French High Command were to group the units then receiving American equipment under Phase I into a task force or expeditionary corps. It will be recalled that the creation of such a force to become part of an Allied overseas expedition had been formally approved by the Allied Commander in Chief as early as 31 January.[26] In the opinion of the JRC, the units currently receiving equipment did not constitute a coherent force capable of operating overseas independently if required. They did not include Engineer, Signal, and Chemical Warfare units, for which equipment was still lacking. Unless another special convoy brought additional matériel, the JRC felt that by 1 July, when the backlog of equipment of the first phase had been received from the United States, General Giraud would have to reshuffle the composition of the task force and, if necessary, reduce the number of units either by combining them or eliminating some. This would mean shifting personnel, reassigning matériel already distributed, slightly modifying division tables of organization, and using some salvaged French equipment. Only in that way could the proposed corps become an efficient task force.[27]

General Giraud was of course eager to rearm more than a limited expeditionary corps. With a total troop strength estimated in mid-April at 16,000 officers and 317,000 men, he had already activated most of the eleven divisions of the ANFA Plan, although some in cadre only. To form these divisions into a self-supporting and coherent force, General Giraud needed 50,000 trained drivers as well as large numbers of technical troops for Ordnance, Signal, Engineer, and Medical units. That meant a large proportion of Frenchmen. On the basis of one Frenchman for two natives, a ratio considered "reasonable" by General Giraud himself, no less than 100,000 Frenchmen would have to be found for the proposed army of 300,000 men. It was doubtful that such a number could be raised. There lay the real bottleneck in a larger rearmament program. The JRC considered that, for the present at least, General Giraud must concentrate on activating, equipping, and putting into the field a small independent task force of the expeditionary-corps size now envisaged, for which troops of all types were available in Africa. Later it might be advisable to incorporate in American or British Army corps such other infantry units up to divisions as were raised and equipped over and above the initial task force. Thus the French would not have to furnish the specialized service troops. The extent to which the North African Army could and should reasonably be expanded beyond the first expeditionary corps soon became the subject of much lively discussion between AFHQ and the French High Command, and lingered as a source of considerable friction for months to come.[28]

Convoys arriving in May, June, and July brought in the backlog of equipment of

---

[26] Dir AG 400/322, AFHQ, 31 Jan 43, AFHQ 0100/12C G–3 Div Ops Fr Rearmt, Vol. II (3).

[27] Memo, Artamonoff for Gardiner, 1 May 43, JRC 902/II Rearmt Plan.

[28] Memo, JRC for Joint Intelligence Collecting Agency, AFHQ, 26 Apr 43, JRC Misc Doc, Item 5–a, Tab K; Interv with Gen Giraud, Dec 48; Memo, JRC for CofS AFHQ, 25 Apr 43, JRC Misc Doc, Item 5–a, Tab M; Memo, Artamonoff for Delaney, cited n. 9.

Phase I.[29] With this matériel the French military authorities completed the equipping of the expeditionary corps as then set up. They had to resort to some juggling to ensure that all units were properly equipped. Thus they were forced to dissolve several units not part of the corps, but to which they had issued some American equipment on the assumption that more was to come from the United States, and to redistribute the matériel so recovered among units on the troop list, especially the 4th Moroccan Mountain Division. At the same time they issued, with the approval of the JRC, to several infantry units already equipped with British or French matériel, a small complement of U.S. equipment, largely infantry weapons and vehicles, and added these units to the troop list. These nonprogram units consisted of one separate brigade of 8,000 men created out of the former Corps Franc d'Afrique (organized in early December 1942), one group of tabors (the equivalent of one regiment of goumiers), and one Shock Battalion (Bataillon de Choc). These troops were to constitute part of the corps reserves.[30] Finally, the French General Staff turned over to the Territorial

forces assigned the task of guarding lines of communication and of maintaining internal security all obsolete equipment available in French stocks as well as some equipment received from the United States.

In late April the U.S. Fifth Army had, with the co-operation of the JRC, launched a training program to instruct the rearmed units in the technical use and care of their new equipment. By June the program carried out under the direction of Brig. Gen. Allen F. Kingman was in full swing.[31]

On 18 June General Giraud informed AFHQ that he was appointing General Juin to command the expeditionary forces designated for participation in forthcoming operations.[32] These operations were the contemplated assault and conquest of Sicily and Italy.

Throughout Phase I, as well as in subsequent phases, the American members of the JRC devoted their efforts, in pursuance of the recommendations of the Allied Commander in Chief himself, to making the units being rearmed a picked force. Their task was not an easy one for their position of buffer between the French High Command and AFHQ made their dealings with both often difficult. To reach the goal of "quality," they had requested and obtained from the War Department the assignment of matériel for units not specifically mentioned in the ANFA Agreement but considered necessary in organizing a balanced modern force. At a meeting held on 14 June, the Deputy Theater Commander,

---

[29] Tonnage of military equipment shipped from the United States between January and July 1943 and turned over to the French as part of Phase I of the program:

Month	Measurement Tons
Total	256,621
January	736
February	1,842
March	a 135,335
April	55,263
May	38,359
June	19,086
July (estimated)	6,000

a Includes 126,151 tons in convoy UGS 6½.

Source: Tab D, Memo, International Div ASF for Gen Clay, 7 Jul 43, JRC 905.6/1 Corres on Statistics of Rearmt.

[30] JRC Rpt 5, 3 Jul 43, JRC Rearmt Rpts. On the organization and equipment of nonprogram units, see pp. 112–13, 158–60, below.

[31] See Ch. XIV, below.

[32] Acknowledging the announcement of this appointment, General Smith pointed out that "the excellent relationship" established between General Juin and his U.S. and British associates during the Tunisian campaign was a "guarantee of effective cooperation in the future." Ltr, Smith to Giraud, 28 Jun 43, AFHQ 0100/12C G–3 Div Ops Fr Corres.

NATOUSA, Maj. Gen. Everett S. Hughes, objected to this procedure. He urged that the ANFA Agreement be followed to the letter and nothing supplied beyond the matériel required for the units listed in the agreement. Should this procedure not be acceptable to the French, he felt that it was up to them to obtain an "interpretation of the agreement on the same level as the agreement itself." [33] In the belief that a clarification of this important matter was required, the JRC urged AFHQ to set forth a definite policy and to advise the French accordingly. On 31 July General Eisenhower directed that the ANFA Agreement be "interpreted" as follows:

a. The object of the Agreement was to create a French force capable of taking part, in conjunction with the Allies, in the liberation of France.

b. Under the terms of the Agreement, Corps and Army Troops and Service organizations will be required. The number of headquarters and the number of service troops will depend upon the use to be made of the French force which is being rearmed and will be a matter of negotiation between the proper French military officials, the JRC, and G–3, AFHQ.

c. Since U.S. T/O's do not exactly fit the French organization and since U.S. TBA's contain many items not suited to French Forces, particularly those composed of native troops, great care will be exercised in submitting requisitions in order that equipment not suitable for the French forces will not be requisitioned from the U.S.[34]

The policy fully upheld the stand already taken by the JRC and gave the committee the necessary authority to proceed with the rehabilitation of the North African Army in such a manner as to make of it a truly effective force.

---

[33] Memo, Artamonoff for CofS AFHQ, 28 Jun 43, JRC Misc Doc, Item 5–a, Tab O.

[34] Memo, CinC for Liaison Sec AFHQ, 31 Jul 43, JRC 902/II Rearmt Plan.

CHAPTER V

Phase II of the Program
(July–August 1943)

Negotiations

In mid-March 1943, long before the matériel of Phase I had been received from the United States, the French military authorities had submitted a proposal calling for a second phase of rearmament to follow immediately on the completion of the first.[1] AFHQ had taken no action on the proposal, largely because the allocation of shipping remained 25,000 tons monthly. The transportation of matériel to complete the first expeditionary corps, of spare parts, of replacement and maintenance items, and of supplies generally necessary for the normal life of the French Military Establishment in North Africa was expected to take up the monthly allocation for the better part of the year. Any equipping of units over and above that of the first corps would therefore require additional shipping, possibly special convoys similar to UGS 6½. As pointed out by G–3, AFHQ, to the JRC on 30 March, no such convoys were contemplated in the near future "although they could be requested if found necessary." [2]

The possibility of using French merchant ships to transport military matériel for the North African forces had already been considered, especially by General Giraud, who fully realized that shipping would determine the tempo of future armament deliveries. In writing to General Eisenhower on 22 February, the French Commander in Chief had outlined the measures taken or contemplated by him to put French merchant shipping to the greatest possible use in the common war effort. He had placed all personnel and cargo ships in the Allied shipping pool, arranged for the rehabilitation of vessels in need of repair, and had slowed down the movement of effectives from West to North Africa so as to release additional tonnage to the Allied shipping pool.[3]

The tonnage promised by Giraud was being turned over very slowly to the pool. Most ships first had to be sent to the United Kingdom for repairs. Refitting in North Africa was almost impossible since dry docks and repair facilities in the area were being used by British and American vessels; the French themselves could use them only at the discretion of the U.S. and British authorities.[4] For some weeks French merchant shipping remained available only on paper.

While General Eisenhower argued that

---

[1] Ltr, Prioux to JRC, 12 Mar 43, JRC Misc Doc, Item 5–a, Tab N.

[2] Memo, Gardiner for CofS AFHQ, 16 Mar 43, JRC Misc Doc, Item 5–a, Tab K; Memo, Rooks for JRC, 30 Mar 43, JRC Misc Doc, Item 5–a, Tab M.

[3] Ltr, Giraud to Eisenhower, 22 Feb 43, JRC 902/II Rearmt Plan.

[4] Msg 6798, Eisenhower to Somervell, 15 Mar 43, JRC Cable Log.

there should be no relation between French shipping and the delivery of arms to the North African forces, both General Marshall and the War Department, with an eye on the global demands on limited cargo tonnage, took the contrary view. Any increase beyond the 25,000-ton rate, Somervell told Eisenhower, would have to depend on the French shipping effectively made available to the united pool.[5]

On 7 April General Béthouart informed General Marshall that French merchant ships representing over 246,000 tons had now been incorporated in, and were operating as part of, the Allied pool.[6] He hoped, therefore, that the War Department would make "appropriate" tonnage available to General Giraud to enable him to plan his program accordingly.[7] General Marshall replied that, although some 163,000 deadweight tons of French cargo shipping allotted to the pool were on the high seas, none of the ships allocated to the United States had yet made an outbound voyage. It would be several months before the ships could make the initial outward trip as much repair work would be necessary once the vessels had reached the United States. As this shipping became available, it might be possible to increase the tonnage allotted for

the transportation of French armament. "In this worldwide war," he concluded, "it it necessary to allocate the material resources of the Allies in such a manner that they will be of the greatest benefit to the common cause regardless of the effect produced on any particular group or nation, and it will be necessary to view the matter in this light at the appropriate time." [8]

It was clear that for the moment at least the French High Command and the JRC would have to continue re-equipping units within the limitations of the 25,000-ton monthly allocation.

Near the end of April, General Leyer, then chief of organization at French headquarters, submitted a new proposal to AFHQ for a second phase of rearmament. Simultaneously he broached the question of a tonnage increase with which to transport the additional equipment. General Giraud, he explained, intended in the near future to make an official request for further tonnage allotments to the extent of 100,000 tons per month for May and June. The object of the proposed second phase, as pointed out by General Leyer, was to increase the number of combat units in the expeditionary corps in order "both to absorb some of the available native manpower, and to make of the Corps a well-balanced, coherent force." The strength of the corps was to be raised to five divisions (three infantry, one mountain, and one armored), elements of a second armored division, and other units.[9]

AFHQ turned down the proposal for a number of reasons, the most important being that the shipping situation was still critical and the additional tonnage could

[5] Msg 6798, Eisenhower to Somervell, 15 Mar 43, JRC Cable Log; Msg 2641, Marshall to Eisenhower, 20 Feb 43, JRC 902/II Rearmt Plan; Msg 4050, Somervell to Eisenhower, 17 Mar 43, JRC Cable Log.

[6] These ships included 9 troopships, 2 tankers, and 19 cargo vessels capable of transoceanic travel. The French were also using 50 cargo vessels for coastwise service representing 170,000 tons. Eventually they furnished a total of 420,000 tons of shipping to the Allied pool. H. H. Dunham, U.S. Army Transportation and the Conquest of North Africa, 1942–43, OCT HB Monograph 9, Jan 45, p. 118, OCT HB.

[7] Ltr, Béthouart to Marshall, 7 Apr 43, OPD 400 France, Sec 1.

[8] Ltr, Marshall to Béthouart, 18 Apr 43, OPD 400 France, Sec 1.

[9] Ltr, Leyer to CofS AFHQ, 25 Apr 43, and Memo, JRC for CofS, 25 Apr 43, JRC Misc Doc, Item 5–a, Tab M.

not be made available. Simultaneously, AFHQ offered a counterproposal with the suggestion that immediate future shipments under the 25,000-ton allocation be utilized to equip, in order of priority, the service units necessary for a corps of three infantry divisions, the mountain division already partly equipped, the balance of a first armored division, as well as additional corps and army troops, especially corps artillery.[10]

On 15 May General Leyer submitted a third, more modest proposal. Its objective was to increase the strength of the expeditionary corps, by 31 July, to four divisions, miscellaneous corps troops, and air units consisting of two pursuit and two dive bomber groups. After pointing out that the final organization and training of this force depended on the nature of its future employment, General Leyer suggested that Generals Eisenhower and Giraud meet without delay to determine the role of the corps "for the campaign of the summer of 1943." [11] AFHQ officials received the suggestion with little enthusiasm for they were still without instructions from the Combined Chiefs of Staff as to the future employment of the French forces. Pending the results of the conference (TRIDENT Conference, 11–27 May) then taking place in Washington, Maj. Gen. J. F. M. Whiteley, Deputy Chief of Staff, AFHQ, informed General Leyer that nothing was to be gained from a discussion between the two commanders in chief at this juncture. He intimated, however, that in the event of such a meeting, it would be well for the French High Command to begin revising further the composition of the expeditionary corps.

He pointed out in particular that the corps was completely lacking in heavy antiaircraft units.[12]

Two days before receiving AFHQ's answer, General Leyer had submitted one more proposal. It called for a second phase of rearmament designed to achieve the following objectives: ground forces—completion of a first armored division around the two armored regiments already in process of re-equipment, nucleus of a second armored division, one mountain division, headquarters for one infantry, one armored, and one expeditionary corps, corps artillery, and additional service units; air forces—additional units representing 300 planes of all types; naval forces—18,000 tons of equipment.[13]

The program being consonant with the suggestions offered by AFHQ on 14 May, the JRC immediately approved it with minor exceptions and recommended its adoption.[14] Subsequently, General Leyer urged that the backlog of Phase I then arriving in North African ports be followed by the matériel of the proposed second phase "without any break." It would be regrettable, he pointed out, if, because of the delay in passing the requests on to the War Department, the small monthly tonnage allotted to the French forces should not be entirely used up.[15]

On 8 June the JRC informed General Leyer that AFHQ had approved with minor modifications the naval and ground force requirements of his proposal. The air part

[10] Memo, Whiteley for Leyer, 14 May 43, JRC 902/II Rearmt Plan.
[11] Memo, Leyer for CofS AFHQ, 15 May 43, JRC Misc Doc, Item 5–a, Tab M.

[12] Memo, Whiteley for Leyer, 22 May 43, JRC Misc Doc, Item 5–a, Tab M.
[13] Ltr, Leyer to JRC, 20 May 43, JRC Misc Doc, Item 5–a, Tab L.
[14] Memo, Gardiner for CofS AFHQ, 23 May 43, JRC Misc Doc, Item 5–a, Tab L.
[15] Ltr, Leyer to JRC, 29 May 43, JRC 902/II Rearmt Plan.

of the program was being put off pending certain major adjustments. General Leyer accepted the proposed modifications and urged that the necessary requisitions be cabled to the War Department without delay to make it possible for deliveries to follow immediately upon the liquidation of the first phase. As no action had yet been taken by 11 June, General Leyer pleaded with the JRC to urge AFHQ not to postpone sending the cable any longer.[16]

Still it was to be nearly four weeks before the requisitions were sent. The delay made sense only in the light of the military and strategic situation in the Mediterranean theater at the time. Since the close of the Tunisian campaign, AFHQ had been engaged in feverish preparations for Operation HUSKY, the invasion and conquest of Sicily.[17] U.S. troops withdrawn from Tunisia had been regrouped in Algeria where they were being re-equipped. Ports in Tunisia were being cleared and restored. The shipping situation had become more critical than ever as more troops and supplies were being brought to the theater from the United States and a large fleet was being made ready for the forthcoming operation. In addition, the CCS decision, reached on 18 May, to rearm the French had made the commitment secondary to the equipping of American and British units. It had moreover established no specific program. French rearmament had become "a hand-to-mouth procedure in which the basic directive was vague and its execution

unmanaged."[18] Not one piece of initial equipment had been assigned since March. The program had reached a state of "definite lethargy."[19]

It was not until 4 July that AFHQ finally cabled the necessary requisitions to the War Department with a request that the matériel be shipped immediately after the liquidation of the first phase and within the 25,000-ton allocation per convoy. Of this allocation, current maintenance needs were expected to take up 4,000 tons and French Navy needs 3,000 tons, leaving a balance of 18,000 tons monthly for the proposed second phase.[20]

The cable reached Washington while General Giraud himself was en route to the American capital. The French Commander in Chief was accepting the invitation extended to him by President Roosevelt, at the time of their meeting at Anfa, to come to the United States for a visit. "Multiple reasons, not the least of which was the stepping-up of French rearmament," had prompted him to undertake the voyage at this juncture.[21]

Anticipating that General Giraud would press for a substantial increase in tonnage to implement a second phase of rearmament, General Eisenhower warned the War Department of the impossibility of handling additional tonnage in North African ports under existing conditions. Limited port capacity, he explained, was further complicated by the present use of berths for loading troops and supplies for Operation HUSKY and for the departure of large numbers of

[16] Memo, Artamonoff for Leyer, 8 Jun 43, JRC Misc Doc, Item 5–a, Tab L; Memo, Leyer for JRC, 8 Jun 43, JRC Misc Doc, Item 5–a, Tab L; Memo, Leyer for JRC, 11 Jun 43, JRC 902/II Rearmt Plan.

[17] The assault on Sicily was launched on 10 July 1943.

[18] Memo, Col Magruder for Director of Opns ASF, 26 Jun 43, ASF Planning Div File A–46–371, Fr Military.

[19] ASF Diary, 23 Jun 43, ASF Planning Div Diary.

[20] Msg W–4078, AFHQ to AGWAR, 4 Jul 43, JRC Misc Doc, Item 5–e.

[21] Giraud, Un seul but, la Victoire, p. 189.

service troops for Sicily. As a result, cargo ships were being held at Gibraltar until inside berths became available in North Africa. Only when the proposed reduction of shipping to Casablanca was effected would an increase in shipments be recommended. The French would then be asked to take over port operations in Casablanca to receive and handle all equipment intended for them. Eisenhower estimated that 1 November was the earliest date at which such a change would be possible, subject of course to the results of HUSKY and post-HUSKY operations.[22]

General Somervell immediately undertook to determine a shipment schedule consonant with General Eisenhower's latest information on port capacity in North Africa. On 6 July he informed General Marshall that the equipment required under the proposed second phase could be made ready for shipment beginning in September at the rate of from 50,000 to 100,000 tons monthly. Although General Giraud might feel that this increase was too conservative, General Somervell considered that, in view of the present port conditions in North Africa, "Eisenhower was correct rather than Giraud." Still, he questioned whether some of the 70,000 additional troops now requested by the Allied Commander in Chief for his operations could not be French. To equip such French forces, he went on to explain, it would be possible to increase shipments, within sixty days, to the 50,000 to 100,000-ton figure provided North African port facilities were made available. The necessary shipping itself was "in sight."[23]

The Army Service Forces had meanwhile completed a thorough study of the French rearmament situation and had drafted a detailed memorandum, dealing in particular with the proposed second phase now on the CCS agenda.[24]

Political Complications

General Giraud was coming to Washington primarily to press for a resumption of armament deliveries. He was also coming for stronger political aid. To understand the full import of his visit and of his relations with the U.S. Army, it is necessary to go back a little to pick up the tangled threads of internal French politics.

It will be recalled that, since the death of Admiral Darlan on 24 December 1942, General Giraud exercised the supreme civil and military authority in French North and West Africa. In London, meanwhile, General de Gaulle continued as president of the French National Committee and chief of the Free French Forces. Some time before the conference at Anfa in January, the two leaders agreed in principle that a union of their respective followers and armed forces was highly desirable. At the close of the Tunisian campaign they decided that the time was ripe for such action. On 30 May General de Gaulle and his associates flew to North Africa with a view to establishing there, in agreement with General Giraud, a central executive body to govern all French areas not under Axis control.

Both men were equally concerned with the restoration of a free, independent France. But they viewed the problem from wholly different experiences, preconcep-

[22] Msg W–4173, Eisenhower to AGWAR, 6 Jul 43, JRC Misc Doc, Item 5–e.
[23] Memo, Somervell for Marshall, 6 Jul 43, Somervell Files, Fr 1943–44, A–46–257, Ser 1.

[24] Memo, International Div ASF for Gen Clay, 7 Jul 43, JRC 905.6/1 Corres on Rearmt Statistics.

tions, and temperaments. Briefly, General de Gaulle and his followers believed that they alone—who, since June 1940, had kept the French flag flying high by refusing to lay down their arms—were entitled to lead the French forces to final victory. In the political field, they envisaged the establishment, after the liberation of France, of a new, more progressive government. General Giraud and his associates, on the other hand, considered that the recognition their leadership had received from the Anglo-American allies in November 1942 conferred upon them the right and duty to control the renascent French forces. Politically more conservative, they favored, after the liberation of the motherland, a gradual return to political freedom. The divergence between the views of the two leaders and the clash between their personalities promised from the beginning not harmony but a political struggle to the death.

After three days of what appear to have been violent discussions and bitter political intrigues, there was established in Algiers, on 3 June, a French Committee of National Liberation (Comité Français de la Libération Nationale—CFLN) composed of members of both factions and with the two generals as copresidents.

Recognition by the United Nations of the CFLN as a *de facto* government of France or, in the narrow field of rearmament, as representing the agency of final jurisdiction in respect to French armament requirements was put off owing especially to President Roosevelt's distrust of the political motives of the Gaullist element in the committee. The British, apparently less reluctant to deal with the CFLN regarding military matters, proposed to the Munitions Assignments Board on 26 June that the existing procedure for assigning munitions to the French

armed forces be revised to include an endorsement by the CFLN of all rearmament requests. This, they felt, was important for both political and financial reasons. They were prepared, however, to block any French request for membership in the MAB on the ground that the French were "customers for arms and not producers." [25] The American members of the MAB, on the other hand, considered that, barring a reversal of the policy regarding recognition of the CFLN, the board had no authority to concur in, or process, the changes in procedure proposed by the British. They felt that, for the moment, existing CCS directives on the assignment of armament to the French should continue to apply. [26] No further action was taken then on the matter. The Allied Commander in Chief kept submitting armament requests for the North African forces since they operated in the American sphere. Demands for other French forces throughout the world followed supply channels of the nation or forces with which such troops were operating.

No sooner had the CFLN been established than General Giraud's authority, already greatly curtailed, was further questioned by General de Gaulle and his followers. They claimed that it was not practicable or advisable for one individual to hold the two posts of Commander in Chief and copresident of the CFLN. The changes which they proposed to effect in the structure of French administration were such that General de Gaulle would in practice assume the control of the armed forces. Apprised of their plan, President Roosevelt, on 17 June, directed General Eisenhower not to permit

[25] Memo, Wing Comdr T. E. H. Birley, Br JSM, for Maj Gen J. H. Burns, Exec MAB, 26 Jun 43, JRC 472 MAB.
[26] Memo, Gen Burns for Maj C. W. Garnett, Br JSM, 9 Aug 43, JRC 472 MAB.

de Gaulle or any other agency not under the complete control of the Allied Commander in Chief to command the French armed forces, and not to tolerate any military or civil direction that might interfere with military operations. The Americans, added the President, would not continue arming any French force in whose co-operation in Allied military operations they did not have complete confidence. Consequently, they would not, at this juncture, allow de Gaulle "personally or through his partisans" to control the French Army in Africa.[27] Complying with these instructions, General Eisenhower, on 18 June, called in the two French leaders for a conference at which he declared that General Giraud must remain as French Commander in Chief as this was "no time for radical changes endangering the Rear." [28]

Four days later, on 22 June, the CFLN reached a compromise solution which they embodied in a Decree on the Organization of the Armed Forces. Under the terms of the decree there was established the Permanent Military Committee of which both leaders and their respective chiefs of staff, General Juin and Maj. Gen. Edgar de Larminat (the latter representing the Free French) were members. This committee, which had full authority over the entire military establishment, was charged primarily with the task of accomplishing the fusion of the two groups of forces. Pending such fusion, each of the two leaders was to retain the command of his respective forces.[29] The arrangement was of little

comfort to General Giraud, whose views on the organization of the High Command as disclosed by him in early June were well known. While agreeing to the principle that the CFLN must control the military establishment, he held to the belief that the Commander in Chief must exercise the command of all forces wherever stationed and that one of his responsibilities must be to allot equipment.[30]

The two-headed organization adopted on 22 June was bound to increase rather than dissipate political friction. The month of July in fact witnessed a rapid deterioration of the situation. While the theater's policy was not to intervene in purely French affairs, the Allied Commander in Chief could not remain indifferent to the potential danger created by the numerous desertions of individuals, even units, of one faction to the forces of the other, as well as by the reported undisciplined behavior of troops currently assigned to guard duty.[31] Secretary of State Cordell Hull became alarmed over the CFLN's leanings toward the political aspirations of General de Gaulle and the lack of sympathy then shown by the committee

[27] Message summarized in William D. Leahy, *I Was There* (New York: Whittlesey House, 1950), p. 168.

[28] Msg 3472, Eisenhower to Sherwood, 22 Jun 43, AFHQ 0100/21 AG Sec.

[29] Decree, CFLN, 22 Jun 43, JRC 320/004 Orgn of Fr Army.

[30] JRC, Note on Giraud's Formula on Organization of Command (*circa* 1 Jun 43), JRC 320/004 Orgn of Fr Army.

[31] "Our policy is not to intervene in squabbles between the Free French and the Giraud French." Statement by DCofS in Memo for G–3, 29 Jul 43, AFHQ 0100/12C G–3 Div Ops Free Fr. When, earlier in the year, mass desertions from Giraudist to Gaullist vessels docked in New York Harbor threatened to cripple the battleship *Richelieu* and other North African naval units, American officials were compelled to intervene and put a stop to the practice on the ground that it endangered the successful conduct of the war. Ltr, Forrestal to Secy Hull, 20 Feb 43, OPD 336.3 France, Sec 1. Seventy-seven incidents involving Free French units with the native population in Tripolitania were reported by the British 10 Corps for the six months ending 31 July. Msg 3D/94156, MIDEAST to TROOPERS, 10 Aug 43, AFHQ 0100/12C G–3 Div Ops Free Fr.

toward the Allies. He even suggested that it might be desirable for the U.S. Government to suspend deliveries of war matériel, at least until the situation was clarified.[32] No such drastic action was taken, for it was only a few weeks since the CCS, on 18 May, had finally reached an agreement on rearming the French. Furthermore, it was hoped that General Giraud's visit in Washington might gain him such material and moral advantages as to strengthen his own authority.[33]

Not only did the 22 June arrangement fail to establish military unity, but it tended to complicate the relationship and channels of communications between the French and AFHQ. An illustration may be found in the efforts of the Free French headquarters, on 1 July, to establish contact with AFHQ with a view to obtaining equipment and, incidentally, representation on the JRC. G–3, AFHQ, urged that these efforts be given no encouragement until French political and military unity had been achieved, and then not until a change of policy had been approved by CCS. General Smith endorsed the recommendation and advised General de Larminat, chief of staff of the Free French Forces, to contact the appropriate sections of General Giraud's headquarters which, he pointed out, had complete information on the organization of the U.S. Army. He then closed the door on the matter of Free French representation in the JRC by explaining to de Larminat that all appointments to the committee had in the past been made by General Giraud and would in all probability be made in the future by the Permanent Military Committee.[34]

The issue was soon reopened by the Free French. On 3 July General de Larminat offered several units from a Free French division for rear guard duty in Tunisia in replacement of American troops about to be relieved, on condition that the division itself be re-equipped by AFHQ within the following two months. Again G–3, AFHQ, recommended that no consideration be given to re-equipping more units except through a unified French High Command. Maj. Gen. Humfrey M. Gale, Chief Administrative Officer, AFHQ, went even further. He proposed that issues of British equipment to the Free French Forces be discontinued inasmuch as "it was assumed" that these would shortly be absorbed in the North African Army. The purpose of his recommendation, he explained, was not to remove a liability from the British, but to simplify the supply and maintenance of the French forces.[35]

In the opinion of Allied officials, therefore, it was essential that the French achieve the fusion of their forces without delay. Only such a step would put an end to the inconsistent arrangement under which some units (those controlled by General de Gaulle) were equipped and maintained by

---

[32] Leahy, *op. cit.*, p. 169.

[33] It was during General Giraud's absence from Algiers that the CFLN, on 9 July, fixed by decree the powers of the newly created Commissioner of Armament, Provisioning, and Reconstruction. Decree, CFLN, 9 Jul 43, JRC 320/004 Orgn of Fr Army. Under the terms of the decree, the Commissioner (Monnet) was charged, *inter alia*, with the task of ensuring—with the co-operation of military authorities—the implementation of rearmament programs as laid down by the Permanent Military Committee.

[34] Ltr, de Larminat to CofS AFHQ, 1 Jul 43, Memo, Rooks for CofS AFHQ, 3 Jul 43, and Ltr, Smith to de Larminat, 4 Jul 43, AFHQ 0100/12C G–3 Div Ops Free Fr.

[35] Ltr, de Larminat to Smith, 3 Jul 43, Memo, Rooks for DCofS AFHQ, 4 Jul 43, and Memo, Gale for ACofS G–3, 6 Jul 43, AFHQ 0100/12C G–3 Div Ops Free Fr.

the United Kingdom through the Middle East Command, while the others were provisioned by the United States through AFHQ. But as General Giraud sped toward the United States, fusion was still in the planning stage.

Implementing Phase II

The French Commander in Chief reached Washington on 7 July and began at once a ten-day round of important conferences with President Roosevelt, Generals Marshall and Somervell, and other officials. On 8 July the CCS invited him to present an account of the French military situation.[36] After describing briefly the part which his forces had played in the battle of Tunisia and the "tremendous moral effect" which the first phase of rearmament had had on them, General Giraud reported that the expeditionary corps was now ready for action. The corps, of a strength of from 70,000 to 75,000 men, included two infantry divisions, one mountain division, and one half of an armored division. He intended to add to it approximately 13,000 goumiers (Moroccan riflemen), "who had given a good account of themselves in Tunisia." General Giraud then outlined his plans regarding a second corps similar to the first, this to be available by September. The second corps, he explained, would serve to relieve the first after the initial phase of operations had ended. To prepare it, he must receive by 1 August the equipment necessary to complete the first armored division and to rearm a second, as well as two additional infantry divisions and general reserve and service troops. He needed also

an allotment of uniforms and shoes for 100,000 men, because his forces, which he estimated then at 417,000 men, were "practically in rags, a factor naturally detrimental to morale."[37] Finally he desired some light escort vessels to be assigned to him for convoy duty between West and North Africa. He was fully aware, he added, of the supply and tonnage implications of his proposal. He urged, nevertheless, that the utmost efforts be made to ensure that the additional divisions and general reserve units would be placed on a fully active footing by September. He felt certain that the CCS appreciated the importance of having a French force "big and powerful enough to seize the opportunity of waging war on French soil." Giraud then spoke of the efficient overhauling and refitting of naval units being effected in the United States "under conditions of great pressure." He expected that a number of vessels such as the battleship *Richelieu*, the cruiser *Montcalm*, and several modern destroyers would shortly be ready to take their place in battle wherever they were most needed. Before concluding, General Giraud urged the CCS to place full trust in the French Army and its command, and to look upon it as a weapon capable of rendering the greatest service to the common cause, especially when operations should extend to the continent of Europe and to French soil.

The CCS immediately took up General Giraud's proposals. General Marshall first pointed out that the U.S. Chiefs of Staff were "in full harmony" with General Giraud's plans and that the details of his requirements were being studied by the Com-

---

[36] General Giraud was accompanied by General Béthouart, Vice Adm. Raymond Fénard, Lt. Col. Albert Le Bel, and Maj. André Beaufre.

[37] This was in addition to a previous request for 100,000 sets of summer clothing from General Eisenhower (Msg 5746, AFHQ to AGWAR, 11 Mar 43, JRC Cable Log).

bined Staff Planners. He then disclosed that War Department officials had decided to suspend the activation of a number of U.S. divisions previously planned for the period between August and the end of the year, in order to make certain that the matériel required by the French would be available to them. All that needed to be done, General Marshall declared, was to implement the requests just submitted by General Giraud. Heretofore, the limiting factor in rearming the French had been a shortage of tonnage and escort facilities. Now the tonnage situation had improved, although the problem of port capacity in North Africa had become rather acute because of forthcoming operations. The U-boat situation likewise had improved, said Admiral King, who added that he was "much in favor" of General Giraud's plan. In his opinion it was clearly an economy of effort to arm the French forces already present in North Africa. The American Navy, he asserted, would continue to do its best on behalf of the French Navy. His view was fully supported by General Arnold who considered it "expedient and economical" to equip the French Air Forces already in the theater. He explained that a recent French request for 300 additional planes was being studied and a proposal for the allocation of this number of aircraft would soon be submitted.[38] On the whole, he concluded, the French squadrons would be equipped with the planes they needed to accomplish their mission. As the meeting broke up, General Giraud expressed his gratitude for the assurances he had been given and added that time was the essential factor to be considered.[39]

The next day, General Giraud called on General Somervell to discuss the details of his proposal. After their conference, General Somervell expressed to General Marshall his confidence that the French request could be implemented. The major items of equipment, he explained, were available for immediate shipment except for the necessary rifles which would have to be obtained as before from the United Kingdom. Shipping could be provided to the extent of 200,000 tons representing approximately twenty-eight ships. These ships would be added to a number of convoys, for the current heavy drain on escort vessels precluded the possibility of a special convoy. The chief stumbling block, Somervell emphasized, remained the limited North African port capacity. It would be well, therefore, if General Giraud were required to obtain Eisenhower's consent to the addition of any shipping before any promises were made in Washington to deliver the matériel before 1 November—the date at which General Eisenhower expected the situation of port capacity to ease up. The 100,000 uniforms, on the other hand, could be shipped at once in July and August as filler cargo. General Somervell then reiterated an opinion he had expressed on earlier occasions. Inasmuch as a successful assault on Sicily would bring increasing demands from General Eisenhower for additional troops to exploit the initial gains, "it certainly would seem desirable to make use of French troops in North Africa rather than to employ troops from America and the additional shipping which their use would entail." He suggested accordingly that the Allied Commander in Chief be asked to review the North African port situation with Giraud after HUSKY had progressed a little further, and to advise the War Department of the

---

[38] The request was contained in General Leyer's memorandum of 20 May.
[39] Min, CCS Spec Mtg, 8 Jul 43.

date when port capacity would become adequate.[40]

The French Commander in Chief then reported to General Marshall the substance of his conference with General Somervell. He stressed the importance he attached to the dispatch of a special convoy to arrive in Africa the latter part of July, a matter which, he declared, he had put before the President.[41] General Marshall informed him that twenty-eight ships probably would be found, although not at one time, but warned him both of the difficulty of finding escort vessels for a separate convoy or for the enlargement of scheduled convoys, and of the congestion in North African ports. He also pointed out that priorities would have to be determined by the Allied Commander in Chief. The War Department, he explained, could not "from this distance" deny General Eisenhower's requests for certain shipments in favor of some others, and at the same time hold him responsible for the success of operations. No final decision therefore could be reached until Giraud had discussed the entire problem with Eisenhower. Turning to the question of the employment of French troops, General Marshall repeated a statement he had made at nearly every CCS meeting at which the matter had come up for discussion: it was the "urgent desire" of the U.S. Chiefs of Staff to have General Eisenhower use French troops wherever possible rather than to import U.S. troops. Thus was highlighted the often-expressed American thesis that the rearmament of the North African forces constituted one of the most economical ways of providing additional troops for

future operations on the European continent. As he took leave of General Marshall, the French Commander in Chief expressed the hope that the promise of another large shipment of supplies and the assurance that his forces would be employed in future operations would have a "tremendous psychological effect" on the political situation in North Africa.[42]

The conversations with General Giraud having come to an end, War Department officials urged the MAB to take immediate action on the latest French demands. Simultaneously, General Marshall informed AFHQ of the plans now under consideration in Washington for Phase II. The President, he pointed out, was naturally desirous of backing Giraud's hand as much as possible and would like to tell him "something encouraging" before his departure from the United States. Could the theater, at this time, give any hint as to what might be done beyond the pessimistic prospect indicated in Eisenhower's earlier report on North African port capacities? [43]

This appeal brought instant, heartening news from the theater. General Smith explained that plans now in effect at Casablanca would free sufficient port capacity to permit the proposed 200,000 tons of additional French rearmament to be unloaded in that port. He recommended, however, that shipments be made after July and at a rate of not more than nine ships a convoy. The monthly 25,000-ton allocation could continue to be delivered in Oran, Casablanca, and Algiers.[44]

---

[40] Memo, Somervell for Marshall, 10 Jul 43, JRC 902/II Rearmt Plan.

[41] Memo, Giraud for Marshall, 10 Jul 43, JRC 902/II Rearmt Plan.

[42] Memo, Marshall for Arnold, Somervell, McNarney, Handy, and Brig Gen Raymond G. Moses, 12 Jul 43, OCS A–45–534 (France).

[43] Msg 2594, Marshall to Smith, 15 Jul 43, JRC 902/II Rearmt Plan.

[44] Msg W–4989, Smith to Marshall, 16 Jul 43, JRC Cable Log.

General Giraud, then in Canada on a four-day visit before his return to Algiers, was apprised by General Marshall of the good news and of the details of the final arrangements just concluded: approximately twenty-seven ships would bring the equipment of Phase II to Casablanca at the rate of nine per convoy.[45] In addition, clothing and accouterments for 200,000 men would be shipped as filler cargo on the regular July and August convoys. Rifles would be ordered from the United Kingdom. Ammunition would continue to be shipped at the customary monthly rate. Such action, General Marshall noted, represented an "immediate substantial compliance" with Giraud's requests. The War Department also proposed, he added, to place the French forces on the same status as U. S. troops in regard to issue and maintenance of uniforms and personal equipment entailing usual replacements.[46]

In the theater, meanwhile, plans were

---

[45] While in Canada, General Giraud was offered, under Canada's lend-lease program, some 200 artillery pieces, including 3.7-inch antiaircraft guns, 100,000 complete sets of clothing, and 1,000 trucks. The guns were to be used for the defense of the principal ports of embarkation, and the trucks largely for the transportation of mobile reserves. General Béthouart having requested the War Department's approval of this offer of assistance, the views of General Eisenhower were sought regarding the matter. The Allied Commander in Chief replied that he saw no objection to the acceptance of the Canadian offer, provided the effect was to reduce the U.S. assignment under the eleven-division program, which he considered of "highest priority." He cautioned, however, against accepting the 3.7-inch antiaircraft guns, as he regarded the introduction of a new caliber undesirable, especially in view of the present shortage of trained French artillery personnel. The French eventually received the 100,000 sets of clothing. Msg 4246, Somervell to Eisenhower, 5 Aug 43, and Msg W–6985, Eisenhower to Somervell, 10 Aug 43, JRC Cable Log.

[46] Msg, Marshall to Giraud, 16 Jul 43, JRC 902/II Rearmt Plan.

being made for the reception of the matériel of Phase II. Since heavy demands for U.S. service troops in other areas were forcing the rapid closing down of all American base activities at Casablanca, it soon would be necessary to turn over to the French the entire responsibility for handling matériel and for operating the motor vehicle assembly in that port. In anticipation of such a move, French authorities were urged to take immediate steps, in agreement with Atlantic Base Section, to make sure that they would become self-sufficient in handling future shipments at Casablanca at the earliest possible date. They were also advised that they, and not SOS, NATOUSA, would be responsible for handling directly from the ships the distribution of uniforms, personal equipment, and maintenance items due to arrive as filler cargo on future convoys.[47]

On 31 July AFHQ requested the War Department to delete from the standard tables of allowance certain corps and army headquarters items which the French did not require. Among the items listed were regimental reference libraries, general-use dictionaries, manual coin-counting machines, American flags, and the like. The arrival of full complements of American flags in earlier shipments had already caused considerable surprise among the French service troops assigned the task of opening boxes containing rearmament. By then the MAC (G) had approved the assignment of 200,000 sets of clothing and of the equipment requested by the theater on 4 July. Phase II was now a reality. Still, no less

---

[47] Memo, CofS NATOUSA for JRC, 17 Jun 43, and Memo, JRC for Leyer, 19 Jul 43, JRC 902/II Rearmt Plan; Msg L–436, SOS NATOUSA to CG NATOUSA, 27 Jul 43, and Msg 5718, CG NATOUSA to CG SOS NATOUSA, 29 Jul 43, JRC Cable Log.

than two months had elapsed between the submission of General Leyer's memorandum of 20 May and the action finally taken by the MAB.[48]

When General Giraud landed in Algiers on 25 July, after a brief stop in England, he could be well pleased with the results of his trip to the American continent. Not only had he succeeded in reviving interest in the rearmament program, but in addition he had the promise that within a few days another substantial shipment would be on its way to North African ports. There was a chance that these positive material gains might help disperse the dark clouds hovering over his political horizon. At any rate, when they became known, these gains acted as a tonic on the morale of French troops. The French, cabled General Eisenhower, were most enthusiastic about the action taken in Washington. They regretted only that the assignment of additional aircraft had been deferred until the next calendar year. As the first ships bringing the equipment of Phase II reached Casablanca in late August, General Giraud seized the occasion to thank General Marshall for his "comprehensive, warm, and effective support in making known to all in America the needs of the French Army."[49]

Fusion of the Giraud and de Gaulle Forces

Fusion of all French armed forces still remained the major problem facing both the French and AFHQ. To expedite fusion, General Eisenhower had, during General Giraud's visit to the United States, submitted to the CCS three important recommendations. He had proposed that thereafter all French forces be controlled through AFHQ; that, pending a final CCS decision on the matter, no further issue of British equipment be made to the Free French; and that General Giraud be requested to include the Free French Forces in the target of eleven divisions due to be re-equipped under the ANFA Agreement. The Combined Chiefs, on 30 July, endorsed the recommendations.[50]

By this time the French themselves had come to the realization that the two-staff arrangement established on 22 June was impracticable and must be done away with. On 31 July, after several weeks of tension, the CFLN finally promulgated two decrees which brought unity of command and made the fusion of forces a reality. All armed forces were to be integrated under one single military administration and placed under the over-all command of General Giraud. In addition, the existing arrangement under which the two copresidents of the CFLN presided alternately was modified: Giraud was to preside over debates whenever they dealt with purely military matters; de Gaulle was to be in the chair when political or economic matters or general policy was to be discussed.[51] The new organization, incidentally, was consonant with the wishes of the Resistance forces in France. Meeting secretly in Paris on 27 May, the National Council of the Resistance had formally rec-

---

[48] Ltr, CinC AFHQ to TAG, 31 Jul 43, JRC 904 Modification of Rearmt; Min, MAC (G) 102d Mtg, 15 Jul 43; Min, MAC (G) 103d Mtg, 24 Jul 43.

[49] Msg W–6517, Eisenhower to Marshall for Arnold, 4 Aug 43, JRC Cable Log; Ltr, Giraud to Marshall, 27 Aug 43, OPD 400 France, Sec II.

[50] Msg, Eisenhower to CCS, 14 Jul 43, NAF 289; Min, CCS 104th Mtg, 30 Jul 43; Msg 3825, CCS to Eisenhower, 31 Jul 43, FAN 176.

[51] See The Kittredge (Capt. T. B., USN) Papers: FRANCE: Political A–2 Aug 43, copy in OCMH; see also, Marey, "Le Réarmement français en Afrique du Nord (1942–1944)," Revue Politique et Parlementaire (October, 1947).

ognized General de Gaulle as the political leader, and General Giraud as the Commander in Chief, of all elements, both within and outside of France, aligned against the Axis.[52]

In the ensuing reorganization of the French High Command, officers from both factions were appointed to key posts: Chief of Army Staff, Maj. Gen. Roger Leyer; Assistant Chief of Staff, Maj. Gen. Pierre Koenig; Chief of Naval Staff, Rear Adm. André Lemonnier; Assistant Chief of Staff, Rear Adm. Philippe Auboyneau; Chief of Air Staff, Lt. Gen. René Bouscat.[53]

A final step toward unification was taken in September with the establishment of a Commissariat of National Defense, a sort of inner war cabinet which replaced the Permanent Military Committee and whose function was to co-ordinate the activities of the three chiefs of staff.

The belated fusion of the armed forces gave rise at once to a number of crucial problems. One was the manner in which the former Free French Forces were to receive further issues of war matériel.

A few days after his return to Algiers, General Giraud was informed of the CCS decision regarding the incorporation of the Free French Forces in the eleven-division program. He then learned "with stupefaction" that, not only would the British-equipped Free French units cease to be a British responsibility, but they were to return to British depots without delay all the matériel in their possession, including cloth-

ing, individual equipment, armament, armored vehicles, and other organizational equipment. In practice the French Commander in Chief was acquiring 13,000 additional combatants, that is to say, 3,000 from the Leclerc Column, and 10,000 from the 1st Free French Division, also known as the Koenig Division, without obtaining a corresponding increase in matériel. He protested, but in vain. Faced with the prospect of having to "sacrifice" two of his own divisions in order to make room for the former Free French, General Giraud announced his intention to revise the composition of the ANFA Plan as follows: 4 armored divisions of the proposed new triangular type, instead of 3 of the old square type (in this manner, the Leclerc Column, trained in tank warfare and now in process of being raised to the strength of a division [the 2d DFL], would be re-equipped as a fourth armored division, thus leaving intact the 3 already activated), and 7 infantry divisions, with an eighth, the British-equipped 1st DFL, remaining for the present at least a British responsibility outside the ANFA Plan.[54]

G–3, AFHQ, immediately objected that the ratio of 7 infantry to 4 armored divisions as proposed by General Giraud constituted an unbalanced force. The deputy theater commander, on the other hand, considered that four armored divisions of the new type would require fewer tanks,[55] therefore less tank maintenance and technical supervision as well as less shipping.[56] Overriding G–3's objection, he urged that the proposed ratio

[52] MS #B–035, Rôle joué par les Forces Françaises de l'Intérieur pendant l'occupation de la France avant et après le débarquement du 6 Juin 1944 (Commandant Rogé, Service Historique de l'Armée, Section Etudes), OCMH.

[53] Memo, Lt Col John C. Knox for Col J. Terrence, 2 Aug 43, AFHQ 0100/26 Liaison Sec Rpts to G–3 on Political Situation.

[54] Interv with Gen Giraud, Dec 48; Memo, Brig Gen Sidney P. Spalding for CofS. AFHQ, 5 Aug 43, JRC Misc Doc, Item 5–a, Tab Q.

[55] 980 as against 1,170 in three old-type divisions.

[56] Memo, Deputy Theater Comdr for CofS AFHQ, 10 Aug 43, JRC Misc Doc, Item 5–a, Tab Q.

be accepted. AFHQ approved Giraud's proposal and the 2d DFL was incorporated in the rearmament program as a fourth armored division. It was then renamed the 2d Armored Division (2d DB), and the former 2d DB, commanded by Brig. Gen. Jacques de Vernejoul, was redesignated the 5th DB.

General Giraud's plan regarding the 1st DFL posed a more delicate problem. As reported by G–3, the further issue of British equipment to that division could be made only at the expense of British troops committed to battle, since shipping limitations precluded for some time to come the shipment to the theater of sufficient British equipment to take care of the unit.[57] It was considered inadvisable, therefore, to maintain the division any longer with British equipment. On 29 August General Smith, after warning General Giraud that the 1st DFL could not begin to receive British issues until after the end of the year (by which time its equipment would be reduced as a result of normal deterioration), urged him to consider making such adjustments in his program as might appear to him expedient.[58]

While discouraging, the above statement was, as later pointed out by G–3, "sufficiently indefinite as to lead the French to live in hopes of finding a solution to the problem within a month or two." [59] The solution which General Giraud adopted was simply the one he had proposed earlier, namely, to keep the British-equipped 1st DFL, now being raised to the strength of a

full division by the addition of a third brigade, as an eighth infantry division.[60] He then announced that it would be employed in Italy "alongside their old comrades of the Eighth Army." To complete its equipment, the French Commander in Chief ordered the other British-equipped unit stripped of its matériel before leaving Tunisia for Morocco, there to receive its new U.S. equipment. Such action had become possible, for the British military authorities had just reversed their earlier policy requiring the Free French Forces to return their British equipment. They had now come to regard this matériel as unserviceable.[61] Soon, however, it became known that the third brigade being added to the 1st DFL was a U.S.-equipped unit. AFHQ authorities immediately pointed out that the idea of having any division take part in active operations with two different types of equipment was "verging on madness." [62] To dispel once and for all the uncertainty then current in French circles, the Deputy Chief of Staff, AFHQ, made it clear to General Giraud that the Eighth Army "no longer regarded the 1st DFL as theirs and would not call it forward." [63] The French Commander in Chief had now no other recourse but to incorporate the division in the rearmament program.

In a letter to General Eisenhower, dated

---

[57] Memo, ACofS G–3 for CofS AFHQ, 25 Aug 43, AFHQ 0100/4 SACS Rcd Sec, Fr Matters, Vol. I.

[58] Ltr, CofS AFHQ to Giraud, 29 Aug 43, signed and mailed 6 Sep 43, AFHQ 0100/4 SACS Rcd Sec, Fr Matters, Vol. I.

[59] Memo, ACofS G–3 for DCofS, 5 Oct 43, AFHQ 0100/12C G–3 Div Ops Free Fr.

[60] The division, organized from the time of its activation on the British model, retained the brigade organization throughout the war. All other French divisions adopted the American organization with only minor modifications.

[61] Memo, CinC for G.O.C. Tunisia District, 9 Sep 43, AFHQ 0100/12C G–3 Div Ops Free Fr.

[62] Ltr, Whiteley to Gruenther, CofS Fifth Army, 17 Oct 43, AFHQ 0100/12C G–3 Div Ops Free Fr.

[63] Ltr, Whiteley to Giraud, 6 Oct 43, JRC 370/002 Employment of Free Fr Divs; Handwritten comment, Whiteley to G–3, 18 Oct 43, on Memo, Rooks for DCofS, 5 Oct 43, AFHQ 0100/12C G–3 Div Ops Free Fr.

26 October, General Giraud proposed a second revision of the ANFA Plan to include the 1st DFL, now renamed 1st Motorized Infantry Division (1st DMI), as an eighth infantry division.[64] The four armored divisions now on the program being practically equivalent to three of the type originally planned, he considered that the number of infantry divisions could be raised from 7 to 8 without increasing the over-all figure of 11 divisions with regard to matériel. The revision, he concluded, would be "within the spirit of the ANFA Agreement." G–3 officials voiced the opinion that General Giraud's proposal was a step in the right direction. The addition of one infantry division, they pointed out, would improve the ratio between infantry and armor. The issue with respect to the 1st DMI could not be settled then and there. Suffice it to say that the division ultimately was re-equipped with U.S. matériel and included among the expeditionary forces for operations overseas.[65]

Results of Phases I and II

By the time the last shipments of Phase II equipment reached North Africa in late September, the French had re-equipped or were in process of re-equipping with American matériel an expeditionary force consisting of four infantry divisions (the 2d Moroccan Infantry, 3d Algerian Infantry, 4th Moroccan Mountain, and 9th Colonial Infantry), two armored divisions (the 1st DB and 5th DB), as well as headquarters, corps troops, and service units. The task of arming these units was complicated by the fact that there had been serious gaps in deliveries of U.S. matériel. No automatic rifles had yet been received. There were shortages in certain types of trucks, signal and medical equipment, tentage, and other items. Equipment for the four Ordnance companies requested in July had not been assigned by the MAB. As a result the French were forced to make substitutions for the missing items from existing French stocks. Already, in August, the JRC had called attention to these facts and had pointed out that because of their expansion the expeditionary forces required a considerable monthly tonnage of spare major items, major assemblies, and spare parts. A plan to furnish them with D and C rations (to which the French had nothing corresponding), as well as ammunition, was under consideration.[66]

Training, meanwhile, was proceeding satisfactorily. The task of General Kingman's French Training Section was made easier by the fact that most of the units being re-equipped consisted of old and battle-tried regiments, a large part of whose personnel had gone through both the 1939–40 and the Tunisian campaigns.[67] In fact there were exceptionally few men who had not had some military training. Hence, the state of preparedness of the expeditionary forces depended upon their capability of becoming acquainted with the new matériel, of learning equipment maintenance and repair techniques, and of training additional drivers for general-purpose vehicles. It was believed that a

---

[64] Throughout the remainder of the war the personnel of the division continued, for sentimental reasons, to refer to their unit as the 1st DFL.

[65] Ltr, Giraud to Eisenhower, 26 Oct 43, AFHQ 0100/12C G–3 Div Ops Fr Rearmt; Memo, Brig Gen William C. Crane, DACofS G–3 for G–3, 1 Nov 43, AFHQ 0100/12C G–3 Div Ops Free Fr; for final re-equipment of 1st DMI, see pp. 116–117, below.

[66] Memo, Artamonoff for Brig Gen Clarence L. Adcock, 2 Aug 43, JRC Misc Doc, Item 5–a, Tab T.

[67] See pp. 230 ff., below.

sufficient number of tank crews with pre- vious experience in French tank units was available for the regiments of the two armored divisions. Most combat units of the four infantry divisions had already acquired a good knowledge of their new matériel, and it was reported that they would shortly be ready for action. The armored divisions on the other hand would not be ready for some months yet, largely because of delays expected in the receipt of signal and ordnance equipment, tools, service trucks, and spare parts.[68]

The status of the rearmament of the air units was less encouraging. The air pro- gram was said to have completely stalled. So far squadrons had been issued only a few planes with the result that their morale was seriously impaired. As for naval units, they had received only a small monthly alloca- tion of supplies.[69]

The effort to rearm the French North African forces was, it can be seen, almost exclusively American, and rightly so since the original commitment, by agreement with the British, was an American one. By

way of comparison, it is interesting to note that the contribution of the British to the rearmament of the ground forces was then estimated at 5 percent in terms of tonnage, and of the air forces at 10 percent in terms of aircraft and related equipment. As for the naval forces, practically the entire fleet was being overhauled and re-equipped in the United States. It was also being sup- plied and maintained chiefly with American matériel in the Mediterranean. The Brit- ish for their part had made temporary re- pairs on vessels harbored in Alexandria, to enable them to reach the United States for complete overhauling.[70] They had also re- paired a number of small craft not capable of crossing the Atlantic. It was estimated that, when the naval program had been completed, the United States would have financed 95 percent and the British 5 per- cent of the cost.[71]

---

[68] Memo cited n. 66.

[69] *Ibid.*

[70] The French fleet harbored at Alexandria since June 1940 had thrown its lot with the North African Naval Forces at the end of April 1943.

[71] Memo, Spalding for Brig Gen A. R. Wilson, 14 Aug 43, JRC 902/II Rearmt Plan. The figures were prepared in reply to a question raised by a senatorial committee as to the relative amount of rearmament furnished by the United States and by the United Kingdom to the French in North Africa.

CHAPTER VI

Phase III of the Program
(Mid-August–November 1943)

The 15 August Plan

The practicability of a third rearmament phase had been examined in Washington long before the ships carrying the equipment of the second had docked in Casablanca. In late June, while waiting for the theater to send in the requisitions for Phase II, War Department agencies were already seeking ways and means to complete the eleven-division program in its entirety. To proceed with intelligent planning, they needed to obtain an accurate picture of the current status of equipment from all sources in the hands of the French or available to them in the theater. To this end, Operations Division requested AFHQ on 1 July to furnish information on (1) the amount of enemy matériel captured in Tunisia likely to become available for French rearmament; (2) the amount of American equipment turned over to the French from American theater stocks over and above that shipped from the United States; (3) the number of units still to be completely or partially equipped and, in the latter case, the list of items already provided; and (4) the amount of matériel required to complete the eleven-division program, with an indication of the earliest dates on which this equipment could be "profitably re-

ceived and assimilated" by the French. The warning was added, as it had been in connection with Phase II, that rifles, some signal equipment, and certain trucks were not available from stocks in the United States.[1]

The desirability of using captured enemy equipment for French rearmament had long been considered by AFHQ. Pursuant to a CCS directive on the disposal of such equipment, the Allied Commander in Chief had, on 16 May, given French requirements fourth priority in the allocation of usable enemy matériel. He had instructed the JRC to handle its issue to the French. In the case of captured equipment and transport of French origin, he had directed the Allied forces in Tunisia to hand over all such items to the French. While enemy equipment, much of which had been left in woods, mountains, and isolated locations, was being collected, removed, segregated, and classified, advance reports indicated that Axis troops had smashed and burned the bulk of their matériel "with their usual thoroughness." Just as Eisenhower had anticipated, when the count was completed, it was found that the total serviceable equipment from this source was very small in-

---

[1] Msg 1453, AGWAR to Eisenhower, 1 Jul 43, JRC Cable Log.

deed. It would not be sufficient to equip even one division.[2]

The situation with regard to U.S. and British equipment loaned to North African troops during the Tunisian campaign was not any brighter. The matériel was now in such poor condition that AFHQ, revising its earlier decision, ruled that it was no longer to be returned to U.S. and British stocks but was to be turned over to Territorial units to supplement the French matériel in their possession.[3] As far as the rearmament program was concerned, this equipment simply did not exist.

In order to answer the other questions raised in the Operations Division query of 1 July, the JRC requested the French High Command to furnish without delay a complete list of the units still to be re-equipped after Phase II had been completed, together with a computation of the ground and air force equipment required for the purpose.[4]

While the French General Staff was preparing the necessary lists, General Giraud, then in Washington primarily to obtain the armament of Phase II, was also pressing for a third phase. General Marshall agreed with him in regarding as a commitment the task of completing the eleven-division program, and so informed General Eisenhower. The U.S. Chief of Staff then dispatched to the theater Brig. Gen. Sidney P. Spalding for the purpose of working out with AFHQ a progressive plan to bring the entire program to completion. At the same time, he requested General Eisenhower to indicate at an early date the rate of shipping and priority of supplies desired for such a commitment.[5]

All together five divisions, several headquarters, and a number of supporting combat and service units remained to be equipped. The task was substantial. To enable the Joint Rearmament Committee to carry it out with greater efficiency, theater officials decided that the committee must undergo some changes. On 7 August they transferred it from the control of Liaison Section, where it had been since 5 June, to that of NATOUSA. The move was a logical one considering that the commitment to rearm the French was almost entirely American. As technical training was inseparable from re-equipping, AFHQ also decided to place General Kingman's Training Section, until then under the control of Fifth Army, directly under the supervision of the JRC. The section became known as French Training Section, JRC. Thus all activities in connection with the re-equipping and training of the North African forces thereafter were co-ordinated and supervised by a single agency, the JRC.[6]

AFHQ then proceeded to give the committee more prestige and authority by appointing a general officer, General Spalding, as its chairman. Similarly impressed by the need for higher-ranking representation, the French military authorities appointed a field-grade officer, Col. Jean Regnault, to head the French Section of the committee. This action on their part indicated clearly that they had come to regard the committee and not the Béthouart

[2] CCS 200/2/D, 23 Apr 43; Dir, Eisenhower To All Concerned, 16 May 43, JRC Misc Doc, Item 5-a, Tab T; Quotation from Ltr, Eisenhower to Giraud, 20 Jun 43, AFHQ 0100/12C Div Ops Fr Rearmt, Vol. II.

[3] Msg W-4636, AFHQ to AGWAR, 11 Jul 43, OPD 400 France, Sec II.

[4] Memo, JRC for Col Blanc, 10 Jul 43, JRC 902/II Rearmt Plan.

[5] Ltr, Marshall to Eisenhower, 17 Jul 43, AFHQ 0100/4 SACS Rcd Sec, Fr Matters.

[6] NATOUSA Staff Memo 74, 7 Aug 43, JRC 320/001 Orgn of JRC.

mission in Washington as the authoritative agency in matters of rearmament. A few weeks later AFHQ established a separate Joint Air Commission (JAC) which it placed under the control of the Mediterranean Air Command. This commission, composed of U.S., British, and French members, was made responsible for handling strictly air armament matters. Problems concerning equipment common to both air and ground units remained the responsibility of the JRC. The closest liaison was established between the two agencies for the discussion of questions that involved their joint attention.[7]

In Washington, meanwhile, the Joint War Plans Committee (JWPC) had concluded a study of the rearmament problem. Its final report, dated 26 July, pointed out that the CCS decision of 18 May to arm the French was merely the "reaffirmation of an indefinite commitment" which avoided the most important issues.[8] In particular, the decision had set no target date, and had given no indication whatsoever as to when the rearmed forces could or would be used in combat. The committee felt that for political as well as military reasons, these issues could no longer be avoided. It was urgent that the commitment to arm the French be carried out and that United Nations strategy be "designed so as to permit taking full advantage of the potential com-

GENERAL ALPHONSE JUIN, *acting French commander in chief.*

bat power of a re-equipped French army in the Mediterranean." [9]

Endorsing the conclusions of the JWPC report, General Marshall, at the next CCS meeting on 30 July, urged that French rearmament be continued, especially now that the shipping situation had improved. Resorting again to the familiar argument that such rearmament would provide over-all economy in the exploitation of Allied resources, he recommended that a more determined effort be made to bring the North African forces into action. So far, he explained, nothing further had been done in this connection than to plan for their employment in an operation against Corsica.[10]

The conquest of Corsica had, indeed, been assigned to the French and was sched-

---

[7] NATOUSA GO 74, 7 Aug 43, JRC 320/001 Orgn of JRC; MAC Hq GO 9, 6 Sep 43, in The History of MAAF: December 1943–1 September 1944, Vol. II, AAF Hist Office Archives; see Ch. XVII, below.

[8] "The re-arming and re-equipping of the French forces in North Africa should be proceeded with as rapidly as the availability of shipping and equipment will allow, but as a secondary commitment to the requirements of British and U.S. forces in the various theaters." Min, CCS 87th Mtg, 18 May 43; see p. 57, above.

[9] JPS 231, 26 Jul 43, OPD CS 381 File 2.

[10] Min, CCS 104th Mtg, 30 Jul 43.

uled to take place at some later date when
the current operations in Sicily came to a
successful end.[11]   But on 21 July, G–3,
AFHQ, also had strongly urged that other
North African forces, possibly one or two
divisions if available, be employed in the
planned invasion of the Italian mainland.
G–3 stressed the advantageous psychological effect which the use of French troops
was likely to have on the Italians.   Three
days later Eisenhower asked General Juin,
acting French Commander in Chief in the
absence of Giraud, then in Washington, to
consider the employment on the Italian
mainland, with the U.S. Fifth Army, of
French units available over and above those
scheduled to take part in the assault on
Corsica.   On 29 July General Smith requested General Juin to indicate how many
such units could be embarked and when.
The further employment of the North
African expeditionary forces, therefore, was
actually under serious consideration, and
energetic plans were being made to bring
them into action as speedily as possible.[12]

General Eisenhower's recommendations
for the completion of the rearmament program reached Washington on 12 August.
They embodied a detailed plan—concurred
in by General Giraud himself—drawn on
the basis of an army of four corps (three
infantry and one armored) consisting of
seven infantry and four armored divisions,
the ratio just approved by AFHQ.[13]   Already a total of four infantry and two

armored divisions, as well as two corps
headquarters had been equipped.   The object of the plan therefore was to obtain the
matériel for the rest of the program.   Under
the plan, which became known as the 15
August Plan, this matériel was to be shipped
in four installments as follows: one infantry
division, one armored division (minus certain elements already outfitted), and one
army corps headquarters in September; one
infantry division in October; one infantry
division and one army corps headquarters
in November; one armored division in December.   Each slice was to include the
matériel to equip all the necessary supporting combat and service units.   Shipments
were to be made to Casablanca, now an
entirely French base.   The total tonnage
required for initial equipment, plus maintenance of major items and assemblies, was
estimated at approximately 180,000 tons
for September, and 150,000 tons monthly
thereafter.   Air and naval requirements, as
well as rations and ammunition, would not
come within this tonnage but would be
shipped under the 25,000-ton monthly
allocation.[14]

Anticipating early approval by the CCS,
the JRC promptly forwarded to the War
Department the priority lists of matériel for
the September slice.[15]   The lists differed
somewhat from those submitted earlier by
the French, especially as to service units.
After some discussion with various AFHQ
sections, the JRC had made some changes
which the French were now reluctant to
accept.   The proposed distribution of
maintenance units, they objected, no longer
corresponded to theirs.   Because of a critical

---

[11] Participating in the Sicilian campaign was one
battalion of goumiers (the 4th Moroccan Tabor),
the only French ground unit then engaged in battle
anywhere.   Its equipment was largely of French
origin, with a sprinkling of U.S. matériel.

[12] Memo, Rooks for Smith, 21 Jul 43, AFHQ
0100/12C G–3 Div Ops Opns in Italy, Pt. II;
Ltrs, Smith to Juin, 24, 29 Jul 43, AFHQ 0100/
12C G–3 Div Ops Fr Corres.

[13] See pp. 87–88, above.

[14] Msg W–7177, Eisenhower to Marshall, 12 Aug
43, JRC 902/II Rearmt Plan.

[15] Msg 7274, AFHQ to AGWAR, 13 Aug 43,
JRC Cable Log.

shortage of technical personnel, they could not, they asserted, commit themselves to follow the proportion as now set up by the JRC for the various maintenance companies within the divisions. Perhaps at a later date, if it proved possible to enlarge the flow of selected men from the Continent, the proposed adjustments might become feasible.[16]

The reluctance of the French High Command to accept the increase in service units as proposed by the JRC raised an important issue. Just who would support the rearmed divisions in combat? The French themselves, or the Allies? The matter had until then been given little attention. Within a few short weeks, it would become the subject of heated debate and a source of considerable friction between the French High Command and AFHQ.

On 16 August General Somervell announced from Washington that the 15 August Plan could in general be met. A large part of the necessary equipment would soon become available in the theater as a result of the expected departure from North Africa of four U.S. divisions. In pursuance of a CCS decision taken in May, these units were shortly to be moved to the United Kingdom to provide a core of battle-tried troops for the cross-Channel operation then under consideration. Their organizational equipment would be transferred and credited to the French program. This would result in a corresponding reduction of the allocation of matériel from the United States and, by the same token, in a considerable reduction of shipping tonnage requirements. Pending a CCS decision on the plan, General Somervell requested his

services to compute at once the items required from the United States and make preliminary arrangements for their shipment.[17]

General Eisenhower's recommendations regarding the 15 August Plan had reached Washington just as the Joint Staff Planners were completing a report entitled Equipping Allies, Liberated Forces, and Friendly Neutrals. Incorporating his proposal in their paper, they recommended that supplies and equipment necessary to implement the plan be authorized for shipment during the period 1 September to 31 December 1943. They urged, however, that the over-all program itself be limited to the obligations of the Casablanca Conference, or seven infantry and four armored divisions as now approved by AFHQ.[18]

To avoid any delay, the U.S. Joint Chiefs of Staff on 18 August submitted the JPS report directly to the CCS, then assembled in Quebec for the QUADRANT Conference (11–24 August). The British members of the committee having expressed their fear, as they had on similar occasions, that the French program might run counter to other commitments, the CCS, on 23 August, amended the American proposal by adding the following proviso: "in so far as this does not interfere with operations scheduled previous to QUADRANT Conference." They then requested the War Department to take appropriate measures to implement the program. Simultaneously the CCS agreed that "such French forces as may be re-equipped and fit for war" would be used in operations in the Mediterranean. This decision, in

---

[16] Memo, Col Blanc for Chief Fr Sec JRC, 19 Aug 43, and Memo, Theater Comdr for AGWAR, 18 Aug 43, JRC 902/II Rearmt Plan.

[17] CCS 242/6, Final Report to the President and Prime Minister, 25 May 43; Memo, Somervell for Marshall, and Msg 2315, Somervell to Styer, 16 Aug 43, Somervell Files, Fr 1943–44, A–46–257, Ser 1, Dr 3.

[18] CCS 317, 18 Aug 43, QUADRANT Conf.

effect, merely formalized the action already taken in the theater to prepare a French expeditionary corps for service in Italy with the U.S. Fifth Army.[19]

Thus, nearly ten months after the landings in northwest Africa, the first definite, Anglo-American rearmament commitment, specific as to scope and time, was finally made. Henceforth all interested Allied agencies as well as the French High Command could look to a clear-cut directive for guidance in rearming the North African Forces.

The QUADRANT Conference, it must be noted, had brought forth another important decision with respect to the French. On 26 August the British, Canadian, and U.S. Governments had agreed to extend limited recognition to the French Committee of National Liberation as representing all Frenchmen fighting the Axis, pending the establishment by the liberated people of France of a government of their own choice. The CFLN therefore was recognized not as a government but as the body administering French Africa and all other territories under its control during the war, and providing the official channels through which all French contributions to the common war effort should be made under the collective responsibility of all its members.[20] The French in North Africa received the announcement of this decision with "enthusiasm and gratification." By 3 September twenty-three other members of the

United Nations had taken similar action.[21]

Recognition of the CFLN did not, for the moment at least, affect the existing relationship between Allied military authorities in the theater and the French High Command. AFHQ continued to handle armament matters directly with the responsible French Army, Air, and Navy staffs or, when co-ordination between the latter was required, with General Giraud or the chief of his personal staff, Brig. Gen. Paul Devinck. These authorities in turn obtained from the CFLN such sanction as was necessary. The procedure had worked well in the past. As pointed out by the chairman of the JRC on 25 August, there was no reason to change it whether or not CFLN was recognized.[22]

Now that the CCS had approved the 15 August Plan, the War Department took steps to put it in effect. General Somervell informed his services on 23 August that the organizational equipment expected to be left behind by the four U.S. divisions when they moved to the United Kingdom in November would be diverted to French rearmament within the limits of General Eisenhower's stated requirements and would be deducted from shipments to North Africa. As a result, October, November, and December shipments to the French would include individual equipment only, such as would be carried by the American divisions going to England. To determine with accuracy the nature and quantities of items remaining to be shipped from the United States, General Somervell requested AFHQ to furnish without delay a detailed list of all matériel likely

---

[19] Memo, COS for CCS, CCS 317/3, 23 Aug 43, QUADRANT Conf; Min, CCS 115th Mtg, 23 Aug 43, QUADRANT Conf; CPS Rpt, CCS 329/2, Implementation of Assumed Basic Undertaking and Specific Operations for the Conduct of the War, 1943–44, 26 Aug 43, QUADRANT Conf.

[20] Memo, Col Knox, Liaison Sec, for G–3, 27 Aug 43, AFHQ 0100/26 Liaison Sec, Rpts to G–3 on Political Situation; see also Sherwood, Roosevelt and Hopkins, p. 746.

[21] Capt. Harry C. Butcher, My Three Years With Eisenhower (New York: Simon and Schuster, 1946), p. 399; Charles de Gaulle, Discours et Messages (Paris: Berger-Levrault, 1946), p. 348.

[22] Personal Ltr, Spalding to Lt Col Roger Jones, MAB, 25 Aug 43, JRC 472 MAB.

to be left behind by the four American divisions.[23]

Meanwhile, the Munitions Assignments Board had approved the transfer to the Commanding General, NATOUSA, of the weapons and matériel constituting the September slice. This would serve to equip a fifth infantry division, the units necessary to complete a third armored division of the three-battalion type, and various service troops.[24]

The French military authorities had long since activated the entire eleven divisions of the program, not counting the British-equipped 1st Motorized Infantry Division which they were retaining as a nonprogram unit. It was now reported that, in addition, they were activating four other infantry divisions, the nucleus of what they hoped would become a second army.[25]

On 26 August General Giraud listed for AFHQ the divisions to be fully rearmed under the 15 August Plan. For each he indicated an approximate date of readiness. The exact date, he pointed out, depended on the reception of the necessary matériel. He warned that in the case of many service troops, such as the maintenance units requested by AFHQ, their activation was bound to encounter great difficulties for lack of trained personnel.[26]

By this time the first ships carrying the equipment of Phase II were being unloaded at Casablanca. When General Giraud wrote to General Marshall on 27 August to express his gratefulness for this new evidence of American intent to rearm his forces, he urged that the effort be continued and the ANFA Plan brought to speedy completion. The men of the remaining five divisions, he explained, were "eagerly awaiting the matériel which had been promised them." He hoped that the entire program would be completed by the end of the year and he counted on the U.S. Chief of Staff to make the necessary arrangements to this effect. "America will not regret it," he asserted in conclusion. In his reply, General Marshall assured the French Commander in Chief that "every practicable effort" would continue to be made to complete the program.[27]

It must be noted in passing that no less than six weeks elapsed between Giraud's letter and Marshall's answer. Records show that at least three drafts were successively prepared by the Operations Division for the Chief of Staff's signature. The first stated that the present goal was to complete the eleven-division program "by the end of the year." The second, somewhat shorter, asserted that the program would be completed "according to schedule." The final draft contained no such assurances. Only an examination of the turbulent French political situation during these six weeks can provide a clue to the delay and the noncommittal wording of General Marshall's answer.

French Political Situation Threatens Program

Just as the implementation of Phase III was about to begin, a recurrence of French political strife in North Africa created a

---

[23] Memo, Somervell for Styer, 23 Aug 43, Somervell Files, Fr 1943–44, A–46–257, Ser 1, Dr 3; Msg 7783, AGWAR to AFHQ, 16 Sep 43, JRC 903 Requests for Units.

[24] Min, MAC (G) 108th Mtg, 26 Aug 43.

[25] Chart, JRC, Plan for Equipment, 26 Aug 43, JRC 902/II Rearmt Plan.

[26] Memo, Giraud for AFHQ Planning Staff, 26 Aug 43, AFHQ 0100/12C G–3 Div Ops Fr Rearmt.

[27] Ltrs, Giraud to Marshall, 27 Aug 43, Marshall to Giraud, 8 Oct 43, OPD 400 France, Sec II.

situation which threatened to put an end to the rearmament program.

Immediately after the limited recognition of the CFLN on 26 August, climaxing a month of truce during which the fusion of all French armed forces had become a reality, General de Gaulle and his followers raised a new issue: the committee's control over French military affairs. In particular they questioned once more General Giraud's remaining authority. The French Commander in Chief had seemingly resigned himself to the fact that he must soon relinquish his post of copresident of CFLN in view of the failure of the two-headed arrangement. He insisted, however, that, by virtue of his recognition by the Allies in November 1942 as the supreme French military commander, he alone had the authority to speak for the French forces. It was his firm belief that the armament furnished by the United States had been given to him in his personal capacity. General de Gaulle and his supporters, on the other hand, were equally insistent that the powers then exercised by General Giraud, except as they confined themselves to the control of expeditionary forces, should revert to the responsible civil authority, namely, the CFLN. In the words of Mr. Murphy, the American political representative in the theater, the controversy had "reached a point where it was threatening the prosecution of the war." [28]

Apprised of the situation, President Roosevelt was tempted at first to order the immediate stoppage of all shipments of equipment and munitions to the French. On second thought he realized it was not necessary to force a showdown. It would come anyway and probably soon. He directed General Marshall to keep in close touch with the situation.[29]

In early October the CFLN reorganized itself, eliminated the two-head arrangement, and elected General de Gaulle as its sole president. General Giraud was thus removed from the political sphere. That accomplished, the CFLN established a National Defense Committee, placed the Commander in Chief directly under the Commissioner of National Defense, and assigned him command of such forces as it made available to him for military operations. As a member ex officio of the National Defense Committee, the Commander in Chief was to share with the president of the CFLN and the Commissioner of National Defense the task of administering and maintaining the armed forces.[30] Although these measures went a long way toward stripping General Giraud of effective control over the French Army, he retained for the moment the title of Commander in Chief. AFHQ officials therefore decided that they would continue to deal directly and only with him regarding rearmament and other military matters. Yet it was clear that he no longer could make decisions that were final and that agreements reached with him would be subject to approval or rejection by other French authorities. General Marshall's reluctance, as evidenced in his letter of 8 October, to make a firm commitment on the completion of the program clearly reflected the trend of the situation

[28] Msg, Murphy to State Dept, 3 Sep 43, OPD 400 France, Sec II.

[29] Memo, President for Marshall, 13 Oct 43, OPD 400 France, Sec II.

[30] Decree on Reorganization of CFLN and Decree Establishing a National Defense Committee, text of both documents in Giraud, *Un seul but, la Victoire,* pp. 262–64.

Implementing Phase III

Two problems of matériel faced the French military authorities during Phase III and, for that matter, long afterward. The first, to which the JRC had briefly referred in its report of 2 August, concerned shortages of items in the hands of units whose re-equipping was supposed to have been completed. The International Division, ASF, had already made a study of it. The MAB likewise had looked into it after learning that the French were requisitioning for supplies which had been assigned and delivered to them.[31]

As explained by General Spalding, chairman of the JRC, on 25 August, shortages existed largely because the French military authorities had distributed among several different units matériel originally assigned for some particular organization. They had done so because of training demands, changes in priority of equipping, transportation difficulties, and various other emergencies. It was up to the French to reshuffle in due time the equipment available to them and to turn it over to the units for which assignments had been made. Where shortages existed because matériel had not been assigned or shipped from the United States, it was urgent that the missing items be sent to North Africa without delay.[32]

The JRC attempted with the help of its French Training Section to determine the extent of shortages by conducting showdown inspections of French units. Similarly, the International Division in Washington began making a check of all shortages in shipments made against Phases I and II. But this check did not take into consideration losses at sea as well as losses, breakage, or diversion on and after arrival in North Africa.[33]

The second problem facing the French was lack of spare parts. In mid-August they reported that they were dangerously short of such items, especially parts for combat vehicles; a large proportion of these, as a result, was reported to be currently deadlined. In answer to repeated appeals from AFHQ, the War Department arranged to have some 11,000 tons of spare parts assigned as part of the September slice of Phase III.[34]

On 19 September AFHQ officials informed the War Department that to maintain properly their American equipment the French needed considerable numbers of major assemblies for replacement and exchange purposes. They pointed out that the one-month supply included in original shipments of matériel was inadequate. They requested that automatic monthly shipments of major assemblies be made for all shipments of organizational equipment, beginning at once and continuing until such time as the French themselves would be in a position to make monthly requisitions.[35]

By then, Army Service Forces had made available for shipment to North Africa practically all the equipment, including spare parts, requested by the theater as part of

---

[31] Memo, International Div ASF, sub: Summary of Status of Equip of Fr Rearmt by Units as of 1 Aug 43, JRC 475 MAB; Personal Ltr 4, Col Jones, MAB, to Gen Spalding, 13 Aug 43, JRC 472 MAB.

[32] Personal Ltr, Spalding to Jones, MAB, 25 Aug 43, JRC 472 MAB.

[33] Memo, Spalding for ACofS G–4, 18 Aug 43, JRC 400.0/009 Sup of Combat Units; Ltr 5, Col Jones, MAB, to Spalding, 27 Aug 43, JRC 472 MAB.

[34] Msg W–7322, AFHQ to AGWAR, 14 Aug 43, and Msg W–8081, 23 Aug 43, JRC Cable Log; Msg 7177, Somervell to AFHQ, 7 Sep 43, JRC 903 Requests for Units.

[35] Msg W–465, AFHQ to AGWAR, 19 Sep 43, JRC Cable Log.

the September slice, with the exception of certain ordnance and signal items then unavailable in the United States.[36] The total amounted to 143,000 tons. Of these, 120,000 tons were to be shipped in September, 5,000 tons in October, and the remainder after October. Tools and equipment for base maintenance shops requested by the theater would be shipped to the extent of 4,000 tons per month under the 25,000-ton monthly allocation.[37]

The sudden arrival, at the end of September, of the large shipment of maintenance equipment created a new and unexpected situation: the French were reported to be unable to handle the avalanche of spare parts presently reaching Casablanca. Cases of equipment were being unloaded by the thousands. Lacking adequate material means, facilities, and personnel, the French Supply Services simply could not segregate, inventory, and make ready for issue the innumerable items of equipment reaching them. Where indeed could they have found the 60,000-odd storage bins necessary for this huge operation? All they could do was to remove wrappings in great haste and distribute sets of spare parts immediately, often right out in the open. "To the great indignation of the Americans," the precious matériel was sometimes lost or damaged.[38]

Aware of this serious situation, the chief Ordnance officer in the theater, Col. David J. Crawford, recommended on 29 September that prompt action be taken to hold up further shipments of parts in all cases in which a large portion of the first six-month quota had been received. He also urged that the JRC and the French Supply Services bend all efforts toward the speedy establishment of an organization responsible for attending to the needs of the French Army for spare parts. He urged further that special attention be given to the development and prosecution of a plan for the supply of the expeditionary forces due to be sent to Italy. In this connection he regarded as essential the "immediate mobilization" of the supplies necessary for these forces by segregating and binning the items at strategically located depots, and the establishment of proper procedures of issue and replenishment by requisitions. Finally, he recommended that replenishment of parts be effected, not by automatic supply likely to result in wasteful accumulation, but by requisition, and then only after the establishment of an initial stockage at what was considered to be a satisfactory level for the troops involved. In line with these recommendations, the JRC requested the War Department to cancel the second 6-month automatic shipment of spare parts but to continue the initial 6-month shipment. The committee then proposed the establishment of a 45-day reserve and a 30-day operating level of Class II and IV supplies. The French had been instructed, and were already organizing, to requisition each month all supplies by item.[39]

---

[36] M5A1 tanks could be sent to the French only at the expense of U.S. troops overseas. Accordingly, M3A3 tanks were being substituted, pending availability of M5A1, for French rearmament as well as for some U.S. troops. Msg 5460, Somervell to Eisenhower, 20 Aug 43, JRC Cable Log.

[37] Msg 7177, Somervell to AFHQ, 7 Sep 43, JRC 903 Requests for Units; Msg 6005, Somervell to Eisenhower, 26 Aug 43, JRC Cable Log.

[38] Marey, "Le Réarmement français en Afrique du Nord (1942–1944)," Revue Politique et Parlementaire (October, 1947), p. 57.

[39] Memo, Col David J. Crawford for G–4 AFHQ, 29 Sep 43, JRC 402 Sup Policy; Msg 1852/3931, JRC to AGWAR, 6 Oct 43, JRC Cable Log. Class II covers supplies and equipment, such as clothing and weapons, for which allowances are established by tables of equipment or allowances; Class IV covers supplies and equipment, such as con-

Before taking action on the matter, the War Department reviewed for the benefit of AFHQ the status of spare parts and major assemblies as seen from Washington in the light of past shipments.[40] AFHQ did not concur in the facts as given by the War Department. As a result a long exchange of correspondence followed which lasted several months and was marked with considerable confusion due largely, it seems, to the different terminology used at both ends.

The ceaseless flow of U.S. equipment into French hands and the readying of units for service in Italy brought the question of technical training to the fore as a preoccupation of theater officials. To increase the scope and efficiency of the program offered by General Kingman's French Training Section, General Eisenhower in mid-August had requested the War Department to send to North Africa 385 additional highly qualified U.S. instructors, including 25 officers. The request had been granted and the men were to be dispatched to North Africa at the end of September.[41]

Meanwhile, the first major engagement of French forces in operations outside northwest Africa, one to which General Marshall had briefly referred in his statement before the CCS on 30 July, was taking place. Operation VESUVIUS, the liberation of Corsica, planned and directed by General Giraud under the over-all supervision of AFHQ, had begun on 13 September at a time when Corsican patriots were already battling the 10,000-odd German troops entrenched on the island. Except for one U.S. Ranger unit and, during the last week of operations, elements of an Italian Army corps, the participating forces—naval, air, and ground—were French. The ground force, commanded by Lt. Gen. Henry Martin and numbering some 15,000 men, included units of the 4th Moroccan Mountain Division, a regiment of goumiers (the 2d Moroccan Tabor Group, or 2d GTM), the Shock Battalion, plus antiaircraft artillery, engineers, and other supporting troops. The 2d GTM and Shock Battalion, not part of the eleven-division program, were equipped with a mixture of French, American, and other matériel.[42] The invading troops, unopposed at first, soon met with stiff resistance as the enemy, suddenly deciding to evacuate the island (as well as neighboring Sardinia), fought a series of rear guard actions to protect his movement toward northeastern ports. Pressing hard on the retreating columns, General Martin, on 30 September, launched a general attack which ended on 4 October with the complete liberation of the island.[43] His forces had suffered some 500 casualties including 100 killed in action.

As the implementation of the first slice of Phase III was coming to an end, Allied military authorities turned their attention to the second, or October, slice. On 7 October the Munitions Assignments Committee (Ground) approved the assignment of signal and individual equipment (less clothing already assigned and rifles, carbines, and pistols to be obtained from the United Kingdom) for a sixth infantry division and twenty-two supporting units, and of all the

---

struction and fortifications materials for which allowances are not prescribed. The others are: Class I, rations; Class III, POL (petrol, oil, and lubricants); Class V, ammunition.

[40] Msg 831, AGWAR to AFHQ, 25 Oct 43, JRC Cable Log.

[41] Msg W-7177, Eisenhower to Marshall, 12 Aug 43, JRC 902/II Rearmt Plan; Msg 8547, Marshall to Eisenhower, 24 Sep 43, JRC Cable Log.

[42] Nonprogram units are treated in pp. 111–13, 158–60, below.

[43] J. Joubert, La Libération de la France (Paris: Payot, 1951) pp. 90–94.

GOUMIERS OF THE 9TH COLONIAL INFANTRY DIVISION *boarding landing craft at Corsica for the invasion of Elba.*

matériel required to outfit units which were not the same as, or comparable to, the U.S. organizations scheduled to move from North Africa to England. The rest of the matériel necessary to equip fully the division and its supporting arms and services was to be provided by the theater from the equipment to be made surplus as a result of the departure from North Africa of similar U.S. units.[44]

Another question came up for discussion during the same period. It concerned the manner in which French forces were to be maintained. In answer to a query from the JRC, the War Department replied on 26 October that NATOUSA was authorized to maintain garrison-trained units on a zone of interior maintenance basis, and units ready and designated for combat service on a combat maintenance basis. The maintenance of all other forces was of course the responsibility of the French High Command. Troops certified and designated for combat service in the theater were authorized the theater level in all classes of supply except Class I (rations).[45] The

issue of maintenance items from U.S. theater stocks was to be made in accordance with existing War Department regulations. These stipulated that, except in case of an emergency, the authority to transfer supplies and equipment to foreign governments must be obtained from the MAB. Lend-lease requirements of foreign governments could not be requisitioned through Army supply channels but must be submitted through normal lend-lease channels.[46]

Near the end of October War Department officials began planning for the third, or November, slice of the 15 August Plan. As they prepared to submit the necessary requisitions to the MAC (G), they requested the theater to forward pertinent information on the amount of equipment expected to become available as a result of the departure of further U.S. units from North Africa.[47] At this point, however, important developments in the theater, long present but increasingly troublesome, had created a situation which forced a suspension of the 15 August Plan and led to a complete re-examination of the program.

---

[44] Min, MAC (G) 114th Mtg, 7 Oct 43; see also Memo, Col George Olmstead for Chmn MAC (G), 4 Oct 43, JRC 472 MAB, Msg W–1282, AFHQ to AGWAR, 29 Sep 43, JRC 903 Requests for Units.

[45] Msg 859, Marshall to Eisenhower, 26 Oct 43,

JRC Cable Log.

[46] WD Cir 220, 20 Sep 43.

[47] Msg 1165, AGWAR to Eisenhower, 29 Oct 43, JRC 903 Requests for Units.

CHAPTER VII

The Program Marks Time
(November 1943–February 1944)

I

"La Bataille des Services"

Nothing, it will be recalled, had been said in agreements and CCS directives regarding the manner in which support of the French forces was to be provided. The ANFA Agreement had been interpreted to mean the rearmament of eleven divisions plus auxiliary troops, without any clear definition of the number and nature of such auxiliary troops. In equipping the first expeditionary corps, the Joint Rearmament Committee had endeavored to make of it a coherent force capable of operating independently. With the much larger ground and air force being outfitted for combat, the problem of support was assuming vast proportions. The 15 August Plan merely aimed at equipping the three infantry and two armored divisions remaining on the ANFA program. It made no provision for army and corps artillery, antiaircraft, and service units; nor did it provide for base units, depots, service installations, repair shops, hospitals, and the like. How, then, were the rearmed divisions and air squadrons to be supported in combat? Where would the support come from?

Just before General Spalding's assumption of office as chairman of the JRC, his predecessor, Lt. Col. George L. Artamonoff, warned that the French lacked the technicians, even semitechnicians, necessary to organize all the service troops required for a modern eleven-division army. He proposed, much as he had done several months earlier, that if maximum use was to be made of the "excellent source of fighting manpower" that was the French Army it should be backed by U.S. Ordnance units. The number of such units would depend upon the number of similar units that the French themselves could not activate from their own resources.[1]

Colonel Artamonoff's proposal had no chance of being translated into action. The possibility of placing U.S. service troops in support of the French had just been ruled out by General Eisenhower himself for the simple reason that his own American forces were short of such troops. Already General Marshall had explained to General Giraud, during their July conversations in Washington, the dilemma then facing the War Department in meeting General Eisenhower's requisitions for service units. He had pointed out that the Allied Commander in Chief had been urged to secure French service troops as these would be required to round out French army corps organization.

[1] Memos, Artamonoff for Delaney, 3 Mar 43, and for Gen Adcock, 2 Aug 43, JRC Misc Doc, Item 5–a, Tabs I, T.

General Giraud had made no comment on that point at the time.[2]

On 31 July Eisenhower made it clear that, as he interpreted the ANFA Agreement, French service organizations would be required. Their number, he indicated, was to be decided by negotiation between the proper French military authorities, the JRC, and G–3, AFHQ. In line with this decision, the deputy theater commander, General Hughes, promptly informed General Spalding that in the build-up of the French Army, adequate provision must be made for complete service organizations and installations. U.S. base sections, he pointed out, were currently being taxed to the maximum to provide mobile service units for U.S. fighting forces; the remaining service troops still had the responsibility of receiving shipments from the United States as well as preparing, transporting, and loading supplies from North African ports to advance elements of American combat forces. It was imperative, then, that the French be required to plan for the huge task of supplying such of their forces as would take part in overseas operations.[3]

There could no longer be any doubt that the French were under obligation to provide, from their own manpower resources, the units necessary to support adequately their combat forces. Yet, in their eyes, the issue was far from settled. A heated debate soon arose between the French High Command and AFHQ. The bitter contest was to last to the end of the war.

The feud began in earnest when General Leyer, on 16 September, informed the JRC

that the proposal to add supporting units to the 15 August Plan was unacceptable. French military authorities, he explained, had been led, by "pressing considerations of a moral, psychological, and political nature, more than military," to set a relatively high figure for divisions at the expense of nondivisional combat and service units. The JRC proposal, he agreed, was a reasonable one, but the increase which it advocated simply was out of question. Even as it stood, the 15 August Plan represented a maximum which could be reached only with considerable difficulties. As for modifying it by lowering the number of divisions in order to activate more service units, the French High Command "flatly rejected the idea." The present program, concluded General Leyer, should stand until the liberation of continental France, either in part or in whole, provided additional manpower. Until then, it was adequate to enable the French Army to play the role likely to be assigned to it "within the framework of the Allied armies and with their assistance." [4]

The last part of General Leyer's letter was a clear indication that the French military authorities still entertained hopes of receiving outside assistance in the form of U.S. or British service units. That they also considered the August Plan in its original form as thoroughly adequate was evidenced by the content of a memorandum from the National Defense Committee dated 18 September. Signed by both Generals de Gaulle and Giraud, and addressed to General Marshall and to the heads of the American, British, and Russian Governments, the communication stressed the committee's intention to carry out "in as complete a manner

[2] Memo, Marshall for Somervell, 12 Jul 43, WDCSA 400 France.

[3] Memo, CinC for Chief Liaison Sec AFHQ, 31 Jul 43, JRC 902/II Rearmt Plan; Memo, Hughes for Spalding, 5 Aug 43, JRC 370/003 Employment of Sv Units.

[4] Ltr, Leyer to Spalding, 16 Sep 43, JRC 902/II Rearmt Plan.

as possible" the program as initially established. In support of this intention, the committee pointed out that the total number of effectives soon to be available was estimated at approximately 500,000 men. Significantly, it was silent on the question of service units.[5]

Just what "pressing moral, psychological, and political considerations" motivated French resistance to Allied demands for a self-sustaining French Military Establishment, General Leyer's letter had not stated. But the reasons had long been clear to AFHQ. The French wanted above all a maximum of combat forces as a means of redeeming French honor on the battlefield and restoring France to its former position as a great nation. The same desire had prompted thousands of men, and was inducing still more, to escape from the mother country, often at considerable personal risk, for service with the overseas forces. To them and to most white elements already in North Africa, the idea of serving in administrative, labor, maintenance, or other service units was repugnant. Their reluctance to pick up the shovel instead of the rifle greatly hampered the organizing of service troops. The white manpower reserve was small to start with, and the native element, although numerous, in general made poor technical personnel. Faced with a dearth of men capable of manning highly specialized units, the French High Command reasoned thus: the Allies had the know-how, the technical skills, and a vast manpower reserve; it was up to them, the Americans in particular, to provide the necessary support and thus make it possible for eleven good combat divisions to get into the firing line as speedily as possible. The French

could cite as precedent for their position the fact that the U.S. divisions engaged in combat in World War I were backed largely by French supporting units.[6] The procedure, adopted then as an expedient to hasten the entry of American troops in battle, had worked well. Why couldn't the practice be repeated at least until such time as the liberation of France provided additional technical manpower?

There were other reasons for the attitude of the French High Command regarding supporting troops. In the judgment of Allied observers, a judgment corroborated after the war by French officers, General Giraud and much of his staff lacked technical knowledge and as a result failed to appreciate the importance of adequate support. Their thinking had not progressed beyond the prewar concept. They suffered from the same incomprehension that had been one of the causes of the French Army's downfall in 1940. The JRC could point to the fact that whenever the French General Staff submitted requisitions they invariably gave last priority to the equipping of service units. The same lack of understanding, it must be noted, persisted long after General Giraud's disappearance from the military scene. The French, consequently, never became fully self-sufficient even when fighting on French soil, and the U.S. Army, in the long run, had no other choice but to provide a large part of the necessary support.[7]

The publication in mid-September 1943 by the French military authorities of a chart giving the contemplated dates of complete activation of the principal service units

---

[5] Ltr and Memo, de Gaulle and Giraud to Marshall, 18 Sep 43, CCS 358/3.

[6] See pp. 3–5, above.
[7] Intervs with Col Artamonoff, Dec 49, Col Gardiner, Apr 50, Brig Gen Harold F. Loomis, Jun and Jul 50, and Lt Gen Jean Valluy, Jun 55.

clearly emphasized their inability, or reluctance, to fulfill their obligations in the matter. According to the chart, no more than a nucleus of personnel for any Engineer unit was to be organized before 1 January 1944. The only Engineer depot company planned for the entire French Army was not to be activated until December and then in cadre only. Except for the three Ordnance depot companies about to be equipped from U.S. matériel already at hand, no other Ordnance units were planned for the remaining months of 1943. General Kingman feared that, as a result, the entire load of heavier maintenance and repair for all units of the French Army—except the expeditionary corps—would be thrown on U.S. Ordnance troops. The same held true of transport, gasoline supply, and base depot services, for which few or no units were contemplated in the near future.[8]

AFHQ officials decided to appeal directly to General Giraud. On 9 October General Whiteley, deputy chief of staff, pointed out to the French Commander in Chief that, while the strength and balance of the expeditionary forces in terms of combat units appeared satisfactory, deficiencies in communications and service troops would constitute a grave weakness in a period of offensive operations. Certain adjustments and additions, he asserted, were necessary to provide a more balanced force and ultimately increase its effectiveness. Repeating the warning that resources presently available to the American forces precluded the possibility of filling existing gaps with U.S. units, General Whiteley urged General Giraud to make every effort to provide the required units from French manpower.[9]

General Giraud did not reply for more than two weeks. Meanwhile AFHQ put forward a number of solutions. General Smith, then in Washington, recommended scaling down the rearmament program to perhaps eight divisions.[10] Brig. Gen. Harold F. Loomis, who on 10 October took over the chairmanship of the JRC in replacement of General Spalding, called to other duties, proposed holding up deliveries of equipment for combat troops until the French activated the required number of service units. He believed that, despite admitted difficulties, the service units could be formed without delay. If trained manpower was not available, then French personnel could be attached to U.S. organizations for instruction. Plans had already been discussed between the JRC, NATOUSA Services of Supply, and the French High Command for training a number of French service units by giving them temporary employment with U.S. bases.[11]

General Loomis was convinced that the time had come to force the French military authorities to adopt "a sound program, not just a program." NATOUSA, however, considered that to hold up further deliveries, as he recommended, was premature and, at any rate, should be delayed until General Giraud had replied to General Whiteley's letter of 9 October.[12]

When General Giraud's letter came, on 26 October, it contained nothing at all on the subject of service troops. Instead it suggested an expansion of the whole program

[8] Memo, Kingman for Spalding, 23 Sep 43, JRC 370/003 Employment of Sv Units.
[9] Ltr, Whiteley to Giraud, 9 Oct 43, JRC 370/003 Employment of Sv Units.

[10] Memo, Handy for CofS, 18 Oct 43, OPD 400 France, Sec II.
[11] Memos, Loomis for CofS AFHQ, 23 Oct 43, and Maj Gen Thomas B. Larkin for CG NATOUSA, 12 Sep 43, and Ltr, Leyer to Loomis, 19 Oct 43, JRC 370/003 Employment of Sv Units.
[12] Interv with Loomis, Jun and Jul 50; Memo, Brig Gen E. L. Ford for Loomis, 26 Oct 43, JRC 370/003 Employment of Sv Units.

from eleven to twelve divisions in order to incorporate the 1st Motorized Infantry Division in the North African forces. General Eisenhower's reaction was immediate and blunt. In a strongly worded letter, he first sought to shatter General Giraud's illusions that U.S. service units might be used in support of French combat troops. He ruled out such an arrangement as being "obviously unacceptable." He explained further that he would not commit French forces "even in Metropolitan France" unless they could operate as self-sustaining units—if necessary at the expense of some of the combat units presently set up on the eleven-division program. Immediate adjustments, he warned, must be made to the extent necessary to ensure that each corps, as it was prepared for active operations, would have its full complement of corps and army service elements on a scale comparable to that recommended for the first expeditionary corps.[13]

Echoes of the feud over service units had by this time reached War Department officials and convinced them that the 15 August Plan was inadequate. Before initiating any further assignments to the French, they sought General Eisenhower's opinion. The Allied Commander in Chief replied that a re-examination of the rearmament program was under way, which had in view the establishment of a balanced army "in increments of self-sustaining army corps." Pending the result of this study, the War Department decided to hold up assignments on the third, or November, slice of the 15 August Plan.[14]

General Eisenhower's reply was the first intimation that AFHQ had reached a decision regarding the future tactical employment of the North African forces. G–3 on 3 November confirmed that French Army corps were to be used in increments as self-sustaining units operating with the Allied forces as soon as these corps were prepared to participate in operations. The decision was important in many respects. It would in particular govern all further rearmament operations. According to G–3's instructions, the French program was to be revised with a view to providing (1) in the immediate future: increments of self-sustaining army corps; (2) ultimately: "a balanced army capable of independent and sustained operations and composed of these successive army corps increments plus whatever additional units were necessary."[15] With this twofold objective in mind, the JRC and other interested AFHQ staff sections undertook, once again, to determine the number and types of units to be added to the program.

Simultaneously, General Loomis decided to have a frank talk with the French and inform them of the plans under consideration. Meeting with General Leyer and Colonel Regnault on 7 November, he outlined the reasons for the sudden "sharp change" in the attitude of the U.S. authorities. With the program well under way, a clearer concept was being developed as to how the French Army was to be employed, and the wide scope of the program was being realized. If in recent days the French

[13] Ltr, Giraud to Eisenhower, 26 Oct 43, AFHQ 0100/12C G–3 Div Ops Fr Rearmt; Ltr, Eisenhower to Giraud, 27 Oct 43, JRC 370/003 Employment of Sv Units; also see pp. 88–89, above.

[14] Memo, Col Robert A. Case, Director Stock Control Div ASF, for Director Sup ASF, 3 Nov

43, OPD 400 France, Sec II; Msg 1464, Marshall to Eisenhower, 2 Nov 43, JRC 904 Modification of Rearmt; Msg W–4199/5981, Eisenhower to Marshall, 3 Nov 43, JRC Cable Log; Msg 2702, Marshall to Eisenhower, 17 Nov 43, JRC 903 Requests for Units.

[15] Memo, Rooks To All Concerned, 3 Nov 43, JRC 370/001 Employment of Units.

military authorities had been required to "justify fully" their requirements from U.S. resources, it was because such requirements must be weighed and their need considered in the light of other United Nations demands. For the French alone, there were, in addition to the eleven-division program, a number of other requirements such as maintenance levels, maintenance of the Territorial forces, and POL (petrol, oil, and lubricants) requirements. The size of the Allies' global commitment was such that it was imperative to keep French requests "within minimum requirements." [16]

On 13 November General Eisenhower rejected General Giraud's proposal for an expansion of the ANFA program to twelve divisions. He then seized the opportunity to remind the French Commander in Chief that previous American appeals for a revision of the 15 August Plan had been unheeded, and to reiterate his warning that U.S. service troops would not be provided to support French combat units. He added:

I am now convinced that you should have the program restudied and revised so that the largest possible balanced force will be re-armed. It must be apparent to all that there is nothing gained in raising divisions which, for lack of adequate supporting arms and services, we are unable to employ in combat. . . . As the revised program will be the basis for the supply of U.S. equipment, I naturally wish to approve it before it is sent to the War Department.

Voicing his belief that only by effecting a cutback of the program would the personnel be found for manning the necessary supporting arms and services, General Eisenhower then revealed his intentions in the matter. He proposed to recommend to the

War Department that the equipment for one infantry and two armored divisions be eliminated from the program. It was his hope that the French Commander in Chief would signify his agreement to the proposal or offer any alternative thereto without delay.[17]

While AFHQ staff sections were revising the program along the lines set forth by G–3 on 3 November, General Eisenhower informed the CCS of his proposal to reduce the number of divisions. In anticipation of Giraud's reply, he urged that he be authorized to determine the appropriateness of any solution which General Giraud might offer and, if necessary, to inform the latter that three divisions would definitely be deleted from the program. Such a reduction, he explained, would free qualified troops for the organization of a balanced army adequately supported by the necessary troops and base units.[18]

The French military authorities, it was then learned informally, were planning to submit a counterproposal calling for the elimination of two divisions only (one infantry and one armored), with the justification that they could properly support in personnel the remaining nine. Hopes were high that a satisfactory agreement could be effected between AFHQ and General Giraud in the near future.[19]

On 20 November the JRC submitted to General Giraud a revised version (known thereafter as the 20 November Plan) of the 15 August Plan. Prepared with the assistance of the general and special staff sections of AFHQ, the new plan represented

---

[16] Notes of Conf, Loomis, Leyer, and Regnault, 7 Nov 43, JRC 902/II Rearmt Plan.

[17] Ltr, Eisenhower to Giraud, 13 Nov 43, AFHQ 0100/12C G–3 Div Ops Fr Rearmt.

[18] Ltr, Eisenhower to CCS, 23 Nov 43, in same file.

[19] Memo, Loomis for G–4, 23 Nov 43, JRC 902 Modification of Rearmt.

a substantial increase in service troops and base section units considered necessary for an army of eleven divisions. It was to be used by the French as a basis in deciding how many increments of self-sustaining army corps they could reasonably activate.[20]

General Giraud's long-awaited reply to General Eisenhower's two communications finally came on 29 November.[21] Contrary to all expectations, the French Commander in Chief merely reaffirmed his determination to implement the 15 August Plan in its original form, meanwhile retaining the 1st Motorized Infantry Division as a non-program unit. In support of his position, he furnished statistics intended to show that sufficient white effectives would be found to provide the necessary technicians and specialists. Service units, he explained, would be set up progressively as matériel and troops became available, and in such a manner that the last unit would be ready by 15 July 1944. The 15 August Plan, he asserted in conclusion, could be achieved in its entirety "with a necessary time lag" between the activation of combat units and the setting up of the corresponding services. As for the 20 November Plan, he had requested his staff to study it and he would send his comments on it shortly. A postscript, penned by the general himself, contained this last plea: "At the present time, the main consideration is to equip the divisions as originally contemplated, for which cadre and fighting personnel are now com-

plete. To delay their rearmament will be an error likely to have grave consequences.[22]

AFHQ officials received General Giraud's communication with considerable apprehension. In the opinion of G–3, the French Commander in Chief either failed to understand the importance of providing an army properly balanced in combat and essential service units, or "purposely ignored" the suggestion made to him by General Eisenhower on 13 November. Not only was the proposal to retain the 1st Motorized Infantry Division as an eighth infantry division regarded as likely to aggravate an already serious deficiency in service units, but it was feared that it would result in setting up a force better adapted to an occupational role than combat against a first-class enemy.[23]

Reluctant to act in a manner that might be construed as arbitrary, General Eisenhower agreed to call a conference with the French, presided over by G–3, for the purpose of re-examining the entire rearmament question. To provide the conference with a working basis on which to draft a program commensurate with available qualified manpower, AFHQ staff sections undertook to prepare alternate tables of the minimum essential supporting service and base units for an expeditionary force of 7 infantry and 3 armored divisions, 7 infantry and 2 armored divisions, or 6 infantry and 2 armored divisions. These tables were to serve as a basis for scaling down, if found necessary, the present 20 November Plan of 7 infantry and 4 armored divisions to whichever of the three combinations would be most practicable in the light of French capabilities.

[20] Chart, 20 Nov Plan, AFHQ 0100/12C G–3 Div Ops Fr Rearmt, Vol. I.

[21] On that same day, incidentally, Allied representatives attending the EUREKA Conference (held at Tehran on 28 November–1 December) heard Marshal Joseph Stalin raise the question of French rearmament. President Roosevelt outlined for his benefit the progress achieved to date and disclosed that "nine" divisions, re-equipped and trained by the United States, would soon be ready.

[22] Ltr, Giraud to Eisenhower, 29 Nov 43, JRC 904 Modifications of Rearmt.

[23] Memo, Rooks for CofS AFHQ, 1 Dec 43, AFHQ 0100/12C G–3 Div Ops Fr Rearmt, Vol. I.

Copies of the tables, once completed, were forwarded to the French for their consideration.[24]

As the month of December opened, the rearmament operations were still bogged down. No action beyond shipment of the October slice of the 15 August Plan had been taken to assign equipment. The prospect of an immediate resumption of shipments was dim. Yet the weeks just ended had not been altogether fruitless. The readying of the first French expeditionary forces had gone on at an accelerated pace. In fact it was about to reach its culmination in an event of significant importance.

On 8 December, two days before the scheduled rearmament conference, a U.S.-equipped North African division was committed to combat in Italy. The action resulted from a decision reached at a meeting of the Commanders in Chief held on 3 November, and in execution of plans drawn in August by AFHQ and the French High Command.[25] The division, the 2d Moroccan Infantry (2d DIM), commanded by Maj. Gen. André Dody and accompanied by a regiment of Moroccan goumiers, the 4th Group of Tabors (4th GTM), constituted the advance party of the French increment expected to be engaged in operations in the Italian theater. For the moment, it was to reinforce, and fight as part of, the U.S. VI Corps, one of the component corps of Lt. Gen. Mark W. Clark's Fifth Army, itself part of the Eighth British Army, commanded by General Sir Bernard L. Montgomery. As General Marshall had pointed out a week before in the course of

the Tehran Conference, the build-up of the French increment was to be effected progressively on the basis of the performance of the first division.[26] Actually, however, another division, the 3d Algerian Infantry (3d DIA), under the command of Maj. Gen. Aimé de Goislard de Monsabert, was already en route to join the 2d DIM in battle. The dispatch of these units was consonant with a decision reached by the CCS themselves at the Cairo Conference on the very eve of the engagement of the 2d DIM. All French troops, they had then agreed, would be given battle experience in Italy before their ultimate employment in operations in continental France.[27]

These and other developments were tangible proof that the rearmament operations, notwithstanding their setbacks, were beginning to bear fruit. The entry of the 2d DIM into combat at this juncture was an excellent case in point. The division had been activated, equipped, schooled in the technical use of its matériel, subjected to extensive and intensive tactical training, briefed, shipped, and brought to the front line, all in just seven months. This was a record that those responsible for French rearmament could well be proud of. In addition to the 2d DIM and the 3d DIA, a third division, the 9th Colonial Infantry (9th DIC), was being readied for shipment overseas, and another, the 4th Moroccan Mountain (4th DMM), was completing its re-equipment in Corsica. Of the armored divisions, two (the 1st DB and 5th DB) were ready; a third (the 2d DB), already trained, was waiting for the rest of its equipment.

The 4th GTM entering the front line

---

[24] Memo, Rooks To All Concerned, 4 Dec 43, in same file.

[25] Field Marshal Sir Harold R. L. G. Alexander, *The Allied Armies in Italy From 3rd September 1943, to 12th December 1944* (London: His Majesty's Stationery Office, 1950).

[26] Min, Plenary Sess, 29 Nov 43, EUREKA Conf.

[27] Min, CCS 138th Mtg, 7 Dec 43, SEXTANT Conf.

GOUMIERS OF THE 4TH GROUP OF TABORS, *Italy, December 1943. Men around the fire have American C rations.*

alongside the 2d DIM was one of several smaller organizations which were not originally planned for under the rearmament program, but which the French had activated and made ready largely at the urging of AFHQ. These nonprogram units, most of which were earmarked for service in Italy, included 4 Moroccan tabor groups corresponding to 4 U.S. light infantry regiments, 8 mule pack companies corresponding to 16 U.S. mule pack companies, 1 brigade of spahis corresponding to 1 U.S. horse cavalry regiment, 1 Commando Battalion and 1 Shock Battalion corresponding to 2 U.S. infantry battalions of the Ranger type, various headquarters, and divisional training centers.

The four Moroccan tabor groups, each consisting of three *tabors,* or battalions, represented a total of approximately 13,000 goumiers. The basic organization of these robust, hardy, fearless mountaineers, most of them Berbers from the Atlas region, was the *goum,* or company, of a strength of approximately 220 men including French cadres of 2 officers and 12 noncommissioned officers, and 16 native noncommissioned officers. Because of its extreme mobility and lightness, the goum was regarded by the French military authorities as a sort of "foot cavalry" unit able to accomplish, over difficult terrain, some of the missions ordinarily assigned to mounted cavalry.[28] In view of the mountainous country in which the U.S. Fifth Army was then operating, Allied and French commanders expected to gain substantial advantage from the employment of goumiers. Already a number of tabors had proved their worth in the Tunisian campaign, in the conquest of Sicily, and in the assault on Corsica. All goumiers were, since 1 July 1943, under the operational command of Brig. Gen. Augustin Guillaume.

The mule pack companies were necessary not only for the support of the French divisions being sent to Italy but, as General Smith pointed out in a letter to General Giraud, for the support of the U.S. Fifth Army as a whole. Several such companies were already in Italy.[29]

Operational developments in Italy had prompted AFHQ, in October, to request General Giraud to nominate a horse cavalry regiment for service with the U.S. Fifth Army. General Giraud had then offered a brigade of spahis (native horsemen) consisting of two regiments, the 7th Algerian Spahis and the 5th Moroccan Spahis, with a total strength of approximately 2,200 men. To equip the brigade, the French General Staff had drawn a substantial amount of American equipment from program units, and obtained additional matériel (vehicles, armament, and technical items) from U.S. theater stocks in answer to an urgent appeal from General Giraud. The brigade, incidentally, never reached

Italy; a subsequent change in the operational situation made its dispatch to that theater no longer necessary.[30]

Both the Commando Battalion and the Shock Battalion had been organized from personnel released after the disbandment of the Corps Franc at the close of the Tunisian campaign. The Shock Battalion, it will be recalled, had participated in the liberation of Corsica. The French General Staff had issued both units some American equipment to complete their French matériel. They were not required for service with the Fifth Army, but were being held in readiness for possible employment in the Mediterranean.

All together the equipping of these various nonprogram units had consumed a substantial amount of American equipment originally intended for program units. As a result, program units were feeling more than ever the pinch of shortages. It was imperative, therefore, that some definite policy be established with regard to the present and future equipping of nonprogram units. The issue, in fact, was one of the many questions on the agenda of the armament conference scheduled for 10 December.

Attending the conference, held at AFHQ, were some twenty U.S. officers representing various AFHQ and NATOUSA staff sections and headed by General Smith. The French delegation included General Devinck, chief of General Giraud's personal staff, Colonel Regnault, chief of the French Section, JRC, and other officers from the French General Staff. Opening the meeting, Maj. Gen. Lowell W. Rooks, Assistant Chief of Staff G–3, AFHQ, reiterated the

---

[28] For information concerning the organization and employment of Moroccan goums, see Memo 2453/EMGG/3/CEF, Gen Juin, 15 Jul 43, AFHQ AG Sec 336.2 (Fr) Foreign Armies.

[29] Ltr, Smith to Giraud, 2 Dec 43, JRC 370/001 Employment of Units—Gen.

[30] Ltr, Whiteley to Giraud, 12 Oct 43, Ltrs, Giraud to Eisenhower, 19 Oct, 4 Nov 43, and Ltr, Hq NATOUSA to SOS, 8 Nov 43, JRC 400.1/003 Equip and Sups for Spahis.

SPAHIS IN NORTH AFRICA

need of creating a balanced French force and asked the conference to determine and agree upon a reasonable basis, fully consonant with French manpower availability, on which to establish a final program. To arrive at such a basis, he pointed out, it might be necessary to reduce the number of divisions from 11 to 10, 9, or even 8.

The conferees first examined the practicability of the larger program as revised on 20 November. Speaking for General Giraud, General Devinck, while readily agreeing to the elimination of a fourth corps and of a twelfth division as proposed by the French Commander in Chief in late October, made a strong plea for the retention of the 15 August Plan. The current activation program as developed by the French General Staff, he explained, was based on the assumption that the August Plan was

firm and final. Implementation of the plan, he pointed out in addition, was proceeding satisfactorily, as evidenced by the arrival of the first combat divisions in Italy. Turning to the troublesome question of service units, General Devinck declared that the activation of these units, although now behind schedule, would be effected in due time because the French General Staff was exerting every effort in that direction. Some of the units, he added, were unnecessary in any case. The French Army could do with fewer service units than the U.S. Army; furthermore, inasmuch as it was destined ultimately to operate on home soil, it would be in a position to use local resources.[31]

---

[31] The French were generally of the opinion that the U.S. Army had an overabundance of services some of which would be of little use to their own frugal forces. As an example they pointed out

Apparently impressed by General Devinck's arguments, the conferees attempted to reach a compromise between the 20 November and 15 August Plans by deleting a number of unnecessary service units. Discussions on the matter were to be resumed four days later.[32]

General Devinck's strong assertion that a program of eleven divisions was practicable must be weighed in relation to the stand then taken by other members of the French High Command. From available evidence it appears that the earlier solidarity of French thought on the subject, as reflected in the de Gaulle-Giraud memorandum of 18 September, had dissipated.[33] In fact Giraud's personal staff, of which General Devinck was the chief, and the French General Staff were in sharp disagreement over the matter. Their divergence of views resulted from a different approach to the problem. General Staff officers felt that it would be next to impossible to find the necessary technicians and specialists for seven infantry and four armored divisions as provided under the 15 August Plan. They reasoned as follows. To activate the entire program would require 403,800 men, 147,500 of whom must be Frenchmen to serve as cadres, technicians, and specialists. The prospects of getting this large number of white effectives were slim. Fewer men than originally anticipated were escaping

from France to North Africa. The integration of the Gaullist forces had yielded a relatively small number of Frenchmen. Even with the application of the contemplated mobilization measures (such as the recall of the 1919–35 classes of reservists, that is, of men twenty-nine to forty-four years of age), it was estimated that a total of not more than 138,000 Frenchmen could be found. The resulting deficit in white effectives would amount to approximately 9,500 for the expeditionary forces alone. To this number must be added the white personnel required to maintain both an adequate reserve pool for the combat troops and the military establishments in the zone of interior. In the opinion of the General Staff, therefore, the 15 August Plan could not be implemented until such time as the liberation of part of the Metropolitan territory had yielded additional French manpower.

General Giraud's personal staff, on the other hand, considered the manpower problem from the standpoint of quantity rather than of quality. According to their calculations, the reserve pool for the eleven-division program could reasonably be reduced from 20 percent as now set to 15 percent of the strength of the expeditionary forces. This would lower the minimum of effectives required to 350,750 men. Since it was anticipated that total resources in North Africa could reach 540,000 men, there would be left 189,250 men for purposes other than the expeditionary forces and the reserve pool. With the needs of zone of interior establishments not exceeding 180,000 men, officers of Giraud's personal staff c o n s i d e r e d that available manpower would be more than sufficient to permit the setting up of the entire program. It is interesting to note, incidentally,

that their divisions had no need for laundry companies since African natives, who formed the bulk of their effectives, were used to washing their own linen. See Marey, "Le Réarmement français en Afrique du Nord (1942–1944)," *Revue Politique et Parlementaire* (October, 1947), p. 56.

[32] Min, Fr Rearmt Conf, 10 Dec 43, AFHQ 0100/12C G–3 Div Ops Fr Rearmt, Vol. I.

[33] See Résumé des Opérations de Réarmement, undated and unsigned, original provided by Gen Devinck, copy in Fr Rcds File 218, OCMH; see also Interv with Gen Regnault, Aug 50; de Gaulle and Giraud Ltr and Memo cited n. 5, above.

that in spite of this claim the French military authorities were already having difficulty in sending to Italy the personnel needed to replace the heavy losses currently being sustained by the 2d Moroccan Infantry Division.

At the end of the conference the delegates agreed to reconvene four days later. It was at this juncture, just when negotiations were proceeding satisfactorily although at a slow pace, that a flare-up in the political tug of war between the French Committee of National Liberation and the French High Command threatened, once again, the very existence of the rearmament program.

The 1st DMI Incident

Having been requested by AFHQ several weeks back to nominate a third infantry division for service with the U.S. Fifth Army in Italy, General Giraud had designated the British-equipped 1st Motorized Infantry Division. The reasons for this selection, as he gave them to General Smith, were military as well as political. The 1st DMI was, in his estimation, well trained and contained a high percentage of Foreign Legion troops of first-class fighting capacity. Moreover, it was an ex-Free French unit. As such, its inclusion among the forces being sent to Italy was highly desirable if only to ward off any possible criticism on the part of the Gaullists.[34]

After much exchange of correspondence, AFHQ informed General Giraud on 1 December that the Commanding General, Allied Armies in Italy, General Sir Harold

R. L. G. Alexander, was not prepared to accept the 1st DMI as then equipped but would welcome it if rearmed with U.S. matériel. This view was shared by General Clark in whose Army the French divisions were fighting.[35]

On 3 December, after restating that the 1st DMI could not be employed as currently equipped, AFHQ requested General Giraud, in view of the urgency of the matter, to nominate at once another infantry division to be ready for embarkation beginning 20 December. General Giraud promptly announced that he was assigning the American-equipped 9th Colonial Infantry Division (9th DIC) in lieu of the 1st DMI.[36]

Apprised of this nomination, the National Defense Committee, acting presumably under authority of the decree of 2 October 1943, rejected General Giraud's decision twenty-four hours after it had been announced.[37] Endorsing General de Gaulle's views on the subject, the members of the committee, excepting of course General Giraud, ordered that the designation of the 1st DMI be maintained. Their action was indicative that the French Commander in Chief no longer held any influence with the committee. To many an observer it seemed but a matter of a short time before he would be relegated to a back seat and possibly forced to withdraw entirely from the military scene. Informal word of the committee's action, followed one day later by offi-

---

[34] Ltr, Smith to Giraud, 18 Nov 43, AFHQ 0100/12C G–3 Div Ops Fr Corres; Hq Fr High Comd, GO 14, 18 Nov 43, quoted in Memo, G–3 Fr CinC's Personal Staff, n. d., copy in OCMH; Msg 6357, Smith to CG 15th Army Gp, 27 Nov 43, JRC Cable Log.

[35] Msg MA–792, Alexander to CinC AFHQ, 30 Nov 43, JRC Cable Log.
[36] Ltr, Giraud to Eisenhower, 9 Dec 43, AFHQ 0100/12C G–3 Div Ops Authority for Control of Fr Exp Forces.
[37] Article 6 of the decree: "Within the scope of the directives of the CFLN, the National Defense Committee shall decide upon the over-all plans concerning the organization, distribution, and employment of the French forces."

cial confirmation from General Giraud, reached AFHQ just as General Devinck was pleading for the retention of the eleven-division program.[38] Its effect could not be anything but detrimental, especially at a time when Franco-American relations were already strained. AFHQ viewed the action with considerable apprehension. G–3 officials in particular regarded it as a threat to the successful prosecution of the war.

Complying with the National Defense Committee's decision, General Giraud ordered the immediate integration of the 1st DMI in the rearmament program as one of the seven infantry divisions, a course of action which elicited a word of praise from General Eisenhower.[39] The length of time required to re-equip and train the division with American matériel was bound to delay its departure for several months. The delay in turn seriously threatened the success of operations in Italy. Later events demonstrated that the threat was real. The 2d DIM and 3d DIA, regrouped in early January 1944 as the nucleus of a separate corps, known thereafter as the French Expeditionary Corps (Corps Expéditionnaire Français—CEF), under the command of General Juin, did not receive a third division until the end of February, instead of mid-January as had been hoped. For lack of reinforcements during the intervening six weeks, General Juin was unable to exploit the successes achieved by his forces north of

Cassino.[40] The third division to join the CEF, it must be noted, was the 4th Moroccan Mountain, commanded by Maj. Gen. François Sevez, ready long before the 1st DMI. The 1st DMI, under the command of Brig. Gen. Charles Brosset, arrived finally in April as the fourth and last division of the CEF.

The committee's action in reversing General Giraud's decision focused attention on an important and delicate issue, present since November 1942, but one that had engaged only the sporadic attention of Anglo-American authorities, namely, the question of the control of French forces. No firm understanding had yet been reached regarding the matter other than the arrangement set forth in the Clark-Darlan Agreement of 22 November 1942. The agreement stipulated that the status, command, functions, employment, rights, and privileges of the French land, sea, and air forces were to remain "under French direction." No basis, therefore, existed on which the Allied Commander in Chief could claim authority to issue orders either to the French Commander in Chief, to the French Committee of National Liberation, or to the latter's military representative, the National Defense Committee, concerning the disposal of French forces. Eisenhower was in fact dependent on voluntary French acquiescence in his proposals. In the past, it had been possible to deal directly with Giraud with reasonable assurance that just demands would be met. The committee's recent action constituted a reversal of the existing arrangement and a dangerous precedent. The time had come to obtain the CFLN's agreement that in the future the troops in-

---

[38] Ltr 924/3.S, Giraud to AFHQ, 11 Dec 43, quoted in Memo, G–3 for CofS, 11 Dec 43, AFHQ 0100/12C G–3 Div Ops Authority for Control of Fr Exp Forces.

[39] In a letter to General Giraud, General Eisenhower praised the French Commander in Chief for "sacrificing" some of his own desires in order "to promote the best interests of the French and a better understanding among the Allies." Ltr, Eisenhower to Giraud, 31 Dec 43, AFHQ SACS Red Sec, Fr Matters, Gen Giraud.

[40] General Marcel Carpentier, *Les Forces Alliées en Italie; la Campagne d'Italie* (Paris: Berger-Levrault, 1949), p. 69.

cluded in the rearmament program would be made available as and when requested, for employment in areas and under commands designated by the Allied Commander in Chief. Divisions, corps, and armies, when employed as such, would of course be under French commanders. Convinced that the practice of dealing directly with the French Commander in Chief was desirable and should be continued, General Rooks suggested that "the onus of getting the required guarantee from the Committee should be placed on him." [41]

In line with this recommendation, Eisenhower requested General Giraud, on 14 December, to transmit to the CFLN the following warning. In view of the National Defense Committee's action, which from the tactical standpoint entailed "grave consequences," the rearmament program would not be continued unless the CFLN gave definite assurance that the use of the rearmed forces would be "governed solely by military considerations and subject to the decisions of the Combined Chiefs of Staff through their representative, the Allied CinC in this Theater." [42] AFHQ immediately cabled a copy of Eisenhower's letter to the CCS and informed President Roosevelt and Prime Minister Churchill of the incident. The President requested General Marshall to keep him abreast of subsequent developments. [43]

General Giraud was now placed in a doubly embarrassing position, for the warning which he was to transmit to the CFLN was the indirect result of one of his own decisions. The committee seized the opportunity to tighten further its grip on the control of French military affairs. By a new decree on the Organization of the High Command, issued on 16 December, the CFLN transferred much of the power heretofore vested in the Commander in Chief to the National Defense Committee. Thereafter the National Defense Committee was to make all decisions concerning the employment and distribution of forces as well as the general armament and organization programs. The Commander in Chief was "appointed by decree of the CFLN." Placed on a level with both the Commissioner of War and Air and the Commissioner of the Navy, he was to "take part" in rearmament discussions and negotiations, and countersign all rearmament requisitions submitted by the individual Commissioners in accordance with the general directives of the National Defense Committee. [44]

To say that the 16 December decree had curtailed General Giraud's functions would be an understatement. By it, the only forces left under his control were the expeditionary forces, and even his control over them ceased the moment they were committed to an overseas operation, for they then passed under Allied command. All other forces were under the direct control of the Commissioners of War and Air and of the Navy. Commenting on the implications of this and other decrees, [45] AFHQ officials

[41] Memo, Rooks for Smith, 12 Dec 43, AFHQ 0100/12C G–3 Div Ops Authority for Control of Fr Exp Forces.

[42] Ltr, Eisenhower to Giraud, 14 Dec 43, AFHQ 0100/12C G–3 Div Ops Authority for Control of Fr Exp Forces.

[43] Msg, Eisenhower to CCS, 15 Dec 43, NAF 548; Msg W–8446, Eisenhower to Marshall, 24 Dec 43, AFHQ 0100/12C G–3 Div Ops Fr Rearmt, Vol. I; Msg WX–5492, Marshall to Eisenhower, 22 Dec 43, OPD Cable Files.

[44] Decree of 16 Dec 43, CFLN, JRC 320/004 Orgn of Fr Army.

[45] Such as the decree concerning the Organization of the Expeditionary Ground Forces, dated 7 January 1943 and signed by General de Gaulle and André Le Troquer, Commissioner of War and Air.

admitted that the authority of the French Commander in Chief was on its way to becoming "negligible." They agreed, however, that since he was being held "responsible for liaison," the practice of dealing with him should continue as before until such time as it would prove ineffective.[46]

Meanwhile, General de Gaulle, as President of the CFLN, had asked for a conference with representatives of the Allied Commander in Chief to discuss the terms of the assurance required of the committee in connection with the control of French forces. The meeting, first planned for 24 December but postponed pending the outcome of another serious French political crisis, was held three days later in General de Gaulle's office.[47] It was attended by General Smith, Edwin Wilson, Minister of the United States, Harold Macmillan, Minister of the United Kingdom, and René Massigli, French Commissioner of Foreign Affairs. Massigli handed to his American and British colleagues the text of a draft agreement prepared by the CFLN setting forth the conditions under which the Allied Commander in Chief could employ the land, sea, and air forces placed at his disposal by the committee. Smith then informed Massigli that a recent CCS decision to undertake an assault on continental France in the near

future envisaged the participation of all French land and air forces, whether American- or British-equipped. The greater part of the land forces, he added, would be employed as a French army in an operation of which he gave the general outline and the approximate location.[48]

The decision to which General Smith referred had been made a fortnight before in the course of the Cairo Conference. The Combined Chiefs had agreed that the cross-Channel attack (OVERLORD), with a target date of 1 May, would be supported by a simultaneous assault on southern France (ANVIL, later DRAGOON). They had decided further that the bulk of the French forces would participate in ANVIL, and only a token force in OVERLORD. The CCS agreement that the rearmed forces would ultimately be employed on French soil was a momentous one. It would tend to reassure the French that their legitimate ambition to participate in the liberation of their homeland would be fulfilled. It would also serve to stimulate interest in French rearmament, for it represented a definite objective on which AFHQ and the War Department could base the next phase. Once the extent of French participation in both OVERLORD and ANVIL had been determined, it would be relatively easy to develop and implement a final program.[49]

Two days after the conference in General de Gaulle's office, Massigli informed the British and American political representatives that General Smith's disclosures regarding the future employment of the French forces had "removed the essential anxieties" of the CFLN. As a result, the

---

[46] Memo, G–3 Opns for G–3 Sec AFHQ, 20 Jan 44, AFHQ 0100/12C G–3 Div Ops Fr Negotiations, No. 1, Vol. II.

[47] Informed that the CFLN was planning to mete out severe punishment in the case of several officials who in the past had shown strong pro-Vichy tendencies, President Roosevelt requested General Eisenhower on 22 December to "direct" the committee to take no action against these individuals at the present time in view of the assistance given by them to the Allied armies during the campaign in Africa. The CFLN complied with the request. Msg 5456, WAR to Algiers (secret and personal from the President for Gen Eisenhower), 22 Dec 43, White House File.

[48] Ltr, Massigli to Wilson, 30 Dec 43, AFHQ 0100/12C G–3 Div Ops Fr Negotiations, No. 1, Vol. II.

[49] Min, CCS 136th Mtg, 4 Dec 43, and CCS 138th Mtg, 7 Dec 43, SEXTANT Conf.

CONFERENCE IN ALGIERS, *November 1943. From left: René Massigli, Andrei Y. Vishinsky, Maj. Gen. Walter Bedell Smith, Harold Macmillan, and Robert D. Murphy. The 27 December meeting was attended by Edwin Wilson, Minister of the United States, and those shown in the photograph except for Mr. Vishinsky.*

committee had decided to place these forces at the disposal of the CCS to be used by the Allied Commander in Chief, in consultation with the French High Command, for the execution of the contemplated operations. While eager not to hinder the conduct of these operations, the committee reserved the right to appeal to the American and British governments, and the right of the French High Command to appeal to the Allied Commander in Chief to ensure that the use of the forces in question would take French interests into account "as completely as possible." [50]

The solution offered by the CFLN for the control of French forces was received by AFHQ with considerable satisfaction. As General Eisenhower had been given to expect by his advisers, the committee had recognized the "reasonableness" of his demands, and in turn was making a reasonable proposal.[51] It now remained for the CCS to settle the issue. For the moment the danger of a serious crisis had subsided. The tension brought about by the 1st DMI episode was rapidly abating. On 4 January AFHQ informed the CCS of the details of the CFLN proposals, adding these comfort-

[50] Ltr, Massigli to Wilson, 30 Dec 43, AFHQ 0100/12C G–3 Div Ops Fr Negotiations, No. 1, Vol. II.

[51] Msg W–8446, Eisenhower to Marshall, 24 Dec 43, AFHQ 0100/12C G–3 Div Ops Fr Rearmt, Vol. I.

ing words: "The equipping of the French forces is continuing." [52]

Cutback of the Program—The 23 January Plan

Staff discussions, meanwhile, had gone on undisturbed. The problems raised in the course of the 10 December conference were taken up again at the second meeting held as scheduled four days later. The conferees examined once more the 20 November Plan and proceeded to reduce it by eliminating certain unnecessary engineer, field artillery, and antiaircraft artillery units. General Devinck then expressed his conviction that the French High Command had the necessary personnel to fulfill the program as now revised. Turning to the question of nonprogram units, he urged that some provision be made for their equipment. These units, he pointed out, had been requested for employment by the Allies and a number of them were already in Italy. After some discussion, the conferees agreed, in part, that (1) the JRC would, as a matter of urgency, examine the revised program in the light of available qualified French manpower, and determine whether or not it could be effectively fulfilled; (2) the French High Command would make available to the JRC all pertinent information needed for such an examination; (3) the schedule for activating and equipping units in the program would be phased so that the forces could be made ready for employment in increments of self-sustaining army corps with proportionate supporting combat and service units for the corps, army and base installations; and (4) some provision would be made for the issue of equipment to nonprogram units.[53]

Immediately after the conference, the French military authorities took steps to force a decision with respect to the provision of equipment to nonprogram units. In their opinion the matter was a serious one, for the issue of U.S. matériel to these units had produced critical shortages in the equipment of program units. To fill these shortages, they announced their intention to submit additional requisitions. Commenting on the proposal, General Loomis declared himself opposed to requisitioning complete initial equipment for the nonprogram units since they were basically French-equipped. He considered that their inclusion on the program for maintenance only would adequately take care of their needs. His recommendation was endorsed by G–3 and G–4, AFHQ, and, for the moment at least, made the basis of the theater's policy on the matter.[54]

General Eisenhower had already informed the War Department that he would soon forward, for submission to the CCS, the final recommendations of the theater on the auxiliary units to be added to the program. He had also indicated that an entirely new project, incidental to the rearmament program and under consideration at AFHQ for some time, was being transmitted to Washington by separate cable, likewise for submission to the CCS.[55]

The new project concerned the provision of matériel to French Communications Zone establishments considered necessary to

[52] Msg W–9307/23731, Eisenhower to CCS, 4 Jan 44, NAF 579.

[53] Min, Fr Rearmt Conf, 14 Dec 43, AFHQ 0100/12C G–3 Div Ops Fr Rearmt, Vol. I.

[54] Memos, Regnault for Loomis, 15 Dec 43, and Loomis for G–3 AFHQ, 15 Dec 43, JRC 904 Modification of Rearmt.

[55] Msg W–7569, Eisenhower to AGWAR, 14 Dec 43, in same file.

maintain the normal life of the expeditionary forces. The question was not a new one. In fact, since February 1943, the War Department had been shipping maintenance materials for these establishments, such as ammunition, petroleum, and subsistence, at the rate of approximately 4,000 tons monthly and on the basis of requisitions submitted by the French Military Mission in Washington.[56] The French, however, had come to regard this assistance as totally inadequate and not commensurate with the expansion of their expeditionary forces. The question of increasing this assistance came up in the fall of 1943 in connection with a study of French maintenance requirements for the future months. In early October War Department officials requested the French military authorities to prepare, with the assistance of the JRC, and submit without delay an estimate of their maintenance requirements for the calendar years 1944 and 1945. This estimate was to be incorporated in the Army Supply Program then under preparation in Washington. It was to include a computation of the maintenance requirements on all matériel, American, British, French, and enemy-captured, other than that sent from the United States under the rearmament program. The War Department, lacking adequate information, delegated the study to the theater. In mid-October General Leyer submitted to the JRC a number of requisitions. At the same time the National Defense Committee produced a long memorandum which the French Military Mission in Washington passed on to General Marshall.[57]

An analysis of these various documents revealed that they envisaged new projects extending far beyond the maintenance of the forces being rearmed under the current program and the Communications Zone troops assigned to the support of expeditionary forces. The new projects included additional units to be activated from manpower resources of the French Union not presently utilized for the build-up of the expeditionary forces, a task force for employment in the Far East, and units to be activated in continental France once OVERLORD and ANVIL had been launched.

American officials promptly turned down these proposals. They regarded them as going "far beyond any possibility of early consideration by the CCS" and, insofar as the Army Supply Program was concerned, as wholly irrelevant.[58] In General Marshall's opinion, the projects, especially the proposal to rearm Metropolitan forces, were matters for decision by President Roosevelt inasmuch as they involved far-reaching questions of policy.[59] On 4 November General Loomis informed General Leyer that the theater would retain, for consideration and processing, only that portion of the requisitions which dealt with the Communications Zone establishments. He pointed out that the French High Command was at liberty to take up all other projects, if it so wished, directly with the War Department through the French Military Mission.[60]

The requisitions submitted by General Leyer on behalf of the Communications Zone troops were quite substantial. To

---

[56] Memo, Loomis for CG NATOUSA, 12 Mar 44, JRC 400.4/002 Maintenance for Territorial Forces.

[57] Ltrs, Leyer to Loomis, 5 Oct, 18 Oct, 20 Oct 43, JRC 907 Rearmt Plan '44–45; Memo, National Defense Committee for Fr Military Mission for Marshall, 16 Oct 43, ABC 091.711 France (6 Oct 43), Sec 1–A.

[58] Memo, Loomis for Deputy Theater Comdr, 4 Nov 43, JRC 907 Rearmt Plan '44–45.

[59] Memo, Marshall for JCS, 2 Nov 43, ABC 091.711 France (6 Oct 45), Sec 2–A.

[60] Memo, Loomis for Leyer, 4 Nov 43, JRC 907 Rearmt Plan '44–45.

justify their validity as well as urgency, he sent to General Loomis, on 10 November, a detailed report. The forces in question, he explained, fell into two categories, namely, Sovereignty and Territorial forces.

Sovereignty forces were the Army units, none larger than a regiment, and service organizations whose functions General Leyer described as follows: to ensure French sovereignty over the North and West African territory after the departure of the expeditionary forces for overseas service, to maintain internal order, and to assume the coastal and antiaircraft defense of the territory as well as the guarding of airfields, depots, and POW camps. These forces represented a total strength then estimated at 103,000 men for both North and West Africa. Of these, 8,000 were already employed by U.S. military authorities as guards in American POW camps.

Territorial forces were the forces responsible for the running of headquarters, training centers, schools, port bases, hospitals, shops, Quartermaster depots, and other similar establishments. Representing a total of some 100,000 men, these troops worked almost exclusively for the support of expeditionary units.

The equipment then in the hands of both Sovereignty and Territorial forces was, explained General Leyer, in deplorable condition. All of it was of old French stock and was now worn out. It was urgent, he concluded, to provide these troops with initial equipment in addition to maintenance materials, lest the expeditionary forces themselves be deprived of proper support in the immediate future.[61]

General Loomis was fully aware of the conditions described by the French Chief of

Staff and recognized the necessity of furnishing equipment at least to the forces and establishments devoting their activities to the support of expeditionary forces. He urged General Smith to consider the preparation of a separate project for submission to the CCS. With this in view, he proceeded to list the Territorial establishments which he considered indispensable, and estimated the personnel necessary to run them at 93,000 men. He then recommended that maintenance only be issued to these establishments, and that no consideration be given, for the moment, to the requirements of Sovereignty forces.[62] Endorsing these recommendations, General Eisenhower requested the CCS to authorize the issue of specific materials, largely nonmilitary, to such Communications Zone establishments as the theater considered necessary. Prompt approval of the project, he pointed out, would ensure the proper support of the expeditionary forces expected to be re-equipped under the rearmament program as currently revised.[63]

The revision of the program was, of course, the main issue still to be solved. The two armament conferences had emphasized the desire of the French High Command to implement the eleven-division program in its entirety. General Giraud had not replied to Eisenhower's proposal, made on 13 November, to reduce the number of divisions to be rearmed. The growing suspicion that he was not prepared to change his views on the subject gained weight when AFHQ officials learned that he had appealed directly to General Marshall.

The American Chief of Staff had, by his

---

[61] Ltr, Leyer to Loomis, 10 Nov 43, JRC 400.4/002 Maintenance for Territorial Forces.

[62] Memos, Loomis for CofS AFHQ, 13 Nov, 29 Nov, 4 Dec 43, and Memo, Loomis for G–4, 4 Dec 43, in same file.

[63] Msg W–7589/13853, Eisenhower to CCS, 14 Dec 43, NAF 546.

attitude and utterances in the course of the preceding months, shown himself to be a firm and constant advocate of French rearmament. General Giraud had not failed to recognize this fact and to express to General Marshall, as he did again in a New Year's greeting, his appreciation.[64] It was to be expected that in his final attempt to retain the original program, Giraud would appeal to the one American official whom he regarded as his stanchest supporter. In a letter submitted on his behalf, Lt. Gen. Paul Beynet, the new chief of the French Military Mission in Washington, assured Marshall that the reluctance of the French military authorities to accept AFHQ's proposal to eliminate three divisions from the program was not due to lack of good will on their part.[65] Rather it resulted from the impossibility of reaching a satisfactory solution to the problem of service troops. To convert into service units, he explained, good combat divisions now trained in the use of U.S. weapons and presently awaiting their final equipment would result in a lowering of morale bound to affect the entire French Army. The conversion, in any case, was not likely to produce efficient service units considering that the personnel so transferred, mostly native, had none of the professional aptitude or skill required to make good mechanics or technicians. In short, to adopt the proposal advocated by AFHQ would merely result in breaking up excellent fightings units and necessitate their replacement by American combat units. The help

of the American services, therefore, was a primary necessity, if only to eliminate the need for a greater number of U.S. divisions.[66]

The argument was one which General Marshall could not dismiss lightly considering his often repeated statement that it was more economical for the United States to rearm available French manpower than to ship both equipment and American manpower overseas. But the decision regarding the composition of the French forces, while subject to CCS approval, rested with General Eisenhower. It was not likely that he and his staff would retreat from the firm position they had taken regarding the necessity for the French forces to become self-sustaining. In his answer to General Beynet, Marshall merely observed that "the present position is that we are awaiting a reply from General Giraud." The French Commander in Chief had still to be heard from regarding Eisenhower's proposal to reduce the program.[67]

The position of the theater had been made unmistakably clear to the French only a few days before by the Allied Commander in Chief himself. About to leave North Africa to take up in London his new post of Supreme Commander for the cross-Channel operation, General Eisenhower had paid an impromptu visit to General de Gaulle. One of the subjects he brought up for discussion was the controversy over service troops. First he offered this sound advice: "We must not be mesmerized by the number of divisions to be rearmed." Professing not to know what this number was, he stressed that it was better to have one division completely organized than several

---

[64] Msg 109 BT, Giraud to Marshall (signed Eisenhower), 31 Dec 43, OCS A–48–11 (091 France Sec 1).

[65] General Beynet was appointed Chief, French Military Mission in the United States, in November 1943, in replacement of General Béthouart, who was recalled to North Africa to take command of an Army corps.

[66] Ltr, Beynet to Marshall, 3 Jan 44, Somervell Files, Fr 1943–44, A–46–257, Ser 1, Dr 3.

[67] Ltr, Marshall to Beynet, 5 Jan 44, in same file.

which were not. General de Gaulle immediately declared himself in agreement with this view. The correct policy was, he recognized, to complete the activation and equipping of some units before trying to form others. He agreed that they must be "made complete above all from the standpoint of Services" even if this meant that their number could not reach that which was at first contemplated. Still, he hoped that it would be possible to arm six infantry and three armored divisions as well as three army corps headquarters and have them ready by 1 April 1944. General Jean de Lattre de Tassigny, under whose command it was intended to place these forces, was to go into the details of their organization. The matter, he agreed, was one to be handled "meticulously and thoroughly." Apparently pleased by these arrangements, General Eisenhower then made clear to de Gaulle that he intended to use a token French force in the cross-Channel operation: "I will not enter Paris without the French at my side." [68]

General de Gaulle's statements were an indication that his concept of armament problems was more realistic than General Giraud's. Granted that he did not feel the moral obligation, as Giraud did, of holding firmly to the ANFA Agreement since he had not been a party to it, his views nevertheless were known to be more in line with those held by AFHQ officials. [69] At any rate, Eisenhower's advice not to be mesmerized by the number of divisions to be re-equipped had accurately identified the chief weakness in General Giraud's reasoning. The French Commander in Chief's insistence on adhering strictly to the original eleven-

division program was understandable from both the psychological and national points of view. Yet it could hardly stand up against the realities of the time. Primarily it was irreconcilable with the firm American decision not to provide troops and services in support of the French expeditionary forces.

Meeting on 31 December, the CCS rejected Eisenhower's proposal of 23 November that he be authorized to determine the appropriateness of any solution of the rearmament problem which Giraud might propose. They felt and agreed that, for the sake of co-ordination on the part of the agencies involved, matters pertaining to French rearmament should continue to be presented for their consideration with the recommendation of the Allied Commander in Chief in the theater. [70] The decision was communicated to General Sir Henry Maitland Wilson, who was succeeding General Eisenhower in the Mediterranean with the new title of Supreme Allied Commander, Mediterranean Theater. [71]

The Munitions Assignments Board had made no assignments to the French since October but was ready to resume them if and when the theater so requested. For some time now, the theater had delayed taking final action on the proposed reduction of the program pending word from General Giraud. [72] AFHQ, however, could wait no longer. The decision to use the bulk of the French forces in the ANVIL operation on 1 May made it necessary to end policy debates. On 1 January AFHQ set the deadline for the readiness of participating French troops at 1 April. With only

---

[68] Min of Interv, Eisenhower with de Gaulle, 30 Dec 43, JRC 908 Policy and Plan—Misc.

[69] Interv with Loomis, Jun 50.

[70] Min, CCS 139th Mtg, 31 Dec 43.

[71] Msg 6133, CCS to AFHQ, 1 Jan 44, FAN 288.

[72] Rpt, MAB to CCS, 31 Dec 43, sub: Status of Fr Rearmt Program, ABC 091.711 France (6 Oct 43), Sec 2–a.

three months left for preparations, there could no longer be any question of devoting further effort to revising the 15 August Plan. Instead it was imperative to determine what units were considered essential for the contemplated operations and whether or not they could be equipped and made ready by 1 April.

Expecting that a firm French troop list for ANVIL would soon be established, AFHQ agreed to resume shipments from the United States. On 1 January the JRC ordered the equipment for those units of the November and December slices of the August Plan which it considered essential for the contemplated operations, and which in its estimation the French could be expected to have trained and ready by 1 April. The JRC eliminated all other units, such as one army corps headquarters, one armored division, one tank destroyer battalion, four shore battalions, and various supporting units for which the French did not have the necessary trained personnel. Furthermore, in anticipation of a reduction of the over-all program, the committee requested the War Department to place the remaining infantry division of the November slice in last priority. On 2 January General Loomis queried the War Department regarding the possibility of equipping eighty-three other supporting combat and service organizations whose addition to the August Plan was considered necessary. No equipment was currently available for these units in North Africa.[73]

On 9 January Lt. Gen. J. A. H. Gammell, successor to General Smith as Chief of Staff, AFHQ, informed General Giraud of the measures being taken by AFHQ as a result of the limited time available for preparations. He urged Giraud to bend all efforts to provide units for which there was urgent need, and to postpone the formation of those not required in the immediate future. Appended to his communication was a list of units on the 15 August Plan no longer considered essential and therefore being deferred, and of those urgently needed by 1 April or immediately after that date for which equipment would be made available if they could be trained and made ready in due time.[74]

General Gammell's letter brought an immediate reply from General Giraud. While signifying his agreement in principle, the French Commander in Chief restated his intention of retaining "as a basis" the 15 August Plan. He confirmed the news that had already reached AFHQ informally that the National Defense Committee had ordered the deactivation of two infantry divisions (the 8th Algerian Infantry and the 10th Colonial Infantry). The action, he pointed out, was expected to make available large numbers of personnel for the creation of supporting units. Giraud then voiced his belief that it would be possible at a later date to set up the units deferred at this time, in particular the fourth armored division.[75]

AFHQ's proposal to eliminate the fourth armored division from the program had greatly distressed General Giraud. In a moving appeal to General Marshall, he explained that he had consented to the elimination of two infantry divisions in order to retain the fourth armored division. He urged Marshall to demonstrate once again

---

[73] Msg 22135/W–9044, Eisenhower to AGWAR, 1 Jan 44, JRC Cable Log; Memo, Loomis for Lutes, 2 Jan 44, JRC 904 Modification of Rearmt; Msg W–9934/27229, Wilson to CCS, 11 Jan 44, NAF 586.

[74] Ltr, Gammell to Giraud, 9 Jan 44, JRC 903 Requests for Units.

[75] Ltr, Giraud to Wilson, 11 Jan 44, in same file.

his "sympathy for France" by pressing for the maintenance of a unit which, for tactical reasons, would be "indispensable" in the forthcoming operations.[76]

The National Defense Committee's decision to abolish two infantry divisions, confirmed in General Giraud's Order 16 of 11 January, had been reached after the committee became convinced that no other step could produce personnel for service units. Even officers of General Giraud's personal staff, who for several months had fought tooth and nail for the retention of the entire program, had finally come to the conclusion that deficits in technical personnel were too great to permit implementation of the program in its entirety. The elimination of two infantry rather than one armored and one infantry divisions had been decided upon by the committee for two reasons. First, it was expected to yield 3,500 more men. Second, it would make it possible, much as Giraud himself had indicated in his last letter to General Marshall, to retain the greatest possible number of armored divisions whose role in the forthcoming operations the committee considered important. The French General Staff was planning to use the 30,000-odd men now made available to fill deficits in two other divisions (the 7th Algerian and 9th Colonial Infantry Divisions), to provide personnel for supporting combat and service units, and finally to complete army corps headquarters and base units.[77]

AFHQ officials did not share the French view on the fourth armored division. In their judgment, terrain in southern France did not favor the employment of armor.

They had fixed the composition of the French-U.S. invading force at two armored to eight infantry divisions. The two armored divisions, they agreed, would be provided by the French, and a third French armored division, if required, would be employed in the cross-Channel operation. They saw no use, therefore, for the fourth armored division (the 3d DB), which the French had already organized and partly equipped.[78] Moreover, they suspected that the French action in deactivating two infantry divisions would result, in practice, in the elimination of only one from the program. Indeed the 1st DMI, heretofore retained as a twelfth nonprogram division, was now being incorporated in the program. There would still be left, in effect, six infantry and four armored divisions, or a total of ten. Such an arrangement hardly accorded with the recommendations of the theater that the program be reduced to eight divisions.

The need for a speedy decision in the matter was becoming increasingly urgent if only for psychological reasons. Uncertainty as to their future was causing a marked lowering of morale among the officers and men of the two divisions whose fate was still in the balance. These were the 3d Armored and the 7th Algerian Infantry. The 3d DB was only partly equipped and trained. The 7th DIA had at one time received most of its American equipment and had done considerable training. In recent weeks some of its matériel had been turned over to the Spahis Brigade; now more of it was being transferred to the 1st DMI.[79]

Once they had eliminated the 8th DIA

[76] Ltr, Giraud to Marshall, 10 Jan 44, OPD 336.2 France, Sec 2.

[77] Résumé des Opérations de Réarmement, Fr Reds File 218, OCMH.

[78] Msg 578, Devers to Marshall, 28 Jan 44, CM-IN 19255.

[79] Memo, Loomis for G–3 AFHQ, 30 Dec 43, JRC 370/001 Employment of Units—Gen.

and 10th DIC, the French military authorities undertook to revise their activation program on the basis of manpower now available to them. On 17 January the National Defense Committee submitted to the JRC a copy of the revised program together with appropriate requisitions for matériel with which to equip new units. The program represented an attempt to effect a compromise between the demands of AFHQ for certain essential supporting units and the French desire to retain units recently deferred by AFHQ. It still included a fourth armored division, although in second priority, as well as a number of units which AFHQ considered no longer necessary. Anticipating that AFHQ would raise objections to their proposal, the committee asked that a conference be held without delay at which representatives of the French General Staff would furnish all pertinent information.[80]

While the French proposal was being studied by the JRC, discouraging news was received from Washington. The CCS, it was learned, had approved only partially the recommendations submitted by the theater in mid-December on behalf of French Communications Zone establishments.[81] They ruled out the provision of organizational equipment and authorized only the issue of certain maintenance materials generally falling into the category of expendable supplies, and of such indispensable items (tools, electrical machines, and so on) as could not be obtained from other sources, provided the French would present sufficient military justification for each request.[82] In

short, the Combined Chiefs were not approving the full amount of even the rather limited quantities of matériel which the theater had requested initially. In a subsequent meeting with Brig. Gen. Auguste Brossin de Saint-Didier, the new chief of the French Military Mission in the United States, about to depart for Washington, General Loomis urged his visitor to take the matter up directly with the War Department. He expressed the hope that a personal approach would succeed where impersonal cables had failed in securing the necessary supplies.[83]

The conference requested by the National Defense Committee was held on 22 January. It was attended by Brig. Gen. William C. Crane, Deputy Assistant Chief of Staff, G–3, Generals Loomis and Leyer, Colonels Blanc and Regnault, and other officers. After much discussion, the conferees drafted a list of the units considered necessary for participation in ANVIL. The list represented in effect the basis of a final rearmament program. It was immediately submitted to the National Defense Committee, which approved it formally on 23 January. The committee agreed that the troops needed to implement the plan, known thereafter as the 23 January Plan, were to be drawn from the 7th DIA and the 3d DB. These two organizations were to be retained in cadre only, in the hope that they would be reactivated and equipped at some later date.[84] As Colonel Regnault pointed out to General Loomis, the action constituted a "painful sacrifice" for the divisions concerned. The French High Command

[80] Ltr, Regnault to Loomis, 17 Jan 44, JRC 903 Requests for Units.

[81] Msg NAF 546 cited n. 63, above.

[82] Msg 7468, CCS to Wilson, 18 Jan 44, FAN 321, as corrected by Msg 8743, AGWAR to Devers, 3 Feb 44; Msg 267, AGWAR to Devers, 20 Feb 44, JRC Cable Log.

[83] Min, Conf Loomis with de Saint-Didier, 12 Feb 44, AFHQ 0100/26 Liaison Sec 337 (Fr) Mtgs and Confs, Vol. I.

[84] Decision, National Defense Committee, 23 Jan 44, Rearmament Plan for Ground Forces, JRC 902/I Rearmt Plan.

would try not to disintegrate their component elements but use them as constituted units within other organizations so as to maintain coherence and efficiency. It was imperative, then, that the necessary equipment be made available to them forthwith. Any delay would result in further lowering morale and reducing efficiency.[85]

Before replying to Giraud's appeal of 10 January for the retention of all four armored divisions, General Marshall sought the views of the theater on the question.[86] Lt. Gen. Jacob L. Devers, who had recently replaced Eisenhower as Commanding General, NATOUSA, reviewed for Marshall's benefit the status of the negotiations to date. He explained how AFHQ had finally established a program aimed at equipping units which the French had the manpower to organize in full and which would be engaged in ANVIL. As for the fourth armored division, General Devers expressed the opinion that it might be advisable to agree to its retention on the program with the understanding that the furnishing of equipment would be deferred indefinitely and that no personnel would be reserved for it. Such a procedure, he explained, would "appease French ambitions and at the same time accomplish our purposes." [87]

The long and irksome struggle over service units appeared over for the moment at least. The victory won by AFHQ had made possible the establishment of a new armament plan, sound and reasonable and therefore workable. When it had been approved by the CCS, an action which they were certain to take, both the French and the Americans would have before them a definite objective: the readying of a specific task force for operations in France. During the final implementation of the program, as many of the units as operationally practicable would be battle-tested beforehand in Italy in accordance with the desires of the CCS. The others would train in North Africa. Ultimately, all would take part in OVERLORD and ANVIL.

The 23 January Plan included in theory six infantry and four armored divisions, and some 245 supporting organizations of which approximately 210 were units of the former 15 August Plan and 35 were additions. Actually, since one infantry division was being retained in cadre only, and one armored division was deferred indefinitely, the program consisted of just five infantry and three armored divisions, or a total of eight divisions. That was the number which General Smith had recommended as a reasonable target in the course of his conversations in Washington back in October 1943.

The French had so far received from U.S. sources the equipment considered necessary for eight divisions and 164 supporting combat and service organizations. To implement the 23 January Plan in full, the task of supplying matériel for approximately 80 supporting organizations remained to be accomplished.

---

[85] Memo, Regnault for Loomis, 25 Jan 44, in same file.

[86] Msg 8180, Marshall to Devers, 26 Jan 44, JRC Cable Log.

[87] Msg W–1489, Devers to Marshall, 30 Jan 44, AFHQ Cable Log.

CHAPTER VIII

The Program Marks Time
(November 1943–February 1944)
II

The French Reorganize Their Supply System

Efforts to induce the French High Command to establish a sound supply system paralleled those which were exerted to prod it into organizing service units. Almost from the beginning of the rearmament operations, AFHQ attempted to push the North African Army into a position where it would ultimately be able to supply and maintain itself properly. As early as 24 March 1943 the chairman of the JRC pointed out informally to his French colleagues on the committee how desirable it would be for the French military authorities to reorganize their supply system along the lines of the American Services of Supply in the theater. Two weeks later, just before the arrival of convoy UGS 6½, the first large-scale shipment of U.S. matériel, he urged the French General Staff, this time in writing, to centralize the control of supply services and to institute material status reports similar to those used in the U.S. Army.[1]

After UGS 6½ was unloaded, reports reached the JRC indicating that U.S. equipment was piling up in ports because the existing French supply system was un-able to keep pace with the rate of deliveries. By September the situation appeared to have worsened considerably. General Kingman, Chief, French Training Section, was expressing deep concern over the apparent incapacity of the French to organize their supply services on a good working basis. On 3 September, General Kingman warned the JRC at length that lack of supply organization was having a serious effect on the efficiency of the entire French ordnance system. Even division ordnance units, he reported, were accomplishing relatively little real maintenance work because they could not obtain spare parts from the responsible supply agencies. As a result, the troops were getting insufficient training. The number of deadlined vehicles in the divisions was slowly increasing, and the supply services were making little effective effort to forward the required spare parts from depot establishments. These and other deficiencies were, in the opinion of General Kingman, unfortunate from the point of view of both morale and training. Nor was the situation due to lack of matériel. The French were at the time receiving large amounts of spare parts, but they were having extreme difficulty in identifying them and had little, if any, knowledge as to what echelon of maintenance the parts should be assigned. Units ap-

---

[1] Memo, Col Ira A. Crump for Loomis, 18 Oct 43, JRC 400.2/002 Stock Control System.

peared not to know what agency or authority they must look to for the satisfaction of their needs. Division ordnance officers had no definite idea where they should go to secure the required parts and no knowledge as to the exact location of depots.[2]

Already War Department officials in Washington had been receiving a "collection of informal reports, rumors, and gossip," tending to show that the French were unable to absorb properly their U.S. matériel and were misusing some items.[3] In the opinion of General Spalding, then chairman of the JRC, the facts as reported to Washington were probably exaggerated. True, there had been "certain accumulations," but the congestion was no more than could be expected under the circumstances. The French, he explained in a letter to a MAB official, were still having considerable difficulty in obtaining space for their depots as the British and U.S. Armies were superimposed on the limited facilities available in North Africa.[4]

Briefly, the inadequacy of the existing French supply system could be ascribed to two causes. First the supply services were handicapped by insufficient storage facilities, a matter soon to be remedied, for the U.S. Army was giving up considerable space especially at Casablanca. Second, their organization, judged by American standards, was totally inadequate. In French Morocco there was as yet no individual officer responsible for over-all supply and maintenance activity in connection with service installations, depots, and central stock control in the area. No stock record cards were being kept of what was available in depots.

At the vehicle assembly plant in Casablanca, personnel rotated so rapidly that the establishment of any efficient organization was impossible. Practically no use was made of the instruction literature sent along with the items; it was often thrown away. Nor was the lack of a supply authority peculiar to French Morocco. JRC officials were convinced that no one in the French Army, either in Algiers or elsewhere, knew what matériel was available or where. They were told that division commanders were visiting depots for the purpose of helping themselves.[5]

The situation called for immediate corrective measures. In the opinion of General Kingman, the time had come for the Americans to undertake a detailed survey of the entire French ordnance organization, then to assign qualified U.S. personnel to the French for the purpose of helping them establish a sound supply system within the shortest possible time.[6]

Endorsing General Kingman's views and recommendations, General Spalding resolved to bring the whole matter up for the consideration of the French. Preferring for the moment not to approach the French General Staff officially, he invited Colonel Regnault to discuss informally with him and his assistant, Colonel Artamonoff, the existing situation, as well as possible corrective measures. AFHQ officials, he pointed out, were eager to learn whether or not the French High Command contemplated adopting the U.S. ordnance system. There was some doubt on their part as to the interest shown by many officers of the Service du Matériel, or Ordnance Department, in Algiers regarding their functions. On the other hand, they were aware of the difficulty

[2] Memo, Kingman for Spalding, 3 Sep 43, JRC 333/001 Inspections—Misc.
[3] Ltr 5, Lt Col Roger Jones, MAB, to Spalding, 27 Aug 43, JRC 472 MAB.
[4] Ltr, Spalding to Jones, 8 Oct 43, JRC 472 MAB.

[5] Interv with Loomis, Sep 51.
[6] Memo cited n. 2.

the French services faced in finding sufficient qualified technicians to carry out their work properly. General Spalding then voiced his own and Colonel Artamonoff's belief that it was highly desirable for the French High Command to reorganize its supply system or at least give it a shot in the arm by applying the U.S. system "in its spirit." There was need, he observed, of building up the morale of Ordnance Department officers at all echelons. Theirs was an essential role. It was possible, concluded General Spalding, that the issuance by the French High Command of a general directive on the responsibilities of the Ordnance Department could improve the situation if it were stringently enforced.[7]

Colonel Regnault immediately conveyed to General Leyer the American desire to see the French establish their own counterpart of the U.S. stock control section then functioning in Oran. Maj. Gen. Thomas B. Larkin, chief of SOS, NATOUSA, had for some time urged the French to establish such a unit in Oran close to the U.S. section. The unit could serve a twofold purpose: provide centralized control of supplies and equipment, and prepare requisitions for the initial equipping of units or their maintenance after departure from North Africa. General Larkin recommended that the unit be operated by the French themselves with such assistance as might be necessary from qualified U.S. Army personnel.[8]

Official French reaction to the American proposal was mixed. The French welcomed the opportunity to establish a stock control unit at Oran, but did not believe it

necessary to give up altogether the existing organization in Algiers.[9] In an effort to prod them into quick action, General Spalding took the matter up directly with the French General Staff. On 27 September he informed General Leyer that both the commanding general of SOS and the deputy theater commander considered the establishment in Oran of a central stock control unit for the French forces to be a necessity. He then outlined the desirable composition and responsibilities of such a unit as envisaged by SOS on the basis of experience acquired through similar earlier undertakings. The unit should be composed of French officers and enlisted men having as much acquaintance as possible with U.S. matériel and with problems connected with requisitions, stock control, and related matters. It should also include a small group of U.S. experts in questions of supply and requisitions to assist in setting up and operating the unit. General Spalding suggested a tentative ratio of one American to four French. He then recommended that the unit be established preferably in a building adjacent to the office of SOS. In this manner, constant, close contact would be maintained with SOS in all matters pertaining to requisitioning of supplies and issue of items to expeditionary corps units. By the same token, unnecessary delays in the exchange of correspondence between Oran and Algiers would be avoided. In the past, such delays had often been the source of considerable annoyance.[10]

General Spalding's recommendation brought forth the desired result. The next day, 28 September, the French High Command ordered the establishment in Oran of

[7] Min Mtg, Spalding, Artamonoff, and Regnault, 4 Sep 43, in Gen Regnault's private papers.

[8] Note 568, Regnault to Blanc, 13 Sep 43, in Gen Regnault's private papers; Msg, Larkin to Devers, 14 Sep 43, AFHQ 0100/12C G–3 Div Ops Fr Rearmt.

[9] Msg 6314, Devers to Larkin, 18 Sep 43, JRC 400.2/002 Stock Control System.

[10] Memo, Spalding for Leyer, 27 Sep 43, JRC 400.2/002 Stock Control System.

a central supply authority known as Service Central des Approvisionnements et Matériels Américains (SCAMA). Its chief was to be an officer of French G–4 responsible directly to the Chief of Staff. Because of limited personnel and material means, however, serious difficulties were anticipated in setting up the unit. Nevertheless, French G–4 was currently preparing a directive on its functioning and mission.[11]

The speedy establishment of SCAMA seemed essential at a time when the first expeditionary units were getting ready to leave for Italy. By the provisions of a plan then under consideration by Allied and French staffs, the French supply system and SOS, NATOUSA, were to share in the responsibility for the supply and maintenance of these units.[12] Effective implementation of the plan required that the French supply agencies be in a position at all times to provide SOS with detailed information as to the quantities available in their depots for each type of supply. General Larkin was insistent that, in addition to organizing a central authority in Oran, the French establish at once in Casablanca a competent administrative agency vested with sufficient authority to act with vigor and promptness in consolidating all French Army supply activity in Morocco. Unless this was done, he warned, the French supply headquarters would not have a stock provisioning system "in any sense of the term."[13]

The first of a series of instructions on stock control was issued by General Leyer on 15 October. It dealt with the organiza-

tion and functioning of the newly created SCAMA. Initially, SCAMA was given the following mission:

To keep the French High Command posted on the exact status of U.S. supplies and equipment of all types, and their distribution at the time, so that the Command can, with full knowledge of the facts, place orders with a view to satisfying, in the shortest possible time and under the best conditions, the needs of the units, and send to the U.S. authorities justifiable requisitions whenever necessary.

Later on, "at a date yet to be fixed," SCAMA was to centralize material and financial accounting operations for all U.S. equipment.[14]

The instruction, although representing a step in the right direction, was wholly inadequate. In the opinion of Col. Ira A. Crump, chief Ordnance officer of the JRC, its provisions were only half measures enacted with little or no conviction of the real importance of the entire undertaking. Centralization, he pointed out, was needed at once, not at a later date. He feared that the French military authorities did not realize the magnitude of the problem with respect to both volume of supplies to be handled and necessity of a rigid stock control, or else they were expecting the U.S. Army to assume part or all of their supply functions. It was all the more urgent, therefore, to press them for a concrete supply plan of their own so that a definite basis for future requirements and assistance could be established. The current situation, he warned, was critical and likely to result in delaying the employment of French units.[15]

Colonel Crump's suspicion that the French military authorities were counting on assistance from U.S. Army supply and

[11] Memos, Leyer for Spalding, 30 Sep 43, and Regnault for Spalding, 30 Sep 43, JRC 400.2/002 Stock Control System.

[12] See below, pp. 138–39.

[13] Msg L–6335, Larkin to Devers, 7 Oct 43, and Memo, Larkin for Hughes, 21 Oct 43, JRC 400.2/001 Admin of Sup—Gen.

[14] Instruction 3751/3/EMGG/4, 15 Oct 43, JRC 400.2/002 Stock Control System.

[15] Memo cited n. 1, above.

ordnance services merely confirmed the feeling that AFHQ had already gained as a result of the feud over French service units. The current lack of interest on the part of the French in reforming their supply system could be construed as one more indication that they expected the U.S. Army to supply, service, and maintain their forces. Yet they had been repeatedly warned not to depend on such assistance and urged to work toward self-reliance by all possible means. In the opinion of AFHQ officials, the time had come to put them in a position where they must take energetic action.

Writing to General Giraud on 20 October, General Whiteley, Acting Chief of Staff, AFHQ, set forth in clear terms AFHQ's position on the matter of supply control. To make it possible for the Commanding General, SOS, NATOUSA, to have accurate and timely information on the status of supply in French installations, the French Army was requested to establish in Oran a central stock control group. This group was to maintain stock records and a central provisioning control on all classes of supply held by depots. Such control was to be based on U.S. Army property accounting and supply control procedure. In addition, the French Army was requested to maintain at Headquarters, SOS, NATOUSA, a liaison group consisting of one senior grade officer, well-qualified and experienced in supply matters and with sufficient authority to act for the French Commander in Chief on all supply problems, and of qualified officers for liaison duty with the various U.S. Army supply services. Finally, the French Army was to make available upon the request of the Commanding General, SOS, NATOUSA, any necessary data to assure complete utilization of stocks

on hand for the maintenance of French forces.[16]

This was no longer a suggestion but a firm request calling for General Giraud's early approval so as to enable AFHQ to issue final directives to the responsible Allied agencies. Five days later, on 25 October, the French Commander in Chief signified his agreement on the various points raised in General Whiteley's letter.[17]

Once again, as in the case of service units, the American concept that the French forces must achieve self-reliance had triumphed over the reluctance of the French to undertake what seemed to them an unnecessary and, in all likelihood, an almost impossible task considering the lack of qualified personnel.

The French General Staff had now no other alternative than to set up an ordnance system patterned after the American SOS. The success of such an undertaking required, first of all, that supply officers at all echelons be fully convinced of the urgency of the proposed reorganization. That they were subsequently won over was largely because of the efforts of Colonel Blanc, then Assistant Chief of Staff for both G–1 and G–4. His energetic intervention succeeded in allaying the reluctance, indeed the hostility, shown by various heads of services to the projected reorganization. Colonel Blanc's own rallying to the American point of view had been the result of the convincing interpretation which the French representatives on the JRC had given him of American views and procedures. Their efforts, coupled with the persistent yet tactful and friendly guidance offered by the

[16] Ltr, Whiteley to Giraud, 20 Oct 43, AFHQ 0100/4 SACS Rcd Sec, Fr Matters, Vol. I.

[17] Memo, Giraud for CinC Allied Forces, 25 Oct 43, JRC 400.2/001 Admin of Sup—Gen.

successive chairmen of the JRC from Colonel Gardiner down to General Loomis, contributed much to bringing about the final meeting of French and American minds on the matter of supply organization.

To assist the French in establishing a sound and efficient supply machinery and more generally to effect liaison with them on all supply matters, SOS, NATOUSA, placed, beginning 4 October, trained personnel at the disposal of SCAMA. The officers and men so detailed soon formed a detachment known as Stock Control Section, JRC. Technically on duty with the JRC, the section, headed by Col. Michael J. Geraghty, acted as a link between SOS, SCAMA, and the JRC.[18]

The early history of SCAMA was marked by unparalleled confusion.[19] For some weeks nothing seemed to get done. But the job was tremendous. SCAMA had to deal with literally hundreds of depots, small warehouses, and storage annexes scattered throughout French North Africa and individually responsible to one of several authorities. Among these was an organization known as Centre de Réception des Matériels Américains (CRMA), set up in the spring of 1943 in Casablanca. It controlled all supplies of American origin and was largely responsible for their distribution. However, it was not co-ordinated in any way with the French Supply Services, which concerned themselves primarily with matériel of French source, and it maintained warehouses separate from those of the services. Controlled from Algiers, CRMA worked in conjunction with a special branch of the General Staff which had been established in Casablanca for the purpose of getting American equipment into the hands of units. CRMA kept no stock record accounts. The other agency at least kept a card for each unit being rearmed. But the card listed only the major items issued; no entry was made of accessories, tools, spare parts, basic loads, allowances of all categories, and individual expendable equipment. Still another branch of the General Staff, functioning in Oran and apparently working independently of the Casablanca branch, was responsible for building up stocks of maintenance supplies for the units preparing to go overseas.

The confusion created by two sets of depots was evident everywhere. Service depots, which frequently received supplies as an overflow from CRMA depots, were actually issuing to units items of equipment no one had any record of having received. Little attempt was being made in either category of depots to account for supplies on hand and very few records of stocks were available anywhere. Such a chaotic situation emphasized the urgent need of setting up SCAMA as the central authority in accounting, recording, and stock reporting.

The lack of qualified personnel served only to aggravate the confusion. Scarcity of personnel can best be appreciated when it is realized that, as late as the end of November 1943, one officer with no assistance whatsoever was handling the Casablanca Pharmacy, a medical depot somewhat similar to the U.S. Medical Issue Warehouse.[20] For several months the manpower problem remained a serious one. Men assigned to

---

[18] For details on the composition, evolution, and technical operation of SCAMA and of Stock Control Section, see pp. 288–93, below.

[19] History of Stock Control Section, JRC, n. d., copy in JRC files: Memo, Geraghty for Loomis, sub: Rpt of Stock Control Sec, 8 Jul 44, JRC 400.2/002 Stock Control System.

[20] Memo, Lt Col A. T. Maxwell, Atlantic Base Sec, for Larkin, 27 Nov 43, JRC 400.2/002 Stock Control System.

SCAMA by the French General Staff were untrained and often untrainable, for they included a substantial proportion of natives unwanted elsewhere and generally ignorant of the French language—in short, of a type unsatisfactory even as common laborers.

Lack of physical means was equally acute. Warehouse equipment, transportation, tools, and covered space were insufficient. Depots even lacked such office supplies as pencils, typewriters, carbon paper, stationery, forms, and filing cabinets. They were using school tablets and scraps of paper on which to record stocks. Their reports to chiefs of services in Algiers or to CRMA were made largely by telephone in the absence of other means. Providing them with a minimum of essential supplies proved at first difficult because SOS was forbidden by NATOUSA from issuing anything to the French without special authority in each case. In mid-October a special initial authorization from NATOUSA enabled SOS to turn over to the depots such stationery and office supplies as were in excess of its own needs. On 4 November NATOUSA approved issue to SCAMA of 200,000 U.S. stock record cards. Within a short time, SCAMA was receiving American catalogues, standard nomenclature lists, tables of organization, tables of equipment, and many other useful publications. It was also able to obtain on loan freight-handling equipment.

Other difficulties hampered the setting up of SCAMA, such as language differences and the frequent impossibility of reconciling French nomenclature as given by warehouses with that used in American catalogues or standard nomenclature lists. And then there were differences in national idiosyncrasies. The easygoing North African natives were not always ready to adopt the American practice of getting things done in a hurry.

More disquieting, especially to Colonel Geraghty who was determined to see the reorganization project through, was the fact that SCAMA, after two months of existence, was still without anything but a very general statement of what it was to accomplish. It had no official standing or place within the French military organization. Three successive directives had failed to vest in SCAMA the authority needed to effect real centralization. Its director, Col. Emile Charpentier, although regarded by his American colleagues as highly qualified for the position he held, could not prevent individual supply services from frequently disregarding his orders.

With SCAMA unable to assert itself speedily and effectively, the general French supply situation was bound to deteriorate further. First to suffer were the troops about to depart or already en route for Italy with incomplete equipment. Their predicament, General Larkin pointed out on 13 November, was indicative of a complete failure of the supply system; the failure precluded any substantial support of the expeditionary forces from French sources. There was no solution but for the U.S. Army to assume the entire maintenance responsibility until such time as the French themselves knew what they had and where it was.[21] Thereupon General Larkin requested and obtained from General Eisenhower the authorization to inspect depots for the purpose of assisting French supply officers in locating items needed by units about to depart, and if necessary to remove and ship any items so found to appropriate

---

[21] Msg L–9908, Larkin to NATOUSA, 13 Nov 43, JRC Cable Log.

destinations.[22] After he had inspected supply installations in Casablanca, General Larkin reported that supplies were being "dissipated through absence of centralized control." He warned that maintenance by the French of their forces would be extremely difficult under the present "loose" organization. He urged once again that SCAMA be given sufficient authority to enable it to carry out its mission.[23]

It was not until 9 January 1944 that the French General Staff, rescinding all prior instructions, issued a new one that greatly extended SCAMA's authority in the supply field. Many of the administrative restrictions which in the past had proved harmful were now removed. Thereafter SCAMA was:

1. to furnish to the French High Command, whenever called upon to do so, the exact status of all stocks of matériel and supply of all kinds; and to do this in such a manner as would permit the French High Command to arrange for the best use of available stocks and to prepare requisitions for submission to the United States;

2. to ensure the proper execution of the High Command's decisions relative to both initial equipping of troops and their maintenance;

3. to maintain close liaison with SOS NATOUSA with a view to settling quickly all questions of shipping or transfer of supplies.[24]

To SCAMA's director, Colonel Charpentier, the instruction delegated specific authority over organization and function. Ac-

tually, organization was not designed by the director, but was thrust upon him by the manner in which activities, previously operating independently, were associated, one by one, with his office. The higher command still seemed reluctant to grant the necessary absolute authority. SCAMA found itself repeatedly hampered by official interference. A case in point was the Casablanca Base. The French High Command had placed all military bases established in the ports of embarkation and debarkation under SCAMA control, either directly or through representatives. Yet the same command did not hesitate to infringe on SCAMA's authority by organizing the Casablanca Base and naming its director. As a result, the base became a source of constant confusion.

Another unsatisfactory feature of the 9 January instruction was that it contained several ambiguous phrases and loose terms which subsequently gave rise to a number of misunderstandings. As late as March 1944 some French agencies were still trying to bypass SCAMA in submitting requisitions. Greatly disturbed over this situation, Colonel Geraghty feared that, unless corrective measures were applied without delay, SCAMA's brave efforts would be futile.

It is interesting to note that, whereas SCAMA remained under the effective control of the French General Staff, at no time was the American Stock Control Section, JRC, the subject of a single order from higher U.S. authority. In fact it had no official existence. Even its name was assumed, having merely been approved by the chairman of the JRC. Colonel Geraghty had been given free hand in running his section as he deemed best. He determined its internal organization, issued the neces-

[22] Msgs L–40, Larkin to CG NATOUSA, 14 Nov 43, 1752, Eisenhower to Larkin, 16 Nov 43, and L–773, Larkin to CG NATOUSA, 22 Nov 43, JRC Cable Log.

[23] Msgs L–2271, Larkin to CG NATOUSA, 5 Dec 43, L–2459, Larkin to JRC, 6 Dec 43, and L–2805, Larkin to JRC, 9 Dec 43, JRC 400.2/002 Stock Control System.

[24] Instruction 340, EMGG/4, 9 Jan 44, JRC 400.2/002 Stock Control System.

sary instructions, and detailed his personnel with a view to providing the French with the maximum assistance. He succeeded in developing a highly efficient system by which French and American technicians were put to work together. This collaboration ultimately made possible the setting up of a sound supply system. To ensure its spread to French depots and installations in other areas, Stock Control Section later opened branch offices in Algiers and Casablanca (February 1944) and in Tunis (May 1944).

In spite of its many handicaps and shortcomings, SCAMA began to grow in stature and efficiency, largely through the excellent co-operation between its personnel and that of Stock Control Section. Recognizing its increasing importance in the supply system, the French General Staff gradually assigned to it additional qualified members, both military and civilian. Numbering some 20 officers and 20 civilians at the end of October, SCAMA could boast, two months later, a total strength of 320 persons, including 65 senior and junior officers, 70 enlisted men, and 185 civilian employees. Issuance of the 9 January instruction definitely accelerated progress by providing the necessary spur. Colonels Geraghty and Charpentier prepared and issued a pamphlet for use by the services as a sort of textbook on all supply matters. By mid-January they had printed and were distributing some three million forms which standardized procedures and made possible "a common language and a common meeting ground for supply interests throughout the Services." An instruction issued by Colonel Charpentier on 26 January set forth the relations to be established between the various echelons of SCAMA, and prescribed the forms to be used throughout the entire sup-

ply system.[25] By this time some progress could be noted in the preparation of stock record accounts and in the reporting of stocks to SCAMA. It was apparent that the recasting of the French supply system had passed the planning stage: the "house of SCAMA" was about to enter the final phase of its organization.

Supply and Maintenance of the Expeditionary Forces

Efficient and timely re-equipping of units was not the only benefit expected from the reorganization of the French supply system. It was hoped in addition that the French military authorities would be better able to supply and maintain their forces in combat, another responsibility which had become theirs as a result of the broad application of the concept of self-reliance.

The development of a supply plan for forces in the field began to receive considerable attention in August 1943 when the decision was reached to use French units in Italy. The basic policy as set forth by Headquarters, NATOUSA, was that French troops, from the moment they departed from North Africa, passed from the supply control of the French General Staff to that of Fifth Army.[26] Fifth Army's responsibility in the matter was limited, however. It consisted merely in ensuring the continuous flow of maintenance supplies into the hands of the French units under its control. The French military authorities themselves were charged with providing

---

[25] Instruction 43/D, SCAMA, 26 Jan 44, in History of Stock Control Section, JRC, copy in JRC files.
[26] Msg 390, CG NATOUSA to CG SOS NATOUSA, 12 Aug 43, JRC 400.4/003 Maintenance for Forces Operating With Fifth Army.

from their own sources, be they of French, American, or other origin, a determined number of equipment items. SOS, acting as the supply agent for Fifth Army, was responsible for making certain that all the necessary items were made available from French sources, or, if necessary, from U.S. sources pending reimbursement by the French, and for effecting their transportation to the theater of operations. Its role was far from negligible and its position between provider and consumer a thankless one. In the last analysis, however, it was on the French General Staff that the chief responsibility fell for furnishing the maintenance supplies for the expeditionary forces.

There remained the task of determining with accuracy the division of responsibility among the three authorities concerned— the French General Staff, SOS, and Fifth Army—and of taking adequate steps to make certain that each was carrying out its respective share of the combined operation. This led to a long series of discussions, conferences, and studies.

At a preliminary conference, held at AFHQ on 29 September 1943, the entire question of the supply of French expeditionary forces was examined. The conference, attended by representatives from the JRC, SOS, the Fifth Army, and the French Supply Services, emphasized two important points. The first was the need for the French authorities to submit, in ample time, requisitions on the United States, through the JRC, for the assignment to them of items not currently available in their stocks. Second, it was urgent for them to accelerate the setting up of the proposed SCAMA system then under consideration in order to guarantee the speedy and continuous flow of supplies to the expeditionary forces.[27]

Three weeks later, General Whiteley, Deputy Chief of Staff, AFHQ, submitted to General Giraud for his concurrence a plan covering all aspects of the supply problem, including completion of initial equipment, transportation of troops and matériel, and maintenance of forces in combat. The recommended policy with respect to maintenance envisaged the following division of responsibility: Fifth Army was to submit to SOS separate requisitions for the maintenance of French units under its control; SOS was to fill such requisitions by placing calls upon the French military authorities; the latter were to deliver the required items from stocks available to them or made available to them through the JRC.[28]

The French Commander in Chief having concurred in the proposal, AFHQ, on 29 October, issued a directive officially charging SOS, NATOUSA, with the responsibility for the mounting and maintenance of the French forces operating with the Fifth Army in accordance with the provisions submitted to General Giraud. AFHQ stipulated, in addition, that essential supplies which definitely could not be furnished from French resources would be provided from U.S. stocks if available, such issues to be reported and accounted for in accordance with established procedures. The French were, of course, to reimburse SOS for the items so transferred as soon as practicable.[29]

The success of the supply plan was de-

---

[27] Min, Conf on Sup of CEF, 29 Sep 43, JRC 400.1/009 Sup of Forces Designated for Combat.

[28] Ltr, Whiteley to Giraud, 20 Oct 43, AFHQ 0100/4 SACS Rcd Sec, Fr Matters, Vol. I.

[29] Ltrs, Giraud to CinC Allied Forces, 25 Oct 43, and AG 381/399 D–O, Hq NATOUSA to CG SOS NATOUSA, 29 Oct 43, JRC 400.2/001 Admin of Sup—Gen.

pendent in a large measure on the extent to which units would manage to complete their initial equipment before embarking. General Whiteley had made this point clear to General Giraud when he requested that departing troops be "completely equipped to authorized allowances under current tables for equivalent organizations of the U.S. Army." Yet, a week later, it was learned that the French military authorities proposed to embark their first division, the 2d Moroccan Infantry, with what appeared to be insufficient winter equipment, such as one coat or one field jacket instead of both items per man, one pair of trousers instead of two, two blankets instead of three, and so on. At the request of General Clark, Commanding General, U.S. Fifth Army, AFHQ impressed upon the French General Staff the desirability of equipping units in accordance with prescribed Fifth Army administrative instructions.[30]

In spite of the warning, it was reported a few days later that the same division had embarked almost completely lacking in basic load requirements of maintenance parts and accessories and short of major items of equipment, including twenty-two 57-mm. guns. Furthermore, when the division reached Italy, an inspection revealed serious shortages, by Fifth Army standards, of winter clothing and equipment. This prompted General Clark to request AFHQ that he be authorized to issue to the division additional blankets and warm clothing on the same basis as for U.S. troops. In fact, without waiting for an answer from Algiers, he ordered the emergency issue of these items.[31]

Investigation showed that the unit in question had received its normal allowance of winter equipment but not the additional items which troops in Fifth Army had been issued under special authorization from NATOUSA. The French High Command, although urged to take similar steps, had for reasons of its own deemed it unnecessary to issue winter equipment over and above the rates prescribed under the current AFHQ tables of allowances. As for the shortages of major items, maintenance parts, and accessories, it was discovered that the division commander and the French General Staff had been working on different tables of organization. NATOUSA immediately brought the matter to the attention of General Leyer with a view to preventing a recurrence of the situation.[32]

The confusion surrounding the equipment of the 2d DIM underlined a grave weakness in the Allied command structure. From the time the French in North Africa had joined the Allies in November 1942, they had been in a peculiar position in which their military establishment functioned parallel to the Anglo-American administrative system, but was at no point, except in the field, fully part of it. This being so, they could be urged, or requested, to take certain measures, but the Allied command was wholly dependent on voluntary acquiescence on their part. They considered themselves free, to a large degree, to decide whether the equipment standards as established by non-French commands, such as Fifth Army headquarters, were practicable or desirable for their own troops. They could, and they did, modify U.S. tables of

[30] Msg 4192, Fifth Army to CinC, 27 Oct 43, JRC Cable Log.

[31] Msgs L–9908, Larkin to CG NATOUSA, 13 Nov 43, 5732, Fifth Army to CG AFHQ, 18 Dec

43, and 5753, Fifth Army to CG AFHQ, 20 Dec 43, JRC Cable Log.

[32] Msgs 2733, CG NATOUSA to Larkin, 18 Nov 43, and 17842, CG NATOUSA to Fifth Army, 22 Dec 43, JRC Cable Log.

equipment to fit what they considered the particular needs of their forces.[33]

To make sure, therefore, that equipment standards of French units operating under American control approached the U.S. counterparts as closely as possible, the utmost co-operation was required between all responsible authorities before the embarkation of troops. Once the troops were in the theater of operations, the issuance of initial equipment to fill shortages or emergency needs entailed a labyrinthine process of requisitioning. If General Juin wished an additional issue of initial equipment, such as winter clothing items for the 2d DIM, his corps G–4 submitted the prescribed requisition to Fifth Army supply sections for clearance and transmission to SOS, NATOUSA. There the French liaison officer, Lt. Col. A. Dufourt, prepared appropriate lists which he forwarded to the French General Staff for examination, first by G–4, then by Rearmament Section. Once approved by the French General Staff, the lists were sent to the French Section of the JRC for submission to the committee, then forwarded to NATOUSA for final decision. Only in "dire emergency" cases was Colonel Dufourt authorized to bypass the French General Staff altogether and request SOS to transmit requisitions to the JRC or to G–4, NATOUSA, for action.[34]

In spite of French urgings that the existing channels of communications be simplified, NATOUSA maintained that these channels were not unduly cumbersome and that they must be adhered to. The position taken by NATOUSA was in accordance

with War Department instructions, which restricted to operational emergency cases the authority of a theater to transfer supplies to a foreign government without prior approval from the MAB.[35] As supplies so transferred were later to be replaced in U.S. stocks by the foreign government concerned, the theater was under obligation to ensure proper and accurate accounting of all transactions. Consequently, the procedure adopted by NATOUSA whereby all requests from the French forces under U.S. control had to be cleared and approved by both the French General Staff and NATOUSA was a logical one. In addition and equally important, such a procedure would tend to prevent wastage in the form of needless expenditures of matériel. French supplies, largely of American origin, were not expendable any more than stocks available to U.S. troops. Sound utilization of resources mattered as much as speed of delivery.

Yet complete observance of the established policy frequently proved impossible. Many cases arose in which operational needs required the issue of equipment to French forces engaged in combat "without regard to strict adherence to the finer points of Lend-Lease bookkeeping."[36] Eager to set the record straight on the matter, AFHQ, on 14 January 1944, informed General Clark that the action he had taken in December in issuing additional winter equipment to the 2d DIM was contrary to the established policy.

It must be emphasized that the initial issue of organizational and individual equipment must occur in North Africa from stocks made available to the French under the rearma-

---

[33] Ltr, Giraud to Allied CinC, 25 Oct 43, JRC 400.4/003 Maintenance for Forces Operating With Fifth Army.

[34] Memos, Regnault for Spalding, 10 Oct 43, and Spalding for Leyer, 11 Oct 43, JRC 400.2/001 Admin of Sup—Gen.

[35] Msg 859, Marshall to Eisenhower, 26 Oct 43, JRC Cable Log.

[36] Ltr, Loomis to Col George Olmstead, 11 Dec 43, JRC 908 Policy and Plan—Misc.

ment program prior to the embarkation of French units for Italy. . . . Where Fifth Army administrative instructions contain prescriptions which can be met by supplies available in North Africa to the French Army, the French authorities will be advised to comply therewith.[37]

In the meantime, NATOUSA had taken steps to effect closer co-operation between the various Allied command and supply echelons on the matter of initial equipment loads. Such co-operation was indispensable if confusion and discrepancies were to be avoided in the future. When Fifth Army instructions or tables of equipment were at variance with those given earlier to the French by the JRC, NATOUSA officials undertook to bring the three interested parties together to solve the problems involved. They also urged the French General Staff once again to verify the completeness of equipment in the hands of units before embarkation and requested General Kingman's French Training Section to give full assistance in this connection. Finally, they asked the JRC to expedite the preparation of requisitions for shortages of equipment as these were reported.[38]

The objective of the supply plan, as put in force on 29 October 1943, could be reached only if the French military authorities were in a position to make available to SOS, on call from the latter or in execution of agreed schedules, the supplies required for the maintenance of their expeditionary forces in Italy. This, incidentally, was only one of their maintenance commitments. They were also responsible for maintaining all troops while in training, forces employed under operational control other than Amer-

ican (such as the units which the French High Command itself had committed to the liberation of Corsica in September 1943), all Territorial and Sovereignty troops, and zone of interior establishments. To carry out these heavy and varied assignments, which the concept of self-reliance as imposed on the French had forced them to assume, required that they establish and maintain considerable stocks of supplies of all types, readily available on a moment's notice, for the support of any of their forces.

AFHQ had long urged the French to accumulate adequate reserves of both American and locally procured supplies. By the fall of 1943 the Americans had the distinct feeling that their urgings had not been heeded, possibly because the French were placing undue dependence on U.S. theater stocks as a reserve. On 7 September General Spalding, chairman of the JRC, warned General Leyer that "such a source could not be taken for granted in the future." He then proposed a number of measures which, if carried out by the French, would enable them to make their Military Establishment self-sufficient. With regard to foodstuffs, he recommended that the responsible authorities exploit North African resources and take energetic steps to increase production to the maximum. He suggested that they prepare a monthly food program and, in case of shortages, make arrangements to obtain the rest from U.S. sources. As for ammunition and all authorized expendable items of American equipment, he urged that they maintain adequate reserves either under their control or available to them in U.S. theater stockages, these to be supported by a flow of supplies from the United States. This operation would require the early establishment, after detailed study, of a sound plan carefully co-ordinated with

---

[37] Msg 28417, CinC AFHQ to Fifth Army, 14 Jan 44, JRC Cable Log.

[38] Msgs 6765, Eisenhower to CG SOS NATOUSA, 5 Nov 43, and L–9158, Larkin to CG NATOUSA, 5 Nov 43, JRC Cable Log.

American and British programs and involve the submission by the French of regular monthly requisitions on the United States for maintaining stocks at established levels. In reply, General Leyer announced that a food program of the sort recommended by General Spalding was in preparation and that the responsible military as well as civilian authorities had already taken steps to increase the production of certain food items both in North Africa and in other French territories. He announced further that, beginning 1 October, the French General Staff would forward monthly requisitions for the procurement of U.S. supplies, such as ammunition and other expendable items. A fortnight later, in the course of a meeting with General Leyer, General Spalding again broached the food question which, he reiterated, required very serious consideration in view especially of heavy demands on U.S. foodstuffs for Soviet and British troops.[39]

The French were to submit to the JRC for necessary action requisitions for all purposes except emergency issues. The requisitions were designed to make possible the establishment and operation of a 45-day reserve of supplies for the maintenance of units dispatched overseas. It soon became evident that the paper work involved was posing for the French insurmountable difficulties. SCAMA was making so little progress that, even at the end of December, it had no accurate information as to the actual supplies on hand and was unable to determine what items it should requisition. To make matters worse, SOS reported, on 1 January, that the French military authori-

ties had replaced in U.S. theater stocks less than 50 percent of the maintenance items advanced as an initial stockpile to their expeditionary forces in Italy. SOS blamed their failure to do so on SCAMA's inability to complete the required 45-day supply reserve, a fact which emphasized, once again, the urgent need for a more efficient French supply system. General Larkin feared that the situation, if allowed to continue, would result in a considerable drain upon U.S. Army reserves since SOS was required to make up for any deficiencies in the French deliveries.[40]

By this time, experience gained from the presence of French units in Italy had shown that the existing system of channeling supplies from the United States to North African depots for reshipment to the combat zone increased movement and accounting operations unnecessarily. In an attempt to simplify the procedure, SOS had recommended earlier in November that Peninsular Base Section (PBS) in Naples be given the responsibility for maintaining the French Expeditionary Corps, and that the French military authorities be required in turn to effect replacements in American depots in North Africa from a stockpile established by them for this purpose. Thus no shipments, except of rations and special items obtainable only from French sources, would be made to Italy for the supply of the CEF, nor would any lend-lease accounting be necessary in Italy.[41] The proposal, a sound one, had been submitted to the various NATOUSA staff sections then considering

---

[39] Memo, Spalding for Leyer, 7 Sep 43, Memo, Leyer for Spalding, 17 Sep 43, and *Aide Mémoire*, Spalding for Leyer, 2 Oct 43, JRC 908 Policy and Plan—Misc.

[40] Msg W–8584/19360, Eisenhower to AGWAR, 26 Dec 43, CM–IN 16426; Msg L–5742, Larkin to JRC, 1 Jan 44, and Memo, Larkin for Loomis, 13 Jan 44, JRC 400.4/003 Maintenance for Forces Operating With Fifth Army.

[41] Memo, DCofS SOS for CG NATOUSA, 28 Nov 43, JRC 400.4/003, Maintenance for Forces Operating With Fifth Army.

steps to improve conditions. The ills which it sought to correct, however, were minor in comparison with others. So damaging were these that the entire supply plan as established on 29 October had become an unworkable arrangement.

In a long message to the War Department on 26 December, NATOUSA outlined the basic weaknesses of the plan in its current form. The chaotic situation of the French supply system made it impossible for the French military authorities to make available to SOS the supplies which they were expected to furnish for their expeditionary forces. It would, in addition, prevent them from preparing and submitting proper requisitions in time to provide any assistance, from the supply standpoint, toward the mounting of Operation ANVIL. NATOUSA then recommended a sweeping change of policy: the responsibility for submitting requisitions for the procurement of equipment and supplies necessary for the maintenance of French units participating in operations under U.S. control should be assumed by SOS, no longer by the French. Otherwise, the large French force designated for participation in ANVIL would not be properly supplied.[42]

War Department officials immediately endorsed NATOUSA's proposal with minor modifications. On 16 January 1944, after further discussions on the matter between the War Department and the theater, SOS issued a new directive on the maintenance of French expeditionary forces.[43] Drafted after consultation with and approval by General Giraud, the directive was applicable to forces specifically operating under

U.S. control whether, as then, in Italy or in future operations in continental France. It set forth in detail the latest policy with regard to the provision of both initial equipment and maintenance supplies.

Initial equipment was to be provided to the greatest extent possible from stocks supplied the French through the rearmament program. Only when items were unobtainable from such sources, was the Commanding General, NATOUSA, empowered to authorize their issue from U.S. theater stocks to the extent available and without jeopardy to the proper supply of U.S. forces. All items so transferred to complete initial equipment were charged against the French lend-lease account in North Africa. As for equipment and supplies required for maintenance of troops in operation, these were, with some exceptions, provided by SOS through the submission to the New York Port of Embarkation of single consolidated monthly requisitions for both French and U.S. troops. Levels of supply furnished were those authorized for the U.S. forces, and combat maintenance provided was computed on U.S. Army replacement factors. Food rations, ammunition, post exchange, and Special Services supplies were excepted from these regulations.[44]

Rations were provided partly from U.S. sources, partly from French sources, as in the case of items peculiar to the French menu, in accordance with agreements reached between NATOUSA and the French General Staff. Post exchange and Special Services supplies were provided entirely by the French. Ammunition was supplied from U.S. stocks in North Africa to the extent available, and the remainder

---

[42] Msg W-8584/19360 cited n. 40.

[43] Cir 7, SOS NATOUSA, sub: SOP on Sup and Maintenance of Fr Forces, 16 Jan 44, JRC 400.4/003 Maintenance for Forces Operating With Fifth Army.

[44] The question of rations, post exchange, and Special Services supplies is treated at some length in Chapter XVI, below.

obtained from the United States through consolidated requisitions for both French and U.S. troops. The French Supply Services were required to replace in U.S. depots, from stocks available to them, the supplies (food, post exchange items, and other materials) which it was their responsibility to provide for the maintenance of participating French units. All items furnished by SOS either by direct shipment from the United States or from U.S. stocks in the theater, and not replaced by the French Supply Services, were charged against the lend-lease account.

The directive contained other important provisions concerning the handling of matériel intended for the expeditionary forces. Supplies furnished from French sources were delivered by the French Army to shipside or to U.S. depots as requested by SOS, and were loaded aboard ship and discharged by the U.S. Army, with French assistance if required. The French liaison group at SOS headquarters was charged with ensuring that complete utilization was being made of French stocks for the maintenance of French forces. To this end, it obtained from SCAMA periodic reports of supplies on hand in French depots.

The advantages gained from the application of the new plan were many and substantial. Supplies were now reaching the base serving the expeditionary forces by direct shipment from the United States or, in the case of a relatively small percentage, by shipment from North African ports, thus saving much valuable time and shipping. More important yet, it now was almost certain that the expeditionary forces would receive in due time all the supplies necessary for their continued support. To make certain that French and Allied agencies responsible for the mounting of ANVIL clearly understood the details of the new policy,

a letter on the subject, which AFHQ addressed to General Giraud on 11 February in the name of the Supreme Allied Commander, was made the basis of an official directive.[45]

In execution of the new policy, SOS, NATOUSA, immediately assumed the responsibility for preparing and submitting, with French assistance, requisitions for the supplies which had to be obtained from U.S. sources for the maintenance of all French forces then, or destined to be, part of an American task force. The French continued to be responsible for preparing and submitting requisitions for the maintenance of all other forces, and for shortages of initial equipment. Subsequently they were urged to consider the submission of requisitions for the replenishment of equipment in the hands of units engaged in combat for some length of time. This matter was expected to present a problem of considerable scope in the not too distant future.[46]

A sound supply plan for the maintenance of French expeditionary forces was now a reality. Its establishment, incidentally, was being effected at a time when the drafting of a workable rearmament plan (the 23 January Plan) was about to be completed. In the last analysis, much of the direction for the supply and maintenance of French troops was now to rest in American hands. This was in line with recommendations from War Department officials who had come to the conclusion and strongly urged that, in the theater, "American management should follow

[45] Ltr, Wilson to Giraud, 11 Feb 44, JRC 400.4/003 Maintenance for Forces Operating With Fifth Army; Dir, AFHQ, AG 400–1 (Fr), 11 Feb 44, sub: Sup and Maintenance of Fr Forces.

[46] Memos, Loomis for Leyer, 15, 22 Jan 44, JRC 400.1/009 Sup of Forces Designated for Combat.

American equipment." Such a course of action, they believed, was a sound development in the lend-lease program and the time was opportune to put it into effect.[47]

Supplies reached the CEF in Italy through Peninsular Base Section, set up in Naples on 1 November 1943 for the support of the U.S. Fifth Army. Long before the arrival of the first North African unit, it had been agreed that the French military authorities would assume their share of the responsibility for the operation of PBS. As early as October, Generals Juin and Clark decided that French Base 901, already activated in North Africa, would join PBS in Naples, there to serve as the supply organization for CEF. Accordingly, an advance detachment from that base was dispatched to Naples where, on 22 November, it set up shop in the G–4 office of PBS.[48] Just then the first division, the 2d DIM, was on its way to the front line.

Headquarters, Fifth Army, having announced, on 23 November, that it was taking over the full responsibility for the supply of the CEF, SOS, NATOUSA, recommended that the French themselves be urged to contribute to the fullest extent possible to the "housemaiding" of their own forces. Since it was expected that three eighths of Fifth Army combat troops would ultimately be French, SOS considered that French service units should be assigned for duty with PBS in approximately the same ratio. On this basis, a list of the required signal, ordnance, quartermaster, transpor-

tation, and medical units was subsequently drawn up and incorporated in the 23 January Plan. The list represented, it was thought, a proper proportion of the total number of base section units required for the support of Fifth Army. AFHQ considered that their assignment would, in addition to helping relieve the acute shortage of U.S. service personnel in PBS, provide them with excellent practical training toward their ultimate employment in ANVIL. General Loomis strongly urged the French General Staff to accelerate the activation of the necessary units. Yet by the end of January, no such troops had been made available. When queried on the matter, General Leyer could only give the assurance that he would "try" to activate as many units as he possibly could and as quickly as practicable.[49]

Such was the situation as the next phase of the rearmament program was about to begin. The blueprint for a French base section to support the CEF had been completed. Running the section now hinged on the ability of the French High Command to assign to it the necessary personnel.

Supply Situation—End of January 1944

By the end of January the long and tedious period of re-examination, begun with the suspension of the 15 August Plan, had come to an end. It had given rise to extensive reorganization in every field of the rearmament operations. A new equipment

---

[47] Ltrs, Col Olmstead, International Div ASF, to Loomis, 6 Nov 43, and Loomis to Olmstead, 11 Dec 43, JRC 908 Policy and Plan—Misc.

[48] Hq, Peninsular Base Section, History of the Peninsular Base Section, North African Theater of Operations, United States Army, Vol. II, Covering the Period 28 August 1943 to 31 January 1944 (Naples, 1944), Ch. IV, copy in OCMH.

[49] The three-eighths ratio was reached at the peak of Fifth Army's strength in May 1944. Of a total of some 13 divisions, 4 plus elements of a fifth were French.

Hq Fifth Army, Admin Dir 12, 23 Nov 43, in Opn Rpts, Fifth Army G–3, Sep 43–Jan 44, and Msg L–4528, Larkin to JRC, 22 Dec 43, JRC Cable Log; Memos, Loomis for Leyer, 29 Dec 43, 29 Jan 44, and Leyer for Loomis, 1 Feb 44, JRC 370/003 Employment of Sv Units.

program, the 23 January Plan, had been drafted which, unlike its predecessors, was considered reasonable, therefore capable of accomplishment. The substantial reduction of the number of combat divisions as agreed to by the French High Command was expected to produce personnel for the activation of supporting arms and services and for the manning of supply installations. A central supply authority similar to the American SOS was attempting, with American assistance, to set up an efficient supply system. A sound plan for the maintenance of expeditionary forces had been put into operation. A program of requisitions had been devised which, it was hoped, would guarantee the continuous flow of supplies from U.S. sources. These and other similar measures had one common purpose, the building up, within the shortest possible time, of a well-balanced French task force adequately equipped and properly maintained in battle.

The need to apply these measures with speed and vigor was emphasized by developments in Italy. Reports currently being received from that theater indicated that French troops were still arriving without their full initial equipment. The two divisions already there, the 2d DIM and the 3d DIA, were said to be fighting extremely well. It was all the more urgent therefore that they and their corps commander, General Juin, be given all the necessary material means with which to maintain their good

record. On 26 January General Kingman voiced to General Loomis the fear that the French had not learned ordnance supply as yet. He then pointed to a curious difference between the respective attitudes of French and American troops regarding supply matters: "Americans howl for what they want. The French anticipate that Higher Command will send what they should have." [50] Yet it was known that CEF authorities themselves had registered their concern over the shortage situation and taken steps to correct it. The Chief of Staff, Brig. Gen. Marcel Carpentier, had urged General Giraud to intervene energetically with the Commissioner of War to ensure that reinforcements reaching Italy would arrive fully dressed and equipped. Unless this was done, he had warned, maintenance stocks available to the CEF would gradually disappear.[51]

Despite these disturbing reports, there were signs that the supply situation would rapidly improve, for the French, bent as they were on assuming as large a share as possible of the fighting, were equally determined to correct errors as they were detected. In addition, the experience being gained as a result of their battle-testing in Italy was expected to be a valuable guide in implementing the next rearmament phase.

---

[50] Memo, Kingman for Loomis, 26 Jan 44, JRC 333/002 Inspections by Gen Kingman.
[51] Msg 182–A, CofS CEF to Giraud, 7 Jan 44, JRC Cable Log.

CHAPTER IX

Phase IV of the Program
(February–October 1944)
I: Background and Objectives

Rearmament Operations Resume

The 23 January Plan for rearming the French forces was formally presented to General Giraud by the Chief of Staff, AFHQ, on 1 February 1944 for his approval of its details. General Gammell reminded Giraud that the plan had been developed after lengthy conversations between French and AFHQ staffs, on the basis of available qualified manpower. The objective, which General Gammell hoped the French Commander in Chief would concur in, was to provide a sound troop list representing a balanced force suitable for the type of combat anticipated in ANVIL.[1] Thus was set forth in precise terms the final rearmament goal which AFHQ was determined to reach.

Three days earlier, General Devers had informed the War Department of the proposed revisions. Pending the final drafting of the plan, he had requested the early shipment of the matériel necessary to equip the remainder of such supporting units on the 15 August Plan as were expected to become part of the new plan. This matériel had already been assigned by the MAB but had not yet been delivered. He had also requested the War Department to fill as completely as possible shortages in previous assignments and shipments.[2]

AFHQ officials were confident that the French part of the ANVIL troop list as represented by the 23 January Plan provided as large and as well-balanced a force as the French military authorities could organize and train within the limitations of time and manpower.[3] The National Defense Committee, it will be recalled, had already approved the troop list. It only remained to obtain General Giraud's final decision. No word had been received from the French Commander in Chief since 11 January, when he had approved in principle the revisions then under consideration while reaffirming his intention of retaining the 15 August Plan "as a basis."

Concern at AFHQ increased when it was learned that Giraud had appealed directly to General Marshall for the retention of a fourth armored division. The U.S

---

[1] Ltr, Gammell to Giraud, 1 Feb 44, JRC Incl to 320/001.

[2] Msg W–1313/44211, Devers to AGWAR, 28 Jan 44, AFHQ Cable Log; Memo, Loomis for Leyer, 29 Jan 44, JRC 903 Requests for Units; Msg 8524, Somervell to Devers, 30 Jan 44, OPD Exec 1, Item 13–A; Msg W–1520, Devers to AGWAR, 31 Jan 44, AFHQ Cable Log.

[3] Memo, Brig Gen Daniel Noce, ACofS AFHQ, for CofS, 1 Feb 44, AFMQ 0100/12C G–3 Div Ops Fr Rearmt 2.

Chief of Staff seized this opportunity to remind him that General Wilson was eagerly awaiting his views on the current restudy of the program, on which to base final recommendations to the CCS.[4]

On 4 February, deciding to wait no longer for a reply from General Giraud, General Wilson cabled to the CCS the full details of the 23 January Plan. His message listed the units of the 15 August Plan to be deleted, those to be added, as well as the nonprogram organizations (Moroccan tabors, mule companies, and so on) for which maintenance only was requested. In a letter of the same date the Supreme Allied Commander recommended that the program be approved and assignments made without delay so that priority of shipments could be established at an early date.[5]

By his action, General Wilson was setting the wheels of the rearmament machinery in motion once again. There was little doubt that the CCS would endorse his recommendations without delay, for the proposed plan involved a relatively small outlay of equipment and its prospect of being carried out successfully was greater than that of any preceding plans. After a three-month period of re-examination, during which no assignments and only a few deliveries of equipment had been made to the French, the rearmament operations were entering a new phase, the fourth and last.

Control Over the French Forces

With the entire French forces expected to be engaged in combat in the near future, the question of their operational control was taking on increased importance. It will be recalled that at a conference held on 27 December 1943, Mr. Massigli, the French Commissioner of Foreign Affairs, had submitted to the U.S. and British political representatives in the theater the draft of a military agreement on the control and employment of the French forces. Two days later he had made known to his American and British colleagues the great interest which the French Committee of National Liberation attached to the speedy conclusion of an agreement.

The entire question was subsequently referred to the CCS who, on 11 March 1944, instructed General Wilson to present to the CFLN a counterproposal they had just approved. Article III of their own draft agreement stipulated that "the French forces to be placed at the disposal of the CCS is a matter for agreement between the CCS and the CFLN, it being understood that the forces placed at the disposal of the CCS will include all French forces which have been rearmed and re-equipped by the U.S. or the U.K." [6]

On 3 April, the CFLN proposed some modifications of the CCS document. The committee held, in particular, that the agreement should be with the two Allied governments and not with the CCS.[7] It was clear that the committee, which regarded itself as a *de jure* government in full possession of its sovereignty, desired that military matters be dealt with at government level. Already French civil authorities had attempted to take over the handling of rearmament negotiations with AFHQ. The Commissioner of War and Air, André Le

---

[4] Ltrs, Marshall to Giraud, 2 Feb 44, and to Devers, 3 Feb 44, OPD 336.2 France, Sec II.

[5] Msg W–1847/47163, Wilson to AGWAR, 4 Feb 44, NAF 597; Ltr, Wilson to CCS, 4 Feb 44, SHAEF 388.3/3 Fr Rearmt, 16 Mar 45, Dr 5418.

[6] Msg 1913, CCS to Wilson, 11 Mar 44, FAN 343; Ltr, Wilson to de Gaulle, 14 Mar 44, AFHQ 0100/12C G–3 Div Ops Fr Corres.

[7] Ltr, CFLN to U.S. and Br Representatives, 3 Apr. 44, AFHQ 0100/12A G–3 Div Ops BIGOT Fr.

Troquer, had requested on 12 January that thereafter all correspondence on armament questions be addressed to him. He had done so in pursuance of the decree of 16 December 1943 which specifically charged the Commissioner of War and Air with the task of implementing the decisions of the National Defense Committee regarding armament matters. But AFHQ officials considered that to deal with Le Troquer through the American and British ministers would be a particularly cumbersome method. Barring a CCS decision to the contrary or new developments in the theater, they agreed to continue to regard the French Commander in Chief as the official link between themselves and the French High Command on all rearmament questions.[8] Although informed of this decision, the commissioner kept writing directly to AFHQ. Replies to his queries were forwarded to him through French headquarters.

As the CFLN kept insisting that military matters be handled on a political level as between governments, General Marshall sought President Roosevelt's advice on the matter. The President informed him on 28 April that it was his desire that military questions which involved the French forces continue to be discussed directly between the Supreme Allied Commander and the French military authorities, and "not as between one sovereign government in full possession of its sovereignty and another government which has no *de facto* sovereignty."[9] This was a restatement of the

policy long advocated by the President, a policy based on his firm conviction that no French government could exist until the liberated people of France themselves established one of their choice. In December 1943 he had specifically informed the Department of State that he wished all military matters to be treated directly between General Eisenhower and the French military authorities and not on a government or committee basis. Later, in March 1944, when the question of establishing British and U.S. military missions to the CFLN was under discussion, the CCS showed, by their action, that they held the same view. They ruled that the proposed missions, if established, should "in no way infringe on the [Supreme Allied Commander's] position as the CCS representative in dealing with the French on military matters, especially French rearmament."[10] Finally, when, at about the same time, General Eisenhower began negotiating with French military authorities in London an arrangement to govern French-Allied relations in the proposed cross-Channel operation, General Marshall restated for his benefit the President's policy.[11]

In mid-May, after AFHQ had carefully examined the French proposal of 3 April, General Wilson cabled the views and recommendations of the theater on the control of French forces. First he outlined the prac-

[8] Memo, Le Troquer for Gen Wilson, 12 Jan 44, Memo, Whiteley for Minister Edwin Wilson, 14 Jan 44, AFHQ 0100/4 SACS Rcd Sec, Fr Matters, Vol. IV; Ltr, Gammell to Le Troquer, 26 Jan 44, AFHQ 400/1 Rearmt.

[9] Memo, President for Marshall, 28 Apr 44, ABC 091.711 France (6 Oct 43), Sec 1–A.

[10] Msg, CCS to Wilson, 28 Jan 44, FAN 329; Msg 890, Wilson to CCS, 20 Feb 44, NAF 623; Msg 197, JCS to Wilson, 29 Feb 44, SHAEF SGS 092 France, Vol. I, Fr Relations; Msg 2500, Marshall to Devers, 17 Mar 44, JRC Cable Log.

[11] Msgs 324, Marshall to Eisenhower, 17 Mar 44, and S–50531, SCAF 15, Eisenhower to CCS, 21 Apr 44, SHAEF SGS 092 France, Vol. I, Fr Relations.

tices then current. Under the terms of a naval agreement to which the French had subscribed, the Allied naval area commander exercised the operational control of all French naval units, rearmed and otherwise. This was consonant with the general policies set forth by the CCS on 4 October 1943 on the subject of French naval vessels.[12] With respect to the air squadrons, on the other hand, no formal agreement existed, the current informal arrangement being that when a squadron was ready, the French Commander in Chief notified the Allied air command in the Mediterranean, which assigned the unit to duty and assumed operational control of it. General Wilson then strongly recommended that a written agreement, similar to the naval agreement, be concluded with the CFLN which would ensure that all French land, air, and sea forces that were rearmed by the United States or the United Kingdom would automatically come under Allied operational control.[13]

By the end of May the control question had not been solved and no agreement was yet in sight. The launching of OVERLORD and ANVIL, in early June and mid-August respectively, would take place without any formal agreement having been reached other than a temporary arrangement concluded by General Eisenhower pending further negotiations with the French.

Reorganization of the French High Command

Meanwhile the showdown between the CFLN and General Giraud, which ob-

servers had long regarded as unavoidable, had come to pass. In spite of continued Allied support, the French Commander in Chief had had his powers so reduced by successive ordinances and decrees that by February he was able to make few, if any, decisions that were final.[14] In early April, a few days after his return to Algiers from a tour of inspection of the French units engaged in Italy, General Giraud was suddenly confronted with a dramatic situation. An ordinance issued by the CFLN on 4 April, apparently without prior consultation with him, announced a reshuffling of the National Defense setup. Invoking the law of 11 July 1938 bearing upon the general organization of the nation in wartime, the ordinance made the president of the CFLN titular Chief of the Armed Forces.[15] It established, in addition to the existing National Defense Committee, a General Staff of National Defense, a sort of war department placed directly under the president. Finally it abolished, although by implication only, the post of Commander in Chief. Feeling that his position was untenable, General Giraud at first declared his firm intention to resign. General Wilson, while concerned over the situation, did not anticipate that immediate serious repercussions would result from the French Commander in Chief's resignation. He was convinced that he could depend upon Giraud loyally to use his influence in favor of continuing the existing Franco-Allied collaboration.[16]

During the following three days, General Giraud deliberated with General Juin,

[12] CCS 358 (Revised), 4 Oct 43, sub: Policies Regarding Fr Naval Vessels.
[13] Msg F–46812, Wilson to CCS, 16 May 44; NAF 701; Memo, Col J. Terrence for Maj Gen Daniel Noce, 30 Jun 44, AFHQ 0100/12C G–3 Div Ops Fr Comd and Liaison 2.

[14] Personal Ltr, Devers to Marshall, 13 Feb 44, Somervell Files A–46–257, Ser 1, Dr 3.
[15] CFLN, Ordinance, 4 Apr 44, AFHQ 0100/12A G–3 Div Ops BIGOT Fr.
[16] Msg F–27715, Wilson to CCS, 4 Apr 44, NAF 661.

whom he had summoned to Algiers, and with various AFHQ officials including the U.S. and British political representatives in the theater. He then decided not to resign. The crisis came to a head on 8 April when General de Gaulle offered Giraud the post of Inspector General whose duties had been defined by a special decree. promulgated the day before.[17]

The reasons for the committee's latest action, as given by de Gaulle in a letter to General Giraud, appear sound when examined in the light of the situation then prevailing.[18] The post of Commander in Chief had lost much of its significance, considering that French expeditionary forces, when engaged in operations, passed under Allied command. It was not likely, moreover, that present and future Allied operational plans offered any chance for General Giraud to assume a field command commensurate with his rank. In addition, the CFLN had come to regard the handling of problems of organization and employment of forces its prerogative. In the opinion of the committee, therefore, the post of Inspector General was a logical substitute, one which General Giraud could fill with greatest advantage to French interests. Giraud, on the other hand, felt that acceptance of the post would entail a lessening of authority which would "prevent him from fully serving his country." Protesting against the decree which he considered arbitrary, General Giraud declined de Gaulle's offer and expressed his intention of continuing to serve as Commander in Chief.[19]

Announcement came on 12 April that Lt. Gen. Emile Béthouart was being appointed by decree Chief of Staff of National Defense. In effect, he was supplanting General Giraud. Thereafter, liaison with AFHQ was to be divided between Béthouart as Chief of Staff, National Defense, and General Leyer as Chief of Staff, Ground Forces. General Béthouart immediately called first on General Gammell, Chief of Staff, AFHQ, then on General Wilson, the Supreme Allied Commander, Mediterranean Theater, to inform them of the latest changes in command.[20]

Two days later, on 14 April, the CFLN, on the ground that General Giraud was unwilling to accept the post to which he had been assigned, decided to relieve him of all command although retaining him on active reserve.[21] The next day, General Giraud issued his last order, a pathetic farewell to the French forces. In it he took occasion to recall how he had obtained from America the armament which now enabled the units in Italy to show their worth.[22]

Whatever the merits or demerits of the CFLN actions that led to General Giraud's removal from the French High Command, it cannot be denied that he played a decisive role in the North African rearmament program. He had been its ardent champion even before his escape from France in October 1942; at Anfa in January 1943 he extracted a promise for arms from President Roosevelt; in July of the same year he went to Washington, there to

[17] Msg F–29518, Wilson to CCS, 8 Apr 44, NAF 669.
[18] Text of letter in Giraud, Un seul but, la Victoire, p. 287.
[19] Ltr, Giraud to de Gaulle, 9 Apr 44, in Giraud, Un seul but, la Victoire, p. 300.

[20] Min Mtgs, Béthouart with Gammell, and with Wilson, 12 Apr. 44, AFHQ 0100/12A G–3 Div Ops BIGOT Fr.
[21] Min Mtg, Béthouart with Wilson, 14 Apr 44, AFHQ 0100/12C G–3 Div Ops Fr Comd and Liaison, Pt. I.
[22] Fr CinC, GO 19, 15 Apr 44, AFHQ 0100/12A G–3 Div Ops BIGOT Fr.

plead for more arms and supplies; for months afterward he relentlessly fought for what he considered to be a major objective: the speedy rearming of a large striking force capable of taking a full share in the common fight against the Axis. At the time of his removal, the undertaking was nearly complete.[23]

Command of the French forces was now vested in the National Defense Committee, with General de Gaulle as its President, and the new General Staff headed by General Béthouart as its executive organ. On 15 April an instruction issued by the committee set forth the respective functions of the president of the CFLN and of the several Commissioners. The President, assisted by the General Staff of National Defense, was responsible for the general organization and distribution of forces as well as the general plans for their employment and equipping. The National Defense General Staff ensured liaison with military and civilian departments and with Allied staffs. The functions of the National Defense Committee and of the Commissioners of War and Air and of Navy remained as defined by the earlier decree of 16 December 1943.[24]

On 4 May General Béthouart outlined the internal organization and the functions of the National Defense General Staff of which he was the chief. One of its duties was to establish and carry out rearmament plans in pursuance of decisions reached by the Commissioners.[25]

Franco-American Relations

The departure of General Eisenhower and some members of his staff from North Africa in early January had brought a reorganization of the Allied command in that theater. As newly appointed officials were assuming their posts, Liaison Section, AFHQ, urged them to start a round of calls on French military authorities. Pointing to the hypersensitivity of which the French had seemed to be the victims since 1940, Liaison Section believed that these courtesy calls would do much to strengthen Franco-Allied co-operation.[26] The first meeting took place on 1 February when General Wilson, the Supreme Allied Commander, called successively on General de Gaulle, Le Troquer, and General Giraud. With the latter, he discussed, in particular, French participation in the Italian campaign. A week later, General Wilson received General de Lattre de Tassigny, commander designate of the French forces assigned to ANVIL, and with him discussed, among other matters, the perennial question of service units.[27]

Since his appointment, on 8 January, to the posts of deputy commander in chief and commanding general of NATOUSA, General Devers likewise was giving close attention to French matters, especially rearmament. Writing personally to General Marshall on 13 February 1944, General Devers outlined the French situation as he had found it upon assuming his command. He dealt largely with the question of Franco-American relations. At a time when increasing numbers of French and American troops were being or would soon be thrown

---

[23] General Giraud received the degree of Chief Commander of the Legion of Merit on 23 October 1943.

[24] National Defense Committee General Instruction, signed by de Gaulle, 15 Apr 44, AFHQ 0100/12C G–3 Div Ops Corres From the Fr.

[25] Memo, Béthouart for Col L. Higgins, Chief Liaison Sec AFHQ, 4 May 44, AFHQ 0100/12C G–3 Div Ops Corres From the Fr.

[26] Memo, Higgins for CofS AFHQ, 11 Jan 44, AFHQ 0100/26 Liaison Sec, Mtgs and Confs, Vol. I.

[27] Min Mtg, Wilson with de Lattre, 7 Feb 44, AFHQ 0100/12C G–3 Div Ops, F–1, BIGOT Fr.

together in combat, the question was taking on considerable importance.

General Marshall, it appears, had been greatly disturbed by the tenor of a confidential report which had recently reached him. Emanating from International Division, ASF, the report implied that Franco-American relations, which had started off so well, had seriously deteriorated, thereby creating "a condition which augured ill for the good of combined operations." The French, explained the report, were ascribing the present "unfortunate trend" to impatience, intolerance, lack of elementary courtesy, officiousness, and a belittling of French effort on the part of U.S. Army officers in the theater when dealing with their French allies.[28] While recognizing that misunderstanding did exist, Devers assured General Marshall that conditions as reported by ASF were grossly exaggerated. Discourtesy, even rudeness, had been present in isolated instances, he admitted. There was no evidence, however, that it was widespread. It would in no case be tolerated.[29]

There is sufficient reason to believe that General Devers' statement reflected accurately the situation prevailing at the time and, for that matter, during the two and one half years of Franco-American collaboration. French and American officers formerly associated with the Joint Rearmament Committee, when queried on the subject since the war, loudly and unanimously discounted the assertions of the ASF report. Several of the French officers so questioned frankly admitted that there had been occasions when an American official, presum-

ably exasperated at French incomprehension of his own views or at French slowness by American standards, had, under the impulse of the moment, acted in a harsh, even scathing manner. But, they quickly admitted, his behavior was generally quite justified, and, at any rate, never unfair. In other instances, they said, American incomprehension of the French viewpoint had caused the French to misinterpret the American position and intentions. They quoted the case of an American general officer who, because he had frequently questioned the validity or soundness of various armament requests submitted by the French, had led the latter generally to believe that he was anti-French. On the whole, they emphasized, American officials had been sympathetic to the French cause.[30]

General Loomis, who for nearly two years supervised French rearmament operations and therefore can speak with authority on the subject, could not, when queried on the matter, recall a single instance of bad feelings other than the alleged anti-French case reported above. He, too, emphasized that, considering the basic difficulties encountered, such as the language barrier and differences in national idiosyncrasies, Franco-American relations were, at the time of the ASF report and thereafter as well, "remarkably good."[31]

Having reduced the allegations contained in the ASF report to their true proportions, General Devers in his letter to Marshall next examined the causes of some of the grievances currently being voiced by the French. Until recently, he pointed out, they had been especially irritated by the very complex

---

[28] Memo, Col Eugene Villaret, International Div ASF, for Director International Div ASF, 21 Jan 44. JRC Misc Doc, Item 5–d.

[29] Personal Ltr, Devers to Marshall, 13 Feb 44, Somervell Files, Fr 1943–44, A–46–257, Ser 1, Dr 3.

[30] Intervs with Lt Col Roland de Beaumont, Jul 50, Brig Gen Jean Regnault, Jul and Sep 50, Col André L'Huillier, Sep 50, Gen Aimé de Goislard de Monsabert, Nov 48, and others.

[31] Interv with Loomis, Jul 50.

procedure through which their armament requests had to pass. He hoped that this particular grievance would soon be dispelled as a result of steps which he had just taken. He had authorized General Loomis to deal directly with General Larkin in all armament matters arising within the framework of established policies. He believed that this change in procedure would be appreciated by the French and would have an immediate favorable effect on relations with them.

Another grievance voiced by the French was that Americans in Washington promised more than Americans in the theater performed. They felt there was contradiction between the decisions announced by the War Department and the restrictions imposed by AFHQ and other Allied agencies. To clear up their misgivings in this connection, General Devers had undertaken to explain to them the existing relationship between the CCS, the War Department, and the theater.

The paucity of equipment available to French communications zone establishments necessary for the support of the expeditionary forces had been another source of friction. No provision had been made at Anfa or since for the issue of supplies to these establishments. It was hoped that the measures recently taken on their behalf would settle the issue to the satisfaction of the French.

General Devers then turned to one final French grievance. In the course of his recent visit to French troops fighting in Italy, he had heard them make one complaint: not enough food. This, he explained, was not the fault of the Americans, but of insufficient planning on the part of the French military authorities themselves.[32] AFHQ,

he pointed out, had taken action to make sure that, thereafter, French troops would get the full U.S. ration.

The 23 January Plan Becomes the Basis of Phase IV

All things considered, Phase IV got off to an auspicious start. A sound over-all program had been drawn up and submitted to Washington for approval. The French were putting their supply system in order. Closer relations with them were being sought. More important, glowing accounts were being received of their fine performance in action in Italy, a tangible proof that American efforts to rearm them were being wisely expended, and a decisive argument in favor of the speedy completion of the rearmament operations.

The general feeling of optimism was enhanced further by the announcement that General Giraud was approving the revisions contained in the 23 January Plan. Writing to General Marshall on 16 February, he declared himself in complete agreement with the principle that "a balance should be brought about between combat forces and service and supply units." In Washington, the Combined Staff Planners had already considered the plan favorably. On 2 March the CCS approved it "insofar as availability of equipment would permit." War Department officials immediately informed General Wilson that the necessary matériel, once assigned, would be shipped in accordance with theater priority. They warned him, though, that shortages were likely to occur in signal equipment, trucks, and artillery.[33]

---

[32] See the discussion on the food and troop ration problem, pp. 254–58, below.

[33] Ltr, Giraud to Marshall, 16 Feb 44, OPD 336.2 France, Sec II; Msg 1255, CCS to Wilson, 2 Mar 44, FAN 340.

On 13 March the MAB assigned all available equipment for the eighty-odd supporting combat and service organizations still to be equipped. Not all the matériel was to be shipped from the United States. Some of it had already been delivered as part of Phase III toward the requirements of the two divisions now deferred. For the rest, as much as possible was to be transferred from stocks available in the theater. At the request of the French, the JRC arranged with NATOUSA to have the locally available items of equipment issued to them before the arrival of the more important shipments. In this manner there would be no sudden congestion of their supply facilities.[34]

Before long, AFHQ and French authorities came to recognize the necessity of subjecting the 23 January Plan to minor modifications. Initially they had drafted the plan with a view to filling specific requirements for an operation, ANVIL, scheduled to take place around 1 May. As time passed, the target date was changed to early June, then to late July, finally to mid-August. Operational requirements were bound to fluctuate accordingly and with them the composition of the French troop list. Headquarters, Force 163, the Allied command organized in early January for the purpose of planning ANVIL, urged from time to time the addition of new units and the elimination of others no longer regarded as essential.

By the end of May the JRC had drawn up a tentative list of the units considered necessary for addition to the plan. All

were supporting service organizations except for two antiaircraft operations detachments and one tank destroyer battalion which American authorities urged the French to include in their troop list. In the case of some of these units, AFHQ felt that maintenance equipment only need be provided. To arrive at a final decision, some thirty-five representatives from AFHQ, NATOUSA, Force 163, and the French General Staff met on 13 June. They drew up a final list of revisions to be submitted first to the French High Command, later to the theater commander. At a second conference, held a fortnight later, the French proposed the further addition of three replacement depots and sixty replacement companies. The proposed revisions having been formally approved by all concerned, General Wilson recommended to the CCS on 17 July their incorporation in the 23 January Plan.[35]

The French, in the meantime, had requested and obtained inclusion in the program of an additional infantry regiment (the 4th Zouaves) for use not in ANVIL but in Corsica to reinforce the Sovereignty forces charged with the defense of the island. General Devers had already authorized SOS to issue the necessary equipment on loan, pending its assignment in Washington and replacement from future shipments.[36]

In early July the French also had urged the addition to the 23 January Plan of two more infantry regiments of two battalions

---

[34] Min, MAC (G) 134th Mtg, 13 Mar 44; Msg 2099, AGWAR to Devers, 13 Mar 44, and Memos, Leyer for Loomis, 29 Feb 44, Loomis for Leyer, 4 Mar 44, JRC 903 Requests for Units; Msg 223, Somervell to Devers, 18 Feb 44, ASF International Div Files, A–45–192.

[35] Min, Conf on Fr Rearmt, 13, 27 Jun 44, JRC 904 Modification of Rearmt; Msg, Wilson to CCS, 17 Jul 44, NAF 752; Memo, Loomis for Leyer, 7 Aug 44, JRC 904.

[36] Ltr, Leyer to Loomis, 21 May 44, Msg F–58925, Devers to Larkin, 13 Jun 44, and Memo, Loomis for Leyer, 21 Jul 44, JRC 903 Requests for Units.

each, to provide for a stronger infantry reserve in the forthcoming operations in southern France. They considered this increase necessary in view of the nature of the terrain and to offset the numerical insufficiency of infantry as compared with tanks in the existing composition of armored divisions. The two regiments were the 9th Zouaves and the 1st Algerian Tirailleurs (1st RTA). Again, on 10 August, the French recommended the addition of a mobile salvage unit to be used in southern France for the salvage and repair of matériel abandoned by the enemy within the French sector of operations. While theater officials were examining these two requests, the CCS, on 13 August, approved the revisions recommended earlier by General Wilson. They directed that the equipment already in the hands of units deleted from the troop list be repossessed and put into U.S. stocks without delay.[37]

By the time of the launching of ANVIL in mid-August, AFHQ officials had come to regard the French troop list as it stood then as quite satisfactory. This was evidenced by the action they took on the French request for two infantry regiments and a salvage unit. In a letter to General Béthouart dated 17 August, General Wilson declared that AFHQ would give no consideration to additional units or equipment until the current program had been completed. He pointed out that the CCS had been "very cooperative" and therefore should not be asked to approve equipment or units unless these were vitally necessary. In the case of the salvage unit in particular, AFHQ considered that there was no need for it in view of the existence of similar Allied organizations.[38]

In spite of General Wilson's warning, the French submitted, on 30 August and again on 22 September, a request for matériel to equip one escort troop and one headquarters company which General de Gaulle considered necessary for his own security and "for reasons of prestige." [39] Deciding against making any further recommendations to the CCS, AFHQ officials informally advised the French to resubmit their request to Supreme Headquarters, Allied Expeditionary Force (SHAEF), then established in Paris.

At the end of August, General Leyer furnished pertinent information on the state of activation of the units now approved for addition to the program. The tank destroyer battalion, for which 3-inch M10 guns had been requested, was organized and had been placed on the troop list. All other units were or would be ready by 30 September at the latest.[40] On 20 October the War Department advised the theater that no equipment for these units had yet been assigned in the absence of information as to the desired priority of shipment and ultimate destination. The theater had, in fact, cabled this information some six weeks earlier but its message had apparently been lost in transit. AFHQ then repeated the content of its first communication and stated that it wished the entire equipment, less the quantities reported earlier as being available in theater stocks, shipped immediately to the port of Oran from which French troops were being embarked for service in southern

---

[37] Ltrs, Leyer to Loomis, 8 Jul 44, and Mr. André Diethelm to Loomis, 10 and 18 Aug 44, JRC 904; Msg, CCS to Wilson, 13 Aug 44, FAN 390.

[38] Memos, Noce for JRC, 23 Aug 44, and Loomis for Leyer, 28 Aug 44, JRC 904.
[39] Ltrs, Leyer to Loomis, 30 Aug and 22 Sep 44, in same file.
[40] Ltr, Leyer to Loomis, 28 Aug 44, in same file.

France.[41] The War Department immediately submitted the necessary bids to the MAB. Once assigned, the matériel was shipped along with the rest of the equipment being furnished under the 23 January Plan.

Secondary Programs

Approval by the Combined Chiefs of the 23 January Plan, including the rider having reference to nonprogram units, came some five to six weeks after other important decisions. On 18 January they had authorized the issue of maintenance materials to a number of French Communications Zone establishments. Ten days later they had also approved an extensive rearmament program for the French Air Force.[42] These various measures were proof that the Anglo-American allies were determined to rehabilitate the North African forces to the fullest extent possible. Moreover, they were evidence of a desire to establish programs consistent with both French manpower and Allied production capabilities. But it soon developed that the French considered the provisions made with respect to nonprogram units and Communications Zone establishments as wholly insufficient, and they reopened the issue.

Nonprogram Units

The letter that General Giraud had addressed to General Marshall on 16 February signifying his general agreement to the terms of the 23 January Plan included an appeal for a more generous provision of matériel to nonprogram units. Under the

plan, they were to receive maintenance supplies only. It was indispensable, he urged, to replace without delay the initial equipment now in the hands of these organizations, as it had been issued at the expense of program units. In his answer, the U.S. Chief of Staff explained that, since the theater itself had originally recommended that only maintenance items be furnished, General Giraud should take the matter of further provision up directly with General Wilson.[43]

AFHQ had, by this time, recognized the necessity of granting the French request so as to make it possible to reduce shortages in program units from which equipment had been diverted. At a conference held on 12 March with General Devinck, chief of General Giraud's personal staff, General Gammell, Chief of Staff, AFHQ, promised that steps would be taken to obtain the necessary equipment. The French General Staff immediately prepared the requisitions and in early April submitted them along with others to the JRC. In transmitting them to the War Department, General Loomis requested that NATOUSA be authorized to transfer at once to the French, as partial fulfillment of the requirements, a number of items then available in theater stocks. Before reaching a decision, War Department officials asked for a justification of the contemplated transfer. General Loomis explained that the transfer was intended not to make up for shortages of assignments or shipments but primarily to replace equipment diverted for the benefit of nonprogram units. These units, he carefully pointed out, had been organized at the

[41] Msgs FX–94554, AFHQ to AGWAR, 10 Sep 44 (repeated in FX–46207, 31 Oct 44), and WX–54256, Somervell to SHAEF Mission to France, 29 Oct 44, in same file.
[42] See pp. 204–06, below.

[43] Ltrs, Giraud to Marshall, 16 Feb 44, and Marshall to Giraud, 4 Mar 44, OPD 336.2 France, Sec II; Msg 1372, Marshall to Devers, 4 Mar 44, JRC Cable Log.

request of the theater commander for service in Italy.[44]

By this time Lt. Gen. Roger Leyer had submitted to the JRC new requisitions for matériel urgently needed by the Shock Battalion and the Commando Battalion, two nonprogram units not intended for service in Italy. These units, each composed of one headquarters company, three combat companies, and one demolition company, and with a combined strength of 1,100 to 1,300 men, were then stationed in Corsica and participating in raids on enemy territory.[45] Their equipment was so inadequate that any further training was considered inadvisable. Also the men were reported to be suffering from such neglect in all spheres (insufficient clothing and food rations in particular) that they lacked energy and showed apathy in their work.[46] The JRC, however, decided that most of the items requested on their behalf by General Leyer had been included in the requisitions sent to the War Department on 17 April and that there was no need for further action.

On 5 May the War Department announced that the transfer of matériel proposed by General Loomis to fill shortages of initial equipment was approved except in cases where such shortages resulted from diversion of matériel to units not authorized initial equipment by the CCS.[47] With this ruling, all hopes vanished, temporarily at least, for the replacement of initial matériel issued to nonprogram units.

It soon became obvious that the diversion of equipment to nonprogram units had created such shortages as to make it impossible for the French military authorities to complete the equipping of program units. Gravely concerned over the situation, General Devers appealed once again to the War Department on 14 June. First he proceeded to justify the operational necessity for the activation and equipping of the nonprogram units. The tabor groups and mule companies, he explained, had been organized by the French at the urgent request of General Clark and with NATOUSA's approval in order to meet unexpected operational requirements presented by conditions of terrain that were unforeseen when the Italian campaign was planned. They had been engaged for several months and had rendered "invaluable support" in the successful operations of the U.S. Fifth Army. The Shock and Commando Battalions were standing ready for the conquest of the Island of Elba (Operation BRASSARD). Divisional instruction centers were considered necessary in view of the French replacement system. The Spahis Brigade had been issued initial equipment as a result of a personal agreement between Generals Smith and Giraud. It was not possible, warned General Devers, to take equipment away from these units nor could the units themselves be withdrawn from present operations or deleted from the ANVIL and BRASSARD troop lists. The promise had been made to the French that the equipment issued these organizations at the expense of program units would be replaced. Failure to fulfill this commitment was bound to jeopardize ANVIL. The only possible course of action, concluded General Devers, was to assign and float the equipment in question without delay.[48]

[44] Msgs F–33327, Devers to AGWAR, 17 Apr 44, WX–26296, Somervell to Devers, 22 Apr 44, and F–36083, Loomis to AGWAR, 22 Apr 44, JRC 400.4/005.

[45] Ltr, Leyer to Loomis, 9 Apr 44, in same file.

[46] Memo, Capt J. McNeil, Officer Commanding Commando Training Teams, for G–3 AFHQ, 27 Apr 44, in same file.

[47] Msg W–32523, Somervell to Devers, 6 May 44, in same file.

[48] Msg F–59425, Devers to AGWAR, 14 Jun 44, ABC 091.711 France (6 Oct 43), Sec 2–A.

Apparently impressed by the strength of General Devers' arguments, War Department officials took immediate action. Four days later they announced that initial equipment for the Spahis Brigade and tabor groups had been assigned. They were, however, referring the entire question to the CCS, the latter being the sole authority in the matter of the provision of initial equipment. In case the CCS turned down the proposal, the matériel already assigned would be deducted from future assignments to program units which had received no equipment, such as the fourth armored division and the remainder of the sixth infantry division.[49]

It was not until 14 July that the CCS finally approved the issue of initial equipment to Moroccan tabors, pack companies, and the Commando and Shock Battalions. With respect to replacement training centers, they approved the issue of a minimum amount of equipment to be used solely for the training of replacements earmarked for expeditionary units. The CCS then warned General Devers to make no further commitments to rearm additional French organizations without their approval. To keep the record straight, Devers replied that, except for the equipment given nonprogram units for operational reasons and that furnished for the purpose of filling shortages in program units alerted for operations, the theater had transferred no serviceable major items of initial equipment to the French without prior CCS approval.[50]

Sovereignty Forces

In the fall of 1943 theater officials, it will be recalled, had recommended against the provision of equipment to Sovereignty forces.[51] This position they maintained for some months but reconsidered it in May 1944 when the question of the responsibility for the ground defense of French North Africa came up for re-examination.

The Sovereignty forces had long taken an important share of the antiaircraft defense of North Africa and, since October 1943, had gradually assumed the entire coastal and air defense of Corsica. When in April 1944 AFHQ suggested that they take over the entire responsibility for the ground defense of North Africa, the French High Command accepted the commitment provided the units charged with the task received additional help in the way of equipment. AFHQ had hoped that they would take on the added responsibility with the equipment already available to them.[52]

Asked to comment on the matter, General Loomis pointed out that the needs of the Sovereignty forces must be assessed in the light of their operational duties. The units charged with the defense of the territory were, in his judgment, sufficiently equipped. Only in the case of those charged with the ground defense of Corsica was there some justification for providing more equipment. Even then, the inclusion in the 23 January Plan of an additional infantry regiment (the 4th Zouaves) for use as reinforcement on the island would probably be sufficient.

---

[49] Msg 53405, AGWAR to Devers, 20 Jun 44, ABC 091.711 France (6 Oct 43), Sec 2–A.

[50] Msg WX–64781, AGWAR to Devers and SACMED, 14 Jul 44, ABC 091.711 France (6 Oct 43), Sec 2–A; Msg F–7307, Devers to CCS, 17 Jul 44, JRC Cable Log.

[51] See p. 123, above.

[52] Two Ltrs, Smith to Devinck, 26 Oct 43, AFHQ 0100/12C G–3 Div Ops Fr Corres; Ltr, Béthouart to Gammell, 1 May 44, AFHQ 0100/12C G–3 Div Ops Corres From Fr; Ltr, Gammell to Béthouart, 14 May 44, AFHQ 0100/12C G–3 Div Ops Fr Rearmt.

It was with respect to the units responsible for maintaining internal security that, in the opinion of General Loomis, the provision of material assistance was wholly justified. He urged that these troops, then inadequately equipped, be furnished sufficient matériel to enable them, should the need arise, to carry out their duties satisfactorily. The forthcoming departure from North Africa of the bulk of the French expeditionary forces made this course of action all the more necessary. AFHQ immediately endorsed General Loomis' recommendation and requested the French military authorities to prepare and submit appropriate requisitions for consideration by the CCS. The new project was intended to provide generally for supplies of an expendable nature to be used for the maintenance of the clothing and equipment, French as well as German and Italian, currently in the hands of the troops concerned and for which U.S. maintenance materials were available. When the French requisitions were received and screened by the JRC, General Wilson cabled a request on 8 June for supplies consisting largely of raw materials and representing a total estimated at from 3,000 to 3,500 tons semiannually.[53]

The French felt that the internal security units needed also more arms. At their request, General Wilson urged the British Chiefs of Staff and the CCS to authorize the transfer to them of 100 Crusader tanks and 30 armored cars, all obsolescent, with sufficient spare parts for six months. The British Chiefs of Staff agreed to the proposed transfer provided the French clearly understood that the British Army accepted no continuing liability for the maintenance of the vehicles once the initial provision of spare parts had been exhausted.[54]

It was not until 1 July that the CCS finally approved the request for the provision to internal security troops of 3,000–3,500 tons of materials semiannually. They made it clear that their approval did not constitute authority for the issue of additional organizational and individual equipment. At the end of the month they authorized the proposed transfer of obsolescent British vehicles, such transfer to take place approximately ninety days before the departure from North Africa of the last British, French, or U.S. unit equipped with tanks and armored cars. As the last Allied unit of this type was due to leave within ninety days, General Wilson recommended and obtained approval that the proposed transfer be effected forthwith.[55]

The French, in the meantime, had requested and General Wilson had subsequently agreed, that the CCS be asked to approve the further transfer of American half-tracks, forty M3's and twenty-four M2's in all, with which to effect the motorization of the units due to receive the tanks. Motorization, they had explained, would enable the units to extend their radius of action and increase their mobility. The CCS approved the proposal on 11 August, with the proviso that the transfer be made concurrent with that of the British tanks and armored cars.[56]

---

[53] Memo, Loomis for Dever, 15 May 44, JRC 902/I Rearmt Plan: Msg F–66424, Wilson to TROOPERS, 30 Jun 44, JRC Cable Log; Msg, Wilson to CCS, 8 Jun 44, NAF 691.

[54] Msg, Wilson to CCS and COS, 15 Jun 44, NAF 714; Msg F–66424 cited in 53; Msg 3256, AMSSO to AFHQ, 22 Jun 44, AFHQ 0100/12C G–3 Div Ops Fr Rearmt.

[55] Msg, CCS to Wilson, 1 Jul 44, FAN 375; Msg, CCS to Wilson, 31 Jul 44, FAN 714; Msg, Wilson to CCS, 6 Aug 44, NAF 757.

[56] Msg, Wilson to CCS, 19 Jul 44, NAF 753; Msg, CCS to Wilson, 11 Aug 44, FAN 388.

The delivery to the security units of the tanks, armored cars, half-tracks, and maintenance materials followed close on the heels of the CCS approval.   With this matériel, the units, within a short time, were in a position considered favorable should they be called upon to engage in operations for the maintenance of internal security.   It is well to note here that throughout the ensuing months their duties remained light.   No development occurred significant enough to warrant their employment, at least while the war in Europe was in progress.[57]

---

[57] Just after the war ended, on 11 May 1945, severe rioting broke out at Sétif, Algeria. Forty Europeans were killed by natives. Rioting was followed by disturbances including the burning of outlying European farms. The Sovereignty forces quickly gained control of the situation. To reinforce them, the French authorities, with the approval of SHAEF, moved a few combat units from France to North Africa. Msg 4237, Lewis to SHAEF, FWD, 11 May 45, AFHQ 0100/12C G–3 Div Ops Fr Movements.

CHAPTER X

Phase IV of the Program
(February–October 1944)
II: Implementation

Equipping the Units on the ANVIL Troop List

While revisions of the 23 January Plan were being effected and secondary programs initiated, implementation of Phase IV was proceeding at a pace that quickened as the launching of ANVIL drew near.

On 18 March AFHQ requested the French High Command to nominate specific units for inclusion in the ANVIL troop list, and to indicate for each the respective U.S. or French table of organization and equipment, its strength in personnel and vehicles, present location, status of equipment, and date of readiness. Within a few days the French General Staff submitted the necessary information on the basis of which AFHQ immediately established and subsequently published, on 1 April, the official French troop list. The troop list actually incorporated all of the units included in the rearmament program. On 17 April the French headquarters informed AFHQ that General de Gaulle had officially appointed General de Lattre de Tassigny to command the French ANVIL forces.[1]

The American ANVIL forces comprised the Seventh U.S. Army, commanded by Maj. Gen. Alexander M. Patch, also Commanding General, Force 163. General Patch, under whose control the French forces were to operate during the initial phase of ANVIL, was watching the progress of their equipping with considerable interest. At his direction, Headquarters, Force 163, on 5 April, instructed NATOUSA to make sure that participating French units would be equipped and maintained on exactly the same scale as corresponding U.S. organizations. All logistical and other plans were being prepared accordingly.[2]

Aware that some U.S. tables of organization and equipment were currently being modified, G–3, AFHQ, voiced the opinion that any attempt at this juncture to change in a like manner the corresponding French tables would result in confusion and delay in readying units for combat. Instead, G–3 recommended that the JRC be asked to determine, with the assistance of all interested staff sections, the minimum requirements of equipment involved in each re-

---

[1] Memo, Gen Noce To All Concerned, 16 Mar 44, ASF Planning Div Files, A–47–192 Theater Br 15––Fr Military NA; Ltr, Gammell to Giraud, 18 Mar 44, JRC 320/004 Orgn of Fr Army (1 Jan 44); Memos, Noce for Liaison Sec AFHQ, 30 Mar

44, and G–3 AFHQ To All Concerned, 29 May 44, AFHQ 0100/12D G–3 Div Ops, Vol. I; Ltr, Béthouart to Wilson, 17 Apr 44, AFHQ 0100/12C G–3 Div Ops Fr Forces in ANVIL, Vol. I.

[2] Memo, Hq Force 163 for CG NATOUSA, 5 Apr 44, AFHQ AG 400–1 Fr Sups.

vised U.S. table, and to establish a method of obtaining the necessary additional equipment for the French. G–4 opposed the proposal on the ground that changes in U.S. tables would bring about a "continual deluge" of requests from the French for additional equipment without their turning in the matériel made surplus also as a result of changes. The JRC, on the contrary, agreed with the recommendation of G–3, and informed the latter that a procedure had already been established by which the War Department, upon the recommendation of the theater commander, obtained from the MAB the assignment of the minimum equipment required.[3]

On 17 June Headquarters, Force 163, indicated the dates by which French units were to be ready and requested NATOUSA to ensure that they would be fully equipped before their release to Force 163. SOS being vitally interested in the matter, its chief, Maj. Gen. Thomas B. Larkin, recommended a number of measures. He suggested that SCAMA, the JRC, and French headquarters be briefed sufficiently in the operation to know what troops must be equipped, in what order of priority, and how soon; that French Training Section be requested to perform thorough showdown inspections of each unit on the troop list; finally, that shortages of equipment be filled, first from French stocks and then from U.S. stocks.[4]

Representatives from G–4, the JRC, NATOUSA, Force 163, and SOS immediately took up General Larkin's recommenda-tions in the course of a series of conferences. They agreed first to brief SCAMA and the French General Staff. General Leyer was handed, on 23 June, a priority list of the units, program as well as nonprogram, to be fully equipped, trained, and made ready. Later General Loomis suggested to him that each organization be asked to submit requisitions for shortages to SCAMA, and that SCAMA be directed to issue all items available in French stocks and to forward consolidated requisitions to SOS for the remaining shortages. He promised that both the French Training Section and the Stock Control Section of the JRC, which he supervised, would furnish all possible assistance in this connection.[5]

Meanwhile, a large part of the equipment ordered from the United States under Phase IV had been assigned and delivered to North Africa. Only a small amount remained to be shipped. In a message dated 23 June, General Devers requested the War Department to float "on highest priority" all the rest of the equipment then awaiting shipment at ports and depots in the United States. The French units, he explained, were to be used in scheduled operations; it was urgent, therefore, that everything be done to reduce their shortages, particularly of critical items not available in theater stocks. The War Department replied that the necessary action was being taken and announced that the MAB had just assigned items omitted from previous assignments because of nonavailability at the time. Simultaneously, NATOUSA turned over to the French, in pursuance of earlier agreements with the War Department, substantial amounts of equipment available in U.S.

---

[3] Memos, Noce for JRC, 3 Jun 44, G–4 for JRC, 6 Jun 44, and Loomis for G–3, 6 Jun 44, JRC 320/004 Orgn of Fr Army (1 Jan 44).

[4] Memo, Hq Force 163 for CG NATOUSA, 17 Jun 44, AFHQ AG 400–1 Fr Sups; Memo, Hq SOS NATOUSA for CG NATOUSA, 19 Jun 44, Hq MTOUSA File, Fr Policy (Feb–Oct 44).

[5] Memo, Loomis for Leyer, 23 Jun 55, Hq MTOUSA File, Fr Policy; Memo, Loomis for Leyer, 6 Jul 44, JRC 400.1/009 Sup of Forces Designated for Combat.

stocks in North Africa, especially items required for the further training of troops.[6]

On 7 July General Béthouart, then on a brief visit in Washington with General de Gaulle, called on General Marshall to discuss with him the general situation of French rearmament. He urged that the rest of the matériel needed to complete the equipment of the fourth armored and the sixth infantry divisions be assigned without delay. The U.S. Chief of Staff promptly referred the matter to General Devers and asked whether it was the theater's intention to order any additional equipment over and above that delivered for the five infantry and three armored divisions. General Devers replied that all essential equipment required for pending operations had been ordered and, in fact, should arrive on time if action already initiated was completed as scheduled. It was true, he explained, that some matériel had not been ordered, but only because of the decision of the theater not to maintain organizations in the program for which the French High Command did not seem to have enough personnel. General Devers then offered a word of caution in connection with the presence in Washington of Generals de Gaulle and Béthouart. The French had just submitted several requests, which AFHQ had ignored, for equipping units to be activated from personnel expected to become available in continental France. It would be well, General Devers recommended, if General Marshall refrained from making any commitments based on statements made by Béthouart or de Gaulle without the theater's comments.[7]

By the beginning of August, no significant items of equipment for which the theater had cabled requisitions to Washington remained unassigned. Moreover, all items assigned had been shipped, received in North Africa, and turned over to the French along with the matériel available locally. Yet, the various inspections conducted in the preceding weeks by French Training Section had revealed some startling and disturbing deficiencies. At a time when the launching of Operation ANVIL was getting dangerously close, some units were reported to be still short an appreciable amount of initial equipment, with the result that much of their personnel had not been trained. Worse yet, several units— all supporting service organizations—had not even been activated. These were indeed serious matters, creating a situation likely to jeopardize the successful employment of the French in ANVIL. The problems involved were familiar ones: lack of technicians and shortages of equipment.

Service Troops and the Lack of Technicians

Activation of the units necessary to implement the 23 January Plan in its entirety was bound to create for the French military authorities insuperable difficulties owing to the continued dearth of technicians and specialists. The elimination of two divisions and the deferment of two more had not produced the expected number of skilled troops. The inability of the French High Command to organize in particular base units for the support of their forces in Italy forced a re-examination of the entire question of service troops.

---

[6] Msgs FX–63398, Devers to AGWAR, 23 Jun 44, and W–57516, AGWAR to Devers, 28 Jun 44, JRC 903 Requests for Units; Msg W–57137, Somervell to Devers, 28 Jun 44, JRC Cable Log.

[7] Memo, Béthouart for Somervell, 6 Jul 44, OPD

400 France, Sec IV; Msg W–61762, Marshall to Devers, 7 Jul 44, JRC 903 Requests for Units; Msg FX–70274, Devers to Marshall, 8 Jul 44, SHAEF Mission to France 475 Rearmt Plan and Policy, Ground, 900–1.

It will be recalled that, by the end of January, the French still had not made available to Peninsular Base Section in Naples any of the units necessary for the operation of Base 901, the French subsection of PBS.[8] On 3 February General Loomis requested General Leyer to nominate at least some of the required units as their presence in Italy was urgently needed. On the same day he complained to General Larkin of continued hesitation on the part of the French in providing units for PBS in spite of several conferences with them on the subject. If his latest communication to General Leyer did not produce immediate results, he intended to take the matter up with General Giraud or General de Gaulle.[9]

General Leyer promptly promised that some units would be made available by the end of February and others activated at a later date. What rendered their organization difficult, he explained, was the extensive reshuffling of personnel and equipment then going on in the army as a result of the application of the January Plan.[10] The Poste de Statistique, or Statistical Branch, of the General Staff was working feverishly to effect the necessary transfers.[11] General Leyer hoped that an accurate report on readiness for combat could be prepared by the end of February, when sufficient adjustments would have been effected.[12]

By this time the French military authorities were making frantic efforts to find qualified service troops for their many commitments. Most of the divisional and corps service units were activated. General Leyer also had succeeded in assigning approximately 8,000 additional effectives for duty with the French bases at Oran and Casablanca. But he still was faced with the problem of activating the army base and other service units provided for under the January Plan, and of assigning additional technicians and specialists to SCAMA, depots, and warehouses. Further aggravating his difficulties, AFHQ was urging him to activate two ordnance maintenance battalions in addition to the ordnance units required under the January Plan. General Loomis informed him that the need for these battalions was urgent; without them, French forces participating in ANVIL would have inadequate fourth and fifth echelon maintenance of artillery and armored vehicles. General Leyer flatly rejected the proposal on the ground that he could not undertake this additional commitment. All present reserves of specialists as well as troops in training and available at a later date, he explained, would be absorbed by service units already on the program.[13]

Intervening directly in the matter, General Giraud, on 3 March, informed General Wilson that the current general lack of service troops made it impossible for his headquarters to assign to PBS as many units as desirable for the support of the French forces in Italy.[14] A few days later, in the course of a meeting with Generals Wilson and Devers, Giraud warned that the same

---

[8] See p. 146, above.

[9] Memos, Loomis for Leyer, 3 Feb 44, and for Larkin, 3 Feb 44, JRC 370/003 Employment of Sv Units.

[10] Memo, Leyer for Loomis, 4 Feb 44, JRC 370/003 Employment of Sv Units.

[11] It had been established in March 1943 for the purpose of allotting U.S. matériel to the units designated for activation in first priority.

[12] Memo, Lt Atlas Cheek, Jr., for Col Crump, 15 Feb 44, JRC 905.6/1 Corres on Statistics of Rearmt.

[13] Memo, Loomis for Larkin, 3 Feb 44, JRC 370/003 Employment of Sv Units; Memos, Loomis for Leyer, 5 Feb 44, and Leyer for Loomis, 11 Feb 44, JRC 904 Modification of Rearmt.

[14] Ltr, Giraud to Wilson, 3 Mar 44, JRC 370/003 Employment of Sv Units.

lack of service troops would prevent the organization of the army and base services required for ANVIL. Reiterating his often-expressed conviction that it was "a pity to waste excellent combat troops by converting them into service units in which duty they were poor," he urged that the U.S. Army make every effort to furnish men for the services, thus permitting him to put more men in combat units. General Devers replied that the U.S. Army itself was short 10,000 men to meet its own service requirements in the theater. He voiced the hope that the French Army, after landing on the Continent, would find competent personnel to meet the requirements for service technicians. In the meantime he recognized that the U.S. Army would have to provide troops for the port and lines of communications, but would provide none for corps services.[15]

In the apparent belief that General Devers' statement left the door open for a more generous provision of U.S. service units, the French High Command, on 17 March, sounded out AFHQ on the matter, only to be told that General Devers had not meant that commitments made in January with respect to the ANVIL troop list were to be modified. The January agreement constituted the basis of the current program. The program itself had been formally acted upon by the CCS; it should therefore be considered as "firm and still binding." [16] The next day General Devers himself clarified his statement in the course of an interview with General Giraud. The U.S. Army, he asserted, would assist to the fullest possible extent in providing certain

port and base service units but it could not do more.[17]

There were sound reasons why General Devers' offer of limited assistance could not be extended further. He had sought, earlier in January, to obtain from the War Department the assignment of some U.S. service units to the French. General Marshall had informed him that the War Department "specifically decided and directed" that service units for support of French troops as requested by him could not and would not be provided.[18]

With the issue now closed, the French High Command endeavored to fulfill its commitments to the limit of available manpower. At the end of March a few service units were ready for movement to Italy. By special agreement between AFHQ and General Giraud, they were being assigned to General Juin's CEF for employment with Base 901. On 23 April the base was placed under the command of a general officer, Brig. Gen. Jean Gross, himself under the operational control of PBS. At the end of May and during the first two weeks of June, more service units were assigned to the CEF for employment, at the discretion of General Juin, with either the corps itself or Base 901.[19]

That the French military authorities did not reopen the issue with respect to technical troops does not mean that they succeeded in activating all the required units. Already at the end of March they had announced that they were unable, for the moment, to organize a number of units,

---

[15] Min Mtg, Giraud and Devinck with Wilson and Devers, 9 Mar 44, AFHQ CAO 1202 BIGOT ANVIL, Pt. I.

[16] Min Mtg, Devinck with Rooks and Noce, 17 Mar 44, AFHQ 0100/12A G–3 Div Ops BIGOT Fr.

[17] Min Mtg, Giraud with Devers, 18 Mar 44, AFHQ 0100/12A G–3 Div Ops BIGOT Fr.

[18] Msgs W–9779, Devers to Marshall, 10 Jan 44, and 2704, Marshall to Devers, 17 Mar 44, OPD Cable Files.

[19] Dir, Hq PBS, 1 Apr 44, JRC 370/003 Employment of Sv Units; CEF Rcds, File 88, OCMH.

among which were three general hospitals then on the 23 January Plan. The order of battle of the CEF as of 22 May 1944, when the corps was at the peak of its strength, shows that the U.S. Army had been forced to place at its disposal a considerable number of supporting units both combat and service. Practically all the corps field artillery and antiaircraft units were American.[20]

At the end of June, with preparations for ANVIL in full swing and the launching of the operation itself only a few weeks away, a report on the equipment status of the service units on the troop list revealed that as many as forty such units had not yet been activated. The French "division slice" was currently being estimated at 32,500 men instead of the required 40,000. On the basis of eight divisions it was feared that the French would lack approximately 60,000 service personnel needed to permit operation as an independent force. There was little doubt that the American Army would be compelled, as it had been in Italy, to make available substantial service troops of its own to the French expeditionary units if the latter were to be supported adequately in operations. In recognition of a situation which the French High Command was not likely to correct in time, the earlier stringent policy as contained in General Marshall's message of 17 March to General Devers was modified on 14 June. The War Department agreed that until French communications zone troops became available, U.S. Army service units could be employed "in indirect support of French combat organizations, but only when

such organizations were employed together with U.S. combat troops in operations under U.S. command, and when such support was incidental to the major mission of supporting U.S. combat units." [21]

Meanwhile, AFHQ officials were redoubling their efforts to induce the French High Command to activate forthwith all the remaining required service units. Their patience was severely tried when they were informed in early August that the French were planning to delay the activation of a number of organizations, mostly truck battalions and ordnance maintenance companies, while at the same time they were requesting equipment for infantry and other units not on the troop list. General Gammell seized the opportunity to remind them that any reduction of the number of service units or any delay in their readiness would have serious repercussions in the pursuit of the war. For this reason no consideration could be given to new requests for armament while such a situation existed.[22]

In mid-August, as ANVIL was about to be launched, the situation with respect to

[20] Msg F–25964, Devers to AGWAR, 1 Apr 44, ASF International Div Files A–45–192 Cables, Vol. IX; Fifth Army History, Pt. V, pp. 251–56.

[21] Memo, Hq Force 163 for SACMED, 21 Jun 44, AFHQ AG 400–1 Fr Sups; Memo, Col J. Terrence for Gen Noce, 30 Jun 44, AFHQ 0100/ 12C Div Ops Fr Comd Liaison 2; Quotation from Msg W–50668, Marshall to Devers, 14 Jun 44, AFHQ 0100/12C G–3 Div Ops Fr Equip.
The "division slice" consists of the total strength of the division plus the number of troops involved in maintaining the division in the field, that is to say, corps, army, army group, and communications zone troops. It is determined by dividing the theater strength (minus air forces) by the number of divisions in the theater. The normal division slice for the U.S. forces operating in Europe in 1944 was estimated at 40,000, made up as follows: 15,000 in the division itself; 15,000 corps and army troops; 10,000 communications zone troops.
[22] Ltr, Gammell to Juin, 15 Aug 44, AFHQ 0100/12C G–3 Div Ops Fr Corres; see p. 157, above.

service units was far from satisfactory. Some units were insufficiently manned, others were only partially equipped and trained, others had not even been activated. There was no alternative but for the U.S. Seventh Army to direct its own service units to assume such support of the French forces as the French High Command was unable to provide.

Shortages of Equipment

As Phase IV opened, the problem of shortages, which had plagued the French for many months, was facing them with undiminished gravity. Reports currently being received from Italy indicated that units were still arriving without essential items of equipment. The reasons were many.

Not all the equipment expected from the United States had been or was being received in North Africa. Some items were unobtainable; others were deleted by the War Department because they were considered nonessential, or because their shipment would jeopardize other commitments. Sometimes, initial equipment arrived without some of the required 30-day maintenance items or 6-month spare parts. At other times, the French failed to submit proper and timely requisitions, or the equipment was ordered by the JRC on the basis of U.S. tables of organization and equipment for units activated on different tables. Furthermore, of the matériel actually received, the French were diverting substantial amounts to equip nonprogram units, run depots and training centers, or maintain units during their period of training, a period extending not infrequently over several months. Finally, and not the least impor-

tant, the order of priority for the readying of alerted units and the corresponding dates of readiness were subject to sudden changes by order of AFHQ.[23]

The French supply system, which still had not progressed to a point where it could handle even routine matters smoothly, was seriously taxed by the unexpected. In spite of considerable juggling of equipment, involving at times the complete and hasty turnover of matériel from one unit to another, the French military authorities were continually faced with the alternative of calling on SOS to complete the initial equipment and basic loads of alerted units or of embarking the units improperly equipped. Greatly concerned over the situation, American officials in the theater undertook to survey its causes with a view to devising adequate remedial measures.

The submission by the French of requisitions for initial equipment still appeared to be a source of considerable difficulty to them. To clear up some of the technical problems involved, a conference, called at the suggestion of the French themselves, was held on 17 February between members of the JRC and French G–4 officers responsible for the submission of requisitions. The conferees discussed and finally agreed on a satisfactory procedure. They agreed further that the requisitions would serve to complete the equipment of the units designated for combat. The matériel to be requisitioned was to replace that previously drawn from program units and diverted for

---

[23] Memo, Charpentier To All Concerned, 21 Feb 44, JRC 400.1/009 Sup of Forces Designated for Combat; Memo, Director International Div for CG North African Theater, 25 May 44, JRC 903 Requests for Units; Memo, G–4 Sup Br for ACofS G–4 SOS, 18 Jun 44, Hq MTOUSA File, Fr Policy.

various purposes; it would also be used to re-equip units after combat.[24]

Having been informed by General Loomis on 19 February that the French had not requisitioned any additional major ordnance items for replacements, General Larkin once again inferred that they were depending on the United States for maintenance of their units in North Africa and elsewhere. The French, he pointed out, still were not providing full initial equipment for departing units, as evidenced by two new cases just reported. One artillery regiment had reached Italy equipped with only one pair of shoes per man, and with three of its twelve 155-mm. guns not in working condition; a training center had arrived short of tents and training equipment. Warning that the Fifth Army stocks would soon be depleted if emergency issues to inadequately equipped troops were allowed to continue, General Larkin urged that the JRC arrange to have every French organization about to depart from North Africa inspected by U.S. officers to ensure completeness of equipment. General Loomis objected that such a procedure was not practicable owing to lack of personnel. He pointed out that the U.S. advisers with French divisions were already submitting weekly reports to the JRC indicating what shortages existed. The attention of the French had been drawn to the matter and he felt certain that the situation would soon improve.[25]

General Loomis immediately informed General Leyer of the great concern currently felt by Generals Larkin and Devers regarding the question of shortages. He reiterated that responsibility for the completion of equipment of units alerted for movement rested solely with the French High Command.[26] Realizing that only energetic action taken without delay could solve the problem, Maj. Gen. Daniel Noce, G–3, AFHQ, called Generals Larkin (SOS), Loomis (JRC), Kingman (French Training Section), and others for a conference on 4 March. General Larkin repeated his earlier recommendation that units be completely inspected before leaving North Africa in order to determine shortages. "Someone has to decide whether they are battle-fit," he insisted. This, explained Generals Loomis and Kingman, was being done. Inspections, however, were in French hands and the responsibility for completeness of equipment, they believed, should remain French. Once in the field, the units reported shortages to the U.S. teams attached to them by General Kingman. In some instances, they claimed to be short certain items of equipment, when in fact the French tables of organization and equipment under which they were equipped did not call for them. In other cases, the responsible authorities had not received the new French table in time. The conferees agreed that efforts should be made to expedite the printing and distribution to all units of the exact table under which each was to operate. After the conference, AFHQ informed General Clark, Commanding General, Fifth Army, that difficulties incidental to shortages appeared to be due largely to lack of knowledge of the

---

[24] Memo, Regnault for Loomis, 7 Jan 44, JRC 402 Sup Policy; Min, Conf AFHQ, 17 Feb 44, JRC 400.1/009 Sup of Forces Designated for Combat.

[25] Msg 53748, Loomis to Larkin, 19 Feb 44, JRC 402 Sup Policy; Msg L–1635, Larkin to Loomis, 20 Feb 44, JRC Cable Log; Msgs L–1603, Larkin to JRC, 20 Feb 44, and 55172, Loomis to Larkin, 22 Feb 44, JRC 400.1/009 Sup of Forces Designated for Combat.

[26] Memos, Loomis for Leyer, 25, 26 Feb 44, JRC 400.1/009 Sup of Forces Designated for Combat.

appropriate tables of organization and equipment under which French units were organized and equipped. Copies of these tables were being prepared in sufficient quantity and would be forwarded to his headquarters without delay.[27]

On 8 March, the War Department issued a directive on the replacement and maintenance of equipment for the French forces. The directive embodied and formalized the several actions taken earlier. It set forth in detail the manner in which shortages of initial equipment and of replacement and maintenance items were to be requisitioned for both combat and noncombat units, and prescribed the accounting procedure to be followed for each category of items. The procedure remained in force until June when it was revised to conform with new War Department policies.[28]

In spite of vigorous action on the part of French and Allied headquarters, the problem of shortages continued to be a thorny one. In early April the U.S. Fifth Army informed General Devers that two pioneer (labor) regiments had arrived in Italy "with such large number of initial shortages as to be impractical to list by cable." In mid-April an inspection of the 1st Motorized Infantry Division about to depart for Italy revealed important shortages of mortars, machine guns, radio sets, trucks, and other items. The division, until recently British-equipped, had been re-equipped with U.S. matériel largely drawn from "nonparticipating" units. These were the units not designated by AFHQ for immedi-

ate participation in operations. Among them were the 1st and 5th Armored Divisions, both program units and both on the ANVIL troop list, but whose presence was not required in Italy. The 1st DMI was still holding some British equipment (such as mortars, Brens, tents, wreckers) besides French and Italian matériel. Fifth Army, having no maintenance facilities, parts, and ammunition for such non-U.S. equipment, requested AFHQ to effect its immediate replacement. It was not until the middle of April that the division, then on its way to Italy, was reported as having all its initial U.S. equipment except antiaircraft weapons.[29]

Simultaneously with the 1st DMI's departure from North Africa, the 2d Armored was being readied for shipment to the United Kingdom, there to be included in the forces designated for the cross-Channel operation (OVERLORD). The CCS had agreed at the TRIDENT Conference in May 1943 that a token French force would participate in OVERLORD.[30] In late January 1944 the Allied command had further decided that French elements would be included among the first troops to enter Paris. The 2d DB had subsequently been chosen for this honor by the French military authorities. This division, like the 1st DMI, was once British-equipped and had now been rearmed with U.S. matériel. It moved to the United Kingdom in mid-April with approximately 100 percent of its initial equipment and basic loads, plus

---

[27] Msg 60678, CinC to Fifth Army, 6 Mar 44, AFHQ 0100/12C G–3 Div Ops Fr Rearmt; Msg 2345, Fifth Army to CinC AFHQ, 21 Mar 44, JRC Cable Log.

[28] Ltr, WD AG 400 (8 Mar 44) to CG NATOUSA and CG N.Y. Port of Embarkation, 14 Mar 44, amended by Ltr, WD AG 400 (7 Jul), 11 Jul 44, JRC 402 Sup Policy.

[29] Msgs 2245, Fifth Army to CG NATOUSA, 3 Apr 44, RFTS 101, Inspection Team to CG Fifth Army, 19 Apr 44, 8321, Fifth Army to CG AFHQ, 10 Apr 44, and F–35027, CinC AFHQ to Allied Armies in Italy, 20 Apr 44, JRC 400.1/009 Sup of Forces Designated for Combat.

[30] Min, 5th Mtg with President and Prime Minister, 24 May 43, TRIDENT Conf.

a 30-day supply of tank replacements.[31] While in the United Kingdom, the division became the supply and training responsibility of the U.S. Third Army, under whose control it was placed, and was maintained in the same manner as U.S. divisions. Third Army determined the exact status of its equipment and submitted requisitions to SOS, ETOUSA, operating in the United Kingdom, for the few existing shortages. These were filled from U.S. Army stocks in the theater and all transfers of matériel were reported by chiefs of services in accordance with current lend-lease directives.[32]

Another division about to depart for overseas duty was the 9th Colonial Infantry. Its destination was Corsica, liberated in September 1943 by French troops, where it was to prepare for future operations in the Mediterranean.

The final equipping of the 1st DMI, 2d DB, and 9th DIC had necessitated the filling of numerous shortages. This had been accomplished by securing the missing items from one of the following sources, in order of precedence: from French sources other than nonparticipating units, that is, from all stocks available to the French; from excess U.S. theater stocks; from nonparticipating units; and from U.S. theater stocks, provided it did not jeopardize the support of U.S. forces. The procedure followed had been that established by NATOUSA on 7 April.[33] SCAMA, SOS, and Stock Control Section, all had shared in the task.

The procedure as set forth by NATOUSA, although simple in appearance, was, when put into application, quite complex because of the many channels of communication involved. As pointed out later by one of the U.S. advisers to the French divisions, to fill a shortage of initial equipment might require no less than twenty administrative steps.[34] Nevertheless, in spite of its complexity, NATOUSA extended its application thereafter to all other units subsequently alerted.

In mid-April the French began submitting, at the request of the JRC, a large number of requisitions designed to complete as fully as possible the initial equipment and basic loads of all remaining units on the troop list. These requisitions were also designed to provide, at least for the second half of 1944, the minimum maintenance requirements of the Territorial establishments necessary for the support of expeditionary forces. The requisitions were first screened by the JRC, then checked against the list of equipment currently available in excess theater stocks, which SOS furnished at frequent intervals. From these lists the JRC extracted the items required and requested the War Department to authorize their transfer. Granting this authorization was a routine matter in itself but necessary for proper co-ordination with supply agencies in the United States. NATOUSA then arranged for the immediate turnover of the equipment. The locally unavailable items were requisitioned from the United States.

Feeling that some French requisitions

---

[31] Msg F–34203, Devers to AGWAR, 18 Apr 44, JRC 400.1/009 Sup of Forces Designated for Combat.

[32] Memos, Hq ETOUSA for CG Third Army and SOS ETOUSA, 10 May 44, and Hq ETOUSA for CG Third Army, 24 Aug 44, SHAEF G–3 091 France, Vol. I.

[33] Ltr, NATOUSA AG 400/466 D–O, 7 Apr 44, JRC 370/001 Employment of Units—Gen.

[34] Memo, Liaison Office Fr Training Sec for JRC, 26 May 44, JRC 400.1/009 Sup of Forces Designated for Combat.

were excessive, General Larkin questioned whether the French Supply Services were exploiting their own resources to the maximum before calling on U.S. theater stocks for equipment. He recommended that, except in cases of actual emergency, only items listed as "excess" in theater stocks be given to the French. The continued issue of other items, he feared, would jeopardize seriously the American supply situation and, in addition, would encourage the French to depend too heavily on the U.S. Army for completion of initial equipment of both alerted and nonparticipating units.[35] General Loomis, likewise, was disturbed by the size of some of the French requisitions, especially those submitted for medical items. He could not help but feel that they were indicative of a desire on the part of the French to build up stocks for ultimate use in continental France either by the civilian population, or by units raised there.[36]

To ensure that the French requisitions were fully justified, the JRC subjected them to more stringent scrutiny and screening. Simultaneously the JRC urged the French once again to exploit their own resources to the limit. In the case of the units which had left North Africa incompletely equipped, General Loomis arranged for the U.S. base section nearest to them to honor the French requisitions as rapidly as possible.

In late May General Leyer forwarded to the JRC a list of requisitions for matériel with which to re-equip the 2d DIM and 3d DIA after their expected withdrawal from the Italian front, in anticipation of their ultimate engagement in ANVIL. General Leyer's action was consonant with a recommendation made several months earlier by

General Loomis. As the requisitions appeared to contain for the most part supplies normally furnished through SOS as maintenance, General Loomis and SOS agreed that they need not be acted upon. They then informed General Leyer that SOS would assume the responsibility for re-equipping all French units operating in Italy before their engagement in ANVIL.[37]

On 16 June Headquarters, NATOUSA, issued a final directive on the readying of French participating units. The directive instructed SOS to see to it that the French completed from their own stocks the initial equipment and basic loads of each unit before it was alerted for movement overseas. As the unit was alerted, SOS would issue to it from U.S. stocks such supplies as were unobtainable from French sources.[38]

The remaining task now was to make arrangements for the adequate and timely provision of the maintenance supplies expected to be required in the course of the following twelve months by forces other than expeditionary units. It will be recalled that on 18 January 1944 the CCS had approved the issue of some maintenance materials to Territorial units and establishments supporting the expeditionary forces and, on 1 July of the same year, the provision of 3,000–3,500 tons semiannually of maintenance materials for the Sovereignty forces. In fulfillment of these decisions, the French, in mid-July, submitted requisitions covering the second half of 1944 and, on 15 September, those for the first half of 1945. Once the requisitions were screened and properly

---

[35] Msg L–17212, Larkin to JRC, 26 Apr 44, JRC 400.1/009 Sup of Forces Designated for Combat.
[36] Memo, Loomis for CofS NATOUSA, 17 Apr 44, JRC 902/I Rearmt Plan.

[37] Ltr, Loomis to Leyer, 22 Jan 44, and Memos, Loomis for McKay, 1 Jun 44, Loomis for Leyer, 21 Jun 44, JRC 400.1/009 Sup of Forces Designated for Combat.
[38] Ltr AG 400/466 D–0, Hq NATOUSA to CG SOS, 16 Jun 44, JRC 370/001 Employment of Units—Gen.

cut down in the case of unnecessary items, the matériel available in the theater was turned over to the French and the rest ordered from the United States.[39]

By the time ANVIL was launched, the situation with regard to shortages had substantially improved. In addition, since some units, especially service organizations, were not expected to land before D plus 25, it was hoped that their shortages would be filled by then. At any rate, General Loomis was satisfied that the French military authorities were making a "real effort" to supply all available items from their stocks. Their task, he recognized, was still greatly handicapped by the dearth of competent supply personnel and the fact that serious shortages and delays in shipments from the United States were placing "a tremendous burden" on them.[40]

SCAMA's Role During Phase IV

Throughout Phase IV, SCAMA, ably assisted by the American Stock Control Section, continued its efforts to assert itself as the supreme French supply authority.[41] Its difficulties, numerous enough from the start, had increased as a result of the application of the decree of 16 December 1943 which divided military responsibility between the Commissioner of War and Air and the Commander in Chief.[42] In January and early February, this responsibility was split fur-ther by the delegation of some authority to the General Staff, the heads of services, and to a smaller extent to the commander-designate of the French ANVIL forces. General Loomis greatly feared that the establishment and continued operation of an effective supply organization were next to impossible. In his judgment the time had come for the French High Command to nominate a general officer armed with sufficient authority to correct a situation likely to affect adversely current and future operations.[43] The French took no such step, but the appointment, later in April, of General Béthouart as Chief of Staff of National Defense did result in a centralization of responsibility.

As SCAMA and supply installations struggled toward standardization, the French General Staff authorized, about 1 February, certain depot and port units for activation one month later. Even though these units never materialized, their authorization served to call attention to the need of reinforcing the personnel in depots and ports. To fill this need, General Leyer recruited additional civilian employees and ordered service units of the expeditionary corps placed on temporary duty with SCAMA while they waited to be shipped overseas. In general, the personnel situation began to improve in early February even though no definite plan had been established.

On 15 February Maj. Gen. Arthur R. Wilson, Commanding General, Mediterranean Base Section, informed General Larkin that all U.S. officers assigned to French depots were reporting notable improvements. Progress was further evidenced by the fact that the French were now replac-

[39] Ltr, Leyer to Loomis, 15 Jul 44, JRC 400.4/006; Memo, Leyer for Loomis, 15 Sep 44, SHAEF Mission to France Requisitions, 1st half of 1945; see pp. 128, 161, above.
[40] Memo, Loomis for G–4 SOS, 12 Sep 44, JRC 400.1/009 Sup of Forces Designated for Combat.
[41] Sources for this section: JRC 400.2/002 Stock Control System; History of Stock Control Section, JRC, copy in JRC Files.
[42] See p. 118, above.

[43] Memo for Rcd, Loomis, 2 Mar 44, JRC 320/004 Orgn of Fr Army (1 Jan 44).

ing in U.S. depots, at an increased rate, the items of equipment issued for the maintenance of their forces in Italy. By early March, SCAMA's director, Colonel Charpentier, felt that "the worst was over." He predicted that the sample inventory scheduled for the second week of March for the purpose of checking the accuracy of SCAMA's records would show a definite improvement. Actually, the inventory did reveal substantial errors, in extreme cases running as high as 80 percent. The discovery shocked the French into realization of the need for still more energetic action.

Meanwhile a publication depot at SCAMA headquarters had been set up. English-French technical dictionaries prepared especially for each service became available. So did a second supply textbook written in both languages. French and American officers on duty with SCAMA were given courses of instruction on the new supply system and the correct use of forms. Once thoroughly schooled, the U.S. officers were posted in French offices and warehouses throughout North Africa to give on-the-spot assistance on all supply matters. Still there were frequent cases where French chiefs of services would issue to their depots directives at variance with the SCAMA textbooks.

By 15 May, when the French were conducting a general inventory of stocks throughout North Africa, it became apparent that rapid strides in warehousing and recording had been made. SCAMA had reached a turning point in its existence. For the first time it had a fairly complete and accurate picture of all stocks on hand, with the possible exception of ordnance and engineer spare parts. In June detailed inspections of all depots conducted by joint Franco-American teams re-

vealed that the SCAMA system was in operation in all warehouses and offices. Establishment of SCAMA as the sole supply authority in the French Army could at last be considered an accomplished fact. The system had become sufficiently entrenched to render almost impossible any return to the haphazard practices of the old days.

SCAMA extended its activities to the entire supply field. It was now responsible for preparing and submitting requisitions to the JRC; for receiving, sorting out, assembling, and stocking matériel in the various depots; for maintaining supply levels, regulating the movement and transport of supplies, and keeping proper accounting of U.S. matériel according to lend-lease regulations. It had full authority to distribute equipment in accordance with priority lists and tables of organization and equipment established by the French High Command. If a unit was called forward before it was completely equipped, SCAMA was empowered to issue to it a "cheque" or bill of credit which enabled it to draw the necessary items from the U.S. base in the theater of its destination. In short, SCAMA had become the SOS of the French Army.[44]

By early July Colonel Geraghty, chief of Stock Control Section, considered that SCAMA could be left to continue its development "along lines natural to the French" and that the presence of his section was no longer needed. On his recommendation, Stock Control Section was disbanded near the end of the month. But SCAMA continued to operate long after the launching of ANVIL, since much work remained to

---

[44] Notes from Col Maurice Labarbarie, Jan 52; Rpt, Col Labarbarie, 18 Jul 44, sub: Functioning and Role of G–1 SCAMA, copy in OCMH.

be done for the supply of the expeditionary forces.

Repossession of U. S. Equipment

Repossession by the U.S. Army of American matériel in French hands took place in a number of cases and for a variety of reasons, all consonant with established policies governing French rearmament and with the theater's responsibility for ensuring the judicious and economical use of all American equipment. Frequently the purpose was to recapture matériel issued in an emergency on the understanding that it would be returned out of subsequent shipments to the French. A case in point is the return to SOS depots of the tools, spare parts, and supplies which SOS had loaned to the French in early April 1943 for setting up and operating their motor vehicle assembly plant at Algiers. In this instance, repossession was effected simply by appropriating the same materials directly from subsequent convoys bringing equipment for the French.[45]

In other cases, particularly numerous during Phase IV, repossession was ordered because the matériel in question was considered "excess" in French stocks for one of the following reasons: it had been delivered by error, it was now in the hands of units once part of approved troop lists, or American officials considered its further use by the French no longer justified. In such cases, repossession involved considerable difficulty, often making it impracticable. The problem became particularly acute in April 1944, when a number of units, not likely to be activated, were stricken off the troop list.

The theater requested from the War Department the authority to instruct the French to return to U.S. depots all ordnance equipment which had then become excess, except general-purpose vehicles of which the French were still short. The authority was immediately granted with the understanding that proper credit reports would be made on all returns and a detailed list of items involved transmitted to the MAB in Washington for information. The French then directed SCAMA to effect the necessary returns.[46]

The operation proved to be more complex than had been anticipated. In the first place, SOS had no knowledge of just what the French were to return. NATOUSA asked the War Department for a detailed list of all equipment that had actually been shipped for the units in question. To complicate matters, the French had used the equipment received on a French table of organization basis with the result that the matériel currently in the hands of the units did not correspond to what had been ordered initially. Finally the French felt that they could not return certain items as they had used them to fill shortages in other units or had given them to training centers. As a result a considerable exchange of correspondence took place during June, July, and August between NATOUSA, SOS, the War Department, and French headquarters. Such items as the French were finally able to return were held in SOS depots pending a decision on their ultimate disposition.[47]

The confusion was further increased by the addition, throughout the early summer

---

[45] Msgs L–2316, SOS to CG Atlantic Base Sec, 15 Apr 43, and L–2317, SOS to JRC, 15 Apr 43, JRC Cable Log.

[46] Msgs F–34037, Devers to AGWAR, 18 Apr 44, and W–26607, Somervell to Devers, 22 Apr 44, JRC 909 Surplus Equip.

[47] Msg F–47011, Devers to AGWAR, 17 May 44, JRC Cable Log; Memo, CG SOS for CG NATOUSA, 2 Jun 44, JRC 909 Surplus Equip.

months, of new units to both the 23 January Plan and the Air Force program. To simplify matters, General Loomis asked the French to transfer to these units the greater part of the items which had become excess as a result of the elimination of others, and to keep him informed of such transfers.[48]

Repossession of U.S. equipment was consonant with the basic principle under which French rearmament had operated from the beginning, namely, that only approved units were entitled to receive and hold Allied equipment. The CCS did not fail to remind the theater commander on 13 August that the French were to return the matériel in the hands of units no longer on approved troop lists.[49]

Disposal of British Equipment

A minor issue raised at the beginning of Phase IV and rapidly settled concerned the ultimate disposal of British equipment still in the possession of the French. On 8 February General Wilson, the Supreme Allied Commander, requested the French military authorities to hand over all such equipment to the British Ordnance Services. The National Defense Committee immediately instructed Le Troquer, the Commissioner of War and Air, to take the matter up with AFHQ and settle it within the framework of the Protocol of Anglo-French Mutual Aid recently signed.[50] The protocol had laid down that the government of the

United Kingdom could, after the cessation of hostilities, ask for the return of "such matériel supplied by it that was not destroyed, lost or worn out." The French military authorities interpreted this to mean that they could continue to use the equipment for the duration of the war. Although not intending to maintain any organizations equipped with British equipment, Le Troquer explained to General Wilson that the French High Command had "various needs closely related to the common war effort" which could not be satisfied from American sources.[51] This was true, he said, of general-purpose vehicles, tank transporters, and spare parts for the maintenance of British equipment. To arrive at a satisfactory solution, Le Troquer suggested that responsible French and British authorities meet to determine what items urgently needed by the British should be handed over. General Wilson having approved the proposal, British and French staff officers drew up a list of equipment to be replaced in British depots and advised General Leyer to complete the agreed transfer at the earliest possible date.[52] With respect to the matériel which the French were to keep, General Wilson pointed out that the British Army could not accept permanent liability for its maintenance now that the French forces were being re-equipped with U.S. matériel. Whenever possible, however, the British supply services would make every effort to furnish spare parts or provide maintenance.

---

[48] Memo, Loomis for Leyer, 5 Jul 44, JRC 909.
[49] Msg, CCS to Wilson, 13 Aug 44, FAN 390.
[50] Memo, Commissioner of War and Air for CinC, 3 Mar 44, AFHQ AG 400–1 Fr Sups.

[51] Ibid.
[52] Memo, SACMED for EMGG, 18 Mar 44, AFHQ AG 400–1 Fr Sups.

CHAPTER XI

The North African Forces in Action

Italy and Other Battlegrounds in the Mediterranean

Vindication of the decisions which had led to the arming of the North African forces came promptly after their commitment to battle. Units of the French Expeditionary Corps, dispatched to Italy as fast as they could be equipped and trained, already were giving a good account of themselves. More would soon be put to the test of combat in anticipation of their ultimate employment in ANVIL.

From a two-division corps in January 1944, CEF had, by 1 May, grown to an oversize corps of a strength equivalent to nearly five divisions. Its component elements were then: the 2d Moroccan Infantry Division, Maj. Gen. André Dody; the 3d Algerian Infantry Division, Maj. Gen. Aimé de Goislard de Monsabert; the 4th Moroccan Mountain Division, Maj. Gen. François Sevez; the 1st Motorized Infantry Division, Brig. Gen. Charles Brosset; the 1st, 3d, and 4th Moroccan Tabor Groups, Brig. Gen. Augustin Guillaume; and general reserve units comprising two regiments of tank destroyers, six battalions of artillery, various services, and Base 901. Total strength of the corps was approximately 105,000 officers and men.[1] This figure represented a division slice only slightly more than half the size recommended for the ANVIL force (40,000), an indication that the French forces still lacked supporting combat and service troops. While no units of the French Air Force were assigned to the direct support of the CEF, some squadrons were actively engaged in operations as part of the Allied air pool in the Mediterranean theater.[2]

Such was the force which, led by General Juin, bore the brunt of the offensive launched in mid-May by General Clark's U.S. Fifth Army for the purpose of breaking through the German troops then solidly entrenched in the Gustav Line. In the words of General Alexander, Commander in Chief, Allied Armies in Italy, the French, on 11 May, attacked with splended *élan* and "drove like the wind" across the mountainous terrain between the Liri River and the Tyrrhenian Sea. Showing themselves quick to exploit each local success, "possibly quicker than U.S. and British troops," they succeeded, "to the surprise and elation of the Allied Command," in overrunning the enemy, forcing him to pay a heavy toll in casualties and prisoners.[3] Within three days they had completed the break-through and outflanked the German positions in the Liri

---

[1] For details on division and regimental organization, fire power, and weapon distribution, see Col. Adolphe Goutard, *Le Corps Expéditionnaire Français dans la Campagne d'Italie (1943–1944)* (Paris: Charles-Lavauzelle, 1947), pp. 5–9.

[2] See Ch. XII, below.

[3] Quotations are from statements made by Field Marshal Alexander to Dr. Sidney T. Mathews during an interview in Ottawa, 10–15 January 1949.

SIENA, ITALY. *French troops moving through the streets of Siena, 3 July 1943.*

valley. Their "sensational advance" [4] had been a major surprise also to the enemy.[5] Greatly pleased with the French performance, General Devers, on 15 May, cabled to General Marshall: "French forces have achieved outstanding victory," a statement followed two days later by a message from General Clark himself, addressed also to the U.S. Chief of Staff: "French troops are fighting splendidly with our American matériel." [6]

Having broken through the Gustav Line, units of the CEF pursued the enemy relentlessly, disorganized German resistance, and continued their rapid advance through the mountains south of Rome. After the capture of that city by Allied units, on 4 June, the French pushed forward to Siena, which they seized on 3 July, and drove in the direction of the Arno River. Just as their first elements were reaching a point only a few miles from Florence, the order was issued for their withdrawal. The rest of the

[4] General Mark W. Clark, *Calculated Risk* (New York: Harper & Brothers, 1950), p. 348. On the same page: "For this performance, which was to be a key to the success of the entire drive on Rome, I shall always be a grateful admirer of General Juin and his magnificent CEF." Again on page 360: "A more gallant fighting organization never existed."

[5] "The French," wrote Field Marshal Albert Kesselring, commander in chief of the opposing German forces, "fought with great *élan,* and exploited each local success by concentrating immediately all available forces at the weakened point." Statement in First Evaluation by the CinC Southwest (Army Group C) of Enemy Tactics During the Offensive Since 12 May 1944, dated 19 May 1944, in Fifth Army History, V, 203.

[6] Msg, Devers to Marshall, 15 May 44, CM–IN 11577; Msg, Clark to Marshall, 17 May 44, OPD 319.1, Sec V, Case 182.

9TH COLONIAL INFANTRY DIVISION *disembarking from LCI's for the invasion of Elba, 17 June 1944.*

corps had already begun, on 20 June, to regroup behind the front line and make ready for the forthcoming assault on southern France.   By 23 July the relief of the CEF by Allied units had been completed. From December 1943, when the first division had been committed, to the final withdrawal, the French had sustained a total of approximately 30,000 combat casualties (of which over a third had been incurred during the three-week period of the May offensive), including 5,900 killed and over 24,000 wounded in action.   They had taken more than 8,000 prisoners.[7]

Meanwhile other French units had been committed to combat elsewhere in the Mediterranean, notably in an amphibious operation, known as BRASSARD, launched against the island of Elba in mid-June 1944.

Conquest of the island had first been advocated by General Giraud in October 1943 but ruled out at the time by the Allied command as premature.   Suggested a second time by the French Commander in Chief, in February 1944, it had then received the approval of AFHQ and planning had begun in April.   The operation was assigned to Gen-

[7] Figures on losses are taken from Lt. Col. P. Santini, "Etude statistique sur les pertes au cours de la guerre 1939–1945," *Revue du Corps de Santé Militaire*, X, No. 1 (March, 1954).   For a detailed account of French participation in Italy for the period March–July 1944, see Sidney Mathews, The Drive on Rome, a volume in preparation for the series UNITED STATES ARMY IN WORLD WAR II; see also Goutard, *op. cit.*

TROOPS ENTERING PORTOFERRAIO, ELBA, *19 June 1944. Destruction was caused by Allied bomb attacks.*

eral Martin, then commanding general of 1st French Corps, with headquarters in Corsica, and was carried out by him under the general direction of General de Lattre de Tassigny, commander-designate of the French forces assigned for participation in ANVIL. General Martin, it will be recalled, had, under General Giraud's direction, commanded in September 1943 the all-French operation for the liberation of Corsica (Operation VESUVIUS).[8]

The ground forces taking part in the assault of Elba were exclusively French. With a strength of 12,000 men, they consisted of approximately two thirds of the 9th Colonial Infantry Division, com-

manded by Brig. Gen. Joseph Magnan, one group of Moroccan tabors (2d GTM), two units of Commandos (Groupe de Commandos d'Afrique and Bataillon de Choc), and supporting antiaircraft and engineer units. Assisting the ground elements were Allied naval forces, largely British but including several French naval vessels, all under the command of Rear Adm. Thomas H. Troubridge (RN), and Allied air units commanded by Col. Thomas C. Darcy (U.S.), among which were two French fighter squadrons. The operation, launched on the night of 16–17 June, rapidly achieved its goal. After two days of severe fighting against well-defended positions, the French overcame the resistance

[8] See p. 101, above.

put up by the German garrison of some 2,700 men. By the evening of 19 June, Elba as well as the neighboring island of Pianosa had been entirely liberated. The assaulting forces had killed several hundred enemy troops, made about 2,000 prisoners, and captured more than 60 pieces of artillery. They had suffered some 900 casualties including 258 killed in action.[9]

Committed to other operations in the Mediterranean under Anglo-American control were French air units and naval vessels. Air squadrons were engaged in convoy and coast protection or in air missions preparatory to ANVIL.[10] Naval vessels, a number of which had been repaired and modernized by the Americans and the British, were carrying out various missions not only in the Mediterranean but in other areas as well. All were under the operational authority of the Allied commanders in the respective theaters of operations.[11]

Yet not all the units on the North African rearmament program had been committed to action. For some, no employment had been found; they were undergoing additional training and were kept in readiness pending their ultimate engagement in OVERLORD and ANVIL.

France

OVERLORD

Of all the ground forces re-equipped under the North African program, only one, the 2d Armored Division, participated in the cross-Channel operation. Since its transfer to the United Kingdom in April 1944, the division had completed its equipping and training. On 31 July, or approximately two months after the launching of OVERLORD, the division, still under the command of Maj. Gen. Jacques Leclerc, was landed in Normandy as part of Third U.S. Army, under Lt. Gen. George S. Patton, Jr. Immediately engaged in battle, the division subsequently took an active part in the pursuit to the Seine. On 23 August Lt. Gen. Omar N. Bradley, commander of 12th Army Group, directed it to push to Paris. The division entered the French capital two days later along with the 4th U.S. Infantry Division. After the liberation of Paris, the 2d DB continued its drive eastward still as a component of the Third Army.[12]

Also engaged in OVERLORD were the British-equipped and British-controlled squadrons of the French Air Force, a number of French naval vessels operating as part of the Allied naval pool, and two paratroop units. These were the 2d RCP (Régiment de Chasseurs Parachutistes) and the 3d RCP. The two units, organized in early 1941 in the United Kingdom and equipped by the British, actually were component battalions (the 4th and 3d) of the British Special Air Service (SAS) Brigade. They were parachuted in June and July respectively to assist the Resistance forces operating in conjunction with OVERLORD.

ANVIL

By early August all alerted French organizations on the ANVIL troop list, includ-

[9] Figures on losses are taken from the Santini article cited note 7. For detailed account of Operation BRASSARD, see Rpts, Adm Troubridge to Adm Sir Andrew B. Cunningham, 24 Jun 44, and Gen de Lattre to Allied CinC, 2 Aug 44, AFHQ 0100/12C G–3 Div Ops BRASSARD; also Général [Jean] de Lattre de Tassigny, *Histoire de la Première Armée Française* (Paris: Plon, 1949), pp. 16–30.

[10] For details on organization, re-equipping, and employment of French air units, see Ch. XII, below.
[11] For details on the refitting and employment of the French naval forces, see Ch. XIII, below.
[12] See Forrest C. Pogue, *The Supreme Command,* UNITED STATES ARMY IN WORLD WAR II (Washington, 1954), Ch. XIII.

ing those that had been withdrawn from the Italian front and those which had taken part in the capture of Elba, were re-grouping in staging areas in southern Italy, Corsica, and North Africa. While waiting for their respective D Days they completed their initial equipment or, in the case of units which had already seen action, drew replacement items from U.S. base sections in the same manner as the American units about to participate in ANVIL. Meanwhile, organizations which remained to be equipped under the 23 January Plan and its subsequent revisions hastily procured equipment in the hope that they would be ready in time for effective participation in the forthcoming operation.

One question was causing considerable concern to American officials in the theater. The French were short, not only of auxiliary troops to support their ANVIL forces adequately, but also of the necessary replacement personnel to maintain them at strength in combat. General Devers estimated that they had replacements for only two months of fighting after landing in France. In a message dated 2 July he had urged General Marshall to impress on General de Gaulle, upon his arrival in Washington where he was expected shortly, the seriousness of the situation and the necessity for planning the recruitment of replacements in continental France after the launching of ANVIL.[13]

The long-awaited assault on the French Mediterranean coast took place on 15 August. Directing the operation was Lt. Gen. Alexander M. Patch, Commanding General, U.S. Seventh Army. Although in the initial stages the attack was led by three American divisions (VI Corps) experienced in amphibious landings, assisted by some

French Commandos and armored elements,[14] the operation was largely backed up by French troops. These formed a task force known as Armée B, under the control of General de Lattre de Tassigny. Within a few days, six French divisions had landed and one by one joined VI Corps in battle. By 31 August, with Marseille and Toulon securely in French hands, the bulk of the French ground forces, then comprising approximately two thirds of the combat strength of Seventh Army, had been committed to battle. Progressively General de Lattre grouped his units into two Army corps—1st Corps under the command of General Béthouart, and 2d Corps under the command of General de Monsabert.[15] In mid-September, when Armée B left the control of the Seventh Army to become a tactically independent organization, it renamed itself Première Armée Française (1st French Army). From this time on, 1st French Army and U.S. Seventh Army were to fight side by side as the two component elements of the U.S. 6th Army Group commanded by General Devers.

At the end of September, after a 450-mile dash northward from Provence through Lyon and Dijon, up to Belfort, 1st French Army had received most of the units on the ANVIL French troop list. These were: five infantry divisions—1st DMI, 2d DIM, 3d DIA, 4th DMM, and 9th DIC; three groups of Moroccan tabors—1st

---

[13] Msg 13244, Devers to Marshall (Eyes Only), 2 Jul 44, OPD Exec 10, Item 52–D.

[14] One combat command from the 1st Armored Division.

[15] General Béthouart was Chief, General Staff of National Defense, until 7 August 1944; he became Commanding General, 1st Corps, on 6 September 1944. General de Monsabert was Commanding General, 3d Algerian Infantry Division, first in Italy, then in France until 2 September 1944, when he was promoted to the rank of lieutenant general and assumed command of 2d Corps.

FRENCH 2D ARMORED DIVISION *passing through a small town near Paris, 25 August 1944.*

MAJ. GEN. JACQUES LECLERC *(left foreground), commanding general of the French 2d Armored Division, is followed by liberated Frenchmen as he walks through the street of a small town on the way to Paris, 23 August 1944.*

STREET FIGHTING IN MARSEILLE, *28 August 1944. By 31 August the city was in French hands.*

REVIEWING FRENCH TROOPS IN LIBERATION CEREMONY, MARSEILLE. *The French Minister of War, Mr. André Diethelm, is followed by General Jean de Lattre de Tassigny (left) and Lt. Gen. Aimé de Goisland de Monsabert, 29 August 1944.*

GTM, 2d GTM, and 3d GTM; two armored divisions—1st DB (commanded by
Maj. Gen. du Touzet du Vigier) and 5th
DB (commanded by General de Verne-
joul) ; and general reserve elements, services,
and base units.

Within a short time, 1st French Army
reached a strength of some 200,000 men
representing nearly all the expeditionary
forces equipped and maintained, or maintained only, by the United States under the
North African rearmament program. Yet
this army, sizable as it was, could not operate as an entirely independent force. Because it still lacked sufficient service units,
it was relying heavily on the U.S. Seventh
Army for a considerable part of its support,
thus creating a situation similar to that
which had existed in Italy with respect to
the former CEF. In addition, few replacements were reported to be available in
North Africa to maintain the existing units
at strength.   Progress toward self-suffi-
ciency could be envisaged, however, for
during its advance through French territory 1st French Army had absorbed considerable numbers of liberated Frenchmen,
40,000 by 20 September, 20,000 more by
15 October.   Still larger numbers were
waiting to be enrolled. Ultimately 137,000
men were mustered in as replacements or
as personnel for new units, thus boosting
the strength of 1st French Army to a peak
of 290,000 men.[16]

Meanwhile the larger part of the French
air squadrons and a substantial number of
French naval vessels had been committed to

action as part of the Allied air and naval
pools operating in support of ANVIL.

Remaining in North Africa were a hand-
ful of expeditionary forces soon to be
shipped to France for use as replacements
or as additional reserve elements of 1st
French Army.   All other forces in the area,
that is, Territorial and Sovereignty troops,
were continuing their normal activities, such
as maintaining the expeditionary forces in
operation or ensuring the defense and internal security of North Africa and of Allied
communications lines.

Logistical Support of the French ANVIL Forces

The same basic principles which had
governed the supply and maintenance of the
CEF in Italy were applied to the logistical
support of the French forces operating in
ANVIL.   The over-all maintenance and
supply responsibility rested with the U.S.
Army.   The U.S. supply services obtained
all maintenance items of American origin
required for the participating French and
U.S. forces by means of combined monthly
requisitions, consolidated these supplies in
U.S. stocks, and saw to their proper distribution.   The French themselves furnished items peculiar to their troops, such
as wine, brandy, and oil, as well as post
exchange and Special Services supplies.
French service units and supply officers assisted in the entire operation.

In early July 1944 a U.S. base section
was organized to support the combined
French-American forces from the time of
their entry on the Continent.   The base,
known as Coastal Base Section (COSBASE)
and commanded by Maj. Gen. Arthur R.
Wilson, was to operate in Marseille as soon
as practicable.   On 27 July Headquarters,

---

[16] These additional effectives being of local recruitment, and consequently not part of the North
African rearmament program, the question of their
amalgamation and equipping is treated in Chapter
XVIII, below, which deals with the rearmament
of the French Metropolitan forces. For final
composition of 1st French Army, see p. 353, below.

SOS, NATOUSA, set forth in detail the policies to be followed by COSBASE with respect to the issue of and accounting for rations and replacement and maintenance supplies to the French.[17]

The French had not yet been able to activate enough service units, especially truck companies, to operate a base section of their own to support their combat forces. In early July they had hastily begun setting up an organization to function side by side with COSBASE. They assigned to it the personnel formerly operating Base 901 in Naples, elements from other French bases, and officers recruited from training centers and elsewhere for the purpose. The base, bearing the old designation "901" and commanded by General Gross, was officially activated on 1 August. Not only was this action belated since the launching of ANVIL was only two weeks away, but the organization of the base itself was, from the start, wholly inadequate. Its personnel was insufficient in number and poorly trained. Few of the officers knew English, a most serious deficiency considering that the base was to work in conjunction with a U.S. base. Material means were almost nonexistent. Consequently, no planning could be done which would effectively guide the base in its future work.

The situation was so serious that by common agreement it was decided to attach Base 901 to COSBASE, thus making General Wilson responsible for the logistical support of both the French and the U.S. forces. As a result, Base 901 became, in practice, a French section of COSBASE and a liaison agency between the latter and the French.

_____
[17] Memo, Hq SOS NATOUSA for CG COSBASE, 27 Jul 44, MTOUSA File, Sup of Fr (Mar–Nov 44).

Landing on 16 August along with the first French combat elements was a small advance party from Base 901. The party was so unprepared for the difficult task of handling vast quantities of personnel and men, and so hampered by lack of physical means, that it could do little valuable work. As a result, the combat elements were forced, during this critical period, to rely entirely on the U.S. Army for their support. It was not until 31 August that the first echelon of the base arrived in Marseille. By this time French combat elements had already reached Lyon, or a point some 200 miles away. The second echelon arrived on 15 September just as 1st French Army was being formed. Two weeks later, when the third and fourth echelons finally reached Marseille, the lines of communications had stretched to such an extent that the base was snowed under with tasks entirely out of proportion to its still meager means—1,200 men and 200 vehicles.

Its work was made even more difficult in early October as a result of the reorganization of the American supply lines. With the ANVIL forces continuing their rapid push northward, the Americans decided to set up an advance base in the liberated town of Dijon, while maintaining the coastal base in Marseille. To conform with this reorganization, Base 901, although still greatly understaffed and poorly equipped, was split into two sections. On 12 October a detachment headed by the new base commander, Brig. Gen. Georges Granier, was sent to Dijon to work with Continental Advance Section (CONAD) commanded by General Wilson, while the remainder stayed with Delta Base Section commanded by Brig. Gen. John P. Ratay. A few days later, on 23 October, General de Lattre announced that CONAD was taking over the direct responsibility for the supply of 1st French Army, and authorized General Wilson to appoint French officers from Base 901 to the various staff sections and commands of CONAD. These provisions were to apply as long as 1st French Army was operating as part of U.S. 6th Army Group and on French soil.[18]

CONAD's responsibility was to supply both component armies of the 6th Army Group. Delta Base Section concerned itself with the operation of the port of Marseille, the base depots, and the maintenance installations in that area. Both sections remained under the control of SOS, NATOUSA, until 20 November when a new headquarters, Southern Line of Communications (SOLOC), commanded by General Larkin, took over the entire American supply system in southern France.[19]

The place of the French within the final American organization was as follows: General Granier, as Commanding General, Base 901, was deputy to General Larkin. French officers were posted at the various U.S. command headquarters, SOLOC, CONAD, and Delta Base Section. At SOLOC and CONAD they were fully integrated in the staffs of these commands, and therefore under the control of the respective U.S. commanding officers. At Delta Base Section the French section was attached to the U.S. organization. For matters of discipline and administration, all French personnel were responsible to General Granier.

Base 901 played a dual role. It was charged with obtaining, largely from North Africa, and distributing supplies drawn from French stocks. In this task it worked independently of U.S. supply agencies and dealt solely with the French High Command. With respect to supplies of American origin, including rations, it assisted U.S. supply organizations in effecting distribution to authorized units, that is, troop list units and their replacements. No U.S. Army responsibility existed for any other French personnel.[20]

The missions assigned to Base 901 were exacting enough considering the limited personnel available. Their execution, however, was made even more difficult from the start as unexpected major problems suddenly arose, in particular, the absorption by 1st French Army of considerable numbers of liberated Frenchmen. Even when this army grew in size, Base 901, whose effectives, according to American estimates, should have amounted to 112,000 for a corresponding eight-division army, never exceeded some 29,000 men. As a result, much of the logistical support continued to be provided throughout the war by American supply lines.[21]

It had been agreed between AFHQ and the French High Command in Algiers that matériel ordered from the United States to complete the equipping of certain units whose presence was urgently needed in southern France would be shipped directly to Marseille. To ensure its proper distribution, SCAMA opened an office in that port on 25 September, and established the necessary liaison between the units concerned

---

[18] GO, Hq 1st Fr Army, 23 Oct 44, in GO 27, Hq CONAD, 27 Oct 44, MTOUSA File, Fr Policy (Feb–Oct 44).

[19] Msg S–66620, Eisenhower to AGWAR, 13 Nov 44, SHAEF Mission to France, 091.711–1 (Fr).

[20] Msg BX–18007, Devers to de Lattre, 17 Oct 44, JRC Cable Log.

[21] For additional information on Base 901, see 1st French Army Report, Maj. Gen. Henri Coudraux, *La Base d'Opérations 901 dans la Bataille pour la Libération de la France, 1944–1945* (Paris: Imprimerie Nationale, 1947).

and COSBASE.[22] In late October SCA-MA's remaining staff in North Africa was ordered to the Continent where it continued to supervise the supply of the French forces.

The North African Rearmament Program Ends

While the fighting was progressing in southern and then in eastern France, rearmament operations were continuing in North Africa. Their object was to complete the equipping and training of the remaining troop list units.

Reports reaching AFHQ immediately after the entry of the first French troops into action emphasized the need of dispatching to the Continent all available French service and base units to ease the burden now thrown on the U.S. Army. Some, it was known, had not yet been activated; others were only partly manned and equipped. At a conference called on 21 August, Brig. Gen. Clément Blanc, of the French General Staff, agreed that all required truck battalions would be activated at once but with only half their personnel, the remainder to be raised later in southern France. With respect to the other units, he insisted that they could not be made ready before the beginning of December for lack of troops.[23]

A week later representatives from SOS, Mediterranean Base Section, the JRC, and SCAMA met to examine the equipment and training status of the units currently alerted for movement to the Continent.

They agreed that, on the whole, the units concerned had made substantial progress. However, they were deeply concerned over the fact that some units, mostly ordnance maintenance organizations and quartermaster truck battalions designated for the operation of Base 901, were so deficient in equipment, personnel, and training that they could not possibly be made ready in time to meet the commitment dates as then set up.[24]

It was not likely that deficiencies in personnel could be remedied in time, if at all, for already there were reports that the caliber of students, both white and native, then attending the French Ordnance Training School at Meknès (Morocco), was far below that of the previous classes as far as mechanical aptitude and experience were concerned.[25] Obviously, the recruiting of technical personnel in North Africa had reached the limit. No improvement could be expected until the liberation of part of France produced additional manpower.

Shortages of equipment were another cause for grave concern both at Allied and French headquarters. The most acute shortage appeared to be that of general-purpose vehicle ($\frac{1}{4}$-, $1\frac{1}{2}$-, and $2\frac{1}{2}$-ton trucks especially), although all necessary vehicles were known to have been assigned in Washington. The shortage was ascribed to unauthorized diversions to nonprogram units and incomplete shipments from the United States. Already SOS had been compelled to draw upon U.S. theater stocks, even to the extent of threatening the maintenance of American units. By 8 Sep-

[22] Msg LX–43235, Larkin To All Concerned, 21 Sep 44, JRC Cable Log; Memo, SCAMA Hq, 29 Sep 44, MTOUSA File, Fr Policy (Feb–Oct 44).

[23] Memos, Knox for Loomis, 21 Aug 44, and Leyer To All Concerned, 24 Aug 44, JRC 370/003 Employment of Sv Units.

[24] Rpt on Conf, SOS, 8 Sep 44, JRC 400.1/009 Sup of Forces Designated for Combat.

[25] Memo, Kingman for Loomis, 10 Sep 44, JRC 353/003 Training Fr Army Personnel.

tember the shortage was estimated at approximately 1,100 vehicles. Since these could not be provided from U.S. stocks, General Larkin r e c o m m e n d e d that NATOUSA redouble its efforts to get the French to withdraw all vehicles from units not entitled to hold U.S. equipment. This recommendation was followed a few days later by a warning to the French that SOS would stop issuing vehicles to them as long as any remained in the hands of unauthorized units.[26]

The warning was accompanied by a request from General Loomis that he be informed by 1 October of the number of vehicles being withdrawn from nonprogram units for re-issue to alerted units. A month later, still without an answer, General Loomis again broached the question. He pointed out to General Leyer that, according to a recent study of assignments and shipments from the United States, French stocks should have, not a shortage, rather a surplus, of some 900 vehicles. It was difficult, he observed, to reconcile this fact with the considerable shortage currently reported. General Leyer replied that figures available to him indicated a "theoretical deficit" of some 560 trucks. However, he was able to report that approximately the same number of vehicles had been returned and would be transferred to troop list units; more would soon be returned. He allowed only schools and training centers to retain their vehicles.[27]

Meanwhile, other shortages, such as various ordnance items, including individual weapons, and signal supplies, were being filled as a result of action by SOS. On 19 September General Larkin explained to the War Department that all possible steps had been taken to complete the equipping of French units from French and U.S. stocks available in North Africa. It was urgent, he concluded, that existing shortages be filled by shipments from the United States in order that the units concerned be made fit for operations.[28] Simultaneously, to make sure that the French were complying with earlier repeated warnings, SOS, NATOUSA, on 21 September, made an important announcement: thereafter, the U.S. Army would issue no major item of equipment as long as any similar or suitable substitute remained in the hands of French organizations not on the troop list or not authorized U.S. equipment by the theater commander. Future requests were to be accompanied by a certificate stating that the equipment could not be supplied from any French source.[29]

Efforts to repossess from the French all items in their hands considered "excess" continued unabated. The matter had become more urgent now that emergency issues of equipment to alerted French units had considerably depleted some American theater stocks. It was expected that as shipments from the United States reached the French, surpluses in their stocks would approximately equal the amounts of emergency items turned over to them initially. It was essential for SOS to repossess such items as well as items in the hands of units once in the program but no longer on the

---

[26] Ltr, Loomis to Leyer, 19 Sep 44, and Memo, Loomis for Leyer, 3 Sep 44, JRC 451/001 Vehicles — Misc; Msg LX–41201, Larkin to NATOUSA, 8 Sep 44, JRC 903 Requests for Units; Msg LX–41818, SOS to JRC, 13 Sep 44, JRC Cable Log.

[27] Ltrs, Loomis to Leyer, 19 Sep 44 and 17 Oct 44, and Leyer to Loomis, 30 Oct 44, JRC 451/001 Vehicles—Misc.

[28] Msg LX–42836, Larkin to CG Pembark, 19 Sep 44, JRC Cable Log.

[29] Msg LX–43288, SOS to MBS, 21 Sep 44, JRC 909 Surplus Equip.

troop list. On 5 September General Loomis requested General Leyer to submit to SOS at frequent intervals an inventory of all initial items of equipment on hand in French depots. He pointed out that the items of U.S. origin currently in training centers had been issued on a loan basis to complete the training of replacements; they were subject to recall by SOS when and if required.[30]

Attempts to repossess the equipment in the hands of a combat unit that had fought brilliantly in Italy, but had subsequently been withdrawn from the ANVIL troop list by the French High Command, precipitated a minor crisis in early September. The unit was the 4th Moroccan Tabor Group. Unlike the other three tabor groups then fighting in France, the 4th GTM had been returned to French Morocco, there to be given some much needed rest. Since it reverted to the status of a Sovereignty unit, it was no longer authorized to retain its American equipment. Repossession in this case posed a delicate problem. Should a victorious unit returning to its native country be stripped of its matériel? American officials finally agreed that, for morale reasons, the regiment would retain its individual equipment including arms. The rest was ordered returned to U.S. depots.[31] The crisis soon came to a head when it became known that the French military authorities had turned over a substantial part of the organizational equipment such as vehicles, weapons, and radio sets to a Commando

unit not on the troop list.[32] General Sir Henry Maitland Wilson expressed to General Juin, then Chief of Staff of National Defense, his dissatisfaction over the French action which, by diverting without authorization equipment to a nonprogram unit, had violated the directives of the CCS.[33]

As repossession frequently tended to interfere with the work of equipping the remaining program units, the JRC decided to try a fresh approach to the problem. General Loomis, on 8 September, recommended a suspension of the repossession operations until such a time as the French had received all equipment due them from the United States. Meanwhile, only critical items would be repossessed as required.[34] That was the procedure adopted and followed for some weeks, during which time the JRC prepared a study on excess stocks in anticipation of the eventual resumption of the recapture operations.

In early October a new situation arose in the theater as a result of operational developments on the Continent. With Paris liberated, on 26 August, the French armed services had already begun to move from North Africa to the French capital on the heels of General de Gaulle's Provisional Government (Gouvernement Provisoire de la République Française), the successor to CFLN since 3 June. Before leaving, General Leyer had submitted plans for the mobilization and equipping of manpower then becoming available as a result of the

---

[30] Memo, Loomis for Leyer, 5 Sep 44, JRC 320/001 Incl: Corres File B.

[31] Msgs LX–39978, Larkin to CG NATOUSA, 1 Sep 44, JRC/176, CG NATOUSA to AFHQ, 3 Sep 44, and FX–91969, CG NATOUSA to Larkin, 4 Sep 44, JRC 370/001 Employment of Units—Gen; Msg FX15252, CG NATOUSA to JRC, 14 Sep 44, JRC 400.1/009 Sup of Forces Designated for Combat.

[32] The Staouelli Commandos, organized at Staouelli, a small town near Algiers; later known as *Commandos de France* during the campaign of France and Germany.

[33] Ltr, Gammell to Juin, 9 Sep 44, JRC 370/001 Employment of Units—Gen; Memo, Loomis for CofS SHAEF, 13 Oct 44, SHAEF Mission to France, 091.711–1 (Fr).

[34] Msg JRC/199, JRC to CG NATOUSA, 8 Sep 44, JRC Cable Log.

VICTORY PARADE THROUGH THE STREETS OF PARIS, *26 August 1944.*
Leading the parade is General de Gaulle, left, and General Pierre Koenig, right; center, rear,
is General Leclerc.

advance of the Allied armies. These and other developments, including the anticipated closing down of U.S. installations in North Africa, prompted AFHQ to question whether it was qualified to act as agent in dealing with French authorities on military matters not directly affecting the theater. General Wilson proposed, on 8 October, that thereafter such matters be dealt with by Supreme Headquarters, Allied Expeditionary Force, in Paris. Already an advance detachment from the JRC, headed by General Loomis, had reached the French capital

on 3 October, and was organizing at SHAEF an agency to handle French armament problems arising within the European Theater of Operations. Pending a decision on the proposed transfer to SHAEF of the over-all responsibility for future rearmament, the rear echelon of the JRC kept functioning in North Africa. It supervised the movement of French Training Section to France where its presence was urgently required, and screened the general supply program requisitions submitted by the French for their Sovereignty and Territorial forces. In these various tasks JRC Rear was assisted by SCAMA and by Mediterranean Base Section (MBS), the Oran port organization serving Delta Base Section in Marseille.[35]

By the end of October the study which the JRC had conducted of excess matériel in French hands had been completed and its findings embodied in a memorandum prepared for the benefit of MBS by Colonel Crump, acting chairman of the committee since General Loomis' departure. Colonel Crump listed the four sources known to possess such matériel: SCAMA stocks, training centers and schools, program units not on current troop lists, and nonprogram units. He pointed out that a portion of the excess items should be repossessed for use in France with the remainder reverting to MBS stocks.[36] Pursuant to Colonel Crump's recommendation, SCAMA proceeded to prepare and submit inventories of items excess in French stocks. These were carefully screened by appropriate theater supply services to determine what items were to be recaptured from the French. Except where large excesses already existed in U.S. theater stocks, most of the items reported by French inventories were finally repossessed by MBS and placed in U.S. depots, and due credit was given the French on theater lend-lease reports.[37]

Throughout the month of November the question of the responsibility for French armament matters continued to be a lively issue. SHAEF was handling entirely new problems arising from the liberation of French manpower in vast numbers and, through ETOUSA, had assumed the support of the French expeditionary forces operating in France. Meanwhile the American command in the Mediterranean, MTOUSA, was supplying the forces, largely Sovereignty and Territorial, operating in that theater. In view of the presence in Paris of the heads of French services, and of the approaching closing down of all U.S. military installations in North Africa, MTOUSA recommended to the War Department that SHAEF be asked to assume the responsibility for the continued support of Territorial and Sovereignty forces in addition to its present commitments. The War Department endorsed the proposal, which fitted with its desire to see a single agency dealing with all French rearmament problems, particularly since the general supply situation had become critical as a result of heavy demands from U.S. troops. SHAEF finally agreed, on 3 December, and from that date on assumed all supply responsibility for the French forces including Sovereignty and Territorial troops, as well as replacements for the expeditionary forces.[38]

By this time most armament activities in North Africa had ceased. On 8 November, JRC Rear had been officially disbanded.[39] So had the remaining echelon of French Training Section whose presence in the theater had become superfluous as a result

[35] Msg FX–35102, Wilson to AGWAR, 8 Oct 44, AFHQ Cable Log; Ltr, Leyer to Loomis, 16 Aug 44, Msgs MF–12547, Lewis to JRC, 5 Oct 44, and JRC/295, Larkin to Loomis, 24 Oct 44, JRC 320/001 Orgn of JRC.

[36] Memo, Crump for MBS, drafted 20 Oct 44, sent 8 Nov 44, in same file.

[37] *Logistical History of NATOUSA—MTOUSA: 11 August 1942 to 30 November 1945*, ed. Col. Creswell G. Blakeney (Naples, Italy: G. Montanino, 1946), p. 372.

[38] Msgs FX–52426, MTOUSA to SHAEF, 14 Nov 44, WX–63198, AGWAR to SHAEF, 15 Nov 44, FX–60290, MTOUSA to SHAEF, 29 Nov 44, and S–69284, SHAEF to MTOUSA, 3 Dec 44, SHAEF Rearmt Div File 900–1.

[39] Memo, Crump for CofS, Fr Ground Forces, 8 Nov 44, JRC 320/001 Orgn of JRC.

of the transfer to southern France of the division and army training centers operating as part of the ANVIL troop list. Such officers and enlisted men of JRC Rear and French Training Section as were needed to reinforce General Loomis' new section at SHAEF had been dispatched to the Continent. SCAMA's rear echelon was on its way to France.

With all equipment problems henceforth the responsibility of SHAEF, the North African rearmament program could be regarded as having come to an end.

All together the contribution to the war effort of French North and West Africa and other French territories then aligned on the side of the Allies had been substantial both in quantity and in quality. Total effectives under arms, as of 1 September 1944, had reached the impressive figure of 560,000 men. Of this number, North and West Africa had furnished approximately 295,000 natives and 215,000 Frenchmen (of whom some 20,000 had escaped from France), or a total of 510,000.

The effort had been greatest in North Africa (Tunisia, Algeria, and French Morocco) where 16.4 percent of the French population had been mobilized (20.5 percent in French Morocco). Natives under arms represented 1.58 percent of the Moslem population, a figure kept necessarily low for lack of sufficient white cadres. Yet, in French Morocco, where natives were not subject to compulsory service and therefore could enter military service only as volunteers, it had been possible to raise two infantry divisions (2d DIM and 4th DMM), four tabor groups, and various cavalry, artillery, and service units.

The operational distribution of effectives, again as of 1 September, was reported

to be as follows: in the expeditionary forces, 260,000 men of whom approximately one half were whites; in the Territorial and Sovereignty forces, 250,000; in the Colonial forces—that is to say, the forces, largely native trooops, maintaining the security of the numerous French colonies throughout the world—50,000.[40]

Equally impressive had been, as already related, the contribution of these forces on the field of battle, a contribution which could only increase as the critical operational situation in the last months of 1944 became more demanding. When, on 1 November, all French forces passed from the control of AFHQ to that of SHAEF, General Wilson, under whose supreme command they had been for approximately ten months, seized the opportunity to express to General Juin his admiration for the "heroic performance" of those French troops who had shared in the campaigns of Italy and southern France. "Their courage in combat, their devotion to duty, their excellent leadership, their sacrifices and successes in battle have brought us to an overwhelming common victory and given mute testimony to the rebirth of French arms."[41] In a similar message to General de Gaulle, also dated 1 November, General Wilson concluded: "Thus it is with certainty that I look forward to new and glorious victories of French arms, in the final crushing of the common enemy. The gallant traditions of French arms live on in safe hands."[42]

---

[40] Memo with statistics, Poydenot To All Concerned, 21 Sep 44, SHAEF Misc Fr 320–2NA, Orgn Fr Army; Colonel Spillman, "L'Armée d'Afrique," Revue Historique de l'Armée (December, 1948), p. 40–41.

[41] Ltr, Wilson to Juin, 1 Nov 44, SHAEF SGS 092 France, Vol. III.

[42] Ltr, Wilson to de Gaulle, 1 Nov 44, in same file.

CHAPTER XII

Rearming the French Air Force

Shortly after the November 1942 landings in North Africa, the French air units then aligned with the Allies began a long period of reorganization and re-equipping.[1] At the time, they fell into two groups: the Free French Air Forces of General de Gaulle, the first elements of which had been organized and engaged in operations as early as August 1940, and the French North African Air Forces then under General Giraud's authority. Both groups of forces continued to operate separately until the summer of 1943, when, with the fusion of the de Gaulle and Giraud forces, all French squadrons became an integral part of a single air force.

The five squadrons of the Free French Air Forces, commanded by Lt. Gen. Martial Valin, had been equipped, maintained, and controlled by the Royal Air Force (RAF). Two were operating from bases in the United Kingdom, one in the Middle East, and one in Africa in conjunction with the Leclerc Column. In October, just before the landings in North Africa, the fifth unit, the Normandie Fighter Squadron, had left for the USSR to be re-equipped with Soviet matériel and engaged under Soviet operational control.[2] In January 1943 two additional fighter squadrons, coming from North Africa, would join the two units already in the United Kingdom.

The North African Air Forces, commanded initially by General Jean Mendigal, included some 20 fighter, bomber, reconnaissance, and transport squadrons scattered throughout Tunisia, Algeria, and French Morocco, and 10 more stationed in French West Africa. Total strength of these units amounted to approximately 12,000–15,000 men, including some 1,500 fully trained pilots and corresponding crews, all of them with wide experience. Most of the pilots had seen action in the 1939–40 campaign of France and had served since then in North and West Africa. Their equipment, largely of French origin with some American planes purchased in 1939, was highly inadequate both in quantity and in efficiency. Of the 700-odd aircraft available on 8 November 1942, a large proportion, approximately two thirds, had been destroyed in action or damaged by sabotage in the course of the brief resistance to the

[1] Except as otherwise noted, the sources for this chapter are: JRC 360/001 Air Force Rearmt Plan and Policy; JRC 360/005 Status and Employment of Units; Hq MAAF, The French Air Force in MAAF, A Preliminary History, 1945, copy in AAF Hist Office Archives; *Les Forces Aériennes Françaises de 1939 à 1945*, Col. Pierre Paquier, ed. (Paris: Berger-Levrault, 1949).

[2] On reaching the USSR in December 1942, the squadron was equipped with the YAK–1, later (July 1943) with the YAK–9, a third time (summer 1944) with the YAK–3, all fighter aircraft of the Red Air Force. The unit, reorganized in early 1944 as a regiment (known after October 1944 as the Normandie-Niemen Regiment) on the model of similar Soviet units, participated in operations around Smolensk, Vitebsk, in eastern Prussia, and finally over Germany.

assaulting American forces, leaving from 225 to 250 planes—some fit for combat, others in various degrees of air worthiness. Most were Dewoitine–520's from which the guns had been removed for use elsewhere. The rest included some Bloch, Lioré, and Potez aircraft and a few American Glenn Martins. The immediate problem now facing General Giraud was to find sufficient equipment to rehabilitate his air units.

Eager to assist the French Commander in Chief was the Joint Rearmament Committee, whose responsibility at the time extended to French air matters. The chairman, Colonel Gardiner, himself a U.S. Air Forces pilot, represented AFHQ, U.S. Army Air Forces (USAAF), as well as G–3 on the committee. Representing French headquarters was Capt. Fernand Rébillon. Little effective assistance, however, could be rendered by the JRC, at least until an overall air rearmament program could be established. For the moment the committee acted as a clearinghouse for French requests and as a liaison agency between French and Allied air force commands and establishments.

During the months of December 1942 and January 1943, most pilots of the North African Air Forces remained idle for lack of flying equipment, and their morale began to sag.[3] Four squadrons were hastily engaged in the battle of Tunisia under various Allied commands. Three were flying their old French equipment. Two of these would be moved to the United Kingdom at the end of the campaign to be re-equipped with British Halifaxes. The fourth unit, known as the Lafayette Squadron, was flying its newly acquired American P–40 Warhawks;

it owed the honor of being the first North African squadron to be re-equipped to the memory of the American pilots who, in 1914–18, had distinguished themselves in the celebrated Lafayette Escadrille. Its re-equipping, effected independently of the JRC, had been arranged by the Allied Air Commander in Chief in Northwest Africa, Maj. Gen. Carl Spaatz.

Meanwhile, in Algeria and French Morocco, other pilots and crews were being trained in U.S. squadrons. In addition, plans were under consideration for sending to the United States a number of selected student pilots for a complete course of instruction, as well as sending transport and bomber crews for a refresher course.[4] Conversely, local USAAF commanders were taking advantage of the presence of experienced French pilots by having them detailed to help train younger American pilots in actual fighting.

Obviously, what the North African air units needed, and quickly, was sufficient modern equipment. It will be recalled that the ANFA Plan of January 1943 envisaged delivery from the United States of 500 fighters, 300 bombers, and 200 transport planes. It was on this basis that General Béthouart, then chief of the French Military Mission in the United States, submitted the first air rearmament program.[5] After a detailed study of the Béthouart proposal, General Henry H. Arnold, Chief of the U.S. Army Air Forces, recommended that the CCS determine without delay the extent, composition, utilization, training, and equipment of the North African Air Forces. His report outlined the advantages, politi-

---

[3] Memo, Maj Paul Chemidlin for Asst Secy of War for Air, 14 Jan 43, ABC 091.711 France (6 Oct 43), Sec 1–A.

[4] Msg 5142, Eisenhower to Arnold, 11 Jan 43, JRC Cable Log.

[5] Memo, Béthouart for Marshall, 3 Feb 43, JRC 902/II Rearmt Plan.

P–40 WARHAWKS FOR THE LAFAYETTE ESCADRILLE, *January 1943.*
Note the squadron's emblem, the head of a Sioux Indian.

cal, psychological, and military, which the re-equipping of these forces would offer. It also listed the disadvantages, such as the diversion of aircraft at the expense of U.S. and British air units, and the likely strain on the command system due, in part, to language difficulties. The report was then submitted to the Combined Staff Planners for study and recommendation to the CCS.[6] Only when the latter had reached a decision could the Munitions Assignments Committee (Air) assign any equipment.

On 14 and again on 27 February 1943, General Eisenhower advised the War Department that the situation of the North African Air Forces was becoming critical. He urged that equipment for at least one light bomber group and one fighter group be shipped without delay, as recommended by General Spaatz and agreed to by General Arnold in the course of his recent visit to the theater.[7] In answer to these appeals, the War Department informed Eisenhower and Spaatz of the steps presently contemplated for furnishing immediate assistance to the French. The training of their pilots in the United States could be arranged to start in June, and an initial shipment of 90 P–39 fighters, 67 A–35 dive bombers, and

[6] Msg 2143, Marshall to Eisenhower, 11 Feb 43, JRC Cable Log.

[7] Msgs 776, Eisenhower to Marshall, 14 Feb 43, and 3271, to Marshall and Arnold, 27 Feb 43, JRC Cable Log.

60 C–78 transport planes would be made beginning late March or early April.[8] Allocation of these aircraft, it must be noted, was being made at the sole initiative of American officials. It represented unilateral action on their part, since the CCS had reached no decision. They felt quite justified in taking such action, pending CCS approval, as the request had come from General Eisenhower, himself the official representative of the Combined Chiefs in the theater.

The responsibility for supplying the necessary aircraft and air force items of equipment rested with the U.S. Army Air Forces. International Division, Army S e r v i c e Forces, on the other hand, was to handle all items common to air and ground forces. The procedure for the assignment, shipment, and accounting of all items was similar to that used in connection with the French ground force program.

In late February Colonel Gardiner undertook a tour of inspection of North African air units. Favorably impressed by their resourcefulness, he reported, on his return to Algiers, that they were doing the best they could with the equipment at their disposal. He pointed out that their Dewoitines, which had proved to be good fighter planes in 1939, were still serviceable but were wearing out fast and needed parts urgently. To assist the French in making maximum use of their equipment, Colonel Gardiner made arrangements with one air service command to issue some spare parts to them.[9]

The month of March 1943 marked the beginning of the gradual integration of the French air forces of North Africa into the Allied air organization then established in that area, known as Northwest African Air Forces (NAAF) and commanded by Lt. Gen. Carl Spaatz. It marked also the beginning of real assistance on the part of NAAF and its component units toward the rehabilitation of the French squadrons. On 13 March, at the request of General Mendigal, authorization was granted by General Spaatz for a first increment of three French squadrons to be placed under the operational control of Northwest African Tactical Air Force (NATAF). A week later, General Spaatz announced that French air units assigned to NAAF were to be supplied by Northwest African Air Service Command (NAASC) in the same manner as any American unit, and that another component of NAAF, the XII Air Force Training and Replacement Command, was to assume the responsibility for the training of French combat crews. Thus were established the basic policies which were to govern thereafter the relationship between the Allied and the French air forces in northwest Africa. In a further effort to achieve close co-operation on matters of supply and service requirements, a first increment of two French junior officers was assigned in April to XII Air Force Service Command (AFSC) as a technical detachment.

In spite of these and other measures taken by the theater, the rehabilitation of the French squadrons was proceeding at an extremely slow pace. Allied deliveries of air equipment were still very small. By the end of March only thirty P–39's had been shipped from the United States, enough to equip one squadron, while the British had,

[8] Msg 2985, Marshall and Arnold to Eisenhower and Spaatz, 27 Feb 43, JRC Cable Log.

[9] Memos, Gardiner for CofS AFHQ, 4 Mar 43, and 5 Mar 43, JRC Misc Doc, "Annexes to History."

UNLOADING P–38 FIGHTER PLANES *for the French, Casablanca, 13 April 1943.*

from local resources, furnished Spitfires for another.[10]

No real progress could be expected until a high-level decision had been reached on the extent and rate of expansion of the air program. Such a decision was not in sight. At the time, it will be recalled, Anglo-American policy makers were in sharp disagreement over the scope of French rearmament, the British expressing the fear that the commitment would jeopardize the interests of both the U.S. and British forces. In their report (CCS 142/1) dated 10 March 1943, the Combined Staff Planners merely recommended that matériel assigned at General Eisenhower's request should not exceed that necessary to equip an air force of 450 planes.

At their meeting of 12 March, the CCS, deciding against action for the moment, simply took note of the deliveries then being made with Eisenhower's concurrence.[11]

By the end of April the French had received approximately 100 planes from the United States. In addition the Lafayette Squadron was undergoing a second re-equipment, this time with P–47 Thunderbolts. On the basis of the fine performance of that unit in the course of the preceding five months, AFHQ officials estimated that combat efficiency of future French air squadrons would approximate that of Allied units, particularly in piloting ability. For this reason they agreed that new combat

---

[10] Msg 4939, Marshall to Eisenhower, 24 Mar 43, OPD Cable Files.

[11] Rpt, CPS to CCS, 142/1, 10 Mar 43. Min and Supplementary Min, CCS 75th Mtg, 12 Mar 43. See p. 54, above.

squadrons should receive only the best matériel, and that old equipment should be used exclusively for training and for transport and liaison duties.[12]

A directive issued on 9 May by Maj. Gen. Delmar Dunton, Commanding General, Northwest African Air Service Command, set forth in detail NAASC's responsibility with respect to the supply and maintenance of French air units. Such combat units as were assigned to NAAF, or attached to the latter for operational control, were, as directed earlier by General Spaatz, to be supplied as were other NAAF units. Squadrons not yet assigned or attached were to obtain supplies by means of requisitions submitted by Headquarters, French Air Service Command, to the JRC.[13]

The 9 May directive, although explicit as far as NAASC was concerned, was insufficient to deal adequately with the entire problem of French supply and maintenance —a problem seriously complicated by the fact that some units had British and some U.S. equipment. In addition, the issue of air items, and of items common to ground and air forces, was to be effected according to widely different procedures. It soon became apparent that proper co-ordination between the various supply agencies had not been established. As late as 7 July base sections had not received orders to honor requisitions submitted by French air units. To clarify the matter, MAC (Air) set forth, on 22 July, the policy to be put into effect at once. Briefly, the new directive stipulated that squadrons not equipped with British or American aircraft were ineligible to receive supplies of British or U.S. origin

unless special authorization was granted by MAC (Air). All other squadrons were to conform to British or U.S. tables of equipment. Such items, other than aircraft and special air force equipment, as were issued to them by NAASC from USAAF or RAF local sources were to be replaced from shipments from the United States effected under the 25,000-ton monthly allocation to the French.[14]

Meanwhile French military authorities had continued to press for an expansion of their air forces. In May General Leyer requested an additional assignment of 300 planes of various types.[15] His proposal, similar to the one submitted on 19 April by General Mendigal to General Spaatz, was held up pending a complete restudy, by the French themselves, of the entire French air position. A reorganization of their air and naval forces was then taking place.[16]

By mid-June the French had received from the United States 126 planes—including 90 P–39's, or enough for four fighter squadrons, 21 A–35's originally intended to form a dive-bomber squadron but later diverted for training and use in police and security squadrons, and 15 C–78's subsequently used for training and communications—as well as most of the necessary ground equipment requested in February.[17]

---

[12] Memo, Chief Air Unit IG for OPD, 22 Apr 43, OPD 336.2 France, Sec 1.

[13] Memos, Spaatz for CG NAASC, 5 May 43, and 65–62, Hq NAASC, 9 May 43, JRC 360/001 Air Force Rearmt Plan and Policy.

[14] Quoted in History of FAF in MAAF, p. 5.

[15] Memos, Leyer for CofS AFHQ, 12 May 43, and SGS for DCofS, 17 May 43, JRC 360/001 Air Force Rearmt Plan and Policy; Ltr, Leyer to JRC, 20 May 43, JRC Misc Doc, Item 5–a, Tab L.

[16] Memo, Deputy Air CinC for DCofS Mediterranean Air Comd, 10 Jun 43, JRC 360/001 Air Force Rearmt Plan and Policy.

[17] The A–35 was so constructed that it required a major overhaul after fifteen to thirty hours of flight. This proved too great a burden on the meager mechanical resources then available to the French. As a result, deliveries of this type of plane were discontinued. Statement in Corres from Col Gardiner, OCMH.

In addition, General Spaatz had given them, from available theater stocks, some 50 P–40's. All deliveries from the United States had been based upon the recommendations of the theater commander. The MAB had assigned to date a total of 217 planes of which 100 still remained to be shipped. No further assignments would be made without a new request from the theater.

With the fusion of the Free French and North African armed forces in July 1943 and the resulting reorganization of the French High Command, General Bouscat was appointed Chief of Staff of the Combined Armée de l'Air (French Air Force—FAF). In a memorandum to Air Chief Marshal Tedder, who, as Commanding General, Mediterranean Air Command, controlled all Allied air forces in the Mediterranean, General Bouscat outlined the steps he was taking to bring the organization of the FAF in line with that of the Allied air force in the theater, and to effect the closest co-operation possible between the two. He then reviewed FAF's position and capabilities and urged that the JRC be instructed to undertake without delay a detailed study of the air rearmament problem. His staff, he pointed out, was preparing a new program which would supersede all previous ones.[18]

Meanwhile the British had made available enough additional Spitfires to equip 2 more squadrons. Allocation of these aircraft had been made entirely on local initiative, as the United Kingdom made bulk allotments to the British air officer commander in chief for redistribution. Only those French squadrons which were stationed in West Africa or in the United Kingdom were included in the War Office program.

By August, excluding the squadrons operating with the Royal Air Force in the United Kingdom, no more than 8 French squadrons had been re-equipped: 3 with Spitfires, 4 with P–39's, and 1 with P–47's. The rehabilitation of the FAF was still painfully slow. To make matters worse, the action taken by the MAB in July, while favorable with respect to the ground forces, did not contemplate any extension of the air part before January 1944. The reasons ascribed for the postponement were the acute needs for aircraft of the Americans and British themselves and shipping difficulties. In the opinion of the chairman of the JRC, the "stalling" was regrettable. The FAF had received only a few planes and its morale was deteriorating.[19] This view was shared by General Eisenhower who, on 4 August, cabled the following warning to the War Department: "The French are much disappointed. . . . The morale of their air units is low. This is unfortunate, for an air force with high morale, even though small, would be of real assistance from a military standpoint. They have many excellent pilots, and personnel skilled in maintenance. General Bouscat has the confidence of both political factions and should make an able leader." The Allied Commander in Chief then recommended, as an emergency measure, that three groups of the Twelfth U.S. Air Force be converted from medium bomber to heavy bomber groups, and the medium bombers thus made available transferred to the French. "The result will be a material increase in our effective strength."[20]

---

[18] Memo, Bouscat for Tedder, 13 Jul 43, JRC 360/001 Air Force Rearmt Plan and Policy.

[19] Memo, Artamonoff for Adcock, 2 Aug 43, JRC Misc Doc, Item 5–a, Tab T.

[20] Msg W–6517, Eisenhower to Arnold, 4 Aug 43, AFHQ 0100/12C G–3 Div Ops Fr Rearmt.

On 8 August a conference on the re-equipping of the French Air Force took place at AFHQ. It was attended by Tedder and his chief of staff, Brig. Gen. Gordon P. Saville, both representing Mediterranean Air Command, General Bouscat representing the FAF, Brig. Gens. Edward P. Curtis and Harold A. Bartron of the NAAF, General Spalding and Colonel Artamonoff of the JRC, and a number of other officials. Opening the meeting, Tedder announced that an Anglo-American committee was being formed for the purpose of handling the rearmament of the FAF. Its first aim would be to make certain that all present French squadrons equipped with British or American equipment, whether operating in the Mediterranean or in the United Kingdom, had sufficient supplies and adequate reserves of airmen and ground crews. In the opinion of Tedder, this objective should be reached before the rearming of other squadrons was contemplated. Speaking for the FAF, General Bouscat disclosed that he had just drawn up a rearmament plan, already approved by Generals Giraud and de Gaulle, based precisely on availability of both airmen and ground personnel. Since June, he continued, French pilots were being trained in the United States at the rate of one hundred monthly. The rest of the training was effected either in the French training center established in Morocco, or under the supervision of the U.S. Air Forces in North Africa. Once ready the French squadrons would be assigned to the Allied air pool for employment, preferably in groups of two or more, under the control of the Air Commander in Chief in the Mediterranean and according to operational requirements.[21]

This was in line with the tacit agreement reached in the earlier days of Franco-Allied collaboration and under which the French placed their squadrons at the disposal of the CCS for employment by the appropriate Allied commanders.

By mid-August, some 230 planes had been shipped from the United States, with 30 more to follow before the end of 1943. Plans as then made by the War Department for the first half of 1944, subject of course to CCS approval, contemplated the shipment of some 700 additional aircraft.[22] In terms of squadrons, total deliveries from the United States for the years 1943 and 1944, if approved and carried out, would provide equipment for 27 squadrons by the end of 1944.[23]

On 29 August General Spaatz informed General Arnold that he was equipping one French squadron with B–26's and would maintain the squadron through 1943 from aircraft assigned to the Twelfth Air Force. He was also giving the French additional B–26's for training to prepare for a second squadron in January. Furthermore, he announced that the rearmament program, then in preparation, would soon be forwarded to Washington for action and that both Eisenhower and Tedder concurred in the steps being taken in the theater to rearm the FAF. To support the squadrons already equipped, AFHQ requested the War Department to provide equipment for eight service units. These were to be in addition to the three for which matériel had been ordered earlier in April.[24]

---

[21] Min, Conf on FAF Rearmt, 8 Aug 43, JRC 360/001 Air Force Rearmt Plan and Policy.

[22] Msgs, AGWAR to Spalding, 5163, 16 Aug 43, 5237, 17 Aug 43, and 5448, 19 Aug 43, JRC Cable Log.

[23] Msg 4752, Arnold to Eisenhower, 11 Aug 43, JRC Cable Log.

[24] Msg W–8617, Spaatz to Arnold, 29 Aug 43, JRC 360/001 Air Force Rearmt Plan and Policy;

On 6 September the Allied committee whose impending creation had been announced by Air Chief Marshal Tedder at the recent AFHQ conference on French air rearmament was formally established in Algiers. The new agency, known thereafter as the Joint Air Commission (JAC), with General Saville as its first chairman, was placed under the control of Mediterranean Air Command. It took over from the JRC, heretofore responsible for all French armament matters, the handling of problems peculiar to the French Air Force. To ensure proper and effective liaison between the two bodies, JAC's chairman was made a member ex officio of the JRC. FAF officers, selected by the French air command and approved by the Allied Air Commander in Chief, were assigned to the JAC.[25]

The Joint Air Commission immediately undertook to work out, in co-operation with General Bouscat, a comprehensive program, taking into account the matériel which had already been ordered and delivered and covering aircraft, crews, and ground units. Functions assigned to the JAC included not only the supervision of the program but the training of units and the upkeep of French air bases, repair depots, training schools, and meteorological stations. The commission, in effect, paralleled for the FAF the functions of the JRC with respect to the ground forces. In it was vested the responsibility for overseeing the administrative preparation of the French air and service units for combat, and making certain that they were adequately trained and equipped

before being turned over to Mediterranean Air Command to take part in operations.[26] Thereafter the War Department would refer to the JAC, for appraisal, co-ordination, and recommendation, all air requests submitted by French military authorities in Washington.

Concerned over the slowness of the air program, Generals de Gaulle and Giraud, on 18 September, appealed directly to General Marshall. It was most regrettable, they stressed, that the 30,000 men constituting the FAF, which contained elements with excellent technical training, were not being utilized to the maximum of their capacity. "In view of the high production capacity of the United States and the United Kingdom," they urged that the program be accelerated.[27] Their communication was immediately referred to the Joint Strategic Survey Committee for study.

Meanwhile, one of the main objectives of both the French and the Allied commands had been to push the training of French air personnel as thoroughly and speedily as possible. Already substantial numbers of pilots, crews, and mechanics had attended Allied air training centers in Africa. In addition the French had opened, mostly in French Morocco, a number of schools of their own, operating largely with American and British assistance in matériel and personnel, the British limiting such assistance to the British-equipped squadrons. Training was reported to be highly effective, students responding readily and well to Allied instruction. Only with respect to technical questions, such as electronics and the assimilation of the U.S. supply system, did they

---

Msg W–7723, Eisenhower to AGWAR, 20 Aug 43, OPD 400 France, Sec II.

[25] Msg W–8409, Spaatz to Arnold, 27 Aug 43, JRC Cable Log; GO 9, Hq Mediterranean Air Comd, 6 Sep 43, JRC 360/001 Air Force Rearmt Plan and Policy. For detailed information on the organization, membership functions, and command of the JAC, see Chapter XVII, below.

[26] MAAF, French Air Force Rearmament Plan, 7 Mar 44, JRC 360/001 Air Force Rearmt Plan and Policy.

[27] Ltr 796, de Gaulle and Giraud to Marshall, 18 Sep 43, ABC 091.711 France (6 Oct 43), Sec 1–A.

seem weak, possibly because of their reluctance to be used as technicians instead of as combatants.[28]

Such squadrons as had completed their training did not remain idle. As fast as they became operational they passed under Allied control and were assigned for duty with the Northwest African Air Forces. The arrangement gave the squadrons exactly the same status in the Allied organization as the British and the Americans: unity of command over all, but separate administration. Allied control over the French squadrons was questioned only once indirectly and briefly in June 1944 when the French were contemplating an operation (CAÏMAN) in support of Resistance forces in central France. Debate over whether or not they might use FAF squadrons for the purpose was cut short by Allied rejection of the whole operation as impracticable.[29]

By agreement with the French High Command, a procedure was established in September 1943 to formalize the assignment of squadrons to Allied control. Thereafter when a unit was ready for operations, General Bouscat notified Mediterranean Air Command, which in time would publish a general order assigning the unit to the appropriate command. The procedure was not always followed to the letter and in January 1944 it proved necessary to trace the assignments of several units far back and make them a matter of record.[30]

Once assigned for operations, units were broken in gradually. Initially they were given relatively easy patrol and convoy duties under Northwest African Coastal Air Force; later, when their flying proficiency had reached a point where they could profitably undertake offensive operations, they were transferred to Northwest African Tactical Air Force. By September 1943 the three Spitfire squadrons had taken part in the support of operations in Sicily, south Italy, and Corsica. Five U.S.-equipped units were employed in convoy and coast protection in the western Mediterranean.

On 29 September the final draft of the air rearmament program was completed. It had been worked out after considerable research and study in the JAC by representatives of USAAF, RAF, and FAF, and under the guidance and supervision of the Air Commander in Chief in the Mediterranean. The program, known thereafter as Plan VII, was designed to provide a small, well-balanced force within the limitations imposed by the scarcity of French technical personnel and by other U.S. and British commitments. Such a force would constitute the nucleus around which the renovated air establishment would subsequently be built. All essential elements of a tactical force were present in the plan.[31] Plan VII contemplated no expansion of French naval aviation, the matter being still under discussion between French and Allied naval authorities.

Under Plan VII the total number of squadrons, including those based in the United Kingdom, was scheduled to be increased from 16 to 21 by the end of 1943, and to 31 (of which 18 would be U.S.-equipped) by July 1944. The plan also contemplated the delivery of matériel neces-

[28] Intervs with Col Gardiner, Apr 50, Col Ervin, Jul 51, and Gen Saville, Jul 51.

[29] History of FAF in MAAF, p. 13.

[30] GO 11, Hq Mediterranean Air Comd, 26 Sep 43, JRC 360/003 Status and Employment of Units; History of FAF in MAAF, p. 12.

[31] Memo, Smith for CCS, 29 Sep 43, AFHQ 0100/4 SACS Rcd Sec, Fr Matters; Memo, AFHQ for Sec CCS, 29 Sep 43, SHAEF Mission to France 091.711 Rearmt (Fr) Air Force 900.2.

sary to equip 1 parachute regiment, 37 service organizations, as well as a number of training centers, depots, and other installations. Priority of build-up for both operational and service units was established on the same level as for the first four Army divisions. Touching upon the question of control, Plan VII merely restated the existing practice, namely, that all FAF tactical units, both combat and service, formed and equipped in North Africa would be assigned to NAAF and be employed as elements of the Allied air force pool of tactical units. Army Air Forces headquarters in Washington approved Plan VII on 1 October and, three weeks later, informed General Eisenhower that it was prepared to include the plan, once it had been approved by the CCS, in the Army Supply Program then under consideration.[32]

Meanwhile the FAF supply situation, far from improving, had become increasingly chaotic. In an attempt to formulate proper remedial action, General Saville, chairman of the JAC, held a lengthy series of conferences with representatives of Mediterranean Air Command, XII Air Force Service Command, AFHQ, NATOUSA, the JRC, and SOS, NATOUSA. Finally he was able to announce, on 2 November, the supply policy and procedure as now agreed to by all agencies concerned.[33] Henceforth priority for distribution of supplies and equipment common to air and ground forces was set as follows: (1) one expeditionary corps of four divisions, (2) air force units already activated and formed, (3) air force units to be activated and formed in accordance with the program recently approved by AFHQ, (4) balance of ground forces. Headquarters, French Air Force, was to requisition from French Ground Forces the matériel needed for Air Force units (initial items and 30-day supplies) and at the same time submit requisitions on the United States for identical supplies for repayment to French Ground Forces. Pursuant to this policy, General Saville submitted to General Loomis, for approval by the JRC and transmittal to the War Department, a first set of requisitions needed to get the supply system working. Thereafter, he thought, it would be a matter of automatic supply.

The problem of automatic supply had already been raised in connection with the maintenance of French ground troops. Queried on the matter, the War Department listed the categories of items for which automatic supply was provided and those for which requisitions were to be submitted. After a further exchange of communications between the theater and the War Department, General Loomis, on 24 January 1944, informed the French of the procedure to be followed by them for the submission of requisitions in cases where no automatic supply was provided. General Bouscat was invited "in the interests of economy" to arrange without delay that items common to the air and ground forces be stocked under the authority and control of the French Army.[34]

So that there would be no doubt as to which FAF organizations were entitled to obtain supplies from U.S. sources, NATOUSA headquarters, on 31 December 1943, listed the Air projects which had been

[32] Msgs 8262, Arnold to Spaatz, 1 Oct 43, 830, Styer to Eisenhower, 25 Oct 43, and W–4465, Eisenhower to AGWAR for CCS, 6 Nov 43, JRC Cable Log.

[33] Memo, Saville for Loomis, 2 Nov 43, JRC 360/001 Air Force Rearmt Plan and Policy.

[34] Msg W–3378, AGWAR to Eisenhower, 25 Nov 43, JRC Cable Log; Memo, Loomis for Bouscat, 24 Jan 44, JRC 360/002 Items Common to Air and Ground; see pp. 99–101, above.

approved by the Allied Commander in Chief. These included the rearmament plan (Plan VII) of 29 September and the maintenance of such establishments (schools, depots, meteorological stations, bases, and airfields) as were considered necessary. NATOUSA stipulated that all requisitions for the projects were to be submitted to the JAC for review, revision, and approval. JAC would then forward the requisitions to the XII Air Force Service Command in the case of supplies and equipment peculiar to the Army air forces, and to the JRC in the case of supplies and equipment common to air and ground forces. It was further directed that XII AFSC and the JRC would forward the approved requisitions, through their respective lend-lease channels, to agencies in the United States for appropriate action.[35] About the same time (26 December), a directive issued by XII AFSC and effective 1 January 1944 changed the Detachment of Technical Liaison (French), assigned to NAASC since April, into French Section, NAASC. The section was charged with, among other duties, the command and inspection of all French air units.[36]

By the end of December, approximately twenty-two squadrons had been re-equipped from U.S. and British sources. (*Table 3*) So had a number of squadrons of the French Naval Air Arm.[37] Finally, the French themselves had equipped and were maintaining, largely with old equipment, four air "security squadrons" for colonial gendarmerie purposes.

It was not until 28 January that the CCS finally approved Plan VII, subject to the

condition that modifications might be made when required by the military situation. Approval of the plan marked the beginning of a new phase in the rehabilitation of the FAF. Until then "at the end of the queue for Allied attention," FAF could now feel reasonably certain that, within a short time, it would become an effective fighting weapon.[38]

TABLE 3—AMERICAN- AND BRITISH-EQUIPPED SQUADRONS OF THE FAF: DECEMBER 1943

Location and Type	Number
Total	[a] 22
North Africa [b]	16
Bomber	3
Light, A–35	2
Medium, B–26	1
Fighter	10
Hurricane	2
P–39	4
P–47	1
Spitfire	3
Transport, C–78	3
United Kingdom [c]	6
Bomber	3
Heavy	2
Light	1
Fighter	3

[a] Plus 1 flight of photographic reconnaissance equipped in North Africa.
[b] American-equipped.
[c] British-equipped.

Source: Memo, Fr Liaison Sec NAAF for A–4 Hq NAAF, 29 Jul 43, and GO 11, Mediterranean Air Comd, 26 Sep 43, JRC 360/003 Status and Employment of Units; Fr Air Force Rearmt Plan, 7 Mar 44, JRC 360/001 Air Force Rearmt Plan and Policy.

Just before the CCS action, a reorganization of the Allied air forces in Northwest Africa had been effected coincidental with that of the over-all Allied command in the theater. In mid-January Lt. Gen. Ira C. Eaker replaced Air Chief Marshal Tedder

---

[35] Ltr, NATOUSA to SOS and JRC, 31 Dec 43, JRC 360/001 Air Force Rearmt Plan and Policy.
[36] History of FAF in MAAF, p. 10.
[37] See Ch. XIII, below.

[38] Min, CCS 143d Mtg, 28 Jan 44; Msg, CCS to Allied CinC Mediterranean, 29 Jan 44, FAN 330; quotation from History of FAF in MAAF, p. 4.

as Air Commander in Chief in the Mediterranean and assumed command of the newly created Mediterranean Allied Air Forces (MAAF) now consolidating and superseding both NAAF and Mediterranean Air Command. One of General Eaker's first steps was to centralize the air service responsibility for all U.S. components of MAAF in a single agency known as Army Air Forces Service Command (AAFSC), Mediterranean Theater of Operations. The latter, commanded by General Bartron, was charged, among other duties, with supervising the supply of the FAF. On 11 February General Bartron issued, on orders from General Eaker, a directive setting forth the basic policy with respect to FAF supply: thereafter all requests for supplies not available in French stocks and needed for immediate consumption (except rations, post exchange and Special Services supplies which were the responsibility of the French themselves) were to be submitted to AAFSC, on the basis of the tables of basic allowances in force for equivalent U.S. units. Appropriate charges were to be made by AAFSC in the monthly lend-lease reports to SOS, NATOUSA. Within AAFSC the unit charged with co-ordinating FAF matters was the French Section which had been taken over from NAASC upon the latter's deactivation.[39]

Immediately after the command reorganization in the theater, the French Chief of Air Staff, General Bouscat, sought and obtained from the Supreme Allied Commander, General Wilson, the definite assurance that French air units would ultimately participate in operations for the liberation of France. Presently the number of squadrons actively engaged in combat had slightly increased. In addition to those operating from bases in the United Kingdom or employed under Mediterranean Allied Coastal Command, in early November an initial increment of two fighter squadrons and one reconnaissance flight had joined the combined Allied air forces in Italy. Six more units were on their way to that theater. Others would follow as soon as they could be made operational.

Meeting with General Wilson on 7 February, General Bouscat reviewed the situation of the FAF at the time. The training of crews and replacements was completed and the necessary maintenance and other supporting services were organized. What was needed to guarantee that units would be ready on time was to speed up the delivery of planes and equipment. "We only await the matériel." The FAF, he assured the Supreme Allied Commander, was eager to carry on the fight against the enemy. General Wilson cautiously replied that the question of equipment deliveries was one for the decision of the CCS who, he reminded General Bouscat, were the final authorities.[40]

It now remained generally to implement that part of Plan VII which applied to the year 1944, the October–December 1943 slice being almost completed. Under the terms of the plan, the United States was to assume the greater share of the task. Of the eleven additional combat squadrons to be re-equipped by 1 July 1944, ten were to receive some 320 American planes of various types. All together, the United States was scheduled to furnish for the entire years of 1943 and 1944, 615 single-

---

[39] Ltrs 65–5, Hq AAFSC MTO, 11 Feb 44, and 65–2, Hq AAF MTO, 3 Jun 44, JRC 360/001 Air Force Rearmt Plan and Policy.

[40] Min Mtg, Bouscat with Wilson, 7 Feb 44, AFHQ 0100/4 SACS Confs—Gen (Fr), Feb 44–Aug 44.

engine and 216 twin-engine planes, or a total of 831 combat and transport aircraft.[41] Deliveries of British aircraft would be limited to equipping, with Spitfires, one additional squadron in the United Kingdom, and maintaining the existing British-equipped squadrons in the Mediterranean, less, however, the two Hurricane units now being converted to P–47's.

Very shortly, shipments of American aircraft and equipment reached North African ports at an increased tempo. Yet between February and August, when Plan VII was to end, deliveries of airplanes fell considerably behind schedule. Shortages of B–26's and P–47's in particular resulted in delaying as much as three months the final re-equipping of several French squadrons. The JAC, headed by Colonel Gardiner (since 9 February), later by Col. R. Gilpin Ervin (after 4 May), grappled with the aircraft shortage problem as best it could, often by obtaining loans from theater stocks pending the arrival of allocations for the French.[42]

In early February a request from General Bouscat, approved by the JAC, for the delivery of 100 additional A–24's for use in training schools and in police and security squadrons was turned down by the MAB because the craft were not available.[43] A second request, this time submitted to the War Department by the French Military Mission in Washington, for 100 primary and 100 basic training aircraft likewise was disapproved "for failure to submit through the JAC and lack of a definite training plan." American authorities in Washington felt that there was no necessity for sending training aircraft to North Africa as long as a training program was continued in the United States. This training program, incidentally, called for a monthly production of some 80 pilots. But the French were reported to be having difficulty in finding the necessary candidates.[44]

Having been informed by the War Department that the B–26's being delivered to the French were not to be equipped with the Norden bombsight, General Eaker, in a letter to Maj. Gen. Barney McK. Giles, chief of the Air Staff in Washington, voiced the opinion that this was a mistake. There was little point in delivering an aircraft that was not fully equipped to do a good military job. Moreover, there could be no question of security since more than a thousand of these bombsights had been left in bombers that had gone down over enemy territory. Two weeks later War Department officials reversed their stand and authorized General Eaker to leave the bombsight on the B–26's allocated to the French.[45]

Apparently feeling that more energetic action should be taken in Washington toward the implementation of Plan VII, now the "accepted guide" in the theater, General Eaker urged General Giles to organize a staff agency which would take prompt action on requests from his command for materiel to equip the FAF.[46] A visit to the French squadron then training in Sardinia with B–26's had convinced General Eaker

[41] Memo, Bouscat for Ervin, 13 May 44, JRC 360/002 Items Common to Air and Ground.

[42] Both Colonels Gardiner and Ervin were Air Corps officers. Colonel Gardiner, it will be recalled, had already served as the first chairman of the Joint Rearmament Committee (16 December 1942 to 5 June 1943).

[43] Msg W–2124, Eaker to Arnold, 7 Feb 44, JRC Cable Log.

[44] Msg AFHQ–604, Arnold to Eaker and JAC, 24 Feb 44, JRC Cable Log.

[45] Ltrs, Eaker to Giles, 29 Feb 44, and Giles to Eaker, 25 Mar 44, History of MAAF, Vol. II.

[46] Ltr, Eaker to Giles, 6 Mar 44, History of MAAF, Vol. II.

that French pilots were "tops." In his opinion, it was essential that the American agreement to rearm French air units be fully carried out. "This program should be pressed to the limit," he asserted in a personal letter to General Arnold. "We ought to give the French the equipment since they have such a fine offensive spirit." General Eaker then praised their willingness to serve as subordinates. "They fit right into our organization willingly and cheerfully and there is never any question about who is in command." All the French wanted, he concluded, was an airplane and a bomb.[47]

By April the number of units available for combat had not increased as substantially as the French had hoped. Yet in May, during the great Allied offensive leading to the fall of Rome, no less than 11 squadrons were operating within the combined Allied air forces. Three more soon were to reach Italy, making a total of 14 divided in 4 groups. From the fall of Rome on 5 June up to 15 August, date of the assault on the southern coast of France (ANVIL), several of the 14 squadrons would be engaged in various pre-ANVIL activities: 3 in coastal protection, 7 in bombing action on German airfields, fortifications, and lines of communication, and 2 flights of 1 squadron in reconnaissance missions.[48] Nearly all crews of the B–26, P–47, and P–38 squadrons had undergone their training at

the "transition school" specially set up for the French by MAAF in early May. The school, located near Tunis and run under the control of the JAC, offered a modified instructional program as the students all had previously received some training.[49]

To enable the squadrons contemplated under Plan VII to maintain their war effort through the second half of 1944, it was indispensable that the needs of French auxiliary organizations in North Africa, such as schools, replacement centers, airfields, and medical and quartermaster services, be properly assessed and filled. To this end, General Bouscat submitted to the JAC, on 14 May, a list of requisitions. He reviewed the composition, purpose, and activities of the various organizations concerned. Their total strength was estimated at 20,250 military and 6,500 civilian personnel. The number of aircraft in use in the training centers was given as 819, of which 322 were of old French design, 181 of U.S. pre-1939 manufacture, 274 of recent American types, and 42 of British design which had been turned over to the French by the RAF since 1942. General Bouscat's requisitions were promptly reviewed by the JAC and transmitted to the JRC for study and approval.[50]

In anticipation of the disbandment of XII Air Force Training and Replacement Command, which had been giving combat training to French bomber crews and fighter pilots, the JAC, JRC, and other theater agencies arranged for the transfer to the French of sufficient equipment to enable them to continue their own training. As no advance trainers were available from U.S. sources, the French, at the suggestion of the JAC, attempted to obtain 25 Harvard

---

[47] Ltr, Eaker to Arnold, 21 Mar 44, History of MAAF, Vol. II.

[48] It was in the course of a reconnaissance mission that the celebrated writer, Maj. Antoine de Saint Exupéry, met with a fatal accident over the Mediterranean on 31 July 1944.

For details on organization, control, and operations of FAF units in the various theaters of operations, see "Les Forces Aériennes Françaises"; General René Bouscat, "L'Armée de l'Air française dans la Campagne d'Italie," Revue de la Défense Nationale (February, 1946), pp. 233–37; History of FAF in MAAF.

[49] Interv with Ervin, Jul 51.

[50] Memos, Bouscat for JAC, 13 May 44, and Ervin for Loomis, 5 Jun 44, JRC 360/002 Items Common to Air and Ground.

planes from the Canadians. The MAB, having no authority to assign Canadian aircraft, advised the French to refer their request to the Canadian Government through British channels. The project was subsequently abandoned. The MAB, however, authorized the transfer of 26 aircraft (including 21 B–26's) used in the French training program and no longer needed by the American air forces in the theater. This was in addition to earlier similar transfers (13 aircraft in October 1943 and 8 more in February 1944) by XII Air Force Training and Replacement Command. Later, in July, the theater would approve one more transfer, also for training purposes, of 90 P–40's which the RAF no longer needed in North Africa.[51]

On 6 June 1944 the powerful Allied armada, which for many months had patiently organized and trained in the United Kingdom, was off on its initial assault of western France. Among the air units engaged in the gigantic undertaking, a small but determined French air force, integrated into the RAF, was playing its part. It was composed of the seven squadrons (4 fighter, 1 light bomber, and 2 heavy bomber squadrons) which had already participated in air operations over western Europe before D Day.

Meanwhile, in the Mediterranean theater, the squadrons engaged in Italy were pursuing their combat and reconnaissance activities, and three others, then in training in North Africa, were making ready to join their comrades at a later date. However, French air participation in operations in that theater would soon cease. In accordance with earlier agreements, all French air squadrons were pulled from Italy along with the units of the French Expeditionary Corps and sent to join the pool of forces being readied for ANVIL.

Headquarters, Force 163, the headquarters charged with the planning and execution of ANVIL, on 28 June published the list of FAF organizations designated for the operation. The list included twelve squadrons and several service units. To ensure that the units would be thoroughly equipped before their release to Force 163, General Eaker requested and obtained from the MAB the authorization to transfer to them such items as were necessary to complete their equipment. Transfers were made on the basis of requests submitted by the French directly to NATOUSA. Meanwhile, the JAC inspected the units to ascertain whether or not they had their full load of equipment.[52]

It soon became evident that, as in the case of the ground forces, the French military authorities had activated too few service units to make the combat squadrons self-supporting. For lack of personnel, they were not organizing all the maintenance units required under Plan VII. The squadrons, as a result, were operating "on a shoestring." To keep them going, MAAF had been compelled to provide, by mid-July, more than 450 American maintenance men.[53]

---

[51] Memo, Ervin for Loomis, 23 Jun 44, JRC 360/002 Items Common to Air and Ground; Msgs W–45370, Arnold to Eaker, 3 Jun 44, and Eaker to Arnold, F–52950, 31 May 44, MX–24412, 13 Jul 44, 25045, 18 Jul 44, and M–25071, 18 Jul 44, JRC Cable Log.

[52] Memo, Hq Force 163 for CG NATOUSA, 28 Jun 44, AFHQ AG 400–1 Fr Sups; Msgs, Eaker to Arnold, M–25502, 21 Jul 44, and M–28515, 18 Aug 44, JRC 360/002 Items Common to Air and Ground; Msg W–86188, Arnold to Devers, 26 Aug 44, JRC Cable Log.

[53] Msg M–23957, Eaker to Arnold, 8 Jul 44, ABC 091.711 France (6 Oct 43), Sec 2–A; Msg M–24150, Eaker to Arnold, 10 Jul 44, History of MAAF, Vol. XXII.

Participating in ANVIL operation, on 15 August, were twelve French squadrons operating from bases in Corsica, Sardinia, and Italy and representing approximately one twentieth of the combined Allied air armada. They were joined later by other French squadrons operating elsewhere in the Mediterranean. Tactically they were employed, at least during the initial phase of the operation, in exactly the same manner as the U.S. and British units engaged in support of ANVIL. They operated directly under the control of XII Tactical Air Command (TAC), commanded by General Saville who, it will be recalled, had served as the first chairman of the JAC. On the recommendation of General Wilson, who felt that for psychological and political reasons French units should be employed in support of French Resistance forces, General Eaker directed XII TAC to put French squadrons, whenever operationally practicable, to such use. While so employed, the units, nevertheless, remained firmly under Allied control.[54]

Also taking part in ANVIL was 1er Régiment de Chasseurs Parachutistes (1st RCP), a parachute regiment equipped under Plan VII as one of the auxiliary units of the FAF. The regiment was to function independently of the other parachute units (2d RCP and 3d RCP) activated and equipped in the United Kingdom and destined to operate as part of the SAS Brigade.[55] Organization and equipping of the 1st RCP were the subject of much discussion and the source of considerable difficulties for many months.

In March, and again in early May 1943,

General Giraud had requested, and AFHQ had subsequently approved, the equipping of a parachute regiment composed of one headquarters company, one service company, and two combat battalions. On 18 May the War Department authorized the delivery of the ground items, the air equipment not being available at the time.[56] Twice in August and September AFHQ requested that the air items be shipped. Not until the end of September did the War Department announce that most of the necessary equipment had been assigned and would reach North Africa shortly. Meanwhile, the unit which until then had been issued only vehicles and clothing had been training with its old French rifles. By October the regiment, with a strength of approximately 1,600 men, had reorganized on a U.S. table of organization and received on loan from SOS some weapons, including M1 rifles, to permit immediate training with U.S. equipment. In November the unit learned the American parachute-jump technique at the Fifth Army Airborne Training Center. It was still expecting its equipment, most of which was said to have already left the United States. Yet by the end of November it had received no parachutes.

The situation of the regiment at the beginning of the year 1944 was not a happy one and held little hope for early employment in combat. The regiment had not completed its training (half of the men had not even fired their M1 rifles). Of the parachute boots issued, 30 percent had been found to be too large. Worse yet, reports indicated that insufficient personnel replacements were available to maintain the unit at

[54] History of FAF in MAAF, pp. 20–21.

[55] The following brief outline draws upon JRC 360/006 Fr Parachute Regt. On 2d RCP and 3d RCP, see p. 182, above.

[56] Msgs W–3, AFHQ to AGWAR, 7 May 43, and 8258, AGWAR to AFHQ, 18 May 43, JRC Cable Log.

strength in case it was engaged in operations. These and other considerations prompted AFHQ officials to decide, on 14 January, that the regiment was unfit for combat and would not be sent to Italy as originally contemplated. Instead it would be held in North Africa for future operations. In April it underwent further training at Fifth Army Airborne Training Center. As the unit was still short of equipment, NATOUSA authorized SOS to issue to it some of the missing items subject to their ultimate replacement by SCAMA. In late May, at the request of the French High Command, the regiment was designated for participation in the conquest of Elba (Operation BRASSARD). On 13 June, four days before the attack, AFHQ announced that, owing to heavy demands for air transport in Italy, no aircraft would be available for the airlift of the regiment.[57] The regiment was finally included in the ANVIL troop list and subsequently transported to southern France, not, however, as a parachute unit, much to the disappointment of its personnel, but as a general reserve infantry organization assigned to 1st French Army. Activated some eighteen months earlier, 1st Parachute Regiment had yet to fire its first shot in combat.

Near the end of August, with the ANVIL forces in fast pursuit of the enemy, Allied commanders agreed that the French air increment operating in France under XII Tactical Air Command should be granted a measure of tactical autonomy. As a first step, there was established, on 1 September, a "French Section, XII Tactical Air Command," the nucleus of what was to become a month later the "1st French Air Corps" commanded by Brig. Gen. Paul Gérardot.

On 13 November 1st French Air Corps, now a full-fledged tactical air command, left the control of XII TAC, and the two organizations were consolidated under the First Tactical Air Force (U.S.). The French component included two B–26 bomber groups and three fighter groups, each consisting of three combat squadrons and one tactical reconnaissance squadron. In order adequately to supply, maintain, and support these units, a French Air Depot group was created with the approval of the CCS, its equipment being provided from matériel available in American stocks in North Africa.[58] Thereafter, 1st French Air Corps was to enjoy, under First Tactical Air Force, a degree of autonomy similar to that enjoyed by 1st French Army within the U.S. 6th Army Group. Its essential mission was generally to act in direct support of 1st French Army.

By November most of the FAF had left North Africa and MAAF's control. Moreover, the JRC and the JAC whose presence was no longer needed in that theater had been disbanded and their key personnel transferred, at General Devers' suggestion and with the concurrence of Generals Eisenhower and Marshall, to the control of SHAEF. Already General Bouscat had moved his staff to Paris.[59]

All twenty-five operational squadrons reequipped under Plan VII were then actively engaged in combat, seven in northern France with the RAF as part of the 2d Tactical Air Force (British), and approximately sixteen, constituting 1st French Air Corps, as part of the First Tactical Air Force (U.S.). Two others were still operating in northern Italy.

[57] De Lattre de Tassigny, *Histoire de la Première Armée Française,* p. 22.

[58] Msg, CCS to Wilson, 23 Oct 44, FAN 441.
[59] Msgs FX–24575, Devers to Marshall, 13 Sep 44, and WX–32283, Marshall to Devers, 17 Sep 44, JRC Cable Log.

After nearly two years of Allied teamwork in the Mediterranean, the rebirth of French military aviation had become an accomplished fact. The North African air rearmament program could now be considered as having come to an end. It had produced a "small but damned good" air force whose performance, "second to none" in the Italian campaign, would for the ANVIL period be remembered "with pride." [60]

Operationally, the undertaking had been highly successful. Morally—and to use the words of one chairman of the JAC—"it would have been a cruel thing, harmful to our international relations, to have neglected the French Air Force. . . . The psychological effect of re-equipping such splendid personnel was most far reaching. . . . It helped greatly the cause of the Allies and played an essential part in the development of the winning team." [61]

---

[60] Intervs with Saville and Ervin, Jul 51. These and other equally favorable statements by Allied field commanders—Generals Alexander and Clark in particular (see pp. 178–79, 179n, above)—are greatly at variance with the curt and disparaging remarks about the French in General H. H. Arnold's *Global Mission* (New York: Harper & Brothers, 1949). His implication that they were playing politics when submitting a particular air equipment request (p. 541) and his statement that, by January 1945, the French Army and Air Force "had not won a battle," although vast quantities of equipment and supplies had been given to them (p. 543), do not appear consonant with the facts.

[61] Statement in corres from Gardiner, OCMH.

CHAPTER XIII

Rehabilitating the French Navy

When the members of the Joint Rearmament Committee assembled for their first meeting on 23 December 1942, they were to consider plans for the rehabilitation of the naval as well as the other French armed forces. The committee confronted a situation unique in the annals of naval history. A month earlier, on 27 November, nearly one half of the entire French Navy, immobilized in the port of Toulon since June 1940, had chosen to scuttle itself, when threatened with German seizure, rather than join the Allies in North Africa. Of the four vessels, all submarines, which had escaped the holocaust by putting to sea, three successfully reached North African ports. Another group of vessels under the command of Admiral René Godfroy, demilitarized and kept under British surveillance in the port of Alexandria since July 1940 as a result of the admiral's unwillingness to join the Royal Navy, was still refusing to rally to the Allies. A third, smaller group, consisting of Admiral Robert's vessels anchored in French West Indies ports, was likewise rejecting Allied appeals to join North Africa.

There was a brighter side. Two French fleets were now at war with the Axis—the Free French Naval Forces of General de Gaulle, which had been in operation since the fall of 1940, and the North African Naval Forces of General Giraud. Both were under Anglo-American operational control, but were acting independently of each other and would continue to do so un-

til the fusion of all French armed forces in late July 1943.

The Free French fleet, commanded first by Vice Adm. Emile Muselier, later, after February 1942, by Admiral Auboyneau, had, from modest beginnings, grown to a well-equipped and seasoned force composed of 5 destroyers, 4 submarines, 13 corvettes and sloops, 1 training ship, and various miscellaneous auxiliary ships.[1] The vessels, some British, the others French or enemy captured, had been operating largely as convoy escorts under the control of the Royal Navy which provided them with equipment and maintenance.

The North African fleet, then commanded by Vice Adm. François Michelier, represented a considerable potential force consisting of some forty-five combat vessels and a number of auxiliary craft. The ships generally were in such poor condition, however, that the question of their employment posed a serious problem. Many had been stripped of armament and equipment during the 1940–42 armistice period; others had been severely damaged in the brief but bloody encounter with Allied naval forces. The French North African authorities had insufficient means and materials at their disposal to make the ships fit for further operation. The few weapons, tools, and parts which they had concealed at great

---

[1] App. 2 to Ltr, Fénard to Leahy, 15 Oct 43, SHAEF Mission to France 900–4 Rearmt Plan and Policy.

FRENCH SUBMARINE, CASABLANCA HARBOR, *joins Allied forces in North Africa, 12 November 1942.*

risk from Italo-German armistice commissions represented only a minor proportion of the matériel required.[2]

The work of rehabilitating the North African Naval Forces began in December 1942. The Anglo-American Allies then agreed to assist them by furnishing materials to carry out relatively minor repairs in French shipyards, by placing Allied shipyards and naval facilities in North Africa at their disposal in the case of more important overhauling, or by sending vessels requiring considerable repairs or refitting, but

---

[2] One French naval official is said to have succeeded in assembling and hiding seventy-five 75-mm. guns, and forty-five 37-mm. guns. Admiral Pierre Barjot, "Le Débarquement," *La France et son Empire dans la Guerre* (Paris: Editions Littéraires de France, 1947), I, 207–34.

able to make the journey, to naval establishments in the United States. The responsibility for co-ordinating these activities was assigned to the JRC upon its creation in mid-December.

At the end of December Admiral Michelier submitted to the JRC a general program of repairs and alterations which he considered necessary for the rehabilitation of the forces and establishments under his command. His proposal involved fitting 8 escort vessels and 6 destroyers with modern antiaircraft armament, asdic (antisubmarine direction indicator) and radar equipment, sending the battleship *Richelieu* to the United States for repairs, and fitting 13 submarines with asdic. It also called for the delivery from Allied sources of a

BATTLESHIP RICHELIEU PASSING UNDER MANHATTAN BRIDGE
heading for drydock at a New Jersey port.

considerable amount of stores and supplies for naval shore establishments, dockyards, and naval aviation.

In forwarding Admiral Michelier's program to the CCS, General Eisenhower pointed out that the provision of secret matériel such as modern radar and fire control equipment would require an early policy decision between Washington and London. He saw no objection to the issue of some form of asdic since several French vessels already had Allied equipment of this type. In his opinion and that of Allied naval officials in the theater, the most urgent problem was to have French convoy escort ships properly furnished with asdic and close-range antiaircraft. The rearmament of the *Richelieu,* reputedly one of the finest battleships in existence at the time, was largely a matter of French prestige; but the vessel, if put into operation, would serve usefully in releasing an Allied battleship from the Atlantic. The French were ready and willing to start immediately on this general program in which Admiral Sir Andrew B. Cunningham, commander of all Allied naval forces in the Mediterranean, concurred.[3]

Pending approval of the program, General Giraud proposed to send to Washington a naval mission, headed by Vice Adm. Raymond Fénard, to cooperate with Allied officials on such matters as the eventual completion of the *Richelieu,* the repair and refitting of other units, and similar questions. The proposal having been endorsed by the Allied Commander in Chief and through him by the CCS, Admiral Fénard left for Washington in late January 1943.[4] The Naval Mission, though separate from

General Béthouart's Military Mission, worked in close collaboration with it.

It was then that a curious and somewhat befuddled situation arose in connection with the payment of French naval personnel. The confusion originated as a result of the dispatch, on 29 December, of a message from Navy Secretary Frank Knox to Rear Adm. John L. Hall, commander of Sea Frontier Forces, Western Task Force. The message authorized and directed the payment by U.S. naval disbursing officers of all personnel of the French North and West African naval units operating with and for the United Nations. Greatly surprised at this offer, which was described to him as emanating from President Roosevelt, Admiral Michelier consulted General Giraud, who in turn registered considerable astonishment since he had already taken the necessary financial measures for the payment from funds available to him of all ground, sea, and air forces under his command. At the direction of the French Commander in Chief, Admiral Michelier explained to Admiral Hall why the offer could not be accepted, and expressed his personal gratitude "for the generosity which had inspired this gesture."[5] Apprised of these negotiations and of the initial offer made without his knowledge, General Eisenhower informed the CCS on 18 January that it would continue to be his policy to respect the apparent desire of the French to maintain their forces in North Africa without recourse to direct financial assistance from the United States.[6] The issue was now closed. The French North African authorities, who had already begun paying their personnel from funds available to them, continued to

---

[3] Msg, Eisenhower to CCS, 2 Jan 43, NAF 78.
[4] Msg, Eisenhower to CCS, 7 Jan 43, NAF 91.

[5] AFHQ Msg (no ref), I Armed Corps (signed Patton) to FREEDOM, 16 Jan 43, JRC Cable Log.
[6] Msg, Eisenhower to CCS, 18 Jan 43, NAF 108.

do so. In the case of crews and other personnel temporarily stationed in the United States, arrangements were made for advances from the Treasury Department subject to repayment from French resources.[7]

Meanwhile, a program of rehabilitation had been worked out after consultation with the French and a conference with Admiral Cunningham and Rear Adm. William A. Glassford, commander in chief of Amphibious Forces, Northwest African Waters. The latter, who had just returned from Casablanca where he had had an opportunity to inspect French naval vessels in that area, submitted to the CCS, on 17 January, the final recommendations of the theater regarding action and priorities for the rehabilitation program. The recommendations were made with a view to putting French ships in operation at the earliest possible date.[8]

The CCS, already assembled for the Casablanca Conference (14–26 January) examined the problem of reconditioning the French fleet in general and the specific program proposed by Admiral Glassford. At one of the meetings attended by General Giraud, Admiral King pointed out that arrangements were well in hand for the refitting in rotation of the French warships. Resources, he explained, would not permit of their being dealt with all at once. Admiral Pound then seized the occasion to welcome the entry of the North African fleet on the side of Allied naval forces. From his experience at the beginning of the war, he was confident that the French Navy would render, once again, substantial and valuable assistance especially in fighting the

U-boat menace.[9] Two days later, on 21 January, the Combined Chiefs informed Admiral Glassford that they approved certain of his recommendations. They also informed him of the respective parts which the United States and the United Kingdom were prepared to play in arming, equipping, and overhauling French naval vessels and installations in North and West Africa. All vessels to be overhauled, such as escorts, submarines, cruisers, and destroyers, were to be sent to shipyards in the United States; none would be sent to the United Kingdom for the moment as it would be impracticable.[10] When, a few weeks later, the first vessels reached U.S. shipyards, the reconditioning program got fully under way. Its progress was not affected by the temporary desertion of crews to Gaullist vessels then anchored in U.S. harbors.[11]

On 27 January, AFHQ formulated a policy to govern the rehabilitation of the North African Naval Forces. The undertaking was to aim at providing forces capable of carrying out the following roles: local defense of ports, escort for coastal convoys, ocean escort, submarine operations. Rehabilitation of course meant repair and refitting of existing vessels. In the eyes of the French it also meant the acquisition of new units. At their request, General Eisenhower urged the CCS, on 1 March, to approve the transfer to them of a number of ships including destroyers, escorts, and tugs, planes and equipment for their Naval Air Arm, clothing and foodstuffs for their personnel, as well as ship repair and construction materials and machine tools for their naval installations. He also recommended

---

[7] Ltr, D. W. Bell to Hull, 26 Feb 43, OPD 336.2 France, Sec I.

[8] Msg, Eisenhower to CCS, 17 Jan 43, NAF 105.

[9] Min, CCS 62d Mtg, 19 Jan 42, Casablanca Conf.

[10] Msg 2226/22, CCS to Glassford, 21 Jan 43, OPD 336.3 France, Sec 1.

[11] See p. 80n, above.

BATTLESHIP JEAN BART AT CASABLANCA *after receiving three direct bomb hits from a carrier-based dive bomber.*

that the Fénard mission in Washington be asked to designate the equipment to be delivered under the shipping allotment reserved by General Giraud for naval units out of the total 25,000-ton monthly allocation. Shipments would be made as agreed upon by Admiral Fénard and Overseas Supply Division of New York Port of Embarkation (and not International Division), the agency responsible for handling naval materials.[12]

On 17 April the CCS examined the various piecemeal recommendations submitted by the theater, then drafted and approved a supply policy for North African naval vessels and bases. The policy determined the extent of the rehabilitation program, the procedure to be followed for the issue of materials, and the respective participation of the United States and the United Kingdom in the commitment. With regard to vessels in operation, the policy stipulated that the United States and the United Kingdom each would supply the necessary ammunition, fuel, and other items to the vessels operating under their control.[13]

[12] Memo, AFHQ (signed Whiteley), 27 Jan 43, AFHQ 0100/4 SACS Rcd Sec, Fr Matters; Msgs 3729, Eisenhower to CCS, 1 Mar 43, and 4498, Eisenhower to AGWAR, 5 Mar 43, JRC Cable Log; Memo, Lutes for Somervell, 8 Mar 43, ASF File 124 Task Force Chronology, 18 Oct 43.

[13] Note, CCS Secretaries to CCS, 16 Apr 43, OPD 400 France, Sec II; Min, CCS 80th Mtg, 17 Apr 43.

By this time a number of ships were being overhauled in various dockyards. In New York, the *Richelieu* was having main armament completed, radar equipment installed, and antiaircraft armament improved. In Casablanca, the battleship *Jean Bart*, badly damaged in November 1942, was undergoing repairs sufficient to enable her to steam to the United States later in the year for final refitting. In Philadelphia, Boston, Hampton Roads, and other American ports, cruisers, destroyers, submarines, and various miscellaneous vessels were undergoing repair, with many more to follow in the near future. Repairs and refitting were also being effected in Casablanca, Algiers, Dakar, Oran, and even Bermuda. Twenty French merchant ships were being issued defensive armament and ammunition. The British were about to furnish twenty Walrus patrol planes for use by the French Naval Air Arm. At all Allied ports in North Africa, French officers were being trained in British and American methods of harbor defense. A French antisubmarine warfare school was functioning at Casablanca. Gunnery schools were in operation at Algiers and Oran. Selected French personnel were being sent to sea in British destroyers escorting convoys to study the latest methods in antisubmarine warfare.[14]

On 30 April, pursuant to the CCS directive issued a fortnight before, the theater forwarded to Washington a revised list of naval items of munitions and warships stores for the French. Two months later General Eisenhower proposed to the CCS that thereafter new requests for ships, proposals for major overhauls, and requests for increases in armament be referred by Gen-

eral Giraud's headquarters to AFHQ for recommendation, leaving matters of detail relating to requests for naval supplies for direct handling between the Fénard mission and appropriate agencies in Washington. Endorsing the proposal, the CCS directed that the French submit their requests for ships and major items of matériel to AFHQ, for recommendation, simultaneously with their requisitions to the MAB in Washington. They stipulated further that no consideration would be given in Washington to items disapproved by AFHQ.[15]

In early July the theater cabled a request for the issue to the French of gun and machinery spare parts and maintenance replacements on a scale comparable to that authorized similar American naval vessels.[16] The request was approved by the CCS a month later.

While the overhauling operations were proceeding, the question of employment of the North African naval vessels and personnel was made the subject of a detailed study by the Combined Staff Planners in full consultation with Admiral Fénard. Until then the operational assignment of vessels had been effected upon a basis of "cooperation" in accordance with the terms of the still valid Clark-Darlan Agreement: "French warships shall operate in close cooperation with the CG, US Army, or Allied representatives acting with his approval."[17] Feeling that there was need for a more precise and orderly arrangement, the CPS recommended that thereafter French naval units, when ready for duty, be assigned to operations areas by the CCS, initially according

---

[14] Memo, Naval Members JRC for Gardiner, 7 May 43: Memo, Gardiner for DCofS, 14 May 43, JRC 905.6/VIII Naval Rearmt.

[15] Msg, Eisenhower to CCS, 25 Jun 43, NAF 245; Msg, CCS to Eisenhower, 10 Jul 43, FAN 156.

[16] Msg, Eisenhower to CCS, 5 Jul 43, NAF 276; Msg, CCS to Eisenhower, 13 Aug 43, FAN 190.

[17] Article VII, Clark-Darlan Agreement, 22 Nov 42, AFHQ 0100/5 CAO/302/1 MAEB.

to a specific detailed plan, later, if changes were required, at the direction of the CCS themselves. On 30 July the CCS approved the recommendations of the CPS but postponed the issuance of a statement on the question of control pending further discussion of the matter.[18]

In late July the long-awaited fusion of the Free French and North African Forces brought into being a single Marine Nationale (referred to hereafter as French Navy) under the supreme command of General Giraud. Admiral Lemonnier was appointed Chief of Staff of the integrated force, and Admiral Auboyneau the Deputy Chief of Staff. The new Navy included also the forces which earlier had refused to join the Allies. In May Admiral Godfroy had finally agreed to rally to General Giraud and arrived in Dakar, via the Suez Canal and the Cape of Good Hope, with his eight ships of which one was the battleship *Lorraine*. In July the seven vessels immobilized in the French West Indies had likewise joined the common struggle after the resignation of Admiral Robert, then High Commissioner for that territory. As a result of these successive additions, the French Navy now represented a large force of some 80 ships including 3 operational battleships,[19] 1 aircraft-carrier, 9 cruisers, 21 destroyers, 22 submarines, and 20 smaller vessels. Besides these, there were about 60 auxiliary craft. Available naval personnel numbered some 45,000 men.

By this time the work of rehabilitation had made substantial progress. Refitting of the *Richelieu* was nearly completed and the vessel was about to be subjected to a period of trials and practice runs in the United States. At Casablanca, temporary hull repairs to the *Jean Bart* were continuing. A number of ships had left U.S. ports upon completion of their refitting and had joined others already operating under the control of the Naval Commander in Chief, Mediterranean. Others were on their way to the United States. The British, for their part, had made sufficient temporary repairs to the ships of Admiral Godfroy's fleet to enable them to sail from Alexandria to Dakar, and eventually to the United States. They also had repaired and refitted in North African ports a number of trawlers, escort vessels, and miscellaneous small craft unable to cross the Atlantic for modernization in American yards. It was estimated that when the program was completed, the United States would have financed approximately 95 percent of the cost of French naval rearmament.[20]

The memorandum on the status of the French armed forces which Generals Giraud and de Gaulle jointly addressed to General Marshall on 18 September contained a plea that the naval rehabilitation program be implemented speedily. Many of the 45,000 sailors constituting the naval forces otherwise would remain unused or poorly used. The two generals also requested new ships: 12 destroyers and 30 escort vessels from the United States, and 3 destroyers, 1 auxiliary aircraft carrier, and 3 submarines from the United Kingdom.[21]

In late September, the CCS consolidated all existing policies with respect to the French Navy into one single memorandum

---

[18] Rpt, CPS to CCS (CCS 207/10), 19 Jul 43, OPD 336.3 France, Sec 1; Min, CCS 104th Mtg, 30 Jun 43.
[19] Two more could not be repaired.

[20] Rpt, JRC Naval Members to Chairman JRC, 1 Aug 43, JRC 905.6/VIII Naval Rearmt; Memo, Spalding for Brig Gen Arthur R. Wilson, 14 Aug 43, JRC 902/II Rearmt Plan.
[21] Ltr and Memo, de Gaulle and Giraud to Marshall, 18 Sep 43, ABC 091.711 France (6 Oct 43), Sec 1–A; see also pp. 105–06, above.

(CCS 358). The memorandum covered all aspects of administration and operational control, such as overhauling, refitting, assignment, and employment; it also proposed a detailed supply policy in connection with repairs and the issue of matériel. The memorandum was subsequently amended on 4 October. The amended version (CCS 358/Revised) became the official policy governing the rehabilitation and employment of the French naval and naval air forces and the basis on which all subsequent programs or revisions thereof were shaped.[22] The provision relating to the assignment of vessels was a restatement of the policy advocated earlier by the Combined Staff Planners in their report of 19 July. With respect to operational control, the directive contained a clause which merely formalized the practice then current: "French ships assigned to any operational area will operate under the operational command of the Allied naval area commander. They will be utilized to the extent of their capabilities and in the same manner as other similar Allied ships in the area, operating normally under subordinate French commanders." Internal administration was to remain, of course, the concern of appropriate French naval authorities. The French immediately endorsed the provisions of the directive and signified unqualified approval.[23]

Now that the French Admiralty in Algiers controlled vessels operating world-wide, many outside of his own theater, the Allied Commander in Chief requested the CCS, on 17 October, to review the procedure with respect to French naval rearmament. He recommended that British and American naval missions operating under the control of the Naval Commander in Chief in the Mediterranean be accredited to the French Admiralty as representatives of the British Admiralty and the Commander in Chief of the U.S. Fleet respectively.[24] The Combined Chiefs replied that they had no objection to the proposal provided the French Admiralty, in compliance with CCS 358 (Revised), took up all policy matters with the CCS through the executive agent of that body, namely, the Commander in Chief of the U.S. Fleet acting in concurrence with the British Admiralty delegation in Washington.[25]

In late November Admiral Lemonnier submitted to the Joint Rearmament Committee a list of requisitions for the year 1944 superseding all previous similar requests most of which had been nullified as a result of the change in supply policy effected by the CCS. The list included a request for ships, aircraft, clothing, medical supplies, and the normal maintenance of vessels. The requisition for clothing was based on a personnel strength of 49,000 men.[26] The request for additional ships had little chance of being granted because the CCS had just decided that it would not be beneficial to the war effort to make further assignments of vessels to the French in the near future.[27]

Another request submitted almost simultaneously by Admiral Lemonnier on behalf of the French Naval Air Arm (Aéronautique Navale) brought the question of the rearmament and maintenance of that force into focus. Four naval air squadrons were

[22] Min, CCS 121st Mtg, 1 Oct 43; CCS 358 (Revised), 4 Oct 43.

[23] Memo, Fénard for Leahy, 15 Oct 43, SHAEF Mission to France 091.711 Rearmt Plan and Policy 900–4.

[24] Msg, Eisenhower to CCS, 17 Oct 43, NAF 472.

[25] Msg, CCS to Eisenhower, 6 Nov 43, FAN 272.

[26] Ltr, Lemonnier to Loomis, 30 Nov 43, JRC 045/001 Plan, Policy, Progress of Rearmt of Fr Navy.

[27] CCS 358/3, approved by CCS 4 Nov 43.

operating under Mediterranean Air Command. Two had been equipped with Sunderlands and Wellingtons by the RAF, one with Walruses by the Fleet Air Arm of the Royal Navy, and one with Catalinas by the U.S. Navy.[28] These units had been rearmed at the initiative of individual Allied commanders without any definite over-all plan and, as a result, the question of their maintenance was presenting serious difficulties.

The advisability of expanding the Naval Air Arm had been the subject of long negotiations in the course of 1943. As early as July the French High Command had requested the War Department to deliver 255 planes to be used for the defense of bases and ports and for the protection of French naval units. The request, although favorably received by General Eisenhower, later was disapproved by the War Department on the ground that it had not been considered by the theater in relation to French Air Force requirements.[29] As the proposed Air program (Plan VII) contemplated no expansion of the Naval Air Arm, the French, in mid-December, made a second attempt to obtain equipment for their naval air units. This time the request, largely a repetition of the first one, was submitted by Admiral Fénard to the U.S. Navy Department.[30] It called for 250 aircraft to equip

naval squadrons "for combat duty under Allied control as may be prescribed by the CCS." The request was referred to General Wilson for advice and recommendation in accordance with the recent CCS decision that all French rearmament matters be cleared by the Allied Commander in Chief in the theater before their submission to the CCS.[31]

On 24 January 1944 General Wilson informed the War Department that no plan had been submitted to him by the French for the rearmament of their naval air squadrons. He urged that no consideration be given to arming such units at the expense of Allied air forces, and added the information that the French were reported to have insufficient trained crews and maintenance personnel either for the activation of new naval air units or for their continued support.[32] In addition, he warned, the theater was having considerable difficulty in solving the supply problem of the four existing squadrons because of the diversity of the responsibilities involved.[33]

Endorsing General Wilson's advice and recommendation, the CCS, on 25 February, disapproved the French request and Admiral Leahy so informed Admiral Fénard.[34] Meanwhile, President Roosevelt, consulted on the matter by General Arnold, had directed that French naval air personnel be employed in the Mediterranean in French

---

[28] Memos, Saville for Loomis, 30 Nov 43, and Loomis for Saville, 16 Dec 43, JRC 045/009 Naval Aviation.

[29] Msgs 3062, Arnold to Eisenhower, 22 Jul 43, W–6872, Eisenhower to Arnold, 8 Aug 43, and 4752, Arnold to Eisenhower, 11 Aug 43, JRC Cable Log.

[30] Admiral Fénard's initial request was submitted to the U.S. Navy and not to the Army Air Forces as indicated by General Arnold in his *Global Mission,* p. 541. Subsequently, however, a second request from Admiral Fénard, dated 7 January 1944 and addressed to Admiral Leahy as Chief of Staff to the Commander in Chief, was forwarded by the

latter to the Army Air Forces for action. Ltrs, Fénard to Navy Dept, 18 Dec 43, and to Leahy, 7 Jan 44, ABC 091.711 France (12 Oct 43).

[31] Msg to AFHQ, 1 Jan 44, FAN 288; Msg 7165, Arnold to Wilson, 14 Jan 44, JRC Cable Log.

[32] Msg W–919, Wilson to AGWAR, 24 Jan 44, JRC Cable Log.

[33] Memos, Saville for Loomis, 30 Nov 43, Timberlake for Loomis, 13 Dec 43, and Loomis for Saville, 16 Dec 43, JRC 045/009 Naval Aviation.

[34] Min, CCS 147th Mtg, 25 Feb 44; Ltr, Leahy to Fénard, 25 Feb 44, ABC 091.711 France (12 Oct 43).

Air Force units equipped and supplied from U.S. sources.[35]

Obviously the matter of expanding the Naval Air Arm was, for the present at least, a closed one, considering in addition that the CCS had just reached an important decision with respect to French military aviation. Indeed, on 28 January, they had finally approved Plan VII, which, in their opinion, represented the maximum objective likely to be reached by the French in the field of aviation during the current war.[36]

In mid-February 1944, the French Admiralty once again attempted to obtain an extension of the naval program. Appearing before the CCS, Admiral Fénard discussed the request for additional vessels submitted by Admiral Lemonnier in November. He explained that some 10,000 naval personnel, including specialists, were currently unemployed for lack of sufficient naval units. A month later the CCS informed Admiral Fénard that existing construction programs for combatant ships, although absorbing all available resources of the United Kingdom and the United States, would be short of the requirements for planned operations during the current year. As a result it was not possible to meet the French request except for some escorts, submarine chasers, mine sweepers and other miscellaneous ships which the Commander in Chief of the U.S. Fleet proposed to transfer to the French Navy as soon as possible.[37] So far the French had received or were about to receive from U.S. sources 6 destroyer escorts, 6 patrol craft, and 6 sub-

marine chasers,[38] and from British sources 4 frigates. During the following months, the transfer of additional Allied vessels, mostly American, such as mine sweepers, sloops, and patrol boats, as well as the refloating and refitting of salvaged French or captured Italian ships, resulted in a substantial increase of the French Navy. By May it was estimated that nearly 100 ships had been added, bringing the total of units to approximately 240.[39]

Meanwhile, such ships as had been overhauled or acquired had not remained idle. For over a year they had been carrying out missions in various theaters of operations under British or U.S. command, as part of the Allied naval pool. In September 1943 a number of submarines, destroyers, and cruisers had temporarily been released from Allied control and placed by Admiral Cunningham at General Giraud's disposal for use in transporting the French ground forces engaged in the assault of Corsica (Vesuvius).[40] In November the *Richelieu* had joined the Home Fleet and four months later had been sent to the Indian Ocean as part of the British Far Eastern Fleet. Other vessels were operating in the Atlantic and Indian Oceans, as well as in the Mediterranean. Several were escorting convoys to Murmansk.

During the coming months of June, July, and August 1944, the reborn French Navy was to furnish its greatest contribution to the Allied war effort and to regain the place of honor it had long occupied. Participating in the cross-Channel operation (Over-lord) as elements of the Allied supporting naval pool, commanded by Admiral Sir

[35] Memo, Arnold for JCS, 9 Feb 44, ABC 091.711 France (12 Oct 43).

[36] For details of Plan VII, see pp. 204–05, above.

[37] Ltr, Leahy to Fénard, 13 Mar 44, OPD 336.3 France, Sec 1.

[38] Rpt, MAB to CCS, 31 Dec 43, ABC 091.711 France (6 Oct 43), Sec 2–A.

[39] André Truffert, "La Marine Nationale," *La France et son Empire dans la Guerre*, II, 188–96.

[40] See p. 101, above.

Bertram H. Ramsay, were a number of cruisers, destroyers, frigates, corvettes, torpedo boats, submarine chasers, and other smaller craft. These vessels, under the command of Rear Adm. Robert Jaujard, were attached to Rear Adm. Alan G. Kirk's U.S. naval force.[41] A week later, on 16 June, several units commanded by Rear Adm. Robert Battet, operating alongside British vessels under the over-all command of Admiral Troubridge (RN), participated in the assault on the island of Elba (BRASSARD).[42]

The most substantial contribution of the French Navy was that given in connection with the landings in southern France (ANVIL). The Allied naval task force, commanded by Vice Adm. Henry Kent Hewitt, included a French increment under Admiral Lemonnier which comprised the battleship *Lorraine,* eight cruisers, a number of destroyers, and many other smaller craft. Like the British and American ships engaged in the operation, the French vessels were given the task of protecting the invading forces and neutralizing enemy coastal defenses. In their after-action reports, Admiral Hewitt and other U.S. naval commanders highly praised the French crews for their excellent seamanship and gunnery, their intrepidity under fire, as well as the fine sportsmanship of their commanding officers.[43]

A word must be said here of the units of fusiliers marins (marines) which the French High Command activated and put to excellent use in operations. Two such units accompanied the French Expeditionary Corps in Italy, the 1st Fusiliers Marins Regiment as the reconnaissance regiment of the 1st Motorized Infantry Division (1st DMI), and the Groupe de Canonniers Marins (Naval Gunners Group) as a general reserve artillery unit of the CEF. Later, in June 1944, the 1st Battalion of Fusiliers Marins Commandos (Marine Commandos) operated as part of the French naval forces engaged in OVERLORD, and the Régiment Blindé de Fusiliers Marins (Armored Marine Regiment) landed in France as the tank destroyer regiment of the 2d Armored Division. All these units, equipped and trained under the North African rearmament program, gave an excellent account of themselves.

Shortly before the launching of ANVIL, General Wilson had recommended to the CCS that the policy contained in CCS 358 (Revised) with respect to the supply of French ships and ports under immediate control of the United States and United Kingdom be extended to the ports expected to be captured in the forthcoming operation and to the French warships and naval personnel likely to be operating outside direct U.S. and British control.[44] In mid-September, a month after the operation had been launched, the CCS approved the proposal provided that the supply of repair equipment and materials, ships, and stores to the French Navy in its home ports and to the ports themselves for their rehabilitation be limited to the extent required for the support of operations.[45]

Soon after, the responsibility for the

---

[41] The old battleship *Courbet* and other ships no longer seaworthy and anchored in U.K. ports since 1940 were brought close to shore, sunk, and used as breakwaters for the protection of artificial harbors.

[42] See pp. 180–81, above.

[43] Ltrs, Vice Adm Lyal A. Davidson, Comdr Task Force 86, 29 Aug and 5 Sep 44, and Hewitt, 3 and 15 Sep 44, to CinC U.S. Fleet, AFHQ Royal Navy Op file, Op DRAGOON, Fr Ships, Rpts.

[44] Msg, Wilson to CCS, 15 Jul 44, NAF 719.

[45] Msg, CCS to Wilson, 21 Sep 44, FAN 424.

supply and maintenance of the French Navy passed, along with that of all other French armed forces, from AFHQ to SHAEF. The rehabilitation of the French Navy, within the limits set forth by the CCS, was nearly completed. The question of further expansion would, thereafter, be a matter for discussion between SHAEF authorities and the French officials in Paris before consultation with the CCS.

CHAPTER XIV

Liaison, Language, and Training Problems

In implementing the North African rearmament program, AFHQ was confronted with a variety of problems affecting, not any one phase in particular, but rather the entire period of operations. Some resulted from human or personal considerations, others involved purely material matters. All resulted from a situation in which the army of one nation was committed to the rehabilitation of another nation's forces having needs peculiar to them, therefore requiring special attention. In general the problems stemmed from lack of sufficient planning or because of unforeseen developments. Their solution depended entirely on the action or arrangements initiated by AFHQ or NATOUSA subject to final approval by the CCS or the War Department.

Liaison and the Language Barrier

Foremost among the factors vitally influencing Franco-Allied relations, particularly in the field of rearmament, were the language barrier and a dearth of qualified liaison officers on both sides.

American as well as French officers agree that, to be successful, a rearmament officer must have certain qualifications. Next to a thorough knowledge of his subject, he must possess a keen understanding of the other fellow's approach to the problem, his personal and national idiosyncrasies, his working habits, and his probable reactions. In short, the rearmament officer must dis-

play a sympathetic attitude. Fluency in the foreign language, although highly desirable, is not the prime qualification required for the position.[1] Judged by such exacting standards, few on either side possessed all the skills required to perform their task adequately. Among the Americans, excepting those officials directly supervising the rearmament and training operations whose sympathetic attitude was fully recognized and appreciated by the French, many were unable to understand the French, usually from lack of preparation for the positions they occupied. Similarly, French officers other than those appointed to key posts frequently lacked technical knowledge, understanding of American organization and methods, and fluency in the English language. Notable among the exceptions were a number of officers recruited in early 1943 among French residents abroad, especially in the United States and Canada. After a period of training in U.S. schools in the use of American equipment, some fifty of these highly qualified bilingual officers were assigned by the French High Command to the JRC, SCAMA, and French depots and supply installations where they rendered valuable assistance.

Fluency in the foreign language, while it may be a secondary qualification for re-

---

[1] Intervs with Col Artamonoff, Dec 49, Col Gardiner, Apr 50, Gen Loomis, Jun and Jul 50, Col de Beaumont, Jul 50, and Gen Regnault, Jul and Sep 50.

armament officers, is obviously of primary importance for liaison officers. When these officers were unable to cope with the finer linguistic problems and, in addition, were not thoroughly familiar with the technical problems involved, their inadequacy led to mistranslations or misinterpretations that often strained inter-Allied relations. A case in point is the serious misunderstanding between AFHQ and French Headquarters brought about by a letter addressed in October 1943 by General Whiteley, then Deputy Chief of Staff, AFHQ, to General Giraud. In his communication, General Whiteley requested that, "whenever necessary, equipment will be *drawn from* non-participating units" in order to complete the re-equipment of units designated for combat. When it became clear, from subsequent French requisitions, that General Whiteley's instructions had not been complied with, the French were accused of willfully disregarding orders received. Resentment on both sides increased until an investigation revealed, nearly three weeks later, that the English text of the paragraph in question had erroneously been translated at French Headquarters as: "equipment will be *drawn from stocks available to* non-participating units." [2]   The very point which General Whiteley had wished to stress, namely, that nonparticipating units should be stripped of their equipment if necessary (a matter of considerable dispute at the time), had been entirely missed. In other instances, misunderstanding resulted from faulty translation by Americans. The following sentence contained in a French directive, "Des forces françaises opérant dans un cadre américain" (French forces operating within the framework of an American

command), was given by a translator at AFHQ as, "French forces operating with American cadres." [3] War Department translators, as well, occasionally missed the particular meaning of a French word. In a letter to General Marshall, General Giraud spoke of a certain armament program "which we have drawn up" (le programme que nous avons *arrêté*). The sentence was rendered, first, as "the program which we have held up," later in a second translation, intended no doubt to improve on the first, as "which we have postponed." [4] The resulting inference that the French Commander in Chief was postponing his rearmament program, when in reality he was fighting for its retention, must have been somewhat of a surprise to those who read the letter. Not all linguistic errors, fortunately, were serious in consequence. Some, by their humorous implications, probably contributed to the relief of tension between Allied and French staffs. In this category can be classed the unexpected statement appearing in the minutes of the 30 December 1943 meeting between Generals Eisenhower and de Gaulle, as drawn up by the French recording officer present. According to the French text, the Allied Commander in Chief is reported to have assured his visitor that he would not fail to include a French "talking force" in the cross-Channel operation. [5]

In addition to being the source of occasional misunderstandings, the language bar-

[2] Ltr, Whiteley to Giraud, 20 Oct 43, AFHQ 0100/4 SACS Rcd Sec. Italics supplied.

[3] Dir 6014, Fr Hq, 8 Dec 43, JRC 400.2/002 Stock Control (SCAMA).

[4] Ltr, Giraud to Marshall, 27 Aug 43, OPD 400 France, Sec. II.

[5] The two words appear in English and in quotations in the French text. Min Mtg, Eisenhower with de Gaulle, 30 Dec 43, AFHQ 0100/26 Liaison Sec, Mtgs and Confs, Vol. I.

rier raised considerable technical difficulties. These might have been greatly reduced had it been possible in the early stages of the rearmament operations to provide the French with translations in their language of U.S. technical manuals and publications, none of which were available at the time. Recognizing the urgency of the matter, the War Department promptly undertook a vast program of translation and began furnishing French texts as fast as they could be prepared and printed. As early as March 1943 thousands of copies of various manuals were sent along with the first large shipments of matériel. Psychological warfare booklets and numerous technical bulletins were subsequently delivered, first through the JRC and French Training Section, later through the French base at Oran, for distribution to troops, depots, and shops. In September of the same year the War Department announced that the translation had been undertaken in the United States of all American technical publications needed for the current rearmament program. Yet, by the beginning of Phase IV in February 1944, much still remained to be done in connection with the translation program.

Even publications in English were not always available to the French when most needed. In the course of the summer of 1943, when the first divisions were being issued their U.S. equipment, the French High Command complained of not having complete sets of standard nomenclature lists as well as the bulletins, circulars, and other publications distributed by the various American services. It was not until October that the first lists were delivered to them.

To ensure that French units would obtain all the necessary technical literature,

whether in English or in French, General Larkin recommended in November that the French High Command organize a central publications depot.[6] The French approved the suggestion and on 1 January 1944 established such a depot (Dépôt français de Publications américaines) at Oran to serve as a clearinghouse for all requests for, and issues of, American publications. These were of two types: War Department publications—such as technical manuals, field manuals, and tables of organization and equipment—and Ordnance technical publications.

By the end of January the French still had not been issued base shop data manuals or lists of maintenance factors. In addition they had received only half of the publications in French promised earlier by the War Department. Without waiting for the rest of the documents to arrive, they had undertaken the translation of a number of U.S. publications. Already in November they had published an English-French lexicon, a most useful manual in view of the scarcity of English-French dictionaries in the theater. Technical dictionaries were and continued to be in great demand. In April 1944 the French General Staff tried unsuccessfully to obtain from U.S. sources in the theater such dictionaries, for use in particular at the Casablanca Vehicle Assembly Line to which women interpreters with no technical knowledge had been assigned. Dictionaries of this sort were not available in U.S. theater stocks and the French were advised to obtain them from the United States through their Military Mission in Washington.

Efforts of War Department and AFHQ officials to provide adequate material both in French and in English continued through-

---

[6] Msg L–1076, Larkin to CG NATOUSA, 24 Nov 43, JRC 461/001 Publications (1943).

out the spring of 1944. That they were ultimately successful is best illustrated by the comments of General Juin, Commanding General, CEF, at the end of French participation in the Italian campaign. On 10 July 1944 General Juin requested the chief of the French Military Mission in the United States to express to the responsible War Department authorities his appreciation of the "great care, accuracy and excellent taste" with which translations of U.S. publications had been prepared.[7]

Training

U.S. assistance in the French training program was limited to technical instruction in the use of American matériel. At no time was tactical training, except in minor infantry tactics and amphibious landings, ever given. By the time that rearmament operations were fully under way, in May 1943, the bulk of the French units consisted of old and tried regiments, a large part of whose personnel had gone through both the 1939–40 and the Tunisian campaigns. Few were the men who had not had some military training. It was felt that French cadres were sufficiently experienced to assume the burden of tactical training. In fact, American commanders frequently sought qualified French officers, especially Air Force officers, to assist in the tactical training of comparatively green American troops.[8]

In the initial phase of Franco-American collaboration, American technical training assistance was extended by local U.S. commanders acting on their own initiative. As early as mid-November 1942 General Patton arranged to have some French technicians as well as fighter pilots trained in handling American equipment.[9] In December, at the request of the French High Command, training materials and instructors were placed at the disposal of the Chantiers de Jeunesse school near Algiers.[10] Schools for instructing French Ordnance and Quartermaster personnel in the use of U.S. weapons and matériel were being organized in various parts of North Africa. As there appeared to be some hesitancy about how far this assistance was to be extended, General Eisenhower, on 30 and 31 December, directed the U.S. Fifth Army and AFHQ to make sure that U.S. troops were giving all possible assistance to the North African forces in their training with U.S. arms and equipment.[11] AFHQ promptly issued an instruction setting forth the purpose and general scope of the training to be given the French and outlining a training plan.[12] Already many French cadres, officers as well as noncommissioned officers, were receiving instruction within American divisions for periods of approximately two weeks in armament, vehicle driving and maintenance, and signal communications.

By mid-March G–3 Training Section, AFHQ, found that the training program was proceeding satisfactorily. The French were reported to have a "keen appreciation of problems, both mechanical and person-

---

[7] Ltr, Juin to Chief Military Mission in Washington, 10 Jul 44, JRC 461/001 Publications (1 Jan 44).

[8] Memo, Artamonoff for G–4 AFHQ, 2 Aug 43, JRC Misc Doc, Item 5–a, Tab T.

[9] Memo, Patton for Eisenhower, 21 Nov 42, AFHQ SAC 000.2–2 NA Political.

[10] On Chantiers de Jeunesse, see pp. 8n, 68n, above.

[11] Ltr, CinC to CG Fifth Army, 30 Dec 42, quoted in Fifth Army History, I, 2; Ltr, AG 353/082 C–M, AFHQ, 31 Dec 42, AFHQ 0100 12C G–3 Div Ops Fr Rearmt, Vol. II (3).

[12] AFHQ Training Memo 1, 1 Jan 43, JRC 353/003 Training Fr Army Personnel.

nel," and to be making great strides. They were supplying personnel for liaison and for instruction, and were expected to take over the brunt of the burden of instruction within a short time.[13] Training equipment had been requisitioned by the theater, assigned in Washington, and would soon be on its way to North African ports.

General Eisenhower on 30 March restated Fifth Army's responsibility in organizing and training the French forces then stationed within its area in French Morocco. In a subsequent directive setting forth the general policies that would govern the process of French rearmament, AFHQ prescribed the manner in which training assistance was to be provided. Basically, the U.S. Army was to assist the French Army in familiarizing its personnel with the technical details of storing, assembly, care, and maintenance of all U.S. types of equipment. To this end, the practice already established of attaching French technical personnel to U.S. service units handling equipment for delivery to the French was to continue. In addition, teams of instructors from U.S. combat and service units were to be attached to French units while they were being re-equipped and for as long afterward as would be necessary. Responsibility in the matter was to be divided. The Commanding General, Fifth Army, was to assist combat and supporting service units being re-equipped in the care and maintenance of their equipment, during both basic training in unit stations and field training, until such time as the French authorities considered assistance no longer necessary. The Commanding General, NATOUSA, on the other hand, was responsible for instructing

supply service units in the technical aspects of handling and maintaining matériel.[14]

In Washington, meanwhile, War Department officials were eager to know how efficiently the French were going to use their newly acquired equipment. On 18 April General Marshall asked approximately how long a time should be allowed after receipt of matériel for complete training of units; also what degree of combat efficiency could be expected of these units after the expiration of the training period. After consultation with General Giraud, the Allied Commander in Chief replied that training would take two months for existing infantry divisions, three months for existing armored regiments and reconnaissance and tank destroyer battalions, and six months for technical units.[15]

To co-ordinate its activities with respect to the French training program, Fifth Army organized, on 23 April, a Rearmament Advisory Section, redesignated on 15 May as the French Training Section (FTS).[16] FTS was charged with the over-all direction and supervision of the training of the French divisions stationed in Fifth Army area. The section, headed at first by Col. Harry A. Flint, consisted of "advisers," assigned one to each of the divisions being rearmed, instructors detailed to teach French instructors in the use and care of U.S. equipment, and staff co-ordination teams whose main function was to observe the training

[13] Memo, AFHQ G–3 (Training) for Col Ross, 17 Mar 43, JRC 353/002 Training of Fr Army Personnel.

[14] Dir AG 322.1/060 CS–M, Eisenhower for CG Fifth Army, 30 Mar 43, JRC Misc Doc, Item 5–a, Tab K; Ltr, Eisenhower to CG Fifth Army and Deputy Theater Comdr NATOUSA, 13 Apr 43, JRC 902/II Rearmt Plan.
[15] Ltr, Giraud to Eisenhower, 28 Apr 43, JRC 902/II Rearmt Plan; Msgs 6213, Marshall to Eisenhower, 18 Apr 43, and 8565, Eisenhower to Marshall, 1 May 43, JRC Cable Log.
[16] For details on composition, organization, and working methods of FTS, see pp. 293–96, below.

FIRING A 105-MM. HOWITZER, *part of the program to train French soldiers in the use of U.S. equipment, North Africa, March 1943.*

and maintenance activities of the units.[17] Three weeks later, on 13 May, General Kingman replaced Colonel Flint (who had been transferred at his own request to combat duty) as chief of the FTS. Thereafter FTS rapidly grew in size and efficiency. Its essential mission became twofold—to give maximum training assistance to the French and to make sure, by means of inspections, that units were adequately trained and properly equipped. In this latter connection, FTS was in a position to render invaluable service to the JRC.

A visit made at the end of May to the units stationed in French Morocco con-

vinced Colonel Artamonoff of the JRC that U.S. instructors should be placed within the units to teach, in particular, preventive maintenance of equipment.[18] At his suggestion, General Kingman immediately spread his personnel among the divisions, but the number of available instructors was too small (150 officers and men by July) to fill the needs of a rapidly expanding army. By August the chief of FTS recognized that the procedure was not satisfactory since it was teaching every soldier only a little about a certain subject and dissipating American instructor personnel through the division. General Kingman then recommended that

[17] Memo, Clark for U.S. Advisers, 23 Apr 43, AFHQ 0100/12C G–3 Div Ops Fr Rearmt.

[18] Memo for Rcd (Artamonoff), 31 May 43, JRC Misc Doc, Item 5–a, Tab V.

U.S. INSTRUCTOR DEMONSTRATING THE USE OF SIGNAL EQUIP-
MENT *to French personnel, North Africa, February 1943.*

division schools be established to which could be sent students selected from all individual units of the divisions. This method, he felt, would make it possible to co-ordinate training within each division.[19] The recommendation was warmly endorsed by General Giraud, who agreed that it would provide better instruction. Pursuant to an order dated 25 August, the French General Staff immediately established divisional technical schools, one for each of the divisions to be rearmed. Each school had the benefit of the collaboration of all the U.S. instructors assigned to the technical instruction of its division. It trained simul-

taneously instructors for the division directly concerned as well as instructors for the division of the same type next to be rearmed.[20] The system proved highly successful and made it possible for U.S. assistance to reach maximum efficiency.

As those divisions that by then had received their equipment in French Morocco and eastern Algeria were being moved to the general vicinity of Oran in order to utilize areas better suited for training, General Kingman, his French deputy, Lt. Col. André L'Huillier, and staff, moved to Oran. Once there, FTS was placed under the con-

[19] Memo, Kingman for Spalding, 9 Aug 43, JRC 353/002 Training Fr Army Units (1943).

[20] Ltr, Giraud To All Concerned, 25 Aug 43, JRC 353/002 Training Fr Army Units (1943).

trol of the JRC and instructed by the latter to prepare to conduct a series of inspection tours.

Meanwhile, a number of small problems had come up in connection with training. Most important had been the establishment of a program in the use of radar equipment. The CCS, on 13 May, had approved the release of such equipment to the French and the disclosure to them, "where cooperation was necessary," of information on any radar equipment in operational use, but none on equipment in research or developmental stages.[21] Meeting on 11 June, the Combined Signal Board, AFHQ, appointed a subcommittee to study and present a definite training plan for the consideration of the board.[22] On the basis of the plan subsequently recommended by the subcommittee, some twenty French officers were sent to the United States in July to receive radar instruction.

By the end of August the various training programs instituted in the United States for French personnel were well under way. Training of pilots at the rate of 100 monthly had begun in June under the direction of Southeast Training Command. A plan had been approved but was not yet in operation for the training of 200 Air Force mechanics at Army Air Forces Technical Training Command installations. At Fort Benning, Georgia, some 200 liaison officers were taking a course in infantry weapons and minor tactics. At Camp Hood, Texas, a number of officers were being given tank and antitank training. Other officers were attending the Quartermaster School at Camp Lee, Virginia. A battalion of 2,000 men from Martinique was undergoing in-

fantry training at Fort Dix, New Jersey. Plans were under consideration for the training of other officers at artillery, armored force, antiaircraft, and engineer schools in the United States. The necessary co-ordination for the assignment of students to these various schools and centers was effected by the French members of FTS. One drawback in the implementation of some of these programs was the fact that a number of officers sent to the United States were not proficient enough in English and, as a result, were having difficulty in absorbing the instruction offered.[23]

Beginning in September and continuing throughout the fall and winter of 1943 and the spring of 1944, FTS, at the request of the JRC, inspected the divisions being reequipped. Inspections were conducted by General Kingman assisted by mixed teams organized by him for the purpose, each team consisting of U.S. members of FTS reinforced, one for one, by French technical officer counterparts. These inspections, it must be emphasized, were not showdown inspections as official memorandums seemed often to imply. They were primarily designed to determine the status of technical training of the inspected units. Only indirectly did they help to complete the action of the JRC whose responsibility it was to make sure that the units were fully activated and fully equipped. After each inspection, General Kingman prepared a detailed report which he forwarded to the JRC.[24]

To expedite the training of service units,

---

[21] Msg, CCS to Eisenhower, 13 May 43, FAN 97.
[22] Min, CSB AFHQ 15th Mtg, 11 Jun 43, AFHQ 0100/4 SACS 337 (SGS) Conf, Military, Naval, and Other.

[23] Memo, G-2 MIS WD for ACofS OPD, 28 Aug 43, OPD 226.2 France, Sec 1; Interv with Lt Claude Tiers, Jul 50; Msg 6934, Marshall to FREEDOM, 12 Jan 44, JRC Cable Log.
[24] Memo, Spalding for Kingman, 15 Aug 43, JRC 333/002 Inspections by Gen Kingman; Intervs with Kingman, Jul 50, L'Huillier, Sep 50, and Tiers, Jul 50.

especially those designated for the support of the expeditionary forces, the French General Staff and the JRC arranged, in early September 1943, to place a number of such units side by side with similar U.S. service units to permit their working together. At the end of the same month NATOUSA directed that five divisions be given amphibious training at the Fifth Army Invasion Training Center located at Port-aux-Poules, near Oran, with the understanding that the French themselves would take over most of the instruction duties as soon as practicable.[25]

By October, General Kingman was able to report that the technical training of the French had reached a satisfactory level. He pointed out that more progress could have been achieved but for shortages of spare parts, cleaning and preserving materials, and the frequent lack of adequate officer supervision. To increase the efficiency of the program, he recommended the following measures: the immediate activation of all French nondivisional units, at reduced strength owing to personnel limitations, and the prompt attachment of the cadres thus assembled to appropriate U.S. service units for training. The French authorities had already been approached on the matter. They were urged to adopt the plan forthwith.[26]

All together, seven divisions were undergoing instruction from U.S. personnel, with one more (the 1st DMI) to be added shortly. Moreover, some 720 officers and 3,500 enlisted men from smaller units were receiving or about to receive individual training. To expand its program, FTS needed more personnel. Although additional instructors were due to arrive shortly from the United States, General Kingman recommended that the training personnel of his section be increased still further.[27]

Reviewing the progress in instruction of units designated for service in Italy, General Carpentier, Chief of Staff, CEF, voiced the belief that the technical preparation and group instruction of the units concerned appeared generally satisfactory, a situation which, he underlined, had been made possible by the assistance of U.S. authorities. He warned, however, that in some instances, training was being hindered or even made impossible by lack of equipment, such as training ammunition, gasoline, mine detectors, and chemical warfare matériel.[28]

By the end of October training of service units still lagged behind schedule. The French had not fully taken advantage of the opportunities offered by AFHQ, such as placing the units alongside similar U.S. organizations. Meeting with a French General Staff representative on 30 October, Lt. Col. John C. Knox, the FTS liaison officer with the JRC, pointed out that "American Service Chiefs would have a better feeling in the matter if the constant pressing and needling for training of services, whether units, cadres or nuclei of future organizations, originated from the French High Command." He then emphasized that American officials were only too ready to examine any reasonable French counterproposals on the matter.[29]

[25] Memo, Leyer for JRC, 8 Sep 43, JRC 370/003 Employment of Sv Units; Memo, CG NATOUSA for Comdr U.S. Naval Forces North African Waters, 24 Sep 43, JRC 353/002 Training Fr Army Units (1943).
[26] Memo, Kingman for JRC, 6 Oct 43, JRC 353/002 Training Fr Army Units (1943).

[27] Memo, Kingman for CG NATOUSA, 12 Oct 43, in same file.
[28] Memo, Carpentier for Leyer, 21 Oct 43, in same file.
[29] Memo, Knox for Kingman, 30 Oct 43, in same file.

By November 1943 the French had organized two types of training centers of their own. At the recruit training center (centre d'instruction), only basic training was given, lasting approximately three months. Recruits were then sent to the nearest replacement training center (centre d'organisation). The replacement training centers prepared replacement battalions to be fed into the regiments of the expeditionary forces. Obviously, instruction in these centers could not go beyond training of the battalion as a unit, and seldom went farther than that of the company. All together, the French organized some forty replacement training centers, as well as a number of miscellaneous replacement depots. They also opened several schools, including one military preparatory school for sons of officers (known as the *Prytanée*), one officers' training school for sons of titled natives, one officer candidate school for French personnel, and a General Staff School.[30] Whenever the French military authorities so requested, General Kingman and members of his staff visited the training centers and schools. At the end of these visits, if individual school commanders desired, General Kingman placed available American officers at their disposal. In this manner complete co-ordination was effected between training conducted by the French themselves and instruction carried out under the FTS program.

Simultaneously, an increasing number of schools or courses of instruction had been or were being opened by the Americans to French personnel. Parachutists were being trained at the Airborne Training Center run by Fifth Army. At L'Arba (Algeria),

Air Force personnel were being instructed in the installation, operation, and maintenance of equipment and facilities required for fighter control and fighter defense. At Meknès (French Morocco), the Americans had established a school to train ordnance personnel. Numerous courses in chemical warfare were being offered. Generally the students attending these various courses were reported to be capable, industrious, and eager to learn.[31]

Throughout January, February, and March 1944, the reports which General Kingman submitted to the JRC at the end of inspections of French divisions had in common one major feature: training was still being impeded by important shortages.[32] The lack of training ammunition being particularly acute, the theater requested and obtained from the War Department, in early January, the shipment of 4,275,000 rounds of .22-caliber long ammunition for the 7,000-odd rifles and 900 machine guns of that caliber in the possession of the French.[33] Other much needed items, such as spare parts, cleaning materials, and training manuals in French, were obtained either from French stocks at the urging of the JRC or through requisitions submitted by the JRC to the War Department.

In early March AFHQ requested the French High Command to forward, each month, a report on the state of training of units likely to be employed at a later date as part of an Allied force. Such information would enable the Supreme Allied Commander to know what units would be avail-

[30] Memo for Rcd, JRC, 25 Nov 43, and Office Memo 4, JRC, 26 Nov 43, JRC 320/004 Orgn of Fr Army.

[31] JRC 353/002 Training Fr Army Units (1943).
[32] Rpts, Kingman to Loomis, 26 Jan, 23 Feb, 1 Mar, 7 Mar, and 30 Mar 44, JRC 333/002 Inspections by Gen Kingman.
[33] Memo, Loomis for G–4 NATOUSA, 6 Jan 44, and Msg 7280, Somervell to Eisenhower, 15 Jan 44, JRC 471/002 Ammunition for Training.

able for employment.[34]   By the end of the month General Kingman and his mixed teams had inspected all major units.   General Leyer expressed to General Loomis his deep appreciation of the assistance rendered thus far by FTS and requested that the section inspect other organizations such as corps and army supporting units, units then in combat, and training centers.[35]   General Kingman immediately arranged for the necessary inspections.

French Air Force training schools, meanwhile, were receiving assistance from American and British air commanders.   A close inspection of these schools by General Eaker in April revealed that they were doing excellent work.   To assist them further, Eaker requested and obtained the assignment in May, June, and July of additional training planes and equipment.[36]

In late April General Kingman accompanied by his French deputy, Colonel L'Huillier, visited the French Expeditionary Corps in Italy to determine on the spot how the units were doing and what further assistance they needed.   By agreement with their commanders, he detached to the divisions a number of single instructors or teams no longer required for the training program in North Africa.   The teams, at reduced strength, usually accompanied the divisions in combat, at least during the early phase of their engagement in operations. The valuable information which General Kingman collected during his visit enabled him, upon his return to North Africa, to improve further the training of the units still in that area.[37]

In May and June, at the request of the French General Staff, practically all French training establishments were inspected by FTS.   Meanwhile, more personnel were being detailed for short periods of instruction to American training schools located in the United States or in the theater, such as the Floating Bailey Bridge School which in June was transferred to French control. Eight officers were attending a special course in sound ranging for artillery at Fort Sill.[38] A tire repair company consisting of approximately 200 officers and enlisted men from Martinique was completing its training in ordnance schools in the United States.[39]

Training, although generally satisfactory, was lagging in some fields.   Instruction in signal communications at regiment level was rendered ineffective by lack of co-ordination.   To effect the unification of the various programs, General Leyer, on 14 June, ordered a centralization of all training facilities.[40]   With respect to chemical warfare, the program had completely bogged down.   This was due to lack of interest on the part of the French military authorities who assumed that chemicals would not be used.   An inspection tour conducted between 12 May and 28 June revealed that practically no chemical warfare instruction was given in the replacement training centers.[41]

An important development took place in mid-May with the establishment in Italy of three training centers to serve the CEF. These centers, one Algerian-Tunisian, one

---

[34] Ltr, Gammell to Devinck, 8 Mar 44, AFHQ 0100/12C G–3 Div Ops Fr Corres.
[35] Ltr, Leyer to Loomis, 3 Apr 44, JRC 353/002 Training Fr Army Units (1944).
[36] See p. 210, above.
[37] Interv with Kingman, Jul 50.

[38] Msg W–49831, Maj Gen James A. Ulio to Devers, 13 Jun 44, JRC Cable Log.
[39] Msg W–45342, Ulio to Devers, 3 Jun 44, JRC Cable Log.
[40] Instruction 835 EMGG/3–T, Leyer, 14 Jun 44, JRC 353/002 Training Fr Army Units (1944).
[41] Memos, CWS for G–3 Training Sec AFHQ, 22 Apr 44, and CWS for Kingman, 4 Jul 44, in same file.

Moroccan, and one Colonial, were constituted by utilizing the personnel from the former divisional technical schools, now discontinued, of the divisions engaged in Italy. Their function was threefold: to supply cadres and enlisted personnel to the CEF by using replacements coming from North Africa and men released from hospitals in Italy; to take charge of replacements coming from rear areas and medical patients released from forward areas until such time as they were reassigned to a unit of the CEF; finally, to train personnel designated for combat units.[42]

With an expeditionary force of nearly five divisions and corps troops engaged in operations, one of the main concerns of the French military authorities was to recruit and train, in North Africa, sufficient personnel replacements. To assist them in this task, and to effect a saving in the amount of training equipment required, General Devers suggested, in late June, that a U.S. camp, preferably situated near Oran and with a capacity of 8,000 to 10,000 men, be turned over to the French complete with housing and utilities. General Larkin having approved the proposal, the American camp located at Chanzy was officially transferred to the French on 30 June.[43]

By this time training activities were being directed more and more toward the readying of the units designated for ANVIL. On 7 July, as these units passed under the control of Force 163, General Patch, Commanding General, U.S. Seventh Army, who was to command them in the initial phase of the operation, assumed the general direction of their training. During the following three weeks Seventh Army inspected the units to determine their state of readiness.

On 14 July the War Department informed General Wilson that the CCS had authorized the issue of a minimum amount of equipment to French replacement centers to be used solely for instructing replacements for the expeditionary forces.[44] In notifying the French of this action, General Wilson requested them to give assurances that the housekeeping and training equipment thus authorized would be used for the purpose for which it was intended. He also urged them to take steps to put into effect, immediately after the landing in France, a sound replacement program to sustain the expeditionary forces in combat.[45] The French had already considered the matter as evidenced by their request, submitted only a few days before, that the permanent cadres of the three infantry training centers then operating in Italy and the Armored Force Training Center still in North Africa be made officially part of the ANVIL troop list.[46]

On 4 August, with the launching of ANVIL only ten days away, Headquarters, Seventh Army, reported to General Wilson on the status of training of the French participating units. Inspections had revealed insufficient technical training owing to shortages of equipment. The remaining basic problem, therefore, was to make sure that such shortages would be filled in time to permit training before the units were engaged in operations. The report then recommended that Seventh Army be relieved of

---

[42] Admin Memo 5997 EMGG/1, Leyer, 9 Jun 44, in same file.

[43] Msgs F–64566, Devers to Larkin, 26 Jun 44, and LX–29481, Larkin to CG MBS, 30 Jun 44, JRC Cable Log.

[44] Msg WX–64781, AGWAR to Devers, 14 Jul 44, ABC 091.711 France (6 Oct 43), Sec 2–A.

[45] Ltr, Gammell (for Wilson) to Béthouart, 30 Jul 44, AFHQ 0100/4 SACS Rcd Sec, Fr Matters, Vol. IV, Jan–Jul 44.

[46] Ltr, Béthouart to Wilson, 26 Jul 44, JRC 400.1/009 Sup of Forces Designated for Combat.

all further responsibility in connection with inspections of French units still in North Africa.[47] The question was examined at a conference on 8 August between General Noce, G–3, AFHQ, and General Loomis. The two conferees agreed to stand fast on the established policy under which Seventh Army was responsible for determining, by means of inspections, the condition of training of the French ANVIL units, and FTS for providing the necessary assistance.[48]

As ANVIL was launched, on 15 August, training operations were going ahead at an increased tempo. In the case of service units instruction still lagged considerably behind schedule. Unable to form all the units in North Africa, the French military authorities were already contemplating their activation from personnel expected to become available in France. As the inspection tour conducted by FTS was coming to an end, General Leyer, with an eye on the future, seized the opportunity to express his gratitude for the valuable assistance General Kingman and his section had been rendering for several months.[49]

On 10 September General Patch broached the question of the responsibility for the training of French replacements. He pointed out to General Wilson that the supervision of this training was not considered the proper function of Seventh Army as personnel was not available and in any case such control would be "resented" by the French. He recommended that the responsibility be turned over to the French themselves with some measure of supervision effected by General Kingman's section.

General Wilson approved the recommendation and advised the French that, thereafter, they were fully responsible for carrying out the training of replacements with the assistance of FTS. Three training centers having already moved with their equipment to southern France in late September, and the fourth being about to follow, personnel from FTS was dispatched to the Continent to assist them in their work. A forward echelon of FTS began operating at Delta Base Section in Marseille on 12 October. The rear echelon continued to function at MBS until about 15 November when all remaining FTS activities were transferred to France.[50]

On 22 October NATOUSA learned with considerable surprise that SHAEF was contemplating recruiting French personnel in France and moving them to North Africa to be equipped and trained as replacements for the 1st French Army. NATOUSA objected that it could not undertake such a commitment inasmuch as instructors, facilities, and equipment would not be available, and pointed out that plans had been made for the resumption, in continental France, of all training activities. Such activities, in fact, were already well under way.

The training of French troops in North Africa under American guidance was now over. Like the rearmament operations, it had been effected on the basis of a program established piecemeal as the situation demanded. On the whole it had been most effective. Collaboration between t h e French and the Americans had been par-

---

[47] Memo, CG Seventh Army for SACMED, 4 Aug 44, AFHQ AG 400–1 (Fr) Sups.

[48] Memo, Foster for G–3 (Orgn), 8 Aug 44, AFHQ 0100/12C G–3 Div Ops Fr Equip.

[49] Memo, Leyer for Loomis, 27 Aug 44, JRC 320/005 Replacement Troops.

[50] Ltr, Gammell to Béthouart, 20 Sep 44, AFHQ 0100/12C G–3 Div Ops Fr Corres; Msgs CP–13330, Patch to Wilson, 10 Sep 44, FX–24103, SACMED to Seventh Army, 12 Sep 44, JRC/235, CG NATOUSA to G–3 AFHQ, 20 Sep 44, JRC Cable Log.

MAJ. GEN. ALEXANDER M. PATCH, *Commanding General, U.S. Seventh Army,
inspecting men of the French Forces of the Interior, August 1944.*

ticularly fruitful. French cadres and personnel had almost without exception appeared to be genuinely eager to receive the assistance of their American comrades of FTS. Relations with French commanders had been most cordial.[51] All signs now pointed to continued mutual respect and understanding during the next phase of rearmament and training activities about to open in continental France.

[51] Intervs with Kingman, Jul 50, Tiers, Jul 50, and L'Huillier, Sep 50.

CHAPTER XV

Controversy Over Substitute Weapons

The ANFA Agreement had stipulated that the French were to receive equipment made up of the most modern matériel. When, in the course of the ensuing months, AFHQ officials undertook to effect certain substitutions, a serious controversy arose between French and AFHQ staffs concerning the legitimacy and desirability of such a course of action. The French, whose attitude in the matter was only human, tended to consider substitutions as meaning inferior equipment and, when applied to weapons, a lowering of fire power. As late as May 1944 they warned that the substitutions imposed on them were "adversely affecting combat efficiency." [1]

In cases where American industrial production was insufficient to fill the needs of both French and U.S. troops, the French resigned themselves, although reluctantly, to receiving substitutes. On the other hand, they reacted strongly when, in the fall of 1943, AFHQ proposed that certain equipment items no longer standard but still serviceable be assigned, because of their availability in theater stocks, against French rearmament requirements in lieu of the standard items. The proposal was made at a time when large stocks had become excess owing to the departure for the United Kingdom of a number of U.S. troops. The

Munitions Assignments Board had ruled that some of these stocks would be utilized toward the partial implementation of the French program. The measure, which General Larkin, Commanding General, SOS, NATOUSA, had strongly urged, was primarily intended to economize shipping.

As the French were showing signs that they would not readily agree to the provision of substitutes for standard issue items, General Loomis sought from the War Department a definite expression of policy. Selecting one standard ordnance item as a test case, the chairman of the JRC, on 4 November, requested Washington officials to indicate whether or not they would authorize the issue to the French of a weapon then available in theater stocks as a substitute for the standard item concerned. [2] Lt. Gen. Wilhelm D. Styer, Chief of Staff, Army Service Forces, replied that since the phrase "equipment of the most modern kind" was interpreted by the War Department as meaning "equipment that had been standard issue in the current war," the substitution proposed was authorized. This and similar substitutions, explained General Styer, could be effected in the case of equipment either still to be assigned from the United States or already assigned but as yet unshipped. [3]

---

[1] Ltr, de Saint-Didier to Marshall, 6 May 44, OPD 400 France, Sec IV; Ltr, Marshall to de Saint-Didier, 24 May 44, OCS A–48–11 France 091, Sec I.

[2] Msg W–4267, Loomis to AGWAR, 4 Nov 43, JRC 400.1/007 Substituting From Theater Stocks.

[3] Msg 2627, Styer to Eisenhower, 16 Nov 43, in same file.

TANK DESTROYER FOR THE FRENCH. *This 3-in. gun motor carriage M10 bears the marking of red, white, and blue stripes stenciled on all equipment for the French.*

Guided by this clarification, General Larkin prepared a report of all equipment in the theater suitable for transfer under the rearmament program. In the case of items not currently standard for U.S. troops, the report included recommendations as to the standard items they might replace.[4] On the basis of these recommendations, substitutions considered desirable by AFHQ were suggested to the War Department, which, in turn, invariably gave its approval. Most important among substitutions effected either as a result of production shortages or because of surplus stocks in the theater were

certain types of artillery guns, tanks, and infantry weapons.

Artillery

The test case selected by General Loomis concerned a proposal to substitute 75-mm. gun motor carriages M3 for the 3-inch M10 guns authorized under the rearmament program for three French tank destroyer battalions. The M3 guns were readily available in theater stocks, whereas the M10's were obtainable only by shipment from the United States.

Apprised of the proposed substitution some weeks before, the French had already

---

[4] Memo, Hq NATOUSA for CG SOS, 22 Nov 43, in same file.

ruled it out as unacceptable "in view of the inferior quality of the M3 gun." In the face of their strong opposition, the various AFHQ sections concerned debated for several months on the advisability of carrying out the proposal. In March 1944, still without information as to the intentions of AFHQ regarding the matter, the French asked that a re-examination of the question be undertaken and a decision reached forthwith. Intervening personally in the matter, General Giraud, in a letter to General Wilson, Supreme Allied Commander in the Mediterranean, restated the French position, namely, that the proposed substitution was not acceptable "as much because of the inferior quality of the M3 as because of the complications resulting from the disparity of the matériel placed in the hands of French units." [5]

Although AFHQ officials regarded the M3 gun as only slightly inferior in combat efficiency to the M10 and, therefore, quite acceptable as a modern weapon, they finally gave in to General Giraud's plea, for they had just learned that M10 guns would soon be available in sufficient quantity to take care of both French and American needs. After five months of debate, French tenacity and American production had settled the case. By 13 May, SOS, NATOUSA, had delivered all 115 M10 guns authorized for the three tank destroyer battalions. [6]

In another instance, a substitution was effected over French objection. On 18 March 1944 General Leyer informed the JRC that he could not agree to the replace-

ment of eight 75-mm. howitzer motor carriages M8 by eight 75-mm. howitzer motor carriages T30 as then proposed by AFHQ for the last of the ten armored reconnaissance battalions to be re-equipped under the program. The substitution had just been authorized by the War Department. General Leyer warned that the replacement would only result in decreasing the combat efficiency of the unit involved. General Loomis replied that AFHQ regarded the T30 as a satisfactory substitute for the M8 and that, in view of the necessity of saving critical shipping space, it did not consider it advisable to recommend that the War Department change its decision. [7]

Once again General Giraud intervened personally in the controversy. He pressed General Wilson for a reversal of the position taken by AFHQ. In addition to lowering the effectiveness of the unit involved, he declared, the proposed substitution would have the serious disadvantage of multiplying needlessly the types of matériel in the hands of the reconnaissance battalions. [8] This last point was a telling one in the eyes of the French who were already plagued with serious maintenance and supply problems. However, their efforts to bring about a reversal of the decision proved futile. On 20 April the theater commander closed the issue by informing General Béthouart, then Chief of Staff of National Defense, that the French request was disapproved. He explained that the T30 was regarded as a "strictly modern weapon . . . superior, in some respects, to the M8." Since, moreover, the T30 was available in

[5] Memos, Leyer for Loomis, 28 Oct 43, and Regnault for Loomis, 13 Mar 44, and Ltr, Giraud to Wilson, 22 Mar 44, JRC 470/002 Substituting 75-mm. for TD's.

[6] Ltrs, Devers to Giraud, 30 Mar, 5 Apr 44, and Memos, Loomis for Leyer, 10 Apr, 13 May 44, JRC 470/002.

[7] Msg 1039, AGWAR to NATOUSA, 29 Feb 44, JRC 400.1/007 Excess Stocks (Mar 44) ; Ltr, Leyer to Loomis, 18 Mar 44, JRC 472/003 Self-propelled Artillery; Memo, Loomis for Leyer, 27 Mar 44, JRC 472/003.

[8] Ltr, Giraud to Wilson, 5 Apr 44, JRC 472/003.

FRENCH TANK CREW WITH U.S. LIGHT TANK M5, *one of the vehicles issued for training purposes, July 1943.*

North Africa in ample quantity, the theater considered it inadvisable to add to the shipping burden by ordering from the United States a large tonnage of M8 carriages.[9]

Tanks

During the Tunisian campaign the British First Army had turned over to the French as an emergency measure sixty surplus Valentine tanks.[10] These vehicles, the first to be issued to the North African forces, subsequently were transferred by the French High Command to Sovereignty troops charged with the defense of the territory. In April 1943, as rearmament operations got under way, the French began receiving American tanks of the same models as those then currently issued U.S. troops—M4A2 and M4A4 medium, and M3A3 light tanks. In the course of the following months, while U.S. forces in the theater were drawing the newer M5A1 light tank, the French continued to receive the M3A3.[11] The M3A3 and M5A1 were quite similar in design. Although the M5A1 provided more armor protection, both had practically the same turret, armament, and hull. The principal difference

[9] Memo, Theater Comdr for Béthouart, 20 Apr 44, in same file.

[10] Background material for this section is located in JRC 470/003 Tanks and Tank Transporters.

[11] Msg 6162, Somervell to Eisenhower, 27 Aug 43, in same file.

between them was in their engines and power trains. Yet operation and maintenance were sufficiently different to require special training.[12] Anticipating that the French would eventually be issued M5A1's, the Americans gave them a few of these vehicles for training purposes. Later, as production of the M5A1 increased, the War Department authorized its issue to the French not in replacement of, but in addition to, the M3A3 toward the fulfillment of the over-all light tank requirements of the rearmament program. As a result the French received tanks of both designs and, incidentally, in approximately the same proportion.

By June 1944 the French had been issued 368 M4A2 and 268 M4A4 medium tanks, and 273 M3A3 and 230 M5A1 light tanks, or a total of 1,139 vehicles.[13] AFHQ regarded this number as sufficient, not only to equip the units on the approved troop list (3 armored divisions, 5 infantry division reconnaissance battalions, and 2 nondivisional reconnaissance battalions), but in addition to provide for combat replacements. In fact some 200 vehicles were considered excess. A number of these were currently being used for training replacement personnel. Others were still in the hands of the 3d Armored Division, an organization in nucleus only which the French High Command still hoped to raise to the status of a fourth armored division. To constitute an adequate replacement reserve for the three authorized divisions, the French in August were requested to release approximately 120 vehicles to Mediterranean Base Section.[14] It was not until

mid-October, after considerable prodding on the part of AFHQ officials, that the French completed the release of all 120 vehicles. The tanks in the hands of the 3d DB had by then all been withdrawn for this purpose.

The French had distributed tanks as the vehicles themselves had become available; as a result, units were not equipped in a uniform manner. The 2d DB enjoyed complete homogeneity of matériel as it had been issued tanks from the earliest shipments, all M3A3's and M4A2's. In the case of the 1st DB and 5th DB, on the other hand, uniformity had been achieved within individual component units, but not within the divisions as a whole. AFHQ had strongly urged the French military authorities to regroup equipment within the two organizations. Judging that such a step would involve a substantial movement of matériel, an additional period of training for crews, and a readaptation of radio equipment, the French chose not to modify the existing distribution. In their opinion, the advantages offered by a regrouping, such as the simplification of spare parts and maintenance problems, would not offset the considerable difficulties involved.[15]

Thus, because of the tank substitution imposed on them, when the 1st and 5th Armored Divisions landed in southern France they were equipped with light vehicles which differed in type from one component unit to another.[16] Yet there is no evidence to indicate that the combat efficiency of these organizations was in any way jeopardized. Nor does it appear that units which received no M5's, such as the

---

[12] Memo, Maj Conrad L. Christensen for Regnault, 21 Aug 43, in same file.

[13] Ltr, Leyer to Loomis, 29 Jul 44, in same file.

[14] Memos, Loomis for Leyer, 5, 9 Aug 44, and Msg JRC–73, Loomis to AGWAR, 8 Aug 44, in same file.

[15] Memos, Leyer for Loomis, 16 Apr, 29 Jul 44, in same file.

[16] See *ibid.*, for exact distribution of tanks in the hands of all French armored units.

2d DB and four reconnaissance battalions, were put to a disadvantage for lack of such vehicles.[17] It must be noted that tanks issued later in the campaign to French armored units included vehicles of newer designs such as were furnished to U.S. units.

Small Infantry Weapons

It was with respect to small infantry weapons, such as rifles, carbines, and automatic arms, that the question of the use of substitutes became an issue of particular seriousness.[18] The French who, by tradition, attached the utmost importance to infantry action were eager to ensure that their infantry units would be provided with adequate fire power.

Rifles and Carbines

The first small arms which the French obtained from Allied sources consisted, it will be recalled, of the 8,000 rifles assigned in November 1942 and delivered to them from the United Kingdom in mid-January 1943.[19] These were .30-caliber M1917 (Enfield) rifles. At the time, French units engaged in Tunisia were equipped with small arms of all descriptions and calibers, particularly of French manufacture, such as the 8-mm. level spring loading rifle (Lebel), and the 8-mm. model 1912–16 *mousqueton* or carbine. One unit, the 1st Free French Division (later renamed the 1st DMI), was using .303-inch rifles of British

manufacture. Meanwhile, training centers and Sovereignty forces charged with the defense of the territory were using, in addition to arms of French manufacture, some 19,000 German rifles of the Mauser and Herstal models, both 7.92-mm., and a number of Italian rifles generally in poor condition, all of which had been collected on battlefields in Tunisia. In May 1943, with more American rifles reaching North African ports, French authorities turned the remaining stocks of French manufacture over to nonprogram units (Moroccan tabors, Commandos, Spahis, and the like).[20]

In addition to the M1917 rifle, which they received throughout the year 1943, the French were also given large quantities of the M1903 (Springfield), likewise .30 caliber. The continued issue to them of these two weapons was being made at a time when the M1903 rifles in the hands of U.S. troops were gradually being replaced by newer and more efficient arms, the .30-caliber M1 rifle and M1 carbine. The French who were not being issued these weapons feared that their units would be less fit than the U.S. troops fighting along with them. American officials, on the other hand, acted on the principle that the M1 rifles and carbines, being scarce at the time, could be made available only at the expense of U.S. troops. They felt justified, as a result, in prescribing acceptable substitute weapons of standard issue during the current war. As both the M1903 and M1917 fell in that category, the former being still used by U.S. troops and the latter by the British, the two weapons became standard issue for the North African program units.

Deliveries were made at a slow and irregular pace because of the over-all short-

---

[17] Two of the five infantry division reconnaissance battalions, as well as the two nondivisional reconnaissance battalions (the 1st and 2d Algerian Spahis Regiments) were equipped with M3A3's exclusively. *Ibid.*

[18] This section draws upon these files: JRC 474/001 Small Arms—Misc, JRC 474/002 .30-cal Rifles, JRC 474/003 Automatic Weapons, and JRC 474/004 Spare Parts for Small Arms.

[19] See pp. 27, 28, above.

[20] Msg 1926, FLAMBO to 15th Army Gp, 19 Dec 43, JRC 474/001 Small Arms—Misc.

age of rifles and in a somewhat erratic fashion as to type depending on availability in the United Kingdom, from where they were shipped to the French. As a result many combat units received both magazine-type rifles. This fact seriously increased spare-part and maintenance difficulties, for although the Enfield and Springfield used the same ammunition their parts were not interchangeable. The French would have preferred to equip all of their combat units with the M1903. This was not possible since the larger part of the rifles issued to them, approximately two thirds, consisted of M1917's. At any rate, they attempted, in the interests of economy and simplicity in the distribution of spare parts and maintenance, to standardize the type of rifle used in each unit. This they were not able to do until January 1944 because they had not been issued grenade launchers for the M1917 rifle and therefore had been forced to retain a number of M1903's in units equipped with the other rifle.[21]

Further aggravating maintenance problems was the fact that a considerable proportion of the rifles (estimated by the French as 10 percent, especially the M1917's) were found to be of a low order of serviceability. This was not surprising for the weapons involved were old. In fact they were part of the stocks shipped by the United States to the British after the evacuation of Dunkerque in 1940 and had served the Home Guard for over two years before being turned over to the French. The latter were forced to effect repairs made possible only by the receipt, in July 1943, of a substantial allocation of spare parts and maintenance materials.[22]

By the end of January 1944 program units engaged on the Italian front were equipped with pistols in lieu of carbines, and with M1903 and M1917 magazine rifles in lieu of semiautomatic rifles such as the M1. The Moroccan tabors and other nonprogram units, on the other hand, were firing their French weapons, thus adding to the complexity of the supply problem and in some instances causing undue hardship on personnel. A U.S. adviser told of the losses sustained by a Moroccan goum when, having exhausted the ammunition for their French weapons, the men were unable to borrow any from adjoining units.[23]

Throughout 1943 American authorities in the theater had recognized the desirability of providing French infantry units with additional arms to compensate for the reduced fire power resulting from the rifle substitutions imposed on them. With this in view they took a number of steps, most important of which consisted in raising the allowance of automatic weapons per infantry regiment.[24] In addition, General Devers recommended, in March 1944, that a portion of the M1 carbines then being earmarked for U.S. service troops in the theater be diverted to French combat units. His proposal was approved and the MAB authorized the lend-lease transfer to the French from U.S. theater stocks of 13,000 carbines.[25] These were to be issued to seven divisions at the rate of 2,000 per infantry

---

[21] Memo, Leyer for Loomis, 30 Oct 43, JRC 474/002 .30-cal Rifles.

[22] Memos, Leyer for Loomis, 16 Jun 44, and Col Villaret for International Div ASF, 31 Mar 44,

JRC 474/002 .30-cal Rifles; Memo, Loomis for Leyer, 28 Oct 43, JRC 474/004 Spare Parts for Small Arms.

[23] Memo, Kingman for Loomis, 26 Jan 44, JRC 333/002ᶦ Inspections by Gen Kingman.

[24] See pp. 250–51, below.

[25] Msgs W–4323, Devers to AGWAR, 5 Mar 44, and 1971, Somervell to Devers, 12 Mar 44, JRC 474/002 .30-cal Rifles.

division and 1,500 per armored division.[26] Priority of issue was to be "above U.S. service troops but below U.S. combat units." [27]

It was then that the publication of a pessimistic report on the fire power of the French infantry, drafted at the end of March 1944 by an ASF officer sent on an inspection tour in the theater, aroused considerable speculation both in Washington and in Algiers and forced a re-examination of the French rifle situation. The report implied that, since the French had been denied M1 carbines and semiautomatic rifles and were using magazine rifles in poor condition, the fire power of their infantry was inferior to that of the enemy and to that of the adjoining U.S. infantry. In consequence, the personnel casualty rate was "prohibitively high" and the functions of the U.S. command were "unnecessarily complicated."

Subsequent investigation revealed that the serious implications contained in the ASF report were grossly exaggerated. G–3, AFHQ, definitely established, on the basis of information furnished by General Juin himself, that the French advances in Italy had been accomplished without undue losses. It was more likely—and the fact has been confirmed since the war—that whatever difficulties French infantry units were, and would later be, experiencing with regard to rifles were not the result of inferior equipment but rather of diversity of equipment. Standardization could have been achieved only by providing all the units concerned with M1 rifles and carbines.

Since the rate of production of these weapons made this impossible, AFHQ decided not to pursue the matter any further.[28]

In July 1944, answering a query from the War Department, General Loomis reviewed the French rifle situation as it stood on the eve of ANVIL. He estimated that the French had received a total of approximately 215,000 rifles including 167,000 M1917's, 47,000 M1903's, 740 M1's, and 13,400 M1 carbines. Of the total, 4,000 rifles and carbines had gone to the French Air Force, and all the M1 rifles to the 1st Parachute Regiment (1st RCP). The over-all figure was considered adequate to cover the needs of the expeditionary forces as well as those of replacements and training centers. To ensure adequacy of fire power during the subsequent months, General Loomis obtained from the War Department the additional supply of 8,000 M1 carbines monthly for the last five months of 1944. This measure was considered all the more necessary since the United Kingdom had just requested that the British obligation to furnish an additional 20,000 M1917 rifles be canceled. The carbines, once assigned, were shipped to Coastal Base Section in Marseille for issue as maintenance to French units operating with U.S. forces.[29]

Subsequent efforts by the French to obtain additional M1 carbines in exchange for M1917 rifles proved unsuccessful.

---

[26] Instead of 6,500 per infantry division and 6,000 per armored division according to the U.S. tables of organization. Memo, Artamonoff for ACofS G–4 AFHQ, 9 Jul 43, JRC 474/003 Automatic Weapons.

[27] Msg 64439, Devers to Larkin, 14 Mar 44, JRC 474/002 .30-cal Rifles.

[28] Memo, Col Villaret for ACofS G–3 WD, 31 Mar 44, JRC 474/002 .30-cal. Rifles. Another report by the same officer concerning Franco-American relations also was regarded as largely unfounded. See p. 154, above.

Memo, Noce for JRC, 22 May 44, JRC 474/002 .30-cal Rifles; Interv with Brig Gen Jean Piatte, former CO 5th Moroccan Tirailleurs Regt, Sep 51.

[29] Memo, Loomis for Leyer, 20 Jul 44, Msgs JRC/72, Loomis to AGWAR, 7 Aug 44, and W–51930, Somervell to Devers, 17 Jun 44, and Memo, Loomis for CofS Fr Ground Forces, 18 Sep 44, JRC 474/002 .30-cal. Rifles.

NATOUSA maintained that French requests to exchange major substitute items of ordnance equipment previously allocated to them by the War Department for standard equipment available in U.S. stocks could be approved only when the items involved were "clearly surplus" to the needs of U.S. troops in the theater. No such surplus stocks existed in the case of the M1 carbine.[30]

The rifle issue was raised again in late August 1944 in connection with battle-loss replacements for the troops engaged in ANVIL. As U.S. stocks of M1917's were rapidly becoming negligible, it was urgent to determine some policy in anticipation of French demands for replacement rifles. NATOUSA ruled, as it had a month earlier, that M1903 rifles would be used as battle-loss replacements for either M1903 or M1917 rifles, but that there would be no wholesale exchange of M1903 with M1917 rifles.[31]

The last discussion concerning rifles took place in mid-September. French military authorities having estimated their over-all requirements at 17,500 rifles and carbines more than the figure established by the JRC, General Loomis asked them to furnish detailed justification for their estimate. He seized this opportunity to request them to withdraw all M1903 and M1917 rifles from units not on the approved troop list. Finally, he informed them that recent requisitions submitted by them for M1 rifles were disapproved, adding a reminder that it was the War Department policy to supply the M1903 and M1917 rifles as substitutes for M1 rifles. He then enjoined them to make no further demands on U.S. supply agencies for M1 rifles, a request which was duly acknowledged, on 27 October, by Brig. Gen. Antoine Poydenot.[32]

To sum up, the French North African forces engaged in the campaign of Italy and later in the campaign of France fought with the M1917 rifle and to a lesser extent with the M1903 rifle and the M1 carbine, in addition to some old rifles of French manufacture. Except for the carbine, they were forced to use substitute weapons as a result of production shortages of the standard items.

Automatic Weapons

As in the case of rifles and carbines, the French used in the Tunisian campaign and for some time afterward the automatic and semiautomatic weapons of French manufacture originally available to them in North Africa.[33] Among these were the 7.5-mm. model 1924–29 (Chauchat) *fusil-mitrailleur*, or automatic rifle,[34] to which they were particularly attached as they considered it far superior to any similar weapon of foreign manufacture, the 7.65-mm. automatic pistol, and the 8-mm. revolver. The British-equipped 1st DFL, meanwhile, continued to use its .303-caliber Bren guns.

As the rearmament operations got under way, program units began receiving American automatic and semiautomatic arms.

---

[30] Msg FX–83584, CG NATOUSA to Larkin, 16 Aug 44, JRC 474/002 .30-cal Rifles.

[31] Msgs L–39826, JRC to NATOUSA, 31 Aug 44, and F–79431, CG NATOUSA to SOS NATOUSA, 5 Aug 44, quoted in Msg F–91987, CG NATOUSA to SOS NATOUSA, 4 Sep 44, JRC 474/002 .30-cal Rifles.

[32] Memo, Loomis for CofS Fr Ground Forces, 18 Sep 44, JRC 474/002 .30-cal Rifles.

General Poydenot was the successor to General Blanc as Assistant Chief of Staff, French Ground Forces in North Africa. Memo, Poydenot for JRC, 27 Oct 44, JRC 474/002 .30-cal Rifles.

[33] Background material for this section is in the file JRC 474/003 Automatic Weapons.

[34] More exactly, machine rifle.

However, deliveries in some cases being considerably delayed by production shortages, a few units retained their French or British weapons with the result that their final equipment included a mixture of armament. In general, program units used, in Italy as well as later in France, American automatic arms, while nonprogram and Sovereignty units used the remaining stocks of French weapons.

In principle, the issue of American automatic rifles and pistols as well as of light and heavy machine guns was to be made in the same ratio as to corresponding U.S. troops. As already pointed out, to compensate for the rifle substitutions additional automatic weapons were added to the French tables of equipment. Thus an allocation of some 900 Thompson .45-caliber submachine guns was authorized in early 1943. In July of the same year, feeling that this allocation was insufficient, the French requested a further issue of 3,500 Thompsons as substitutes for a like number of M1 rifles and carbines. The request was disapproved by Ordnance, AFHQ, on the ground that the proper substitute for these weapons, as used by U.S. troops themselves, was the M1903 rifle.[35]

By August of the same year AFHQ officials themselves became aware of the critical situation of the three divisions already rearmed with respect to automatic weapons. As they explained to the War Department, of the 1,769 Browning automatic rifles (BAR's) authorized for these divisions under the approved French Table of Organization of 18 January 1943, only 253 had been made available for shipment due to shortages of that weapon in the United States.[36] This was a serious matter for, in the opinion of the French, no weapon could adequately take the place of an automatic rifle, much less of their own version of that weapon, the fusil-mitrailleur. Their whole conception of minor tactics was predicated on the use of the automatic rifle as the basic weapon of the combat group. To deprive a combat group of such a weapon was tantamount to destroying its effectiveness in action. The substitution previously offered by the War Department, namely, the provision of 724 light machine guns M1919A4, was termed inadequate, the weapon being considered unsatisfactory because of weight. Theater officials feared that divisions, if equipped with M1903 and M1917 rifles instead of M1 rifles and carbines, and largely with M1919A4 machine guns instead of BAR's, would have considerably reduced combat efficiency. They urged, on 29 August 1943, the early assignment of additional automatic rifles or satisfactory substitutes to bring the units up to authorized table of organization.[37] Three days later they also requested the immediate allocation of 200 additional submachine guns, preferably Thompsons, per infantry regiment, the request being based on the fact that in each regiment 2,728 M1903 rifles had been substituted for 1,128 M1 carbines and 1,600 M1 rifles. They also asked for a further allocation of submachine guns, 972 for the Moroccan goumiers, then num-

---

[35] Ltr, Blanc to Artamonoff, 4 Jul 43, Memo from Ordnance Office appended to draft cable from JRC to AGWAR, 9 Jul 43, and Memo, Artamonoff for Blanc, 9 Jul 43, JRC 474/003 Automatic Weapons.

[36] The French Table of Organization referred to was T.E.G. (Tableau d'Effectifs de Guerre) 48, established on the basis of the old U.S. Table of Organization of 1 August 1942. On 21 November 1943 the French adopted a new table, T.E.G. 5465, based on the U.S. Table of Organization 7–11 of 1 March 1943.

[37] Msg W–8568, Spalding to AGWAR, 29 Aug 43, JRC 474/003 Automatic Weapons.

bering 12,000 men, and 125 for the 1,100 commandos.[38]

On 8 September the War Department informed AFHQ that the Thompson submachine guns could be made available without delay as requested. A subsequent message advised that since BAR's were still in short supply only 1,000 could be furnished. To compensate for this deficiency, additional Thompsons were being offered "in some ratio greater than one for one" if desired. To this, the theater replied that the deficiency could be best met tentatively by additional Thompsons in a ratio of one to one, with the supply of BAR's to be completed as rapidly as production would allow. Such was the line of action taken. In November, the French military authorities having reduced the allowance of BAR's per infantry regiment from 189 to 81 to conform with the new U.S. table of organization,[39] it was expected that sufficient BAR's could soon be made available to them under the reduced ratio.[40]

In December 1943, as the first division (the 2d Moroccan Infantry) reached the Italian front, each of its infantry regiments was equipped with the following automatic weapons: 81 BAR's, 150 Thompson submachine guns, 31 light and 24 heavy .30-caliber machine guns, and 34 .50-caliber machine guns.[41] Except for the Thompsons, which were intended to make up for rifle deficiencies, the number and types of automatic weapons in the hands of the division corresponded almost exactly to those furnished similar U.S. organizations. Incidentally, the division had received its BAR's only five days before leaving North Africa with the result that instruction in the use of that weapon had been practically nil. The BAR being much more complicated than the fusil-mitrailleur, the natives were reported to be experiencing considerable technical difficulties in handling and maintaining the rifle; in particular they were said to be consistently mislaying the bipod.[42]

Later divisions to reach Italy were similarly equipped, although their armament still included some non-U.S. automatic weapons. Thus the 3d Algerian and the 4th Moroccan Mountain arrived with 335 and 686 French automatic rifles, respectively, and the 1st Motorized Infantry Division with its full load of Brens. Ammunition for the latter was provided entirely by the British forces in Italy. As for Moroccan tabors, they, like other nonprogram units then in process of organization, were using their 7.5-mm. fusils-mitrailleurs, 8-mm. carbines and revolvers, and 7.65-mm. automatic pistols. In March 1944 the French General Staff undertook the gradual replacement of these weapons with U.S. arms, since the supply of spare parts and ammunition for the French calibers was rapidly diminishing. An earlier French proposal that the United States undertake the manufacture of 115 million rounds of 7.5-mm. ammunition for the 1,600-odd fusils-mitrailleurs still in active service had been turned down, in December, as impracticable. In the opinion of the French General Staff, therefore, it was urgent to receive as speedily as possible the number of

---

[38] Msg W–8954, Spalding to AGWAR, 2 Sep 43, in same file.

[39] Table of Organization 7–11, Mar 43.

[40] Msgs, Somervell to Eisenhower, 7149, 8 Sep 43, and 7258, 9 Sep 43, and W–681, Spalding to AGWAR, 22 Sep 43, JRC 474/003 Automatic Weapons.

[41] Memo, Leyer for Rearmament Sec Fr Gen Staff, 13 Jan 44, in same file.

[42] Memo, Kingman for Loomis, 26 Jan 44, JRC 333/002 Inspections by Gen Kingman.

BAR's assigned under the rearmament program as well as the repayment of U.S. arms loaned to equip nonprogram units.[43]

In April the War Department offered for use by the French some 10,500 Johnson semiautomatic rifles, and 1,500 Johnson light machine guns, both .30 caliber, remaining undelivered from old Netherlands contracts taken over by the United States Government in 1942. The French requested the rifles for the Sovereignty troops. No favorable action appears to have been taken by the MAB in this connection.[44]

Throughout the spring of 1944 and right up to the time of the launching of ANVIL, the French concentrated their efforts on trying to obtain an increase in the allocation of BAR's for their combat units. On 19 June General Leyer informed the JRC that he wished to effect the replacement of 1,155 fusils-mitrailleurs still in use by an equal number of BAR's. In the absence of a decision on the matter, he submitted, four weeks later, a request for the immediate allocation of 117 additional BAR's for the 4th Moroccan Mountain Division, this in spite of the fact that, by this time, the French had received enough BAR's to raise the allowance of that weapon per infantry regiment from 81 to 93 and in some cases to 110. The request, General Leyer pointed out, was motivated by tactical considerations and the fact that the 4th DMM possessed characteristics of a special nature. NATOUSA turned down the proposal and advised General Leyer to redistribute the BAR's already in the hands of the other

divisions if he wished to carry out his intentions with regard to the 4th DMM.[45]

Another attempt made later by the French met with a similar fate. On 18 July they offered 200 fusils-mitrailleurs for use by the Resistance forces in France, in exchange for a like number of BAR's for issue to expeditionary units. After a lengthy examination of the various problems involved, the JRC advised them that no BAR's would be made available for such an exchange.[46]

By this time it was obvious that AFHQ would not consent to an increase of BAR's, the opinion being that the total number of these weapons furnished both as initial equipment and as maintenance was sufficient to fill all needs including those of nonprogram units.[47] The matter could now be considered closed.

In September the French General Staff requested that nonprogram units be issued 1,500 .45-caliber Colt automatic pistols in exchange for a like number of 7.65-mm. automatic pistols and 8-mm. revolvers in their possession, for which the supply of ammunition was now nearly exhausted. Once again their request was denied because of the current shortage of Colt pistols, but the JRC submitted a requisition to the London Munitions Assignments Board for the allocation of 8-mm. and 7.65-mm. ammunition then available in the Middle East. In view of the more limited supply of 7.65-mm. ammunition, however, the French were urged to replace the 7.65-mm. pistols in the hands of combat units with 8-mm. revolvers for which ammunition was available in suf-

---

[43] Memo, Leyer for Loomis, 10 Mar 44, JRC 474/004 Ammunition for 1st Exp Corps; Memos, Leyer for Loomis, 16 Nov, 7 Dec 43, JRC 471/001 Ammunition—Misc.

[44] Msg W–21454, Somervell to Devers, 11 Apr 44, and Memo, Leyer for Loomis, 7 Jun 44, JRC 474/003 Automatic Weapons.

[45] Memos, Leyer for Loomis, 19 Jun 44, Loomis for Devers, 20 May 44, and Loomis for Leyer, 24 Jul 44, JRC 474/003 Automatic Weapons.

[46] Memos, Leyer for Loomis, 18 Jul 44, and Loomis for Leyer, 31 Aug 44, in same file.

[47] Memo, Loomis for G–4 AFHQ, 21 Jun 44, in same file.

ficient quantity. The French chose to withdraw from stocks reserved for Sovereignty forces the 7.65-mm. pistol ammunition needed by expeditionary troops.[48]

Considering that French infantry regiments received the normal complement of other standard U.S. weapons,[49] the few substitutions imposed on them, while increasing their supply and maintenance problems, did not impair in any appreciable manner their fire power. It can reasonably be said that they were really at no disadvantage when compared with corresponding U.S. units.[50]

[48] Memos, Poydenot for Loomis, 2 Sep 44, Loomis for Poydenot, 30 Sep 44, and Crump for JRC Advance, 20 Oct 44, in same file.

[49] Such as hand and rifle grenades, 27 60-mm. mortars, 18 81-mm. mortars, 18 57-mm. antitank guns, and 6 105-mm. howitzers.

[50] Intervs with Loomis, Jun and Jul 50, and Piatte, Sep 51.

CHAPTER XVI

Other Material Problems

Food

It will be recalled that General Devers, in a letter of 13 February 1944 to General Marshall discussing Franco-American relations, referred to the inadequacy of the rations served to the troops fighting in Italy as an important French grievance.[1]

The food problem had long been a major preoccupation of both Allied and French military authorities. From November 1942 to the fall of 1943, the French had assumed the entire responsibility for feeding their own forces; with the exception of some minor food items procured from U.S. sources, French troops had subsisted on locally produced foodstuffs. With the forthcoming departure of the first expeditionary units for overseas operations, the question of the responsibility for their subsistence was re-examined.

It was then agreed that the French military authorities would make available to SOS, NATOUSA, as in the case of other supplies, all food items needed for such of their forces as would operate under U.S. command. SOS would then issue, through the appropriate U.S. command, to the units in operation rations based on a predetermined menu. Since a large percentage of the troops was made up of Moslems (50 percent by March 1944),[2] two types of rations were established, the Moslem ration

differing from the French menu largely in that it included no pork products.[3]

French authorities then promised to furnish the items peculiar to the French diet, such as brandy, wine, and cooking oil, as well as all items produced in North and West Africa: dried vegetables, dried fruit, lentils, sardines, flour, macaroni, and coffee. To build up a large reserve of these foodstuffs, the JRC, it will be recalled, had urged General Leyer in September and October 1943 to proceed at once with the establishment of a comprehensive food program. It was agreed that what the French could not procure from local sources they were to obtain by requisitioning on the United States through the JRC.[4]

In anticipation of the huge demand for nonperishable foods likely to result from the expected increase in the size of the expeditionary forces, the French submitted in September an initial requisition for such types of food since these were not available from local sources. This led to a re-examination of French capabilities and to a restatement by AFHQ of the policy with regard to the division of responsibility between the Americans and the French. On 12 October NATOUSA reiterated that the French were to furnish an agreed list of items, the U.S. Army being responsible for

---

[1] See pp. 153–55, above.

[2] 32 percent in armored units; 54 percent in other units. Msg F–24631, Devers to AGWAR, 29 Mar 44, JRC Cable Log.

[3] Memo 493, Leyer for Spalding, 19 Aug 43, and Memo, Hq NATOUSA for SOS NATOUSA, 15 Sep 43, JRC 400.1/061 Subsistence for Fr Army.

[4] Memo, Hq NATOUSA for SOS NATOUSA, 12 Oct 43, in same file. See pp. 142–43, above.

providing all other components necessary to complete the agreed ration scale. In addition, the U.S. Army was to supply all emergency rations.[5]

Such were the arrangements made in October with respect to the subsistence of French troops. Barely two or three months later, at a time when the first units of the CEF were reaching the battle line in Italy, the JRC reported that the French military authorities were submitting requisitions for flour, macaroni, fruit juice, and canned fruit, all items which they previously had agreed to furnish in full. Their inability to keep to their agreement was ascribed to a variety of reasons. With respect to some items, the food-raising and -collecting program had not been pursued with sufficient energy. In other cases, physical causes beyond their control had prevented the French from accumulating the required reserves. Some harvests had not yielded the expected returns. Materials needed for canning, storing, packaging, and transporting perishable foodstuffs had been unobtainable. A request submitted by General Leyer on 13 October for an allocation of 10,000 sacks was expected to relieve the situation with respect to the packing of flour.[6]

The French, meanwhile, had given serious consideration to the shipment to North African ports of the foodstuffs reported to be available in substantial quantities in other French territories, especially in Madagascar. Quartermaster, NATOUSA, had supported their attempts in this direction on the ground that such shipments would save like amounts of tonnage from the United States. But the North African Shipping Board declined to make the necessary shipping available and the French were advised to requisition, through the North African Economic Board, the items which they would otherwise have obtained from Madagascar. General Giraud's personal appeal to General Eisenhower in December was likewise fruitless. Nor did the special conference called on 5 February 1944 produce any satisfactory arrangement. The necessary shipping was not available. Furthermore, the bulk of the food production of Madagascar was being absorbed by the Allies for the supply of other theaters of operations.[7]

These and other factors had, by the end of 1943, precipitated a serious food crisis with the result that a larger share of the responsibility for feeding French combat troops was now being thrown in the lap of American supply agencies. On 16 January 1944 General Devers advised both SOS, NATOUSA, and the Commanding General, Fifth Army, that the U.S. Army would not furnish any of the ration items which the French had agreed to provide wholly from their own sources. Only in the case of items listed for partial supply from French sources would deficiencies be met from U.S. stocks. The French Army would then be required to replace the items so furnished.[8]

In addition to the difficulties encountered by the French in fulfilling their part of the subsistence program, it soon developed that the rations as currently fed the units of the

[5] Memos, Hq NATOUSA for SOS NATOUSA, 12 Oct 43, and for Gen Leyer, 28 Oct 43, in same file.

[6] JRC 400.1/051 S.A.A. of QM Items—Gen-Misc.

[7] Memos, QM for M and Tn NATOUSA, 6 Oct 43, Loomis for Leyer, 6 Nov 43, and Ltrs, Giraud to Eisenhower, 9 Dec 43, Leyer to Loomis, 4 Mar 44, JRC 400.1/062 Food From Madagascar and West Africa.

[8] Msg 29668, CG NATOUSA to CG SOS NATOUSA, 16 Jan 44, JRC 400.1/061 Subsistence for Fr Army.

2D MOROCCAN INFANTRY DIVISION MEN UNLOADING AMERICAN
RATIONS *from a mule train on the slopes of Mount Pantano, Italy, December 1943.*

CEF were not only insufficient in quantity but seriously deficient in nutritive elements, sugar and fats especially. The French High Command strongly suspected that ration deficiencies were partly responsible for the abnormal number of cases of frozen feet (440 in the 2d Moroccan Division alone in December). In a memorandum to General Clark, General Juin pointed out that the present ration inadequacy was prejudicial to the physical condition of his troops. It was necessary, he urged, to provide CEF units with a diet similar to the U.S. ration because of the severe climate conditions. The double standard was also affecting their morale. They felt "less well treated than their American comrades-in-arms." Simultaneously, General Giraud appealed to General Wilson with a request that CEF troops be issued rations similar to the American B ration with some minor differences, such as French bread instead of U.S. bread and French tinned meat for natives instead of U.S. tinned foods containing pork.[9]

That the French and Moslem rations were low by American standards was made apparent in a study conducted by Headquarters, Fifth Army. Comparative figures indicating the number of pounds of daily ration per man were given as follows:

American_____ 4. 89
French_____ 3. 61
Moslem_____ 3. 09

The modification requested by the French was designed to increase the French ration

---

[9] Ltr, Devinck to CG AFHQ, 12 Jan 44, Memo, Juin for Clark, 12 Jan 44, and Ltr, Devinck to Wilson, 12 Jan 44, AFHQ Liaison Sec 420 France.

to 4.77 pounds and the Moslem ration to 3.68 pounds. Fifth Army recognized that CEF troops were not getting enough food and urged AFHQ to take immediate action to bring about an adjustment which would be satisfactory to them.[10]

The food crisis came to a head when, on 22 January, General Leyer disclosed that supplying foodstuffs to the French armed forces was now encountering insurmountable difficulties. These had been aggravated by a recent SOS decision whereby the French Quartermaster was to stock up in Italy a 90-day reserve of foodstuffs for the CEF. Considering that, in addition, the French Quartermaster had been directed to constitute stocks for the units designated for participation in ANVIL, the huge amount of supplies thus to be assembled within a three-month period was much more than available resources permitted. General Leyer flatly stated that, thereafter, the subsistence of the CEF could be assured only on condition that the Allied command would undertake the responsibility "either without compensation in kind from the French or with repayment in kind within the limitations of French stocks under Reciprocal Aid procedure." [11]

The serious implications contained in General Leyer's announcement were made the object of a detailed study by the JRC. In a memorandum to G–4, AFHQ, General Loomis described the unsatisfactory features of the existing arrangement governing the supply of rations to French units operating as part of a U.S. force. He recommended, in the interests of simplicity and of assuring proper subsistence for the troops involved, a modification of the arrangement closely akin to General Leyer's own proposal. He suggested that SOS requisition the entire ration, substituting additional flour for certain components deemed unnecessary; that the French furnish the additional components which they required but which were not part of the U.S. ration; finally, that the French replace in U.S. stocks such food items as SOS would make available to their forces.[12]

While General Loomis' recommendations were being studied, General Giraud, on 9 March, pointed out to General Wilson that the diet as then served to the CEF was so monotonous as to result in a marked lack of appetite among the troops. He urged that French units be "admitted to the benefits of the substitution of fresh or frozen meat," such as were enjoyed by American troops of the Fifth Army. Four days later General Leyer also referred to the monotony factor, which he blamed on the fact that the French and Moslem diets were based primarily on canned foods. He warned that the reduction of the cooking oil rations as then contemplated by SOS would be most unfortunate since French units were receiving neither butter nor margarine, and oil was the only fat component of their diet. At the time, cooking oil was scarce in the United States. Since olive oil was available in North Africa, the War Department asked the theater to provide salvage containers in sufficient quantity for transporting this oil to Italy. Subsequently, the theater made available to the French 25,000 five-gallon water cans for use as cooking oil containers.[13]

---

[10] Memo, Hq Fifth Army for CinC AFHQ, 26 Feb 44, JRC 400.1/061 Subsistence for Fr Army.

[11] Ltr, Leyer to Loomis, 22 Jan 44, in same file.

[12] Memos, Loomis for G–4 AFHQ, 7 Feb 44, and for Leyer, 7 Mar 44, in same file.

[13] Ltr, Giraud to Wilson, 9 Mar 44, and Memo, Leyer for Loomis, 13 Mar 44, in same file; Msgs 2653, Somervell to Devers, 19 Mar 44, and L–27933, Larkin to Devers, 22 Jun 44, JRC Cable Log.

General Giraud's proposal concerning fresh meat, of which troops of the CEF received none, was taken up by NATOUSA. Quartermaster officials reported that no such meat could be furnished the French, as the only source of supply was the United States, and the number of available reefer ships was limited. However, in April the French authorities and NATOUSA were able to arrange for the shipment to Italy of 5,000 live sheep from local sources, or enough for one month's supply of fresh meat. Soon after, General Leyer informed the JRC that shipments of this nature could not be continued without disrupting the supply for civilians and for Territorial troops. Quartermaster, NATOUSA, then pointed out that General Leyer's statement was greatly at variance with the definite assurance given earlier by French civil authorities that sufficient sheep could be found in North Africa to fulfill all French commitments. Incidentally, the same authorities were reported to have informally offered to sell fresh meat from North Africa to the U.S. Army. In addition, they were said to have requested the return of cold-storage facilities then used by Allied forces, thus indicating a desire to provide a greater supply of fresh-frozen meat. The question of the further provision of fresh meat to the CEF was finally dropped, especially when it became known that the French command in Italy had made arrangements to purchase fresh meat locally and no longer needed live sheep from North Africa.[14]

On 19 April General Devers informed General Clark that to improve French ra-

tions authority had been secured from the CCS to furnish the entire French and Moslem rations with the exception of wine and brandy. Yet it was not until 1 June, after final agreement between AFHQ, the War Department, and the CFLN, that the SOS assumed full responsibility for feeding the French forces fighting with the Fifth Army. The change-over did not affect the composition of the French and Moslem rations, which remained the same. Simultaneously, the MAB in Washington allocated to the French Army 4,800 tons of canned corned beef, and 12,000 tons of frozen meat then available in Madagascar.[15]

From the time the new subsistence policy became effective, food ceased to be a problem. Thereafter, the units of the French Expeditionary Corps in Italy received adequate rations. The policy was subsequently extended to the French forces participating in Anvil.

Clothing

Soon after the start of the rearmament operations, it became known that the French were unable to use a considerable proportion, in some instances as high as 25 percent, of the clothing items of U.S. manufacture delivered to them. This was because of size differences, the average stature of the French soldier being smaller than that of the American soldier. The differences were particularly notable in the case of overcoats, coats, trousers, shirts, coveralls, and service shoes.[16] In order to clothe

[14] Memos, QM for JRC, 26 Mar, 27 Apr 44, Leyer for Loomis, 23 Apr 44, and G–4 for QM, 26 Apr 44, JRC 400.1/061 Subsistence for Fr Army; Msgs F–57630, Devers to Clark, 10 Jun 44, and 4904, Clark to Devers, 22 Jun 44, JRC Cable Log.

[15] Memos, Devers for CG Fifth Army, 19 Apr 44, Hq NATOUSA for CG Fifth Army, 12 May 44, and Msg F–48500, Devers to Fifth Army, 20 May 44, JRC 400.1/061 Subsistence for Fr Army; Memo for Rcd, Office of CofS, 28 Apr 44, and Memo, QM AFHQ for AG OPS, 16 May 44, AFHQ 0100/4 SACS Rcd Sec, Fr Matters, Vol IV.

[16] Size differences were not limited to items of

their men properly, French unit commanders were compelled to arrange locally with U.S. supply organizations or with the French Quartermaster for the exchange of unusable items. The seriousness of the situation can be best appreciated when it is realized that in the case of one unit of 1,600 men (the 1st Parachute Regiment), no fewer than 600 pairs of service shoes, 110 parachute boots, 1,250 coveralls, and 1,200 pairs of woolen trousers had to be exchanged. In November 1943 the French Military Mission in Washington requested the War Department to lower the U.S. tariff by one size when assigning clothing to French troops. Later, in June 1944, the French military authorities supplied the War Department with their own size tariff to be used in the case of all subsequent shipments of clothing.[17]

Something should be said of the many problems raised in connection with the provision of clothing for the women serving in the French armed forces.[18]

By the end of 1943 the African Army included 3,100 women in uniform, all volunteers. A few of these were employed as technicians in the Signal Corps or as nurses in the Medical Corps. The rest were serving as secretaries, social workers, interpreters, drivers, and the like. Mobilization of

women having been decreed, another 1,700 women were in process of induction. Expecting that more would be recruited within the first few months of 1944, the French High Command set the goal at approximately 11,000. This number never was reached, partly because AFHQ urged that conscription of the numerous women already employed in Allied services throughout North Africa be deferred. SOS, NATOUSA, in particular, was eager to retain its civilian female employees so as not to disturb the progress of its activities. The French High Command agreed to place all such personnel on special assignment to the Allied agencies concerned.

So far the French Supply Services had received 5,800 sets of women's clothing or enough for the effectives then in active service. The uniforms and clothing items were of the type issued members of the U.S. Women's Army Corps (WAC). It was understood that uniforms were to be worn with French buttons and insignia. When it was reported that a number of French nurses were wearing WAC uniforms with U.S. buttons and insignia, the theater commander directed the JRC to inform the French that the practice must be stopped at once.[19]

The wearing by French Army women of the WAC cap with visor, an item which had been issued to them along with the rest of the uniform, precipitated a minor crisis. American officials in the theater decided that, because of its style, the cap was a distinctive article of the U.S. uniform, and that its wearing even with French insignia would result in confusion. Whereupon NATOUSA requested the War Department to discontinue further shipments of the item to the French, and at the same time

---

clothing for troops. In the case of animals, differences in shoe size caused considerable difficulty. In June 1944 AFHQ requested the War Department to discontinue all further shipments of horse and mule shoes to the French Army as the conversion of U.S. shoes to conform to French requirements resulted in excessive waste. Thereafter, metal only would be requested, if needed, for fabrication of shoes locally. Msg F–54092, AFHQ to AGWAR, 2 Jun 44, ASF International Div Files, A–45–192 Cables, Vol. X.

[17] Memo, Bouscat for Loomis, 18 Nov 43, JRC 360/002 Items Common to Ground and Air; Memo, NATOUSA for WD, 21 Jun 44, OPD 400 France, Sec IV.

[18] JRC 400.1/076 Women's Clothing.

[19] Memo, Loomis to Leyer, 30 Nov 43, in same file.

asked the French to return to U.S. stocks the caps already delivered to them.[20] Soon French Army women were observed in the streets of Algiers without any hat at all, no provision having been made for a substitute. The JRC then hurriedly submitted a requisition for 5,000 garrison caps which SOS subsequently was authorized to deliver from stocks in the theater. Much to their chagrin, the French women returned the cap with visor and donned the less elegant garrison headgear.

On the assumption that mobilization would achieve the expected goal, the French Military Mission in Washington, in February 1944, obtained the assignment of another 6,500 sets of women's clothing. By this time the French had received all together 11,500 sets (8,000 U.S. WAC uniforms and 3,500 U.S. Army Nurse Corps obsolete blue uniforms). This was over twice as many as they needed, for even by August 1944 no more than 4,815 women had actually been recruited (3,465 in the Army and 1,350 in the Air Force). Of these, 1,745 were serving with the expeditionary forces. Out of an expected total of 1,335 nurses, only 635 had been recruited. The French, as a result, lacked 100 nurses for their expeditionary forces, and 500 for the Territorial forces.

On 26 April 1944 the French Army women were reorganized as the Auxiliaires Féminines de l'Armée de Terre, or AFAT. Shortly after, their Director, Maj. H. Terré, submitted to AFHQ a request for 3,000 sets of British clothing "on sentimental as well as practical grounds." She explained that the first women to be recruited had been organized in the United Kingdom where they had been issued the uniform worn by the women of the British Army (Auxiliary Territorial Service). She now wished to have all AFAT units dressed in that fashion. In her opinion the British uniform was more suitable for the heavy duties which the French women were performing as drivers and mechanics. Moreover, the British allotment included "under-garments unobtainable in North Africa and not included in the American equipment." [21] The request was rejected on the general principle that the provision of clothing to the AFAT was just as much an American responsibility as was the equipping of other French personnel. Throughout the war, except for the few women still stationed in the United Kingdom, the AFAT continued to be supplied from American sources.

Special Supplies

One problem closely related to the food ration question caused considerable difficulties and endless confusion, particularly throughout Phase IV of the rearmament program. It concerned the distribution to French troops of special supplies considered essential from the standpoint of health, morale, and combat efficiency.

These supplies fell into three categories: (1) "gratuitous components," items such as candy, cigarettes, and the like, which in the U.S. Army are normally issued free to the troops in the forward zone; (2) "post exchange" supplies, also called "resale articles," such as candy, toilet articles, smoking components, clothing, and other items handled by Army Exchange Service and sold in post exchange stores to military personnel for cash usually on a ration schedule; and (3) "Special Services" supplies,

[20] Msg W–6706, JRC to AGWAR, 1 Dec 43, in same file.

[21] Ltr, Maj Terré to Maj Gen Beaumont-Nesbitt, Liaison Sec AFHQ, 8 Jun 44, in same file.

FRENCH WACS ASSEMBLING ON THE BEACH *after landing at St. Tropez, France, 17 August 1944.*

such as athletic kits, libraries, and other recreational items, distributed to units by Special Services Division, ASF.

In the summer of 1943, as the first expeditionary units were getting ready for combat duty outside of northwest Africa, the French military authorities gave serious consideration to the question of special supplies. AFHQ urged them to stockpile the necessary items, first by drawing to the maximum extent possible on local French sources, then by lend-lease cash purchases effected on the basis of requisitions submitted to, and screened by, the JRC, and finally, when necessary, by direct cash purchases in the United States through the French Military Mission in Washington. The last procedure was to be followed particularly in the case of Special Services sup-

plies.[22] When, in mid-October, the French requested for their expeditionary units an allocation of boxing gloves, rugby balls, and basketballs, all items then unavailable in North Africa, they were advised to buy them in the United States on a cash basis.

Later, on 21 October, the theater approved an initial global requisition covering post exchange supplies for 125,000 French Army and Air Force troops, plus 90 days' maintenance. Distribution of the resale items was to be effected by the French High Command through military co-operatives set up on the pattern of the American post exchange stores. In a subsequent

---

[22] Memos, Spalding for Leyer, 20 Aug 43, and Loomis for Leyer, 23 Oct 43, and Msg 2034, Somervell to Eisenhower, 9 Nov 43, JRC 400.1/051 PX Sups.

message to the War Department dated 24 December, AFHQ recommended that the French be required to make cash payment in the United States for the supplies involved, and that shipment of the items be included in the 25,000 tons allocated monthly to the French military. The War Department approved the recommendation with the proviso that the French Military Mission would arrange for the shipment of supplies through the War Shipping Administration.[23]

Such was the situation at the opening of Phase IV in February 1944. The French were still eagerly awaiting the supplies ordered in October. Anticipating that their needs would increase as their expeditionary forces grew, they submitted new requisitions. These, although approved at first by the JRC, were rejected as excessive by the North African Economic Board. The French were then asked to scale down their demands and resubmit requisitions, this time with appropriate justification and the assurance that the items involved could not be obtained locally.[24]

In an effort to ward off any possible misunderstanding on the part of the French with respect to the transfer to them of post exchange supplies shipped from the United States, General Loomis, on 10 February 1944, reiterated the policy as determined earlier by the War Department, namely, that the transaction was to be "on a cash basis outside of Lend-Lease procedure" and that payment was to be effected in the United States. To establish a definite pro-

curement procedure, General Loomis then asked General Leyer to agree that French requests for post exchange supplies would be submitted by French representatives in the United States directly to the appropriate U.S. agency.[25]

Pending arrival of the first supplies ordered from the United States in the fall of 1943, AFHQ authorized and later completed several cash transactions in the theater. These concerned items then considered theater excess stocks, such as pipe tobacco available in large quantities in British depots and substantial amounts of American "off-brand" cigarettes not desired by U.S. troops. These sporadic transactions were not sufficient to improve the situation greatly. By April the French military authorities were still forced to ration stringently the post exchange type of supplies which they were distributing to their troops.

In a memorandum to the Joint Air Commission dated 14 April, General Bouscat, Commanding General, French Air Force, described the plight of the air squadrons then stationed in Sardinia and operating under U.S. command. Personnel of the units were limited to the following rations: 10 ounces monthly of soap of poor quality, one package of cigarettes daily, and some shoe polish at irregular intervals. No other items were provided. Considering that the men of these units were forbidden by the Allied command to buy from the local shops and were not allowed the use of American post exchange stores, they had no way of supplementing their meager rations. This, General Bouscat stressed, was bad from the standpoint of morale as it created

---

[23] Memo, Hq NATOUSA for CG SOS NATOUSA, 21 Oct 43, in same file; Msgs W-8440, Eisenhower to AGWAR, 24 Dec 43, and 6188, Somervell to Eisenhower, 2 Jan 44, JRC Cable Log.

[24] Memo, Loomis for Leyer, 3 Feb 44, JRC 400.1/051 PX Sups.

[25] Memo, Loomis for Leyer, 10 Feb 44, in same file.

among the men the regrettable feeling that they were less well treated than their American comrades. Couldn't access to the U.S. post exchange stores be extended to the troops concerned? General Bouscat's request, opposed at first by G–4, NATOUSA, on the ground that the responsibility for providing post exchange supplies rested entirely with the French High Command, was subsequently granted by order of General Devers. This action was not to be taken as a policy but as an emergency measure. Meanwhile, the supplies ordered in November were still under procurement in the United States. It was not until 30 April 1944 that they were finally shipped. They began reaching North African ports in June.[26]

The entire question of special supplies came up again for discussion apropos of the gratuitous components then turned over to the units in Italy. On 23 May the War Department reminded AFHQ that such supplies were to be paid for in cash by the French. A month later the French advised the theater that they were unable to pay cash and requested that the issue to them of the items be made under the Lend-Lease Act as in the case of all other supplies of U.S. source. Queried on the matter by AFHQ, the War Department replied that it was up to the State Department and the Foreign Economic Administration to determine whether supplies furnished the French by the War Department were for cash or on credit. Pending final arrangements on the matter, the issue of gratuitous components

as currently made to CEF units in Italy was approved.[27]

It was not until 20 July that the French finally answered General Loomis' letter of 10 February concerning the question of post exchange "resale items." General Leyer's reply disclosed that, as in the case of the gratuitous components, the Finance Commissioner was now unable to provide the necessary funds in dollars for cash payment in the United States of the resale items. Nor, he added, could the Commissioner pay in French francs each time such supplies were procured. This was because receipts from post exchange sales remained in unit treasuries and did not return to any general post exchange fund, as was the practice in the U.S. Army, thus making it impossible to purchase additional resale articles. He then proposed that the supply of such items to the forces whose maintenance was a U.S. responsibility be authorized as a lend-lease transaction. All items so obtained would be sold on a cash basis to the troops concerned.[28] NATOUSA endorsed the proposal and, with the agreement of the International Division, established, on 12 August, a policy to govern the provision of post exchange resale items and gratuitous components to the French. Thereafter SOS issued gratuitous components to such Army and Air Force troops as were serving with the U.S. forces outside the continental limits of Africa, and reported the transfers to International Division for financial accounting. SOS also made available to the same troops,

[26] Memos, Gardiner for Loomis, 20 Apr 44, Adcock for CofS NATOUSA, 10 May 44, and Loomis for G–4 AFHQ, 7 May 44, and Msgs F–46396, CG NATOUSA to Brig Gen Robert M. Webster, 16 May 44, and WX–43037, Somervell to Devers, 29 May 44, in same file.

[27] Msgs WX–40295, Somervell to Devers, 23 May 44, and FX–62567, Devers to AGWAR, 21 Jun 44, JRC Cable Log; Msg WX–57756, Somervell to Devers, 29 Jun 44, JRC 140 Accounting.

[28] Memo, Leyer for Loomis, 20 Jul 44, JRC 400.1/051 PX Sups.

stocks permitting, a limited number of post exchange resale items to be sold for cash only. The War Department and NATOUSA determined together, on the basis of availability, what quantities of the approved items could be delivered without jeopardizing the welfare of American troops.[29]

In mid-August, SOS turned over to the French approximately 40,000,000 books or boxes of matches and 6,500,000 packages of pipe tobacco then available in theater stocks. In the case of cigarettes, War Department officials informed NATOUSA that because of the current severe shortage of tobacco in the United States, cigarettes could be supplied up to 50 percent of the U.S. allowance and only if off-brands were acceptable to the French.[30]

On 8 October SOS urged the War Department to secure the items requisitioned in August as most were necessary to maintain the health and morale of the French troops serving with the U.S. Army. Fifty percent of the normal allowance was considered a minimum requirement. In the case of cigarettes, General Larkin suggested that off-brand cigarettes be supplied to the French before being offered for sale to prisoners of war.[31]

As the equipment responsibility for the French forces passed from NATOUSA to ETOUSA in the fall of 1944, the same general policy continued to apply with respect to special supplies. French troops on the Continent kept receiving, as they had in the Mediterranean theater, a min-

imum of items which could not be increased because of U.S. production limitations.

Miscellaneous Equipment

The French in North Africa also were almost destitute with respect to a number of articles of common use, especially manufactured goods, generally available in healthy national economies and indispensable for the efficient running of a large military establishment. The critical situation which French military authorities had faced in this connection during the year 1943 became more acute as their troops were being committed to combat in Italy at the close of that year.

In late December 1943 the Surgeon, AFHQ, reported that a large percentage of the CEF troops engaged on the Italian front were infested with lice, apparently because they lacked the necessary sanitary facilities and supplies. Since it was essential that troops be kept free from lice if epidemics of typhus fever were to be prevented, AFHQ requested the War Department to provide the French armed forces with 1½ million cans of body insect powder, 750,000 ampoules of methyl bromide, and 6,000 ethocel fumigation bags. The requisition was established on the basis of 300,000 troops. The methyl bromide being available in U.S. stocks in the theater, SOS delivered 750,000 ampoules at the end of January 1944. At the urging of the War Department, the requisition for insect powder was reduced to 645,000 cans. These were subsequently assigned and their shipment arranged at the rate of 215,000 monthly for the three months of March, April, and May 1944. To assist further the French High Command in taking proper sanitary measures, various cir-

[29] Msg FX–82228, Devers to International Div, 12 Aug 44, JRC Cable Log.
[30] Msg 41292, AGWAR to NATOUSA, 16 Sep 44, in same file.
[31] Msg LX–45177, Larkin to Pembark, 2 Oct 44, in same file.

culars and pamphlets issued by the Surgeon's Office, NATOUSA, were translated into French, and in February 1944 lectures and demonstrations on typhus control were given to French personnel under the direction of American medical officers.

From 1944 on, miscellaneous French requests increased sharply in number. In February, General Leyer asked for 200 barber kits. The requisition, at first rejected by MAC (G), was finally granted in March. A first shipment of 100 kits was authorized, with the rest to follow at a later date. Also approved during the same month were requests for 6,000 canteen covers to be used by combat troops as grenade carriers, and for needles for the shoe-stitching machines which had been delivered earlier with an insufficient number of replacement needles.

In April the French asked for a special allocation of 6,000 to 9,000 canteens to be used by the Senegalese troops of the 9th Colonial Infantry Division. The request was based on the fact that such troops required approximately four liters of water per day, or double the normal ration, to maintain their efficiency. On 28 April SOS, NATOUSA, effected the lend-lease transfer of 7,000 canteens.

Again in April the French requested, through their Military Mission in Washington, the issue of 60,000 packages of dried blood plasma for use by their expeditionary forces engaged in Italy. This quantity was to tide them over until the opening of a blood collection center in North Africa which they then had under consideration.[32] On 29 April the War Department authorized the issue of blood plasma to all French troops operating as part of a U.S. force outside of North Africa with the un-

derstanding that U.S. Army stocks in the theater would be replenished by the French themselves through purchases in the United States of commercially procured plasma. This procedure was intended to prevent a conflict with the American Red Cross blood donor program.[33]

The question of the issue of penicillin to French hospitals in North Africa came up for discussion at about the same time. French troops operating with and supplied by the U.S. Army were issued penicillin on the same basis as U.S. personnel. However, many casualties were evacuated to French hospitals in North Africa where penicillin was not available. For the benefit of these hospitals, the theater requested the shipment without delay of a first allocation of 1,000 ampoules. The War Department promptly granted the request and directed the theater to prepare thereafter monthly requisitions for submission to the War Production Board.[34]

For the printing of identification tags furnished to them under the rearmament program, the French had been authorized, in March 1944, to use an electric embossing machine then available at Peninsular Base Section. When it was realized that this procedure overtaxed the limited U.S. facilities, General Devers, in July, requested the War Department to furnish the French with two such machines. The War Department replied that no electric equipment could be made available at the time, but offered to deliver a hand-operated machine instead. This machine was shipped in October 1944

---

[32] Msg W–20933, Somervell to Devers, 9 Apr 44, JRC 400.1/033 Plasma, Human Normal, Dried.

[33] Msgs, Somervell to Devers, 2667, 20 Mar 44, and W–29823, 29 Apr 44, and Ltr, Loomis to Leyer, 12 May 44, in same file.

[34] Msgs WX–47401, Somervell to Devers, 7 Jun 44, F–64807, Devers to AGWAR, 26 June 44, and W–59483, Somervell to Devers, 3 Jul 44, JRC 400.1/030 Medical Sups and Equip.

to Base 901 in Marseille, the base then serving 1st French Army.

The problem of the protection of clothing in storage was one which the French had difficulty in solving for they lacked antimoth products. In the fall of 1944 they requested an allocation of twenty tons of naphthalene. The War Department promptly arranged to have 42,200 pounds of naphthalene delivered through the Foreign Economic Administration.

Throughout the year 1943, some equipment had been turned over piecemeal to the French Army Geographic Service in North Africa for which no provision was made under the rearmament program. This equipment was wholly inadequate and the service was unable to perform any valuable work. On its behalf, General Leyer submitted, from February 1944 on, a series of requisitions for materials and machinery of all types, such as overlay paper, maps, paper and equipment for printing maps, presses, photographic supplies, and even common-use items such as glue. In practically all cases, NATOUSA authorized the lend-lease transfer, from U.S. Army theater stocks, of the materials requested. As a result the Geographic Service gradually improved its efficiency and in the pre-ANVIL period succeeded in doing much valuable work.

One last problem of some importance should be mentioned. It concerns the inability of the North African authorities to secure from local sources the chemicals needed for the treatment of malaria, a disease prevalent in many areas of French North and West Africa and the source of considerable annoyance to the troops stationed in these territories. Atabrine, the medication used by the U.S. Army for this purpose, was then in great demand for Allied troops operating in the various theaters

of operations. In 1943 the French had already requisitioned and obtained from the United States an adequate supply of the precious curative, or approximately 12 million tablets, on the basis of a troop strength of 270,000 men. This had enabled them to control the disease during and until the end of the malarial season (November). In January 1944 they estimated their requirements for the coming year at about 25 million tablets, a figure which U.S. theater authorities reduced to 20 million. A first shipment of 15 million tablets was made in June and the rest shipped soon after. Contending that their West African forces had not been included in the over-all 1944 requisition, the French requested an additional allocation of 4 million tablets which NATOUSA reduced to 1,250,000. This latter quantity was subsequently approved in Washington and assigned for shipment in July. Thanks to the substantial shipments of atabrine from the United States and the energetic prophylactic measures taken by all theater medical agencies concerned, malaria failed to cause any undue hardship on the North African forces.

Accounting

No attempt is made in this volume to examine the many legal and financial aspects of the North African lend-lease operations owing, in part, to the fact that the important matter of the supply of the civilian population has been entirely left out as being irrelevant. Nor is a study made of the problems peculiar to "reverse" lend-lease, such as the procurement by the U.S. forces of goods and services available in North Africa (a matter involving, incidentally, the thorny tax issue) and the signing of an agreement with the French on reciprocal aid. These and other similar problems are matters for lend-lease historians.[35] One question, however, requires some treatment at this juncture, not only because of its close connection with the rearmament operations, but also because the issue involved was the source of a serious controversy lasting some two and one half years, as a result of which insuperable difficulties were added to the already heavy burden of supplying the French with munitions of war. It concerns the manner in which transfers of American equipment were recorded and charged against the French for payment under the Lend-Lease Act.

Under the terms of the Lend-Lease Act of 11 March 1941, the War Department was required to maintain complete records of all defense articles, facilities, information, or services transferred to foreign governments. In the case of the French, materials were transferred to them either in the United States or in the theater.

Transfers effected in the United States involved largely the issue of initial equipment under the approved rearmament programs. They were reported and charged against the French lend-lease account in the United States. Such accounting, in itself a simple procedure, should have been wholly adequate had it not been for the fact that shipments to the French were made, not directly to them, but to the American commanding general in the theater for subsequent transfer, hence their designation of Commanding General Shipments. Thus was the responsibility of the commander involved since he was given control over French matériel to the extent that he could, if he so wished, divert part or all of it for purposes other than French rearmament. As a result the theater was placed in a position where it had to keep strict accounting of the deliveries it made to the French of initial equipment obtained through Commanding General Shipments.[36]

Responsibility for the accounting of theater transfers, that is, transfers effected at the direction of the U.S. commanding general in the theater or at the order of U.S. commanders in the field, obviously was that of the theater itself. Such accounting was effected in accordance with directives issued from time to time by the theater on the basis of policies established by the War Department. Transfers were recorded at the time of issue on shipping tickets signed by duly authorized French officers. The tickets were then priced in terms of dollars and, until September 1944, consolidated by the base section or Air Forces service command concerned. After 30 September 1944 they were consolidated by the Special Staff section concerned in Headquarters, MTOUSA, for ground force items, and the Air Forces service command for air force technical items. In this manner more uniformity in pricing and reporting could be achieved. Finally, the reports, once consolidated, were forwarded to the theater fiscal director for inclusion in the bimonthly report to the War Department.[37]

To lessen the burden of lend-lease accounting which it was required to assume and for which it had insufficient personnel, NATOUSA sought to obtain at least a

---

[35] See, for example, Leighton and Coakley, *Global Logistics and Strategy: 1940–1943.*

[36] Msgs 7162, Eisenhower to AGWAR, 17 Mar 43, and 4663, Somervell to Eisenhower, 26 Mar 43, JRC Cable Log.

[37] Admin Memo 12, Hq NATOUSA, 19 Sep 43, MTOUSA 400.114 Misc Aug–Nov 43; Cir 5, AFHQ, 10 Jan 43, JRC 400.2/001 Admin of Sup—Gen; *Logistical History of NATOUSA-MTOUSA,* p. 369.

simplification of the procedure with respect to Commanding General Shipments. In a message to the War Department dated 30 March 1943, NATOUSA strongly urged that receipts be signed by the French in Washington and not in North Africa, with the understanding that any diversion of equipment subsequently made in the theater would promptly be reported.[38] War Department officials having turned down the proposal, the theater then sought ways and means to lighten the task of SOS, NATOUSA. To make it unnecessary, in particular, to open thousands of packages in order to inventory their contents, the French military authorities in Algiers were asked if they would be willing to sign receipts based on ships' manifests. This they agreed to do. Thereupon, those American base sections expecting large shipments of French lend-lease equipment issued a standing operating procedure setting forth the manner in which shipping tickets were to be prepared and receipted.[39]

The issue was reopened in late August 1943 in connection with a new directive from the War Department redefining the policy with regard to lend-lease transfers. The directive stipulated that all transfers were to be recorded and reported, except in the case of Commanding General Shipments when only diversions from the latter needed to be reported.[40]

In the belief that this provision at last exempted the theater from receipting ship-

ments which were definitely consigned for transfer to the French, NATOUSA announced its intention of discontinuing the practice. Whereupon the War Department directed that the theater was to continue to obtain signed receipts from the French upon transfer of matériel either from theater stocks or from Commanding General Shipments.[41]

Meanwhile, accounting of theater transfers was running into considerable difficulties for a number of reasons. The theater was unable to obtain complete price catalogues to cover the wide variety of parts and supplies released to the French. Shipping, handling, and other miscellaneous costs accruing to supplies furnished could not always be computed with accuracy. Soon after the entry of French troops on the Italian front, many of the large number of transactions made necessary for their maintenance were taking place in forward areas thus often precluding the possibility of obtaining and pricing itemized signed receipts for all transfers. In addition, it was frequently impossible to distinguish between initial and maintenance issues.[42] From December 1943 on to July 1944 new difficulties were experienced. The accounting policies established by the War Department for each category of transfers, such as subsistence, battle-loss replacements, petroleum, ammunition, were frequently changed. Piecemeal emergency transfers from theater stocks to fill large shortages of initial equipment, as well as attempts to recapture U.S. equipment from French stocks, complicated the situation further.

[38] Msg 173. Eisenhower to AGWAR, 30 Mar 43. JRC Spalding Cable Log.

[39] Msg 5032, Somervell to Eisenhower (Eyes Only), 31 Mar 43, JRC Spalding Cable Log; Msgs L-1595, MBS to Gardiner, 3 Apr 43, and 1548, Eisenhower to MBS, 4 Apr 43, JRC Cable Log; Admin Memo 47, Atlantic Base Sec, 8 Apr 43, JRC 402 Sup Policy.

[40] Memo W5-12-43, WD, 30 Aug 43, JRC 140 Accounting.

[41] Msgs W-944, Eisenhower to AGWAR, 25 Sep 43, and 8890, AGWAR to Eisenhower, 29 Sep 43, JRC 140 Accounting.

[42] Logistical History of NATOUSA–MTOUSA, pp. 373–76.

By July 1944 accounting of theater transfers had reached such a state of confusion that SOS officials recommended a radical change in procedure for the sake of simplification "even at the sacrifice of a certain degree of accuracy." They proposed that the French be charged for all supplies and services furnished by the theater on a "per man per diem" basis, with the charge made effective at a date to be agreed upon between the French and SOS. General Devers endorsed the proposal and strongly urged the War Department to approve its immediate adoption. Meanwhile, SOS proceeded to determine the amount to be charged per man per diem, on the basis of the average cost of maintaining one U.S. soldier for one day in the North African theater. To this average cost, 25 percent would be added for overhead, transportation, and accessorial charges, the percentage having been tentatively set, on 29 August, by War Department authorities themselves. On 11 September 1944 ASF accepted the principle of the per man per diem accounting procedure, but directed that, pending the approval of a definite rate, accounting be continued in accordance with existing policies. A month later, SOS, NATOUSA, forwarded to Washington all pertinent data likely to assist the War Department in establishing a final rate and, on 16 November, recommended a charge of $8.54 per man per day.[43]

As the supply responsibility for the French forces passed from NATOUSA to ETOUSA, the War Department, on 18 November, informed ETOUSA of the accounting policy to be followed thereafter. The policy resembled closely the one established earlier under War Department Memorandum 35–44 of 22 September 1944, and made no reference to the per man per diem proposal. Throughout the months of December 1944 and January 1945, the War Department kept insisting that the existing policy be strictly adhered to. But the policy was not workable; it had not produced records "even approaching reasonable accuracy" on which future charges could be made. On 15 January General Somervell, then on a visit on the Continent, was made aware of the difficulties in complying with the complicated system prescribed by the War Department, especially in view of the lack of qualified personnel in the theater. Recognizing the desirability of adopting a simpler method, he urged the War Department by cable to put into effect the per man per diem method.[44]

Discussions on the per man per diem procedure continued for several months. In April 1945 the War Department dispatched a special committee to study the status of lend-lease accounting in both the Mediterranean and European theaters. It was not until the end of May, after the cessation of hostilities in Europe and, incidentally, after ten months of correspondence between the two theaters and the War Department, that the latter, acting on the recommendations of the special committee, established a firm

[43] Ltr, SOS NATOUSA to AG WD, 29 Jul 44, and Msgs FX–85245, Devers to AGWAR, 20 Aug 44, and LX–47559, Larkin to AGWAR, 16 Oct 44, JRC 140 Accounting; Ltr, Hq ASF, APLIC CO8 Accounting (3 Aug 44), 11 Sep 44, and 3d Ind, Hq MTOUSA, AG 400.3295/414 D–O, 16 Nov 44, quoted in *Logistical History of NATOUSA-MTOUSA*, p. 379.

[44] Msg WX–66076, Somervell to Eisenhower, 18 Nov 44, ASF International Div A–45–192 Cable Log, France–Out; Msgs E–90834, Lee to AGWAR, 26 Jan 45, and E–86634, Somervell to AGWAR, 15 Jan 45, SS and P Planning Div Files.

accounting policy.[45]   All prior charges and credits were to be canceled and, in their place, the French were to be charged: (1) for the complete equipment of all units included in the approved rearmament programs on the basis of tables of organization and equipment for similar U.S. units; (2) for the supply and maintenance of their expeditionary units at the per man per diem rates of $6.56 (for MTOUSA) and $6.67 (for ETOUSA), retroactive to the date when such units had become part of a U.S. force and terminating on 31 May 1945; and (3) for ammunition, petroleum and lubricants, and other special items not covered in the above per man per diem rates.[46]

Thus a simple accounting procedure had finally been adopted, a method not as accurate, to be sure, as the item per item system which the War Department had vainly tried to enforce, but one considered fair enough to all concerned.   Such was the basis on which the cost of equipping and maintaining the French was estimated at the time of the final settlement of lend-lease obligations.

---

[45] Msgs WX–88427, AGWAR to MTOUSA, 26 May 45, and WX–38215, AGWAR to ETOUSA, 26 Jul 45, quoted in *Logistical History of NATOUSA–MTOUSA,* pp. 380–81.

[46] International Div, Lend-Lease as of September 30, 1945, II, 1212–14, MS copy in OCMH; *Logistical History of NATOUSA–MTOUSA,* pp. 379–81.

CHAPTER XVII

Agencies Handling Rearmament

The various wheels of the machinery set up to initiate, implement, and supervise the rearming and training of the French North African forces have been introduced in the preceding chapters. The justification for the creation of the JRC, JAC, SCAMA, Stock Control Section, and French Training Section, the directives responsible for their establishment, the functions assigned to each, their successes or failures — all these matters have been related at some length as they arose. It remains to outline briefly the composition and internal organization of these agencies, their respective position in the theater staff structure, their operational practices, the tools at their disposal as well as those which they forged.

The Joint Rearmament Committee

Composition and Position in the Theater Staff Structure

When, in early December 1942, creation of an agency to supervise the rearmament of the French North African forces was first envisaged, the most directly concerned AFHQ staff sections—namely, the G–4 and Liaison Sections—made the following recommendations. T h e contemplated agency should be established as a special staff section of AFHQ; it should be composed of American representatives from G–1, G–3, G–4, the Air and Naval Sections of AFHQ, and of representatives from the French General Staff; finally, its functions should be so set forth as to require it to refer matters of policy to the Chief of Staff, AFHQ, for instructions, and other matters to the particular staff sections concerned for both discussion and action.[1]

These and other recommendations were embodied in AFHQ Staff Memorandum 52, issued on 16 December 1942, instituting officially the Joint Rearmament Committee. The memorandum set forth in detail the responsibilities and functions of the new agency. In addition it made the JRC directly responsible to the Chief of Staff, AFHQ. This arrangement was of fundamental importance to the committee for it determined the nature of its internal organization, of its activities, and of its dealings with other agencies.[2]

That the committee had not been placed under the control of Liaison Section, the agency previously set up to serve as an intermediary between AFHQ and the French, is not surprising. The technical nature as well as the scope of the assignment required the establishment of a separate agency with a permanent membership responsible for its

[1] Memo, Col Julius C. Holmes for CofS AFHQ, 5 Dec 42, JRC 320/001 Orgn of JRC; Memo, Holmes for CofS AFHQ, 11 Dec 42, AFHQ 0100/12C G–3 Div Ops Fr Equip.

[2] AFHQ Staff Memo 52, 16 Dec 42, AFHQ 0100/12 G–3 Div Ops Fr Equip; see p. 25, above.

own internal organization. As such, it fell definitely into the special staff category.[3]

The JRC having no power of decision, its authority was limited. It managed, however, to circumvent this intrinsic handicap by establishing personal friendly relations with outside officials and agencies most interested in its activities such as the deputy chief of staff, G–3, G–4, Ordnance, and other technical and administrative services, both American and British.[4]

The eight original appointees to the committee assembled for their first meeting on 23 December 1942 at the Hotel St. Georges in Algiers. The four U.S. members and the AFHQ sections they represented were Col. William Tudor Gardiner (G–3 and Air), Col. John Morrow (G–4), Capt. Jerauld Wright (Naval Staff), and Maj. George L. Artamonoff (Ordnance). The four French delegates were Maj. Jean Morel (Army), Capt. Fernand Rébillon (Air), Capt. Roland de Beaumont (Army), and Lt. Comdr. R. Poincelet (Navy).[5]

In accordance with the 16 December memorandum, the senior officer representing AFHQ, in this case Colonel Gardiner, took over the chairmanship of the committee. The posts of vice chairman, executive secretary, and vice secretary went to Major Morel, Major Artamonoff, and Captain de Beaumont, respectively, thus giving the appearance of a truly "joint" (in the sense of inter-Allied) agency.

Of the four U.S. members, two, Colonel Gardiner and Major Artamonoff, were destined to play a major role in the subsequent activities of the committee. Colonel Gardiner, a pilot on loan from the Air Forces, was highly qualified for his new assignment. His experience with military matters accrued from two years' service in World War I, during which he had served as interpreter because of his excellent knowledge of French. During the years 1929 to 1933, he had been governor of the State of Maine. He was to remain with the committee as chairman until 2 June 1943.[6] Major Artamonoff, also a veteran of World War I, served first as executive secretary, later as chairman, replacing Colonel Gardiner. His fluency in the French language and an excellent background in organization and supply problems qualified him admirably for the discharge of his important functions.[7]

Membership in the JRC varied from time to time. Already by mid-February 1943 there had been a number of changes. Colonel Morrow had been replaced by Lt. Col. Douglas N. Lawley. Comdr. André Stourm of the French Navy had replaced Commander Poincelet, who had been transferred to other duties. Earlier, in late December, the advisability of appointing to the committee a British ordnance representative had been given serious consid-

[3] Memo, R. G. Lewis for Director of Ordnance Svs (Br), 22 Dec 42, JRC 320/001 Orgn of JRC; Gen Crane and Col William S. Biddle, discussion of CofS Mtg, 24 Dec 42, JRC 320/001 Orgn of JRC; Memo, Gen Rooks for Col Gardiner, 30 Dec 42, AFHQ 0100/12C G–3 Div Ops, Ser 623.

[4] Notes from Col Artamonoff, Dec 51; Interv with Gen Loomis, Jun 50.

[5] Min, JRC Conf, 23 Dec 42, JRC 320/001 Orgn of JRC; AFHQ SO 86, 26 Dec 42, copy in Gardiner's private files.

[6] For his contribution to the success of the North African rearmament operations, the French awarded him, in July 1943, the Order of the Legion of Honor (Chevalier), a singularly fine gesture toward the United States considering that, a few months earlier, the American Army had awarded him the Silver Star for meritorious service in the course of the 8–10 November 1942 operations against the opposing French forces.

[7] Order of the Legion of Honor (Chevalier) and Croix de Guerre (with Palm and Gold Star), June 1945.

MEMBERS OF THE JOINT REARMAMENT COMMITTEE, *Algiers, April 1943. Left to right: Maj. Jean Morel, Col. Clément Blanc, Capt. Roland de Beaumont, partially visible behind Col. William Tudor Gardiner, Lt. Col. George L. Artamonoff, Capt. François Rébillon, Capt. Jerauld Wright, Comdr. André Stourm. The officer behind Captain Rébillon is not identified.*

eration, since French troops then fighting in Tunisia were receiving equipment from British as well as U.S. sources. However, after the Casablanca Conference in January 1943, when it became clear that the rearmament of the French Ground Forces was to be a wholly American commitment, the presence of a British Army representative hardly seemed necessary. It became even less so as time went on for, with the fusion of the de Gaulle and Giraud forces in late July 1943, the two British-equipped divisions (the 1st and 2d DFL) were re-equipped with American matériel. The Royal Navy, on the other hand, had been represented on the committee since January by Capt. Geoffrey Barnard. In practice, neither he nor the U.S. naval representative was a full-time member. They were called in only when naval matters had to be discussed and acted upon. For all practical purposes, therefore, the JRC could be regarded as a Franco-American committee with only occasional British participation.

The position of the JRC in the theater staff structure was altered three times. The first change, which occurred on 5 June 1943, was brought about by a number of important considerations. With the battle of Tunisia ended and the considerable amount of equipment brought over on the April convoy sorted out and distributed, the various Allied agencies responsible for rearming the French were turning their attention to the task of developing the North African Army into an efficient fighting force. As it was anticipated that AFHQ would some day move from northwest Africa, leaving the rearmament operations the exclusive responsibility of NATOUSA, it appeared necessary to review the relationship of these two agencies with the French. Liaison Section, AFHQ–NATOUSA, voiced the opinion that the time was opportune for centralizing under a single authority the handling of all French problems arising both within the lines of communications and in the forward zone. Its chief, Col. Julius C. Holmes, recommended that a special French section be set up within Liaison Section to handle, for both AFHQ and NATOUSA, all policy, organizational, and technical questions concerning the French armed forces, including rearmament. On the assumption (an erroneous one, as demonstrated by later developments) that the work of the JRC was becoming "more and more a routine G–4 problem," Colonel Holmes further recommended that the committee be consolidated, at least for the present, into this proposed French section.[8] Only part of his proposals was accepted; no separate section was constituted, but, on 5 June 1943, the JRC passed under the control of Liaison Section.[9]

Concurrently with the transfer of JRC

from the control of the Chief of Staff, AFHQ, to that of Liaison Section, Colonel Gardiner was replaced by Lt. Col. George L. Artamonoff as chairman.[10] A few weeks later, on 19 July, General Spalding, who had recently arrived in the theater to undertake a survey of the French supply situation, was appointed both chief of Liaison Section and chairman of the JRC, with Colonel Artamonoff reverting to the post of executive secretary of the committee.[11]

JRC's position in the staff structure underwent a second change in August 1943. By that time supervision by Liaison Section had proved inadequate. The various tasks performed by the committee had turned out, after all, to be more than G–4 routine work. The technical aspects of the problems involved were unfamiliar to the members of Liaison Section who, in addition, were too busy with matters of their own. Considering, furthermore, that the rearmament of the French had become an almost exclusive American responsibility, it appeared logical to transfer the committee to the jurisdiction of NATOUSA. Action to this effect was taken on 7 August 1943.[12] JRC was made responsible to the Deputy Theater Commander, NATOUSA, then General Hughes.

The added responsibility which the JRC began assuming with respect to the training and supply of the French expeditionary forces quickly brought about changes as well as increases in personnel. Chairmanship changed hands once again when General Loomis replaced General Spalding on 10 October. As of 15 October, member-

---

[8] Memo, Holmes for CofS AFHQ, 24 May 43, JRC 320/001 Orgn of JRC.

[9] AFHQ Staff Memo 45, 5 Jun 43, in same file.

[10] Colonel Gardiner was recalled to duty with the Air Forces.

[11] AFHQ GO 42, 19 Jul 43, in same file.

[12] NATOUSA Staff Memo 74, 7 Aug 43, in same file.

ship of the committee was approximately as follows:

JOINT REARMAMENT COMMITTEE

(Asterisk denotes officers who remained with the JRC until the end of rearmament operations in North Africa)

Chairman: Brig. Gen. Harold F. Loomis*
Executive Officer: Lt. Col. George L. Artamonoff (1)

Policy Section

U.S. Army member: Col. Ira A. Crump* (2)
U.S. Air member: Brig. Gen. Gordon P. Saville (3)
U.S. Navy member: Capt. Francis P. Old (4)
Royal Navy member: Capt. Geoffrey Barnard (5)

Executive Section
(all U.S. officers)

Lt. Col. John C. Knox* (representing FTS), Training
Maj. E. S. De Long,* Quartermaster and Medical
Maj. Conrad L. Christensen,* Ordnance, Engineer, and Chemical Warfare Service
Maj. J. R. Qualls, Ordnance
Lt. John L. Dexter,* Engineer and Ordnance
Lt. Atlas L. Cheek, Jr.,* Statistics
Lt. John W. Buckley,* Training
Lt. John S. Edmonston,* Engineer
Lt. Gordon H. Buter,* Office Administration
Maj. John W. Ames,* Liaison with French for Air
Lt. (jg) J. Lodge, Liaison with French for Navy

French Section

Chief: Col. Jean Regnault*
Army member: Capt. Roland de Beaumont (6)
Air member: Maj. Gilbert Mondin
Naval member: Comdr. André Stourm*
Two interpreters

(1) Left the committee on 5 November 1943. Shortly after, he was transferred to the U.S. Fifth Army in Italy where he took over the command of

the 53d Ordnance Group which included one French ordnance battalion supporting the CEF.
(2) Replaced Colonel Artamonoff as executive officer on 5 November 1943.
(3) Also chairman of the Joint Air Commission. See pp. 203, above, 285–86, below.
(4) Replaced Captain Wright on 7 October 1943. Was replaced by Capt. D. D. Dupre, USN, in June 1944.
(5) Replaced by Capt. M. B. Laing, RN, in January 1944.
(6) Left for Italy on 1 January 1944.

NOTE.—Other officers were subsequently assigned to the committee. Among the French members so assigned, three (Maj. Plat, Lt. René Lehman and Lt. Guy de Biran) remained to the end of the JRC's existence.

The committee had now under its jurisdiction both the French Training Section since the end of August and Stock Control Section since the beginning of October. It had become a sizable organization with a total strength of approximately 600 officers and men.

The third and last change in the committee's position in the staff structure came about in February 1944. (*Charts 2 and 3*) Simultaneously with the command reorganization then effected in the theater, the JRC was transferred from the jurisdiction of the Deputy Theater Commander, NATOUSA, an office which had just been abolished, to that of the Commanding General, NATOUSA, now General Devers.[13]

In July, with the arrival in North Africa of the first elements of the Brazilian Expeditionary Force, NATOUSA directed the JRC to provide assistance in the training of these troops before their departure for Italy. The committee set up a Brazilian Training Section similar to the section organized for the French and placed it under the command of Lt. Col. Robert J. Shaw, himself

[13] History of Allied Force Headquarters and Headquarters NATOUSA: Part Three, December 1943–July 1944, Sec. 1, pp. 697–99, copy in OCMH.

BRIG. GEN. HAROLD F. LOOMIS, *center, and two of his associates of the JRC, Brig. Gen. Allen F. Kingman, left, chief of French Training Section, and Brig. Gen. Jean Regnault (then a Colonel), chief of French Section.*

an officer from French Training Section who had served more than a year with the 3d DIA as its senior instructor. Such was the extent of the responsibility assumed by the JRC with regard to the Brazilian Expeditionary Force.[14]

At the end of the same month, with the departure, of NATOUSA headquarters from North Africa and the gradual closing down of U.S. installations, the chairman of the JRC, General Loomis, was designated representative of the theater commander in the Algiers area, as well as Commanding General, Headquarters, North African District, the successor to NATOUSA. As this

meant a broadening of the committee's responsibilities and functions, these were redefined by Headquarters, NATOUSA, on 14 August.[15]

Meanwhile, a field echelon of the committee (JRC Advance) had gone to Italy to assist in the last-minute preparations of the French units designated for ANVIL and to keep the committee informed of the latest developments in this connection.

After the launching of ANVIL on 15 August 1944, the JRC continued to operate but its strength gradually decreased as its various activities diminished in importance.

In late August, with Paris and a large part of France liberated, the French proposed and Allied authorities agreed that an agency to supervise the rearmament of the Metropolitan forces should be set up in the French capital. By agreement between Generals Eisenhower and Devers, it was decided to use for the purpose selected members of the personnel heretofore assigned to the JRC. On 9 September orders were issued directing the transfer to Supreme Headquarters, Allied Expeditionary Force, of General Loomis and four or five officers of his choosing, requests for the remaining personnel to be made after General Loomis had reached Paris. Leaving a rear echelon in North Africa, General Loomis and his party arrived at SHAEF on 3 October and were assigned for duty with Rearmament Division, SHAEF Mission to France, the successor to the JRC on the Continent.[16]

With some of its members now in Italy

---

[14] Interv with Loomis, Sep 51.

[15] Headquarters, NATOUSA, AFHQ, and other Allied Headquarters moved to Caserta, Italy, on 20 July 1944. Ltr AG–370.5 A–0, Hq NATOUSA, 7 Jul 44, and Memo, NATOUSA for CG SOS NATOUSA, 28 Jul 44, and Staff Memo 32, Hq NATOUSA, 14 Aug 44, JRC 320/001 Orgn of JRC.

[16] Msg 12547, Loomis to JRC, 5 Oct 44, in same file.

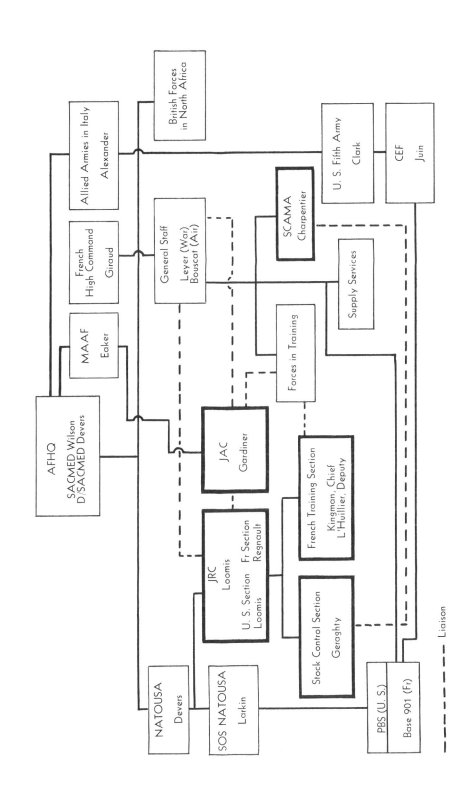

CHART 3—INTERNAL ORGANIZATION OF THE JOINT REARMAMENT COMMITTEE: 1 APRIL 1944

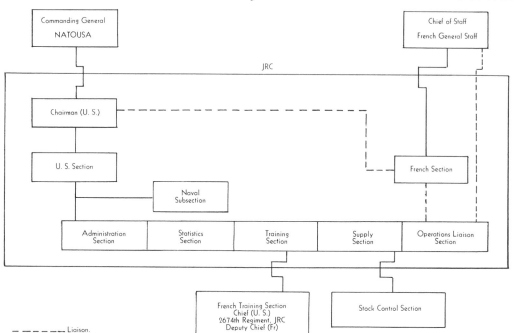

or France as part of JRC Advance and some transferred to other duties, the JRC had, by this time, been reduced to a skeleton organization. The responsibility for the remaining rearmament activities having been assigned, on 10 October, to Headquarters, Communications Zone, NATOUSA, JRC Rear was officially disbanded on 1 November, although it continued to operate one week longer.[17]

French Participation

All available organizational charts give an erroneous impression that the French enjoyed equal representation on the JRC.

They did not, either in authority or in numbers.

That the French representatives were never considered as copartners in the fullest sense of the term is not surprising. Their position reflected the fact that the North African army was not integrated with the Anglo-American military establishment. Having neither the right to cast a vote nor the power to exercise control over U.S. or British personnel, French representatives could act only as liaison officers. In addition, it seems certain that, had equal participation been originally possible, it would have been ruled out as inopportune on the ground that the French were customers for, not producers of, war matériel. For this reason possibly more than any other, American supremacy in the committee was firmly established from the

[17] Hq NATOUSA, GO 104, 11 Oct 44, in same file; Memo, Capt Graham for Loomis, 14 Nov 44, SHAEF Mission to France, Rearmt Div 320-1 Orgn and Function of Rearmt Div.

outset with the provision of the 16 December 1942 directive that the senior U.S. member of the committee was to be the chairman.

Surprisingly, the French military authorities themselves did not seem eager to obtain equal participation in the JRC, at least during the first year of its existence. Possibly that was because, discounting the value of the JRC, they were content that their representatives should remain without real authority. General Giraud, it will be recalled, had banked heavily on the Béthouart Military Mission, which he had dispatched to the United States in late December 1942. In the apparent belief that the mission would adequately represent him in Washington, the fountain of all supply, and from there expedite the flow of rearmament matériel, he had tended to attach little importance to negotiations at theater level. It was his opinion, not an unreasonable one considering the limitations placed on the JRC, that it was little more than a liaison agency. In detailing officers to represent him on the committee, he expected them simply to interpret for the benefit of the American and French commands the views of each regarding rearmament matters. It must be noted here in passing that the Military Mission in Washington established and subsequently maintained close relations with the French members of the JRC, through the channel of the Rearmament and Technical Studies Section of the French General Staff.

Unequal representation on the JRC was made more apparent by the fact that the French members were, particularly during the first eight months, of a rank not commensurate with their responsibilities and duties and inferior to that of their American colleagues. Possibly because of their aloofness toward the committee, French authorities were content to let the situation continue for some time, any change being made difficult by the fact that promotions were more or less frozen. In spite of their lower status, however, at no time did the French members feel subjected to undue inconvenience and embarrassment except possibly in their dealings with other Allied agencies. Within the committee, they were treated on the basis of function, not of rank. The feeling of inferiority which they suffered occasionally was due solely to the limited authority vested in them by their own superiors.[18]

The French Section remained small largely because qualified men were hard to find. The demands for officers with linguistic skill and technical knowledge were so pressing from the field and from the services that the section never had a chance to expand. Even such officers as were appointed from time to time were subject to instant recall for duty elsewhere.

Their American colleagues have spoken highly of Major Morel and Captain de Beaumont, emphasizing that, in the early period of the rearmament operations, these two officers were among the few Frenchmen who appeared to understand thoroughly the problems involved. Before the North African landings, Major Morel had gained considerable ordnance experience by serving as assistant to General R. Poupinel then in charge of matériel; in particular he had played an important part in the French efforts to hide equipment from the Axis. Although technically he ceased to be a member of the committee in August 1943, he

[18] Intervs with de Beaumont, Jul 50, Artamonoff, Dec 49, Gardiner, Apr 50, and Loomis, Sep 51; Notes from Gardiner.

continued to handle rearmament problems at G–4, French Headquarters.

Before his appointment to the JRC, Captain de Beaumont had been called to Algiers on 20 November 1942 by General Leyer to serve as assistant in charge of rearmament. Considering that he remained at JRC's headquarters, whereas his colleague Morel operated largely from G–4, French Headquarters, it can be said of Captain de Beaumont that he assumed the greater part of the burden of representing the French High Command at JRC, a task which he appears to have filled with complete satisfaction. He was relieved of this responsibility at the time of the appointment of his successor in August 1943, but he continued to serve on the committee in a different capacity until January 1944 when, at his request, he was transferred to active service with the CEF in Italy.

The work of both Major Morel and Captain de Beaumont was immensely facilitated by the cordial relations established early between the JRC and members of the French General Staff, Col. Clément Blanc in particular. The latter, then serving as both G–1 and G–4, although not a member *de jure* of the committee, kept in constant touch with it. His frequent ex officio presence at JRC meetings, which he attended at the invitation of the American members, and his informal, almost daily contacts with the various members of the committee, made it possible for much constructive action to be taken which otherwise would have been delayed because of the lack of authority vested in the French members. At one time a classmate of General Loomis at the Ecole de Guerre, Colonel Blanc was highly esteemed by American rearmament officers who regarded him as the top French authority in the field of equipment and training. He

was promoted to the rank of brigadier general in April 1944. By then his superior, General Leyer, Chief of General Staff, had delegated much of his authority to him in dealing with Allied staffs.

The arrangement by which the chairman of the JRC or his representative directly approached Colonel Blanc or General Leyer worked admirably. It was maintained even after the CFLN vainly attempted to vest in the Commissioner of War the responsibility for handling rearmament problems. Both General Leyer and Colonel Blanc continued to work closely with the JRC to the very end of the North African rearmament operations. Another French official, Mr. Jean Monnet, contributed much to the good relations between the French and the JRC. The MAB, it will be recalled, had arranged for his dispatch from Washington to North Africa in early 1943 to assist General Giraud on financial and armament matters.

By the summer of 1943 the French military authorities had come to recognize in the JRC the only effective machinery through which their demands could be met. Feeling the need for more substantial representation on the committee, they appointed on 13 August a higher-ranking officer, Col. Jean Regnault, to the post of chief of the French Section, held until then by Major Morel.

Colonel Regnault's appointment proved to be a most fortunate one. A combat officer who, a few months before, was leading an infantry regiment in Tunisia, he had had no prior training in armament matters. Yet, thanks to his qualities of adaptability and open-mindedness, his thoroughness in handling technical details, an excellent knowledge of English, and a genuine friendship for Americans, he soon succeeded in strengthening further the co-operation between the French and American elements of the JRC, and between the latter and the French General Staff.[19]

It must be noted that the amount of authority vested in Colonel Regnault other than the power which his rank carried did not exceed that enjoyed by his predecessors. Officers of the French High Command continued to feel that, as long as the aim and scope of the rearmament program were still to be determined, they alone could effectively deal with such matters. Meanwhile, the American position with respect to French participation in the committee remained unchanged.

Together with the French officers subsequently appointed to assist him, such as Lt. René Lehman who displayed an especially keen understanding of rearmament problems, Colonel Regnault carried out the duties assigned to the French Section with the utmost efficiency. He remained with the JRC until its disbandment in September 1944. He was then transferred to Paris to occupy a similar post in the newly created Rearmament Division of SHAEF Mission to France.[20]

Internal Organization

From the moment it was activated, the JRC was left free to develop its own structure.[21] During the initial phase, little internal organization was needed. The committee was then devoting its entire attention to the emergency provision of equipment to the units engaged in Tunisia. Not that the 16 December directive establishing the com-

mittee restricted the latter's functions to such duty. On the contrary, the directive specifically empowered the JRC, in addition, to develop an over-all rearmament program. The French members had brought with them such a program based on the Mast Plan. Their American colleagues, however, had come with "no plan at all, merely an idea of rearmament."[22] In the absence of clear instructions from AFHQ as to what a program should consist of and as to how far the Allied command was prepared to go, the U.S. members strongly felt that the committee's most immediate task was to assist the units in Tunisia in getting the equipment they needed so urgently. They maintained this position even after the Casablanca Conference, pending the receipt of definite instructions regarding the long-range program. During this entire stopgap period the members worked as a group, each specializing in one particular field and the executive secretary keeping the necessary records and statistics.

It was when the French submitted their first requisitions, in the spring of 1943, that the question of the division of responsibility arose which soon led to a functional organization of the committee. The requisitions, before being transmitted to the responsible AFHQ staff sections, required considerable processing and redrafting, for the French, unfamiliar with the U.S. classification system and tables of organization and equipment, or with technical nomenclature in English, were submitting them according to their own classification system and in their own language. To present these requests in proper form, the JRC obtained the assignment of several assistants qualified in armament matters. The requests were screened

[19] Interv with Loomis, Sep 51.

[20] Just before his transfer to Paris, Colonel Regnault was awarded the Legion of Merit with the rank of Officer.

[21] Memo for Rcd, JRC, 27 Dec 42, JRC 320/001 Orgn of JRC.

[22] Intervs with Artamonoff, Dec 49, and Gardiner, Apr 50.

and broken down according to service and type of item, then translated into English.

As the scope of its activities increased, the JRC secured other assistants whose duty it became to disseminate technical information to the French, supervise the delivery to them of equipment, and establish liaison with the several AFHQ staff sections involved in the rearmament operations.

Soon the JRC began grouping these assistants into sections. The Statistics Section collected and assimilated information on the amount of matériel furnished. The Administration Section handled reports and correspondence passing through the U.S. members of the committee. The Operations Liaison Section controlled all liaison matters with the French.

The successive transfers of the JRC, first to the control of Liaison Section, AFHQ, in June 1943 and later to that of NATOUSA in August of the same year, brought no substantial changes in internal organization. In the fall of 1943, however, as the committee became involved with the supply, maintenance, and training of the first expeditionary units about to depart for combat overseas, the number of sections had to be increased. The Supply Section was created to handle technical matters pertaining to all services and to act as liaison with the Stock Control Section when the latter passed under the control of the committee. Similarly, when the JRC extended its jurisdiction over the French Training Section, a special Training Section was set up to act as intermediary.

By February 1944, the beginning of the fourth and last phase of the North African rearmament program, the Joint Rearmament Committee had reached its full growth. Its internal organization, established piecemeal as conditions had war-

ranted, was now completed. It must be noted that, with the creation of the Joint Air Commission in September 1943, the committee was no longer concerned with air matters except in the case of items of equipment common to both air and ground forces. It was, on the other hand, still handling a number of problems arising in connection with the rehabilitation of the French Navy. The three naval representatives were responsible for initiating plans for miscellaneous projects, and for screening requests for new ships, major overhaul of ships, and increases in armament. Other naval matters were handled through other theater channels.

Operating Procedures

In order to achieve maximum efficiency and to keep abreast of the changing situation, JRC, from the outset, adopted flexible methods of work. Most of the business at hand was handled through individual action, and only a few formal plenary meetings were held.

During the stopgap period, no system existed that would provide the committee with accurate information on what equipment the French needed most and on what could be made available to them from Allied sources. For lack of such a system, the committee as a whole agreed that individual members should, whenever possible, go after this information, using their own devices and means.

A few isolated examples, gleaned at random, are given of this individual effort to "go and get things done." Early in January 1943, two members, Major Artamonoff and Captain de Beaumont, visited the units engaged on the Tunisian front to determine for themselves what items of equipment were most urgently needed. Meanwhile, the chairman discussed with U.S., British, and French officials the possible emergency release of equipment. During the winter months, various members toured Allied agencies and establishments throughout northwest Africa with a view to locating matériel likely to be of use to the French. Some of these trips were made by air, the necessary aircraft being borrowed for the purpose from American or even French sources.

In April, when arrangements were being made with Colonel Suttles for the setting up of the vehicle assembly line at Algiers, the chairman again borrowed an airplane from the Northwest African Troop Carrier Command and flew to Rabat to pick up an advance party of twenty mechanics from the U.S. 2d Armored Division for employment on the new project.[23]

Later, after the fall of Tunis in May, the chairman rushed to Tunisia to survey the availability of captured enemy equipment. The venture, incidentally, proved unprofitable, for what little matériel the Germans had not destroyed the theater planned to distribute not only to the French but to other Allied forces as well. It was also through individual action that the necessary technical troops were gradually secured and assigned for duty with the JRC. When he learned of a surplus of French-speaking G–2 officers at General Patton's headquarters in Casablanca, Colonel Gardiner immediately approached the responsible authorities and obtained the assignment of two.[24]

After the cessation of hostilities in Tunisia, the committee faced a multitude

of new problems arising from the implementation of the long-range rearmament program. It was then that Colonel Artamonoff conducted a survey of French ordnance units to determine how they were handling their newly acquired equipment. Without such information no sound rehabilitation program could be pursued. Later, in August, when the French Training Section passed under the operational control of the committee, its chief, General Kingman, undertook at JRC's request to inspect certain units and report on the completeness of their equipment and training. Thus the committee was able to inform with accuracy both French and Allied commands on the state of readiness and the degree of efficiency of these units.

Again, when in the late summer of 1943 it became obvious that the French supply system was totally inadequate, the JRC instructed a special party headed by Colonel Geraghty to make a thorough investigation of the situation. Colonel Geraghty's report, it will be remembered, led to the establishment of Stock Control Section, the agency which so successfully assisted the French in overhauling their supply system.

Although the committee was not empowered to make decisions affecting policy, its members, especially the chairman and the executive secretary, frequently participated in conferences, some called at their own initiative, with representatives from the policy-making echelons. It was at such a conference held at the end of March 1943 in the office of the Deputy Theater Commander, NATOUSA, that the chairman discussed with General Clark the advisability of bringing the Fifth Army into the rearmament picture, as well as the procedure to be followed in case this was done. Conferences were also held with staff sections or indi-

---

[23] Statement in Notes on Fr Rearmt by Gardiner, 10 Apr 50, copy in OCMH files.
[24] *Ibid.*

viduals of the French High Command. On 31 March Colonel Artamonoff discussed with General Leyer and Colonel Blanc plans for the forthcoming reception of the first large-scale shipment. Two days earlier Colonel Gardiner, together with other Allied officials including Brig. Gen. William F. Tompkins from Operations Division, had examined the problem with General Giraud, General Leyer, and Mr. Monnet. Meetings with the French were for the most part informal and, as already stated, held as often as necessary.[25]

To deal effectively with the more technical problems, the JRC frequently borrowed civilian and military experts from other headquarters. One of the first experts to be called in was Lt. Col. Howard J. Lowry. Because of his thorough knowledge of enemy equipment, he was assigned to the JRC from May to October 1943 for the purpose of handling the various problems connected with the transfer of such equipment to the French.[26] Civilian technicians on loan from American industrial plants gave the JRC the benefit of their firsthand knowledge of U.S. equipment. They conducted inspections of French base shops and maintenance and combat units, and reported to the JRC the degree of technical efficiency of these units. In addition, they organized classes for the benefit of French personnel in which they taught the correct use and maintenance of American equipment, especially vehicles. Among the civilian technical observers called upon to assist the JRC were William E. Burnett and Charles F.

Dye, Jr., representing respectively the Cadillac Motor Car and the Fisher Tank Divisions of General Motors, and Thomas A. Demetry of the Chrysler Tank Corporation.[27]

A word should be said about the reports issued by the JRC. When the initial allocations of matériel arrived in North Africa at the end of January 1943, AFHQ directed the JRC to maintain an up-to-date schedule showing how the French authorities were assigning the items received and how they intended to make future assignments.[28] The committee then began issuing a semimonthly report to keep the Chief of Staff, AFHQ, informed of the quantity of matériel turned over to the French in response to emergency and training requirements. Simultaneously the JRC issued a weekly record of its day-to-day activities. With the arrival of the first large-scale convoy in April, the semimonthly report was replaced by a progress report designed especially to give accurate information regarding the distribution of equipment among units. This information was obtained largely through personal contact with the French General Staff, through visits to units by either regular JRC members or temporarily attached personnel, and through the exchange of communications between the JRC and Colonel Blanc. It included valuable data on the equipment status of units, reasons for delaying their rearmament, changes in tables of organization and equipment as effected by the French, exact tonnage of equipment arriving on the various convoys, and so forth. Copies of the progress report were sent to the responsible AFHQ staff sections including the chief of staff himself,

[25] Memo, Hughes for Clark, 26 Mar 43, AFHQ 0100/12C G–3 Div Ops Fr Rearmt; Memo, Artamonoff for CofS SOS NATOUSA, 1 Apr 43, JRC 902/II Rearmt Plan; Weekly Rpt No. 1, JRC, 27 Mar 43, AFHQ 0100/26 Liaison Sec 319.1/1 (Fr–B) Ser 93.

[26] SO 99, Hq NATOUSA, 15 May 43, JRC 210.3 Assignment and Transfer of Officers.

[27] JRC 353/001 Training Rpts, Tech Observers.

[28] AFHQ Ltr AG 400/322 A. M., 31 Jan 43, AFHQ 0100/12C G–3 Div Ops Fr Rearmt.

NATOUSA headquarters, American and British Ordnance Sections, the U.S. Fifth Army, and the lend-lease representatives in the theater. The last of such reports was issued in September 1943.

There is no question of attributing to the JRC the entire credit for the success of the rehabilitation of the French North African forces. The role played by other Allied agencies cannot be minimized, nor can the impressive achievements on the part of the French themselves in setting up an armament machinery of their own be underestimated. In addition to establishing SCAMA, the French High Command organized two special staff sections to deal with rearmament problems. The first of these was the Rearmament and Technical Studies Section, headed by Lt. Col. Charles Chanson. This section, with the assistance of 1st and 2d Bureaux (G–1 and G–2) and under the general direction of Colonel Blanc, prepared the over-all rearmament programs and determined the composition of the successive phases, as well as the general plans of distribution of equipment. The other section was the Poste de Statistique, created in March 1943 for the purpose of working out the details for the distribution of U.S. equipment to the units designated for activation in first priority.[29]

Yet there is little doubt that the JRC did represent the driving force which rallied and co-ordinated all individual efforts and guided them to a sound and fruitful accomplishment. It is likely that when they first met in December 1942 the original members of the committee did not grasp the full significance of the undertaking they were embarking upon, or foresee the scope of the

task that lay ahead. Neither could they visualize the ultimate, impressive results of the rearmament operations. From a stopgap committee with no plan but only an idea, the JRC, in spite of its limitations, had become in early 1944 a real power extending its arm into many fields of endeavor. Together with the other related rearmament agencies, it had built up an efficient and indispensable machinery ready to undertake and, as later events amply proved, quite able to effect the final forging of the North African forces. Both the French and the Americans would long be grateful to the JRC for the major role it had played in making it possible for these forces to assume their rightful share of the struggle against the common foe and, incidentally, in strengthening Franco-American friendship. They would also, in the fall of 1944, draw from the record of its experience valuable lessons on which to base their plans for the second chapter, then opening, in the rehabilitation of the French forces in World War II: the rearmament of the Metropolitan forces.

The Joint Air Commission

Shortly after he was appointed Air member of the Joint Rearmament Committee on 24 August 1943, General Saville, Chief of Staff, Mediterranean Air Command, came to recognize two important points. First, the establishment of a separate committee to handle French air matters independently of the JRC must be expedited. Such a committee, in fact, was already in process of organization.[30] Second, sufficient authority must be vested in the air committee to enable it to function from the start with the maximum efficiency. To ensure that

---

[29] Marey, "Le Réarmement français en Afrique du Nord (1942–1944)," *Revue Politique et Parlementaire* (November, 1947), pp. 139–40.

[30] See p. 202, above.

the agency when established would enjoy such authority, General Eaker, Commanding General, Mediterranean Air Command, decided to make its relationship with his own command the closest possible one. Consequently, he delegated his chief of staff, General Saville, to represent Mediterranean Air Command on the Joint Air Commission when the latter was officially established on 6 September 1943.[31]   No better kinship between the two organizations could have been devised.   The assignment of a key staff officer to a staff section would, as later events amply proved, make for efficiency and speed in the carrying out of important business.

JAC's position in the staff structure remained unchanged throughout the commission's existence.   When, in mid-January 1944, Mediterranean Air Command and Northwest African Air Forces were jointly replaced by Mediterranean Allied Air Forces, the JAC merely passed under the control of the latter.

The orders establishing the JAC had stipulated that it was to be composed of three air officers: one American, as chairman, one British, and one French.   Initially, the three members were General Saville, chairman, Col. André Hartemann, representing the French Air Force, and Group Capt. J. Rock de Besombes, representing the Royal Air Force.   The French and British membership remained unchanged throughout the commission's existence.   G e n e r a l Saville left the JAC on 3 January 1944, to assume the command of XII Tactical Air Command, and turned the chairmanship over to Brig. Gen. Patrick W. Timberlake who incidentally had already succeeded him as Chief of Staff, Mediterranean Air Com-

mand, three months earlier.   General Timberlake remained on the commission only one month, until 9 February when he was replaced by Colonel Gardiner.[32]   After two requests for Colonel Gardiner's services with G–5, SHAEF, in London, Generals Eaker and Devers consented in mid-April 1944 to relieve him but only after he had indoctrinated Colonel Ervin, who had come from the United Kingdom with General Eaker and was to become the fourth and last chairman of the JAC.   Colonel Ervin officially replaced Colonel Gardiner on 4 May 1944 and remained on the commission up to its disbandment in September 1944.[33]

Assisting the JAC was, initially, one secretary whose duty it was to prepare action on the basis of agreements reached by the three members.   The first officer to serve in that capacity was Flight Lt. A. L. W. R. Henry (RAF), himself a staff officer of the Establishment Section of the Mediterranean Air Command.   He was replaced, in November 1943, by Lt. Paul C. Sheeline (U.S.) who remained on the commission to the end of its operations.   For several months it was felt that nothing more than the one-man executive staff was required. When in need of assistance, the chairman merely drew from personnel resources available to Mediterranean Air Command. Thus American and British instructors, liaison officers, and technicians were assigned, from time to time, to the French Air Force.   As JAC's activities increased, especially in the spring of 1944, it was deemed necessary to enlarge the executive staff.   At the time of the dissolution of the commis-

---

[31] GO 9, Hq Mediterranean Air Comd, 6 Sep 43, JRC 360/001 Air Force Rearmt.

[32] Since his departure from the JRC, Colonel Gardiner had been serving as A–2 with the 51st Troop Carrier Wing in Sicily.

[33] Statements in Notes on Rearmt of FAF by Gardiner, 6 Jul 51, copy in OCMH.

sion, the staff had reached a strength of eleven officers and enlisted men, Americans for the most part. Meanwhile the practice of using personnel from MAAF as instructors and technicians had continued.

The wide scope of the activities carried out by the JAC can be best estimated by examining the journal kept by one of the chairmen.[34] In the field of training, they covered such problems as the allocation of training planes, material assistance and visits to training centers, the sending of pilots and mechanics to schools in the United States. In the field of supply, JAC handled such questions as the issue of post exchange items, the issue of the Norden bombsight, the inadequacy of the food ration, at one time reported to be a factor in the high rate of accidents, the supply of equipment to the Naval Air Arm. Among the administrative problems handled by the JAC were the operational assignment of squadrons, the assignment of U.S. liaison officers to FAF units and of French staff officers to Allied air commands, finally, the advisability of making available to the French the air intelligence weekly summaries.[35]

In the course of their meetings which they held at regular intervals, the three members of the commission, having obtained beforehand the views of their respective commands, discussed the plans to be established or the measures to be taken. As each member enjoyed the double advantage of having the full confidence of his two colleagues and sufficient authority from his own superiors, the JAC as a whole could reach decisions promptly and take proper action without having to refer constantly to higher command echelons. In this connection, the American member was in a most enviable position. General Saville, as well as his successor General Timberlake, could, by virtue of the fact that they served in the dual capacity of Chief of Staff, Mediterranean Air Command, and chairman of the JAC, obtain the speedy implementation of the decisions reached by the commission. For them it was merely a matter of "picking up one's hat in one place and putting it down in another." [36] The pattern was somewhat altered with the arrival of Colonel Gardiner. But the latter immediately established the policy, in agreement with Brig. Gen. Charles C. Chauncey, the new Chief of Staff, Mediterranean Allied Air Forces, that the JAC would have authority to make all minor decisions, submitting for approval matters of importance or affecting policy.[37] With the last chairman, Colonel Ervin, who directly represented General Eaker on the commission and therefore enjoyed fuller authority than his predecessor, the original pattern was re-established.

In contrast with his compatriots on the JRC, the French member of the JAC was in a most favorable position. He enjoyed a considerable degree of authority, for General Bouscat, Chief of Staff, FAF, had made him his personal representative on the JAC with full power to speak for him. As a result, his American and British colleagues regarded him as a partner member of equal standing. Yet it would be inaccurate to describe the commission as being entirely tripartite in character, for policy matters remained an exclusive Anglo-American responsibility. When such matters needed

[34] Gardiner, Journal, 9 Feb–4 May 44, in Gardiner's private files.
[35] The British appear to have objected strongly to making these reports available to the French. At the insistence of the Americans, they finally relented.
[36] Interv with Saville, Jul 51.
[37] Statement in Corres from Col Gardiner, 1951.

to be cleared with higher French authorities, they were brought directly to the
attention of General Bouscat who, frequently, was invited to come and present his
views in person before the commission.
The bonds of friendship established early
between him and the members of the JAC
made possible the speedy conclusion of
agreements. The co-operation which the
French Chief of Air Staff extended so willingly proved especially useful in the initial
period. After three days of frank and
thorough discussions regarding the capabilities and needs of the FAF, Generals
Saville and Bouscat came to a complete
understanding as to the goal to be achieved:
"not a lot of squadrons but an efficient air
force." [38] This meeting of minds between
the two Chiefs of Staff, each stating freely
what his respective command was in a position to contribute, got the JAC off to an
excellent start.

Relations between General Bouscat and
General Saville's successors continued on
the same cordial and fruitful plane. By
the time of Colonel Ervin's chairmanship,
collaboration between French air command
and JAC was so firmly established that the
commission could reach most decisions on
Colonel Hartemann's sole recommendations without further reference to General
Bouscat. The several American members
consulted since the war on the matter have
highly commended the manner in which
Colonel Hartemann acquitted himself of
his functions. Likewise they have been
unanimous in their praise of the co-operative
spirit displayed by all responsible French
air authorities. [39] Within the commission
itself, perfect teamwork on the part of men

naturally endowed with widely divergent
national idiosyncrasies and representing
three different air forces resulted in greater
efficiency and prevented dissipation of effort.

Co-operation with the JRC was established from the outset. This was essential
considering the role which the JRC
was expected to play in relation to the
JAC. With the JRC rested the responsibility for ensuring the shipment from the
United States of the air equipment ordered
by the JAC, and for requisitioning all
items common to air and ground forces
requested by the commission. The necessary co-operation was achieved simply by
making the chairman of the JAC the ex
officio air member of the JRC. Co-operation was further strengthened by the fact
that the JRC liaison officer with the French
Air Force, Maj. John W. Ames—who, incidentally, had a desk at General Bouscat's
headquarters—also worked closely with the
JAC.

SCAMA and Stock Control Section

Both SCAMA and Stock Control Section, JRC, worked toward the same goal,
the establishment of a French central supply authority similar to the American SOS.
It is fitting therefore that, after a brief
study of the organization and evolution of
each, an account be given of their common
operating procedures. [40]

Organization of SCAMA

In establishing SCAMA the directive of
15 October 1943 made the agency directly

[38] Interv with Saville, Jul 51.
[39] Intervs with Saville and Ervin, Jul 51; Corres
from Gardiner, 1951.

[40] For the background of their establishment
and an account of their achievements, see pp.
132–38, 174–76, above.

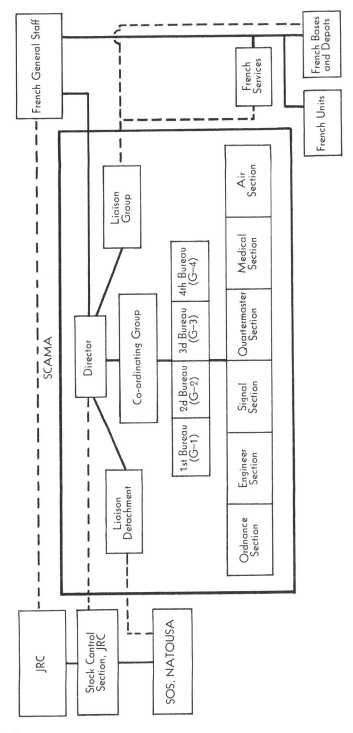

----- Liaison

Source: JRC 400.2/002 Stock Control System (SCAMA) 25 May 44.

responsible to 4e Bureau (G–4) of the French General Staff. In this manner SCAMA was to enjoy a status equal to that of the services. Its high position in the chain of command was expected to enable it to deal authoritatively with other agencies. Such would have been the case had the services extended their full co-operation. As pointed out earlier, it was not until SCAMA's authority had been redefined in stronger terms, especially by the 9 January 1944 directive, that the necessary co-operation was gradually effected.[41]

The 9 January 1944 directive also prescribed the internal organization of SCAMA, although, by a curious contradiction, it empowered the director to set forth its composition, internal co-ordination, and functioning.[42] The director, Col. Emile Charpentier, himself appointed by General Leyer, had no alternative but to follow the pattern established in the directive.

When its organization was completed, SCAMA included a central agency and field echelons. (*Chart 4*) At the head of the entire system was the director, stationed in the headquarters of the central agency set up in Oran in proximity with SOS, NATOUSA. The central agency was composed of a clerical staff, a co-ordinating group, four bureaus whose functions corresponded approximately to those of a general staff in the American Army, and five sections each representing one of the French services, namely, Ordnance, Engineers, Medical, Signal, and Quartermaster. A sixth section was

eventually added to handle air matters. Also considered operationally part of the central agency was the Stock Control Section.

The field echelons comprised the military bases in the ports of embarkation and debarkation, a liaison detachment with SOS, a mobile group for technical liaison with depots and warehouses, and various representatives with the services and the General Staff. Over all of these echelons SCAMA had exclusive authority. In addition its jurisdiction extended, but only insofar as the movement of matériel and supplies and the keeping of records were concerned, to all service establishments.

Thanks to this intricate but necessary organization, SCAMA was able to keep a finger on the pulse of the entire French supply system.

Organization of Stock Control Section

Stock Control Section, JRC, was organized on 5 November 1943 under the command of Colonel Geraghty.[43] As SOS, NATOUSA, had given him no instructions as to what specific duties his section was to fulfill, Colonel Geraghty merely set out to meet problems as they were presented by the French and to "assume responsibilities growing out of these problems as a matter of course."[44]

When he had recruited enough specialists to begin operations, Colonel Geraghty organized them into five branches corresponding to the five sections of SCAMA—

---

[41] See p. 137, above.

[42] Dir 3751–3 EMGG/4, 15 Oct 43; Dir 5499–3 EMGG/4, 25 Nov 43; Dir 340 EMGG/9, 9 Jan 44, JRC 400.2/002 Stock Control Section.

[43] Unless otherwise indicated, this section is based upon Col Michael Geraghty, The History of the Stock Control Section, JRC, copy in JRC Files.

[44] Memo, Geraghty for Larkin, 8 Jul 44, JRC 400.2/002 Stock Control System, SCAMA.

Engineer, Ordnance, Medical, Signal, and Quartermaster. Each branch was then subdivided into four groups—requisition, stock control, technical, and warehousing. Assisting the commanding officer was an executive officer and the Administrative Branch. Close liaison with the JRC was maintained through Colonel Crump, a member of the committee.

Finding sufficient trained personnel constituted one of the major problems facing Colonel Geraghty. During the first four months his section hardly increased in numerical strength because U.S. Army replacement depots could furnish few officers and enlisted men with adequate supply experience. It was not until February 1944, with the arrival from the United States of a substantial number of personnel dispatched at the request of Colonel Geraghty, that the situation began to improve. Eventually the section grew to a strength of some 50 officers and 100 enlisted men.[45]

Another major difficulty confronting the section was its inability, in spite of repeated efforts, to secure official status and to obtain a table of organization. For this reason the officers and men employed by the section were "loaned" from replacement centers and placed on detached service with, or assigned as overstrength to, French Training Section, or more accurately, 2674th Headquarters Company, JRC (Provisional). They were attached to the service company of Mediterranean Base Section for rations and quarters, with the understanding, however, that they were to be employed by Stock Control Section. Lack of official recognition made each administrative detail a major problem for the solution of which various commands had to be approached. The section found it par-

ticularly difficult to obtain the vehicles which it needed to carry out its duties. Thus efficiency and progress were frequently retarded.

The function of the officers and men of each of the five technical branches was to assist their French counterparts in SCAMA by imparting to them their knowledge of supply. This method of placing U.S. personnel side by side with corresponding French personnel proved to be the most advantageous way of giving maximum on-the-spot assistance and advice to the French. In spite of its inherent limitations, Stock Control Section succeeded in reaching its goal. There is little doubt that without its fine performance, the "SCAMA system" might well never have been firmly established.

Stock Control Section ceased to function in late July 1944.

Operating Procedures

SCAMA and Stock Control Section followed three basic principles in carrying out their operations. These principles, which corresponded to three major goals to be reached, were embodied in Colonel Charpentier's operational instruction dated 26 January 1944.[46]

First, and to quote from the instruction, all records maintained by SCAMA were to be based on the actual existence of stocks in warehouses. To apply this principle required that a complete physical inventory be conducted of all matériel and supplies in French hands. As already stated, such an inventory proved impracticable for many months owing especially to lack of sufficient

---

[45] Ibid.

[46] Gen Instruction on Functioning of SCAMA, 26 Jan 44, in Geraghty, History of Stock Control Section, App B, JRC Files.

trained personnel in French establishments. In fact it did not take place until 15 May 1944. Only then did SCAMA have, for the first time, a fairly complete and accurate picture of stocks on hand throughout North Africa.

Second, a "common language" had to be established. The 26 January instruction itself provided a number of definitions for words currently used in French and American services. This was a welcome step, for misunderstandings had frequently resulted from differences in French and American definitions of the same words. In using the term *requisition,* for instance, the French meant a delivery order given to a depot by a qualified authority, or an approved requisition. The Americans, on the other hand, were using it to mean a request submitted by a unit within the limits of its rights of allowances. For this and other similar terms, definitions in simple and clear language were established once and for all. Thus a common technical vocabulary, including such English words as *tally-in, tally-out, bin cards* and French terms such as *gestion, demande de réquisition, réserve d'entretien,* was compiled for compulsory use by all personnel concerned, French as well as American. Much later, in 1944, SCAMA published a complete French-English technical dictionary which was made available throughout the various interested agencies and armies.

Third, information as collected within the SCAMA system was to be given on convenient, thoroughly understood, standard forms for use by all concerned. To achieve this objective, Colonels Geraghty and Charpentier first proceeded to eliminate some of the thirty-odd forms and cards then in use throughout the French services. They finally adopted six standard forms,

three stock cards, and one stock identification tag, or ten in all.

Obviously the common aim of these principles was to achieve standardization. To make it as nearly 100-percent complete as possible, Colonels Geraghty and Charpentier took other steps. They agreed that every article, whether it be a unit containing minor items, an assembly of various parts, or a part detached and considered separately, was to be designated by the American stock number and nomenclature.[47] They also prescribed a method for tagging and identifying U.S. equipment at all echelons and made its application compulsory. Finally, they issued definite instructions illustrated by charts on the procedure for the reception and handling of American matériel from debarkation base to warehouses and on to units in process of re-equipping. Briefly the procedure was as follows. Upon the arrival of the cargo ship, the base commandant checked the French shipment against the ship's manifest, separated the matériel according to service, and forwarded it to the designated place of storage. He then sent a detailed report of this phase of his activities to SCAMA. At the storage plant, boxes and bales were turned over to the services where they were classified and inventoried. The entry of every item into magasins (warehouses) was recorded on a tally-in card. A bin card describing the item, its location, and stock number was then made and filed in the warehouse office, and a bin tag giving the description as well as the English and French name of the item was prepared for identification in the warehouse. A tally-out card was filled after an item had left a warehouse. All officers in charge were warned that periodic inspections by French

---

[47] *Ibid.*

and U.S. officers would be made to determine the accuracy of all information so
recorded.

As a result of the application of these various measures and procedures, SCAMA, in
due time, was placed in a position where it
had an accurate record of (1) arrivals of
equipment at the port, (2) actual receipts
of items in warehouses, (3) actual issues of
items from warehouses, and (4) physical
inventories. Thus could SCAMA fulfill
one of its main missions, that of keeping
the French High Command informed at all
times of the exact status of American matériel available in French hands.

French Training Section

The formal activation of French Training Section as an agency of the U.S. Fifth
Army occurred on 13 May 1943, concurrently with the appointment of General
Kingman as its chief.[48] The section was
the successor to the Rearmament Advisory
Section established earlier in April. Stationed at first at Oudjda, French Morocco,
FTS moved in August to Oran, Algeria,
where General Kingman set up headquarters and remained for the following fourteen
months.[49]

FTS retained close contact with the various agencies which, before its own activation, had taken part in the French training
program, such as G–3 and G–4, AFHQ,
SOS, NATOUSA, and to a limited extent,
the JRC. As these agencies continued to

maintain an interest in certain aspects of
the program, General Kingman reported
frequently to them on the progress of his
own activities. The JRC, however, gradually assumed a more extensive role of co-
ordination and, within a short time, gave
more attention to the activities of the FTS
than the other agencies. General Kingman and the JRC began working in closer
association. They exchanged information
on their day-to-day activities, and together
planned the over-all training program, JRC
often acting as intermediary between FTS
and the French High Command.

Soon after the distribution of the first
substantial allocations of American equipment in May–June 1943, the JRC recognized the need of giving units immediate
instruction in the proper use and maintenance of their newly acquired matériel. As
the official clearinghouse for all rearmament matters, the committee felt that its
own activities and those of FTS must be
integrated to provide maximum assistance.
By August, with the equipment ordered as
part of Phase II then on its way, integration
of JRC and FTS seemed so logical to General Kingman himself that he suggested the
transfer of his section from the control of
Fifth Army to that of NATOUSA, and
recommended that his personnel be made
available for use under the general supervision of the JRC.[50] General Kingman's
proposal was accepted, and on or about 14
August his section passed under the control
of the JRC. Thereafter it was known officially as the French Training Section, JRC.

A few days later, on 25 August 1943, by
NATOUSA order, the personnel of FTS
was organized into the 2674th Headquarters Company, JRC (Provisional). The

[48] This section draws upon the JRC Files: 330/
001 Inspections—Misc, 330/002 Inspections by
Gen Kingman, 330/003 Rpts of FTS, 350/001
Training Rpts of Observers, 350/002 Training Fr
Army Units, 350/003 (Continuation of 350/002);
and SHAEF Mission to France, Rearmt Div Files:
320–1 Orgn and Function, 353–1 Training.
[49] See pp. 231 ff., above.
[50] Ltr, Kingman to Spalding, 9 Aug 43, JRC
353/003 Training Fr Army Personnel.

company, which enjoyed the unique distinction of being commanded by a brigadier
general, was placed under the administrative control of Headquarters, Mediterranean Base Section, and assigned for operational duty with the JRC. Shortly after,
in September, the personnel of Armored
Force Detachment, which had been
brought over in June from the Middle
East to instruct French armored units, was
organized into the 6704th Armored Force
Training Company and placed under the
administrative control first of MBS and in
May 1944 of SOS, NATOUSA. The two
units merged, later in the year, as the 2674th
Regiment, JRC, the administrative unit for
the FTS. By this time, FTS had reached a
strength of some 50 officers and 400 enlisted men. Because of the highly technical
nature of the armored force training program, and the fact that a large number of
armored units were still to be trained, FTS
underwent another change in organization
just before the end of training operations
in North Africa. It was split into the two
original component organizations, namely,
the 2674th Company, JRC, and the 6704th
Armored Force Training Company. In
October 1944 the two components, with a
total strength of 643 officers and men,
moved to Marseille. Soon after, the 2674th
Company, JRC, was disbanded and, on 1
November, the remaining unit was reorganized as the 6834th Training Regiment,
JRC.[51]

The arrangement by which FTS had
been placed under the control of JRC was
not designed to decrease the authority of
the former or to subordinate it in any way

to the JRC, rather to obtain the greatest
co-operation possible between the two
agencies. Although the chairman of the
Joint Rearmament Committee issued orders
to the FTS, these were usually initiated at
the instigation and always with the complete
concurrence of General Kingman. Liaison
was effected by Colonel Knox who served
as the FTS representative on the JRC.
Colonel Knox continued in this capacity
until the end of the North African rearmament operations.[52] Possibly because of the
technical requirements involved and of the
need for continuity in the program, the key
personnel of FTS changed very little. General Kingman and his American and French
assistants carried on this assignment during
almost the entire period.

General Kingman's selection as director
of FTS appears to have been due to his
knowledge of U.S. equipment, especially
armor, his knowledge of the French language and of the French Army, which he
greatly improved while attending the Centre
d'Etude des Chars de Combat at Versailles
in 1923–24, and the fact that as a general
officer he held a rank commensurate with
the functions involved. French officers in-
terviewed since the war have been unanimous in their praise of General Kingman's keen understanding of the training
and material problems then facing the
French Army, and of his ability in developing a sound and effective program.[53]

General Kingman's deputy was Colonel
L'Huillier of the French Army. His official

---

[51] Much later, on 11 January 1945, the regiment,
renamed 6834th Rearmament Regiment, served as
the training organization for the Rearmament Division, SHEAF Mission to France. See pp. 386, 387,
below.

[52] As a vice consul in Algiers, Colonel Knox had
taken an active part in the secret preparations for
the Allied landings of November 1942.

[53] Intervs with L'Huillier, Tiers, Devinck, Regnault. In recognition of General Kingman's work
in training the North African forces, the French
Army awarded him the Order of the Legion of
Honor (Chevalier) in September 1944. See also
p. 388n, below.

title was Chief, French Liaison Section with FTS. Before his appointment to that post on 18 August 1943, he had been assistant to his predecessors, Col. Raoul Bonvalot and later Lt. Col. René Préclaire, each of whom served only a short term. Colonel L'Huillier's main responsibility consisted in effecting the necessary spadework before each inspection conducted by the FTS. Assisting the deputy were several French officers, among them Lt. Claude Tiers, who participated in the activities of FTS from July 1943 to the end of the North African rearmament operations.[54]

The officers whom General Kingman detailed as senior advisers to the divisions contributed greatly to the success of FTS. Not only did their daily presence among the troops help the latter considerably during the training phase, but their gallant conduct under fire, in the case of those who accompanied the divisions to Italy, drew from the French no small degree of admiration. These senior advisers were: 1st DB, Capt. Henry Jacobson, later, Lt. Col. Everett A. Luckenbach; 2d DB, Maj. Robert M. Luminaski; 5th DB, Lt. Col. Robert W. Burke; 1st DMI, Lt. Col. W. C. Parnell (in North Africa only) and Lt. C. S. Campbell (who accompanied the Reconnaisance Regiment in Italy); 2d DIM, Lt. Col. Roy Stephens; 3d DIA, Lt. Col. Robert J. Shaw; 4th DMM, Maj. Archibald W. Green; 9th DIC, Lt. Col. C. H. Cheatham. No advisers were attached to the Moroccan tabors, only teams, none of which, however, accompanied them to Italy.

The success of the program instituted by the FTS, attested to frequently by French and U.S. military authorities both dur-

---

[54] Lieutenant Tiers was awarded the Bronze Star Medal in December 1945.

ing and after World War II, is due largely to the manner in which the section itself was organized and the way it operated. Having sensed that the closest co-operation between his staff and the French must be effected in arranging for the instruction and inspection of units, General Kingman resolved to make of the FTS a mixed French-U.S. organization. Not only did he see to it that the teams sent to inspect units were bipartite in nationality, but, in addition, he requested and obtained the assignment to the section of French officers and made the French senior officer his own deputy. This system had many obvious advantages. Not only did Colonel L'Huillier participate in the planning and implementation of the training and inspection programs, thereby ensuring that these would be consonant with French capabilities and desires, but he was able to act as liaison between FTS and French unit commanders. In addition, if it became necessary to consult the French High Command before reaching a decision affecting policy, he could judiciously advise General Kingman on how best to approach the responsible officials, General Leyer and Colonel Blanc in particular.

The responsibility for making all necessary arrangements with French commanders regarding the training and inspection of their respective units rested largely with the deputy. To him also fell the task of preparing, on the basis of individual after-inspection reports submitted by the various teams, the synthesis which General Kingman used for the drafting of his final report to the Joint Rearmament Committee.

In June, July, and August 1944, French Training Section inspected nearly all French training establishments to determine the degree of efficiency of the training program and to check on the state of preparedness of units being trained. At the end of August, as the North African program was drawing to an end and the French themselves were assuming the responsibility for the training of replacement troops, plans were made for moving FTS to the Continent. On 25 September an advance party consisting of a few officers and enlisted men reached Marseille. Another party arrived soon after, General Kingman meanwhile remaining in North Africa to instruct and inspect the last program units. On 8 October General Kingman and Colonel L'Huillier left Oran for Marseille, turning over the supervision of the remaining FTS activities in North Africa to Col. Richard F. Fairchild. Shortly after his arrival in France and while at Headquarters, 6th Army Group, en route to 1st French Army, General Kingman, Colonel L'Huillier, and personal staff were ordered to Paris to establish a French Training Section there. The rear echelon commanded by Colonel Fairchild was composed of about six officers and fifteen enlisted men. As these men also moved to France on or about 15 November, all FTS activities ceased in North Africa.[55]

---

[55] Msg LX–46516, Larkin to CG MBS, 11 Oct 44, JRC 320/001 Orgn of JRC.

PART TWO

THE METROPOLITAN FORCES

CHAPTER XVIII

Initial Assistance

Even while they were supplying arms to the North African ground, air, and naval forces, Allied officials as well as the French High Command gave considerable attention to two other important logistical problems connected with French participation in the war. One was the continuance of material assistance to the increasing number of patriots engaged in subversive operations against the German forces occupying the mother country. The other was the eventual provision of equipment to the forces likely to be raised upon the liberation of any part of France.

Supplying arms to the French Resistance began before the North African rearmament operations and continued simultaneously with them. Until the cross-Channel operation (OVERLORD), the commitment was largely a British one. From OVERLORD on, the United States, which by that time was assuming an increasing share of the burden, was more seriously concerned, as was Britain, with the larger aspect of the problem, namely, the equipping of French liberated manpower. Indeed, plans as formulated by SHAEF contemplated that, as fast as Resistance groups were overrun by advancing Allied armies, they were to be incorporated, as all other liberated manpower recruited for service, into regular Army or labor units. It appears logical, therefore, in view of the U.S. role in the matter, to consider the two problems—material assistance to the Resistance and provision of equipment to liberated

manpower—as part of one single undertaking, the rearmament of the Metropolitan forces.

Supply of the Resistance Forces

Organization

In the fall of 1940 two agencies were established in London for the purpose of maintaining in France a will to resist the enemy, and of providing patriots with material means for conducting subversive operations against the occupying forces. One of these agencies was a staff section of General de Gaulle's headquarters, known first as Service de Renseignements (SR), later as Bureau Central de Renseignements et d'Action (Militaire) (BCRA). The other was a British organization, known as the French Section of Special Operations Executive (SOE), the latter being responsible to the Ministry of Economic Warfare.[1]

Although the BCRA enjoyed a substantial measure of autonomy, it was, nevertheless, entirely dependent upon SOE for obtaining the material means with which to carry out its operations. As a result the brunt of the task of assisting the Resistance rested on SOE and the other British agencies (the Ministry of Economic Warfare, the War Office, the Admiralty) upon which SOE itself was dependent for support. Be-

---

[1] The French Forces of the Interior, MS, I, 3, copy in OCMH. See Bibliographical Note.

ginning with the spring of 1941, SOE, together with BCRA, infiltrated into France
British as well as British-trained French
leaders, agents, radio operators, intelligence
officers, and saboteurs. Most were
dropped by parachute, although some went
by sea. SOE also dropped such small
amounts of equipment and supplies as were
permitted by meager air transport facilities.
Working in collaboration with SOE, from
1942 on, was a special Committee on Equipment for Patriot Forces appointed by the
British Chiefs of Staff to consider the problems of equipment for Resistance groups
and liberated manpower.

In the summer of 1942 a Special Operations branch of the American Office of
Strategic Services (OSS) was set up in
London, bringing into being an American
counterpart of SOE which, although independent of the British organization,
worked in close collaboration with it.
This co-operation led to the unification of
the operational control of the London
group of SOE and the Special Operations
branch of OSS-London, and to the establishment, during the last months of 1943,
of a single headquarters known first as
SOE/SO and later, on 1 May 1944, as
Special Force Headquarters (SFHQ).
Such activities of SOE/SO as fell within
the sphere of the Supreme Commander for
western Europe were placed under the operational control of his chief of staff.[2]

Determined that fuller assistance should
be given to the French Resistance, Prime
Minister Churchill organized, in January 1944, a special informal committee
headed by Lord Selborne, Minister of Economic Warfare, and composed of representatives of SOE, OSS, BCRA, and the Air

Ministry. The committee was instructed
to devise ways and means of increasing the
flow of military equipment, because airlift
rather than availability of matériel was still
the limiting factor in supplying Resistance
groups.[3]

Finally, to complete the organization of
assistance to the Resistance, a Mediterranean counterpart of SFHQ was established on 14 May 1944 under the name of
Special Project Operations Center
(SPOC). Its function was to implement
SHAEF's control over Resistance groups in
southern France.[4]

Meanwhile, the BCRA was continuing its
relatively independent existence. With
the approach of the cross-Channel operation, the need was felt for more co-ordination, not only between the Resistance
groups and Allied agencies engaged in their
support, but also between the activities
themselves of the various agencies involved.
As a preliminary step, on 6 June the Resistance forces, renamed officially Forces Françaises de l'Intérieur (FFI), or French
Forces of the Interior, were placed under
the command of Lt. Gen. Pierre Koenig,
who was to operate directly under the command of Supreme Headquarters, Allied Expeditionary Force. Two weeks later, at the
insistence of the French, SHAEF approved
the constitution of a tripartite headquarters
and staff to co-ordinate all Allied activities
in support of the FFI. The staff, called
Etat-Major des Forces Françaises de l'Intérieur (EMFFI), with headquarters in
London and commanded by General Koenig, was composed of representatives from
SFHQ, BCRA, SOE, OSS, and other

---

[2] SHAEF G–3 Ops C 322–7 (2 and 3) SFHQ
Orgn and Terms of Reference.

[3] Msg B–270, Eisenhower to Marshall, 14 Mar
44, ABC 400.3295 (2 Aug 43), Sec 2–A.
[4] Memo, Wilson To All Concerned, 14 May 44,
AFHQ History of Special Operations, Mediterranean Theater, 1944–45, DRB AGO.

agencies. Finally on 8 July, in anticipation of the launching of ANVIL, the command of the FFI in southern France was vested in Maj. Gen. Gabriel Cochet under the supreme command of General Wilson.[5]

American Contribution

Before the establishment of SOE/SO (hereafter referred to as SFHQ) in the fall of 1943, the effort to arm the French Resistance had been solely British. Even for a short period afterward, the effort continued to be largely British. Except for three planes operating from North Africa, U.S. air force commands were reported to be unable to place the necessary aircraft and specially trained crews at the disposal of SFHQ. The sum total of Anglo-American assistance was still inadequate, this at a time when some 50,000 Frenchmen who had fled to mountainous and wooded areas were said to be organizing into Maquis, or guerrilla groups. With many thousands more expected to join, it was imperative that Allied effort to supply them with arms and equipment be sharply increased. Already the men in the Maquis were reported to be growing impatient, even indignant at what they regarded as Allied unwillingness to keep promises. U.S. political representatives in Algiers were warning that the situation was fraught with military, psychological, and political dangers.[6]

It was not until January 1944 that, at the direction of the British Prime Minister, who had just discussed the matter with General de Gaulle, substantial additional temporary British airlift was made available to SFHQ. By February the British were carrying out their commitment with the utmost vigor and were reported to be giving very high priority to the undertaking.[7]

In the meantime, the first American transport planes to be permanently assigned to SFHQ for operation from the United Kingdom had, in January 1944, begun to fly supply missions over northern France. Attempts by the chief of OSS, Brig. Gen. William J. Donovan, to get an increased allotment of American aircraft were unsuccessful. As the Combined Chiefs of Staff were informed in February, the U.S. Army Air Forces warned that it could not for the present divert any more airplanes to SFHQ. It could only authorize local air commanders to use such aircraft as in their opinion could be spared for the purpose.[8]

By March the disproportion between the British and the American efforts was so great (approximately ten to one) that the impression was reported to be gaining credence among French officials in North Africa and in the United Kingdom that, not only was the undertaking an entirely British one, but the United States was even opposed to arming the French underground for political reasons.[9] Eager to counteract the unjustified comment being directed against the U.S. Government, the Secretary of State, Cordell Hull, sought the views of the U.S. Chiefs of Staff on the matter. On 17 April General Marshall furnished Hull

[5] The French Forces of the Interior, II, 425, copy in OCMH; Memo, Wilson To All Concerned, 8 Jul 44, AFHQ History of Special Operations, Mediterranean Theater, 1944–45, DRB AGO.

[6] Msgs, Edwin C. Wilson to Cordell Hull, 110, 11 Jan 44, and 129, 12 Jan 44, and Memo, McCloy for OPD, 27 Jan 44, ABC 400.3295 (2 Aug 43), Sec 2–A.

[7] Msg ML–382, Donovan, OSS, to Eaker, 11 Feb 44, AFHQ 0100/12A G–3 Div Ops BIGOT Fr.

[8] Min, CCS 145th Mtg, 11 Feb 44; Memo, JPS for JCS, 13 Apr 44, ABC 400.3295 (2 Aug 43), Sec 2–A.

[9] Memo, Cordell Hull for Leahy, 20 Mar 44, in same file.

with information which, he hoped, would help in dispelling "any impression that may exist that the U.S. is less aware than the British of the potential importance of the French Resistance groups, and less willing than the British to utilize the very valuable aid the underground can render to our operations." Marshall explained, first of all, that the committee organized in London by the Prime Minister was, according to General Eisenhower himself, working "in full cooperation with and under the general supervision of" the Supreme Commander. As for the supplies dropped to French Resistance groups, they were, in a large part, furnished by the United States. General Marshall then reminded Secretary Hull that the United States had been engaged for some twelve months in equipping a French expeditionary force "comparable in size to our own peace-time army," an undertaking, he added, to which the British had made no substantial contribution.[10]

At the same time the French Committee of National Liberation had approached both the American and British Governments with the suggestion that a special conference be held in London for the purpose of increasing further the flow of military equipment into France. The U.S. Chiefs of Staff seized the occasion to clarify the American position on the matter by pointing out to the CCS that the special committee already functioning in London rendered the French suggestion inopportune. Such was the substance of a message which, at the request of the JCS, the CCS addressed to General Eisenhower on 24 April 1944.[11]

It was then that a disquieting report reached Secretary Hull which quoted General de Gaulle as having expressed, in the course of a press conference given in Algiers on 21 April, his satisfaction at British efforts to supply the Resistance, efforts which, he implied, were solely British.[12] Such a statement, in the opinion of the Secretary of State, could not remain unanswered.[13] Apprised of the incident, the JCS agreed with Hull's suggestion to draw the matter to the immediate attention of the responsible American military and civil authorities in Algiers and in London. In the belief that it could be more effectively handled at CCS level, JCS drafted a message for General de Gaulle and proposed to the representatives of the British Chiefs of Staff in Washington that it be delivered to him via General Wilson.[14] The communication, intended to clarify the apparent misunderstanding indicated by General de Gaulle's statement to the press, pointed out that the arming of the Resistance had, for some three months past, been a joint U.S.-British effort, not an exclusive one of either nation; that the matériel dropped in France was being drawn from a common pool; finally, that the entire operation itself was under the control of both the Supreme Commander, Allied Expeditionary Force, and the Supreme Allied Commander in the Mediterranean. This message, incidentally, never was sent. The British Chiefs of Staff having subsequently indicated informally that they did not in-

---

[10] Memo, Marshall for Hull, 17 Apr 44, in same file.

[11] Msg FACS 18, CCS to Eisenhower, 24 Apr 44, in same file.

[12] The exact words of General de Gaulle were: "Je puis vous dire avec beaucoup de satisfaction que, depuis trois mois, les efforts de nos alliés britanniques—car ce sont eux qui en ont le mérite—pour armer la Résistance française ont été grands et couronnés de succès." Text in de Gaulle, *Discours et Messages,* p. 434.

[13] Memo, Hull for Marshall, 26 Apr 44, ABC 400.3295 (2 Aug 43), Sec 2-A.

[14] Memo, JCS for Hull, 29 May 44, in same file.

tend to take any action on the issue, the JCS decided, in August, to withdraw their original proposal.[15]

General Eisenhower, meanwhile, had taken the matter in his own hands. In a message to the JCS dated 1 May, supplemented by a personal letter to General Marshall, he reviewed the situation with respect to American material assistance to the Resistance forces. He recognized that, in the past, the effort had been predominantly British since no U.S. aircraft had been made available for airlift to France until 1 January 1944, and only a very few thereafter. But the situation had changed considerably in recent weeks. Exclusive of aircraft operating from North Africa, the number of planes as then permanently allotted to SFHQ in the United Kingdom was 32 American as against 22 British. The British, it was true, had made available to SFHQ supplementary airlift averaging approximately 65 aircraft per month since February. Plans were afoot to increase the permanent U.S. allotment by 25 aircraft. In addition. U.S. supplies were being drawn upon by SFHQ at an increasing rate. Given adequate personnel and means both in the United Kingdom and in North Africa, the United States would shortly be in a position to "equalize" its effort with that of the British.[16]

A few days later, General Devers, commanding general of the U.S. forces in North Africa, likewise reported on the situation as it related to his theater. Judging from the figures he quoted in a message to General Marshall, the American contribution in terms of tonnage of supplies delivered was still greatly inferior to that of the British. But an improvement was in sight, for 9 U.S. aircraft had just been added to the 3 operating from that theater.[17]

A compilation of the data contained in the messages from Generals Eisenhower and Devers was immediately forwarded by General Marshall to President Roosevelt. The memorandum assured the President that the U.S. Chiefs of Staff had the matter "under continuing review" and that General Eisenhower had advised that he would explain fully to the French in London the position of the U.S. Government in the matter.[18]

By mid-May the American effort had sharply increased and General Eisenhower was able to report that, under the current allotment of aircraft to SFHQ, the Americans could now deliver 160 tons a month as against 132 tons from the British. Furthermore, an additional allotment of U.S. aircraft, just granted, would make it possible to raise the figure for the American effort to 280 tons by 1 July 1944.[19] That this was not wishful thinking, but a firm intent to expand American participation in the combined commitment, was amply substantiated by later events.

Meanwhile, units of the French Forces of the Interior, particularly active since the beginning of the year, were redoubling preparations in anticipation of the forthcoming Allied landings. From 6 June, when OVERLORD was launched, to the end of July, the period of the battle in Normandy, they embarked on large-scale

[15] CCS 492/4, 29 May 44, JCS Memo, 3 Jul 44, and other papers, in same file.

[16] Msgs S–51066, Eisenhower to JCS, 1 May 44, and S–51396, Eisenhower to Marshall, 6 May 44, in same file.

[17] Msg, Devers to Marshall, 5 May 44, CM–IN 3917.

[18] Memo, Actg CofS for President, 8 May 44, ABC 400.3295 (2 Aug 43), Sec 2–A.

[19] Msg S–52023, Eisenhower to Marshall, 17 May 44, SHAEF SGS 475/1, Vol. I, Policy.

guerrilla and sabotage operations. To co-ordinate their effort with that of the assaulting Allied forces, assist further in their organization and supply, and strengthen their fighting potential, EMFFI dispatched to them by parachute, from the United Kingdom and North Africa, several thousand American, British, and French Commandos, liaison officers, and other troops. The Commandos included 11 U.S. Operations Groups, each composed of 4 officers and 30 men, and the British Special Air Service (SAS) Brigade, of which two battalions were French—the 2d and 3d Parachute Regiments. The liaison troops comprised some 90 three-men teams (called "Jedburgh" from the name of the small town in southern Scotland), each composed of 1 American or British officer, 1 French officer, and 1 non-commissioned officer acting as signalman. Other personnel included individual agents (organizers, leaders, sabotage experts) and missions (command staffs, medical teams), all drawn from the ranks of the three nations.

In some areas, the FFI acted spontaneously and without sufficient co-ordination with the Allied High Command. In southern France the revolt against the German forces gathered too much momentum to be checked. General Donovan feared that failure to support the FFI troops in that area on a sufficient scale to prevent their liquidation by the enemy would not only destroy a valuable military asset but produce unfavorable political repercussions.[20] With this in view, OSS arranged to have additional U.S. aircraft assigned for a mass daylight supply drop, the first such undertaking in the European Theater

of Operations. The venture, which took place on 25 June, was highly successful. Five combat wings of the 3d Bombardment Division, U.S. Eighth Air Force, representing 180 bombers, delivered to some 20,000 guerrillas scattered over four separate areas in southern France more than 300 tons of supplies, mostly American, all packed in some 2,000 American containers by personnel in OSS packing stations. It had been a "100-percent-American show" and the Prime Minister was then urged to put on a similar British performance. A week later, General Donovan, writing to General Marshall, prefaced his account of the operation as follows: "It is now possible to publicize our aid to the French Resistance and thus to cultivate for the U.S. the good will of the French people." The chief of OSS then voiced the belief that the daylight operation had been "a tremendous morale builder" and had generated gratitude from the FFI. One Maquis leader had expressed his feelings in these words: "The Maquis' thanks to the U.S. Air Force for damned good show! When is the next?"[21] The next was to follow soon; in fact it took place on 14 July, Bastille Day. It, too, was a 100-percent-American operation.

On 22 July General Donovan summed up for the benefit of the U.S. Chiefs of Staff the American effort expended since 1 January to assist the French Resistance. In addition to infiltrating about 70 U.S. agents, American planes had dropped all together some 6,000 containers and 2,000 packages packed by OSS, representing 1,000 tons gross weight of arms and equipment.[22]

By then, the FFI had grown by leaps and

---

[20] Memo, Donovan for Marshall, 9 Jul 44, ABC 400.3295 (2 Aug 43), Sec 2–A.

[21] *Ibid.;* Rpt, OSS Opn ZEBRA, 24 Jul 44, in same file.

[22] Memo, Donovan for JCS, 22 Jul 44, in same file.

FRENCH FORCES OF THE INTERIOR *at a staging area in southern England, about to receive American clothing and equipment before returning to duty in France, October 1944.*

bounds to an approximate strength of 200,-000 men. Even with the limited armament at their disposal, these men were rendering considerable assistance to the advancing Allied armies by fighting the enemy behind his own lines. They were blowing up bridges, cutting rail lines and wire communications, and setting up roadblocks and ambushes, all so effectively that enemy units, even armored divisions, were hopelessly cut off and, in the case of some, unable to reach the battle area in time or in a condition to fight. As both the War Department and the War Office were having difficulty in supplying equipment on a scale much larger than originally contemplated, General Eisenhower requested and obtained from the CCS the authorization to issue to Resistance forces on a temporary basis captured enemy matériel, largely small arms.[23]

Throughout the summer, areas containing the scattered groups of FFI were, one by one, overrun by the victorious Allied troops. By October, with most of France liberated, some 60,000–75,000 Maquis were still actively engaged against the German pockets

---

[23] Msgs, SCAF 59, Eisenhower to CCS, 2 Aug 44, and FACS 56, CCS to Eisenhower, 15 Aug 44, ABC 091.711 France (6 Oct 43), Sec 5.

entrenched on the Atlantic coast, or were behind the front lines in eastern France. Supply of these groups continued to come from the United Kingdom until November when EMFFI, the Resistance headquarters in London, closed down. Meanwhile, the other "liberated" groups of FFI had for the most part chosen to continue the fight alongside the Allied armies and were being incorporated either in the 1st French Army or in units organized by the French High Command at the direction of SHAEF. From that point on, their rearming was but one aspect of the larger problem of equipping French liberated manpower.[24] For the part they had played in the liberation of their country, the FFI had paid heavily. The number of men and women killed in action or executed by the enemy up to October 1944 has been estimated at 24,000.[25]

Employment of French Liberated Manpower

The question of employing French liberated manpower against the Axis had come up for brief discussion just before the landings in North Africa. In October 1942 first General de Gaulle, then General Giraud, anticipating an early Allied assault on continental France, had submitted proposals for raising troops on French soil and requests for armament. The Allies having chosen instead to land in North Africa, de Gaulle and Giraud devoted their efforts thereafter to rearming the forces available in that territory. For months afterward the Allies carefully avoided making any commitments with respect to equipping a French continental army either upon the liberation of France or after victory was won. But as time passed it became evident that, sooner or later, they would have to face the problem of employing liberated manpower once an assault had been successfully launched on continental France.[26]

In August 1943 the U.S. Joint Staff Planners submitted a report on the general question of "equipping Allies, liberated forces and friendly neutrals." With regard to France, they pointed out that, for purely military and logistical reasons, no units formed from liberated manpower could be employed for from ten to thirteen months after an initial assault on continental France. They recommended that the equipping of liberated manpower be confined to forces required for garrison or guard duties and that no attempt be made to organize assault forces. Endorsing these recommendations, the CCS agreed that, for the present, the re-equipping of army units would be limited to the obligations of the North African rearmament program.[27]

Meanwhile, the Committee on Equipment for Patriot Forces had submitted a memorandum to the Combined Staff Planners for examination and report to the CCS. The committee recommended that the equipment ordered for both Resistance groups and Patriot forces (the latter being defined as "forces which may be embodied in areas liberated by Allied armies to fight on the side of the UN") be pooled for allocation among countries in accordance with the strategic situation. The committee then pointed out that equipment requirements

---

[24] For partial list of equipment delivered by OSS to the French Resistance, see Table 4.

[25] Lt. Col. P. Santini, "Etude statistique sur les pertes au cours de la guerre 1939–1945," *Revue du Corps de Santé Militaire*, X, No. 1 (March, 1954).

[26] Rpt, JPS to JCS, JCS 201/1, 20 Mar 43. See pp. 12–13, above.

[27] Rpt, JPS to JCS, CCS 317, 18 Aug 43, QUADRANT Conf; Min, CCS 115th Mtg, 23 Aug 43, QUADRANT Conf.

TABLE 4—QUANTITIES OF EQUIPMENT PACKAGED BY OSS IN THE UNITED KINGDOM AND
AIRDROPPED INTO FRANCE: JANUARY–OCTOBER 1944 [a]

Type	Quantity
Weapons	
Bayonet, M1, With Scabbard, M7	15
Carbine, .30-caliber, US, M1, With Sling, Oiler, and Magazine	16,807
Carbine, .30-caliber, US, M1A1, With Sling	498
Gun, .45-caliber, Thompson, 1918A2, Submachine, Complete	2
Gun, 9-mm., Marlin, Submachine	2,405
Gun, .30-caliber, Machine, M1919A4, Aircooled, Complete	3
Knife, Fighting, OSS	121
Pistol, .45-caliber, M1911A1, Automatic, With Two Magazines	15,692
Pistol, .32-caliber, Colt, Automatic	14
Pistol, .22-caliber, Automatic, Various Makes	17
Rifle, .30-caliber, US, M1	56
Rocket Launcher, 2.36-inch, M1A1, With Sling and Muzzle Deflector	2,266
Rocket Launcher, 2.36-inch, Antitank, M9A1, Complete	350
Ammunition (Cartridge Data in Rounds)	
.50-caliber Cartridge, Ball, in Metal Links	25,000
.45-caliber Cartridge, Ball, Pistol, M1911	1,030,900
.38-caliber Cartridge, Ball, Revolver	4,000
9-mm. Cartridge, Ball, Parabellum	829,000
.32-caliber Cartridge, Ball, Short Revolver	350
.32-caliber Cartridge, Ball, Pistol	1,050
.30-caliber Cartridge, Ball, M2 (Eight-Round Clips in Bandoleers)	10,272
.30-caliber Cartridge, Ball, M2, MLB, Machine Gun, Tracer 9–1	81,750
.30-caliber Cartridge, Ball, Carbine	5,403,500
.22-caliber Cartridge, Ball, Long Rifle	750
Cap, Blasting, Nonelectric	294,838
Composition C (in Pounds)	323,029
Cord, Detonating, PETN (in Feet)	1,025,000
Rockets, HE, 2.36-inch, Antitank, M6A1	43,892
Food and Clothing	
Cap, Wool, Olive Drab	94
Jacket, Field, Wool, Olive Drab	13,380
Ration K	10,920
Ration X	10,263
Other Equipment	
Barrel, Spare, Marlin	240
Belt, Web, Pistol	2,380
Blanket, Wool, Olive Drab	19
Bulb, Launcher, Rocket	2,588
Container, Serial, Plastic	5
Cosh, Spring	6
Eyeshield, M1	2,588
Holster, Shoulder, Pistol, .32-caliber	14
Kit, Cleaning Carbine	8,376
Magazine, Assembly, Carbine, .30-caliber	63,220
Magazine, Assembly, Double, Marlin	4,800
Magazine, Assembly, Single, Marlin	7,200
Magazine, Pough, Assembly, Double, Marlin	2,400
Magazine, Pough, Assembly, Single, Marlin	2,400
Mount, Tripod, Machine Gun, .30-caliber, M2, 1919A4	10
Sling, Gun, Marlin, Submachine	2,400
Truck, ¼-ton, 4 x 4	2

a Excludes equipment dropped into France by OSS-Algiers.
Source: Statistics furnished by OSS-Paris, Nov 45, to Fr Gp, Hist Sec, ETOUSA.   Copy in OCMH.

for European countries had been formulated in London and that action had already been taken to allocate matériel for Patriot forces while continuous deliveries were being made to Resistance groups.[28]

Reviewing the various aspects of the problem on the basis of the findings and recommendations of the JPS and the Committee on Equipment for Patriot Forces, the British Chiefs of Staff pointed out to the CCS that, in their opinion, there were three separate commitments to be considered: equipment to Allied forces and neutrals, equipment for forces useful in winning the war (Resistance groups and Patriot forces), equipment for postwar armed forces. The last of these commitments, they explained, was being made the object of a study by the Post-Hostilities Planning Committee, also established in London.[29] There the matter rested for several months.

In the meantime, French military authorities in North Africa were giving increased attention to the question of liberated manpower. Hampered as they were in their efforts to organize service and specialized units by the lack of technicians in North Africa, they were heavily counting on this new source of manpower, which they expected to be large, for the fulfillment of their commitments. Actually, they were relying on it also for the discharge of other obligations which they had set for themselves: "to fight the Axis powers in Europe to the finish, to contribute to the occupation of Axis territories and the maintenance of security in Europe, to assist in the war against Japan, and to restore French sover-

eignty to all territories of the French Union." In the belief that they could not carry out these commitments without additional forces, they were contemplating a vast conscription program for the years 1944 to 1946. In a memorandum addressed to the War Department on 16 October 1943, the National Defense Committee estimated that sufficient liberated manpower could be found to extend the 11-division North African program by the end of 1945 to 36 divisions (23 infantry, 10 armored, and 3 airborne) with reserves and services, and to expand the air force to 2,800 first-line aircraft. The committee then urged the War Department to consider without delay the assignment of the equipment necessary for the additional forces and for the rehabilitation of military establishments in France.[30]

On 20 October General Leyer forwarded, for inclusion in the U.S. Army Supply Program for 1944–45, requisitions for the 25 divisions to be raised from liberated manpower. A few days later, General Bouscat, chief of staff of the French Air Force, submitted a detailed plan calling for the equipping of new air combat and auxiliary units during 1944, 1945, and the beginning of 1946. If the new program was much larger than the original ANFA Plan, General Béthouart explained to General Marshall, it was because of the will of the French people to make the maximum contribution to the liberation of their country.[31]

The proposal was received by War Department officials with considerable

[28] Rpt, Committee on Equipment for Patriot Forces and Resistance Groups, 31 Aug 43, ABC 400.3295 (2 Aug 43), Sec 1–A.

[29] Memo, COS for CCS, 12 Oct 43, ABC 400.-3295 (2 Aug 43), Sec 1–A.

[30] Memo, National Defense Committee, 16 Oct 43, ABC 091.711 France (6 Oct 43), Sec 1–A.

[31] Memos, Bouscat for JAC and JRC, 2 Nov 43, and Leyer for JRC, 20 Oct 43, JRC Misc Doc, Item 5–b, Fr Liaison 5; Memo, Béthouart for Marshall, 30 Oct 43, ASF Planning Div Files.

skepticism, even some hostility,[32] for it was being made at a time when the North African program itself appeared unattainable in its entirety for lack of adequate manpower and was about to be re-examined with a view to scaling it downward. Moreover, AFHQ officials definitely felt that the CFLN was empowered to concern itself only with the North African forces and that some sort of an agreement must be reached at government level before plans for Metropolitan French forces could be considered. Both Generals Leyer and Bouscat had been aware of this fact when they submitted their respective requisitions. They pointed out that neither the Joint Rearmament Committee nor the Joint Air Commission was in position to take any action until a decision of principle was reached on a governmental level. Washington held the same view. Discussing the French proposal in a memorandum to the U.S. JCS, General Marshall expressed the opinion that the question of arming the French over and above the ANFA commitment was one of national policy. It involved such issues as the attitude of the U.S. Government toward the CFLN insofar as matters outside North Africa were concerned, the attitude of the U.S. Government toward the rearmament of French units to be used in the present war, and, finally, the American policy on the establishment and maintenance of military forces by France after the war. These matters clearly were for the decision of the President.[33] At General Marshall's sug-

gestion, the French proposal was referred to the Joint Strategic Survey Committee for study and appropriate recommendations to the JCS on which the latter might advise the President.

In their report, the members of the Joint Strategic Survey Committee expressed the belief that the current North African rearmament program would enable the French to assist in the war against Germany to the full extent of their capabilities. They considered it undesirable at this time to promise an increase in armament for purposes other than winning the war in Europe. They recommended therefore that no additional U.S. military assistance and equipment be offered to the French beyond that already contemplated.[34] Endorsing this recommendation, the JCS agreed that "generally, except for minor readjustments from time to time to utilize trained French personnel," the current program would not be extended.

Theater officials greatly doubted that substantial forces could be raised on French soil, as the Germans were draining the country of able-bodied men for employment in Germany. They felt that no great expansion of the French forces could be contemplated before the capitulation of the enemy.[35]

At the end of December 1943 the French military authorities, who had received no answer to their October proposal, instructed the chief of their Military Mission in Washington, General Beynet, to query the War Department as to the intentions of the American Government on the matter. General Marshall could only assure General

---

[32] From the chairman of the MAC (G) the proposal elicited a curt "Nuts," which he penciled in the margin of a report on the proposed French plan adressed to him by the secretary. Memo, Secy MAC (G) for Chmn MAC (G), 27 Dec 43, ASF Planning Div Files.

[33] Memo, Marshall for JCS, 2 Nov 43, ABC 091.711 (6 Oct 43), Sec 2–A.

[34] Memo, JSSC for JCS, 8 Nov 43, in same file.

[35] Memo, Timberlake Med Air Comd for Deputy Theater Comdr, 7 Nov 43, JRC 907 Rearmt Plan, 1944–45.

Beynet that the desire of the French to participate in all phases of the operations in their homeland was fully appreciated and that it was planned to make the fullest possible use of the French forces in this crucial phase of the war.[36]

Meanwhile, the CCS had referred to the Combined Staff Planners for study both the JPS 18 August memorandum recommending that no attempt be made to organize assault forces from French liberated manpower and the British memorandum of 12 October regarding the equipping of Resistance and Patriot forces. To enable the CPS to formulate plans for arming liberated manpower, the CCS requested General Eisenhower to determine the total number and breakdown by nationalities of the liberated manpower which he desired to have equipped.[37] On 9 March General Smith communicated to the CCS, on behalf of the Supreme Commander, a proposal for the employment of French and other western European liberated manpower. It was now assumed that a large reservoir of manpower, estimated for the French alone at five and a half million men, would become available. A study of what proportion of this manpower should be equipped had led to the following conclusions. Since a French task force was being equipped and trained in North Africa to take part in the defeat of the German land forces, the Supreme Commander's operational requirement in liberated manpower did not extend beyond troops to relieve British and U.S. fighting forces from lines of communications duties and to garrison liberated territory for internal security

reasons. The need was for units no larger than battalions, 175 (a total of 140,000 men) to be raised by France, 40 by Holland and Belgium. It was essential that the arming of these battalions be completed by D plus 300. The figure of 140,000 men for France did not include members of Resistance groups whose equipment was the concern of SFHQ in London. Nor did it include mobile labor elements for which clothing was to be provided by the army group headquarters concerned, or static labor elements to be used for military and civil affairs purposes and whose equipment was to be furnished under a civil affairs plan.[38]

On 14 April the Combined Chiefs approved General Eisenhower's proposal. They reached no decision, however, on the question of tables of organization and equipment, nor did they stipulate from what source, how, and when the necessary equipment was to be furnished.[39]

The plan reckoned without French views. These were made clear in May when Brig. Gen. Charles Noiret, chief of the French Military Mission in London, told SHAEF that the French military authorities were determined to reconstitute the metropolitan army, using members of the Resistance forces as cadres, and the existing territorial system for mobilization and administration. Their plan was first to muster available Resistance personnel into battalions or regiments for immediate participation in operations alongside the Allied armies, later to convert these units into larger organizations. In the meantime they would mobilize and train several classes of young men and assign Territorial units made up of older

---

[36] Ltrs, Beynet to Marshall, 27 Dec 43, and Marshall to Beynet, 7 Jan 44, OPD 400 France, Sec III.
[37] JSM 1426, CCS to Eisenhower, 16 Jan 44, ABC 400.3295 (2 Aug 43), Sec 1–A.

[38] Ltr, Smith to CCS, 9 Mar 44, in same file.
[39] Min, CCS 155th Mtg, 14 Apr 44; Msg WX–25272, Marshall to Eisenhower, 19 Apr 44, ABC 400.3295 (2 Aug 43), Sec 1–A.

classes to lines of communications and internal security duties. For reasons of morale, they considered it highly desirable that all this personnel be suitably equipped and armed as soon as practicable. General Noiret then proffered this warning—to use Resistance groups merely in the role presently contemplated for them by Allied authorities and not as combatants was to risk serious repercussions.[40]

That the French were determined to rebuild their metropolitan army was substantiated to some degree by reports received from North Africa. General Loomis, then chief of the JRC, had just expressed his suspicion that the unduly large requisitions currently being submitted to the JRC by the French military authorities in Algiers were intended for purposes other than the North African forces. It was quite possible that the French were desirous of building up stocks for use in continental France either for the civilian population or for new units to be organized there.[41] On the assumption that Allied planning included adequate provision for these purposes, General Loomis recommended that the French be advised accordingly so as to put an end to their "futile attempts" to obtain supplies which the JRC had no authority to provide.[42]

On 6 June the Anglo-American Allies entered France in the great OVERLORD attack still without any firm policy on the use of liberated manpower. A step toward compromise with the French desire for combatant troops had been made in late May by a SHAEF suggestion to train French Commando and Ranger units soon after the beginning of operations. These would use only a small number of men and would require only light equipment.[43] The French, however, had not agreed to this proposal. No concrete plan meanwhile had been made to provide equipment for the security and labor units authorized by the CCS. The Supreme Commander had only the assurance of the British Chiefs of Staff, given on 11 May, that they would make every effort to place at his disposal British and U.S. equipment in sufficient quantities.[44]

General Eisenhower, on 13 June, urgently asked the CCS for a policy decision. He pointed out that western European Allies were contemplating the reconstitution of their national armies and submitting requirements ranging, in some instances, "from musical instruments to heavy equipment." It was "not impossible," he explained, "that Governments of the U.N. might cloak their desire for large post-war armies by pleading that they want to give maximum assistance to OVERLORD." From an operational point of view, he did not consider it necessary to arm and equip any forces beyond those already authorized for security and garrison duties, and the forces required for various types of labor. Nonetheless, it might be necessary, in order to satisfy the French, to equip a few Commando-type units for immediate action. It might also be desirable to form French training centers in the United Kingdom where liberated manpower might train, under French arrangements, to become reinforcements for the units raised in North

---

[40] Min, Confs with Fr Military Mission, 2 and 9 May 44, SHAEF SGS 475 France, Vol. I.

[41] See p. 173, above.

[42] Memo, Loomis for CofS NATOUSA, 17 Apr 44, JRC 902/I Rearmt Plan.

[43] Memos, Lt Gen A. E. Grasett for SHAEF G–3, 21 May 44, and Lt Col M. D. Molloy for Chief Plans and Opns Sec G–3, 25 May 44, SHAEF G–3 091 France, Vol. I.

[44] Memo, COS for SAC, 11 May 44, SHAEF SGS 475/1, Vol. I, Policy.

Africa. SHAEF needed an early statement of policy on which to base its answer to the proposals submitted by the various military missions concerned.[45]

It soon became evident that the concession which General Eisenhower was willing to make to the French would not satisfy their ambitions. Writing to General Marshall on 14 June, General Béthouart, then Chief of Staff of National Defense, reaffirmed the desire of his government to enlist in the Army, once they had been cleared and screened, all able-bodied men, whether or not they had been enrolled in the Resistance forces. This, he explained, was the best way to avoid internal disorder and to provide the strongest possible support to Allied m i l i t a r y action.[46] General Béthouart's memorandum having been communicated to the CCS, the latter referred it to General Eisenhower for comment on which to base a reply. Speaking for the Supreme Commander, General Smith pointed out on 27 June that General Eisenhower, while fully conscious of the valuable assistance rendered to his operations by the Resistance forces, had made it clear to the French that his operational needs must take priority over any reconstitution of the French Army. In this connection, General Eisenhower wished to remind the CCS that he had referred to them for decision the whole question of the reconstitution and arming of national armies of liberated Allies. Lack of guidance from them was proving embarrassing to him in his discussions with the various Allied military missions. A firm decision on the matter was urgently required.[47]

On 8 July General Béthouart, who had accompanied General de Gaulle to Washington, called on a number of War Department officials. The purpose of these visits was to renew the requests submitted some nine months earlier by the National Defense Committee for equipment to arm an additional 25 divisions and to expand the air force before the end of 1945. With the liberation of France under way, the government, he declared to General Marshall, wished to increase the size of the Army in proportion to the liberation of the territory itself. Béthouart then handed the director of the International Division, ASF, an armament program calling for the equipping, initially, of 30 infantry battalions, 72 artillery batteries, 3 tank battalions, and other miscellaneous units. All these units would be formed with some 100,000 men from the Resistance and would constitute the nucleus of 1 armored, 1 airborne, and 3 infantry divisions. On the same date General Béthouart requested of General Arnold, chief of the U.S. Army Air Forces, the equipment to arm 25 combat squadrons in addition to the units already re-equipped under the North African program.[48]

Both proposals were immediately examined in the light of equipment availability and of other commitments. After a preliminary conference between officers of the French Military Mission and representatives of International Division, ASF, Maj. Gen. LeRoy Lutes, director of Plans and Operations, ASF, expressed the belief that the

[45] Msg SCAF 51, Eisenhower to CCS, 13 Jun 44, OPD Cable Files.

[46] Memo, Béthouart for Marshall, 14 Jun 44, SHAEF SGS 475 France, Vol. I.

[47] Ltr, Smith to CCS, 27 Jun 44, ABC 091.711 France (6 Oct 43), Sec 5.

[48] Memo, National Defense Committee, 16 Oct 43, ABC 091.711 France (6 Oct 43), Sec 1–A; Memo, Béthouart for Marshall, 6 Jul 44, ABC 091.711 France (6 Oct 43), Sec 5; Memo, Fr Military Mission for Director International Div ASF, 8 Jul 44, ASF Planning Div Files; and Msg WX–62001, Arnold to Eaker, 8 Jul 44, JRC Cable Log.

matériel for the 5 divisions could be made available with some exceptions.[49] Before taking any action, both Generals Arnold and Marshall sought the views of theater officials on the matter.

General Eaker promptly informed General Arnold that, in his opinion, it would be a grave error to allow the French in Washington to present an air rearmament plan and obtain its approval without full theater concurrence. He doubted that the French High Command could furnish at an early date the men to form the contemplated units. "We must insist that they show us definitely a manpower capacity for another unit before we authorize and equip it." [50]

General Eaker's skepticism confirmed the impression which General Marshall had already gathered from information available to him. In asking Generals Devers and Eisenhower to comment on the latest French proposals, Marshall expressed his own views. It was doubtful whether French Resistance groups and other liberated personnel would provide sufficient effectives to furnish replacements for 1st French Army, to make up for shortages of supporting troops, to activate security and lines of communications battalions, and to organize new combat units as well. However, since the Resistance forces were reported to be effective not only in guerrilla action but in large-scale operations as well, it might be desirable to consider the possibility of organizing them forthwith into combat units. Meanwhile, other available liberated personnel would be utilized to form replacements, security battalions, and noncombat units. It might be practicable to start with a program of modest proportions and build up toward the

total indicated in the French proposals, depending on manpower availability and operational developments. Such a course of action would mean greater strength for OVERLORD and would help to eliminate any shortage of combat troops on the Western Front which might occur should the war continue to the middle of 1945. The matter of equipment would depend on whether or not the decision was made to form additional U.S. divisions and on operational requirements as currently estimated. Matériel for new French units would be drawn from the strategic reserve. On the present commitments, it would be possible to equip at least some of the five divisions proposed by the French for activation in 1944. The arming of these units would, of course, be handled in the same way as that of the divisions re-equipped under the North African program.[51]

The first to answer General Marshall's query was General Devers. The French, he explained, had shown a marked aptitude for organizing and training combat units and had demonstrated their "outstanding ability in combat." But, because of their slowness in organizing supporting combat and service units, it had been necessary to place U.S. troops of this type at their disposal on an appreciable scale to ensure their success. The French proposal therefore was not consonant with current policy. The rearmament program was designed to equip an expeditionary force for operations on the Continent and not to furnish supplies for liberated areas in France nor to build up a postwar French army.[52] Yet, Devers admitted, a true appreciation of French capabilities and limitations "dic-

---

[49] Memo, Lutes for ACofS OPD WD, 8 Jul 44, OPD Exec 10, Item 52–E.

[50] Msg M–23957, Eaker to Arnold, 8 Jul 44, ABC 091.711 France (6 Oct 43), Sec 2–A.

[51] Msg WX–62685, Marshall to Eisenhower and Devers, 9 Jul 44, OPD Cable Files.

[52] Msg FX–70274, Devers to Marshall, 9 Jul 44, AFHQ 0100/12C G–3 Div Ops Fr Equip.

tated" that Resistance troops be organized and equipped by the most expeditious means possible into small combat units, ultimately divisions, so as to enable them to continue to fight in a more efficient manner. Such a course of action would necessitate that supporting combat and service requirements be met from other sources, most likely American. Furthermore, to reduce supply problems, it would probably be advisable to equip and maintain the new units through U.S. base sections. In conclusion, General Devers recommended that the 150,000–200,000 Frenchmen expected to become available in AFHQ's zone of responsibility be employed, in order of priority: (1) to establish a replacement pool sufficient to carry the North African units through the rest of 1944, (2) to make up for the existing shortages of French supporting combat and service troops currently estimated at 60,000 men, (3) then and only then, to organize one infantry division (the sixth on the North African program but never activated) and one armored division (the fourth likewise on the program but deferred indefinitely).[53]

General Eisenhower, in his answer to General Marshall's query, first restated his own requirements in French liberated manpower, namely, essential labor units and internal security and lines of communications troops. The Supreme Commander then recommended that manpower available over and above his requirements be used in combat units on the assumption that the war in Europe "might continue well into 1945" and in the light of the fact that the French themselves were eager to have

units fighting alongside British and U.S. troops in northern France. He did not consider it advisable, as suggested by General Marshall, to organize the Resistance forces into combat units. While excellent in a guerrilla role in their own native area, they were likely to be ineffective if engaged in combat alongside U.S. or French regular units in a strange territory. In fact they could become an administrative encumbrance. The most advantageous manner of using this "prolific and first-rate source of manpower" was to take the best of them for recruits and form the remainder, already armed, into internal security and lines of communications units. In conclusion he recommended that French liberated manpower be employed, in order of priority: (1) to fill requirements of the Supreme Commander, Allied Expeditionary Force; (2) to fill requirements of the Supreme Allied Commander, Mediterranean; (3) to activate three divisions, two in southern France and one in northern France, complete with administrative and service elements, for use in European operations in 1945; and (4) to form a limited number of Ranger or Commando-type units to be quickly trained in the United Kingdom. The organization of these smaller units would, he believed, satisfy French eagerness to participate fully in the European campaign.[54]

By this time War Department officials were convinced that the question of the use of French liberated manpower was becoming entirely too complex and, as pointed out in a memorandum from OPD to the Joint Logistics Committee (JLC), "would have to be tied together in order to be handled

---

[53] Memo, Devers for Marshall, 11 Jul 44, AFHQ 0100/12C G–3 Div Ops Fr Rearmt, Vol. II; Msg BX–13549, Devers to Marshall, 11 Jul 44, OPD Exec. 10, Item 52–E.

[54] Msg FWD 12414, Eisenhower to Marshall, 18 Jul 44, AFHQ 0100/26 Liaison Sec LX 320, Order of Battle.

intelligently." The recent communications from Generals Eisenhower, Devers, and Eaker, letters from Generals Béthouart and de Gaulle, a talk by General Donovan before the JLC in which he had urged that Resistance groups be issued heavy equipment, each had stressed one phase or another of the problem and often expressed conflicting views. To arrive at some sound solution, General Marshall directed that all papers, radios, and letters be turned over to the JLC for a comprehensive study of the most effective use of liberated manpower. He emphasized that the committee was to give no consideration to the development of a postwar French army but was to proceed on the assumption that only those troops should be equipped and armed which could participate in the war at an early date.[55]

Most eager to see some sort of a decision reached on the matter were, of course, the French themselves. On the ground that the "reorganization of the metropolitan army" was already raising a considerable number of problems, General Noiret proposed, on 1 August, to attach to SHAEF the Rearmament Section of his staff headed by Colonel Chanson, who in the past had dealt with similar problems in connection with the North African rearmament operations. A few days later General Noiret and representatives of SHAEF reached an agreement on the division of responsibility between SHAEF and French headquarters in the United Kingdom for handling problems arising in connection with liberated manpower, such as availability and allocation of personnel, submission of requisitions, and distribution of matériel.[56]

On 2 August 1944 the CCS finally took action on the matter of the reconstitution and equipping of armies of liberated nations. They communicated to General Eisenhower, who had been waiting since 13 June, a policy statement to guide him in his discussions with Allied military missions. The statement merely confirmed their earlier decision authorizing the formation of security units totaling not more than 172,000 men for western Europe (140,000 for the French).[57] It shed no light on the subject of labor units (not included in the 172,000-man ceiling) or of French combat units. It simply directed the Supreme Commander to inform Allied military missions that any requests from them considered by him to include, in effect, requirements for postwar armies, should be taken up "as between governments and not on the military level." Moreover, the statement provided no clue on the question of the provision of equipment.

With operations in progress on the Continent, the Supreme Commander was eager to proceed with the organization of the labor and security units necessary for the conduct of the war. The question of the provision of equipment needed to be settled without further delay. Yet the CCS still had not given any indication as to what proportion of the equipment required was to come from U.S. and what from British sources. In a memorandum to the British Chiefs of Staff, dated 8 August, General Smith urged that, pending a CCS decision on the matter, the requirements of the British 21 Army Group for mobile labor units and internal security units, as well as the requirements of the U.S. forces for internal security up to D plus 90, be met from British sources, that is, from

[55] Memo, Brig Gen Patrick H. Tansey for JLC, 20 Jul 44, ABC 091.711 France (6 Oct 43), Sec 2–A.

[56] Memos, Noiret for SHAEF, 1 Aug 44, and Whiteley for Noiret, 9 Aug 44, SHAEF G–3 091 France, Vol. II.

[57] Msg FACS 49, CCS to Eisenhower, 2 Aug 44, ABC 400.3295 (2 Aug 43), Sec 1–A.

stocks held by the War Office for liberated manpower. The War Office replied that the equipment requested would be released at once except for some items that were unavailable. However, the release would be made on the assumption that the figure of 172,000 (140,000 for the French) represented both security and labor units. If the Supreme Commander wished to increase the total beyond 172,000 in order to include labor units, he was advised to put the necessary proposals up to the CCS.[58]

On 9 August General Eisenhower informed the War Department that his combined requirements for static and mobile French civilian labor units were estimated at between 140,000 by D plus 60 and 468,000 by D plus 240. These units were over and above the 175 French battalions authorized earlier in April by the CCS for assignment to internal security and lines of communications duties. New, additional requirements were for the Garde Mobile (about 6,000 men), abolished by Vichy but whose reorganization he considered necessary, the Gendarmerie (approximately 10,000 men), and fire-fighting personnel (2,500 men). Also, it was intended to form another French Special Air Service (SAS) parachute battalion (in addition to the two activated earlier in the United Kingdom) for service behind enemy lines, and two Ranger battalions. The formation of these three units was essential in view of the attitude of the French. "While they are anxious to assist us to the greatest degree, they must for morale reasons be given an opportunity to fight." These several requirements concerned only the French. There were other Allies to consider. It was

imperative, then, that an early decision be reached on the question of allocation of responsibility for equipping all the units involved. Most of these were operationally required and none could be raised in the absence of a directive from the CCS.[59]

Such was the situation as ANVIL got under way on 15 August. Already large groups of Frenchmen, including Resistance units, had been liberated as a result of the progress of OVERLORD. No commitment had yet been made regarding their employment other than the formation of security and lines of communications units. Even for these, the question of equipment had not been settled.

It was difficult to see how the French liberated manpower question could be solved to the satisfaction of the three allies concerned considering the conclusions each had reached on the matter after months of negotiations.

For the French military authorities in Algiers, liberated manpower could be best used by enrolling it without delay in new combat units. They had already completed plans to this effect and were about to submit appropriate requisitions. On 16 August, just as the first North African divisions were landing on the beaches near St. Tropez, General Leyer asked the JRC what Allied agency would examine and process the requisitions. General Loomis could only reply that the CCS had the whole question of employment of Allied liberated manpower under consideration.[60]

For the British Chiefs of Staff, the question involved not only the immediate fulfillment of the Supreme Commander's re-

[58] Memos, Smith for COS, 8 Aug 44, and COS 1425/4, Office of War Cabinet for CofS SHAEF, 15 Aug 44, SHAEF SGS 475 France, Vol. I.

[59] Msg FWD 12731, Eisenhower to AGWAR, 9 Aug 44, OPD Exec 10, Item 52–E.

[60] Memos, Leyer for Loomis, 16 Aug 44, and Loomis for Leyer, 18 Aug 44, JRC 320/001 Orgn of JRC.

quirements, but, in view of the French position on the matter, the early building up of a nucleus of forces to assist in the occupation of Germany. Such a concession would, in their opinion, make the French more "amenable" to the wishes of the Supreme Commander and appease their understandable desire to organize more than internal security troops and Commandos.[61] On 22 August they broached the subject in a memorandum to the CCS. The British, they explained, desired strongly that the western European Allies have forces available for use in the period immediately following the cessation of hostilities in Europe and after the resumption of effective control by indigenous governments. Such forces would be required for the maintenance of internal security within the Allied territories concerned. In addition, by contributing to the occupation of Germany, they would assist in alleviating the British manpower situation and permit the United Kingdom to play a greater role in the war against Japan. As for their equipping, the British Chiefs of Staff considered it highly undesirable that the French or any other European Allies adopt a policy of accepting arms of enemy make as this could lead to a continued demand for spare parts, replacements, and ammunition. In their opinion, the responsibility for arming the forces in question should be divided as follows: pending the re-establishment of French industry, a "clearly military desirable" objective in itself, the United States would undertake to furnish the French with the needed equipment; the equipping of other western Allies would remain a British commitment. These proposals, they emphasized, were put forward on "purely military grounds," their

belief being that it was "in the vital strategic interest of both the U.S. and U.K. that the forces of our Western Allies should be closely integrated with our own." They estimated that the size of the French contingents required for the occupation of Germany would be eight divisions at the end of twenty-four months.[62]

For the Americans, the urgent question, as emphasized by a report just published by the JLC, was not the organization of post-armistice armies, but the best and most expeditious possible employment of liberated manpower during the current hostilities in Europe. Armed forces formed from liberated manpower in excess of those authorized for operations in the sphere of the Supreme Commander were, in effect, postwar armies which should be the subject of agreement between the governments concerned.[63] Commenting on the British Chiefs of Staff memorandum of 22 August to the CCS, General Handy, Assistant Chief of Staff, OPD, voiced the opinion that their proposal was a purely postwar matter and urged the U.S. Chiefs of Staff to approach it carefully and to make no commitment without the approval of the President.[64]

On 29 August the U.S. Chiefs of Staff submitted to the CCS a long memorandum (CCS 661) setting forth their latest views and recommendations. Ruling out the organization of forces over and above the requirements of the Supreme Commander as being postwar armies, they proposed that both he and General Wilson, the Supreme Allied Commander in the Mediterranean,

---

[61] Memo Washington COS (W) 180, COS for JSM, 19 Aug 44, SHAEF SGS 475 France, Vol. I.

[62] Memo, COS for CCS, CCS 653, 22 Aug 44, ABC 400.3295 (2 Aug 43), Sec 1–A.
[63] Rpt, JLC 140/3, 16 Aug 44, ABC 091.711 France (6 Oct 43), Sec 2–B.
[64] Note, Handy, 23 Aug 44, ABC 400.3295 (2 Aug 43), Sec 1–A.

be asked to determine, on the basis of operational considerations, the priorities for the use of French liberated manpower within their respective areas. Any new combat units organized by them would be equipped by the United States. Internal security battalions, on the other hand, would be equipped by the United Kingdom. Taking into consideration the desire of the French for a more active part in the fighting, the U.S. Chiefs of Staff then recommended the formation of new combat units not exceeding, for both theaters, 27 infantry battalions, 9 105-mm. artillery battalions, and three engineer combat battalions, all to be put in action as speedily as possible. Only such units should be re-equipped which were "essential to the completion of approved operations" and which were "likely to be trained and equipped in time to take part in operations." [65]

Thus was the American position made quite clear. In essence it had not varied since 18 July when General Eisenhower had proposed that the formation of new French combat units be restricted to three infantry divisions (or the equivalent of the battalions now recommended by the U.S. Chiefs of Staff), in addition to a limited number of Ranger or Commando-type units for immediate participation in operations.

By the end of August, as the CCS were examining the latest U.S. proposal, the French still were without a clear statement as to what material assistance they could expect from the Allies in equipping their liberated manpower.

[65] Memo, JCS for CCS, CCS 661, 29 Aug 44, ABC 091.711 France (6 Oct 44), Sec 2–B.

CHAPTER XIX

Arming Liberated Manpower

Interim Organization and Equipping of Labor and Internal Security Units

The spectacular speed with which the liberation of France progressed from the beginning of August through September 1944, as a result of the lightning advance of the Allied armies from both west and south, raised for the French military authorities insuperable problems of personnel and equipment. With more of the territory freed from enemy forces each passing day, larger numbers of Resistance troops, reservists, volunteers, and liberated prisoners of war became available. The French High Command was faced with one of two alternatives: to incorporate these men into regularly constituted units or to give them immediate employment in the civilian economy. With national resources exhausted, industry and commerce at a standstill, communications and transportation paralyzed, and a territorial military establishment completely disorganized, the constitution of new units was in itself a difficult task. It was made more troublesome as a result of the natural desire of a large part of the liberated men to resume the fight against the enemy rather than serve as laborers or guards in rear areas. Adding to the confusion was the absence of a clear indication of Anglo-American intentions with regard to the ultimate employment of liberated manpower, thus forcing the French High Command to take piecemeal measures in an effort to solve at least the short-term aspect of the problem.

The most serious question was what to do with the former FFI forces. Immediately after the liberation of Paris on 26 August, the irresponsible behavior of some of the units in the capital and vicinity became the source of grave concern to French and Allied authorities, as it constituted a threat to the security of the rear. In an attempt to regain control of the situation General de Gaulle decided to weed out and disarm the disaffected elements and to put the rest into uniform without delay. With this in view, he requested and obtained from General Eisenhower the emergency issue of 15,000 sets of clothing and some armament. Another request from General Koenig, then military governor of Paris, for arms and equipment to enable the Paris Gendarmerie to maintain order in the capital was likewise granted.[1] The situation quickly deteriorated, however. Armed, undisciplined groups were reported wandering through Paris and country towns, seriously threatening order. General Koenig, technically still the commander in chief of all FFI, estimated that, by this time, some 200,000 armed men and boys, and possibly another

---

[1] Memo, Smith for G–4 SHAEF, 28 Aug 44, SHAEF SGS 475 France, Vol. I; Msg (unnumbered), SHAEF Mission Paris to SHAEF FWD, 5 Sep 44, SHAEF SGS 475 France, Vol. II.

200,000 unarmed but organized into bands, were at large in the liberated areas. Responsible French authorities were said to be reluctant to disarm or disband them in view of the services they had rendered. Furthermore, it was unlikely that they could be absorbed into civilian life for several months. In General Koenig's opinion, serious trouble would be forestalled only if 100,000 of them were promptly mustered into the Army or given employment.[2]

It was largely in an attempt to reduce the FFI problem that the French military authorities then launched their mobilization program. As a first step, they began organizing two infantry divisions, one in the north, one in the south. In Washington General de Saint-Didier, chief of the French Military Mission, explained to General Marshall that the new units were two of the three divisions whose organization Generals Eisenhower and Devers had "approved." Anticipating that their status would be debated for some time, General de Saint-Didier urged that, in the interim, consideration be given forthwith to the supply of clothing and equipment for the 30,-000 men involved. Such a step would help to speed up their employment and thereby maintain their morale. In referring the matter to Eisenhower and Devers for advice, Marshall pointed out that since the U.S. Chiefs of Staff had approved as a general principle the equipping of "such French units as could be used at an early date against the enemy," the Supreme Commander might wish to consider the desirability of granting the request. Pending a reply from the theater, General Marshall advised General de Saint-Didier that the

present plan as approved by the U.S. Chiefs of Staff did not contemplate equipping complete additional divisions but "permitted a charge for clothing and equipment to be made against the plan should it prove desirable."[3]

Meanwhile, the organization of security battalions and labor units was getting under way. In Brittany, ten battalions formed from FFI personnel were being employed in mopping-up operations. They were being issued fuel and food, as well as captured German weapons and ammunition. Similar measures were being taken to equip the security battalions being organized in southern France also from FFI personnel.[4]

To meet SHAEF's requirements for security battalions and labor units, the French High Command agreed on 23 August to make available at once, as a first increment, 100,000 men distributed as follows: 53,000 in the U.S. zone of communications, 26,000 in the British zone, and 21,000 in their own zone. SHAEF promptly initiated action to obtain from the War Department and the War Office the matériel necessary to equip these men. Without waiting for the CCS to determine the source of equipment for liberated manpower, the British Chiefs of Staff agreed to the immediate release of the equipment needed for the security units being activated within both the British and the U.S. zones. Simultaneously, General Marshall assured the Supreme Commander that War Department officials were making every effort to meet the requirements for

---

[2] Msg FWD 14014, SHAEF to State Dept, 6 Sep 44, SHAEF SGS 475 France, Vol. II.

[3] Memos, de Saint-Didier for Marshall, 2 Sep 44, and, Marshall for de Saint-Didier, 6 Sep 44, OCS A–48–11, 091 France, Sec I; Msg WX–25757, Marshall to Eisenhower and Devers, 5 Sep 44, OPD Exec 10, Item 52–E.

[4] Msg FWD 13729, Eisenhower to Somervell, 4 Sep 44, SHAEF SGS 475 France, Vol. I; Memo, Gammell for CofS Fr Ground Forces, 8 Sep 44, AFHQ 0100/12C G–3 Div Ops Fr Equip.

civilian labor in support of the U.S. forces.[5]

By early September plans had been completed for activation of the units required by SHAEF. Tables of organization and equipment had been determined for each category: military mobile labor companies, civilian mobile and static labor units, and security battalions. Pending a CCS decision regarding the responsibility for the procurement of equipment, the War Office had offered to provide an initial 40,250 individual sets of clothing and equipment from the pool of equipment for 172,000 men which it was holding.[6]

At the request of the French, plans also were made to rehabilitate the Territorial Command, the organization normally charged with recruitment and administration. The nineteen military regions and ninety subregions comprising this command being completely depleted of material resources, arrangements were made to provide them with a minimum of equipment drawn from British, Canadian, and U.S. sources.[7]

In the belief that a decision on the long-term aspect of the liberated manpower question could be postponed no longer, General Juin, Chief of Staff of National Defense since his return from Italy in early August, appealed directly to General Marshall on 7 September. Liberated effectives, he explained, were now available in large numbers. Their immediate absorption into the Army, most desirable at this time, could be effected only under strict military discipline and by integration into divisional units. On the hypothesis, which he considered "plausible," of a very rapidly approaching cessation of hostilities, it would be sufficient to organize, as already started, security units equipped with light matériel. Later, as the necessary heavier matériel was made available, these units could be formed into divisions to be used as a "supplementary security force" for maintaining order within the country. General Juin "assumed" that the principle of arming five such new divisions had been accepted by War Department officials as a result of their conversations with Generals Béthouart and de Gaulle in July. He hoped that the U.S. Chiefs of Staff would approve his proposal, since the French military authorities needed their agreement to guide them in planning the reorganization of the metropolitan army.[8]

General Juin's conviction about the need of building up a large security force of the size of five divisions was not shared by General Devers. The latter, in fact, was now reversing his earlier stand with respect to the use of French liberated manpower in the light of the current operational situation. Answering General Marshall's message of 5 September, he not only questioned, from a military viewpoint, the necessity of organizing the 175 security battalions for which equipment had been requested, but declared himself no longer in favor, as he

[5] Msg FWD 14795, Eisenhower to SHAEF Mission to France, 14 Sep 44, SHAEF G–3 091 France, Vol. III; Msg FWD 13217, FWD SHAEF to CG COMZONE and CG 12th Army Gp, 24 Aug 44, SHAEF G–3 091 France, Vol. II; Msg EX–45523, CG ETOUSA to WD, 28 Aug 44, OPD 400 France, Sec 4; Memo, SHAEF for CG COMZONE ETOUSA, 30 Aug 44, SHAEF SGS 475 France, Vol. I; Msg WX–23756, Marshall to Eisenhower, 30 Aug 44, ASF International Div File Cable Log OUT A–45–192, France, Aug–Nov 44.

[6] Memo, SHAEF for CG COMZONE, 6 Sep 44, SHAEF G–3 091 France, Vol. III.

[7] Memos, Bull for CofS SHAEF, 18 Aug 44, and Smith for CG COMZONE ETOUSA, 21 Aug 44, SHAEF SGS 475 France, Vol. I; Ltr, Noce to Director Liaison and Munitions WO, 18 Sep 44, AFHQ 0100/12C G–3 Div Ops Fr Equip.

[8] Ltr, Juin to Marshall, 7 Sep 44, ABC 091.711 France (6 Oct 43), Sec 2–B.

had been in July, of activating new divisions on the ground that they would not be ready before the spring of 1945. He recommended instead the formation of a maximum of five infantry regiments, amounting to approximately 15,000 men, for use as replacements for the existing North African divisions currently engaged in operations. The maintenance of these divisions at effective combat strength was, in his opinion, the most urgent problem to be considered.[9]

The British Chiefs of Staff, on the other hand, were more convinced than ever, also in the light of the current operational situation, that discussions on the employment of French liberated manpower should not be restricted to the period preceding the cessation of hostilities. Elaborating on their earlier statement of 22 August, they urged the CCS, on 10 September, to examine the long-term aspect of the problem and to do so "in a realistic manner." While agreeing with the U.S. Chiefs of Staff that SHAEF must have priority in calling French manpower for immediate essential duties, they pointed to the "very real need of encouraging the creation of substantial French forces to assist in the occupation of Germany." They felt that what was required was the establishment of a broad plan to equip forces of all western European Allies including the French, in which due consideration would be given to the employment of manpower during the earlier posthostilities stage as well as before the cessation of hostilities.[10]

The stand taken by the British Chiefs had already been made the subject of a study by the U.S. Joint Logistics Committee upon the receipt of their first memorandum. The JLC had come to the conclusion that any discussion concerning the build-up of post-hostilities internal security armies must be tripartite, that is, it must include the USSR. This course of action was indispensable in order to promote the confidence of that country and to avoid strained relations likely to result from any steps toward the establishment of a military bloc in whose creation the USSR had not been consulted.[11] No solution appeared yet in sight which would reconcile the divergent positions now taken by the British, Americans, and French.

On 22 September General Marshall, answering General Juin's proposal of 7 September, informed him that because of the scope and importance of the question, it was one to be ultimately decided by the CCS. No action could be taken by them until the British Chiefs of Staff had been heard from. General Marshall then referred to what he called General Béthouart's "apparent misunderstanding" on the question of additional divisions. The present intention of the U.S. Chiefs of Staff was to equip 3, not 5, new infantry divisions thereby bring the original ANFA commitment of 11 divisions to completion.[12]

In the theater, the equipping of security and labor units was proceeding at a much slower pace than originally contemplated. The French military authorities were reported to be showing "great unwillingness" to meet the requirements for labor units. Concerned over the situation, SHAEF reminded them of their agreement of 23 August to place a specific number of men at the disposal of the Allied command and

[9] Msg BX–16065, Devers to Marshall, 9 Sep 44, OPD Cable Files.

[10] Memo, COS for CCS, CCS 653/1, 10 Sep 44, ABC 400.3295 (2 Aug 43), Sec 1–B.

[11] Rpt, JCS 1039, JLC to JCS, 6 Sep 44, in same file.

[12] Ltr, Marshall to Juin, 22 Sep 44, OCS A–48–11, 091 France, Sec 1.

warned that if the agreement was not carried out the Supreme Commander would be compelled to revise the commitments already undertaken to equip the men.[13]

All things considered, it appeared to be not so much a case of unwillingness on the part of the French military authorities as of quasi impossibility for them to require the former members of the Resistance to drop their rifles in exchange for shovels.[14] Already large numbers of the FFI (40,000 by 20 September) were swelling the ranks of 1st French Army, meanwhile raising, for the latter, considerable equipment and maintenance problems. To the French General Staff it was clear that the labor and internal security program was not, in itself, sufficient to solve satisfactorily the liberated manpower problem.

Eager to co-operate with the Supreme Commander, General Juin immediately contacted the responsible Allied headquarters only to be told that the 40,000-odd individual sets of clothing and equipment promised by the War Office as a first allocation for labor and security units were still in the United Kingdom. Earlier messages from Communications Zone, ETOUSA, to the War Office requesting information on where and when to obtain the matériel had not yet been answered. Thus the already difficult task of forming the required units became even more troublesome, as the U.S. and British Armies could make only piecemeal emergency issues pending the replacement of matériel from War Office stocks.[15]

Partly as a result of the slowness with which the labor and security program was progressing, but mainly because of the currently favorable operational situation, SHAEF authorities were gradually reversing their earlier stand in favor of activating additional French divisions. In spite of French pressure, it appeared no longer desirable or feasible, as it did in July and early August, to form any unit larger than a battalion from liberated manpower. It was no longer to be assumed that the war would last well into 1945. The total number of French nationals suitable for full military service had not reached the expected figures. Shipping commitments w e r e severely strained. Furthermore, if French divisions were formed, a large portion of available manpower would thus be lost for immediate and direct assistance to the Allied Expeditionary Force, thereby greatly aggravating the labor and internal security problems. On 22 September General Eisenhower informed General Marshall that he desired to form only internal security units (including the Gendarmerie), labor units, ten Ranger-type battalions, and certain administrative units, for all of which plans were going forward and full details were being communicated to the CCS for decision. He stressed that no unit larger than a battalion was required at that time. With this pronouncement, the issue with respect to additional French divisions was to rest for some weeks to come.[16]

To co-ordinate the various equipment problems then involving the French, such as the continued maintenance of their expeditionary forces engaged in combat and the implementation of the current labor and security program, as well as of any future

---

[13] Msg FWD 14795, Eisenhower to SHAEF Mission to France, 14 Sep 44, SHAEF G–3 091 France, Vol. III.

[14] Interv with Regnault, Sep 50.

[15] Ltr, Juin to Smith, 17 Sep 44, and Memo, SHAEF Mission to France for Smith, 19 Sep 44, SHAEF SGS 475 France, Vol. I.

[16] Memo, Bull for CofS, 14 Sep 44, SHAEF SGS France 475/2, Vol. I; Msg FWD 15331, Eisenhower to Marshall, 22 Sep 44, OPD Cable Files.

armament program, the decision was reached, at the urging of the French themselves and of Allied authorities in the Mediterranean theater, to establish a central armament authority similar to the North African JRC. Soon after the organization, on 15 September, of the SHAEF Mission to France to act as a channel through which the French Provisional Government could raise matters with SHAEF, the latter authorized the setting up of a Rearmament Division within the mission. Selected American, French, and British personnel from the various agencies heretofore charged with supervising the rearmament and training of the North African forces gradually were transferred to the Continent for the purpose of staffing the division. By 16 October Rearmament Division, SHAEF Mission to France, headed by General Loomis, was in full operation.[17]

Meanwhile, the question of the disposition of former Resistance personnel was becoming increasingly acute. Within the area of 1st French Army, sufficient elements had become available to form twenty security battalions over and above those which the French authorities were organizing for combat. Equipping the security battalions offered no great problem since the necessary matériel was provided by the War Office on call. It was with respect to combat battalions that difficulties were being experienced. Neither 1st French Army nor U.S. 6th Army Group had excess stocks available for the purpose. The French General Staff then turned to SHAEF for assistance and

submitted a request for equipment. SHAEF replied that if General Devers, Commanding General, 6th Army Group, wished to employ FFI combat battalions as part of 1st French Army, their equipment would have to be drawn from captured war matériel, at least temporarily, or from other 6th Army Group resources. Whereupon General Devers pointed to the considerable confusion which existed regarding the matter and urged that the responsibility for equipping and maintaining FFI combat battalions be made to rest solely with the French High Command. Pending final settlement of the question, the Supreme Commander authorized Devers, on 2 October, to equip at his discretion such units as he considered necessary to assist in military operations, using for the purpose captured war matériel and local French resources.[18]

By then the situation had reached a critical point. General Devers reported on 7 October that some 52,000 former FFI troops had enlisted in the French Army for the duration of the war. Of this number, approximately 12,000 were already in combat. To provide them with adequate equipment was beyond the means of 6th Army Group. With respect to weapons, the French authorities expected to have sufficient German, Italian, British, and French rifles to meet the requirements. But no clothing was available. Because of this, there was danger of these men returning to their homes where their presence might result in public disturbances. It was

[17] Ltr, Juin to Smith, 20 Sep 44, SHAEF Mission to France 091.711–3 (Fr); Msg NAF 783, Wilson to CCS, 16 Sep 44, OPD Cable Files; Msg 14930 SCAF 83, SCAEF to CCS, 15 Sep 44, JRC Cable Log. For additional information on the Rearmament Division, see Chapter XXIII, below.

[18] Msgs, Eisenhower to Devers, FWD 15582, 24 Sep 44, and FWD 15887, 26 Sep 44, SHAEF SGS 475 France, Vol. I; Msg BX–16780, Devers to SHAEF FWD, 27 Sep 44, SHAEF SGS 475 France, Vol. I; Msg FWD 16836, Eisenhower to Devers, 3 Oct 44, SHAEF SGS 475 France, Vol. II.

essential that the clothing problem be settled without delay.[19]

General Smith promptly advised General Devers to submit a request to the CCS, through SHAEF, for the necessary clothing and equipment for the 52,000 men if he wished to use them. He then requested General Devers to remind the French in his area that the size and composition of the French Army was a matter for the decision of the CCS. SHAEF itself was not in a position to authorize the French High Command to enlist personnel for the national army in excess of units provided for under the current approved programs.[20]

The next day, 12 October, Mr. André Diethelm, Minister of War, whose previous requests had been turned down and who had been advised by General de Saint-Didier in Washington not to entertain the hope that combat units drawn from FFI personnel might be equipped, appealed directly to General Eisenhower. It was essential, he urged, that for military, moral, and political reasons a few at least of the FFI units then engaged in operations be issued a minimum amount of modern equipment. The forces in question amounted to some 112,000 men, 52,000 of whom were fighting as part of 1st French Army and the rest, or 60,000, were engaged in operations on the Atlantic coast. The conditioning of these forces would interfere in no way with the labor and security program. Mr. Diethelm's request was no more fortunate than his earlier proposals. The Supreme Commander directed SHAEF to inform him that no consideration would be given French requests until

SHAEF's requirements in labor and security units had been met.[21]

Answering General Smith's letter of 11 October, General Devers submitted his plan for the employment of the 52,000 FFI personnel now incorporated in 1st French Army. It contemplated the organization of 1 infantry regiment, 2 infantry battalions, and 3 armored battalions; the activation of relief and rest battalions for each of the existing infantry regiments, or a total of 19 battalions; the building up of a replacement pool of 12,000 men for 1st French Army; finally, with the coming of cold weather, the replacement of all Negro troops in the 9th Colonial Infantry Division (9th DIC) and 1st March Infantry Division (1st DMI).[22] These Negro elements, largely from Senegal and amounting to approximately 15,000 men, were already being withdrawn and moved to southern France.[23]

With the approach of winter the problem of clothing liberated effectives swelling the ranks of the French armed forces was becoming serious. The Allies were providing clothing only for the security battalions, none for the ill-clad FFI troops currently engaged in operations. To those FFI units fighting on the Atlantic coast, the French High Command was able to allocate 72,000 French uniforms recovered in a depot at

---

[19] Msg B–17326, Devers to SHAEF FWD, 7 Oct 44, SHAEF SGS 475 France, Vol. II.

[20] Memo, Smith for Devers, 11 Oct 44, in same file.

[21] Ltr, Diethelm to Eisenhower, 12 Oct 44, SHAEF Mission to France 421–1 Combined; Memo, SCAEF for SHAEF Mission to France, 19 Oct 44, SHAEF G–3 091 France, Vol. III.

[22] This was the former 1st Motorized Infantry Division, known before September 1943 as the 1st Free French Division.

[23] Memo, G–3 SHAEF for CofS, 21 Oct 44, and Msg S–63760, Eisenhower to AGWAR, 24 Oct 44, SHAEF SGS 475 France, Vol. II; Msg S–65011, SCAEF to AFHQ, 1 Nov 44, SHAEF Mission to France 091.711–1 (Fr); Msg SCAF 130, Eisenhower to CCS, 13 Nov 44, ABC 380 France, Sec 1–A.

Troyes after the withdrawal of the Germans. But for those in 1st French Army area, it could only provide 25,000 sets from Canadian clothing stocks then in Algiers. This quantity was woefully insufficient.[24]

In an effort to solve the problem of clothing and equipment for FFI personnel, representatives of SHAEF, Communications Zone, Rearmament Division, and other agencies met on 25 October. They agreed that changes in liberated manpower requirements brought about by new conditions on the Continent necessitated review and a fresh approach to the CCS for the purpose of obtaining both an increase of the equipment allotments to SHAEF and a covering authority for equipment commitments entered into without previous sanction of the Combined Chiefs. The latest such commitment concerned the various Allied Resistance forces currently estimated, for the French alone, at 105,000 men, for whom neither clothing nor equipment was available. It was essential that the provision of matériel to them be fitted into a long-term program for equipping liberated manpower.[25]

Organization and equipping of labor and internal security units, meanwhile, were lagging behind schedule. The French military authorities were not making available all the manpower necessary to meet SHAEF's requirements. In addition, matériel was slow in coming from the United

Kingdom because of the very limited port and shipping facilities and the fact that shipment of the equipment was competing with that of other matériel considered essential to the further advance of the Allied armies. The French themselves were responsible for activating the units, for distributing to them matériel issued through army groups or Communications Zone channels, and for their training which was conducted with the assistance of Inspection Group, the Rearmament Division's training section headed by General Kingman. Once ready, the units passed under Allied operational control, the French High Command retaining full disciplinary powers.[26]

While the launching of the labor and security program was making some headway, the issue with respect to additional combat forces was no nearer solution. The only new development in the controversy was that the British had given up, in the face of American opposition, their earlier proposal to equip liberated manpower units for posthostilities occupation duties. In late September the Joint Strategic Survey Committee had advised against arming such forces because at that juncture they would be of no advantage to the United States and the United Kingdom. The committee urged the JCS to adhere to the position that any discussion of the British proposal must be held at government level in order to include the USSR, since it was not an appropriate subject for consideration by the CCS.[27] The JCS promptly informed the CCS that, in their opinion, the subject

---

[24] The 25,000 were part of 100,000 sets originally intended for Territorial forces in North Africa. In late October the Canadian Government offered a further 100,000 sets and 20,000 greatcoats. Msgs WX–47757, Somervell to SHAEF, 17 Oct 44, and S–64381, Eisenhower to AGWAR, 27 Oct 44, and Memo, SHAEF Mission to France for SCAEF, 8 Oct 44, SHAEF Mission to France 421–1 Combined.

[25] Min, Mtg at SHAEF Main, 25 Oct 44, SHAEF Mission to France 091.4 Liberated People.

[26] Memo, Smith for Juin, 27 Sep 44, SHAEF SGS 475 France, Vol. I; Memo, SHAEF AG–400–1 (Fr), 4 Oct 44, SHAEF G–3 091 France, Vol. III; Ltr, Hq COMZONE to Sec Comdrs, 27 Oct 44, SHAEF Mission to France 091.711–1 (Fr).

[27] Rpt, JSSC to JCS, JCS 1039/1, 28 Sep 44, ABC 400.3295 (2 Aug 43), Sec 1–B.

of re-equipping postwar forces must be divorced from the question of equipping additional French forces for early participation in active operations against Germany. They urged the British Chiefs of Staff to approve their 29 August proposal without delay so as to permit its early implementation. Ten days later, in the absence of a reply from the British Chiefs of Staff, the JCS submitted a second memorandum to the CCS, reiterating their belief that the British counterproposals involved long-term matters of policy requiring decision and agreement not at CCS but at government level. They were therefore referring the matter to the U.S. Government and recommending that an agreement be reached on a governmental level or through the European Advisory Commission "since it would appear that tripartite control of occupation of Germany is involved." A few days later, on 21 October, the British Chiefs having decided to pursue the matter no further, the controversial proposal was removed from the CCS agenda by secretarial action.[28]

The French of course had not given up hope for the equipping of new combat units. Told on several occasions that the matter was one to be taken up directly with Washington on a governmental level, General de Gaulle had, in early October, considered sending General Juin to Washington with full authority to explain the French point of view to General Marshall and the CCS. Informed of the proposed visit, OPD officials urged General Marshall to tell the French that matters would be expedited if concrete proposals, cleared beforehand with

General Eisenhower, were submitted by General Juin to the CCS before he arrived in Washington. General Juin's trip did not materialize, for in the meantime General Marshall had flown to the Continent where he had an opportunity to discuss the rearmament issue with General Juin. On his return to Washington, he was handed a memorandum from General de Saint-Didier restating the position of the Provisional Government. The French recognized that General Eisenhower was above all justly concerned with the conduct of operations now in progress and the security of his armies, but they were "under obligation" to take into account requirements of national import, such as the incorporation of FFI units into the army to enable them to fight in a normal way as an integral part of large units. France owed it to herself to have more than 8 divisions in action to pursue the war and at the same time to "satisfy her domestic needs and those of occupation." The French hoped that the equipment necessary for the 5 divisions requested by General Juin, or at least for the remaining 3 on the ANFA program, would be authorized.[29]

At that very moment SHAEF was submitting to the French in Paris for their concurrence the draft of an agreement between their government and the Supreme Commander to regulate the command of labor, internal security, and other units raised for service with the Allied Expeditionary Force. Examination of the document prompted General Juin, on 31 October, to make two important observations. To achieve the rapid success of future operations as well

---

[28] Memos, JCS for CCS, CCS 653/2, 11 Oct 44, and Leahy for Hull, 11 Oct 44, ABC 400.3295 (2 Aug 43), Sec 1–B; Memo, JCS for CCS, CCS 661/1, 29 Sep 44, ABC 400.3295 (2 Aug 43), Sec 2–B.

[29] Ltr, de Saint-Didier to Marshall, 24 Oct 44, ABC 091.711 France (6 Oct 43), Sec 2–B; Ltr, de Saint-Didier to Marshall, 6 Oct 44, ABC 091.711 France (6 Oct 43), Sec 5; Memo, OPD for Marshall, 19 Oct 44, in same file.

as to permit the French to play the part which they desired to play, it was necessary that the Allies facilitate the development of the French Army. The Provisional Government, moreover, could not envisage the creation of auxiliary units as required by SHAEF except within the framework of a reconstituted army requiring, first of all, the equipping of a certain number of large units.[30]

The situation was reaching an impasse. Ten weeks after the launching of ANVIL, the CCS were no nearer a decision on the French liberated manpower question. The British Chiefs of Staff still had not answered th U.S. proposal of 29 August calling for the equipping of some additional French combat battalions. Now the French were renewing their demands for the reconstitution of their metropolitan army.

Yet, in the course of the preceding weeks, some progress had been noted in the rehabilitation of the French war machine. Arrangements had been made for the supply of French ports not under immediate U.S. or British control. At the request of the French, SHAEF had authorized the organization of a French tactical air command to give air support to 1st French Army. Particularly noteworthy had been the efforts of the French to rehabilitate part of their armament industry. The manufacture of automatic pistols and rifles was under way, and it was expected that within a few months production could be expanded considerably to include machine guns, mortars, vehicles, and other items. The French were also planning to reopen shortly their ordnance depots for the repair of French ordnance matériel, including vehicles.[31]

The Liberated Manpower and Metropolitan Programs

Bridging the gap between the respective positions taken by the three allies on the matter of French liberated manpower came rather suddenly as a result, not of the weakening of any of the stands taken, but because of the unexpected turn of military events.

The summer dash of the Allied armies through France, which had brought with it high hopes for a not-too-distant cessation of hostilities, had slackened toward the end of September. The slowing-down period, in fact, had just begun at the time of the Supreme Commander's intimation, given on 22 September, that he desired no new French combat units larger than a battalion.[32] The Germans had managed to stop their hasty retreat and appeared determined to dig in for a prolonged defense. In a message to the CCS dated 31 October, General Eisenhower disclosed that events of the past few weeks were causing him to review the situation with respect to the employment of French liberated manpower. He believed that, in addition to the current labor and security program for which he was sending final recommendations in a separate communication, some divisions could be made ready in time to be of use provided the necessary equipment and shipping were made available. The units raised in North Africa had fought well in Italy and France, he explained. Arming them with U.S. matériel had resulted in saving thousands of American and British lives. After the long campaigns in which they had been involved, some of them needed to be withdrawn and replaced. In lieu of the ten Ranger battalions recommended earlier, Eisenhower now proposed the activation and equipping of two addi-

---

[30] Ltr, Juin to SHAEF Mission to France, 31 Oct 44, ABC 091.711 France (6 Oct 43), Sec 2–B.

[31] SHAEF Mission to France, Appendix to Fortnightly Rpt 15–31 Oct 44, SHAEF SGS 475/3 France.

[32] Msg FWD 15331, Eisenhower to Marshall, 22 Sep 44, OPD Cable Files.

tional infantry divisions to be used as replacements. He believed that the French could provide the necessary personnel and organize and train the two units to be ready for combat by 1 March 1945.[33]

In a second message of the same date, the Supreme Commander reviewed for the CCS the whole question of SHAEF's requirements in Allied liberated manpower and recommended that, in the light of the experience gained to date and of the current operational situation, the ceiling be raised from 172,000 men (as estimated in March of the same year and approved by the CCS on 9 July) to 460,000 men. For the French, this meant an increase from 140,000 to 243,000 men. This revision upward was essential to take care of additional commitments, such as Territorial Command headquarters, Gendarmerie, and Garde Mobile, which, in the absence of specific authority, SHAEF had undertaken to assume for operational reasons. There were, in addition, 48,000 FFI troops which 6th Army Group desired to equip and organize in light infantry battalions. Matériel for these various additional requirements had been drawn from the War Office pool of equipment for 172,000 men. This pool was now nearly exhausted. So far, the supplies released from British sources had been sufficient to equip 108,000 men out of the authorized 140,000. General Eisenhower then broached the question of the division of responsibility between the United States and the United Kingdom for providing the matériel to outfit the 460,000 men required under the revised program. He proposed that the United States be asked to furnish all vehicles and other types of equipment which the British normally obtained from the Americans.[34]

The Supreme Commander's views, together with General Juin's communication of 31 October on the reconstitution of the French Army, were transmitted to the CCS by General Loomis, then on a short visit in Washington. In a personal memorandum, the chief of the Rearmament Division informed the CCS that General Juin's letter had filled Supreme Headquarters with considerable apprehension. The letter appeared to be in effect a declaration by the French that they considered the reconstitution of their Army as taking precedence over aid to the Allies in winning the war. Such a proposal was inacceptable to SHAEF. In fact General Smith's first reaction had been to consider the withdrawal of the recommendations already made for additional equipment and the cancellation of orders. This course of action had now been ruled out in favor of immediate discussions with the French. In the forthcoming negotiations with them, the Supreme Commander's hand would be greatly strengthened if he had the authority of the CCS to furnish equipment for such units as could be agreed upon to fill SHAEF's requirements. The authority, if granted, would be used only if the French agreed to provide units of a type and priority required by SHAEF for current operations. Should no such agreement be reached, it might then be desirable to stop further issues of equipment to the French and utilize Polish, Czechoslovakian, and other sources of Allied manpower.[35]

[33] Ltr, Eisenhower to CCS, CCS 661/2, 31 Oct 44, ABC 091.711 France (6 Oct 43), Sec 2–B.

[34] Ltr, Smith to CCS, CCS 627/4, 31 Oct 44, in same file.

[35] Memo, Loomis for CCS, 6 Nov 44, ABC 091.-711 France (6 Oct 43), Sec 2–B; Memo for Rcd, SHAEF G–3, 13 Nov 44, and Memo, SHAEF G–3 for CofS, 14 Nov 44, SHAEF SGS 475 France, Vol. II.

During this time the two communications of 31 October from the Supreme Commander had been referred to OPD and the JLC with a view to weighing his proposals in the light of availability of equipment and shipping space. On the recommendation of the JLC, the U.S. Chiefs of Staff informed the CCS on 23 November that as far as France was concerned, General Eisenhower's requirements could be met in general under the provisions of their earlier memorandum of 29 August (CCS 661) which, incidentally, was still awaiting British action.[36]

To settle the liberated manpower issue, General Smith, at a meeting held at Supreme Headquarters on 18 November, invited Generals Juin and Leyer to present the French point of view. The discussion resulted in complete agreement. After paying tribute to the efforts exerted by SHAEF to equip the French armed forces, General Juin outlined the progress of French action in meeting the Supreme Commander's requirements. He pointed out that a number of labor units as well as 120 security battalions had already been activated. His recommendations on the control, functions, and equipping of the security battalions appeared satisfactory to General Smith and his associates, who, after some discussion, expressed their complete approval. General Juin then turned to the subject which his government had most at heart, the reorganization of the metropolitan army. The French, he explained, were most anxious to participate in the war with more than 8 divisions in the line. They wanted, in fact, 8 more divisions—6 infantry, 1 mountain, and 1 armored—grouped

in 2 army corps. Even if there could be no guarantee of equipment, the military authorities were determined to proceed with the organization of these new units and to equip them progressively. At the invitation of General Smith, General Leyer then explained how the French General Staff hoped to equip these 8 new divisions.

The proposed plan, entirely separate from, and in addition to, the current security and labor program, contemplated three phases, as follows: Phase I, 1 mountain and 2 infantry divisions, equipped largely with French matériel in order to save on shipping; Phase II, 1 infantry and 1 armored division, equipped entirely with matériel of Allied source; Phase III, 3 infantry divisions equipped also with French matériel.

General Smith pointed out that the program was an excellent one but that the possibility of its implementation would be determined by two factors: the fulfillment of other priority commitments and availability of equipment and shipping. After some discussion, the conferees agreed upon the following armament priorities: (1) completion of the security and labor program, (2) Allied equipment to complete Phase I of the proposed French plan, (3) instructional equipment for Phase II. They further agreed that the FFI would be completely absorbed in the plan and that all details of implementation would be worked out between the French military authorities, the Rearmament Division, and other responsible SHAEF staff sections.[37]

One factor apparently not discussed at the meeting but bound to condition the speed of implementation of the plan was that of manpower. Figures which the Ministry of War had just released on 10

---

[36] Memos, OPD for Col George A. Lincoln, 9 Nov 44, and Hull for Marshall, 14 Dec 44, ABC 091.711 France (6 Oct 43), Sec 1–B.

[37] Min, Rearmt Conf, 18 Nov 44, SHAEF 388.3/3 Fr Rearmt.

November indicated that 382,000 liberated men were then available. Of these, 52,000 were at the disposal of 1st French Army and 36,000 were engaged in operations on the Atlantic c o a s t, leaving approximately 294,000 men. SHAEF's own requirements being estimated at 216,000, the net excess numbered only 78,000 men. Since the 8-division proposal required over 200,000 men, it was apparent that its implementation could be effected only very gradually as the units of the labor and security program reverted to French control. The mobilization of additional effectives could hardly be considered at this juncture as all civilian manpower was urgently needed for the rehabilitation of the national economy and the maintenance of existing public services.[38]

Two days after the French had outlined their intentions, they held a conference with British military authorities to determine the extent to which the United Kingdom could assist in providing equipment for the proposed new divisions. Lt. Gen. Sir Ronald Weeks, representing the Imperial General Staff, informed General Leyer that some surplus stocks of equipment in the United Kingdom could be made available. At his suggestion, the French Chief of Staff agreed to send a team to tour British depots and determine what items would be acceptable and in what quantities. It was then decided that all subsequent negotiations on the matter would be channeled through the Rearmament Division.[39]

To ensure closer co-ordination with SHAEF on armament matters, in anticipation especially of an approval of their new program, the French military authorities merged their Armament Liaison Section, currently attached to G–3, SHAEF Mission to France, with the French Section already operating with General Loomis' Rearmament Division. They placed the new section, called French Group of the Rearmament Division, SHAEF Mission to France, under the command of Colonel Regnault and gave it full authority to represent them at SHAEF.[40] Meanwhile, SHAEF undertook to determine the procedure and responsibilities for processing the detailed plan which the French General Staff was preparing in pursuance of General Juin's proposal.[41]

The final plan was submitted by Mr. Diethelm on 30 November. Known thereafter as the 30 November Plan, it consisted of three separate projects: Liberated Manpower (or SHAEF) Program, Far East Program, and Metropolitan Program. The Liberated Manpower Program, to be completed at a pace to be determined by SHAEF, consisted of 120 security battalions grouped in 40 regiments, 34 labor groups of 4 companies each, Gendarmerie and Garde Mobile units, and 10 Ranger battalions. The Far East Program, which had already been submitted to General Marshall on 1 October, contemplated the activation of units amounting to 18,000 men. The Metropolitan Program envisaged the constitution of 8 divisions and 213 supporting army corps and general reserve units, with a combined total strength of 207,000 men. Its implementation, according to Mr. Diethelm, was conditioned, not by availability of manpower which, he stressed, was adequate, but to a great extent by the output of French industry, as 6 of the divisions were

[38] Rpt, Fr War Ministry, 10 Nov 44, SHAEF Mission to France 091.711–1 (Fr).

[39] Min, Mtg on Fr Rearmt, 20 Nov 44, SHAEF Mission to France 091.711–3 (Fr).

[40] See p. 386, below.

[41] Memo, SHAEF Mission to France for G–3 SHAEF Main, 24 Nov 44, SHAEF G–3 091 France, Vol. IV.

to be equipped largely from French sources. The 5 divisions of Phase I and Phase II, of which 3 were already activated, were to be made ready by 1 May 1945, and the 3 divisions of Phase II by 1 August of the same year.[42]

Apprised of the French intentions, the British Chiefs of Staff expressed the fear that the proposed Metropolitan Program was in conflict with the recommendations submitted on 29 August (CCS 661), recommendations which, incidentally, were still awaiting British concurrence. General Loomis assured General Weeks that there was no conflict between the two proposals. CCS 661 had urged the equipping of a number of infantry, artillery, and engineer battalions equivalent to three of the infantry divisions now requested by the French. These could be considered as representing the balance of the old ANFA program.[43]

After a careful study of the 30 November Plan, SHAEF concluded that it contained implications requiring further examination. In particular, the Metropolitan Program, as it stood, did not include sufficient service troops. It contemplated the activation of divisions on the basis of a 25,000-man division slice, a much lower figure than the corresponding U.S. slice of 40,000 and even lower than the current 1st French Army slice of 32,500.[44]

In transmitting a copy of the plan to the CCS on 18 December, General Smith limited his comments to the Metropolitan Program since the Liberated Manpower Program was already before the CCS for their consideration, and the Far East Pro-

gram was obviously not the concern of the Supreme Commander in western Europe. He explained that the French planned to equip six of the new divisions largely from their own sources, either from stocks already on hand, or from local manufacture provided they obtained raw materials and other commercial products from the outside. It was the opinion of SHAEF officials that the Metropolitan Program or any portion thereof would be of great value to the Allied forces. The program was a reasonable one, although it would require considerable revisions. Smith then urged the CCS to approve it without delay.[45]

The British Chiefs of Staff, meanwhile, had finally taken action on CCS 661 nearly four months after its submission. On 16 December their representatives in Washington informed the CCS that they were prepared to agree to the issue to the Supreme Commander of authority to proceed with the program recommended by the JCS on 29 August. They were doing so on the understanding that such authority would in no way prejudice the reconsideration of the whole question of French rearmament upon the receipt of the Supreme Commander's latest proposal, which, they understood, was shortly to be submitted. The British Chiefs of Staff had also taken simultaneous action on the over-all liberated manpower program submitted by General Eisenhower on 31 October. While agreeing to the higher ceiling proposed by the Supreme Commander, they considered that the equipment load should in the future be shared on a "more equitable basis." To this end they proposed that the War Department be made to assume the responsibility for procuring

[42] Ltr, Diethelm to Eisenhower, 30 Nov 44, SHAEF Mission to France 091.711 (Fr).
[43] Memo, Loomis for SHAEF G–3, 5 Dec 44, SHAEF Mission to France 091.711–3 (Fr).
[44] Memo, Hull for Smith, 15 Dec 44, SHAEF SGS 475 France, Vol. II.

[45] Ltr, Smth to CCS, CCS 752/1, 18 Dec 44, SHAEF SGS 475 France, Vol. II.

equipment required by the liberated manpower controlled by the U.S. forces.[46]

British approval of CCS 661, in practice, merely formalized the action already initiated by the War Department to begin equipping the 27 infantry, 9 artillery, and 3 engineer battalions recommended by the JCS. In proceeding with shipments, American officials had acted on the justification that the battalions in question represented the completion of the old ANFA program.

Apparently warned that U.S. industrial output was currently falling far short of requirements in a number of items, War Minister Diethelm advised General Eisenhower of the steps contemplated by the French High Command to reduce to a minimum the requirement for U.S. matériel. The survey just completed of depots in the United Kingdom had revealed the existence of excess British stocks probably sufficient for six divisions. Although much of the matériel was in poor condition, the French would accept it and use it as "transition equipment" pending its ultimate replacement. In this manner, the United States would be called upon, for the present at least, to furnish only a comparatively small but essential amount of equipment unobtainable from either British or French sources.[47]

The equipment situation of the Resistance forces fighting on the Atlantic coast and to a lesser degree of those forces absorbed by 1st French Army had, by this time, dangerously deteriorated. Returning from an inspection tour through eastern and southern France, a representative of G–3, SHAEF, reported that these forces were in general poorly equipped and using whatever clothing and arms were available. The disparity between their equipment and that of 1st French Army was causing considerable ill feeling among the men. With the unusually cold weather then prevailing, it was urgent to furnish them at least boots or shoes and overcoats or jackets. To improve their lot, the Supreme Commander directed, on 16 December, that, pending their absorption into civilian life or into authorized military units, they were, when employed on operationally necessary duties, the responsibility of SHAEF with respect to maintenance, clothing, and, if need be, equipment. He urged, however, that all steps be taken to expedite their early disbandment.[48]

As the French military authorities had received no reply to their 30 November proposal, they instructed their representative in Washington to try to obtain a decision from the CCS. In a preliminary conference held on 18 December with General Marshall, General de Saint-Didier outlined the aims and implications of the proposed Metropolitan Program and pointed out that General Eisenhower himself had "seemed interested" in its operational possibilities. He then listed the heavy matériel and the technical items of lighter equipment which would be required from the United States. The French, on their side, would provide from their own resources the necessary light infantry weapons, mortars, machine guns, most of the engineer equipment, and other

[46] Memo, COS for CCS, CCS, 661/3, 16 Dec 44, ABC 091.711 France (6 Oct 44), Sec 2–C; Memo, COS for CCS, CCS 627/6, 16 Dec 44, ABC 400.3295 (2 Aug 43), Sec 1–B.

[47] Ltr, Diethelm to Eisenhower, 17 Dec 44, ABC 091.711 France (6 Oct 43), Sec 2–C.

[48] Memo, Lt Col D. K. Griffith for ACofS G–3 SHAEF, 16 Dec 44, SHAEF G–3 091 France, Vol. IV; Ltr, SCAEF to Comdrs Concerned, 16 Dec 44, SHAEF SGS 475/1, Vol. I.

miscellaneous items.[49] General de Saint-Didier then communicated to the CCS, in advance of his appearance before them, a memorandum setting forth the background and aims of the Metropolitan Program. It was not a postwar plan, but one designed to increase to the maximum France's war effort. General Eisenhower had not reached a decision but "seemed to have been greatly impressed." [50]

On 19 December the Supreme Commander, postponing his comments on the 30 November plan until further study, proposed to the CCS that, in the event a rearmament program was implemented for any country in western Europe, his headquarters be made the co-ordinating authority and, where necessary, the responsible agency for processing, formulating, and implementing the program, subject of course to CCS approval. Such a procedure would tend to avoid any conflict likely to result from the fact that present demands for rearmament were diverse and might compete with SHAEF's operational requirements for personnel and equipment. Simultaneously, he requested that the scale of equipment for liberated manpower be increased, as he now considered it inadequate. Finally, his deputy chief of staff for air, Air Marshal James M. Robb, transmitted a proposal calling for an extension of the French Air Force. The plan envisaged the activation of new air and ground units and, if approved, was to go into effect on 1 January and be completed by 30 June.[51]

In the hope of prodding SHAEF into quick action, Mr. Diethelm called on General Smith on 20 December and urged him to take steps for the speedy issue of the matériel that would have to be delivered from the United States under the new eight-division program. He explained that Prime Minister Churchill had agreed in the course of his recent visit to France that some obsolete equipment then in the United Kingdom would be turned over to six of the infantry divisions awaiting equipment.[52] This would be a makeshift solution pending reception of the modern U.S. equipment "promised" earlier by General Smith. He then requested that SHAEF approve the transfer to the French forces of the captured war matériel then stocked up at Trun in Normandy.[53]

The scheduled appearance of General de Saint-Didier before the CCS took place on 22 December. The French representative briefly outlined the details of the Metropolitan Program. The French High Command expected to complete it by 1 May 1945, for the British had just given assurances that sufficient used British matériel would be made available earlier than originally anticipated. Admiral Leahy, after paying tribute to the combat record of the French forces in Italy and France, assured General de Saint-Didier that the CCS would consider the proposed program with sympathy but warned him that the recent operational events on the western European front had increased the difficulties of delivering military equipment even to the U.S. armies in

[49] Min Conf, Marshall and de Saint-Didier, 18 Dec 44, and Memo, Marshall for Hull, Somervell, and Handy, 18 Dec 44, OCS A–48–11 091 France, Sec I.

[50] Memo, de Saint-Didier for CCS, CCS 752, 19 Dec 44, ABC 091.711 France (6 Oct 43), Sec 2–C.

[51] Msg SCAF 148, Eisenhower to CCS, 19 Dec 44, OPD Cable Files; Msg SCAF 147, Eisenhower to CCS, 19 Dec 44, ABC 400.3295 (2 Aug 43),

Sec 1–B; Ltr, Robb to CCS, 19 Dec 44, ABC 091.711 France (6 Oct 43), Sec 2–C. See discussion in Chapter XXII, below.

[52] The Prime Minister visited France in October and again on 11 November.

[53] Min Conf, Smith and Diethelm, 20 Dec 44, SHAEF SGS 475 France, Vol. II.

France. After the meeting, the CCS referred the matter to the Combined Administrative Committee for comment and recommendation.[54]

In Paris, examination of the Metropolitan Program was continuing. As an interim measure, G–3, SHAEF, on 24 December recommended that the Supreme Commander approve the French proposal to use British matériel available in the United Kingdom and acceptable to them, and that the CCS be urged to approve the transfer. Meanwhile, 43,000 FFI personnel had been issued equipment from sources in the theater. In addition, matériel for eleven infantry battalions had been received or was en route to the Continent as a result of the action initiated by the War Department.[55]

The impatiently awaited comments of the Supreme Commander finally reached the CCS on 28 December. Clearly, they reflected the operational developments of the preceding few days. The situation on the western front had taken a sudden turn for the worse. The Ardennes offensive launched by the Germans on 16 December had met with considerable initial success. Within ten days the enemy had advanced over fifty miles. Although the momentum of the German drive had slowed by 26 December, the situation was still critical. Under the circumstances, Eisenhower was now eager to make the maximum use of liberated manpower—Belgian, Polish, but more especially French. No quicker, more economical, or more effective way to increase Allied fighting power could be found, he explained to the CCS,

than by furnishing the equipment for at least 5 of the proposed 8 divisions. He added that it would be a great help if 2 divisions equipped with excess British matériel apparently acceptable to the French could be placed at the disposal of Field Marshal Montgomery, then in command of the British 21 Army Group. The Supreme Commander then turned to the labor and security program. The War Office pool of equipment was exhausted. Some 43,000 FFI troops were fighting on the Atlantic coast, for whom SHAEF was unable to provide anything. Although sympathetic to their plight, the War Office was hampered by lack of authority from the CCS. It was essential that the Liberated Manpower Program be given prompt approval.[56]

The CCS lost no time in taking action. With the prospect of a longer war, the realization that the Germans were stronger than it was thought earlier and the knowledge that the dearth of U.S. infantry replacements, already felt before the Ardennes offensive, was critical, the CCS quickly endorsed General Eisenhower's recommendations. Within twenty-four hours, they approved the eight-division Metropolitan Program, the Liberated Manpower Program, and the French Air Force Program. They then directed the Combined Administrative Committee to determine the responsibility for the provision of the necessary equipment.[57]

The question of the employment of French metropolitan manpower was at last solved in a manner which, it was hoped, would satisfy the wishes of all concerned.

---

[54] Min, CCS 180th Mtg, 22 Dec 44, ABC 091.711 France (6 Oct 43), Sec 2–G; Memo for Rcd, MIS WD, 27 Dec 44, OCS A–48–1 091 France.

[55] Memo, Hull for Smith, 24 Dec 44, SHAEF SGS 475 France, Vol. II; Memo, Hull for Smith, 27 Dec 44, OCS A–48–11 091 France, Sec I.

[56] Msg SCAF 159, Eisenhower to CCS, 28 Dec 44, OPD Cable Files.

[57] Min, CCS 181st Mtg, 29 Dec 44, ABC 091.711 France (6 Oct 43), Sec 5; Msg FACS 120, CCS to Eisenhower, 29 Dec 44, ABC 091.711 (6 Oct 43), Sec 2–C.

The Liberated Manpower Program provided, for the Supreme Commander, a sufficient force to maintain the security of the rear and a labor force to assist in the physical support of his armies. The Metropolitan and Air Programs would give him, by the spring of 1945, a substantial increase of his fighting force and, at the same time, would satisfy the long-felt desire of the French to reorganize their national army. To some French authorities, on the other hand, the Metropolitan Program as it stood was only a beginning. In General de Gaulle's opinion, France could do much more than activate eight divisions from her liberated manpower. Apparently impressed by the speed with which the CCS had acted on the eight-division program (barely a month had elapsed since the submission of the program on 30 November), and in the belief that he must strike while the iron was hot, the French leader wasted no time in trying for a much larger program.

In a personal letter to President Roosevelt, dated 1 January 1945, de Gaulle, after expressing his gratefulness for the agreement reached three days earlier to rearm 8 divisions, declared that his government could have before the end of 1945 "about fifty good divisions" if it had the means to equip them. Should the President give a favorable reply in principle, he would send General Juin to Washington at once to discuss all technical arrangements. General de Gaulle's letter did not clearly indicate whether the 50 divisions were to be in addition to the 8 already equipped under the North African program and the 8 to be rearmed under the recently approved program. Even assuming that these 16 units were included in the total, this meant a further increase of 34 divisions by the end of 1945, still a sizable figure. The proposal at any rate was referred immediately to the JCS and the JLC for examination and recommendations, and three weeks later to General Eisenhower for comment. Meanwhile the State Department dispatched a noncommittal reply to the U.S. Ambassador in Paris for delivery to the Minister of Foreign Affairs.[58]

General Somervell, then in Paris, was discussing with Supreme Headquarters the details and implications of the new 8-division program. He and theater officials had already agreed that the program would require considerable revisions in view of its insufficiency in service units. In fact, SHAEF's Rearmament Division was busy drafting a revised program in which the necessary service units would be placed on a higher priority than most of the divisions themselves. On 30 January General Eisenhower informed General Marshall that in his opinion the recently approved program represented "the maximum effort which the French could make in time to be of use in operations" in his theater. French rearmament industry, he explained, was still directly dependent upon import of raw materials largely from U.S. sources. As for manpower, it was doubtful that enough of it could be made available to fulfill all existing commitments including the 8 new divisions, much less the activation of 34 additional divisions as proposed by General de Gaulle.[59]

A few days later the JLC reported that existing and expected shortages of essential equipment, present requirements placed on U.S. production which exceeded produc-

[58] Ltr, de Gaulle to President, 1 Jan 45, and Msg, Grew to U.S. Ambassador Paris, 27 Jan 45, ABC 091.711 France (6 Oct 43), Sec 2–C.

[59] Msgs CM–OUT 26436, Marshall to Eisenhower, 25 Jan 45, and S–77124, Eisenhower to Marshall, 30 Jan 45, in same file.

tion capabilities, and a strained shipping situation ruled out the provision, in 1945, of further equipment to meet General de Gaulle's request. On the basis of this conclusion and of the recommendations of the Supreme Commander, the Joint Chiefs of Staff decided that, since the French could not provide the necessary personnel and the United States could not furnish the necessary equipment, the commitment to rearm the French should be limited to the 16 divisions and supporting troops approved under the North African and Metropolitan Programs. Such was the tenor of the letter which President Roosevelt himself addressed to de Gaulle on 24 March. "In view of all the factors involved," he concluded, "you will appreciate the fact that attempts at French rearmament beyond the commitments which can clearly be met by France and the U.S. would interfere with the prosecution of the war." [60]

Any implication that the American rejection of the de Gaulle proposal was based on a veiled desire to crush French ambition for the future, as then rumored among the French, must be dismissed if one considers the position which American officials had taken with respect to French military power. This position had been made unmistakably clear only a few weeks before by the State-War-Navy Coordinating Committee, the highest American policy-making agency. In briefing President Roosevelt on the proposal made earlier by the British to reorganize the French and other Allied postwar armies, the committee had this to say:

Our present policy toward the French is based on the belief that it is in the best interests of the U.S. that France resume her traditional position as a principal power capable of playing a part in the occupation of Germany and in maintaining peace in Europe. The recruiting and equipping of French land forces would be a natural corollary of this policy, and politically such a move could be portrayed as a further evidence of American friendship for France and a proof of our desire to see her as a strong nation.[61]

That, in the light of such a statement, the U.S. Chiefs of Staff had now come to reject the latest French proposal could be explained only by motives of a sound, practical, military nature such as were given in the reply to General de Gaulle. Shortages of U.S. matériel were known to exist, a fact which the JLC had emphasized in their 9 February report. But more serious was the situation with respect to French manpower availability itself.

As matters stood, 1st French Army, with a reported strength of 241,000 men, was already short some 58,000 supporting troops—lines of communications personnel for the most part—thus throwing a considerable burden on the U.S. forces. In addition, its regiments were short from 700 to 800 white effectives each. They had in fact received no replacements from liberated France. Without wishing to prejudice the plans currently being made for the activation of new divisions, largely from the former FFI, General de Lattre, Commanding General, 1st French Army, had urged General de Gaulle on 18 December to place at his disposal without delay the 8,000 to 10,000 young Frenchmen needed to restore to his Army "its initial moral equilibrium" and "fighting qualities." [62] The new 8-

[60] Memos, JLC for JCS, 9 Feb 45, and Leahy for Secy War and Secy Navy, 2 Mar 45, in same file; Ltr, President to de Gaulle, 24 Mar 44, ABC 091.711 (6 Oct 43), Sec 2–D. See also Memo, Daly for Craig, 11 May 45, OPD 336.2 France, Sec V.

[61] Memo, State-War-Navy Coordinating Committee for President, 28 Dec 44, ABC 091.711 (6 Oct 43), Sec 2–D.

[62] Ltr, de Lattre to de Gaulle, 18 Dec 44, quoted in de Lattre, *Histoire de la Première Armée Française*, p. 337.

division program as planned by the French called for a total of 205,000 men with a division slice of only 25,600 men, a level regarded by SHAEF as totally inadequate. The Liberated Manpower Program, meanwhile, was still in process of implementation and absorbing considerable effectives. It was difficult to see how the French could raise, in addition to these various commitments, 1,275,000 men for 34 new divisions before the return and rehabilitation of prisoners of war then detained in Germany, or without extensive mobilization. So far only the class of young men twenty-one years of age had been called to the colors. Even if the necessary effectives were raised, General Eisenhower did not consider it likely that they could be equipped and trained in time to participate in operations. His skepticism regarding the de Gaulle proposal was shared by those who, at Supreme Headquarters, were grappling with the armament problem. The Americans regarded it as an example of "utter folly." Their French colleagues, when apprised of it, registered considerable embarrassment.[63]

The action taken by the CCS at the end of December had firmly established the principle of two separate armament commitments (if one considers the new Air Force Program as part of the Metropolitan Program) involving French liberated manpower, with one, at least in the eyes of the Allied comand, having priority over the other. The French, while agreeing to this distinction, regarded the Liberated Manpower Program rather as a transition program, one forced upon them and one in which they saw no advantage to themselves other than the formation of units to be absorbed as speedily as possible in the Metropolitan Program. Judging from the enthusiasm they had shown consistently since November 1942 for the activation of combat divisions at the expense of service units, it was to be expected that they would now likewise throw all their energy into expediting a program from which they were to gain additional combat units, meanwhile devoting less attention to the organization of labor and security troops.

---

[63] Msg S–77124, Eisenhower to Marshall, 30 Jan 45, ABC 091.711 France (6 Oct 43), Sec 2–C; Intervs with Loomis, Jun 50, with Regnault, Sep 50.

CHAPTER XX

The Liberated Manpower and Metropolitan Programs in Operation

Implementing the Liberated Manpower Program

Implementation of the Liberated Manpower Program, begun long before the CCS approval on 29 December, had already produced some tangible results. By 15 January the French had activated or were in process of activating approximately 45 security battalions, as well as 23 transport and 13 labor units.[1] Equipping of these units was effected as follows. First G–3, SHAEF, indicated to G–4 the priorities in which equipment was to be released and to what units it was to be allocated. G–4 then obtained the release of equipment from U.S. or U.K. sources. Shipments involved questions of over-all priority as they tended to compete with the maintenance and build-up requirements of armies in the field. Equipment arriving on the Continent was unloaded at either Le Havre or Rouen. As there were no depots available in these two ports, the matériel was transported to the French reception center at Caen where it was held until distributed to the units. Once equipped, the units were inspected by General Kingman's Inspection Group for the purpose of determining completeness of equipment. After this inspection, they were subjected to an initial training period by the military region commands, at the end of which the latter informed SHAEF Mission to France that the units were ready for operational employment. SHAEF Mission then notified the appropriate headquarters and co-ordinated the issue of instructions placing the units under the command or at the disposal of British or U.S. forces. As Inspection Group and the French War Ministry did not always agree on dates of readiness, the Rearmament Division acted as a check on statements by these authorities. One of the principal difficulties encountered appeared to be insufficient liaison between the War Ministry and the military regions. Another resulted from the fact that the French were simultaneously reorganizing Metropolitan Program units, a process which involved a constant reshuffling of units. Thus within 6th Army Group area, it was not always too clear which battalions were security battalions and which were units intended for the Metropolitan Program.[2]

Adding to the difficulties in setting up the units required under the Liberated Manpower Program was the fact that the program itself included no service troops. Logistical support of these units, especially the security battalions, could not be im-

[1] Memo, SHAEF Mission to France G–3 for SHAEF Main, 15 Jan 45, SHAEF Mission to France 320–2–NA Orgn of Fr Army.

[2] Min, Conf at SHAEF Main, 16 Jan 45, SHAEF Mission to France 091.4 Liberated People.

posed upon U.S. service troops and installations as these were already working to capacity and in any case were not organized to service British equipment. Arrangements were finally made in mid-January with commanders of the military regions and of the battalions themselves for the activation of French service units. Equipment for these was drawn from that issued to the battalions or from other French sources.[3]

In Washington, the question of the division of responsibility between the United States and the United Kingdom for providing equipment for labor and security units was still unsolved. The U.S. members of the Combined Administrative Committee were now recommending that the British be asked to supply all the requirements and that they be urged to indicate specifically what they could or could not do so that the United States would know the extent of its obligation.[4]

By the end of January, the equipment situation of Liberated Manpower Program units had become critical. Already three months had elapsed since the submission of the original request to the CCS and the latter had so far given only an approval in principle. Resources were dwindling rapidly while demands for liberated manpower had risen. Equipment could be obtained only for certain limited and specific requirements approved by the War Office. It was therefore not possible for the theater to keep any phased program to meet requirements for the Allied Expeditionary Force as a whole. Lack of approval of the pro-

posed increased scale of equipment added to the seriousness of the situation. Units were being employed under the most exacting weather conditions and many were reported to be suffering serious sickness rates. Additional equipment, especially clothing, was urgently needed. SHAEF was in a position neither to provide adequately for existing units nor to meet further requirements.[5]

In a message dated 30 January the Supreme Commander brought these facts before the CCS. He urged them to approve forthwith an increase in the scales of equipment, such as a second pair of boots, a fourth blanket, and a second set of battle dress. These increases were particularly essential where units were serving with U.S. or U.K. forces, as they had no facilities for the rapid replacement of soiled or damaged clothing. Resources were exhausted, warned the Supreme Commander, and the British War Office was unwilling to make further issues pending the decision of the CCS. The whole program had come to a standstill thus "tying up" U.S. and British combat troops.[6]

When, on 2 February, the CCS met to discuss General Eisenhower's recommendations, they were faced with a difficult decision. The operational situation had greatly changed for the better in the past few days. The Allied drive eastward, resumed after the Ardennes setback, was gaining momentum. On the Eastern Front, the Russian offensive launched on 12 January had brought the Red Army deep into the Reich. These successes were reviving hopes for an early end of hostilities. Preferring not to reach a decision on the provision of equip-

---

[3] Msg EX–80374, Lee to Base Secs, 31 Dec 44, SHAEF Mission to France 091.711–1 (Fr) ; Memo, Loomis for Regnault, 5 Jan 45, SHAEF Mission to France 091.4 Liberated People.
[4] Memo for Info, CAdC, 25 Jan 45, ABC 091.711 France (6 Oct 43), Sec 2–C.

[5] Memo, Bull for Smith, 27 Jan 45, SHAEF SGS 475 France, Vol III.
[6] Msg SCAF 193, Eisenhower to CCS, 30 Jan 45, OPD Cable Files.

ment for the Liberated Manpower Program until they had received the report they were expecting from the Combined Administrative Committee, the CCS merely ordered, in the interim, a reduction of the over-all program from 460,000 to 400,000 men.[7] This forced a revision downward of the French part of the program. The 20,000-odd effectives of the military regions, Gendarmerie, and Garde Mobile, who had been issued only a small fraction of the equipment initially promised them, were stricken off the program. The number of security battalions and labor units was reduced to 103 and 30 respectively.

On 21 February the Supreme Commander and the French Provisional Government reached an agreement on the general subject of the command and employment of the units raised under the Liberated Manpower Program. The agreement formalized an earlier informal understanding reached on 18 November 1944. Signed by Maj. Gen. John T. Lewis, Chief, SHAEF Mission to France, and General Juin, it stipulated that when employed within French territory the units concerned were commanded by the military region commanders who in turn received their missions from army and army group commanders in the zone of armies, or from the Commanding General, Communications Zone, in the zone of interior. When operating in Germany, the units were to be organized in task forces consisting of a minimum of five to ten battalions and commanded by French officers, the latter in turn receiving their missions from the army and army group commanders concerned.[8]

Finally, the agreement authorized the limited transfer of men, but for replacement purposes only, from Liberated Manpower Program to Metropolitan Program units. On 24 March General Lewis reminded General Juin that men so transferred were to leave behind clothing and individual equipment so as to prevent the loss of this matériel to labor and security units.[9]

Pursuant to the agreement, the French were requested to organize 7 headquarters to command a corresponding number of task forces for operation in Germany. The headquarters were tentatively allocated on the basis of 1 to 12th Army Group, 4 to 6th Army Group, and 2 to Communications Zone. Each task force was to include six battalions and some service units, a list of which was subsequently forwarded to the French military authorities.[10]

The Combined Administrative Committee finally submitted on 24 March its over-all study of the rearmament programs for western European Allies. The committee recommended in part that the United Kingdom be made to assume the equipment responsibility for the 400,000 labor and security troops required by SHAEF [11] "without upward revision of the present U.K. requirements against the War Department." It also offered an important recommendation affecting all western European rearmament programs, namely, that any units which had not been equipped by the time active hostilities with Germany ceased should not be equipped.[12] Two weeks later,

[7] Min, CCS 185th Mtg, 2 Feb 45, ABC 400.3295 (2 Aug 43), Sec 1–C.

[8] Text of Agreement in Memo AG 091.711–5 (Fr) GCT–AGM, SCAEF To All Concerned, 2 Mar 45, SHAEF G–3 091, Vol. VI.

[9] Memo, Lewis for Juin, 24 Mar 45, SHAEF Mission to France 421–1 Combined.

[10] Msgs EX–21116 and EX–22400, SCAEF to SHAEF FWD, 15 and 18 Mar 45, SHAEF G–3 091 France, Vol. VI; Ltr, Lewis to Juin, 30 Mar 45, SHAEF Mission to France 091.711–1 (Fr).

[11] As well as for six Belgian infantry brigades.

[12] Rpt, CAdC to CCS, CCS 768/7, 24 Mar 45, ABC 400.3295 (2 Aug 43), Sec 1–C.

on 6 April, the CCS, by informal action, approved the recommendations of the committee and advised the Supreme Commander accordingly.

By the beginning of April implementation of the Liberated Manpower Program had made but little progress. Of the 103 French security battalions required under the revised program, 49 only were equipped and operational or about to become operational—18 in Communications Zone area, 24 in 6th Army Group area (of which 12 were administered by 1st French Army), none in 12th Army Group area, and 7 in the British zone. Fifty-four battalions had not yet been activated or, if activated, had not been equipped. As for labor groups, of the 30 units required, no more than 6 were operational, all in the British zone, leaving 24 still to be formed and equipped.[13]

The program, obviously, had bogged down. The reasons ranged from lack of personnel, suitable clothing, and organizational equipment to lack of interest by key French officers. In some instances, it was reported that battalion commanders had not inspected or visited companies under their command for periods of three to six weeks.[14] In addition, considerable confusion appeared to exist in 6th Army Group area in connection with security battalions. General Devers reported that the 24 battalions assigned to his command had "gotten out of hand" and were being absorbed by the French for employment in other than lines of communications duties. SHAEF immediately took steps to recover the control of these units so that they could be used as

originally contemplated and not for combat.[15]

It was then that the French, by injecting a political note into the matter, precipitated a crisis which brought the implementation of the program to a sudden end. In late March General Juin had been requested by SHAEF to assign additional security battalions for service with Allied armies operating in Germany. Writing to General Lewis on 5 April, he announced that, with the exception of the 12 battalions then at the disposal of 1st French Army, no other battalions would be assigned to the Allied Expeditionary Force in Germany until the French zone of occupation had been determined. An additional 45 battalions would then be made available but for employment in that zone only.[16]

This announcement could not fail to bring forth a violent reaction from SHAEF. Maj. Gen. Harold R. Bull, Assistant Chief of Staff, G–3, considered that the restrictions proposed by the French were in violation of the understanding reached between Generals Smith and Juin on 18 November and the formal agreement signed on 21 February. He recommended that if the French remained adamant in their position, the Supreme Commander should be asked to order a suspension of the Liberated Manpower Program.[17]

In an attempt to ward off such drastic action, General Smith requested the French Chief of Staff to clarify his earlier statement as well as French intentions. "As this headquarters," he went on to explain, "is concerned only with operations for the defeat

---

[13] Tab D to Memo, Bull for CofS, 7 Apr 45, SHAEF SGS 474 France, Vol. III.
[14] Memo, Theater Comdr ETOUSA for Lewis, 18 Apr 45, SHAEF Mission to France 091.711–13 (Fr).

[15] Memo, Bull for Chief Orgn and Equip Sec SHAEF, 6 Apr 45, SHAEF G–3 091 France, Vol. VI.
[16] Ltr, Juin to Lewis, 5 Apr 45, SHAEF SGS 475 France, Vol. III.
[17] Memo, Bull for Smith, 7 Apr 45, in same file.

of Germany and has nothing to do with political questions such as the delimitation of the French zone of occupation, it is difficult for me to understand the connection between the two matters. . . . It is possible that I have misinterpreted your meaning." [18]

On 9 April, as no word had been received from General Juin, then on a tour of inspection of the troops engaged on the Atlantic coast, the Supreme Commander directed that initial issues of equipment to French security and labor units be suspended pending clarification of the conditions under which the units were to be employed in Germany.[19] This action, taken, ironically enough, only three days after the CCS had approved the program itself, brought immediate response from the French. The agreement of 21 February, General Juin assured General Smith, was not questioned at all by the French military authorities; what was involved at the moment, he explained, was a discussion of the "specific arrangements." In support of this contention he referred to a paragraph of the agreement which, as quoted by him, stipulated that "separate and specific arrangements must be made with respect to the place and time of employment of the security battalions." He urged that the matter be discussed at once between General Smith and himself.[20]

In the course of a meeting held on 11 April, General Smith pointed out that the paragraph quoted in General Juin's letter referred, as worded in the agreement, only to the organization and *not* to the employment of the units. It was not clear, he

added, why the French authorities considered that any discussion was justified at this juncture. General Juin replied that his government was concerned with the political aspects of the question. The employment of the French forces in Germany was tied up with basic political questions, such as the ultimate problem of occupation and of French security. The French Government was being "kept in the dark" concerning the attribution of a zone of occupation to France and could not be expected to agree to the use of its forces as mere "colonial auxiliaries." French authorities, General Juin stated flatly, had no part in the direction of the war although they remained at all times ready to contribute within the full limits of their resources to the defeat of Germany.

Replying to these and other arguments, General Smith emphasized that he was concerned with and must be guided by strictly military considerations. If no other solution could be found, SHAEF would, however reluctantly, have to dispense with the French battalions. These would be replaced by U.S. troops and additional units now being offered by the Belgian and Netherlands Governments. Having made unmistakably clear SHAEF's position in the matter, General Smith then, on a conciliatory note, asked General Juin to consider the following solution: the employment under Allied control of French battalions up to a total of 52 for lines of communications duties in the area west of the Rhine, with the understanding that no rigid restrictions would be placed on their employment later in other areas should this become necessary. In return, three Metropolitan Program divisions, the 1st, 10th, and 36th Infantry, would be placed at the disposal of the French High Command; the first two would

---

[18] Ltr, Smith to Juin, 7 Apr 45, in same file.
[19] Msg FWD 18819, SCAEF to COMZONE, 9 Apr 45, in same file.
[20] Ltr, Juin to Smith, 10 Apr 45, in same file.

be assigned to the maintenance of security in the Strasbourg and Saar areas, and the third would be moved to the Franco-Italian border to replace the 1st DMI. The latter would then become available for employment with 1st French Army.[21]

After he had consulted General de Gaulle, the French Chief of Staff announced that the plan proposed by General Smith was satisfactory. The French Government consented, for the time being, to placing at SHAEF's disposal initially 24 battalions organized in 8 regiments and later, other units, all under the command of a French general officer, Lt. Gen. Henri Préaud, provided they be employed in the territory lying between the 1939 French border, the Rhine, and a line running from Aachen to Cologne both inclusive.[22] Two weeks later, on 30 April, with the issuance of equipment still suspended, the French authorities reiterated that they were prepared to place 24 battalions (10 at once, 14 after they had been equipped) at the disposal of the Allied command but only during the period of active operations against organized German forces.[23] Thereafter their employment would be made the subject of a new agreement.

This latest French note brought to the fore a question already under consideration for some time, namely, the employment of Liberated Manpower Program units after the signing of an armistice in Europe. The Supreme Commander, anticipating an early end of hostilities, had requested the CCS, on 24 April, to authorize him to continue to equip, for employment in Germany, such

units as would be required for up to a maximum of one year.[24] His requirement in French security troops was estimated at 47 battalions (13 for the British zone and 34 for the U.S. zone), of which 22 only were currently equipped and available. Without waiting for a reply from the CCS, General Smith informed the French on 7 May that the issue of further equipment to security and labor units was not justified unless these units could be operationally employed under Allied Expeditionary Force command for a period of six months.[25]

On the same day the German forces were surrendering to the Western Allies and to the USSR. In pursuance of the directive from the CCS, all rearmament programs in western Europe were to terminate. Yet the end of hostilities brought no change in the status of the French programs. Implementation of the Liberated Manpower Program already had been suspended and the question of its resumption was now before the CCS. The Metropolitan Program had suffered a similar fate a week before the cessation of hostilities.

Implementing the Metropolitan Program

By the time the Metropolitan Program had been approved on 29 December 1944, its implementation had made some headway as a result of action taken in anticipation of a favorable CCS decision. It will be recalled that the War Department had already shipped equipment for eleven infantry battalions, that the British War Office was prepared to deliver stocks of old matériel acceptable to the French, and that the

[21] Min Conf, Smith and Juin, 11 Apr 45, in same file.
[22] Ltr, Juin to Smith, 14 Apr 45, in same file.
[23] Ltr, Sevez to Smith, 30 Apr 45, SHAEF SGS France 475/2, Vol. II.

[24] Msg SCAF 304, Eisenhower to CCS, 24 Apr 45, ABC 091.711 France (6 Oct 43), Sec 2-D.
[25] Ltr, Smith to Sevez, 7 May 45, SHAEF G-3 091 France, Vol. VII.

French themselves had activated several of the eight divisions scheduled to be re-equipped.

As the CCS signified approval, implementation went into high gear. Yet the prospects of success did not look too encouraging. Considering the implications of the program itself and, in the light of experience gained in North Africa, the factors on which it was dependent for its progress, it appeared almost certain that the undertaking would face serious obstacles and might well make no more than a limited start.

From the standpoint of materiel, there were a number of unfavorable factors, such as the multiplicity of sources from which equipment was to come—British, American, Canadian, French, and enemy-captured; the fact that French industry was experiencing considerable difficulties, not likely to be solved for some time, in reaching production goals especially with respect to clothing requirements; finally, the current and anticipated shortages of U.S. equipment. From the manpower standpoint, two problems had to be considered: the competitive requirements of the two French programs and the possibility of insufficient numbers of trained men for the required service units.

Finally, there were psychological and political factors. Should the tempo of operations be stepped up again and the cessation of hostilities appear closer at hand, as in August of 1944, a corresponding slackening of interest in the program on the part of the Allies would probably result. Should, in addition, political complications arise between Allied and French authorities, as they had on occasions during the North African rearmament operations with regard to command or employment of troops, the program might well be dealt a death blow. Fewer such complications, it was hoped, were likely to arise as a result of a political step taken by the Allies a few months back. On 23 October 1944 they had finally recognized the Provisional Government of the French Republic, headed by General de Gaulle.[26] On 1 January 1945 Mr. Henri Bonnet presented to President Roosevelt his credentials as French Ambassador to the United States and signed the United Nations Declaration in the name of his government. France had now joined officially the fraternity of nations aligned against the Axis.

On 6 January 1945 the CCS approved the transfer of British equipment requested by the French for their new divisions. They stipulated that all items of U.S. lend-lease origin were to be turned over to the theater commander and by him transferred to the French on behalf of the United States. The transaction involved a much smaller volume than the amount initially offered by the British, for the matériel available was largely obsolescent. Items transferred included machine guns (light, medium, and heavy), automatic rifles, ammunition, miscellaneous vehicles, all to be used for training purposes and as part of the equipment for the six divisions of Phases I and III.[27] Further French-British conversations led to new French demands for other British items, such as 150 Cromwell tanks, armored cars, and a number of miscellaneous trucks not in running order but repairable. The French wished to use the tanks and armored

[26] The United States and the French Provisional Government signed, on 28 February 1945, the Lend-Lease and Reciprocal Aid Agreement which, in practice, continued in force the agreements reached earlier with the former French Committee of National Liberation. *Twentieth Report to Congress on Lend-Lease Operations, August 30, 1945.*

[27] Msgs SCAF 162, Eisenhower to CCS, 30 Dec 44, and FACS 122, CCS to Eisenhower, 6 Jan 45, OPD Cable Files.

cars to equip the six reconnaissance regiments of the six infantry divisions.[28]

In the opinion of Allied officials, the one factor likely to determine the success of the new program more than any other was availability of manpower. On 31 December they had requested General Juin to submit an estimate of effectives available for the following purposes: replacements for the divisions of 1st French Army then reported to be considerably understrength, the Liberated Manpower Program, the Metropolitan Program, and "any other program which the French might be considering and about which SHAEF had not been informed." [29] In his reply, General Juin assured Supreme Headquarters that while no estimate, even approximate, could possibly be made at the moment of the manpower available for each of the various commitments, there would be no difficulty in obtaining the needed personnel. The essential problem that remained was matériel. The Allies should "stick firmly" to the program as it stood, not depart from it, and bend all efforts to provide forthwith as much of the necessary equipment as possible.[30]

An important conference, meanwhile, had been held in Washington at which some thirty representatives from the International Division, Ordnance, Operations Division, and Army Air Forces discussed the two problems of supply and accounting for the Metropolitan Program. They agreed that, because the program involved many different sources of equipment and the time

schedule was short, the commanding general in the theater should have the maximum amount of latitude in equipping the new units. With this in view, they set forth a new method of effecting supply and accounting to replace the existing Commanding General Shipments system.[31]

Under the new procedure, in which both SHAEF and the French subsequently concurred, matériel shipped thereafter to the French from the United States was sent through U.S. Army supply channels to U.S. supply depots in the theater. Co-ordination between the theater and the International Division was assumed by General Loomis' Rearmament Division. The latter and other SHAEF agencies concerned were responsible for determining what units should be activated and the time at which it would be possible to do so. In addition they surveyed the various sources of supply to determine the amount of equipment needed to be furnished from the United States. The War Department forwarded the necessary requisitions to the MAB which allocated the matériel to the U.S. Army on the basis of operational urgency. All accounting was, of necessity, accomplished in the theater.

The new system represented a complete departure from the one followed formerly in North Africa. Whereas equipment used to be shipped to the French even before their units were organized, now it was delivered to them only after theater officials were satisfied that units were ready to receive it. Thus the theater was given complete control over the rearmanent operations. Under this system it would feel no reluctance in pushing any program which it deemed reasonable and necessary. As a

---

[28] Memo, Leyer for Eisenhower, 5 Jan 45, SHAEF SGS 475 France, Vol. III.

[29] Memo, Lewis for Juin, 29 Dec 44, SHAEF Mission to France 091.711–13 (Fr) ; Memo, Lewis for Juin, 31 Dec 44, SHAEF Mission to France 091.711–3 (Fr).

[30] Ltr, Juin to Lewis, 7 Jan 45, SHAEF Mission to France 091.711–3 (Fr).

[31] Min Conf, 4 Jan 45, ABC 091.711 France (6 Oct 43), Sec 2–C.

result of the change in procedure, the Rearmament Division became, more than ever before, the central authority and the source of all information with respect to French rearmament.[32]

By 5 January Army Service Forces had already completed a detailed analysis of requirements of U.S. matériel for the Metropolitan Program. Of the entire 1,600-odd items needed, nearly 1,400 could be furnished in accordance with the desired schedule without significant interference with other estimated demands and without major additional encroachments upon existing deficiencies, if any, in stock levels in the United States. Of the remainder, only fifty critical items, including artillery, ammunition, tanks, and certain categories of trucks, could not be furnished from the United States except at the expense of U.S. demands in the theater. To fill the French program as completely as possible, Army Service Forces took immediate steps to increase American production in all cases where necessary. On 8 January ASF informed the theater that the War Department had authorized the shipment of available items. Simultaneously, General Marshall urged the theater to consider the use of available enemy-captured equipment.[33]

The first shipment of matériel was due to leave U.S. ports within a few days in two ships bound for Marseille. It contained first-priority items, such as clothing and individual equipment, and matériel for the first three divisions and supporting units. Deliveries were being made on the basis of the phasing established for the divisions by the Supreme Commander in his letter of 15 December, and for the supporting units by the French Military Mission in Washington.[34] General Loomis then informed the French that the shipment of available equipment for Phase I would be substantially completed by 1 May. He also advised them that revisions of the troop basis of the program and of the shipping schedule were in progress and would be discussed with them soon.[35]

Meanwhile, the first of the new divisions, the 10th Infantry (or Paris) Division, assembled and organized in September primarily from FFI troops in the Paris area and commanded by Brig. Gen. Pierre Billotte, was being moved to 6th Army Group area. Its strength was approximately 14,000 men. Its matériel, consisting largely of enemy-captured equipment of assorted types, was wholly inadequate. American inspecting officers considered that the unit would not be in a condition to be used in an offensive role until it had received suitable equipment and had been trained for a period of not less than four months.[36] The division was one of the several units which General Juin had offered, on 30 December, to put into the Strasbourg area in an effort

---

[32] Interv with Loomis, Jun 50; Memo, International Div ASF for Col Delalande, 30 Jan 45, SHAEF Mission to France 475–10 Equip of Troops Metropolitan Program; Msg S–75501, Eisenhower Personal to Marshall, 18 Jan 45, SS and P Planning Div Files.

[33] Memo, Maj Gen W. A. Wood for Somervell, 5 Jan 45, sub: Analysis of Requirements for Fr Rearmt Program, SHAEF Mission to France 091.-711 (75) Analysis; Memo, Styer for Chiefs of Tech Servs, 12 Jan 45, SS and P Planning Div Files A–46–371; Msg W–88550, Styer to Eisenhower, 8 Jan 45, SS and P Planning Div Files, Fr Rearmt, A–46–371, Dr 2407; Msg W–89078, Marshall to Somervell, 9 Jan 45, SS and P Planning Div Files.

[34] Msg WX–20034, Styer to Lee, 12 Jan 45, International Div Cable Log, A–45–192.

[35] Memo, Loomis for Regnault, 16 Jan 45, SHAEF Mission to France 091.711–3 (Fr).

[36] Msg BX–22426, Devers to SHAEF Main COMZONE, 6 Jan 45, SHAEF Mission to France 091.711–2 (Fr); Memo, Hinton for DACofS G–3, SHAEF G–3 091 France, Vol. V.

to retain control of that city at a time when the Supreme Commander was contemplating the possibility of its abandonment.[37] French authorities, incidentally, were planning to move other units into 6th Army Group area, such as six infantry regiments of two other newly activated divisions, apparently without prior consultation with either SHAEF, SHAEF Mission to France, or 6th Army Group itself. Fearful that the unauthorized movement of these units would place an unbearable burden on his already strained supply facilities and resources, General Devers urged SHAEF to warn the French against such action.[38]

By mid-January the only equipment readily available in the theater for Metropolitan Program units was captured enemy matériel and a limited number of French items. Considering that British and American matériel would not arrive for some weeks to come, SHAEF officials revised their estimates as to the dates of readiness of the new divisions. They came to the conclusion that only three would be ready some time in June (and not 15 April as originally contemplated), the rest in July and August.[39] The French were naturally getting impatient. The Office of War Information was reporting a growing bitterness in France over the alleged inability of the United States to equip French divisions with American arms, and a tendency among the French to believe that the United States did not want France to become a strong power.[40] To dissipate such misgivings,

SHAEF considered the possibility of holding a press conference at which information on the American effort to rearm the French would be released. The conference was postponed pending the drafting of pertinent reports by the Rearmament Division and other responsible agencies.

Revising the Metropolitan Program

It will be recalled that the Metropolitan Program consisted initially of 8 divisions and 213 supporting combat and service units. In submitting the program to the CCS on 18 December, General Smith had warned that it would require revisions as it contained no base service or lines of communications units. If implemented in its original form, it was feared that it would place an unbearable burden on the U.S. Army. The latter was already heavily committed to the support of 1st French Army. As General Somervell, then in the theater, pointed out in a message to the War Department, Communications Zone did not have enough American service units for the U.S. forces, much less to support the French. By building up some extra French service units, he explained, "we will be doing ourselves a favor." [41] In line with this contention, the theater drew up for addition to the program a list of 915 supporting combat and service units for both the 1st French Army and the new divisions, thus increasing the Metropolitan Program to a total of 8 divisions and 1,128 supporting units. In submitting the revised program to Washington on 17 January, the theater recommended an entirely new phasing in which the supporting units

---

[37] Memo, Whiteley for G-4 SHAEF, 30 Dec 44, SHAEF G-3 091 France, Vol. IV; Pogue, *The Supreme Command,* pp. 398–402.

[38] Msg BX-22565, Devers to SHAEF Main, 8 Jan 45, SHAEF Mission to France 091.711–2 (Fr).

[39] Memo, Col H. A. Twitchell for Chief Plans Sec G-3 SHAEF, 12 Jan 45, SHAEF G-3 091 France, Vol. V.

[40] Memo, Director Bureau of Public Relations WD for Asst Secy War, 10 Jan 45, OPD 336.2 France, Sec V.

[41] Statement by Somervell in telephone conversation with Gen Wood, 23 Jan 45, SS and P Planning Div Files.

would be given first priority over the divisions. The perennial issue over service troops had, once again, come to the fore.[42]

Apprised on 27 January of the contemplated revisions, the French military authorities promptly objected that "in spite of their insistence" they had not been given an opportunity to discuss the matter with American officials. They pointed out that, since the plan as originally submitted by them had been accepted by the CCS, they had gone ahead with their activation program and they could not at this juncture accept any changes likely to delay the equipping of the larger units.[43]

War Department officials meanwhile had informed the theater that the complete revision of the phasing as now proposed would disrupt the procurement program and cause delays in the shipment of available matériel.[44] They recommended that the phasing suggested by General Somervell on 5 January be adhered to with only such modifications as would be required for the incorporation of additional supporting units. The recommendation was endorsed by the theater. Pending a conference which he planned to hold with General Leyer in the near future, General Loomis outlined the plan now under consideration for the French Chief of Staff. The War Department, he explained, would ship the equipment already set up except that the matériel for the last five infantry divisions would be withheld to the extent that this could be done without disrupting the schedule. The next phase would then consist of the equipment for such additional supporting units

as would be considered necessary for both the 1st French Army and the first corps of three divisions of the new program, plus supporting corps troops as well as an appropriate share of army and base units. Only when substantial progress had been made in the equipping, organization, and training of these units would SHAEF authorize the arming of further divisions.[45]

By this time the French had designated the units to be activated under the program. They included 2 new corps (3d and 4th), 6 infantry divisions (the 10th DI, 1st DI, 36th DI, 19th DI, 14th DI, and 25th DI), 1 mountain or Alpine division (the 27th DIA), and 1 armored division (the 3d DB).[46] The first three units scheduled to receive U.S. and British equipment under the program were the 10th DI, 1st DI, and 27th DIA. The 10th DI, although poorly equipped, had been operational since 7 January. It was to be withdrawn as soon as practicable into the zone of interior where it would receive its new matériel. The 27th DIA, commanded by Col. Jean Vallette d'Osia, had a strength of 20,500 men comprising mostly former FFI troops from the Alps area and some North Africans. It was equipped almost entirely with French matériel. So was the 1st DI (not to be confused with the 1st March Division, or 1st DMI, then part of 1st French Army), activated on 1 February from various FFI groups and commanded by Brig. Gen. Jean Callies.

Toward the end of January the Supreme Commander came to the conclusion that it would be inadvisable, as he had recom-

---

[42] Msg S–75390, Eisenhower to AGWAR, 17 Jan 45, SS and P Planning Div Files.
[43] Memo, Leyer for Regnault, 28 Jan 45, SHAEF Mission to France 091.711–3 (Fr).
[44] Msg W–23517, Styer to Eisenhower, 19 Jan 45, SS and P Planning Div Files.

[45] Memo, Loomis for Leyer, 31 Jan 45, SHAEF Mission to France 091.711–3 (Fr).
[46] Memo, SHAEF Mission to France for SCAEF, 23 Jan 45, SHAEF Mission to France 091.711–1 (Fr).

mended earlier, to place 2 of the 8 new divisions at the disposal of the British 21 Army Group, largely because of the supply complications likely to result. He felt, and so recommended to the CCS, that it would be better both tactically and logistically to combine the 16 French divisions in two French armies operating alongside each other in the American sector.[47] On the basis of this and other considerations, the U.S. members of the Combined Administrative Committee recommended, on 25 January, that the United States be asked to underwrite the entire Metropolitan Program.[48]

While the French were studying the proposed revision of the program, implementation of Phase I had begun and, by the end of the first month, had made substantial progress. American equipment for 2 infantry divisions and 46 supporting units was currently leaving U.S. ports and due to arrive in Marseille at the end of February. A second shipment consisting of matériel for the mountain division and its supporting units was scheduled to leave in early March.

British training equipment as well as matériel for 3 divisions was about to be shipped to Cherbourg. Deliveries were to include .30-caliber M1917 rifles, Browning automatic rifles (BAR's), .30-caliber machine guns, 40-mm. and 3.7-inch antiaircraft artillery, 57-mm. antitank guns, and various other items all available from British sources and therefore not required from the United States.

The French themselves were to furnish, depending on their ability to manufacture them, 60-mm. and 81-mm. mortars, some 155-mm. howitzers, pistols, and other equip-

ment. To enable their war industries to resume production, a military import program had been set up, supplementary and parallel to a civilian import program, through which they obtained raw materials from the United States. All requirements for the purposes were channeled to the War Department for appropriate action.[49] Production of a number of items being slower than originally contemplated, it was expected that these would now have to be furnished from Allied sources.

Stocks of captured enemy matériel offered many items but, because of the maintenance and replacement problems involved, they could only be used for training purposes. As for Canadian equipment, only a few items were readily available. The French, with an eye on the second phase of the program, proposed to submit to the Canadian Government a request for the entire equipment for two infantry divisions. Apprised of this intention, the Canadian Chiefs of Staff, on 22 January, approached the CCS on the matter. When, on 6 April, the CCS finally acknowledged the Canadian inquiry, it was too late for action to be initiated.[50]

After a detailed study of the contemplated revision of the program, the French military authorities notified General Loomis on 7 February that only about one half of the supporting combat and service units newly proposed by SHAEF were acceptable to them. SHAEF officials promptly expressed their disappointment. "This is the same old story as in North Africa," General Smith pointed out. "French officers who have participated in modern battle realize

---

[47] Msg SCAF 186, Eisenhower to CCS, 24 Jan 45, OPD Cable Files.
[48] Memo cited n. 4.

[49] Msgs E–92846, Eisenhower to Somervell, 31 Jan 45, SS and P Planning Div Files.
[50] Ltr, Maj Gen H. F. G. Letson to CCS, 22 Jan 45, ABC 091.711 France (6 Oct 43), Sec 2–C; Memo, CCS for Letson, 6 Apr 45, ABC 400.3295 (2 Aug 43), Sec 1–C.

the necessity for these services and maintenance units, but such officers are few.   The remainder are perfectly naive and cannot comprehend the necessity." The chief administrative officer, Lt. Gen. Sir Humfrey M. Gale, urged that SHAEF insist on the French providing adequate service troops of their own. "Why should the U.S. do all the housemaiding for the French due to the faulty organization of the latter?" [51]

In an attempt to reconcile the French and SHAEF's points of view, General Leyer submitted a counterproposal listing the maximum supporting units which the French military authorities could organize within the time limits established in the original program.   The reduction, which amounted to one half of the units proposed by SHAEF, was legitimate, explained General Leyer, since the French forces were not in the situation of an expeditionary corps fighting overseas but, on the contrary, were "supported to an ever-increasing extent by a territorial organization whose effectiveness was expected to grow daily."   Judging from General Leyer's statement, the French were assuming that the CCS, in approving the Metropolitan Program, had prescribed a time limit for its implementation.   The CCS, in fact, had done no such thing; their approval had been one in principle only. In submitting to the CCS the troop list and shipment priorities as now revised by SHAEF, General Smith urged them, on 15 February, to consider a new course of action. The French being unable to activate more supporting units than the number indicated in their counterproposal, he recommended that only such combat divisions for which

they could provide adequate support be equipped by the Allies.[52]

In notifying the French of this recommendation, SHAEF emphasized that the Supreme Commander reserved the right to defer the provision of equipment for combat units which could not be furnished adequate support and which therefore could not be employed in the prosecution of the war against Germany.   Thus were the prospects of an early build-up of a second army of eight divisions greatly reduced.   SHAEF was now inclined to believe that no new divisions could possibly be equipped and trained before June, and their employment even at this date might well be impracticable for lack of adequate supporting troops.[53]

Meanwhile, SHAEF was seriously concerned over the fact that 1st French Army was still considerably understrength.   The slow push toward Colmar throughout January had whittled down its effectives. The replacement program instituted with a view to maintaining the divisions at strength appeared to have broken down in its initial phase.   Under the program, 10,000 men recruited in France were to be moved to 1st French Army training centers in January and 4,500 monthly thereafter.[54]

By 5 February only 2,500 men had reported for instruction.   In addition the program was short 1,600 North African

---

[51] Memo, Lutes for Crawford, 7 Feb 45, and Notes by Smith and Gale, 8 Feb 45, SHAEF SGS 475 France, Vol. III.

[52] Ltr, Leyer to Loomis, 9 Feb 45, SHAEF Mission to France 091.711-3 (Fr); Memo, Bull for Smith, 15 Feb 45, SHAEF SGS 475 France, Vol. III; Ltr, Smith to CCS, CCS 752/3, 15 Feb 45, ABC 091.711 France (6 Oct 43), Sec 2-D; Msg S-79317, Eisenhower to AGWAR, 16 Feb 45, SS and P Planning Div Files.

[53] Memo, Lewis for Leyer, 19 Feb 45, SHAEF Mission to France 091.711-3 (Fr); Rpt, SHAEF Main G-3, 16 Feb 45, SHAEF SGS 475/2 France, Vol. II.

[54] Ltr, Leyer to Lewis, 24 Jan 45, SHAEF Mission to France 091.711-13 (Fr).

LES INSIGNES DES GRANDES UNITÉS DE LA PREMIÈRE ARMÉE

1: Irᵉ Armée Française. – 2: Iᵉʳ Corps d'Armée. – 3: 2ᵉ Corps d'Armée. – 4: 2ᵉ Div. blindée. – 5: Groupements de Tabors Marocains – 6: 2ᵉ Div. d'inf. marocaine. – 7: 10ᵉ Div. d'infanterie. – 8: 4ᵉ Div. marocaine de montagne. – 9: Irᵉ Div. blindée. – 10: Irᵉ Div. française libre – 11: 3ᵉ Div. d'inf. algérienne. – 12: 9ᵉ Div. d'inf. coloniale. – 13: 5ᵉ Div. blindée. – 14: 14ᵉ Div. d'Infanterie.

INSIGNIA OF 1ST FRENCH ARMY AND ITS MAJOR COMPONENTS,
15 February 1945, except for the 27th DIA and the 1st DI.

natives. The situation greatly worried General Devers who was constantly being informed by French division commanders of personnel shortages in their units. To maintain 1st French Army at strength, General Devers estimated that a pool of no less than 12,000 reinforcements (80 percent infantry) must be maintained at all times in the training centers. In his estimation, efforts by the French High Command to carry out a satisfactory replacement program were not energetic enough. He considered that proper support of 1st French Army should be secured before any French manpower was allocated to future rearmament programs. His views were upheld by the Supreme Commander, who on 14 February directed SHAEF Mission to France to inform the French that it was not sound policy to form and equip new units when at the same time operational forces were becoming inefficient due to lack of reinforcements.[55]

The French War Ministry attempted to remedy the situation by establishing a replacement program based on General Devers' recommendations.[56] But the program was not put into effect until 1 April with the result that the personnel situation of 1st French Army did not materially im-

---

[55] Msg BX–23931, Devers to SHAEF, 5 Feb 45, and Memo, SCAEF for Lewis, 14 Feb 45, in same file.

[56] Ltr, Leyer to SHAEF, 17 Mar 45, in same file.

prove during the remaining weeks of hostilities. The deficiency in divisional personnel was partially offset by the gradual addition to the Army reserves of light infantry battalions and of Metropolitan Program divisions.

The 1st French Army as of 15 February 1945 comprised the following corps and divisions:

Commanding General: General Jean de Lattre de Tassigny

*1st Corps	Lt. Gen. Emile Béthouart, from 6 September 1944
*2d Corps	Lt. Gen. de Goislard de Monsabert, from 2 September 1944
*1st DMI	(1re Division de Marche d'Infanterie) Brig. Gen. Pierre Garbay, from 21 November 1944, in replacement of General Brosset killed in line of duty on 20 November 1944
*2d DIM	(2e Division d'Infanterie Marocaine) Maj. Gen. Marcel Carpentier, from 25 November 1944, in replacement of General Dody; replaced by Brig. Gen. François de Linarès on 12 April 1945
*3d DIA	(3e Division d'Infanterie Algérienne) Maj. Gen. Augustin Guillaume, from 2 September 1944, in replacement of General de Monsabert
*4th DMM	(4e Division Marocaine de Montagne) Maj. Gen. René de Hesdin, from 13 December 1944, in replacement of General Sevez
*9th DIC	(9e Division d'Infanterie Coloniale) Maj. Gen. Louis Morlière, from 26 December 1944, in

replacement of General Magnan; replaced by Brig. Gen. Jean Valluy on 10 March 1945

*1st DB	(1re Division Blindée) Brig. Gen. Aimé Sudre, from 6 December 1944, in replacement of General du Vigier
*2d DB	(2e Division Blindée) (assigned to 1st French Army from 5 to 31 December 1944 and from 20 January to 21 February 1945) Maj. Gen. Jacques Leclerc
*5th DB	(5e Division Blindée) Brig. Gen. Jacques de Vernejoul, replaced by Brig. Gen. Guy Schlesser, 23 April 1945
**10th DI	(10e Division d'Infanterie) (activated 30 September 1944) Brig. Gen. Pierre Billotte
**27th DIA	(27e Division d'Infanterie Alpine) (activated 17 November 1944; under control of 1st French Army until 1 March 1945; thereafter part of Détachement d'Armée des Alpes under the control of U.S. 6th Army Group) Col. Jean Vallette d'Osia

Two other divisions activated in February 1945 were assigned to 1st French Army in early April:

**1st DI	(1re Division d'Infanterie) Brig. Gen. Jean Callies
**14th DI	(14e Division d'Infanterie) Brig. Gen. Raoul Salan

Note: Five U.S. divisions were assigned to 1st French Army at one time or another during operations on the Western Front: 3d Infantry, 28th Infantry, 36th Infantry, 75th Infantry, and 12th Armored Divisions.

*Equipped under the North African Rearmament Program.

**Equipped under the Metropolitan Program.

Carrying Out the Revised Program

The progress of the Metropolitan Program by the end of February 1945 can be summarized as follows. The revisions prepared by SHAEF and submitted to Washington were awaiting CCS action. The French had raised a total of five infantry divisions, largely from FFI personnel. The 1st DI and 10th DI were being moved to the Châteauroux area where they were to receive their new equipment and undergo training. The intention of the French High Command was to use these two units together with the 2d Armored Division (2d DB) to form a third army corps. The 27th Alpine Division was still being employed in a defensive capacity on the Alps front. The 36th and 14th Infantry Divisions were the latest units to the activated, the latter from FFI battalions in 1st French Army area.[57] Considering that FFI troops had, in addition to being absorbed in these divisions, been used also to form security battalions, to replace Negro personnel in the 1st DMI and 9th DIC, and to organize replacement infantry regiments for the battle-weary North African program divisions (at the rate of one per North African division), it was expected that they shortly would be completely liquidated. Liquidation of the FFI in the 1st French Army area had strongly been urged by General Devers, who wanted all troops in that area to be placed on a "recognized status" and be maintained adequately.[58]

The first shipment of U.S. matériel had reached Marseille on 21 February. It was consigned to Communications Zone with special markings to indicate the intent of ASF in shipping the equipment. From arrival at quayside to final distribution, the matériel was processed according to a relatively simple method. All items, with the exception of boxed vehicles and ammunition, were loaded directly in rail cars on the pier and moved over U.S. lines of communications to a depot located at Lyon. Boxed vehicles were taken on trucks to a motor vehicle assembly area two miles away from the pier where they were assembled before being convoyed to Lyon. Ammunition was taken directly from shipside to U.S. ammunition depots where it was held earmarked for the French. Assisting in the handling of equipment at Marseille were several French service units organized for the purpose and for which Communications Zone had furnished equipment and clothing.[59]

The depot at Lyon, called Delta Base Section Depot for Rearmament, was, in theory, an integrated French-American organization. Actually it was a U.S. depot maintaining stock records and the equipment was part of U.S. theater stocks until issued to the French. Lend-lease accounting was, as a result, based on shipping tickets issued by the depot. This arrangement necessitated the use of American clerical, technical, and supervisory personnel until French personnel could be trained and taught sufficient familiarity with American equipment to take over their share of the work. The French service units at the Lyon depot formed a base called Base du Sud. Their activation being too slow, only very

[57] Memo, Regnault for Loomis, 21 Feb 45, SHAEF Mission to France 091.711–1 (Fr); Ltr, Juin to Eisenhower, 21 Feb 45, SHAEF SGS 475/2 France, Vol. II; Memos, SHAEF Mission to France for Juin, 6 Feb 45, and Juin for SHAEF Mission to France, 9 Mar 45, SHAEF Mission to France 091.711–13 (Fr).

[58] Msg BX–23958, Devers to SHAEF, 5 Feb 45, SHAEF G–3 091 France, Vol. VI.

[59] Memo, Loomis for Regnault, 19 Jan 45, SHAEF Mission to France 091.711–1 (Fr).

few had been made available to the depot by the end of February.

The entire plan for the receipt, storage, and distribution of matériel was considered adequate except for the shortage of French personnel. It was a much simpler system than the one used in North Africa under which the equipment was turned over at shipside to French supply agencies for issue to units. More important, it marked the beginning of a new era during which American management assumed the entire responsibility for distributing U.S. equipment, since Communications Zone controlled rigidly both priorities and flow of equipment.[60]

British equipment also had begun to arrive. A first shipment consisting of training matériel had reached Cherbourg on 8 February. Three other shipments, with the first to arrive 8 March, were scheduled to bring matériel for the initial three divisions. Shipments would then be postponed until further advice from SHAEF. The British were placing a Port Ordnance and Workshop Detachment at the disposal of the French to assist in handling equipment both in Cherbourg and at the French depot in Le Mans. They were particularly concerned over the risk of damage to vehicles at the hands of the "Paris taxi driver" type of French workman currently taking them over on discharge from the ships. The British were also offering training teams to instruct the French in the proper use of British equipment.[61]

All things considered, the responsibility for the implementation of the Metropolitan Program was divided generally between the Americans and the French. The French were charged with the provision and issue of French and British items, while the U.S. Army was responsible for the provision and issue of Canadian and captured enemy items as well as matériel of U.S. source. Co-ordinating all activities was the Rearmament Division which obtained from the French themselves reports of initial issues of equipment not provided by the United States.

In spite of the abundance of sources of equipment, some shortages were anticipated or already being felt which, it was feared, would threaten the combat effectiveness of the new units. General-purpose vehicles, for the most part, were reported to be unavailable. In addition, a number of items which the French had agreed to furnish immediately could not be produced by their industry. The Rearmament Division succeeded in obtaining from the United States a number of the missing items. In the case of clothing, however, its efforts were unsuccessful.

A serious shortage of clothing was hampering the efforts of the French High Command in calling up classes of recruits for the Metropolitan Program. General Juin currently estimated the immediate requirements at 130,000 sets of uniforms. As no new clothing was provided for recruits inducted under the program, SHAEF directed Communications Zone to survey the availability of worn surplus or salvaged U.S. clothing. Communications Zone reported that all available stocks of such clothing were required to meet "anticipated needs for prisoners of war expected to be taken in the near future" and for other commit-

---

[60] For additional information, see Rpt with illustrations, SHAEF G–4 FWD to Loomis, 11 Mar 45, SHAEF Mission to France, Rearmament.

[61] Msg, SHAEF G–4 to Crawford, 1 Mar 45, SHAEF Mission to France 475–10 Equip of Troops Metropolitan Program; Memos, Weeks for Loomis, 26 Feb 45, and Loomis for Weeks, 4 Mar 45, SHAEF Mission to France 091.711–3 (Fr).

ments.[62]   With this source of supply closed to the French, the latter would have to turn elsewhere for assistance.

On the basis of the progress achieved in two months and on the premise that it would continue unabated, General Loomis estimated that two infantry divisions should be ready for operations in a secondary role sometime in April and a third sometime in May.   All three should be ready for offensive operations as part of a corps, with adequate supporting and service troops, late in August or early in September.[63]

As the third month of implementation opened, the French, while declaring themselves in agreement with the priorities recommended by SHAEF on 15 February, urged the Allied authorities to speed up the distribution of matériel to the units of the first phase, and not to delay the launching of the second phase.   Only complete unity of action, General Leyer wrote to SHAEF on 3 March, would make it possible to secure, within the desired time limit, the benefits of the efforts agreed to by all concerned.[64]

During the four weeks of March matériel continued to arrive from the United Kingdom and the United States.   By the end of the month, the British had delivered training equipment, maintenance supplies, and replacement items for the whole eight-division program, as well as matériel for the

first three infantry divisions.   Subsequent shipments were being held up in order to phase the arrival of British equipment with that of American matériel for later priority divisions.   It was expected that shipments would be resumed in June.

General-purpose vehicles and clothing still remained the most critical items.   Some improvement in the vehicle situation was in sight as the British now were offering 5,200 trucks which, if found serviceable, might replace corresponding U.S. vehicles then in short supply.   With regard to the provision of clothing for newly inducted men, little progress had been made.   Efforts to obtain surplus uniforms from the British War Office had been unsuccessful.   The War Department, also approached on the matter, had given no encouragement other than promising to ship to France the rest of the 200,000 sets of Canadian clothing originally intended for Sovereignty troops in North Africa.[65]   In answer to their repeated appeals, including a formal request for 130,-000 sets submitted directly to the War Department, SHAEF reminded the French that critical shortages in both British and U.S. stocks were so acute, in the case of woolen clothing, shoes, and blankets, that the initial issue of these items to Metropolitan Program units would be made only with the greatest difficulty.   SHAEF then explained to them that their requirements with respect to newly inducted men could be filled only by taking every advantage of existing French stocks, Canadian clothing, French manufacture, and materials sup-

---

[62] In informing Colonel Regnault of the substance of Communications Zone's report, General Loomis wisely refrained from making any reference to the "anticipated needs for POW's," a statement which might well have angered the French. Memos, Loomis for Regnault, 4 Mar 45, Lewis for CG COMZONE, 21 Feb 45, and CG COMZONE for Lewis, 1 Mar 45, SHAEF Mission to France 421–1 Combined.

[63] Memo, Loomis for SCAEF, 8 Mar 45, SHAEF Mission to France 091.711–3 (Fr).

[64] Ltr, Leyer to SHAEF, 3 Mar 45, in same file.

[65] French industry was reported to be currently producing, since January, not more than 45,000 sets monthly. These sets were incomplete and adequate only for men in training. Furthermore, production was not expected to continue after April. Memo, Regnault for Loomis, SHAEF Mission to France 421–1 Combined.

plied under the civilian import program.[66] Incidentally, American officials also urged them, as they had once in connection with the North African Rearmament Program, to replace all U.S. buttons and insignia by French ones on American clothing turned over to program units "so as to permit ready identification and in the interest of esprit de corps." [67]

In Washington, War Department officials were still examining the revised program of eight divisions and 1,128 supporting units. ASF had undertaken an analysis of availability of equipment and, on 13 March, reported that, with the exception of some items, the program could generally be met. The Combined Administrative Committee meanwhile had pursued its study of the division of responsibility between the United States and the United Kingdom for the provision of matériel to meet the various western European rearmament programs. In the report which it finally submitted to the CCS on 24 March, the committee made no commitment with respect to the Metropolitan Program as the latter was still not firm. It merely recommended that unfilled portions of the Metropolitan Program and of all other rearmament programs be canceled effective V-E Day.[68]

The same recommendation, it will be recalled, had been made earlier, in August 1944, by the U.S. Chiefs of Staff in a memorandum to the CCS (CCS 661). It had already led ASF to develop a procurement schedule in which no provision was made for the shipment of the rest of the equipment required to complete the Metropolitan Program upon the cessation of hostilities. Such action was based on the premise that the program itself would then become postwar in character.[69] Incidentally, it was the same stand which had guided the U.S. Government, only four days before the publication of the Combined Administrative Committee's report, in its decision to reject a certain request from the British. The latter had, earlier in February, approached the State Department regarding a proposal they had received from the French for the manufacture in France of aircraft of the British Mosquito type. The matter involved an immediate U.S. commitment for the allocation of certain materials. Deciding that the proposal was in the nature of a postwar enterprise, the State Department informed the British, on 20 March, that the United States Government could not concur in it.[70]

At the end of March the War Ministry announced a reorganization of the French rearmament services. SCAMA was being abolished and its work taken over by a new army headquarters section called Mission de Réarmement. Simultaneously, a Rearmament Inspection Section was created whose function was generally to ascertain, in co-operation with Inspection Group of SHAEF's Rearmament Division, the completeness of equipment of the units being rearmed.[71] Both organizations were placed

[66] Msg WX–57738, Somervell to Eisenhower, 22 Mar 45, ASF International Div Cable Log A–45–192; Ltr, Lewis to Juin, 21 Mar 45, SHAEF Mission to France 421–1 Combined.

[67] Memos, Theater Comdr for SHAEF Mission to France, 17 Mar 45, and Lewis for Juin, 12 Apr 45, SHAEF Mission to France 421–1 Combined.

[68] Rpt, Availability Study of Fr Rearmt Program, 13 Mar 45, and Memo, Lutes to SCAEF for Loomis, 22 Mar 45, SHAEF Mission to France 091.711, File 92, Analysis of Availability; Rpt, CAdC to CCS, CCS 768/7, 24 Mar 45, ABC 400.3295 (2 Aug 43), Sec 1–C.

[69] Memo, Somervell for Marshall, 25 Mar 45, OPD 336.2 France, Sec IV–A.

[70] Aide Mémoire, Secy State to Br Ambassador, 20 Mar 45, ABC 091.711 France (6 Oct 43), Sec 2–D.

[71] Dir 1756/EMA/CAB, 26 Mar 45, SHAEF Mission to France 091.711–9 Combined.

under the command of General Granier who, it will be recalled, had been serving as commanding general of Base 901, supporting 1st French Army, and was now being replaced in that capacity by Col. Henri Coudraux. Assisting General Granier was Lt. Col. Maurice Labarbarie who had been associated with SCAMA for over a year and in recent months had served as SCAMA's deputy director.[72]

The equipment status of Metropolitan Program units was then as follows. Pursuant to a decision which, for operational reasons, SHAEF had made in mid-March in agreement with the French, three infantry divisions, the 1st, 10th, and 36th, were now scheduled to be re-equipped in first priority. Detachments from the first two were currently being ordered to the Lyon depot where they were to receive U.S. initial equipment beginning on or about 4 April. Very little organizational equipment was available for the 36th DI as shipments from the United States of matériel for a mountain division had started before the action had been taken to replace the 27th Alpine (27th DIA) by an infantry division. Except for British training matériel, the remaining divisions, being second and third priority units, were not scheduled to receive equipment until the Supreme Commander gave his approval. Two of them, the 19th and 25th Infantry, were currently employed on the Atlantic coast, and two others, the 3d Armored and 14th Infantry, although activated, were not expected to be fit for employment for a long time.[73]

The French military authorities were also in process of organizing the service units required in first priority. These included both the units needed for employment with Base du Sud operating in support of 1st French Army and those necessary for the support of the first three Metropolitan Program divisions. It was the firm intention of Rearmament Division to continue to exercise rigid control by not authorizing equipment for the next group of divisions until reasonable progress had been made in the organization of all first priority service units.[74]

By the end of March the operational situation on the Western Front was most favorable. General Eisenhower's armies were already deep in German territory. With the prospect of an early cessation of hostilities and in view of the relatively small progress of the Metropolitan Program, SHAEF re-examined the question of employment of the new units. Both the U.S. 6th Army Group and U.S. 12th Army Group were requesting two or three French divisions each for occupational duties under their control with a view to relieving U.S. divisions for employment elsewhere. In the belief that the presence of partially equipped and insufficiently trained divisions among units of 1st French Army might result in considerable confusion, SHAEF temporarily ruled out the employment of new divisions under 6th Army Group. SHAEF, on the other hand, approved the request from 12th Army Group and asked General Juin to nominate the 1st and 36th

---

[72] In November, Labarbarie had replaced Colonel Charpentier, who had become gravely ill and whose death took place in early 1945. Colonel Charpentier was posthumously awarded the Legion of Merit (degree of Officer) in April 1945.

[73] Msg MF–13626, Loomis to AGWAR, 10 Mar 45, and Memo, Lutes for Crawford, 2 Apr 45,

SHAEF Mission to France 091.711 Rearmt Plan and Policy 900–5; Memo, Bull for Smith, 31 Mar 45, SHAEF SGS 475/2 France, Vol. II.

[74] Memos, G–4 SHAEF FWD for Crawford, 10 Mar 45, and Loomis for Kingman, 17 Mar 45, SHAEF Mission to France 091.711 Rearmt Plan and Policy 900–5.

Infantry to serve under U.S. Fifteenth Army (itself part of 12th Army Group) in an occupational capacity while continuing their equipping and training, and to consider similar action in connection with the 10th DI.[75] The latter, incidentally, had been earmarked for operations on the Atlantic coast. The 27th DIA, although still poorly equipped, was to be maintained on the Franco-Italian border.

In early April, pending approval by the CCS of the revised program of eight divisions and 1,128 supporting units, the War Department prepared to effect the shipments scheduled to take place during that month for the units of the first priority. Simultaneously, the Combined Administrative Committee submitted to the CCS a report on its study of the revised program. In it, the committee recommended that the program be approved in spite of shortages of equipment, and that the United States be made responsible for the supply of initial equipment as well as replacement and maintenance supplies. The committee then reiterated its earlier recommendation, made on 24 March, that the unfilled portion of the program be canceled effective V-E Day.[76]

Taking immediate action on the report, the CCS, on 6 April, approved its recommendations. They formalized, and so notified General Eisenhower, the action already taken by the United States to supply the initial equipment as well as replacement and maintenance items to the first incre-

ment of three divisions and 167 supporting units. At a later date they would advise the Supreme Commander of the decisions taken with respect to the size of the program. Finally, they directed, as recommended by the committee, that any units which had not been armed by the time active hostilities with Germany had ceased would not be equipped. Four days later, after the War Department had completed its analysis of the revised troop list proposed by General Smith on 15 February, the CCS approved the list. The action of the Combined Chiefs, it must be noted, was taking place five weeks after they had approved the French Air Force Program. The latter included the same proviso directing the cancellation of the incompleted portion of the program upon the cessation of hostilities.[77]

Among the currently reported shortages of equipment for the new program, the most important was still that of clothing. In view of the critical situation in the United States of woolen clothing and of blankets in particular, the French were urged once again to investigate the possibility of manufacturing these items and to arrange with responsible American authorities in the theater for the delivery from the United States of the necessary raw materials.[78]

In Washington, ASF estimated that of the equipment scheduled to be shipped for the Metropolitan Program in January, February, and March, 99, 98, and 94 percent, respectively, had been floated. The French Military Mission was now pressing for ship-

---

[75] Ltr, Smith to Juin, 4 Apr 45, SHAEF Mission to France 091.711–12 Combined.

[76] Msg WX–64492, Somervell to Eisenhower, 5 Apr 45, International Div Files Cable Log; Rpt, CAdC to CCS, CCS 768/10, 5 Apr 45, SHAEF Mission to France 091.711 Rearmt Plan and Policy Rpt.

[77] Msg FACS 172, CCS to Eisenhower, 6 Apr 45, SS and P Planning files; Msg FACS 175, CCS to Eisenhower, 10 Apr 45, ABC 091.711 France (6 Oct 43), Sec 5; Msg FACS 147, CCS to Eisenhower, 1 Mar 45, ABC 091.711 France (6 Oct 43), Sec 2–C. See pp. 374–75, below.

[78] Ltr, Loomis to Juin, 10 Apr 45, SHAEF Mission to France 421–1 Combined.

ments due to be made in April and May.[79]

As three infantry divisions and certain corps troops had by this time already received much of their standard combat equipment, most of it American, some of it British, plans were made to begin their training. A considerable quantity of British matériel, the greater part of which had not been accepted as standard equipment, was available for the purpose. A training program was drafted which contemplated making the best possible use of existing resources and of U.S., British, and French training personnel, within the shortest possible time.[80]

On 20 April, with hostilities seemingly about to end, the U.S. Chiefs of Staff agreed that equipment intended to complete the Metropolitan Program but not likely to be used against the German forces would not be shipped from the United States. They then requested the theater on 26 April to review the whole rearmament question in the light of their decision and to submit to the War Department a list of units for which initial equipment need no longer be provided. Their request was consonant with

General Marshall's recommendation made a few days earlier that the choking off of the program should not be done automatically, effective V-E Day, but rather should be reexamined by the General Staff in consideration of the probable French requirement for occupation forces.[81]

In anticipation of the cessation of hostilities, SHAEF was preparing a plan to transfer the supply responsibility for the French forces from ETOUSA to the French Government. The proposed plan envisaged the establishment of a French Advance Section charged with the supply, maintenance, and movement of French troops. It also contemplated a new requisitioning procedure under which the French would submit monthly requisitions to be forwarded through military lend-lease channels to the MAB in Washington.[82]

It was then, near the end of the month of April, hardly three weeks after the Liberated Manpower Program had been suspended by order of the Supreme Commander, that a serious political complication subjected the Metropolitan Program to a similar fate.

---

[79] Memo, ASF for Director Plans and Opns, 18 Apr 45, SS and P Planning Div Files A–46–371; Msg WX–69225, Somervell to Loomis, 18 Apr 45, SHAEF Mission to France 475–10 Equip of Troops Metropolitan Program.

[80] Memo, Loomis for Regnault, 14 Apr 45, SHAEF Mission to France Training 353–1; Memo, Loomis for Leyer, 19 Apr 45, SHAEF Mission to France 091.711–1. Also, see below, p. 390.

[81] Memo, JCS for ACofS OPD, 20 Apr 45, OPD 336.2 France, Sec IV–A; Msg WX–73760, Marshall to Loomis, 26 Apr 45, OPD Cable Files; Memo, Lincoln for Policy Sec OPD, 21 Apr 45, ABC 091.711 France (6 Oct 43), Sec 2–D.

[82] Memo, SHAEF G–4 FWD for Crawford, 27 Apr 45, SHAEF Mission to France 091.711 Rearmt Plan and Policy 900–5.

CHAPTER XXI

The Rearmament Operations End

Suspension of the Metropolitan Program

For a question of national prestige, the French unwittingly were about to throw the armament operations out of gear. On 24 and again on 26 April, General Devers had directed General de Lattre to evacuate the city of Stuttgart then occupied by units of 1st French Army. The city was in the operational zone of the U.S. Seventh Army and was urgently needed as a link in the supply and communications system supporting the current military operations of that army. On instructions from General de Gaulle, the French commander refused to comply with General Devers' order.

In a strongly worded letter dated 28 April, the text of which was immediately communicated to the CCS, General Eisenhower called General de Gaulle's action in issuing orders directly to 1st French Army a violation of existing agreements. French divisions armed and equipped by the United States were under the control of the CCS representative in the theater. It was with complete faith in this understanding that he, as Supreme Commander acting for the CCS, had "so long and so earnestly" supported the French request for matériel to equip new divisions. In the present circumstances, he had no other alternative but to inform the CCS of the incident and to point out to them that he could no longer count with certainty upon the operational employment of any French forces which

they might contemplate equipping in the future.[1]

On the same date General Eisenhower informed the Joint Chiefs of Staff that, in line with their suggestion of 26 April, the shipment of any equipment not yet floated could be stopped, and that he was revising the list of units for which equipment need not be furnished.[2] Simultaneously and apparently without prior notification to French headquarters, the Supreme Commander directed that all issues of equipment to Metropolitan Program units be suspended. In informing the French as well as the British of this decision, SHAEF made no reference to the Stuttgart incident, but gave the following reasons for the action. With the approaching end of the campaign in Europe, the need no longer existed for equipping additional French units as the Allies had sufficient divisions on hand to liquidate pockets of resistance and to police occupied areas. Furthermore, all American matériel in Europe was destined for use in the Far East theaters.[3]

---

[1] Msg SCAF 319, Eisenhower to CCS, 29 Apr 45, OCS A–48–1 091 France.

[2] Msg MF–14139, Eisenhower to Marshall, 28 Apr 45, SHAEF SGS 475/1 France, Vol. IV.

[3] Msg FWD 20357, Eisenhower to WO, 1 May 45, SHAEF SGS 475/1, Vol. II; Ltr, SHAEF to Juin, quoted by de Saint-Didier in Conf with Marshall, 3 May 45, Min Conf, ABC 091.711 France (6 Oct 43), Sec 2–D; Memo, Loomis for Leyer, 30 Apr 45, SHAEF Mission to France 475–10 Equip of Troops Metropolitan Program.

In replying to General Eisenhower's communication on the Stuttgart episode, de Gaulle used some of the arguments that General Juin had advanced in connection with the controversy over the control of security battalions. The French Command, he pointed out, had no representation in the CCS, and, as a result, decisions reached by the latter did not take into account French "national requirements," thus forcing him personally, although to his "great regret," to "step in" sometimes either with respect to plans or their execution. He explained further:

> You are certainly aware that while agreeing to placing French operational forces in the Western Theater under your supreme command, I have always reserved the right of the French Government eventually to take the necessary steps in order that French forces should be employed in accordance with the national interest of France which is the only interest that they should serve. I have, naturally, never made any distinction with respect to French forces which have had the benefit of American equipment. I should, moreover, call your attention to the fact that this armament has been turned over by the United States on the basis of Lend-Lease agreements by virtue of which France and the French Union provide on their part, and in accordance with their means, important services for American forces. On this point, I note with much regret that, as of the present moment, no new French division has been completely equipped by the United States since the beginning of operations in Western Europe in spite of all that had appeared to have been understood a long time ago.[4]

General de Gaulle's letter brought this brief acknowledgment from the Supreme Commander. ". . . I understand your position, and while I repeat my regret that you find it necessary to inject political con-

siderations into a campaign in which my functions are purely military, I am gratified to know that you understand my situation and attitude." [5]

With the issue apparently closed in the theater, the French immediately took steps to reopen it in Washington with a view to obtaining a resumption of equipment deliveries. Calling on General Marshall on 3 May, General de Saint-Didier, chief of the French Military Mission, sought, in behalf of General Juin who had just advised him of the deadlock, assurances that the United States would complete the equipping of the first three divisions and of certain supporting units. He pointed out that the action taken by the Supreme Commander was "not in accord with the supply agreement of 30 December 1944 or with the personal letter of President Roosevelt to General de Gaulle dated 24 March 1945." What General de Saint-Didier probably meant by the "supply agreement" was the message dispatched to SHAEF by the CCS on 29 December advising that they had accepted in principle the Metropolitan Program. The CCS, however, had made no further commitment. As for the President's letter to de Gaulle, nothing in it implied that a promise had been made to complete the program. Replying to General de Saint-Didier, General Marshall explained that he had not been informed that SHAEF had ordered a stoppage of issues. He would look into the matter at once before discussing it with General Juin on the latter's return from the United Nations conference then taking place in San Francisco.[6]

In the meantime, War Department offi-

---

[4] Ltr, de Gaulle to Eisenhower, 1 May 45, SHAEF SGS 094 Stuttgart.

[5] Ltr, Eisenhower to de Gaulle, 2 May 45, and Msg SCAF 328, Eisenhower to CCS, 2 May 45, SHAEF SGS 094 Stuttgart. See p. 337, above.

[6] Min Conf, Marshall with de Saint-Didier, 3 May 45, ABC 091.711 France (6 Oct 43), Sec 2–D.

cials had informed General Loomis that, in accordance with the Supreme Commander's recommendation, they were canceling the unshipped balance of initial equipment for both the Metropolitan and Air Force Programs.[7] SHAEF then advised the French that the two programs were being re-examined to determine what units, if any, could be equipped in time to operate against German forces, and that pending revision issues of matériel were being suspended.[8] On 6 May the Supreme Commander submitted to the War Department the list of some twenty-two organizations, all service units, which the theater considered operationally necessary and desired to equip fully. He then took this opportunity to discuss the fate of the first three divisions on the program. Inasmuch as it had been agreed that they should be employed as soon as they were operational, the question now arose, "as a matter of good faith," as to whether or not it might be desirable to complete their equipping. The units in question had been issued approximately one third of their authorized U.S. equipment, and had made considerable progress in training. The rest of their equipment could be provided from matériel likely to become available at the time of redeployment following the cessation of hostilities. If not contrary to the policy of the U.S. Chiefs of Staff, this course of action, if authorized, would result "in postponing, rather than in entirely eliminating," the equipping of the three divisions.[9]

The cessation of hostilities on 7 May found 1st French Army deployed in enemy

territory over a wide area which included parts of western Austria and southwestern Germany. The long dash from the French coast was now completed. All together the campaign of France and Germany had cost the French ground forces (excluding the FFI troops before their integration in regular units in October 1944) some 74,000 casualties, including nearly 15,000 killed in action.[10]

The end of the campaign also found the implementation of both the Liberated Manpower and Metropolitan Programs already suspended pending a review of the theater's requirements for the postarmistice period. Fully or partially equipped units were being furnished maintenance but no replacements for equipment used. This provision was extended to the units of 1st French Army on 8 May, when the Supreme Commander directed Communications Zone to discontinue immediately the issue of initial equipment and of major replacement items, but not of maintenance.[11]

By then the status of the Metropolitan Program was as follows. Three infantry divisions and only approximately 40 supporting units, representing a total of some 50,000 men, had been partially equipped. They had received the greater part of their British equipment, almost no French ma-

---

[7] Msg WX–76320, Hull to Loomis, 1 May 45, SS and P Planning Div Files.
[8] Msg FWD 20647, Eisenhower to AGWAR, 5 May 45, ABC 091.711 France (6 Oct 43), Sec 2–C.
[9] Msg FWD 20723, Eisenhower to AGWAR, 6 May 45, SS and P Planning Div Files.

[10] The breakdown of casualties per major ground force component is estimated as follows:

	Killed in Action	Wounded in Action
Total	14,900	59,307
1st French Army (excluding the 2d DB)	12,439	51,882
2d DB	1,205	3,500
Army Detachment of the Atlantic	456	1,425
Army Detachment of the Alps	800	2,500

Source: Lt. Col. P. Santini, "Etude statistique sur les pertes au cours de la guerre 1939–1945," Revue du Corps de Santé Militaire, X, No. 1 (March, 1954).

[11] Msgs FWD 20723, SCAEF to AGWAR, 6 May 45, and FWD 20921, SCAEF to COMZONE, 8 May 45, SHAEF SGS 475/1 France, Vol. IV.

tériel as the French themselves had been unable to provide it, and about one third of the U.S. equipment shipped to France for them. All together they had been issued most of the required individual and housekeeping items, but only one quarter of their organizational equipment. Outstanding shortages were in clothing items, signal equipment, and general-purpose vehicles.[12]

The Joint Logistics Committee meanwhile had studied the Supreme Commander's request that the equipping of the first 3 divisions and of 22 selected supporting units be completed. In its final report the committee approved the proposal as it related to the supporting units, but urged that the question of the further issue of equipment to the divisions be taken on a governmental level as being a postwar armament problem. In a review of the Supreme Commander's request and of the recommendations contained in the JLC report, Maj. Gen. Howard A. Craig, Deputy Assistant Chief of Staff, OPD, urged General Marshall to exercise the utmost caution in his forthcoming meeting with General Juin. He advised him to make no commitment regarding the rest of the equipment for the 3 divisions in view of the probable difficulty in making such equipment available, and to limit any discussion of supporting units to the 22 organizations currently under consideration. He then furnished some data to enable Marshall to review for General Juin's benefit the extent of military aid provided the French to date.[13]

Pressed to comment further on the ad-

visability of completing the equipment of the three divisions, General Eisenhower pointed out that, although inadequately equipped, the 1st DI and 10th DI had been used in operations. The 10th DI had been committed at the edge of the Colmar Pocket in January and in the Bordeaux area in April; the 1st DI had served in an occupational role first west of the Rhine during April, later in early May east of the Rhine. It was feasible to equip these two divisions, as well as the 36th Infantry which had not yet served under Allied control, up to a scale suitable for occupational purposes by using equipment available in the theater. The Supreme Commander then urged that he be authorized to carry out his proposal, subject to operational needs for other theaters and to availability of stocks. Such an undertaking, he declared, would be "an act of good will."[14]

In the course of his conference with General Marshall on 11 May, General Juin spoke of his government's hope that some means would be found to complete the equipping of the three divisions. He suggested that this be done by using the equipment which U.S. divisions would leave behind before moving to the Pacific theater. General Marshall replied that, for the moment, it was impossible to promise the definite delivery of specific items by any fixed date. Feeling certain that some sort of an arrangement could be worked out, he recommended that General Juin on his return to France contact the Supreme Commander with a view to arranging the details of a possible allocation of matériel. The financial aspects of the problem would of course have to be handled by the civil rather

---

[12] Msg MF–14197, Lewis to SHAEF FWD G–4, 6 May 45, SHAEF SGS 475/1 France, Vol. IV; Msg FWD 20888, Eisenhower to Marshall, 7 May 45, ABC 091.711 France (6 Oct 43), Sec 2–D.

[13] Rpt, JLC 1012/8, 9 May 45, and Memo, Craig for Marshall, 9 May 45, OPD 336.2 France, Sec IV–A.

[14] Msg FWD 21192, Eisenhower to Marshall, 11 May 45, SHAEF SGS 475/2 France, Vol. II.

than the military agencies of both governments.[15]

On 12 May the Supreme Commander informed the Combined Chiefs of Staff that, in accordance with the policy they had established on 6 April, he was directing SHAEF as well as the British War Office to stop initial issues of equipment to all units of the French air and ground rearmament programs with the exception of twenty-two service units already partially equipped. He then instructed SHAEF Mission to France to notify the French War Ministry of his decision.[16] Implementation of the programs, heretofore suspended, was now stopped.

At the conference which General Smith held the next day with Minister of War Diethelm, the latter sought some indication concerning the future of the three partially equipped divisions. His government eagerly hoped that the equipping of these units would be resumed as early as possible as they would be required for occupational tasks in Germany. The order to discontinue deliveries of equipment had had a harmful effect on the morale of the troops involved. General Smith replied that the program, originally conceived as an operational commitment, was no longer so considered now that hostilities had ceased. SHAEF's authority did not extend to the consideration of the broader problem of the restoration and re-equipment of a French national army. This was a matter for intergovernmental negotiations. The Supreme Commander, he added, was fully aware of the French point of view and was urging the JCS to authorize delivery of the rest of the equipment for the three divisions.[17]

Meanwhile, the question of the continued logistical support of the French forces had been restudied. Because of the anticipated early redeployment of U.S. service units and streamlining of the U.S. lines of communications, it was imperative that the French authorities be made to assume the administrative support of their forces as soon as possible. With this in view, on 16 May the theater submitted to the War Department a supply plan contemplating the transfer to the French, in two stages, of the responsibility for the maintenance of their troops. Under the proposed plan the War Department was ultimately to furnish the authorized maintenance on an automatic basis with the French assuming the complete responsibility for shipment, reception, storage, and distribution.[18]

As the question of the delimitation of a French zone of occupation was still pending, War Department officials favored another solution of the maintenance problem. They felt that, until the French had formally taken over their zone of occupation, the issue to them of maintenance supplies should be done on a military lend-lease basis. Thereafter, the issue of such supplies should be regulated under a new program to be negotiated by the French Government and the appropriate civil agencies of the U.S. Government. The whole matter being properly one for decision by the Joint Chiefs, it was referred to them on 22 May.[19]

The question of whether or not it was

---

[15] Min Conf, Marshall with Juin, 11 May 45, ABC 091.711 France (6 Oct 43), Sec 2–D.

[16] Msg SCAF 387, Eisenhower to CCS, 12 May 45, ABC 091.711 France (6 Oct 43), Sec 2–C; Msg FWD 21251, Eisenhower to WO, ETOUSA, SHAEF Mission to France, 12 May 45, SHAEF SGS 475/3 France.

[17] Min Mtg, Smith with Diethelm, 13 May 45, SHAEF SGS 475/2 France, Vol. II.

[18] Msg 21662, SHAEF to AGWAR, 16 May 45, ABC 091.711 France (6 Oct 43), Sec 2–C.

[19] Memo for Rcd, OPD, 22 May 45, OPD 336.2 France, Sec V.

desirable to complete the equipment of twenty-two supporting units as requested earlier by the Supreme Commander was still under study. There appeared to be considerable disagreement among the members of the JCS as to whether these units were essential to the American war effort and could be properly considered as a military lend-lease requirement, or whether they were of "postwar benefit" to the French and should then be supplied through civilian lend-lease on a governmental level. On 25 May the JCS finally agreed to authorize the Supreme Commander to finish equipping the units from theater stocks. The decision with respect to the three divisions was being withheld pending further information from the theater.[20]

The status of the Liberated Manpower Program had not changed to any appreciable degree. The question of its resumption was still under consideration by the CCS. It will be recalled that on 24 April the Supreme Commander had requested that he be authorized to form and equip such security and labor units as might be required for a period not exceeding one year after V-E Day. On 12 May General Eisenhower reminded the CCS of this request and informed them that pending their approval SHAEF planned to continue the formation of labor and security units if the governments concerned agreed to the proposal. Some progress had been made toward solving the controversial issue of the control of French units. General Smith and War Minister Diethelm, meeting on 13 May, had discussed the matter and come to an agreement. The agree-

ment, confirmed in writing by General Juin on 31 May, stipulated that the Supreme Commander was to continue to control for six months, beginning 1 June, the 25 security battalions and 6 labor groups then employed under Communications Zone and 21 Army Group. An additional 20 battalions were to be made available to him as soon as they would be equipped. None of the units were to be employed outside French territory.[21]

At the end of May SHAEF was taking steps to complete the equipping of the 22 service units approved by the JCS at least up to the scale required to accomplish their assigned mission. These units were already being employed by Communications Zone and army groups to release corresponding U.S. units required to support forces under U.S. command. Three additional French units (2 railway operating battalions and 1 railway grand division), proposed by SHAEF in early May as operationally necessary, had still not been authorized by the JCS. As for the three divisions, the decision to complete their equipping was being withheld by the JCS, pending receipt from the theater of a detailed list of the items required. The Lyon depot meanwhile was being maintained in operation and the matériel stocked there for the French was being held in reserve, except in the case of items in critical short supply required for U.S. troops in process of redeployment.[22]

[20] Msg W–87143, Marshall to Eisenhower, 24 May 45, SHAEF SGS 475/1 France, Vol. IV; Msg WX–87996, JCS to Eisenhower, 25 May 45, ABC 091.711 France (6 Oct 43), Sec 2–D.

[21] Msg SCAF 387, SCAEF to CCS, 12 May 45, ABC 091.711 France (6 Oct 43), Sec 2–C; Ltr, Juin to Lewis, 31 May 45, SHAEF G–3 091 France, Vol. VII.

[22] Msg FWD 22447, Eisenhower to Marshall, 27 May 45, OPD Cable Files; Msg FWD 21005, SHAEF to AGWAR, 8 May 45, ABC 091.711 France (6 Oct 43), Sec 2–D; Msg FWD 22658, Eisenhower to COMZONE, 29 May 45, SHAEF SGS 475/1 France, Vol. IV.

Political Developments Doom Rearmament

The hope, which the French still entertained, that the first phase at least of the Metropolitan Program would be completed was suddenly shattered, once again as a result of a political complication arising in the theater. The incident, more serious than any of those preceding, threatened to bring Franco-American co-operation to an end.

In the spring of 1945 German forces still occupied a narrow strip of French territory west of the Franco-Italian border. Facing them were French units reorganized since 1 March as the Détachement d'Armée des Alpes commanded by Lt. Gen. Paul Doyen, who was under the operational control of the U.S. 6th Army Group. The detachment included then the 27th Alpine Infantry Division (27th DIA) still poorly armed, the U.S.-equipped 1st March Infantry Division (1st DMI) temporarily detached from the 1st French Army, and a number of units of FFI origin. All together it represented a strength of some twenty infantry battalions with several artillery and engineer units. The detachment was to launch an attack in co-ordination with the planned offensive of the 15th Army Group in Italy. By direction of Field Marshal Sir Harold R. L. G. Alexander, then Supreme Allied Commander in the Mediterranean, the French units were not to go beyond a line extending from the Swiss frontier to the Ligurian Gulf.

The attack came on 9 April. The French successfully drove the Germans off French territory, and continued their push eastward. They had nearly reached the restraining line when, on 27 April, 15th Army Group informed 6th Army Group that any further advance by the French detachment could have no appreciable effect on operations in Italy. The next day General Devers ordered General Doyen to halt and prepare to withdraw to the Franco-Italian border. This border delimited the boundary between the Mediterranean and European theaters. The withdrawal of the French was necessary as Alexander was establishing Allied military government within his theater including all of liberated Italy. Doyen ordered his troops to halt but declined to bring them back to the border without instructions from his government. By the end of May the French detachment had still not withdrawn in spite of repeated orders from Devers.[23]

The situation was reminiscent of the Stuttgart episode in which another French commander, General de Lattre, on orders from de Gaulle, had refused to comply with instructions from his superior. It was all the more regrettable considering that General Juin, on 11 May, had given assurances to American officials in Washington that there would be no recurrence of the Stuttgart affair.

Allied officials learned that, for reasons of prestige and honor, the French were not prepared to evacuate the disputed area largely in the belief that such a move would appear to the Italians as a retreat on the part of France. They learned moreover that France was planning to annex part of the area. Determined to carry out the establishment of Allied military government even in the territory occupied by French troops, Field Marshal Alexander urged SHAEF to make strong representations to the French Government with a view to obtaining prompt compliance with General Devers' orders.

---

[23] Hq Fifth Army, "The French-Italian Border Problem," Sec II, Chronological Summary, DRB AGO.

On 30 May General Doyen wrote to his immediate superior, Maj. Gen. Willis Crittenberger, Commanding General, U.S. IV Corps, then on his way to assume control of the area occupied by the French detachment. Doyen protested against Allied attempts to establish military government in the Province of Cuneo, which his government had ordered him to occupy and administer. The installation of any Allied administrative agency in that area being incompatible with his mission, he would be compelled to oppose it. Any insistence in this direction "would assume a clearly unfriendly, even hostile, character, and could result in severe consequences." [24] Two days later the French commander informed General Crittenberger that General de Gaulle had instructed him to make it as clear as possible to the Allied Command that he was to prevent the establishment of Allied military government in the territories occupied and administered by French troops "by all necessary means without exception." [25]

Alexander immediately apprised the CCS of the impasse now reached with the French High Command and recommended that he be allowed to complete the occupation of northwestern Italy and establish Allied military government there, using force if need be. Informed of the situation, President Truman on 6 June cabled to General de Gaulle his deep concern over the action of the French Army in ignoring orders issued by representatives of the CCS. General Doyen's letter of 30 May contained the "unbelievable threat" that the French might fight the Americans. Pointing out that the American people would be shocked if they were apprised of this threat, the President urged General de Gaulle to reconsider his stand in the matter. In the meantime, he had no alternative but to order the stoppage of issue of military equipment and munitions. [26]

In the belief that, largely as a result of the prompt and effective intervention of General Juin and Foreign Affairs Minister Georges Bidault, the matter was about to be settled in a satisfactory manner, General Smith recommended to the War Department that execution of the stoppage order be delayed a day or two pending clarification of the situation. He feared that, if action were taken at once, the French might give the incident considerable publicity. [27] General Marshall replied that the order remained in effect. Further, it was to apply also to the labor and security units supplied from U.S. sources. Excepted from the order were rations and sufficient quantities of gasoline to maintain the normal life of troops and to allow for such movements as might be required. In anticipation of an acceptable answer from General de Gaulle, the Supreme Commander was to prepare for the resumption of the issuance of supplies but "only upon specific instructions" from the War Department. [28] In a second message of the same date, General Marshall informed General McNarney, Commanding General, U.S. Forces in the Mediterranean

[24] Ltr, Doyen to Crittenberger, 30 May 45, Fifth Army Files, "The Fr-Ital Border Question," No. 20, DRB AGO.

[25] Msg 44/CEM, Doyen to Crittenberger, 2 Jun 45, in same file.

[26] Msg NAF 1002, Alexander to CCS, in same file; Msg W–12923, Marshall to Eisenhower and McNarney, 6 Jun 45, Staff Message Center Cable Log.

[27] Msg FWD 23981, Smith to Handy, 8 Jun 45, SHAEF Cable Log, Fr Forces, A–49–70 TS.

[28] Msg W–13700, Marshall to Eisenhower, 8 Jun 45, SHAEF Cable Log, Fr Forces, A–49–70 TS; Msg WX–14512, AGWAR to ETOUSA and MTOUSA, 8 Jun 45, ABC 091.711 France (6 Oct 43), Sec 2–E.

Theater of Operations, that military lend-lease support of the French Sovereignty and Territorial forces in North Africa was being terminated forthwith. Only such matériel as had been floated would be delivered.[29] This action was being taken on the ground that support of these forces was no longer justified militarily now that hostilities had ceased in Europe.[30]

In compliance with the presidential decision, the Supreme Commander ordered the cessation, as of 9 June, of all issues of equipment, except rations and some gasoline, to all French forces, including air, whether in North Africa or in Europe. The next day Alexander received word from General Juin that de Gaulle had consented to the withdrawal of French troops west of the 1939 Franco-Italian border. French and Allied commanders, meeting on 11 June, agreed that the relief of all French troops from the disputed area was to be accomplished progressively and completed by 10 July. No publicity was to be given to these arrangements and no communiqué issued by any military headquarters concerned. The operation was to be referred to as a "normal military relief" and the use of the word "withdrawal" was to be avoided.[31]

In an attempt to obtain the rapid lifting of the ban on the further issue of equipment, Ambassador Bonnet called on State Department officials on 13 June and urged that lend-lease shipments be resumed. He was told by John J. McCloy that the matter was in the President's hands and would have to be taken up with him. The President, in fact, had just been sounded out and had indicated that he was prepared to lift the ban "in a few days." [32] His policy appeared to be that the embargo order would be rescinded only after completion of the planned withdrawal of French troops from northwestern Italy. This was made clear in a message from General Marshall requesting General McNarney to keep him informed of French preparations for and progress in withdrawal, so that he could recommend to the President the appropriate time for the resumption of supply to the French forces. General McNarney then urged that he be authorized to tell General Juin that deliveries would be resumed upon completion of the French withdrawal. General Marshall replied that the matter rested entirely with the President, since it was he who had made the original decision to stop the supply of equipment.[33]

While the ban imposed on 9 June continued in force, the War Department examined its implications. On 18 June the International Division pointed out that should all military lend-lease to the French be definitely ended, it would mean the stoppage of the further issue of replacement and maintenance supplies to the forces now equipped, of rations to approximately

---

[29] Msg WX–14512, AGWAR to McNarney, 8 Jun 45, ABC 091.711 France (6 Oct 43), Sec 2–E.
[30] Memo, McFarland for de Saint-Didier, 9 Jun 45, in same file.
[31] Msg FWD 24154, Eisenhower To All Concerned, 9 June 45, SHAEF SGS 475/3, Vol. I; Msg NAF 1008, Alexander to CCS, 10 June 45, SHAEF Cable Log, Fr Forces, A–49–70 TS; Msgs NAF 1009, Alexander to CCS, 11 Jun 45, and NAF 1010, Alexander to CCS, 11 Jun 45.

[32] Memo, McCloy for Marshall, 14 Jun 45, ABC 380 France (7 Aug 44), Sec 1–A.
[33] Msgs FX–94233, McNarney to Marshall, 16 Jun 45, WX–18779, Marshall to McNarney, 18 Jun 45, and FX–13943, McNarney to Marshall, 27 Jun 45, AFHQ Cable Log; Msg WX–20076, Marshall to McNarney, 21 Jun 45, SHAEF Cable Log; Msg FX–98608, McNarney to AGWAR, 24 Jun 45, Staff Message Center Cable Log; Msg (unnumbered), Marshall to CG U.S. Armed Forces in Med, 28 Jun 45, ABC 091.711 France (6 Oct 43), Sec 2–E.

300,000 troops, of matériel to complete the first three divisions of the Metropolitan Program, as well as the nondelivery of 100 airplanes then en route to Europe. It would also spell the end of the current negotiations regarding the equipping of the forces offered by the French for employment in the Far East. Finally, it would have far-reaching implications with respect to the civilian import program.[34]

One problem, meanwhile, had come up for examination, namely, the ultimate disposition of the units equipped under the Liberated Manpower Program. The advisability of maintaining in operation under U.S. control the thirty-five security battalions and two labor groups furnished by the French was seriously being questioned. Communications Zone, which regarded the units as "the least efficient of all Allied liberated manpower units," felt that their maintenance placed a heavy load on the U.S. supply system. On 8 June Communications Zone urged that they be released to French Government control without delay.[35]

As new commitments were being thrown in the lap of the U.S. Army, such as the feeding of large numbers of prisoners of war and displaced persons, the supply situation of the theater was being severely strained. It was becoming increasingly essential that national governments be made to assume the supply responsibility of their respective forces at the earliest practicable date. With this in view, SHAEF advised the French High Command on 23 June that the requirements of the U.S. forces for security and labor units had been revised. It was no longer proposed to raise

and equip any new units of this type. In addition, ten security battalions were being returned forthwith to French control. On 29 June SHAEF officials informed the CCS that they were gradually releasing all liberated manpower units except a few truck companies. They then proposed, in anticipation of the termination of combined command, that thereafter matters connected with Liberated Manpower Program units be handled by American and British commanders—with the War Office for the issue of initial equipment and maintenance, and with the national governments concerned regarding the employment and movement of units.[36]

By early July all liberated manpower units, with the exception of a few truck companies, had been returned to French control. As the French military authorities were proposing to disband the units no longer considered necessary, SHAEF was satisfied that they would have sufficient surplus equipment to maintain the others in operation, including military regions headquarters, the Gendarmerie, and the Garde Mobile.[37]

The embargo on the issue of equipment to the French never had a chance of being lifted. On 5 July President Truman announced in a directive to the Joint Chiefs of Staff that thereafter the issue to Allied governments of lend-lease military equipment would be limited to that which would be used in the war against Japan exclu-

---

[34] Memo, Lt Col Don G. Shingler for Asst Secy War, 18 Jun 45, OCS A–48–1 091 France. See Ch. XXIV, below.

[35] Memo, G–3 COMZONE for CofS, 8 Jun 45, SHAEF G–3 Orgn and Equip Sec 091, Vol. III.

[36] Msg EX–59933, COMZONE to SHAEF, 21 Jun 45, SHAEF G–3 Orgn and Equip Sec 091, Vol. III; Memo, Lewis for Juin, 23 Jun 45, SHAEF Mission to France 091.711–12 (Fr) Combined; Msg S–93960 SCAF 468, Tedder to CCS, 29 Jun 45, ABC 091.711 France (6 Oct 43), Sec 2–E.

[37] Memo, Bull for OCofS, 5 Jul 45, SHAEF SGS 475/1, Vol. II; Memo, SHAEF for CG COMZONE, USFET, and SHAEF Mission to France, 7 Jul 45, SHAEF Mission to France 091.4 Liberated People.

sively.[38] While leaving the door open to further negotiations on the French proposal to equip an expeditionary corps for the Pacific, the directive put an end to the possibility that at least the first phase of the Metropolitan Program would be completed. The French would find only small comfort in the decision reached by the War Office on 9 July to resume the delivery of British items of equipment to fill shortages existing at the time of initial shipments, and of supplies required for the maintenance of equipment currently in the hands of French units.[39]

As a result of the presidential decision, the activities of the rearmament depot at Lyon came to an end and all equipment stored there was ordered returned to U.S. theater stocks. All records of the depot were subsequently moved to Delta Base Section.[40]

With the termination of the combined command and SHAEF's dissolution on 13–14 July, 1st French Army reverted to French control. Simultaneously the responsibility for the remaining U.S. activities in connection with French armament and training passed to the new U.S. command in the theater, United States Forces, European Theater, the successor to ETOUSA. The British, meanwhile, organized an agency of their own for the purpose of handling matters of interest to the War Office.[41]

The presidential directive of 5 July had hardly been put into effect when it became apparent that its provisions were too restrictive. In the case of the French, their occupation forces would not long maintain their normal life unless the issue to them of U.S. rations and gasoline was resumed for some time at least. The matter, which was of equal concern to the British forces of occupation, was discussed by President Truman and Prime Minister Churchill in the course of the Potsdam Conference (17 July–2 August).[42]

On 29 July President Truman communicated to the JCS an "interpretation" of his original directive. The continuation of lend-lease aid was authorized when, in the opinion of the JCS, such aid was to be used in direct support of American or Allied redeployment in the war against Japan. Also authorized was the issue to U.S.-equipped French units, on a military lend-lease basis, of rations until 31 August 1945 and of replacement and maintenance items (including lubricants) until 30 September of the same year. The interpretation authorized further the supply for all other purposes of maintenance items for U.S. equipment now in the possession of Allied armies "against payment under such terms and conditions as may be determined by the State Department and the Foreign Economic Administration in accordance with established procedure." [43]

Pursuant to this clarification, General Eisenhower issued, on 2 August, an instruction to all headquarters under his command defining the extent and nature of further material assistance to the French.[44] The latter were then advised by United States

---

[38] Directive communicated to CG USFET in Msg W–28135, 6 Jul 45, repeated in WX–41696 of 30 Jul 45, ABC 091.711 France (6 Oct 43), Sec 2–E.

[39] Rearmament Division, Notes for Conference, 10 Jul 45, in SHAEF Mission to France Rearmt Div, Misc Papers "Notes for Conferences."

[40] Msg EX–73131, Lee to Delta Base Sec, 26 Jul 45, SHAEF Mission to France 475–10 Equip of Troops Metropolitan Program.

[41] See pp. 387–88, below.

[42] International Div, ASF, Lend-Lease, I, 315.

[43] Msg VICTORY 407, 29 Jul 45, CM–IN 29906.

[44] Msg S–15196, Eisenhower To All Concerned, 2 Aug 45, SHAEF SGS 475/3, Vol. I.

Forces, European Theater, Mission to France, of the terminating dates of lend-lease issues as prescribed by the President.

On 5 September, three days after the surrender of the Japanese forces, President Truman issued a second directive on military lend-lease to become effective V-J Day. Although virtually ending lend-lease by the War and Navy Departments, the directive stipulated that aid could be furnished to Allied forces in the form of rations, shelter, medical supplies, and services, where these could not be reasonably furnished by the foreign government concerned and where denial would work immediate hardship on Allied forces, or on U.S. forces which were dependent upon continued support by elements of Allied forces. Such aid was to be considered as a liquidating measure and, in any case, was to terminate within six months, or in March 1946.[45]

Except for minor transfers of maintenance items, ammunition, and training matériel, effected purely as a liquidating measure, the rearmament operations had come to an end, much to the chagrin of the French. Subsequent efforts on their part to purchase surplus American equipment proved unsuccessful, the State Department having established the policy that the sale of combat materials in an undemilitarized state was not authorized.[46] The matter, in any case, being of a strictly postwar nature, exceeds the scope of the present study.

---

[45] Msg WX–59961, OPD WARCOS to CG USAFMEDTO, 5 Sep 45, OPD Cable Files.
[46] Memo for Rcd, OPD, 30 Nov 45, OPD 400 France, Sec 4.

CHAPTER XXII

Re-equipping the French Air Force and French Navy

The Air Force

It will be recalled that in October 1943 the French military authorities had submitted an extensive rearmament program for the years 1944, 1945, and 1946 based on the premise that a large reservoir of manpower would become available as the liberation of France was undertaken. The air part of the program contemplated the activation by May 1946 of a total of 172 squadrons with 2,800 first-line planes and the corresponding ground and service troops. It was to be an extension of Plan VII then being implemented in North Africa. The Allies had declined to examine the program at the time as they considered it premature. Later, a few weeks before the launching of ANVIL, the French resubmitted their proposal. General Arnold seemed more disposed to consider it provided that it had General Eaker's approval and that equipment could be furnished largely from theater stocks. There the matter rested.[1]

In the fall of 1944, as the liberation of France progressed, the French military authorities then established in Paris renewed their proposals. Implementation of Plan VII was virtually completed. Additional effectives were available in France. At the end of November the French High Command estimated that 20,000 former aviation personnel needing but little refresher training could be put to useful employment provided they were given the necessary clothing, equipment, and aircraft. The new French Chief of Staff for Air, General Valin, approached Allied air officials in the theater. They in turn instructed the newly created Air Section of Rearmament Division, SHAEF Mission to France, to draw up a second air program.[2]

In the meantime, the units equipped under Plan VII were actively pursuing the missions assigned to them as component elements of Allied air pools. They included 1st French Air Corps operating under the control of the U.S. First Tactical Air Force and the seven British-equipped squadrons operating under the British 2nd Tactical Air Force or under RAF Bomber Command. In addition, other nonprogram squadrons, equipped by the French in North Africa largely with obsolete matériel, were

---

[1] See pp. 308–09, above. Memo, Bouscat for JAC and JRC, 2 Nov 43, JRC Misc Misc Doc, Item 5–b; Msg W–62001, Arnold to Eaker, 8 Jul 44, JRC 360/001 Air Force Rearmt Plan and Policy.

[2] General Valin's predecessor, General Bouscat, was now inspector general of the French Air Force.

Air Section was headed first by Colonel Ervin, former chairman of the Joint Air Commission in North Africa, later by Brig. Gen. Jack W. Wood. For details on Air Section and its successor, Air Component, SHAEF Mission to France, see pp. 384–85, below.

operating in the Middle East and in French West and Equatorial Africa as police and security units. The 1st Parachute Regiment, equipped and trained in North Africa, was currently engaged in operations as a general reserve infantry regiment of 1st French Army. The British-equipped 2d and 3d Parachute Regiments had been severely decimated during the summer operations. They had returned to their base in the United Kingdom for regrouping, refitting, and further training in anticipation of new missions. They would still operate as battalions of the British Special Air Service Brigade.[3]

U.S.-equipped squadrons and service troops were being maintained through American supply channels in the same manner as corresponding American units, all supplies furnished being incorporated in monthly theater lend-lease lists. British-equipped units were maintained by the RAF except for clothing and some items of equipment which were provided from U.S. sources in the interests of uniformity.

To provide an adequate reserve of combat crews, French students were still being sent to schools in the United Kingdom and the United States. In late September the number of students undergoing training in the United States was approximately 300 officers and 1,600 men.[4]

Such was the situation of the French Air Force as Air Marshal Robb, Deputy Chief of Staff for Air, SHAEF, on 19 December

submitted to the CCS details of the program proposed by Air Section of Rearmament Division, SHAEF Mission to France. The program, prepared in collaboration with the French Air Ministry and concurred in by Allied air and other officials in the theater, was in the nature of a "complement" or extension of Plan VII. Scarcity of trained aviation specialists in North Africa had prevented the formation of a French tactical force as independent and efficiently organized as a comparable U.S. or British force. To fill existing gaps, it was now proposed to add to Plan VII the following units: (1) 9 combat squadrons (8 to be provided with equipment by the United States, 1 by the United Kingdom), thus bringing U.S.-equipped "groups" and British-equipped "wings" currently composed of 3 squadrons up to the normal complement of 4 squadrons as in corresponding U.S. and British organizations; (2) a number of headquarters units to enable the French to operate on their own, as well as service units to ease the load on U.S. and British service facilities. The plan, if approved, was to go into effect on 1 January 1945 and be completed by 30 June.[5]

On 29 December the CCS accepted the program in principle and requested the Combined Administrative Committee to work out the responsibility for the provision of equipment. It was not until 1 March that the CCS, endorsing the recommendations of the committee, announced the policy to be followed with respect to the new program, thereafter known as Extension of Plan VII (CCS 350/7). SHAEF was given the entire responsibility for its implementation. It was charged with establish-

---

[3] The 2d and 3d RCP were dispatched to northern Holland by parachute in early April 1945 to operate in support of the 21 Army Group. Chief de bataillon Rocolle, *L'Arme aéroportée clé de la victoire* (Paris: Charles-Lavauzelle, 1948), I, 102–15. Memo, Fr Military Mission AFHQ for Liaison Sec AFHQ, 30 Nov 44, sub: FAF Order of Battle, AFHQ 0100/4 SACS Rcd Sec, Fr Matters, Vol. VI. See pp. 182, 211–12, above.

[4] International Div, ASF, Lend-Lease, II, 774.

[5] Memo, Air Marshal J. M. Robb for CCS, 19 Dec 44, ABC 091.711 (6 Oct 43), Sec 2–C.

ing the priorities for the supply of equipment strictly on the basis of operational factors and in co-ordination with other rearmament programs in the theater. It was also to observe the rule established for all programs: any unit of the new air program which had not been equipped by the time organized hostilities with Germany ceased would be deleted.[6]

As in the past, Army Air Forces headquarters was to provide U.S. aircraft and items peculiar to air, following their assignment by the MAB. Organizational equipment and spare parts were to be shipped directly to U.S. Air Forces depots in the theater, and their issue to the French was to be controlled by the United States Strategic Air Forces in Europe (USSTAF). Aircraft were to be shipped directly to French depots in Marseille where the FAF had adequate assembly facilities. International Division, ASF, meanwhile, was to handle and ship items common to air and ground in the same manner as for the ground rearmament program. Shortages were to be filled from U.S. theater stocks wherever possible. All units, once equipped, were to be placed under the operational control of the Supreme Commander and employed in the Allied pool of air units.[7]

By the end of March 1945 a priority list of units for which the French could furnish the necessary personnel had been drawn up jointly by the French Air Ministry, SHAEF Air Staff, and Air Component of SHAEF Mission to France, the successor

to Air Section of Rearmament Division. The list, submitted to and approved by First Tactical Air Force, included the units as desired by months. The new phasing no longer corresponded to that originally contemplated. The program was now to start in April with the delivery of equipment for several headquarters and four combat squadrons and terminate in September–October.[8]

Throughout the month of April a detailed procedure was worked out under the general supervision of Air Component of SHAEF Mission to France for the activation and equipping of units upon the reception of matériel due to arrive from the United States. By the end of the month none had yet reached the Continent, however, and, as the Supreme Commander decided on 28 April to suspend all further shipments of equipment to the French as a result of the Stuttgart episode, only the matériel for the April phase was on its way from the United States. On 1 May War Department officials informed the theater that, in accordance with the Supreme Commander's request, shipment of the remaining equipment was being canceled with the exception of aircraft which would continue to be delivered until further advice from the theater.[9]

After a rapid re-examination of the program in the light of the current operational situation, the theater informed the War Department that a number of units in the April and May priorities were being eliminated

[6] Msgs FACS 120, CCS to Eisenhower, 29 Dec 44, and FACS 147, CCS to Eisenhower, 1 Mar 45, ABC 091.711 France (6 Oct 43), Sec 2–C.

[7] Memo, Twitchell for Gen Bull, 20 Dec 44, SHAEF Mission to France 091.711 Rearmt (Fr) 900–2; Msg FWD 19714, Schlatter to Arnold, 19 Apr 45, SHAEF SGS 475 France, Vol. III.

[8] Memo, Ervin for Loomis, 28 Mar 45, SHAEF Mission to France 091.711 Rearmt (Fr) Air Force 900–2.

[9] Memo, Ervin to U.S. Component SHAEF Air Staff, 20 Apr 45, SHAEF Mission to France 091.711 Rearmt (Fr) 900–2; Msg WX–76320, Maj Gen John E. Hull to Loomis, 1 May 45, SS and P Planning Div Files. See pp. 361 ff., above.

as no longer required, leaving others, already operational but only partially equipped, still on the program. With respect to these, SHAEF planned to complete their initial equipment insofar as possible from U.S. theater stocks and by using matériel currently afloat. No further initial equipment was desired from the United States as no other units were to be activated and equipped.[10]

Throughout the winter 1944–45 and the following spring months, units of the FAF had continued in operation on various fronts. The squadrons of 1st French Air Corps acting in co-operation with 1st French Army and for the benefit of U.S. Seventh Army had participated, under the control of First Tactical Air Force, in the liberation of Alsace, the reduction of the Colmar Pocket, the crossing of the Rhine, the bombing of German communication centers, and the final drive eastward through enemy territory. The British-equipped squadrons, still under either the 2d Tactical Air Force or the RAF Bomber Command, had been active in support of operations carried out by the British and Canadian Armies. Other units had been engaged on the Atlantic coast front and on the Franco-Italian border. The Russian-equipped Normandie Squadron had continued to operate as part of the Red air forces.

By 7 May, as hostilities ended in Europe, the air program was still suspended except for the few units which the theater commander wished to be equipped for operational reasons. With the embargo ordered by President Truman on 6 June as a result of the northwest Italy incident, French hopes for a resumption of the pro-

gram fell off sharply. They vanished completely when it became known that the Allied commander in the Pacific, General Douglas MacArthur, on 2 June, had expressed his opposition to the use of French air squadrons in his theater.[11]

With the dissolution of SHAEF in mid-July, all FAF units reverted to French control as did the rest of the French armed forces. To enable them to carry out their mission in occupied Germany, U.S.-equipped units continued to be dependent on American supply installations for spare parts and maintenance items. British-equipped units remained dependent on the RAF for almost all their service facilities.[12] After President Truman's second directive of 5 September, virtually ending all lend-lease aid, such U.S. assistance as was still required by the FAF for the maintenance of its units during the immediate posthostilities period was made the subject of negotiations between the French and U.S. Governments.[13]

As estimated by General Loomis at the end of August 1945, the results of the efforts expended by the United States between December 1942 and May 1945 toward the rehabilitation of the FAF had been far from negligible. All together the French had received from American sources the complete initial equipment for 19 combat squadrons and 60 supporting units, representing a personnel strength of some 30,000 men, for which the United States had also furnished the entire necessary maintenance. The

---

[10] Msg FWD 20564, Eisenhower to Arnold, 4 May 45, SS and P Planning Div Files.

[11] See pp. 368, above, and 397, below.
[12] Memo, Loomis for CG USFET, 23 Aug 45, SHAEF Mission to France 370–1 NA Employment of Units.
[13] Transfers of supplies effected after that date, as well as requests by the French submitted in mid-September for a further expansion of the FAF, are postwar in character and exceed the scope of the present study.

supporting units had been used to form an air defense wing, an air depot group, 3 service groups, as well as suitable command headquarters. The British, for their part, had equipped a total of 10 squadrons.[14]

The Navy

The vast rearmament program for the years 1944 and 1945 submitted in Algiers by the National Defense Committee in mid-October 1943 envisaged the further build-up not only of the ground and air forces, but of the Navy as well. The entire program, it will be recalled, was based on the assumption that considerable numbers of effectives would become available as a result of operations in continental France. The part relating to the Navy contemplated a substantial increase in the number of destroyers, aircraft carriers, cruisers, submarines, and other types of smaller vessels. The request was considered to be a postwar project and, like the rest of the program, had been turned down as inopportune.[15]

When, in mid-September 1944, the first French naval vessels re-entered the battered port of Toulon, the earlier program initiated in December 1942 for the rehabilitation of the French Navy was nearly completed. A few ships were still being overhauled in North African dockyards under the general direction of French, British, and American naval authorities in the Mediterranean.

The more important problem now was that of restoring ports and naval installations in France, some of which had been greatly damaged before and during the landing operations. Toward the end of 1944, as the entire French territory passed under the control of SHAEF, the latter became responsible for assisting the French in carrying out this difficult assignment. SHAEF also became responsible for the maintenance and supply of such French ships as were operating within its sphere, AFHQ meanwhile maintaining a similar responsibility for French ships and naval installations in its area. The old supply policy, CCS 358 (Revised), put in force on 4 October 1943 and applicable to the French Navy while it was based on North Africa, was no longer adequate. There was need of coordinating the activities between the two theaters and between them and the French, and of determining the share of responsibility of the United States and the United Kingdom.

After some discussion between officials of both theaters, the task of co-ordination was finally vested in Vice-Adm. Alan G. Kirk, deputy for Navy, SHAEF. Admiral Kirk carried out this assignment through the Naval Division established for the purpose at SHAEF Mission to France in December 1944 and functioning parallel to the Rearmament Division and the Air Component.[16] In this manner, Admiral Kirk and Naval Division, composed of U.S. and British officers, were able to deal effectively with the French Admiralty in Paris, now the sole authority in French naval rearmament matters, and to co-ordinate American and British responsibilities with respect to French naval problems arising in the two theaters. To achieve further co-ordination, Admiral Fénard, chief of the French Naval Mission in the United States, was directed to refer all requests for equipment to be used in French port operations to SHAEF for consideration. No action would be taken

---

[14] Memo, Loomis for CG USFET, 23 Aug 45, SHAEF Mission to France 370–1 NA Employment of Units.

[15] Memo, National Defense Committee for WD, 16 Oct 43, OCS 45–466 France 1942–43. See pp. 308–09, above.

[16] See p. 385, below.

BATTLESHIP STRASBOURG, *Toulon Harbor, September 1944. Note four lower turret guns, the ends of which were cut off when the French scuttled the ship in November 1942.*

in Washington without SHAEF's recommendations.[17]

Thanks to the efforts of Naval Division, the French obtained until the end of the campaign in Europe substantial amounts of equipment, such as cranes, derricks, barges, and other materials, for the rehabilitation of their ports, Brest and Cherbourg in particular. French naval vessels continued to operate throughout the world as part of the Allied naval pool. In April 1945 a number of them were released from Allied control for participation in the combined land, air, and sea operations launched, under the direction of Lt. Gen. Edgar de

Larminat, for the purpose of reducing the German pockets of resistance on the Atlantic coast. Together with a flotilla of British mine sweepers, the French vessels, which included the battleship *Lorraine*, one cruiser, three destroyers, and several escorts and mine sweepers, were grouped into a naval task force commanded by Rear Adm. Joseph Rue.

By the time operations in Europe ended, the French Navy had increased further in size as a result of the acquisition of additional Allied ships and the refitting of salvaged French ships. The number of its vessels was now estimated at 350 including auxiliary craft, its air arm at 10 squadrons, and its effectives at close to 100,000 men.

---

[17] Msg W–20574, Styer to Loomis, 13 Jan 45, International Div Files, Cable Log, A 45–152.

Its fighting power was regarded as being nearly equivalent to that of 1939.[18]

In June 1945 Admiral Fénard submitted to the JCS a detailed list of machinery, tools, and other materials still needed for the restoration of ports and naval yards. Although the French Government was prepared to pay for the equipment on the basis of 20 percent cash and the balance within 30 years, the CCS turned down the request. Now that hostilities had ended in Europe, the materials involved were needed in other theaters and could not be spared for French naval installations.[19]

Other requests from Admiral Fénard had likewise been denied by the CCS. They had been submitted throughout the fall and winter of 1944 in connection with attempts by the French military authorities to set up an expeditionary force for participation in operations in the Pacific. It was not until June that the CCS took into consideration some of Admiral Fénard's proposals. By this time it was too late for any constructive program to be put into effect before the cessation of hostilities in the Pacific.[20]

It will be recalled that in the winter of 1943–44, the French had unsuccessfully attempted to obtain equipment and planes for the rehabilitation of their Naval Air Arm (Aéronautique Navale). The CCS had turned down their requests largely because of the dearth of trained personnel.[21] When, in the fall of 1944, the liberation of part of France produced a substantial increase in naval effectives, the French renewed their requests for equipment.

On 29 September 1944 Admiral Fénard submitted to Admiral King a plan for the complete rehabilitation of Aéronautique Navale. The plan contemplated the re-equipping of existing squadrons, the formation and equipping of new units, and the rehabilitation of the naval air bases whose equipment and facilities had been destroyed in the course of operations. The existing number of squadrons had been raised from 4 in 1943 to 10. They included 2 dive bomber, 2 fighter, and 6 coastal command squadrons. Except for 2 coastal command squadrons equipped with U.S. aircraft and the 2 fighter squadrons equipped with P–47's and Spitfires and currently engaged in operations as part of the FAF, the units were using obsolescent or obsolete French and British equipment. To standardize equipment and simplify maintenance problems, the program submitted by Admiral Fénard envisaged the utilization of American equipment exclusively. It contained also a request for clothing, tools, ground handling and ground training equipment, and other miscellaneous materials.[22]

Admiral Fénard's proposal was immediately referred to the Joint Strategic Survey Committee for study. On the recommendations of the committee, the JCS urged the CCS, on 31 October, to reject the proposal. The French plan, they pointed out, contained no substantial military advantage in the prosecution of the war or in the solution of immediate postwar problems in Europe. In addition it would have an adverse effect on the prosecution of the war in the Pacific to the extent that it involved the diversion of U.S. resources and

---

[18] Lemonnier, "La Marine Nationale," *La France et son Empire dans la Guerre.*

[19] Memos, Fénard for JCS, 22 June 45, and CCS for Fénard, 17 Jul 45, ABC 091.711 France (6 Oct 43), Sec 5.

[20] See pp. 393, 395–96, below.

[21] Min, CCS 147th Mtg, 25 Feb 44; see pp. 222–24, above.

[22] Ltr, Fénard to CinC U.S. Fleet, 29 Sep 44, ABC 091.711 France (12 Oct 43).

effort.[23]   Endorsing this view, the CCS disapproved Admiral Fénard's request on the
ground that it contained implications re-

garding postwar rearmament.   The issue
was definitely closed and the French were
forced to continue operating their Naval
Air Arm with the equipment already on
hand.

[23] Ltr, JCS to Cordell Hull, 31 Oct 44, in same
file.

CHAPTER XXIII

Rearmament Division, SHAEF
Mission to France

Membership, Organization, and Operation

When, on 3 October 1944, General Loomis arrived at Supreme Headquarters, Allied Expeditionary Force, he was appointed deputy chief of a special staff section organized two weeks earlier for the purpose of handling all matters involving the French. The section, known as SHAEF Mission to France, was commanded by General Lewis. As problems of French equipment were arising in increasing number, General Loomis was directed to take over the responsibility for their solution. With the party of officers from the Joint Rearmament Committee whom he had brought along from North Africa, he organized a rearmament division within the mission, giving it a structure somewhat similar to that of the former JRC. The division began operating at once under the name of Rearmament Division, SHAEF Mission to France. Within a short time SHAEF directed General Loomis to extend the division's activities to include the rearmament of other western European Allied nations as well, including Belgium, Holland, and Denmark. Only the role played by the division in connection with French rearmament will be presented.

The Rearmament Division's position in the staff structure and its relationship to other SHAEF agencies and sections concerned with French armament matters did not vary until July 1945 when SHAEF itself was disbanded and a reorganization of Allied command and headquarters took place. (*Chart 5*). The transformation which the Rearmament Division underwent then and the role that it played for a short time thereafter are matters treated separately at the end of the chapter.

During its relatively short existence the division was made responsible, first for the continued implementation of the North African program, later for the initiation, establishment, and implementation of the Liberated Manpower and Metropolitan Programs. In carrying out these assignments, it effected the necessary co-ordination with all French and Allied agencies concerned, kept SHAEF informed of the status and progress of the units being re-equipped, directed the operations of the U.S. instructor personnel assigned to Inspection Group, and co-ordinated with SHAEF all questions arising in connection with units not included in approved rearmament programs.[1]

Membership

The British having assumed most of the commitment with respect to the Liberated

---

[1] Memo, SHAEF Mission to France for Chief Rearmt Div, 30 Nov 44, and Memo, SHAEF (Brig Gen T. J. Davis, Adj Gen) for SHAEF Mission to France, 22 Dec 44, SHAEF Mission to France 320–1.

REARMAMENT DIVISION, SHAEF MISSION TO FRANCE. *Seated in center, wearing glasses, is General Loomis; left of him is General Kingman; General Regnault is on the right.*

Manpower Program and a small part of that for the Metropolitan Program, the Rearmament Division was made, from the outset, a U.S.-British agency with French representation. As the work of the division progressed, the number of U.S. and British members varied in proportion to the respective participation or interest of the United States and United Kingdom in the rearmament operations being carried out.[2] The French members, meanwhile, operated as they had under the JRC—as a liaison group.

[2] Memo, Loomis for Lewis, sub: Proposed Plan for Fr Rearmt, 5 Oct 44, SHAEF Mission to France 320–1.

U.S. Members. The division began functioning with a nucleus organization consisting of approximately twelve officers, all Americans and formerly members of both the JRC and the Joint Air Commission. U.S. membership fluctuated very little. Its increase was slowed down as a result of the difficulties encountered by SHAEF Mission to France in securing from AFHQ, and from agencies controlled by the latter, additional personnel formerly assigned to the JRC and now needed for service with the Rearmament Division. It had been agreed in September 1944 by Generals Eisenhower, Devers, and Marshall that all JRC personnel was to be held for transfer

CHART 5—POSITION OF REARMAMENT DIVISION IN SHAEF: 1 JANUARY 1945

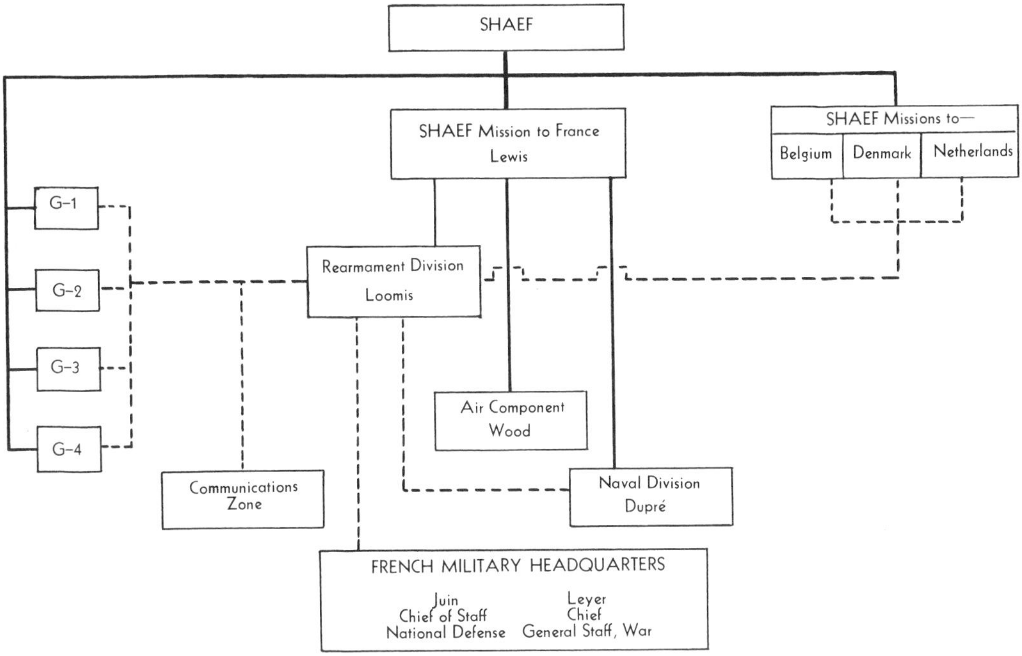

Source: Ltr AG/091.112–2 GCT–AGM, SHAEF To All Concerned, 29 Dec 44, SHAEF Mission to France 320–1 Rearmt Div, Orgn and Functions, Annex A.

to SHAEF if and when required. Apparently fearing an undue reduction of its own personnel strength, AFHQ showed considerable reluctance in authorizing the transfers requested by General Loomis. This produced an intertheater tug-of-war lasting over a period of four months.[3]   All together not more than six U.S. officers were added to the initial roster.

British Members. The appointment of British members was not effected as speedily as it had been hoped, with the result that British membership never reached the expected ratio. The first officer to join the division, Lt. Col. R. G. Fullerton, was given the post of deputy executive officer shortly after his appointment in November.[4] Later, in March 1945, he was joined by two other officers.

Internal Organization

During the period in which the Rearmament Division was an agency of SHAEF Mission to France (October 1944–July 1945), its internal organization went through two different phases. In the initial period, which lasted to the end of December, the Rearmament Division comprised an Executive Staff, Ground, Air, and Naval Sections, a French Group, and a training section known as Inspection Group,

[3] Msg S–78109, SHAEF Main to MTOUSA for Nelson, 7 Feb 45, in same file.

[4] Memo, SHAEF Mission to France Rearmt Div (Lt Col Conrad L. Christensen), 1 Nov 44, in same file.

CHART 6—THE REARMAMENT DIVISION, SHAEF MISSION TO FRANCE: MARCH 1945

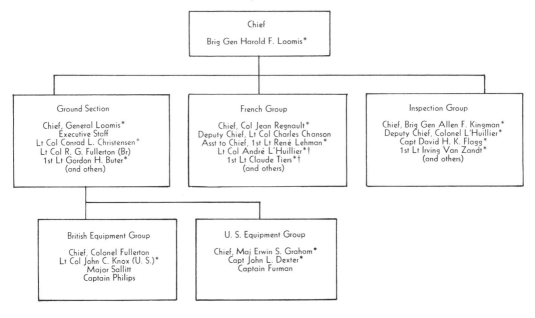

*Officers formerly with the JRC in North Africa.
†Attached to Inspection Group.
Source: SHAEF Mission to France 320–1 Rearmt Div, Orgn and Functions, Annex A.

all under the command of General Loomis. The arrangement whereby the various sections dealing with French armament matters were consolidated in one single agency had been adopted to facilitate the transfer to France of personnel and records from the former North African JRC and JAC, and to speed up the launching of the new organization. However, when the armament programs began to crystallize and multiply toward the end of December 1944, it was felt advisable to set the air and naval sections apart from the rest of the division, leaving the latter responsible for ground force armament matters only. (*Chart 6*)

Until then, the Naval Section, although established in principle, had remained unstaffed and inoperative. The Air Section, on the contrary, had done considerable work in supervising the continued implementation of the North African air rearmament program and in planning for an extension of that program on the basis of manpower then available in continental France. It was composed of six U.S. officers, formerly members of the North African Joint Air Commission. It was headed, first by Colonel Ervin, who, it will be recalled, had served as the last chairman of the JAC, later after 1 December, by Brig. Gen. Jack W. Wood. In carrying out its mission, the section co-ordinated all air armament matters between appropriate agencies of the French Air Force, the Royal Air Force, and the U.S. Army Air Forces, recommended approval or disapproval of French requests for matériel, made suggestions on the employment of units, and maintained liaison with U.S. Strategic Air Forces and with the 1st French Air Corps created in the fall of 1944.[5]

When the two sections left the division, on or about 1 January 1945, there were created parallel to the Rearmament Division and under the jurisdiction of SHAEF Mission to France an Air Component under the command of General Wood, and a Naval Division under the command of Capt. D. D. Dupre (USN), the representative of Admiral Kirk, Deputy for Navy, SHAEF. The Air Component took over the duties of Air Section, and the Naval Division was given the task of carrying on the rehabilitation of the French Navy under the general direction of Admiral Kirk.

In its final stage of organization, the Rearmament Division included three of the original sections, namely Ground Section, French Group, and Inspection Group.

Ground Section. In matters of equipment, the Ground Section constituted the central authority. Placed under the direct control of General Loomis, it was composed of an executive staff, a British Equipment Group under the command of Colonel Fullerton, and a U.S. Equipment Group under the command of Maj. Erwin S. Graham, the two equipment groups working in close coordination. The section was responsible for initiating programs and implementing them once they had been approved by the CCS. In the discharge of this function, it worked in full and constant collaboration with the French Group.

The problems faced by the Ground Section and by the division as a whole were fewer than those encountered by the JRC in North Africa. This was largely because most of the responsibility for the rearmament operations was now vested in the division, French agencies no longer being involved in the handling and distribution of equipment. Yet the task of the section was somewhat complicated by the fact that it was dealing with three separate programs and that the American commitment was not as clearly defined as under the ANFA program when the United States had undertaken to furnish all the matériel for the French Ground Forces. To expedite action, General Loomis or members of the Ground Section held frequent conferences with outside American, British, and French officials and agencies. They maintained close contact with the British War Office and the London Munitions Assignments Board, both of which, on several occasions, sent representatives to discuss matters of common interest. When, in the fall of 1944, it was urgent that the War Department reach a decision on the Metropolitan Program, General Loomis flew to Washington to present the case and soon returned with a promise of speedy action.

French Group. Shortly after the organization of SHAEF Mission to France, the French military authorities in Paris detailed a liaison section, headed by Colonel Chanson, to work with the G–3 Section of the mission on armament problems in which they and SHAEF had a common interest. Before his transfer to the French capital, Colonel Chanson had served briefly in General Noiret's headquarters in London as chief of the Rearmament Section. Earlier he had headed the Rearmament and Technical Studies Section at the French General Headquarters in Algiers. In October another French section, composed of Colonel Regnault and several officers formerly associated with the JRC, began operating as

---

[5] Memo, Air Sec for Loomis, 26 Oct 44, SHAEF Mission to France 320–1 Orgn and Function, Rearmt Div.

part of Rearmament Division. To ensure closer co-ordination on armament problems and prevent duplication of efforts, the French military authorities decided, on 21 November, to merge the two sections into one thereafter known as French Group, Rearmament Division, SHAEF Mission to France. The group, placed under the command of Colonel Regnault with Colonel Chanson as his deputy, became the official representative agency of the French High Command empowered to deal with SHAEF on matters pertaining to armament.[6] In addition to Colonels Regnault and Chanson, the group included approximately ten officers, most of whom had contributed earlier to the success of the North African rearmament operations.

The specific duties of the French Group were to work out with Rearmament Division questions concerning matériel from U.S., British, enemy-captured, and French sources, as well as problems of activation, organization, maintenance, and training of French units. All such matters, whether they involved the National Defense headquarters, the Ministry of War, the General Staff, or any other commands, were channeled through the French Group. Other questions were handled directly between SHAEF Mission and the French headquarters concerned.[7]

To effect closer liaison with the War Office on questions involving the shipment of British equipment to France, Colonel Regnault detailed one officer to London. Likewise, to keep both SCAMA, then established in Marseille, and the base in Cherbourg informed of British deliveries, he dispatched to London another officer whenever required.[8] No French Air Force or Navy officers were appointed to the group, as all air and naval rearmament matters were handled by the appropriate French headquarters directly with the Air Component and Naval Division of SHAEF Mission to France.

By establishing almost daily contact with Generals Leyer and Blanc, chief and deputy chief of General Staff, Ground Forces, and by holding frequent informal meetings with General Loomis or with individual U.S. or British members of Rearmament Division, Colonel Regnault was able to maintain the cordial and fruitful co-operation which had existed between French and Allied Headquarters in North Africa.

Inspection Group. Commanded by General Kingman, assisted by his French deputy, Colonel L'Huillier, Inspection Group was composed of American and British instructors.[9] American instructors were organized as the 6834th Rearmament Regiment, SHAEF (the former 6834th Training Regiment, JRC). The regiment, after being based for some months in the Marseille area, was moved near Paris early in 1945. A small group of officers headed by General Kingman posted themselves in the French capital in proximity to the other components of the Rearmament Division. British personnel did not join Inspection Group for some months. Initially the War Office placed a small number of instructors directly at the disposal of the French soon after the first deliveries of British matériel. In April 1945 three officers were assigned to Inspection Group for the purpose of setting up a training program in the use and

---

[6] Memo 701 EMGG/CAB, 28 Nov 44, SHAEF Mission to France 091, 711-9 (Fr) Combined.
[7] *Ibid.*

[8] Memo 1396, EMGG/LA, Leyer for Regnault, 6 Feb 45, SHAEF Mission to France 320-12.
[9] Colonel L'Huillier was awarded the Legion of Merit with the degree of Officer on 25 January 1946.

care of British equipment and of arranging the assignment to Inspection Group of a detachment of British instructors. The detachment ultimately grew to a size of 100 officers and enlisted men.[10]

During the first few months of its existence, beginning October 1944, Inspection Group devoted its activities to assisting the training centers run by 1st French Army. With the arrival in February 1945 of British training matériel for the units of the Liberated Manpower and Metropolitan Programs, Inspection Group found its responsibilities greatly increased. It was given the task of inspecting all units scheduled to be equipped to make sure that they were fully activated and organized on appropriate U.S. tables of organization and equipment, the intent being that any unit failing to meet the requirements was denied matériel. Once the units were equipped, Inspection Group assisted them in their technical training. Later it inspected them once again to determine their fitness for operations.[11] Inspection Group also undertook to provide assistance in the form of training teams to the French troops engaged in operations along the Atlantic coast. The training teams effected the necessary liaison between the units involved and the U.S. 66th Infantry Division assigned to their support.

Posthostilities Period

AFHQ officials had long recognized that even after the termination of the Supreme Command there would still be French rearmament problems of mutual interest to

the United States and the United Kingdom. As early as April 1945 General Loomis proposed that upon the dissolution of SHAEF the Rearmament Division either remain a joint British-American unit operating as agent for the CCS, or be split into two separate sections functioning under their respective chiefs of staff.[12] The second of these suggestions was accepted by SHAEF and made the object of a directive.[13]

On 13–14 July, as SHAEF was dissolved and ETOUSA became USFET, all American responsibilities toward the French passed from SHAEF Mission to France to USFET Mission to France. Part of the U.S. personnel of Rearmament Division was then transferred to the new mission as a staff section known as the Rearmament and Operations Division. This agency simply took over the work heretofore performed by its predecessor except that it confined its activities to matters involving the United States. It co-ordinated with the British such matters as were of common interest to both America and the United Kingdom. General Loomis headed the division until 12 September. He was then replaced by Colonel Christensen. Attached to the division were a French Group headed by Colonel Regnault, brigadier general since May, and an Inspection Group commanded by General Kingman and composed of personnel of the 6834th Rearmament Regiment. The regiment was active until 1 November 1945, when it was disbanded. Meanwhile, air and naval matters continued to be handled separately by the air and

---

[10] Informal Routing Slip, SHAEF Mission to France (Col Alden K. Sibley, ACofS) to Chief Rearmt Div, SHAEF Mission to France 353–1 Training; Interv with Kingman, Jul 50.

[11] Interv with Loomis, 51; also International Div, ASF, Lend-Lease, II, 1217.

[12] Memo, Loomis for SHAEF G–3, 9 Apr 45, SHAEF Mission to France 320–1.

[13] Ltr, SHAEF AG 400–1 (Fr) GCT–AGM to CG ETOUSA, 22 Jun 45, SHAEF Mission to France 091.711 Rearmt Plan & Policy 900–5.

naval components of the USFET Mission to France.[14]

The British also had organized a Rearmament Division of their own which included the personnel heretofore part of their training teams and ordnance and engineer detachments. The division, placed under the direct control of the War Office, was charged with completing existing commitments with respect to British equipment and training.[15]

Considering the late start of the armament programs enacted and carried out in continental France, the intricacies of their implementation traceable largely to the multiplicity of equipment sources and the frequent revisions made necessary by the fast-changing operational situation, and finally the time element involved, the Rearmament Division and its successors achieved substantial results. These were made possible, as in North Africa, by the excellent co-operation between the British, American, and French members of the division, and between the division itself and outside Allied agencies.

---

[14] Memo, Rearmt and Opns Div (Christensen) for SGS, 17 Jul 45, SHAEF Mission to France 320–1.

In 1945 the French Government conferred on General Loomis the grade of Officer in the Order of the Legion of Honor, and awarded him the Croix de Guerre (with Palm). The U.S. Government conferred on him the Distinguished Service Medal (May 1945) and the Legion of Merit (October 1945). General Regnault was promoted to the degree of Commander in the Order of the Legion of Merit on 15 June 1945. General Kingman was promoted to the grade of Officer in the Order of the Legion of Honor and simultaneously awarded the Croix de Guerre (with Palm) (October 1945).

[15] Memos, RDB/A/11, Fullerton GSO–1 Br Sec Rearmt Div SHAEF for Chief Rearmt Div, and Fullerton Br Sec Rearmt Div SHAEF for Maj Gen Harold Redman, 1 Jul 45, SHAEF Mission to France 320–1.

Training Under Inspection Group

When the four French Army training centers which had been operating in North Africa and Italy reached France in the fall of 1944, they began training the replacements earmarked for 1st French Army.[16] For some weeks thereafter, training operations on French soil were limited largely to the instruction given in these centers with the technical assistance of U.S. instructors detailed by General Kingman from his Inspection Group. Training in the United States, meanwhile, was still being offered to selected groups of French students. As of 20 September 1944, some 2,100 officers and men, mostly Air Force personnel, were reported to be attending schools in the United States.[17]

The inability of the training centers to provide the number of replacements required to maintain the units of 1st French Army at authorized strength has already been related. By the end of December three of the centers were still furnishing too few replacements, the fourth none at all. The assignment to them of insufficient numbers of trainees was not the only reason for the unsatisfactory situation. The centers were reported to be lacking adequate matériel largely as a result of the decision of the French military authorities to reserve what equipment was still available in North African training centers for use in centers being set up in France to train Metropolitan Program units. In spite of SHAEF's repeated objections to such an arrangement, the French continued to maintain that they had no other alternative, at least not until the arrival of equipment expected to be shipped

---

[16] For training during the North African rearmament operations, see Ch. XIV, above.

[17] International Div, ASF, Lend-Lease, II, 774.

from the United Kingdom and the United States.[18]

Within a short time, SHAEF officials came to the conclusion that the existing replacement system, by which 1st French Army itself was charged with the induction and training of reinforcements for its units, was not satisfactory. They felt that the provision of replacements was a responsibility for the French zone of interior and so advised the French General Staff. The latter replied that the system could not be changed as the zone of interior lacked adequate facilities and personnel to train both Metropolitan Program units and replacements for 1st French Army.[19] Until the end of hostilities, 1st French Army retained its replacement system and, in an attempt to meet requirements, even raised the number of its training centers from four to eight. It must be noted that, in addition to these army centers, there existed divisional training centers, one for each division, constituting pools of personnel from which reinforcements could be made readily available to the divisions.[20]

Meanwhile the launching of the Liberated Manpower and Metropolitan Programs had sharply increased the scope of training activities and raised for the French many difficult problems. Among these were creation of new schools and camps, rehabilitation of those few not utilized by the Anglo-American forces, provision of training personnel and matériel, and establishment of programs of instruction.

The training of security battalions and labor groups constituted a relatively small commitment, so it was made the responsibility of military region commanders. The training of personnel recruited under the Metropolitan Program, on the other hand, represented a substantial undertaking. To carry it out in an orderly and efficient manner, the French War Ministry put into effect in late November 1944 a detailed procedure. Infantry, artillery, and armored instruction was given at basic level by the military regions, at advanced level (for specialists and cadres) in replacement training centers. Training for other branches, (Engineer, Signal, Transportation, Antiaircraft Defense, Ordnance) was given at recruit training centers. Initially, instructional matériel used was that then available in France or in the centers formerly operating in North Africa. All centers, whether recruit training or replacement training, were under the control of the Ministry of War. Army training centers, meanwhile, remained under the direct control of the Commanding General, 1st French Army.[21]

In early December some consideration was given by G–3, SHAEF, to the possibility of sending FFI personnel sufficient for two divisions to the United States for training. The project was abandoned, for it involved too many difficulties and the scope of the Metropolitan Program had not yet been firmly determined.[22] Similarly, in March 1945, a proposal to organize courses

---

[18] Memo, Kingman for Loomis, 30 Dec 44, SHAEF Mission to France 091.711–13 (Fr); Msg L–18152, SOLOC to Loomis, 22 Dec 44, and Memo, Regnault for Loomis, 21 Feb 45, SHAEF Mission to France 400–3 (Fr).

[19] Memo, Lewis for Juin, 25 Feb 45, and Ltr, Leyer to SHAEF, 5 Mar 45, SHAEF Mission to France 091.711–13 (Fr); Ltr, Lewis to Leyer, 26 Apr 45, SHAEF Mission to France 353–1 Training.

[20] Memo, SHAEF Mission to France for CG COMZONE, 16 Apr 45, SHAEF Mission to France 353–1 Training.

[21] War Ministry Dir 1782 EMGG/4–1, 29 Nov 44, SHAEF Mission to France 320–2 NA Orgn of French Army.

[22] Memo, ACofS G–3 for Reber, 18 Dec 44, SHAEF G–3 091 France, Vol. IV.

in the United Kingdom for training French personnel in the use of British equipment was abandoned. Instead, the War Office dispatched to France a detachment of instructors which was placed at the disposal of General Kingman's Inspection Group.

In mid-April 1945, when the first three divisions (the 1st, 10th, and 36th Infantry) and some corps troops of the Metropolitan Program had received a proportion of their standard equipment, Generals Kingman and Loomis worked out and put into effect a detailed plan to assist the units in their training. General Kingman arranged, much as he had done in North Africa, to detail to each of the divisions a U.S. senior adviser, initially to serve as liaison between Inspection Group and the division commander, later to determine the number of instructors to be assigned to the training of the division. The training program was primarily the responsibility of French instructors supplemented by U.S. and, where necessary, British instructors. It raised no more problems than had the program established earlier in North Africa since most of the personnel being called to the colors had had prior military training. Hence, for most of the troops the object of training was familiarization with new weapons more than basic training In addition to detailing teams of instructors to the three divisions, General Kingman also assigned teams to various French specialist centers and, incidentally, several to other western European Allied armies.[23]

Upon the dissolution of SHAEF in mid-July, the responsibility for assisting the French in the technical training of their forces was split between Inspection Group of USFET Mission to France and the newly created British Rearmament Division. When U.S. deliveries of initial equipment, already suspended since May, came definitely to a stop as a result of the cessation of lend-lease aid, U.S. training assistance similarly was cut off. Only the three teams assigned to French divisions were allowed to continue in operation until October, when their mission was completed. French air personnel no longer could be sent to the United States for instruction. Several training projects which the French wished to continue or initiate, such as the dispatch of students to airborne schools and centers in the United Kingdom and the United States, were turned down by the theater. For all practical purposes, these were postwar projects and as such were matters to be taken up by the French directly with the War Department and the War Office.[24]

By 1 November 1945 all U.S. technical training assistance to the French had been terminated.

---

[23] Memos, Kingman for Regnault, 5 Mar 45,

Fullerton for Kingman, 14 Apr 45, and Capt David H. K. Flagg for Kingman, 6 Apr 45, SHAEF Mission to France 353–1 Training; Memo, Loomis for Leyer, 19 Apr 45, SHAEF Mission to France 091.711–1 (Fr).

[24] Ltr, Foreign Liaison Office WD to Maj Gen Charles Luguet, 25 May 45, ABC 091.711 France (12 Oct 43); Ltr, Juin to Lewis, Incl to Memo, Lewis for CG USFET Main, 31 Aug 45, SHAEF Mission to France 320–2 NA Orgn of Fr Army.

CHAPTER XXIV

French Plans for a Far East Expeditionary Corps

From the earliest days of Franco-Allied collaboration in North Africa, the French military authorities entertained a strong desire to participate in operations in the Far East, primarily for the purpose of liberating Indochina which the Japanese had occupied since July 1941. Their desire was legitimate, the more so considering they had American assurances, given in November 1942, that French sovereignty would be reestablished "as rapidly as possible in all territories over which the French flag waved in 1939," [1] and that French forces would "aid the United Nations in restoring integrally the French Union." [2]

By the fall of 1943 the French desire had crystallized and led to a decision by the National Defense Committee to organize, equip, and train an expeditionary corps for the Far East. On 20 October, when General Leyer submitted to AFHQ the over-all armament requirements for the calendar years 1944–45, he included a tabulation of the matériel which he considered necessary for the proposed corps. [3] The corps, later designated Corps Expéditionnaire Français

d'Extrême-Orient (CEFEO), was to include two brigades—one recruited in Madagascar, the other in West Africa—plus naval and air units to be added, all to be ready by the fall of 1944. Simultaneously, the French representative in Washington, General Béthouart, handed General Marshall a memorandum indicating the intention of the French military authorities to petition for representation in the Pacific War Council as they considered themselves "eminently qualified to assist the allies in the preparation of operations with their own counsels." [4]

It was becoming increasingly evident that the French were going to insist upon a decision both as to the principle and the extent of their participation in the war in the Pacific. To determine a policy in this regard, the Joint Chiefs of Staff, on 2 November, referred the various French notes on the matter to the Joint Strategic Survey Committee and to the Joint Staff Planners for collaboration in preparing recommendations. [5]

If there remained any doubt as to the French position and determination, the doubt was soon dispelled once and for all as a result of a trivial incident involving a high-

---

[1] Ltr, Murphy to Giraud, 2 Nov 42, text in Langer, *Our Vichy Gamble,* p. 133.

[2] Preamble, Clark-Darlan Agreement, 22 Nov 42, AFHQ 0100/5 CAO/320/1 MAEB.

[3] Ltr, Leyer to Loomis, 20 Oct 43, and Memo, Loomis for CofS AFHQ, 29 Oct 43, JRC Misc Doc, Item 5–b.

[4] Ltr and Memo, Béthouart to Marshall, 28 Oct 43, ASF Planning Div Files, A–47–192 Theater Br, 15–Fr Military NA.

[5] Memo, Handy for CofS, 4 Nov 43, OPD 336.2 France, Sec II.

ranking figure of the U.S. Government. In a public statement which he delivered in late December regarding the war in the Pacific, Vice President Henry A. Wallace made no mention of France when listing the countries expected to take part in that theater once Germany had been defeated. Apprised of the fact, the French Committee of National Liberation promptly directed General Beynet in Washington to express to General Marshall its "legitimate surprise" at an omission which it regarded as "unfair . . . even if it did not represent a definite stand." The committee did intend to wage war against the Japanese, who now occupied a part of the French Union, and it intended to do so with all its might and will. The committee moreover wished to remind the U.S. Chief of Staff of the measures already taken by the French High Command to organize an expeditionary corps and of the requests for armament submitted earlier on behalf of the corps. Lacking a policy on which to base a firm answer one way or another, General Marshall merely acknowledged his satisfaction that the CFLN was "so keenly aware of the requirements for forces in all theaters of war." [6]

By May 1944 the French still had no word from the War Department. The British War Office, more responsive to the French proposals, not only had promised to help, but were already sending equipment, in limited quantities, to the Madagascar Brigade. The French had none with which to outfit the other brigade then in process of organization in North Africa. At first they had planned to equip it with British matériel withdrawn from the 1st

Motorized Infantry Division (1st DMI), but at the request of AFHQ they were compelled to return a considerable part of this to British stocks. Faced with a dilemma, the French High Command on 4 May urged General Wilson, the Supreme Allied Commander in the Mediterranean, to intervene with Washington and London with a view to obtaining the speedy equipping of the two brigades. Ten weeks later AFHQ informed the French that the War Office had agreed to deliver some additional matériel including general-purpose vehicles, as well as signal and radio equipment for five infantry battalions and one artillery group. [7]

As late as August 1944 no high-level decision had yet been communicated to the French with respect to the major issue of the problem, namely, whether or not they were to participate in Far East operations, especially in Indochina. The fact was that no decision had been reached because of the divergent views held by American and British statesmen. President Roosevelt was reported to be increasingly opposed to a return of the French in Indochina in the belief that their administration of the colony in the past had been a total failure. [8] The British Foreign Office, on the contrary, considered French aspirations in the matter with sympathy. They were prepared in fact to grant a recent French request for the accreditation of a French military mission to Headquarters, Southeast Asia Command, and the establishment in India of some of the expeditionary troops already assembled in North Africa. Lord Halifax sounded out the State Department on these matters; Secretary Hull decided that, al-

[6] Ltrs, Beynet to Marshall, 26 Jan 44, and Marshall to Beynet, 12 Feb 44, OCS A–48–11 091 France, Sec II.

[7] Ltr, Béthouart to Wilson, 4 May 44, AFHQ 0100/12C G–3 Div Op Corres From the Fr; Memo, Gammell for Béthouart, 14 Jul 44, AFHQ 0100/12C G–3 Div Ops Fr Equip.
[8] The Memoirs of Cordell Hull, II, 1596–1601.

though ostensibly military in character, they had wide political implications. He then referred them to President Roosevelt for decision.[9]

By the time Paris had been liberated in late August, the question was still in suspense, with the result that no plan was yet in sight for the provision of equipment to the CEFEO. General Loomis, chief of the JRC, who had long been aware of French efforts to organize their Far East corps, had watched these efforts primarily because of the possibility of diversion of U.S. equipment, as well as diversion of personnel, at the expense of the units of the North African rearmament program. As far as he had been able to ascertain, the CEFEO was made up of a headquarters company, two brigades, and some supporting elements, with a total actual strength possibly not exceeding 1,300 men.[10]

No sooner had the French military authorities moved to Paris in September than they reopened the Far East issue. Thus far only the British had shown a definite interest in their plans to the extent of beginning deliveries of matériel, but the attitude of American officials remained polite and noncommittal. Militarily, Indochina, the Far Eastern territory where the French with their knowledge of the country could be of most assistance, was in the China theater of operations and, as such, in an area of U.S. strategic responsibility. American strategy, however, did not contemplate any operations in that territory. Politically, President Roosevelt's apparent determination to keep French administration from returning to Indochina constituted the

major stumbling block in the path of equipping a French expeditionary corps.[11]

As the liberation of France progressed and the victorious outcome of the war in Europe appeared a certainty, the French once again focused their attention on what they regarded as the next commitment of their armed forces and renewed their attempts to obtain Anglo-American approval of their participation in the Far East. First they sounded out U.S. officials in Washington. Writing to Admiral King on 19 September 1944, Admiral Fénard, chief of the French Naval Mission in the United States, urged that serious consideration be given to the employment of the French Navy in the war against Japan, a war in which France was "anxious to take her part." [12] Without waiting for a reply, Admiral Fénard, a few days later, submitted a request for four long-range submarines, a request promptly turned down on the ground that no submarines were available in excess of U.S. naval requirements.[13]

The French, meanwhile, were stepping up preparations even to the extent of increasing the size of the expeditionary corps. On 13 September the National Defense Committee decided to create two divisions in addition to the light task force (Corps Léger d'Intervention) and the brigade (Brigade d'Extrême-Orient) already activated. One division was to be of the U.S. Marine Corps type, with a strength of from 17,000 to 20,000 men. The other was to be of the British two-brigade type, with a strength of 26,000 men. On 1 October

---

[9] Memo, State Department for President, 26 Aug 44, ABC 380 France (7 Aug 44), Sec 1–A.
[10] Memo, Loomis for G–3 AFHQ, 22 Sep 44, JRC 370/001 Employment of Units—General.

[11] Memo, Gen Hull for Marshall, 14 Dec 44, ABC 091.711 France (6 Oct 43), Sec 2–C; *The Memoirs of Cordell Hull,* II, 1596–1601.
[12] Memo, Fénard for King, 19 Sep 44, ABC 091.711 France (6 Oct 43), Sec 5.
[13] Memos, Fénard for King, 30 Sep 44, and King for Fénard, 7 Oct 44, in same file.

General de Gaulle informed General Eisenhower that he intended to transfer to the two divisions a large part of the 15,000 Negro troops then being withdrawn from the 1st French Army in anticipation of the cold season. Both new units were to be assembled in southern France. If equipped, they could be made ready by January and March 1945 respectively.[14] The augmented CEFEO was being placed under the command of Lt. Gen. Roger Blaizot.

Apparently thinking that a direct approach to the War Department would speed matters up, de Gaulle instructed the French representative in Washington to broach the subject to General Marshall. When he called on the Chief of Staff on 22 October, General de Saint-Didier submitted a memorandum outlining in great detail the National Defense Committee's plan and pressed for an early decision.[15] His memorandum was then forwarded to the CCS, who in turn handed it over to the Combined Staff Planners for study and recommendations.

General Eisenhower already had communicated to the CCS his views regarding the French proposal. The formation, equipping, and maintenance of additional divisions, with the attendant demand on strained transportation facilities, were likely to interfere with planned operations in Europe by detracting from the main effort of the 6th Army Group currently being supplied from French ports in southern France. For these and other reasons, General Eisenhower could not concur in the proposal.[16]

In a report submitted to the CCS on 29 November the Combined Staff Planners, fully supporting the Supreme Commander's opinion, recommended that the French request be rejected. They could not see the value of the proposed divisions in the light of current Allied strategy in the Far East; nor could they agree to providing the necessary shipping and equipment at the expense of U.S. and British forces.[17]

By then, President Roosevelt had been informed that a large French military mission headed by General Blaizot had arrived in Ceylon where it was said to have received American approval and official recognition, with the same status as other Allied missions to the Southeast Asia Command. In a memorandum to Navy Secretary James V. Forrestal dated 17 November, the President directed that no American approval be given to any French mission being accredited to that command and that no U.S. military or civilian representatives be authorized to make decisions on political questions with the mission or with anyone else.[18] Six weeks later Roosevelt reiterated his position in a memorandum to the State Department. He still did not want to "get mixed up" in any Indochina decision, nor did he want to get mixed up "in any effort toward the liberation of Indo-China from the Japanese." He had made this clear to Mr. Churchill. Action at this juncture was, in his opinion, premature from both the military and civil point of view.[19]

With regard to U.S. material assistance to the Resistance forces, French and native,

---

[14] Ltr, de Gaulle to Eisenhower, 1 Oct 44, SHAEF G-3 091 France, Vol. III.

[15] Memo, de Saint-Didier for Marshall, 20 Oct 44, ABC 380 France (7 Aug 44), Sec 1-A.

[16] Msgs SCAF 106, Eisenhower to CCS, 16 Oct 44, and SCAF 117, Eisenhower to CCS, 1 Nov 44, in same file.

[17] Rpt, CPS to CCS, CPS 147/1, 29 Nov 44, ABC 091.711 France (6 Oct 44), Sec 2-B.

[18] Memo, President for Forrestal, 17 Nov 44, ABC 380 France (7 Aug 44), Sec 1-A.

[19] Memo, Stettinius for Forrestal, 11 Jan 45, ABC 384 Indochina (16 Dec 44).

engaged in guerrilla operations against the Japanese on Indochinese territory, the President already had ruled out such aid.[20] Not until February 1945 would he modify somewhat his position on the matter and agree to extend help to the underground in Indochina. And even then such aid would be extended provided that it did not interfere with planned operations in the area, that it would be limited to what was necessary for the defeat of the Japanese forces, and that it would not be construed as an official U.S. recognition of the French interests in Indochina.[21]

In mid-December Admiral Fénard, still without reply to his long communication of 19 September, submitted a letter, this time directly to the CCS, setting forth the views of his government concerning the conditions under which French land, sea, and air forces could bring the maximum possible assistance to the Allied forces engaged against Japan. Significantly, he made no reference to Indochina and even emphasized the French Government's agreement that whatever French forces the Combined Chiefs chose to employ against Japan would be utilized by them in whatever way they deemed best. Appended to the letter were five memorandums, one of which was a copy of General de Saint-Didier's communication of 20 October, also still unanswered.[22]

In the replies which they addressed first to General de Saint-Didier on 4 January 1945 and a few days later to Admiral

Fénard, the CCS expressed their deep appreciation of the "generous offers" to assign French forces to operations in the Far East. But because of considerable logistical commitments in Europe, they were compelled to forego the diversion at this juncture of critically needed equipment and shipping for use by such forces. Nor could they determine at present the time when it would be feasible to employ them in the Far East.[23]

In the belief that the operational situation in western Europe had sufficiently improved during the month of December to warrant a re-examination of the question, Admiral Fénard, on 19 January 1945, again approached the CCS. He requested, as an initial step toward the program "to which the French Government had pledged itself," the supply of equipment for use in the training of a Marine division to be formed from colonial infantry troops. The division could be used "under American command in any operational theater where Marine forces were in action." The Joint Logistics Committee examined the proposal and concluded that the reasons which had prompted a refusal to equip new French divisions for the Far East applied equally to the provision of training matériel. The United States, the JLC pointed out, had just undertaken to equip eight more divisions under the recently approved Metropolitan Program and could accept no further commitments. Endorsing the recommendations of the committee, the CCS informed Admiral Fénard on 28 March that, as Allied resources had been further taxed by the sharply increased requirements of the war against Germany "as evidenced by the new Metropolitan and

[20] *The Memoirs of Cordell Hull,* II, 1598.

[21] Memos, Gen Hull for Wedemeyer, 9 Feb 45, and McFarland for Marshall, 13 Mar 45, Msg WX–55402, Wedemeyer to Chennault, 19 Mar 45, and other papers, in F.I.C. Book I, China Theater Files, DRB AGO.

[22] Memo, Fénard for CCS, 18 Dec 44, ABC 380 France (7 Aug 44), Sec 1–A.

[23] Ltr, CCS to de Saint-Didier, 4 Jan 45, ABC 380 France (7 Aug 44), Sec 1–A; Ltr, CCS to Fénard, 10 Jan 45, ABC 091.711 France (6 Oct 43), Sec 5.

Liberated Manpower programs," his request could not be met.[24]

Still determined to carry out their plans, the French reopened the issue in April, when the cessation of hostilities in Europe appeared to be near at hand. The French Government, Admiral Fénard explained to the CCS, believed that the time was ripe to reach a decision on the proposal to equip two divisions. The units were ready to be put at the disposal of the CCS "to be used wherever they would think it advisable" against the Japanese.[25]

No action on the matter had been taken when, a week after the armistice in Europe, General Juin, then on a visit to the United States, called on various officials to discuss French military problems. In the course of the interview which he held with General Marshall, General Juin raised the question of France's participation in the war against Japan. The U.S. Chief of Staff could give him no encouragement. The matter, he explained, would have to be decided "on the highest levels." His own view was that the matériel and shipping necessary to equip and transport two divisions to the Pacific war front could not be spared until after the defeat of Japan when it would be too late. The United States, he pointed out, had sufficient well-trained and battle-tested troops to defeat Japan alone, "although it would prove difficult and costly." Furthermore, it might well be that there would be no need to fight in Indochina as it was his opinion that the Japanese would evacuate the area so as to

concentrate their forces in north China to meet a Red Army advance.[26]

General Juin's conversation with Admiral Leahy offered a slight ray of hope. Leahy first questioned him about the recent Stuttgart incident in which a French commander had refused to comply with orders from his American superior. General Juin assured him that there would be no repetition of such a situation. In this connection he intended to make it clear to General de Gaulle that French divisions would be accepted by the Allied command for action in the Pacific only if their disposition remained "wholly a U.S. function." Admiral Leahy declared that, under these conditions, he was prepared to recommend to the American members of the CCS that they approve the French proposal. He added that the final decision rested with the heads of governments and that any ultimate agreement would have to be reached between them.[27]

A week later, on 18 May, Foreign Affairs Minister Georges Bidault, also on a visit to the United States, called on the President. Mr. Truman signified his acceptance in principle of French participation in the Far East, but carefully indicated that the determination of whether or not such participation would be practicable and helpful would be left to General Douglas MacArthur, the Allied commander in the Pacific. Elaborating on the President's statement, State Department officials made it clear to Mr. Bidault that the question was to be judged on its military merits, and that General MacArthur would decide "just how much and where" the French contribution

---

[24] Ltr, Fénard to CCS, 19 Jan 45, and Memo, CCS for Fénard, 28 Mar 45, ABC 091.711 France (6 Oct 43), Sec 2–C; Memo, Craig, JLC, for Handy, 6 Feb 45, OCS A–48–1 091 France.

[25] Memo, Fénard for CCS, 7 Apr 45, ABC 091.711 France (6 Oct 43), Sec 5.

[26] Min Mtg, Marshall with Juin, 11 May 45, ABC 091.711 France (6 Oct 43), Sec 2–D.

[27] Min Interv, Juin with Leahy, 11 May 45, ABC 091.711 France (6 Oct 43), Sec 2–D.

could be best utilized. Such was the tenor of a message which General Marshall addressed to General MacArthur. In it the Chief of Staff outlined the French offer of four air squadrons and a corps of two divisions with supporting combat and service units to be commanded by General Leclerc. "The French," he pointed out in conclusion, "have, when well led and where political considerations were not involved, fought well in this war." [28]

General MacArthur replied that he had the greatest admiration for the fighting qualities of the French and would be glad to include in his command the corps offered by them. He felt that because of language and other difficulties, the French divisions, if used, should be employed with the reinforcement echelons, just as was contemplated for the Canadians, and not in the initial stages of operations. As for the air squadrons, he considered that the introduction so late in the campaign of units of non-English speaking personnel would run counter to the intimate co-ordination and teamwork so essential in operations. For these reasons, he urged that the offer of air squadrons be declined. [29]

General Eisenhower also had been requested by General Marshall to submit his views on the French proposal. In his reply, he first commented on the composition of the corps. The French were offering the 9th Colonial Infantry (9th DIC), commanded by Brig. Gen. Jean Valluy, and the 1st Colonial Infantry (1st DIC), commanded by Brig. Gen. Georges Nyo, the two divisions to be placed under General Leclerc as corps commander. The Supreme Commander pointed out that only the 9th DIC

was suitable, the other division being a newly created organization which had no combat experience. As a second division he suggested the 3d Algerian Infantry commanded by Maj. Gen. Augustin Guillaume, which had distinguished itself in Italy, France, and Germany. He also recommended that Maj. Gen. Marcel Carpentier [30] be named corps commander. Turning to the more important issue, that of the manner in which the proposed corps should be employed, General Eisenhower urged that a detailed written agreement be negotiated beforehand with the French Government covering all major aspects of the question. He recommended, among the points to be agreed upon, that the organization and equipping of units be made to conform to U.S. tables of organization and equipment; that a firm troop list providing a self-sufficient corps be drawn, and a sound replacement program established; that the corps be placed under complete operational control of the U.S. commander; and that its supply and maintenance be effected on the same basis as for U.S. forces. [31]

No more valuable commentary could have been furnished those officials of the War Department then engaged in planning for the introduction of French forces in the Pacific theater. It represented a comprehensive policy, established on the basis of experience, which, if followed, would tend to prevent a recurrence of the often difficult problems raised in the course of some two and a half years in connection with the rearmament and deployment of the French. In a letter to the Joint Chiefs of Staff General Smith amplified the Supreme Com-

---

[28] Msg W–10226, Marshall to MacArthur, 1 Jun 45, ABC 380 France (7 Aug 44), Sec 1–A.

[29] Msg C–17621, MacArthur to Marshall, 2 Jun 45, in same file.

[30] CofS, CEF, in Italy; CofS, 1st French Army, until 15 Sep 44; CG, 2d DIM, from 25 Nov 44 to 12 Apr 45.

[31] Msg FWD 24298, Eisenhower to Marshall, 9 Jun 45, ABC 380 France (7 Aug 44), Sec 1–A.

mander's comments, urging in particular that the detailed written agreement with the French be executed on a governmental level with copies furnished to the interested commanders.[32] This insistence regarding a firm agreement was no doubt the result of the unfortunate recurrence, in the first days of June, of the situation in which a French commander had refused to comply with orders from his American superior. At that time the possibility of a clash between French and Allied troops in northwestern Italy had caused President Truman promptly to order a complete stoppage of issue of matériel to the French. When Ambassador Bonnet called on Assistant Secretary of War McCloy on 13 June, his first words were to confirm that a satisfactory agreement had just been reached in the matter. Broaching the question of the expeditionary forces for the Far East, he declared that French officials were prepared to give "any assurances that were required" that these forces would have no relationship to Indochina and that they would fight under an American command wherever decided by the latter.[33]

On 26 June General de Saint-Didier once again appealed to the Combined Chiefs and urged them to reach a decision so that preparations and training could get under way. He emphasized that further delay was harmful to the morale of the troops, who, with the full support of the nation, had eagerly awaited for several months their opportunity to participate in the Far East operations against the common enemy. Then on 6 July General de Saint-Didier informed General Marshall of the steps already being taken with regard to the setting up of the ex-

peditionary corps. Without waiting for the American command to make known its desires in the matter of supporting units, the War Ministry, he declared, was in process of activating and training a number of such units. The corps, as currently planned, would total 62,000 men, all volunteers and all white.[34]

President Truman's directive of 5 July, limiting thereafter the issue of war matériel to Allied governments to that which was to be used in the war against Japan, gave the French a slight ray of hope that their project might still come to realization. What was required was a policy statement from the CCS. With events now moving swiftly in the Far East, and with the prospect that far-reaching decisions would be taken at the Potsdam Conference then opening, the fate of the French proposal was hanging by a thread. On 19 July the CCS finally took action. They agreed, and so notified the French, that they accepted in principle their offer of a corps on the understanding that (1) the corps would serve under U.S. or British command, in an area to be determined later; (2) final acceptance of the corps would involve an agreement with the governments concerned on basic matters including command, combat efficiency, replacements, and logistical support; (3) maximum use would be made of equipment delivered under the North African and Metropolitan Programs; (4) because of pressing shipping and other requirements, it would not be possible to commit the corps to operations before the spring of 1946.[35]

While pleased with the CCS acceptance

---

[32] Ltr, Smith to JCS, 9 Jun 45, in same file.
[33] Memo, McCloy for Marshall, 14 Jun 45, in same file.

[34] Memos, de Saint-Didier for Leahy for CCS, 26 Jun 45, and de Saint-Didier for Marshall, 6 Jul 45, in same file.
[35] Min, CCS 196th Mtg, 19 Jul 45, and Memo, CCS for de Saint-Didier, 19 Jul 45, ABC 380 France (7 Aug 44), Sec 1–B.

in principle, the French, through General de Saint-Didier, promptly pointed out that to equip the corps with matériel in the hands of North African and Metropolitan Program divisions would not be satisfactory. For one reason, a large part of this equipment had deteriorated both during the campaigns in Italy, France, and Germany and since then as a result of the presidential order of 8 May stopping the further issue of maintenance. In addition, the French Army needed its present equipment to continue operating in occupied Germany.[36]

There the matter rested. It had made no progress by 2 September, the day of the Japanese surrender. With the armistice, nearly three years of fruitless negotiations were coming to an end. A few days later the CCS informed General de Saint-Didier that they did not intend to take further action on his last memorandum, and that military problems relating to the area of the Southeast Asia Command thereafter were to be taken up directly with the British Chiefs of Staff in London.[37] The question of the return of the French to Indochina, still unsolved, was now clearly a matter for the decision of the governments. More than that, it was a postwar problem.[38]

---

[36] Memo, de Saint-Didier for CCS, 3 Aug 45, in same file.

[37] Memo, CCS for de Saint-Didier, 13 Sep 45, in same file.

[38] For an account of the political and military problems arising in Indochina in the immediate postwar period, see History of U.S. Forces in China Theater, Ch. XV, MS in OCMH Files.

Conclusion

The rehabilitation of the French armed forces in World War II constitutes an unprecedented achievement if one considers the results attained in relation to the difficulties encountered. The undertaking had one aim—to enable the resurgent military power to assume as large a share as possible of the United Nations' war effort against the Axis. On this there was complete agreement between the three parties directly involved: the French themselves, whose position made them entirely dependent on outside assistance; the British, who initiated the rehabilitation process when they equipped the Free French; and the Americans, who rearmed the North African forces and, along with the British, supplied first the Resistance groups operating underground on French soil, then the forces of liberated France.

The first major difficulty arose with the re-entry of French North Africa into the war, when the three partners disagreed as to the extent of rehabilitation. The French, understandably, wanted the greatest number of their troops equipped and readied for combat and this as speedily as possible. The Americans, while sympathetic with this ambition, reasoned that only those units should be rearmed that could be made self-sustaining in combat. The British, while they bore only a small portion of the burden of rearming the French, shared with the Americans control of allocation of matériel to all United Nations forces, and in this capacity objected that too large a program would cut across existing commitments—such as those made to the USSR and China—and interfere with the planned equipping of U.S. and U.K. forces. With both the Americans and the British standing firm on their respective positions, the French had no alternative but to scale down their initial expectations and let their rearmament proceed at a pace determined by global demands for implements of war. Such was the basis on which the successive rearmament programs were established and carried out. Still the French continued to press for fuller re-establishment of their national military power.

The diversity of the forces re-equipped, each with its respective needs, constituted a serious hindrance. Some were Free French; others, the majority, were the forces raised in North Africa. A large proportion were natives, with distinctive language, habits, and physical constitution. To complicate matters, the bulk of the troops emerged outside their national home base and therefore lacked the logistical support normally provided by a zone of interior.

Difficulties were multiplied by temporary or permanent deficiencies of one sort or another. The language barrier was one problem. Others arose from differences in customs, dietary habits, and clothing tariff sizes, especially where non-European troops were involved. Most acute were shortages of various kinds: of Allied shipping, of port facilities for receiving, stocking, and distributing equipment; and of French technical personnel necessary to man depots, repair shops, and base units and to provide combat and service support troops. Then there was the lack of familiarity on the part of the French with the newer weapons and with American technology and working methods. For these or other reasons the French were persistently reluctant to accept fully the importance of logistics and by the same token found themselves excessively dependent on American logistical support in combat. The reluctance was so persistent as to suggest that the French Army had forgotten, or not learned, the importance of logistics in a period in which logistics had become more than ever vital to the effective conduct of war.

But the difficulties, seemingly insuperable at first, were overcome, one by one, by dint of good will and mutual respect, hard work, and an unflagging determination to complete the assigned task. In record time a sizable French force was equipped, trained, and put in battle on land, in the air, and on the sea. While this force never succeeded in becoming self-sustaining and the U.S. Army was compelled to provide a large part of the necessary support, once in combat it proved to be highly effective and its contribution to final victory was impressive.

The War Department furnished equipment to the French largely through theater transfers (66 percent) and Commanding General Shipments (33 percent), and a small proportion (1 percent) through direct shipments, that is, by ships flying the French tricolor. All items delivered, whether initial equipment, combat maintenance supplies, or petrol, oil, and lubricants, were charged to the French lend-lease account for settlement at the end of the war.

At first deliveries were made on the basis of units to be equipped under approved rearmament programs, the French themselves being responsible for distribution as they saw fit. Later the system was revised to give the U.S. commanding general in the theater complete control over the distribution process, and units were furnished equipment only after they were fully activated. Thus American management followed American matériel. Once the units were equipped, U.S. personnel provided the necessary technical training in the use, care, and maintenance of matériel.

In terms of units and men, the United States furnished full initial equipment as well as complete maintenance for 8 divisions and 300 supporting units raised in North Africa, a total of 250,000 men. It provided partial equipment (approximately one third of the table of organization and equipment) and all the maintenance on the equipment issued for 3 more divisions and some 40 supporting units activated in continental France and totaling about 50,000 men. The United States also furnished full equipment for 19 air squadrons and 60 supporting units representing another 20,000 men. It carried out an extensive repair and refitting program for the French Navy. To Sovereignty and Territorial forces in North Africa, numbering over 200,000 men, it furnished old clothing, construction materials and machinery, and certain expendable supplies. Finally, the United States provided rations for all effectives re-equipped under the various armament programs (approximately 360,000 as of 1 March 1945). All together these commitments represented about 3,250,000 measurement tons. To draw up a detailed schedule of the myriad individual items furnished by the United States would serve no useful purpose. By way of illustration, however, a list of selected items is given in Table 5.[1]

---

[1] Memo, Craig for Marshall, 9 May 45, OPD 336.2 France, Sec IV–A; Memo, Loomis for CG USFET, 23 Aug 45, SHEAF Mis Fr 320–NA Org of Fr Army.

TABLE 5—MAJOR ITEMS OF EQUIPMENT
FURNISHED BY THE UNITED STATES TO
THE FRENCH FORCES

Item	Quantity
Weapons (Except Combat Vehicles)	
Heavy Field Artillery	85
Light Field and Antitank	851
Antiaircraft Guns	758
Mortars	1, 504
Small Arms	
Machine Guns	10, 731
Submachine Guns	20, 856
Rifles	69, 129
Carbines	96, 983
Combat Vehicles	
Tanks	1, 406
Light	651
Medium	755
Other *a*	3, 941
Ammunition (Rounds)	
Heavy Field Artillery	11, 580
Light Field and Antitank	531, 079
Antiaircraft	368, 500
Mortar	169, 172
Small Arms	50, 173, 000
Trucks	27, 176
Light and Medium	20, 282
Light-Heavy and Heavy-Heavy	6, 894
Trailers and Semitrailers	16, 034
Other Vehicles	1, 523
Aircraft	1, 417
Medium and Light Bombers	330
Fighters	723
Other	364

a Includes carriages for self-propelled weapons.

Source: Theodore E. Whiting *et al.,* Statistics, a volume in preparation for the series UNITED STATES ARMY IN WORLD WAR II, Lend-Lease. MS in OCMH.

In terms of dollar value (value at the time of delivery), the supplies and services furnished by the United States to the French Army, Air Force, and Navy have been estimated at about $1,527,000,000, $457,000,-000, and $310,000,000, respectively, or a total of $2,294,000,000. Of the total, the War Department furnished $2,039,474,000; the remainder, representing items such as vessels and special supplies, was furnished by the Foreign Economic Administration. Comparative figures show that France came third in the list of recipients of War Department lend-lease shipments and transfers: [2]

	Percent
British Commonwealth (excepting Canada)	58
USSR	23
France	8
China	7
Others (approximately 45 countries)	4

In addition the United States furnished the French civilian economy, up to V-J Day, supplies representing another $548,000,000. Thus, for the period 11 November 1941 (when the benefits of lend-lease were first extended to the French) to 2 September 1945 (V-J Day), the total French military and civilian lend-lease account amounted to approximately $2,842,000,000.[3] The account for the immediate postwar period of September 1945 to September 1946 amounted to a further $391,000,000. The French, in return, made available to the U.S. armed forces as reciprocal aid goods and services amounting to $868,000,000.

By agreement reached in Washington on

[2] Theodore E. Whiting *et al.,* Statistics, a volume in preparation for the series UNITED STATES ARMY IN WORLD WAR II. Lend-Lease. MS in OCMH.

[3] Unsuccessful efforts were made to obtain from the British War Office statistics on the British contribution to French rearmament. The only figures available are those published by the French Ministry of Finance and Economic Affairs in "Le Prêt-Bail et l'Aide Réciproque Franco-Alliée," *Notes et Etudes Documentaires* (Paris, 2 and 3 November 1949), which states that the French received from the United Kingdom supplies and services estimated at approximately $435,000,000, and from Canada matériel to the amount of $25,000,000.

28 May 1946, the governments of the United States and France disposed of the accounts for lend-lease and reciprocal aid and settled all outstanding claims arising out of the conflict. After credit for $232,000,-000 already paid by France during the war years for goods supplied through lend-lease procedures, the settlement figure stood at $420,000,000, subject to some adjustment to cover additional post-V-J Day transactions. Such was the sum which France agreed to pay, with interest at 2 percent, beginning 1 July 1951.[4]

All things considered, America received good value for the money and effort it expended in rearming the French, a value difficult to assess in quantitative terms but none the less real. True, the undertaking posed a host of baffling problems, which absorbed the attention of countless persons. But it made it possible for the United States to reduce its outlay of combat manpower in the Mediterranean and European theaters by eight to ten divisions and nineteen air squadrons, possibly more, considering that American troops used in lieu of the French would have been relatively inexperienced. By the same token, the U.S. forces incurred fewer losses in these two theaters. There the French themselves suffered, from the beginning of the Tunisian campaign to the end of the war in Europe, losses estimated

for the ground forces alone at 23,500 killed and 95,500 wounded in action.[5]

Without American assistance in World War II, it is unlikely that France would have assumed its present important position in the North Atlantic Treaty Organization and the Western European Union, so vital to American policy. American insistence on French self-reliance in supply matters definitely consolidated the French position. Whereas in 1943–44 this insistence was construed by some French military men as a manifestation of unreasonable autocracy, in postwar years it was referred to as a blessing in disguise For, it was then argued, had the French Army not been compelled to organize its supply services properly, what would its prospects of survival have been in May 1945 when, with the cessation of hostilities in Europe, it found itself suddenly cut off from further U.S. assistance and left to its own devices? As it was, it had forged, albeit the hard way, an adequate if not perfect maintenance and

---

[4] Memorandum of Understanding Between the French and U.S. Governments, signed by Léon Blum and James F. Byrnes, 28 May 46, in files of Department of State. "French Lend-Lease Settlement," *Twenty-Third Report to the Congress on Lend-Lease Operations,* H. Doc. 41, 80th Cong., 1st Sess., January 3, 1947. For subsequent revisions of the settlement figure to cover all post-V-J Day transactions, see *Twenty-Eighth Report to the Congress on Lend-Lease Operations,* H. Doc. 263, 81st Cong., 1st Sess., July 18, 1949, and *Thirty-Second Report to the Congress on Lend-Lease Operations,* H. Doc. 227, 82d Cong., 1st Sess., October 3, 1951.

[5] Casualties (deaths only) incurred by the French armed forces during the entire 1939–45 period are estimated as follows:

Total	212,114*
Army (excluding FFI before Oct 44)	172,613
(1) Killed in action	114,613
1939–40 Campaign of the West	90,000
1940–45	24,613
a. Middle East and Northeast Africa (Free French)	1,158
b. Tunisia (excluding Free French)	2,300
c. Italy, Corsica, and Elba	6,255
d. France and Germany	14,900
(2) Died of wounds or illness	14,000
(3) Died while in POW camps or upon release therefrom	44,000
Air Force**	5,089
Navy**	10,412
French Forces of the Interior (before Oct 44)**	24,000

*Excepting the 1,200 casualties suffered by "Armistice Army" units in the course of operations against Allied forces (Syria, Jun–Jul 41; Northwest Africa, Nov 42).

**No breakdown available.

Source: Lt. Col. P. Santini, "Etude statistique sur les pertes au cours de la guerre 1939–1945," *Revue du Corps de Santé Militaire, X,* No. 1 (March, 1954).

supply machinery. The advantages it had gained in so doing were such as to make it unlikely it would soon forget the techniques, not to mention the "jargon of the trade," learned from the American Army in the formative years of 1943–44.[6]

Far more important, of course, is that the American undertaking made it possible for the French armed forces to regain the honored position they had long occupied but momentarily lost. True, the small band of General de Gaulle's followers had kept the French flag flying high during the dark months which followed the June 1940 armistice. But only a large-scale re-entry of the French into the common struggle, as took place in mid-November 1942, could regain for them the esteem of the Allies and a place among the democratic nations of the world.

Seen in retrospect, French participation in the major campaigns of northwest Africa and Europe underwent definite changes. In a sense, the Tunisian campaign proved to be the testing ground for French loyalty and French determination to fight. Engaged in battle on greatly unequal terms, French troops achieved only

---

[6] Interv with Col de Beaumont, Jul 50; with Gen Regnault, 50.

limited military objectives. But they succeeded in winning American confidence, in overcoming British skepticism, and in restoring faith in themselves. These intangible gains, more than actual victories, amply justified the large investments in matériel and effort then being made on their behalf by the United States.

The Italian campaign was the testing ground for French ability to make the fullest use of modern weapons in combat. Then fighting on equal terms, the French quickly demonstrated that they possessed this ability and moreover could match a formidable enemy. Their achievements were such, in fact, as to convince the Americans that the rearmament program, then in progress, must be completed without delay.

The campaign of France and Germany marked the end of the testing period and the beginning of a new phase: the rebirth of France as a military power. The new French Army, proud of its equipment and of its skill in the use of modern weapons, and determined to give the full measure of its will to fight, had reached the stature of a full-fledged, independent force. Side by side, Americans and French marched forward, along with the other Allies, to reap the fruits of victory. Side by side, today, they stand ready to defend the free world.

Bibliographical Note

Rearming the French is based almost entirely on documents now in the possession of the Department of the Army. These sources have been supplemented by documents made available by the French Service Historique de l'Armée, by interviews with American and French officers who participated in the rearmament operations and by documents from the latter, by published memoirs and histories, and finally by detailed comments on the manuscript by persons mentioned in the volume.

Primary Sources

I

The two most important single collections of documents used in the preparation of this volume are those of the Allied Force Headquarters (AFHQ) and Supreme Headquarters, Allied Expeditionary Force (SHAEF). From these collections must be singled out, respectively, the files of the Joint Rearmament Committee (JRC) and those of the Rearmament Division of SHAEF Mission to France. Both of these files include letters, cables, memorandums, reports, minutes of conferences, plans, drafts of plans, and miscellaneous papers.

Details of high-level planning on French rearmament are based largely on the formal record of the wartime proceedings of the Combined Chiefs of Staff and the U.S. Joint Chiefs of Staff. This record contains minutes of their meetings, together with papers embodying the proposals which they formally considered. The record also includes minutes of the plenary conferences presided over by President Roosevelt and Prime Minister Churchill. War Department records contain message files of cables and letters between the CCS and JCS and the Supreme Commander, between the War Department and the North African and European theaters, and between Allied commanders and Allied planners. Supplementing these are letters and cables exchanged by General Marshall and General Eisenhower.

The author also has drawn on documents made available by the Service Historique de l'Armée and by French officers who took an active part in the rearmament operations.

The sources have been supplemented by interviews conducted by the author with French and American officers in the period 1948–55. (See list at end of bibliographical note.)

II

The principal document collections used in this volume are as follows:

ABC files. A collection kept by the Strategy and Policy Group of OPD (q.v.).

AFHQ files. Records of Allied Force Headquarters. The collection consists of separate files for each of the general and special staff sections. For the present work the richest file is that of the JRC, the section most directly concerned with the rearmament of the North African forces. The files are held by the Departmental Records Branch, Adjutant General's Office. (DRB AGO.)

ASF files. Especially important on the subject of French rearmament are the International Division files, the Planning Division files, and the Somervell file. Among the records of the International Division are the minutes and papers of the Munitions Assignments Committee (Ground) and a virtually complete file of those of the Munitions Assignments Board. Located in DRB AGO.

CCS. Combined Chiefs of Staff papers and minutes of meetings. All of these may be found in the OPD collection (q.v.). The collection includes memorandums, reports, and copies of cables and letters prepared by the British or U.S. Chiefs of Staff or their subordinate agencies. Minutes of the meetings are not stenographic. Notes were kept by British and U.S. secretaries. The minutes in final form were specifically and individually approved by each of the Combined Chiefs.

C/S file. Contains documents from wartime files of the Office of the Chief of Staff, War Department. Now held as a separate collection by Departmental Records Branch, AGO.

ETO file. Files of Headquarters, European Theater of Operations, U.S. Army (ETOUSA). Now held by Organizational Records Branch, Records Administration Center, AGO.

JCS. U.S. Joint Chiefs of Staff papers and minutes of their conferences. Copies of all JCS documents cited can be found in OPD files (q.v.). The JCS collection is located in G–3 Records, Department of the Army.

JPS. Joint Staff Planners (U.S.) papers and minutes of meetings. Copies of JPS documents are in OPD ABC files, which include in most cases not only the planners' final memorandums, but OPD drafts, discussions, and working papers.

JWPC. Joint War Planning Committee (U.S.) papers, many of which were reissued as JPS or JCS documents. All documents cited are in OPD files.

NATOUSA and MTOUSA files. Files of Headquarters, North African Theater of Operations, U.S. Army, and Mediterranean Theater of Operations, U.S. Army, respectively. Now held by Organizational Records Branch, Records Administration Center, AGO.

OCMH files. A miscellaneous collection containing documents prepared or collected by the author or members of the Office of the Chief of Military History staff. Some of the material cited in this volume consists of interviews, answers by former members of French and U.S. staffs to special questionnaires, and certain French documents not found in U.S. files.

OPD files. Collection of cables and papers of the Operations Division, War Department. The division at present is a part of the G–3 Division.

SHAEF files. Records of the Supreme Headquarters, Allied Expeditionary Force. One of the basic sources for this volume. The collection consists of separate files for each of the general and special staff sections. For the present work the richest file is that of the Rearmament Division of the SHAEF Mission to France, the division most directly concerned with the supply of war matériel to the French Metropolitan Forces. Files are held by DRB AGO.

WD Cable files. A large collection of cables which cleared through the War Department Message Center, filed by date in incoming and outgoing books.

Secondary Sources

Unpublished preliminary historical studies by Army, Navy, and Air Force historians:

Hq, Mediterranean Allied Air Forces. The History of MAAF: December 1943–1 September 1944; Vol. II. April 1945. AAF Hist Office Archives.

Hq MAAF, The French Air Force in MAAF, A Preliminary History, 1945, copy in AAF Hist Office Archives.

Rôle joué par les Forces Françaises de l'Intérieur pendant l'occupation de la France avant et après le débarquement du 6 Juin 1944. Commandant Rogé, Service Historique de l'Armée, Section Etudes, 21 May 1946. Copy in OCMH.

Fifth Army History (in nine volumes): 5 January–6 October 1943; 1 April–4 June 1944: Part I, From Activation to Fall of Naples; Part V, The Drive to Rome. DRB AGO.

History of Allied Force Headquarters and Headquarters, NATOUSA: Part Three, December 1943–July 1944. Copy in OCMH.

AFHQ Commander-in-Chief's Dispatch. North African Campaign: 1942–1943. Copy in OCMH.

History of Allied Force Headquarters, Mediterranean Theater of Operations. Copy in OCMH.

Résumé des Opérations de Réarmement. Undated and unsigned. Original provided by Maj. Gen. Paul Devinck. Copy in French Records File 218, OCMH.

Hq, Peninsular Base Section, Naples. History of the Peninsular Base Section, North African Theater of Operations, United States Army: Vol II, Covering the Period 28 August 1943 to 31 January 1944. Copy in OCMH.

International Div, ASF. Lend-Lease as of September 30, 1945. Copy in OCMH.

The French Forces of the Interior, a 1,500-page history prepared in the European Theater of Operations under the direction of Col. S. L. A. Marshall by Capt. Lucien Galimand, Capt. Marcel Vigneras, Maj. R. A. Bourne-Paterson, Capt. Harry S. Griffiths, and Lt. Louis Kervran, based on documents of the French Resistance and the Allied agencies dealing with these forces. Copy in OCMH.

Dunham, H. H. U.S. Army Transportation and the Conquest of North Africa, 1942–43. OCT HB Monograph 9, Jan 45, OCT HB.

Mathews, Sidney T. The Drive on Rome, a volume in preparation for the series UNITED STATES ARMY IN WORLD WAR II.

Published Sources

World War I

Ayres, Col. Leonard P., Chief of Statistics Branch of the General Staff. *The War With Germany: A Statistical Summary*. Washington: Government Printing Office, 1919.

Chambrun, Col. Jacques de, and Capt. Charles de Marenches. *The American Army in the European Conflict*. New York: The Macmillan Company, 1919.

Clarkson, Grosvenor B. *Industrial America in the World War*. Boston and New York: Houghton Mifflin Company, 1923.

Crowell, Benedict. *America's Munitions: 1917–1918.* Washington: Government Printing Office, 1919.

Crowell, Benedict, and Robert Forrest Wilsom. *The Armies of Industry,* I, *Our Nation's Manufacture of Munitions for a World in Arms: 1917–1918* New Haven: Yale University Press, 1921.

Historical Branch, War Plans Division, General Staff. *Organization of the Services of Supply, American Expeditionary Forces.* Monograph 7. Washington: Government Printing Office, 1921.

Historical Division, Department of the Army. UNITED STATES ARMY IN THE WORLD WAR: 1917–1919, III, *Training and Use of American Units With British and French.* Washington: Government Priting Office, 1948.

Historical Division, Department of the Army. UNITED STATES ARMY IN THE WORLD WAR: 1917–1919, XIV, *Reports of Commander-in-Chief, A.E.F., Staff Sections and Services.* Washington: Government Printing Office, 1948.

Military Board of Allied Supply. *Report of the Military Board of Allied Supply.* Washington: Government Printing Office, 1924.

Pershing, John J. *My Experiences in the World War.* New York: Frederick A. Stokes Company, 1931. 2 vols.

———. *General Pershing's Story of the American Army in France;* Report of General Pershing to the Secretary of War, November 20, 1918. New York: John H. Eggers Company, Inc., 1919.

Réquin, Lt. Col. Edouard. *America's Race to Victory.* With Introduction by General Peyton C. March, Chief of Staff, U.S. Army. New York: Frederick A. Stokes Company, 1919.

World War II

Alexander, Field Marshal Sir Harold R. L. G. *The Allied Armies in Italy From 3rd September 1943, to 12th December 1944.* London: His Majesty's Stationery Office, 1950.

Arnold, General H. H. *Global Mission.* New York: Harper & Brothers, 1949.

Bajot, [Admiral] Pierre. *Le débarquement du 8 Novembre 1942 en Afrique du Nord.* Paris: J. de Gigord, 1948.

Bouscat, Général René. "L'Armée de l'Air française dans la Campagne d'Italie," *Revue de la Défense Nationale* (February, 1946.

Butcher, Capt. Harry C. *My Three Years With Eisenhower.* New York: Simon and Schuster, 1946.

Carpentier, Général Marcel. *Les Forces Alliées en Italie; la Campagne d'Italie.* Paris: Berger-Levrault, 1949.

Clark, General Mark W. *Calculated Risk.* New York: Harper & Brothers, 1950.

Maj. Gen. Coudraux, [Henri]. *La Base d'Opérations 901 dans la Bataille pour la Libération de la France, 1944–1945.* Paris: Imprimerie Nationale, 1947.

Crusoë. *Vicissitudes d'une Victoire.* Paris: Les Editions de l'Ame Française [1946].

Gaulle, Charles de. *Discours et Messages.* Paris: Berger-Levrault, 1946.

Giraud, Général [Henri]. *Un seul but, la Victoire.* Paris: R. Julliard, 1949.

Goutard, Col. [Adolphe]. *Le Corps Expéditionnaire Français dans la Campagne d'Italie (1943–1944).* Paris: Charles-Lavauzelle, 1947.

Howe, George F. *Northwest Africa: Seizing the Initiative in the West,* UNITED STATES ARMY IN WORLD WAR II. Washington: 1957.

Hull, Cordell. *The Memoirs of Cordell Hull.* New York: The Macmillan Company, 1948. 2 vols.

Joubert, [Lt. Col.] J. *La Libération de la France.* Paris: Payot, 1951.

Langer, William L. *Our Vichy Gamble.* New York: Alfred A. Knopf, Inc., 1947.

Lattre de Tassigny, Général [Jean] de. *Histoire de la Première Armée Française.* Paris: Plon, 1949.

Leahy, Adm. William D. *I Was There: The Personal Story of the Chief of Staff to Presidents Roosevelt and Truman Based on His Notes and Diaries Made at the Time.* New York: Whittlesey House, 1950.

Leighton, Richard M., and Robert W. Coakley. *Global Logistics and Strategy: 1940–1943,* UNITED STATES ARMY IN WORLD WAR II. Washington: 1955.

Les Forces Aériennes Françaises de 1939 à 1945. Ed. Col. Pierre Paquier. Paris: Berger-Levrault, 1949.

Logistical History of NATOUSA–MTOUSA: 11 August 1942 to 30 November 1945. Ed. Col. Creswell G. Blakeney. Naples, Italy: G. Montanino, 1946.

Marey, Georges. "Le Réarmement français en Afrique du Nord (1942–1944)," *Revue Politique et Parlementaire* (October, November, 1947.

Matloff, Maurice, and Edwin M. Snell. *Strategic Planning for Coalition Warfare: 1941–1942,* UNITED STATES ARMY IN WORLD WAR II. Washington: 1953.

Ministère des Finances et Affaires Economiques. "Le Prêt-Bail et l'Aide Réciproque Franco-Alliée," *Notes et Etudes Documentaires* (Paris, 2 and 3 November 1949).

Mouilleseaux, Louis, Ed. *La France et son Empire dans la Guerre.* Paris: Editions Littéraires de France, 1947.

Pogue, Forrest C. *The Supreme Command,* UNITED STATES ARMY IN WORLD WAR II. Washington: 1954.

Richard, René, and Alain de Sérigny. *L'Enigme d'Alger.* Paris: Librairie Arthème Fayard, 1947.

Rocolle, Chef de bataillon breveté, *L'Arme Aeroportée Clé de la Victoire.* Paris: Charles-Lavauzelle, 1948. 2 vols.

Santini, Lt. Col. P. "Etude statistique sur les pertes au cours de la guerre 1939–1945," *Revue du Corps de Santé Militaire,* X, No. 1 (March, 1954).

Sherwood, Robert E. *Roosevelt and Hopkins: An Intimate History.* New York: Harper & Brothers, 1948.

Spillman, Colonel. "L'Armée d'Afrique," *Revue Historique de l'Armée* (December, 1948).

Suttles, Col. E. A., Ed. *A Photographic Story of the Assembly of T.U.P. Motor Vehicles by the New French Army in the North African Theater of Operations.*

Weygand, Général [Maxime]. *Mémoires: Rappelé au Service.* Paris: Flammarion, 1950.

Interviews

Col. George L. Artamonoff

Col. André Beaufre

Col. Roland de Beaumont

Brig. Gen. Paul Devinck

Col. R. Gilpin Erwin

Col. William Tudor Gardiner

General Henri Giraud

Lt. Gen. Augustin Guillaume

General Alphonse Juin

Brig. Gen. Allen F. Kingman

General Jean de Lattre de Tassigny   Brig. Gen. Jean Piatte
Col. André L'Huillier   Brig. Gen. Jean Regnault
Brig. Gen. Harold F. Loomis   Brig. Gen. Gordon P. Saville
Lt. Gen. Aimé de Goislard de Monsabert   Lt. Claude Tiers
Brig. Gen. Marcel Pénette   Lt. Gen. Jean Valluy

List of Abbreviations

AAF	Army Air Forces
AAFSC	Army Air Forces Service Command (MTO)
ACofS	Assistant Chief of Staff
Actg	Acting
Admin	Administration
A.E.F.	American Expeditionary Forces (World War I)
AFAT	Auxiliaires Féminines de l'Armée de Terre (French counterpart of WAC)
AFHQ	Allied Force Headquarters
AFSC	Air Force Service Command
AGWAR	Adjutant General, War Department
Asdic	Antisubmarine direction indicator
ASF	Army Service Forces
BAR	Browning automatic rifle
BCRA	Bureau Central de Renseignements et d'Action (Militaire)
Br	British
CCS	Combined Chiefs of Staff
CEF	Corps Expéditionnaire Français (French Expeditionary Corps)
CEFEO	Corps Expéditionnaire Français d'Extrême-Orient (French Far East Expeditionary Corps)
CFLN	Comité Français de la Libération Nationale (French Committee of National Liberation)
CG	Commanding general
CinC	Commander in Chief
CM-IN	Classified Message, Incoming
CM-OUT	Classified Message, Outgoing
CofS	Chief of Staff
Comd	Command
Comdr	Commander
Conf	Conference
Corres	Correspondence
COS	British Chiefs of Staff
CPS	Combined Staff Planners
CRMA	Centre de Réception des Matériels Américains (Reception Center for American Equipment)
DAD	Defense Aid Division (to 1 Oct 41), Defense Aid Director
DB	Division Blindée (Armored Division)
DFL	Division Française Libre (Free French Division)
DI	Division d'Infanterie (Infantry Division)

DIA	Division d'Infanterie Algérienne (Algerian Infantry Division), or Division d'Infanterie Alpine (Alpine Infantry Division)
DIC·	Division d'Infanterie Coloniale (Colonial Infantry Division)
DIM	Division d'Infanterie Marocaine (Moroccan Infantry Division)
Dir	Directive
DMI	Division Motorisée d'Infanterie, or Division de Marche d'Infanterie (Motorized Infantry Division)
DMM	Division Marocaine de Montagne (Moroccan Mountain Division)
DRB AGO	Departmental Records Branch, Adjutant General's Office
EMFFI	Etat-Major des Forces Françaises de l'Intérieur
EMGG	Etat-Major Général, Guerre (General Staff, War)
ETOUSA	European Theater of Operations, U.S. Army
Exp	Expeditionary
FAF	French Air Force (Armée de l'Air)
FFI	Forces Françaises de l'Intérieur (French Forces of the Interior)
Fr	French
FTS	French Training Section
GO	General Order
G.O.C.	General-officer-commanding (British)
GPF	Grande Puissance Filloux
GTM	Groupe de Tabors Marocains (Moroccan Tabor Group)
Hq	Headquarters
Interv	Interview
JAC	Joint Air Commission
JCS	U.S. Joint Chiefs of Staff
JLC	Joint Logistics Committee
JPS	Joint Staff Planners
JRC	Joint Rearmament Committee
LMAB	Munitions Assignments Board (London)
Ltr	Letter
MAAF	Mediterranean Allied Air Forces
MAB	Munitions Assignments Board
MAC (G)	Munitions Assignments Committee (Ground)
MAC (A)	(Air)
MAC (N)	(Navy)
MBS	Mediterranean Base Section
MLB	Metallic link belt
Msg	Message
Mtg	Meeting
MTOUSA	Mediterranean Theater of Operations, U.S. Army
NAAF	Northwest African Air Forces
NAASC	Northwest African Air Service Command
NATOUSA	North African Theater of Operations, U.S. Army

OCMH	Office of the Chief of Military History
OCT HB	Office of the Chief of Transportation, Historical Branch
OPD	Operations Division, General Staff
Opns, Ops	Operations
OSS	Office of Strategic Services
PBS	Peninsular Base Section
PETN	Pentaerythritol tetranite
POL	Petrol (gasoline), oil, and lubricants
POW	Prisoner of war
RAF	Royal Air Force
Rcd	Record
RCP	Régiment de Chasseurs Parachutistes (Parachute Regiment)
Rearmt	Rearmament
RTA	Régiment de Tirailleurs Algériens (Algerian Tirailleurs Regiment)
SACMED	Supreme Allied Commander, Mediterranean
SAS	Special Air Service
SCAEF	Supreme Commander, Allied Expeditionary Force
SCAMA	Service Central des Approvisionnements et Matériels Américains (Central Office of American Supplies and Equipment)
SFHQ	Special Force Headquarters
SHAEF	Supreme Headquarters, Allied Expeditionary Force
SO	Special Order
SOLOC	Southern Line of Communications
SOS	Services of Supply
SR	Service de Renseignements (Intelligence Service)
Sup	Supply
Sv	Service
TAC	Tactical Air Command
TAG	The Adjutant General
USAAF	U.S. Army Air Forces
USSTAF	United States Strategic Air Force
WAC	Women's Army Corps
Wac	A member of the Women's Army Corps
WD	War Department
WO	War Office

Glossary of Code Names

AFLOC
: A trans-Africa supply route for the supply of vehicles and equipment to the Middle East and east Africa.

ANAKIM
: A large land operation for the reopening of the Burma Road and an amphibious operation for the recapture of Rangoon.

ANFA
: Sometimes used by OPD officers as a code name for the Casablanca Conference of January 1943.

ANVIL
: The planned 1944 Allied invasion of southern France in the Toulon-Marseille area. (Later DRAGOON.)

BIGOT
: Special security procedure for OVERLORD.

BOLERO
: Build-up of troops and supplies in the United Kingdom in preparation for a cross-Channel attack.

BRASSARD
: Operation to liberate the Island of Elba, June 1944.

CAÏMAN
: Proposed operation in support of Resistance forces in central France. Allies rejected the whole operation as impracticable.

EUREKA
: Tehran Conference, 28 November–1 December 1943.

FLAMBO
: AFHQ Advance Administrative Echelon, established at Naples, October 1943.

FREEDOM
: Code designation for radio station at Algiers.

HUSKY
: Allied invasion of Sicily in July 1943.

OVERLORD
: Plan for the Allied invasion of northwest Europe, spring 1944.

QUADRANT
: First Quebec Conference, August 1943.

SEXTANT
: Cairo Conference, 22–26 November and 3–7 December 1943.

SYMBOL
: Conference at Casablanca, January 1943.

TORCH
: Allied invasion of North and Northwest Africa, November 1942.

TRIDENT
: Washington Conference, May 1943.

VESUVIUS
: Operation to liberate Corsica, September–October 1943.

United States Army in World War II

The multivolume series, UNITED STATES ARMY IN WORLD WAR II, consists of a number of subseries which are tentatively planned as follows: The War Department, The Army Air Forces, The Army Ground Forces, The Army Service Forces, The Defense of the Western Hemisphere, The War in the Pacific, The European Theater of Operations, The Mediterranean Theater of Operations, The Middle East Theater, The China–Burma–India Theater, Civil Affairs, The Technical Services, Special Studies, and Pictorial Record.

The following volumes have been published or are in press:*

The War Department
Chief of Staff: Prewar Plans and Preparations
Washington Command Post: The Operations Division
Strategic Planning for Coalition Warfare: 1941–1942
Global Logistics and Strategy: 1940–1943

The Army Ground Forces
The Organization of Ground Combat Troops
The Procurement and Training of Ground Combat Troops

The Army Service Forces
The Organization and Role of the Army Service Forces

The War in the Pacific
Okinawa: The Last Battle
Guadalcanal: The First Offensive
The Approach to the Philippines
The Fall of the Philippines
Leyte: Return to the Philippines
Seizure of the Gilberts and Marshalls
Victory in Papua

The European Theater of Operations
The Lorraine Campaign
Cross-Channel Attack
Logistical Support of the Armies, Volume I
The Supreme Command

*The volumes on the Army Air Forces, published by the University of Chicago Press, are not included in this list.

The Mediterranean Theater of Operations
  Northwest Africa: Seizing the Initiative in the West

The Middle East Theater
  The Persian Corridor and Aid to Russia

The China–Burma–India Theater
  Stilwell's Mission to China
  Stilwell's Command Problems

The Technical Services
  The Transportation Corps: Responsibilities, Organization, and Operations
  The Transportation Corps: Movements, Training, and Supply
  The Transportation Corps: Operations Overseas
  The Quartermaster Corps: Organization, Supply, and Services, Volume I
  The Quartermaster Corps: Organization, Supply, and Services, Volume II
  The Quartermaster Corps: Operations in the War Against Japan
  The Ordnance Department: Planning Munitions for War
  The Signal Corps: The Emergency
  The Signal Corps: The Test
  The Medical Department: Hospitalization and Evacuation, Zone of Interior

Special Studies
  Three Battles: Arnaville, Altuzzo, and Schmidt
  The Women's Army Corps
  Rearming the French

Pictorial Record
  The War Against Germany and Italy: Mediterranean and Adjacent Areas
  The War Against Germany: Europe and Adjacent Areas
  The War Against Japan

Index

Aachen, Germany, 344

Accounting, 28, 141, 143, 144, 145, 266–70, 346, 354. *See also* Lend-lease.
  of British equipment, 63
  cash payments, 262, 263, 265
  of Commanding General Shipments, 267, 268
  per man per diem procedure, 269–70
  of theater transfers, 267, 268–69

Admiralty (Br.), 222, 299

Admiralty (Fr.). *See under* French Navy.

Aéronautique Navale. *See under* French Navy, Air Arm.

AFLOC, 53n

African Army. *See under* North African Forces.

Air Commander in Chief in the Mediterranean. *See* Tedder, Air Chief Marshal Sir Arthur W.

Air forces, Allied tactical
  First Tactical Air Force, 212, 373, 375, 376
  2d Tactical Air Force (Br.), 212, 373

Air forces, U. S. *See* Eighth Air Force; Twelfth Air Force; U. S. Strategic Air Forces (USSTAF).

Air Ministry (Br.), 300

Air Ministry (Fr.), 374, 375

Air Service Command (Fr.), 200

Alexander, Field Marshal Sir Harold R. L. G., 116, 369
  on French combat performance, 178, 213n
  and Franco-Italian border incident, 367, 368

Alexandria, Egypt, 90, 90n, 214, 221

Algeria, 11, 14, 194, 195, 196, 233

Algiers, 25, 63, 65, 84, 85, 131, 132, 135, 136, 138, 140, 151, 152, 188, 191n, 198, 203, 220, 230, 248, 260, 268, 272, 276, 280, 294n, 301, 302, 316, 326, 377, 385
  Allied landings at, 16
  celebration at, 59–60
  French Committee of National Liberation established at, 79
  vehicle assembly line at, 67–69, 67n

Allied Armies in Italy, 116

Allied Commander in Chief, 18, 49, 52, 53, 55, 62, 63, 71, 72, 79, 91, 117–18, 119, 120, 125. *See also* Allied Force Headquarters (AFHQ); Eisenhower, Gen. Dwight D.

Allied commander in the Pacific. *See* MacArthur, Gen. Douglas.

Allied Force Headquarters (AFHQ), 123, 142, 169, 180, 188, 314, 382, 383. *See also* Allied Commander in Chief; Eisenhower, Gen. Dwight D.; Gammell, Lt. Gen. J. A. H.; Mediterranean theater; Smith, Lt. Gen. Walter Bedell; Wilson, Gen. Sir Henry Maitland.
  and ANFA Plan, 40
  and assistance to the French, 65, 67
  and composition of French expeditionary forces, 87–88, 109, 110, 125–26, 127, 148, 157, 171
  and control of French forces, 117–18, 119, 120, 149, 150–51, 194, 225
  and employment of French forces, 108, 111, 112–13, 116, 117, 159, 212, 259
  and equipping French expeditionary forces, 140, 141–42, 163–64, 170
  establishment, 25
  and French Committee of National Liberation, 149–50
  and French forces in ANVIL, 163, 164
  and French High Command, 96, 153, 228
  and French naval forces, 218, 220, 377
  and French rearmament, 46n, 62–63, 70, 71, 75–76, 77, 81–82, 84, 85, 88, 91, 92, 94, 96, 97, 101, 109, 110, 111, 113, 120, 121, 125, 126, 129, 148, 155, 156, 161, 165, 177, 199, 202, 205, 211, 227, 229, 241, 242–43, 244, 245, 248, 250, 251, 252, 258n, 260, 261–62, 281, 391, 392
  and French service troops, 104–05, 107, 108, 109–10, 124, 128, 146, 166, 167, 168, 202
  and French supply system, 130, 131, 133–34
  and fusion of French armed forces, 81–82, 86
  and Giraud, 98, 118–19, 150, 151–52
  and the JAC, 93
  and the JRC, 25, 92, 271, 272, 284
  Liaison Section, 271, 274, 282
  and maintenance of French expeditionary forces, 139, 145, 155, 254, 257, 258, 261, 262, 263, 264
  and Metropolitan Forces, 192, 309
  movement to Caserta, 276n
  and nonprogram units, 121, 158
  and training of French troops, 28, 230, 231, 235, 236, 293

Allied Military Government, Italy, 367, 368

Alps, operations in the, 349, 354, 363n, 367